Education for All by 2015
Will we make it?

S0-AYZ-587

Education for All by 2015
Will we make it?

UNESCO Publishing

OXFORD
UNIVERSITY PRESS

The analysis and policy recommendations of this Report do not necessarily reflect the views of UNESCO. The Report is an independent publication commissioned by UNESCO on behalf of the international community. It is the product of a collaborative effort involving members of the Report Team and many other people, agencies, institutions and governments. Overall responsibility for the views and opinions expressed in the Report is taken by its Director.

The designations employed and the presentation of the material in this publication do not imply the expression of any opinion whatsoever on the part of UNESCO concerning the legal status of any country, territory, city or area, or of its authorities, or concerning the delimitation of its frontiers or boundaries.

OXFORD
UNIVERSITY PRESS

Great Clarendon Street, Oxford OX2 6DP
Oxford University Press is a department
of the University of Oxford.
It furthers the University's objective of excellence
in research, scholarship, and education by publishing
worldwide in Oxford New York Auckland Cape Town
Dar es Salaam Hong Kong Karachi Kuala Lumpur
Madrid Melbourne, Mexico City Nairobi New Delhi
Shanghai Taipei Toronto
With offices in Argentina Austria Brazil Chile
Czech Republic France Greece Guatemala Hungary
Italy Japan Poland Portugal Singapore South Korea
Switzerland Thailand Turkey Ukraine Vietnam
Oxford is a registered trade mark of Oxford University
Press in the UK and in certain other countries
Published jointly by the United Nations Educational,
Scientific and Cultural Organization (UNESCO),
7, place de Fontenoy, 75007 Paris, France, and
Oxford University Press, Great Clarendon Street,
Oxford OX2 6DP, United Kingdom.

© UNESCO, 2007
First published 2007
Published in 2007 by the United Nations Educational,
Scientific and Cultural Organization
7, Place de Fontenoy, 75352 Paris 07 SP, France

Graphic design by Sylvaine Baeyens
Layout: Sylvaine Baeyens and Hélène Borel
Maps: Hélène Borel

Library of Congress Cataloging in Publication Data
Data available
Typeset by UNESCO
Printed on acid-free paper by Rotolito Lombarda SpA
OUP ISBN 978-0-19-953263-6
UNESCO ISBN 978-92-3-104058-0

Foreword

Seven years ago 164 governments, together with partner organizations from around the world, made a collective commitment to dramatically expand educational opportunities for children, youth and adults by 2015.

Participants at the World Education Forum in Dakar, Senegal, endorsed a comprehensive vision of education, anchored in human rights, affirming the importance of learning at all ages and emphasizing the need for special measures to reach the poorest, most vulnerable and most disadvantaged groups in society.

This sixth edition of the *EFA Global Monitoring Report* assesses the extent to which these commitments are being met. There is clearly a 'Dakar effect', evidence that rallying around common goals can mobilize countries to empower individual lives. Partly because of the abolition of tuition fees, more children are enrolled in school than in 2000, with the sharpest increases in the regions farthest from the goals set in Dakar. Many governments have introduced targeted strategies to reach the poorest households and to encourage girls' schooling. A growing number are conducting national assessments to measure pupils' learning achievement, valuable evidence for improving education quality. Though a recent downturn is cause for concern, aid to basic education has increased rapidly since 2000.

As education systems expand, however, they face more complex and more specific challenges. They must address the increasing number and diversity of student populations by ensuring that all children and youth, regardless of their backgrounds, gain access to a quality education. They must act upon the challenges of our era: rapid urbanization and the HIV/AIDS pandemic, the demands of knowledge societies. Any failure to deliver on these obligations breaches our commitment to universal basic education.

We are steering the right course but the years ahead will require unwavering political will to consistently ensure that education from early childhood onwards is a national priority, to engage governments, civil society and the private sector in creative partnerships, and to generate dynamic coordination and support from the international community. Time is of the essence: for the 72 million children out of school, for the one in five adults without basic literacy skills and for the many pupils who leave school without acquiring essential skills and knowledge.

The *EFA Global Monitoring Report* offers an authoritative reference for comparing the experiences of countries, understanding the positive impact of specific policies and recognizing that progress happens when there is political vision and commitment. I urge every development and education stakeholder to use this report as a guide and impetus for bold and sustained action. We cannot afford to fail.

Koïchiro Matsuura

Acknowledgements

This Report could not have been prepared without the kind assistance of many people and organizations.

At UNESCO, we are very grateful for the advice and support of individuals, Divisions and Units within the Education Sector and in the field. In particular the International Institute for Educational Planning in Paris and in Buenos Aires, the International Bureau of Education and the UNESCO Institute for Lifelong Learning, and UNESCO's Regional Office for Education in Latin America and the Caribbean, and UNESCO Bangkok provided helpful advice on country-level activities and helped facilitate commissioned studies.

The Report profited enormously from the advice and support of the international Editorial Board and its chair, Ingemar Gustafsson. Consultations on the outline of the Report (online and among UNESCO colleagues) strengthened the report. Comments from the online consultation can be viewed at www.efareport.unesco.org

We are also grateful to the many experts and colleagues who took time to actively participate in a special on-line consultation on the literate environment, which enriched the team's understanding of the different conceptual and monitoring approaches to the literate environment.

The EFA Report depends greatly on the work of the UNESCO Institute for Statistics. Director Hendrik van der Pol, Saïd Belkachla, Michael Bruneforth, Brian Buffet, Alison Kennedy, Weixin Lu, Patrick Lucas, Adriano Miele, Albert Motivans, John Pacifico, Juan Cruz Persua, José Pessoa, Pascale Ratovondrahona, Ioulia Sementchouk, Saïd Ould Voffal and their colleagues contributed significantly to this Report, particularly in the preparation of chapter 2 and the statistical tables.

Special thanks to all those who prepared background papers for the Report:
Abdulrahman Al shaer, Rashid Aderinoye, Massimo Amadio, Katy Anis, Caroline Arnold, Ildikó Balazsi, Dennis Banda, Madumita Bandopadhyay, Masooda Bano, Angeline Barrett, Karima Barrow, Kathy Bartlett, Aydagül Batuhan, Claudie Baudino, Hazel Bines, Lyndsay Bird, Rae Blumberg, Gabrielle Bonnet, Teresa Bracho González, Vladimir Briller, Rhona B. Caoli-Rodriguez, Diem Chau Lam, Lisa Chauvet, Roshan Chitrakar, Paul Collier, Marcelo Cortes Neri, Lisa Deyo, Marta Encinas-Martin, Claudia Flores-Moreno, Jude Fransman, Marcela Gajardo, Joseph Goodfriend, R. Govinda, Carolina Guerrero, El Mostafa Hddigui, Nadia Hillard, Wim Hoppers, George Ingram, Timothy D. Ireland, Najwa Andraos Kefayeh, Nestor Lopez, Xin Ma, Ian Macpherson, Tonic Maruatona, Karen McGregor, Katharina Michaelowa, Amit Mitra, Elhadji Ngom, Angela Owusu-Boamong, Francis Owusu-Mensah, Steve Packer, Jeffrey M. Poirer, Emilio Porta Pallais, Abby Riddell, François Robert, Alan Rogers, Pauline Rose, Aisha Sabri, Zia Sabur, Mona Sedval, Amanda Seel, Tammy Shel, Joel D. Sherman, Fary Silateka, Wisanee Siltragool, Kishore Singh, Gita Steiner-Khamsi, Nelly Stromquist, Celia Swann, Chie Takahashi, Erin Tanner, David Theobald, Nhung Truong, Paul Vachon, Nora von Buttlar, Peter Wallet, Anke Weber, Hu Wenbin, Babette Wills, Eric Woods, Aigly Zafeirakou, Jing Zhao and Madeleine Zuniga.

We also thank the Academy for Educational Development's Educational Policy and Data Center, the American Institutes for Research, the Aga Khan Foundation, the Associés en Recherche et Éducation pour le Développement (ARED) and Save the Children UK for facilitating commisionned studies.

We are grateful to Desmond Bermingham and Luc-Charles Gacougnolle in the Fast Track Initiative secretariat, and to Julia Benn, Valérie Gaveau, Cecile Sangare and Simon Scott in OECD/DAC for their continuing support and helpful advice on international cooperation and aid data.

Special thanks to Lene Buchert, Francois Leclerq, Steve Packer and Ramya Subrahmanian for their valuable comments on draft chapters, and to Francois Leclercq for his editorial input.

The production of the Report benefited greatly from the editorial expertise of Rebecca Brite. Wenda McNevin also provided valuable support. We would also like to thank Nino Muños Gomez, Sue Williams, Enzo Fazzino, Agnes Bardon and Stephen Roberts and Ian Denison and his colleagues from the UNESCO Bureau of Public Information. Rudi Swinnen, Jean-Paul Kersuzan and their colleagues from UNESCO's Document Section helped with production of other language versions. Thanks also to Anne Muller, Judith Roca, Lotfi Ben Khelifa, Marc Leibnitz and their colleagues in the UNESCO Education Knowledge Management Services for their valuable support and assistance. Special thanks also to Fouzia Jouot-Bellami, Richard Cadiou, Igor Nuk and Fabienne Kouadio who facilitated the on-line consultation.

The EFA Global Monitoring Report Team

Director
Nicholas Burnett

Nicole Bella, Aaron Benavot, Mariela Buonomo, Fadila Caillaud, Vittoria Cavicchioni, Alison Clayson, Catherine Ginisty, Cynthia Guttman, Anna Haas, Keith Hinchliffe, Anaïs Loizillon, Patrick Montjourides, Claudine Mukizwa, Delphine Nsengimana, Ulrika Peppler Barry, Paula Razquin, Isabelle Reullon, Yusuf Sayed, Suhad Varin.

For more information about the Report, please contact:
The Director
EFA Global Monitoring Report Team
c/o UNESCO
7, place de Fontenoy, 75352 Paris 07 SP, France
e-mail: efareport@unesco.org
Tel.: +33 1 45 68 21 28
Fax: +33 1 45 68 56 27
www.efareport.unesco.org

Previous EFA Global Monitoring Reports
2007. Strong foundations – Early childhood care and education
2006. Literacy for life
2005. Education for All – The quality imperative
2003/4. Gender and Education for All – The leap to equality
2002. Education for All – Is the world on track?

Any errors or omissions found subsequent to printing will be corrected in the online version at www.efareport.unesco.org

Contents

Foreword i

Acknowledgements ii

List of figures, tables, text boxes and maps vi

Highlights of the Report 1

Overview 5

Chapter 1 The enduring relevance of Education for All 11

Introduction 12
Education for All as endorsed at the Dakar World Education Forum 13
Achieving EFA in a changing world 17
The 2008 *EFA Global Monitoring Report* 28

Chapter 2 The six goals: how far have we come? 31

Overview and main findings 32
Early childhood care and education: still not comprehensive 34
Universal primary education: nearer but not close 41
Secondary education and beyond also contribute to EFA 56
Are the learning needs of young people and adults being met? 59
Literacy and literate environments: essential yet elusive 62
Quality: the continuing challenge 66
Gender parity and equality: not there yet 79
Overall Education for All achievement 91
Taking stock 95

Chapter 3 Countries on the move 97

Monitoring country efforts 98
Developing enabling institutions 100
Comprehensive approaches 107
Expanding equitable access 108
Improving learning 123
Restoring education in difficult circumstances 136
Access and quality are mutually reinforcing 137

| Chapter 4 | Progress in financing Education for All | 139 |

Introduction 140
Changing national financial commitments to EFA since Dakar 141
Contribution of external aid to EFA since Dakar 154
What progress within the Framework for Action? 172

| Chapter 5 | The way forward | 177 |

Introduction 178
Trends and prospects for 2015 178
Financing the EFA goals to 2015 185
Towards an agenda 191

Annex 197

The Education for All Development Index 198
Prospects for the achievement of EFA by 2015: methodology 206
National learning assessments by region and country 208
National policies to advance Education for All in thirty countries 221
Statistical tables 232
Aid tables 373
Glossary 390
References 396
Abbreviations 417
Index 420

List of figures, tables, text boxes and maps

Figures

1.1: Global political and civil rights, percentage of countries by status, 1990-2006 20

1.2: Total official development assistance, net disbursements, 1992-2005 21

1.3: Regional distribution of total official development assistance, 1999-2000 and 2004-2005 22

2.1: Changes in pre-primary gross enrolment ratios between 1999 and 2005 in countries with GERs below 90% in 2005 ... 38

2.2: Comparison of pupil/teacher ratios with ratios of pupils to trained teachers in pre-primary education, 2005 40

2.3: Gross intake rates to primary education in countries with GIRs below 95% in 1999, 2005 or both 42

2.4: Distribution of new entrants into primary education relative to official age, 2005 43

2.5: Change in primary net enrolment ratios between 1999 and 2005 in countries with NERs of 95% or lower in both years 45

2.6: Subnational geographic disparities in net enrolment ratios, pre- and post-Dakar 46

2.7: Average annual change in the rural/urban ratio of net attendance rates for thirty-nine countries 47

2.8: Strength and direction of the association between the prevalence of poor households and primary net attendance rates, post-Dakar period 48

2.9: Distribution of out-of-school children by educational experience and region, 2005 51

2.10: Repetition and dropout in primary education by grade and area of residence, Guatemala, 2005 52

2.11: Situation of countries in terms of access to schooling and survival 54

2.12: Survival rates to last grade and cohort completion rates, 2004 56

2.13: Proportion of youth and adults whose reported highest educational attainment level was achieved in non-formal education, 2000 61

2.14: Percentage of countries in each region that carried out at least one national assessment between 1995–1999 and 2000–2006 69

2.15: Distribution of student performance in Hungary, by residence, 2006 70

2.16: Rural-urban disparities in language and mathematics achievement in grade 5 or 6 based on national assessments, various years 72

2.17: Median yearly instructional time in grades 1-6, based on total number of intended hours, by region 73

2.18: Ratio of pupils to trained teachers in primary education, 1999 and 2005 78

2.19: Changes in gender disparities in access to primary schooling, by region, between 1999 and 2005 81

2.20: Gender parity index of primary GERs by region, 1991, 1999 and 2005 81

2.21: Changes in gender disparities in secondary gross enrolment ratios by region, 1991, 1999 and 2005 84

2.22: Change in gender disparities in tertiary gross enrolment ratios by region, 1999 to 2005 86

2.23: Percentage of female teachers by level of education and region, 2005 87

2.24: Gender differences in language and mathematics in grade 6 as reported in national student assessments 90

2.25: Female participation in various fields of study in tertiary education, 2005 92

2.26: The EDI in 2005 and change since 1999 94

4.1: Change in total public expenditure on education as % of GNP between 1999 and 2005 (percentage points) 144

4.2: Total public expenditure on education as % of GNP in sixteen sub-Saharan African countries, 1991–2005 145

4.3: Average shares of public current expenditure on education by level, by income group, 2005 147

4.4: Relative proportions of public, household and other private expenditure on education institutions 150

4.5: Mean annual public and household current expenditure per pupil in public primary schools 151

4.6: Components of total aid commitments to education and to basic education, 1999–2000 and 2004–2005 155

4.7: Total aid commitments to education and to basic education, 1999–2005 156

4.8: Aid to education and to basic education (disbursements), 2002–2005 157

4.9: Distribution of total aid to education and to basic education by income group (commitments), 1999–2005 157

4.10: Distribution of total aid to education and to basic education by region (commitments), 1999–2005 157

4.11: Aid commitments to basic education and out-of-school children, 2005 158

4.12: Aid commitments to basic education and income per capita, 2005 158

4.13: Breakdown of aid commitments to education by level, 2004 and 2005 average 162

4.14: IBRD loans to education (commitments), 1991–2005 163

4.15: Regional distribution of IBRD loans to education (commitments), 1991–2005 163

4.16: Share of aid commitments to education and to basic education, all countries,
by type of aid, 1999–2000 and 2004–2005 165

4.17: Share of aid commitments to basic education by type of aid, by income group, 1999–2000 and 2004–2005 165

4.18: Changes in the share of GNP devoted to education in twenty-one FTI-endorsed countries, 1999–2005 174

4.19: Annual growth rates of domestic expenditure and aid for education
in thirty-two low-income countries, 1999–2005 175

Tables

1.1: Selected international human rights treaties relevant to the EFA goals 16

1.2: Fragile states, 2005 21

1.3: The Gleneagles aid commitments, 2005 23

1.4: Changes in compulsory education laws since Dakar (to 2005) 25

1.5: National definitions of basic education 26

2.1: Pre-primary enrolment and gross enrolment ratios by region, 1999 and 2005 36

2.2: Pupil/teacher ratios in pre-primary education by region, 1999 and 2005 40

2.3: New entrants into grade 1 and gross intake rates by region, 1999 and 2005 41

2.4: Primary enrolment by region, 1991, 1999 and 2005 44

2.5: Changes in country-level enrolment ratios and in educational geographic disparity, pre- to post-Dakar 47

2.6: Percentages of children with and without disabilities not attending school in seven countries (various years) 48

2.7: Estimated number of out-of-school children by region, 1999 and 2005 49

2.8: Estimated number of out-of-school children worldwide, 1999 to 2005 (thousands) 49

2.9: Number of out-of-school children in selected countries, 1999, 2002 and 2005 51

2.10: Enrolment ratios in secondary education by region, 1991, 1999 and 2005 58

2.11: GERs in lower and upper secondary education by region, 1999 and 2005 59

2.12: Tertiary gross enrolment ratios by region, 1999 and 2005 59

2.13: Comparison of self-assessment and direct assessment of adult literacy by gender, 2006 62

2.14: Estimated number of adult illiterates by region, 1985–1994 and 1995–2004 63

2.15: Estimated adult literacy rates by region, 1985–1994 and 1995–2004 63

2.16: Percentage of grade 3 and 6 pupils in Uganda reaching defined competency levels, by subject, 1999 to 2006 69

2.17: Changes in learning outcomes based on national assessments, various years 71

2.18: Total teaching staff in primary and secondary education by region, 1999 and 2005 75

2.19: Pupil/teacher ratios in primary and secondary education by region, 1991, 1999 and 2005 76

2.20: Contract and civil-servant or government teachers in thirteen francophone countries of sub-Saharan Africa 79

2.21: Distribution of countries according to distance from the gender parity goal in primary, secondary and tertiary education, 2005 80

2.22: Gender disparities in survival rates to the last grade of primary education, 1999 and 2004 83

2.23: Gender differences in school subjects and grade levels as reported in recent international and regional student assessments 89

2.24: Countries with the largest gender differences in learning outcomes in the latest regional and international student assessments 90

2.25: Distribution of countries by EDI scores and region, 2005 93

3.1: Summary of strategies in the Expanded Commentary on the Dakar Framework for Action 99

3.2: Cash-transfer programmes targeting poor households with school-age children in fourteen countries 115

3.3: Examples of policy approaches to address child labour and school attendance 119

4.1: Total public expenditure on education as % of GNP and as % of total government expenditure, selected countries, 2005 142

4.2: Total public expenditure on education as % of GNP, by income group, 2005 143

4.3: Annual compound rates of growth in total real public expenditure on education and GNP, 1999-2005 146

4.4: Public current expenditure on primary education per pupil as % of GNP per capita in selected countries, by region, 2005 148

4.5: Distribution of benefits of public spending on education to poorest and richest households in selected countries 149

4.6: Household expenditure on public primary schooling, by type of expenditure 151

4.7: Education expenditure as a share of household expenditure, selected countries 152

4.8: Priority given to education and to basic education (commitments), 1999–2000 and 2004–2005 156

4.9: Changes in aid to basic education in the main recipient countries (commitments), 1999–2005 159

4.10: Aid commitments to education and to basic education by donor, 2004–2005 average and change since 1999 161

4.11: Number of major donors to the education sector in sixty-eight low-income countries, 2003–2005 165

5.1: Country prospects for achieving universal primary enrolment by 2015 180

5.2: Country prospects for achieving adult literacy by 2015 182

5.3: Country prospects for achieving gender parity in primary and secondary education by 2005, 2015 and 2025 184

5.4: Primary school teacher needs between 2004 and 2015 by region (millions) 185

5.5: Real per capita GDP growth in low-income countries, selected periods (% per year) 185

5.6: Prospects for bilateral aid to education and basic education in 2010 for all developing countries (commitments) 187

5.7: Allocation of aid for basic education to the low-income countries most at risk of not achieving UPE, 1999-2000 and 2004-2005 190

Text boxes

1.1: The EFA perspective 14

1.2: The Dakar EFA goals 15

1.3: The Dakar EFA strategies 15

1.4: The emerging concept of 'fragile states' 21

2.1: What is the age of children entering school? 43

2.2: China: population data issues pose a UPE monitoring challenge 51

2.3: Repetition and dropout in Guatemala 52

2.4: Diversification of secondary education reflects changing interests and social needs 57

2.5: EFA goal 3: the hardest to define and monitor 60

2.6: Direct literacy assessment: the Kenya National Adult Literacy Survey 62

2.7: Education quality and equity in Central and Eastern Europe: new evidence 68

2.8: Teachers, HIV/AIDS and absenteeism 76

2.9: Boys' underparticipation in secondary education: background and identity issues 84

2.10: Sex education: hindered by gender stereotypes 89

3.1: Burkina Faso: capacity is a major constraint on EFA achievement 102

3.2: The Global Campaign for Education: linking national, regional and global advocacy 102

3.3: National EFA coalitions find a voice around the world 103

3.4: Scorecards in Latin America 104

3.5: Compensatory programmes in Mexico 107

3.6: Involving civil society in building and rehabilitating schools in the Philippines 110

3.7: Imbalance of opportunities: internal migration in Mongolia 111

3.8: Transfer programmes for orphans and vulnerable children 117

3.9: Access and quality measures reinforce each other in Cambodia 123

3.10: The 'rainbow spectrum' in the Philippines 129

3.11: Recruiting female teachers in Ethiopia and Yemen 129

3.12: Cluster-based mentoring in Pakistan 130

3.13: HIV/AIDS education 132

3.14: Facilitating early literacy in Zambia 133

3.15: India – a revolution in distance education 134

3.16: SchoolNets on the rise 135

3.17: Home-based classrooms in Afghanistan 137

3.18: Education for child soldiers in southern Sudan 137

4.1: The fluctuating nature of education expenditure in sub-Saharan Africa since the Jomtien Conference 144

4.2: Assessing total contributions to the education sector 155

4.3: Non-concessional loans for education 163

Maps

2.1: Pre-primary gross enrolment ratios, 2005 37

2.2: Primary education NER and out-of-school children, 2005 50

2.3: Survival rates to the last grade of primary education, 2004 55

2.4: Adult literacy rates and number of illiterates, 1995–2004 64

2.5: Gender parity index in primary gross enrolment ratios, 2005 82

2.6: Gender parity index in secondary gross enrolment ratios, 2005 85

3.1: Countries abolishing primary school tuition fees since Dakar (2006) 112

3.2: Primary school tuition fees and gross enrolment ratios since Dakar, with pupil/teacher ratios in 2005 113

Highlights of the EFA Report 2008

Major developments since 2000

■ Primary school enrolment rose from 647 million to 688 million worldwide between 1999 and 2005, increasing by 36% in sub-Saharan Africa and 22% in South and West Asia. As a result, the number of out-of-school children declined, with the pace of this decrease particularly marked after 2002.

■ Rapid progress towards universal enrolment and gender parity at the primary level for example in Burkina Faso, Ethiopia, India, Mozambique, the United Republic of Tanzania, Yemen and Zambia shows that national political will combined with international support can make a difference.

■ The cost of schooling remains a major obstacle to education for millions of children and youth despite the abolition of primary school tuition fees in fourteen countries since 2000.

■ The gender parity goal has been missed: only about one-third of countries reported parity in both primary and secondary education in 2005, with only three reaching it since 1999.

■ An increasing number of international, regional and national assessments report low and unequal learning outcomes, reflecting the extent to which poor education quality is undermining the achievement of EFA.

■ National governments and donors have favoured formal primary schooling over early childhood, literacy and skills programmes for youth and adults despite the direct impact of these on achieving universal primary education and gender parity.

■ Illiteracy is receiving minimal political attention and remains a global disgrace, keeping one in five adults (one in four women) on the margins of society.

■ Aid to basic education in low-income countries more than doubled between 2000 and 2004 but decreased significantly in 2005.

Where the world stands on the six EFA goals

● Out of 129 countries, 51 have achieved or are close to achieving the four most quantifiable EFA goals,[1] 53 are in an intermediate position and 25 are far from achieving EFA as a whole, the EFA Development Index shows. The lowest category would be larger still if data were available for a number of fragile states, including conflict or post-conflict countries with very low levels of education development.

1. Early childhood care and education

● Although child mortality rates have dropped, a majority of countries are not taking the necessary policy measures to provide care and education to children below age 3.

● The provision of pre-primary education for children aged 3 and above has improved but remains scarce across sub-Saharan Africa and the Arab States.

● Early childhood care and education programmes generally do not reach the poorest and most disadvantaged children, who stand to gain the most from them in terms of health, nutrition and cognitive development.

1. The EFA Development Index reflects progress towards the goals of universal primary education, adult literacy, gender parity and education quality.

1

Measures to promote quality

- use incentives to attract new recruits to the teaching profession, provide adequate teacher training and professional development;

- assure sufficient instructional time and a textbook development and distribution policy;

- create safe and healthy learning environments;

- promote gender equality through teacher training, the curriculum and textbook contents;

- recognize the importance of mother tongue instruction in early childhood and the first years of primary school;

- develop constructive partnerships between government and the non-state sector to increase access to quality education.

Measures to improve capacity and financing

- maintain or, where necessary, increase public spending, noting that unit costs are likely to rise for enrolling the most disadvantaged and marginalized;

- increase financing for early childhood, literacy and quality, especially teacher training and professional development;

- strengthen management capacity at all levels of government;

- coordinate early childhood and adult literacy programmes with all involved ministries and NGOs;

- formally engage civil society in EFA policy formulation, implementation and monitoring;

- invest in capacity to collect, analyse and use data on education systems.

Civil society

- further strengthen civil society organizations that enable citizens to advocate for EFA and to hold government and the international community to account;

- engage with national governments in the development, implementation and monitoring of education policies;

- encourage training in education policy analysis and finance.

Donors and international agencies

- Increase aid to basic education sharply to meet the annual external financing need of US$11 billion by 2010.

- Raise to at least 10% the share of basic education in bilateral sectoral aid.

- Improve governments' capacity to use larger amounts of aid effectively.

- Ensure that aid is:

    more targeted, to reach the countries most in need, especially fragile states and countries in sub-Saharan Africa;

    more comprehensive, to include early childhood, youth and adult literacy and skills programmes, and capacity development in policy, planning, implementation and monitoring;

    more focused on EFA rather than post-secondary education;

    more predictable, to support long-term national education plans;

    more aligned with government programmes and priorities.

Overview

Chapter 1
The enduring relevance of Education for All

 This edition of the *EFA Global Monitoring Report* marks the midway point in an ambitious international movement to expand learning opportunities for every child, youth and adult in the world by 2015.

In April 2000 in Dakar, 164 governments together with partner institutions adopted a Framework for Action focusing on the achievement of six Education for All goals pertaining to the expansion of early childhood care and education, the achievement of universal primary education, the development of learning opportunities for youth and adults, the spread of literacy, the achievement of gender parity and gender equality in education and improvements in education quality.

The EFA agenda rests on a belief that public policy can radically transform education systems, given adequate political will and resources. The global prospect for achieving EFA is also influenced by trends in demography, urbanization, migration, health, and economic and political systems. By 2008, for example, more than half the world's population (about 3.3 billion people) will live in urban areas, nearly one-third of whom will live in slums. Due to continued population growth, the least developed countries, which are furthest from universal participation at primary and secondary level, especially in sub-Saharan Africa, will face increasing enrolment pressure in coming decades. Among health concerns, HIV/AIDS, tuberculosis and malaria are having a devastating impact on school systems, especially in sub-Saharan Africa.

Real per capita income growth was sustained in sub-Saharan Africa and South Asia between 2000 and 2005, and remained high in East Asia and the Pacific. But despite reductions in the number of people living in absolute poverty, there has been rising inequality between rich and poor. Unless policies targeting poor and disadvantaged children are introduced, existing socio-economic inequality may be worsened through poor education and differentiated school systems.

Strengthening and supporting 'fragile' states has been an emerging priority on the EFA agenda since 2000. Such states are characterized by weak institutions, prolonged economic hardship and/or conflict, with a direct negative impact on education development. More than half a billion people are estimated to live in thirty-five fragile states.

Official development assistance from bilateral donors grew by 9% annually between 1999 and 2005, but preliminary data indicate a downturn in 2006. In 2005, the G8 countries made commitments to increase aid substantially through a variety of means, including traditional development assistance and debt relief. Yet donors need to accelerate plans to scale up aid to Africa if their promises are to retain credibility.

Recent research confirms the developmental benefits of expanding education systems, but points to a need for complementary policies to offset inequality and improve learning. The right to education has been enforced through measures such as compulsory education laws, passed by an increasing number of countries since 2000.

At international level, initiatives have focused on specific targets (literacy, girls, HIV/AIDS) and on improving the quality of aid. The convergence of such initiatives, however, will be vital for the full range of education for all goals to be achieved.

Chapter 2
The six goals: how far have we come?

This chapter provides a systematic assessment of progress towards EFA since Dakar, comparing data which pertain to the school year ending in 2005 with corresponding 1999 figures. It focuses on the regions and countries that face the greatest challenges in achieving the goals by 2015 and draws attention to inequities within countries.

Early childhood care and education programmes improve children's health, nutrition, well-being and cognitive development. They offset disadvantage and inequality and lead to better achievement in primary school. The comprehensive care and education of children below age 3 remains a neglected area. Meanwhile, access to pre-primary education for children aged 3 and above has improved, but remains very uneven. Many developing countries still have limited or non-existent pre-primary education systems.

Access to and participation in primary education have sharply increased since Dakar, and the number of out-of-school children dropped from 96 million to 72 million between 1999 and 2005. The Arab States, sub-Saharan Africa, and South and West Asia have shown substantial increases in enrolment ratios. However, progression through the primary grades and school completion remain important concerns nearly everywhere. Most countries, even those with relatively high primary enrolment ratios, need to address equity issues.

The learning needs of young people and adults remain woefully undocumented. This goal has been particularly neglected, in part because of the difficulty of defining and monitoring it. Many young people and adults acquire skills through informal means, or through a great variety of non-formal literacy, equivalency, life-skills and livelihood programmes.

Adult literacy remains a serious global issue: 774 million adults (of whom 64% are women) still lack basic literacy skills. Three regions (East Asia, South and West Asia, and sub-Saharan Africa) concentrate the vast majority of the one in five adults around the world still denied the right to literacy. Except in China, there has been little progress during the past decade in reducing the large number of illiterate adults.

The goal of eliminating gender disparities in both primary and secondary education by 2005 has been missed in a great majority of countries. While about 63% of countries with data have managed to eliminate gender disparities in primary education, only 37% have done so at secondary level.

Progress towards gender equality remains elusive. Sexual violence, insecure environments, and inadequate sanitation in schools disproportionately affect girls. Physical violence, by contrast, mainly affects boys. Gender-biased teacher attitudes, perceptions and expectations are common, and textbooks often reinforce stereotypes of gender-specific roles of adult men and women. Academic performance of boys and girls is converging, but fields of study and occupational orientations continue to be clustered by gender.

International and regional assessments, and a growing number of national assessments conducted since 1999 show that poor learning outcomes in language, mathematics and other subjects still characterize many countries worldwide. More than 60% of countries allocate fewer than 800 yearly hours of instruction in grades 1–6, even though recent research confirms positive correlations between instructional time and learning outcomes. Many developing countries, especially in sub-Saharan Africa, have crowded classrooms, poor school infrastructure and inadequate learning environments. Acute shortages of teachers are common, especially in sub-Saharan Africa, and South and West Asia, and even greater shortages of trained teachers in some countries restrict quality teaching and learning.

The EFA Development Index, calculated for 129 countries, points to multiple challenges in 25 countries that are far from achieving EFA as a whole, several of them characterized as fragile states. Two-thirds are in sub-Saharan Africa, but the group also includes some Arab States and countries of South and West Asia. Data are lacking for many countries, among them a number of fragile states, which are likely to suffer from limited education development.

Chapter 3
Countries on the move

This chapter focuses on three policy areas to illustrate how countries are developing and strengthening education systems in order to meet the basic learning needs of all children, youth and adults: the importance of having an institutional environment that promotes and supports education; strategies that countries have followed to expand access to education, especially for the poorest and most disadvantaged groups; and measures countries are taking to improve teaching and learning. Information is based on a review of policies and strategies adopted since 2000 by a selected group of thirty developing countries.

Governments' efforts to develop national education sector plans have gained momentum since 2000 but weak management capacity is a major barrier to progress in many low-income countries. Although civil society has played a much more visible advocacy role since Dakar, opportunities to engage with government in setting national education agendas remain limited.

Two other institutional trends are the increasing prominence of non-state providers, especially in countries where enrolment has risen sharply since 2000, and the decentralization of financial, political and administrative responsibilities for education. A common problem with decentralization is confusion about new roles and responsibilities, and there is a risk of making subnational inequality worse.

The Dakar Framework calls on governments to ensure that education systems explicitly identify, target and respond to the circumstances of the poorest and most marginalized populations. The need for a comprehensive approach not limited to universal primary education is a hallmark of the Dakar agenda.

Early childhood care and education has moved up on policy agendas, especially pre-primary education, but problems persist: not enough focus on under-3s; a lack of holistic approaches encompassing care, health and nutrition in addition to education; a poorly trained workforce; and a lack of coordination among providers.

The Dakar goal of halving the illiteracy rate by 2015 will not be met without a substantial scaling up of programmes. Although some governments in recent years have made efforts to develop national frameworks for meeting the needs of youth and adults, programmes remain marginal and underfunded.

Fourteen countries have abolished tuition fees for primary school since 2000. Evidence suggests that this measure encourages enrolment of the most disadvantaged children. In several countries where girls' enrolment has increased sharply since 1999, governments have taken special measures to increase their participation: improving school infrastructure, encouraging the recruitment of female teachers and making learning materials free.

More targeted approaches are needed to reach the most vulnerable and marginalized children. A number of countries in Latin America have introduced programmes transferring money directly to marginalized households that enrol their children. In Asia, stipend programmes have encouraged the transition of girls to secondary school. Flexible schooling, non-formal equivalency courses and bridging courses are among options being taken to provide for the learning needs of working children and youth.

To varying degrees, all countries need to improve the quality of education. There is no single strategy, but key elements include health and safety at school, enough learning time and textbooks, skilled and motivated teachers, and effective teaching methods. To address teacher shortages and limit costs, many governments are hiring teachers on temporary contracts. In the long term, governments need a policy framework assuring the integration of contract teachers with regular teachers into one career stream.

Classroom practices and curricula influence teaching and learning. Of particular importance are the use of children's mother tongue, regular assessment, enough textbooks, and access to information and communication technology. Many countries are moving towards a system of continuous pupil assessment. While there is a long way to go in promoting multilingualism and mother-tongue initial instruction in primary education, progress is being made.

Although the number of armed conflicts around the world is in decline, most wars continue to be fought in the developing world, with civilians suffering the most casualties. By investing in education in post-conflict situations, governments and the international community send out a forceful message about building a more peaceful future.

Chapter 4
Progress in financing Education for All

The ultimate responsibility for achieving EFA lies with governments, but for many countries, especially the poorest, progress also relies on support from donors.

While a majority of governments, particularly in the least developed countries and most noticeably in sub-Saharan Africa, have increased the financial priority given to education, too many countries continue to allocate very low shares of GNP and total government expenditure to education.

Education for All Global Monitoring Report

2008

Even when tuition fees have been abolished, costs of schooling remain an obstacle for the poorest families, although some governments have been innovative in devising ways to reduce the financial burden of schooling on households.

The overall amount of external financial support for basic education grew consistently between 2000 and 2004, particularly benefiting low-income countries, but declined in 2005. The amount and distribution of aid remain inadequate: too many donors are giving greater priority to higher levels of education, too high a share of education aid continues to go to middle-income rather than low-income countries, and levels of assistance to the latter vary widely by country.

The movement to improve the effectiveness of aid through greater harmonization between donors and alignment between donors and governments has accelerated since 2000. The Fast Track Initiative is one illustration of this, with education sector plans of thirty-one countries now endorsed. Multiple donors have been giving growing support for sector-wide programmes with sectoral budget support, including for education.

External aid for basic education does not automatically lead to improvement in educational outcomes. Quantitative studies suggest that the impact is positive, though less than generally anticipated, and more qualitative evaluations indicate that some objectives are much easier to reach through external funding than others.

Some major initiatives to increase levels of debt relief for highly indebted poor countries have been taken since 1999, first for bilateral debt and since 2005 for debt to multilateral institutions; these initiatives appear to have benefited basic education. In some countries governments and donors have worked well together since Dakar and been able to increase financial resources for basic education significantly. In others, however, this has not happened. Such countries, where education development is low, no strong reform programmes are in place and donor interest is lacking, are in the greatest danger of not fulfilling the goals set at Dakar.

Chapter 5
The way forward

As we move beyond the midway point from Dakar to 2015, key questions arise. What are the prospects for achieving the goals, and how can governments and actors at every level accelerate the movement towards quality education for all?

Projections suggest that, without accelerated efforts:

- 58 of the 86 countries that have not yet reached universal primary enrolment will not achieve it by 2015;

- 72 out of 101 countries will not succeed in halving their adult illiteracy rates by 2015;

- only 18 of the 113 countries that missed the gender parity goal at primary and secondary level in 2005 stand a chance of achieving it by 2015.

Countries making significant progress towards universal enrolment in primary education have tended to increase their education expenditure as a share of GNP. In countries where the progress has been slower, the share has decreased.

The analysis also signals that, although early childhood care and education is receiving increasing attention, participation rates remain relatively low in all developing regions except Latin America and the Caribbean. Sub-Saharan Africa, and South and West Asia, the two regions with the lowest literacy rates and the highest number of out-of-school children, need to pay much stronger attention to the inclusion of youth and adults in basic education through literacy and other programmes.

Across the world, more than 18 million new teachers will need to be employed by 2015. Sub-Saharan Africa faces the greatest challenge. To reach universal primary education the stock of teachers will have to increase from 2.4 million in 2004 to 4 million in 2015, in addition to the 2.1 million new teachers required to replace those leaving the teaching workforce.

Growth in per capita income across all low-income countries creates the potential for higher government expenditure on EFA, as does the increasing share of national income that governments across Asia and sub-Saharan Africa allocate to EFA. But governments face the need to spend more on secondary and tertiary education, as well as on basic education.

The amount of aid to basic education for low-income countries in 2004 and 2005 – an average of US$3.1 billion year – is clearly well below the estimated annual US$11 billion required to reach the EFA goals. If donors fulfil their pledges, annual bilateral aid to basic education will reach US$5 billion by 2010.

Overall, the thirty-two low-income countries identified as having the lowest levels of education development received one-third of total aid to basic education in 2004–2005, roughly the same as before Dakar; six of them received below-average amounts of aid to basic education per primary school-age child.

Towards an agenda to make EFA happen

At global level:

■ All stakeholders need to ensure that EFA remains a priority in the face of other emerging issues such as climate change and public health, and that the focus is not just on universal primary education.

■ Policy and implementation must emphasize inclusion, literacy, quality, capacity development and finance.

■ The international architecture for EFA needs to be made more effective.

National governments must:

■ take full responsibility for all the EFA goals, even if all services are not delivered through the public sector;

■ include the poorest and most marginalized children, youth and adults through better school infrastructure, elimination of tuition fees, provision of additional financial support to the poorest households and flexible schooling for working children and youth;

■ ensure that progress towards gender parity is maintained sustained and that gender equality is pursued;

■ recruit and train teachers on a vast scale;

■ greatly expand adult literacy programmes;

■ make sure pupils master basic skills by paying particular attention to teacher training, safe and healthy learning environments, mother tongue instruction and sufficient learning resources;

■ maintain public spending on basic education and expand it where necessary;

■ engage with civil society organizations in policy formulation, implementation and monitoring.

Bilateral and multilateral agencies alike need to:

■ increase the amount of aid they provide and deploy it differently;

■ make long-term commitments, to enable finance ministers to approve major policy initiatives;

■ pay special attention to sub-Saharan Africa and fragile states;

■ continue efforts on aligning aid behind country-led sector plans.

The evidence since Dakar is clear: determined national governments have made progress in all regions and increased aid has worked to support this progress. This momentum must be maintained and accelerated in the short time left to 2015 if the right to education at every age is to be fulfilled.

Discovering
the world:
a schoolgirl
examines
a globe in
Djibouti.

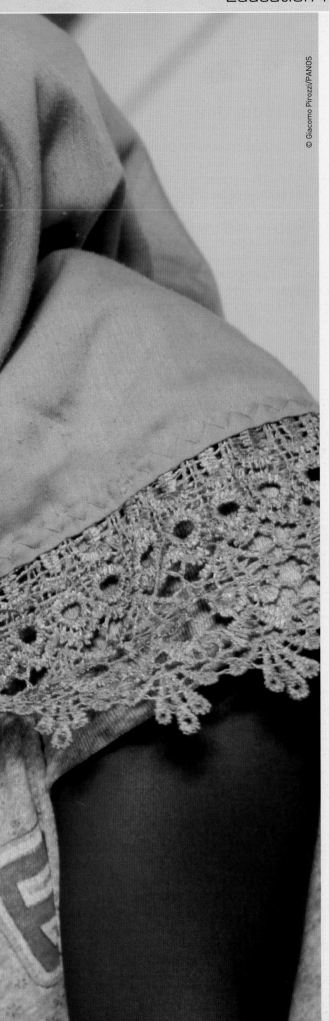

© Giacomo Pirozzi/PANOS

Chapter 1

The enduring relevance of Education for All

This edition of the Education for All *Global Monitoring Report* marks the midway point in an ambitious international movement to expand learning opportunities for every child, youth and adult by 2015. At the World Education Forum in 2000, 164 governments, 35 international institutions and 127 non-government organizations adopted the Dakar Framework for Action, promising to commit the necessary resources and effort to achieve a comprehensive and inclusive system of quality education for all. This introductory chapter examines the many developments occurring within education since 2000, and reflects on how these and other changes outside education have affected the Education for All vision.

Introduction 12

Education for All
as endorsed at the Dakar
World Education Forum 13

Achieving EFA
in a changing world 17

The 2008 *EFA
Global Monitoring Report* 28

Introduction

Ten years after the World Conference on Education for All held in Jomtien, Thailand, in 1990, many stakeholders maintained that insufficient progress had been made towards the realization of Education for All (EFA) and that a renewed commitment was necessary. The World Education Forum in Dakar, Senegal, adopted a Framework for Action focusing on the achievement by 2015 of six EFA goals. Gender parity, defined as equal figures for both genders in key education indicators at the primary and secondary levels, was meant to be achieved even earlier, by 2005.

The *EFA Global Monitoring Report* was established with the 2002 edition to monitor progress towards the EFA goals. Subsequent editions have each focused on a specific goal. Data are now available for 2005 and they show definitively that a large number of countries[1] did not achieve the gender parity goal. Halfway between 2000 and 2015, this *Global Monitoring Report* assesses the progress of the EFA movement since 2000 and identifies implications for the achievement of the Dakar agenda:

■ Have national governments followed up on their commitment to the EFA goals?

■ Has the international community provided adequate support to national governments?

■ Is the world, as a result, progressing towards EFA by 2015 and, if not, which are the goals that have been neglected and the countries or regions in greatest difficulty?

This Report emphasizes that:

■ The gender parity goal set for 2005 has been missed. Only 59 out of 181 countries with data have no gender disparities in both primary and secondary education. Most of these countries had already reached gender parity by 1999. Only three countries eliminated gender disparities between 1999 and 2005.

■ Very significant progress has been made in terms of enrolment in primary and lower secondary school, especially for girls and in

---

1. Throughout the Report, the word 'countries' should generally be understood as meaning 'countries and territories'.

Education for All Global Monitoring Report 2 0 0 8

some of the regions and countries that were facing the greatest challenges in 2000. A major equity challenge remains: to enrol and retain all children, especially the poor and disadvantaged, and those living in fragile states.[2]

■ Fields as important as early childhood care and education (ECCE) and learning opportunities for youth and adults, including in literacy, have suffered because of continued neglect from national governments and the international community. This is a further aspect of the equity challenge: giving all people an educational start (through ECCE) and compensating for past failures to do so (via youth and adult programmes, especially literacy).

■ The quality of education is increasingly perceived as the pervasive issue, across the world. Systematic assessments of learning outcomes, which have become more frequent in recent years, show problematically low and/or unequal levels of learning in most countries. Although the proportion of an age cohort entering the first grade of primary education is high or has increased in most developing countries, many children do not complete the primary cycle and even fewer master basic literacy and numeracy skills.

■ Reforming classroom teaching and learning, and the management of schools, so as to reduce gender inequality and improve the quality of education has proved difficult and not easily amenable to global policy prescriptions.

■ The flow of external financial support for basic education grew consistently between 2000 and 2004, but declined in 2005 and remains totally inadequate overall, compared to needs, in terms of both level and allocation.

■ The vision of EFA has tended to be reduced to an emphasis on provision of formal schooling at primary level, which is necessary but insufficient to achieve education 'for every citizen in every society'. This limited vision has particularly been reinforced at the international level, where the Millennium Development Goals (MDGs), with their focus on primary education, are dominant and with the growth of the Fast Track Initiative (FTI), which also largely limits itself to primary education, albeit in a broader sectoral context.

This introductory chapter presents Education for All as it was envisaged in Dakar in 2000 and reflects on developments both within and outside the education sphere that have since affected its realization. It then explains how the subsequent chapters will assess the EFA movement.

Education for All as endorsed at the Dakar World Education Forum

From the Jomtien Declaration to the Dakar Framework

In March 1990, the World Conference on Education for All, in Jomtien, Thailand, adopted the World Declaration on Education for All, which stated that 'everyone has a right to education', recognized the setbacks suffered by the education systems of many developing countries during the 1980s, and proclaimed a commitment to meeting the basic learning needs of every citizen in every society (Box 1.1). This concept of 'Education for All' meant much more than the expansion of existing formal school systems to foster economic growth through the spread of basic cognitive skills. It implied reflection on the nature and purpose of education in each society, given that it stressed basing education expansion on the actual needs of children, youth and adults, especially the excluded, as well as promoting culture and empowering citizens.

By the late 1990s, it was felt that, despite the emphasis on basic education repeated at many international conferences that followed Jomtien, the EFA agenda had essentially been neglected. An EFA Assessment conducted in 1999–2000, involving six regional conferences, revealed that, 'at the start of the new millennium':

(i) Of the more than 800 million children under 6 years of age, fewer than a third benefit[ted] from any form of early childhood education.

(ii) Some 113 million children, 60 per cent of whom [were] girls, [had] no access to primary schooling.

(iii) At least 880 million adults [were] illiterate, of whom the majority [were] women (UNESCO, 2000a, Commentary, para. 5).

The concept of EFA implies reflection on the nature and purpose of education in each society

2. See Box 1.4 on fragile states.

Box 1.1: The EFA perspective

Article 1 of the World Declaration on Education for All adopted at Jomtien defined the purpose of EFA as meeting basic learning needs:

1. Every person – child, youth and adult – shall be able to benefit from educational opportunities designed to meet their basic learning needs. These needs comprise both essential learning tools (such as literacy, oral expression, numeracy, and problem solving) and the basic learning content (such as knowledge, skills, values, and attitudes) required by human beings to be able to survive, to develop their full capacities, to live and work in dignity, to participate fully in development, to improve the quality of their lives, to make informed decisions, and to continue learning. The scope of basic learning needs and how they should be met varies with individual countries and cultures, and inevitably, changes with the passage of time.

2. The satisfaction of these needs empowers individuals in any society and confers upon them a responsibility to respect and build upon their collective cultural, linguistic and spiritual heritage, to promote the education of others, to further the cause of social justice, to achieve environmental protection, to be tolerant towards social, political and religious systems which differ from their own, ensuring that commonly accepted humanistic values and human rights are upheld, and to work for international peace and solidarity in an interdependent world.

3. Another and no less fundamental aim of educational development is the transmission and enrichment of common cultural and moral values. It is in these values that the individual and society find their identity and worth.

4. Basic education is more than an end in itself. It is the foundation for lifelong learning and human development on which countries may build, systematically, further levels and types of education and training.

Source: UNESCO (1990).

The state of education was particularly problematic in the countries of sub-Saharan Africa and South Asia, in the Arab States, in the least developed countries and in countries in conflict or undergoing reconstruction. In addition, several areas of concern were identified: the impact of the HIV/AIDS pandemic on education systems, the lack of early childhood education opportunities, school health, the education of girls and women, adult literacy and the provision of education in situations of crisis and emergency.

In April 2000, at the World Education Forum in Dakar, 164 country governments, together with representatives of regional groups, international organizations, donor agencies, non-government organizations and civil society, reaffirmed the Jomtien perspective on EFA and adopted a

Framework for Action designed to deliver on the commitments made since 1990, with the aim of achieving Education for All within a generation and sustaining it thereafter.[3]

EFA goals and strategies

There are three key elements of the Dakar Framework for Action. The first is a set of six goals to be achieved by all countries by 2015 (Box 1.2). The fact that part of the fifth goal – eliminating gender disparities in primary and secondary education (defined as disparities in key education indicators such as enrolment and completion ratios) – was to be achieved within five years rather than fifteen may have been more an expression of strong commitment to female education than a realistic target.

The MDGs, approved by world leaders at the United Nations Millenium Summit in 2000 and reaffirmed at the UN World Summit in 2005, form an agenda for reducing poverty and improving lives, and for the activities of many aid agencies. Two of them echo EFA goals 2 and 5:

- MDG 2. Achieve universal primary education. (Target: ensure that by 2015 children everywhere, boys and girls, will be able to complete a full course of good quality primary schooling.)

- MDG 3. Promote gender equality and empower women. (Target: eliminate gender disparity in primary and secondary education, preferably by 2005, and at all levels of education no later than 2015).

In addition, MDG 8 is to 'Develop a global partnership for development', encompassing the target of addressing the least developed countries' special needs through 'more generous official development assistance for countries committed to poverty reduction' (United Nations, 2001a).

The second element of the Dakar Framework for Action is a set of twelve strategies to be followed by all participants in the World Education Forum, whether governments or others (Box 1.3).

The Dakar Framework reaffirms the prominence of national governments in the expansion of education opportunities: 'The heart of EFA activity lies at the country level' (UNESCO, 2000a, Framework, para. 16). Governments are to implement national

3. Five international agencies jointly convened the Dakar forum: UNDP, UNESCO, UNFPA, UNICEF and the World Bank.

Box 1.2: The Dakar EFA goals

Paragraph 7 of the Dakar Framework for Action defines the EFA goals the governments, organizations, agencies, groups and associations represented at the World Education Forum pledged themselves to achieve:

1. expanding and improving comprehensive early childhood care and education, especially for the most vulnerable and disadvantaged children;

2. ensuring that by 2015 all children, particularly girls, children in difficult circumstances and those belonging to ethnic minorities, have access to and complete, free and compulsory primary education of good quality;

3. ensuring that the learning needs of all young people and adults are met through equitable access to appropriate learning and life-skills programmes;

4. achieving a 50 per cent improvement in levels of adult literacy by 2015, especially for women, and equitable access to basic and continuing education for adults;

5. eliminating gender disparities in primary and secondary education by 2005, and achieving gender equality in education by 2015, with a focus on ensuring girls' full and equal access to and achievement in basic education of good quality;

6. improving all aspects of the quality of education and ensuring excellence of all so that recognized and measurable learning outcomes are achieved by all, especially in literacy, numeracy and essential life skills.

Source: UNESCO (2000*a*).

Box 1.3: The Dakar EFA strategies

Paragraph 8 of the Dakar Framework lists twelve strategies:

1. mobilize strong national and international political commitment for education for all, develop national action plans and enhance significantly investment in basic education;

2. promote EFA policies within a sustainable and well-integrated sector framework clearly linked to poverty elimination and development strategies;

3. ensure the engagement and participation of civil society in the formulation, implementation and monitoring of strategies for educational development;

4. develop responsive, participatory and accountable systems of educational governance and management;

5. meet the needs of education systems affected by conflict, natural calamities and instability and conduct educational programmes in ways that promote mutual understanding, peace and tolerance, and that help to prevent violence and conflict;

6. implement integrated strategies for gender equality in education which recognize the need for changes in attitudes, values and practices;

7. implement as a matter of urgency education programmes and actions to combat the HIV/AIDS pandemic;

8. create safe, healthy, inclusive and equitably resourced educational environments conducive to excellence in learning, with clearly defined levels of achievement for all;

9. enhance the status, morale and professionalism of teachers;

10. harness new information and communication technologies to help achieve EFA goals;

11. systematically monitor progress towards EFA goals and strategies at the national, regional and international levels; and

12. build on existing mechanisms to accelerate progress towards education for all.

Source: UNESCO (2000*a*).

A key element of the Dakar Framework constitutes an international pledge

plans of action for EFA (analysed in the 2006 Report: UNESCO, 2005*a*, pp. 76-84), integrated into their broader poverty reduction and development strategies, and developed in partnership with civil society (see, for example, UNESCO, 2006*a*, pp. 175-7).

The third key element of the Dakar Framework has to do with resources and constitutes an international pledge. Budget priorities should be altered as far as necessary to achieve the goals, and the international community promises to support countries that lack the necessary resources: 'Political will and stronger national leadership are needed for the effective and successful implementation of national plans in each of the

countries concerned. However, political will must be underpinned by resources. The international community acknowledges that many countries currently lack the resources to achieve education for all within an acceptable time-frame. ... We affirm that no countries seriously committed to education for all will be thwarted in their achievement of this goal by a lack of resources' (UNESCO, 2000*a*, Framework, para. 10).

Both the Jomtien
Declaration and
the Dakar
Framework for
Action draw on
the Universal
Declaration of
Human Rights

EFA as a human right

Both the Jomtien Declaration and the Dakar
Framework for Action draw on the Universal
Declaration of Human Rights (United Nations, 1948)
and subsequent international treaties. These
treaties establish the right to education and to
non-discrimination, and have the force of law
for the governments that ratify them. Specific
provisions in these conventions emphasize free
and compulsory primary education, and they also
provide a backbone for the other EFA goals (Table 1.1).

Table 1.1: Selected international human rights treaties relevant to the EFA goals

Instrument	Components relevant to Education for All	Ratifications[1]
International Bill of Human Rights:	Free and compulsory elementary (primary) education. Accessibility to higher levels of education on the basis of merit. No discrimination.	
• Universal Declaration of Human Rights (1948)		
• International Covenant on Civil and Political Rights (1966)		160 (17)
• International Covenant on Economic, Social and Cultural Rights (1966)		156 (14)
Convention concerning Discrimination in Respect of Employment and Occupation [No. 111. Adopted by ILO, 1958]	Protection of all persons in vocational training and employment from discrimination (based on distinction, exclusion or preference) made on the basis of race, colour, sex, religion, political opinion, national extraction or social origin.	166 (26)
Convention against Discrimination in Education [Adopted by UNESCO, 1960]	Free and compulsory primary education. Governments shall formulate, develop and apply a national policy tending to promote equality of opportunity and of treatment. No discrimination in access to or quality of education.	94 (7)
International Convention on the Elimination of All Forms of Racial Discrimination (1965)	Right to education and training with no distinction as to race, colour or national or ethnic origin. Adopt measures, particularly in the field of teaching, education, culture and information, to combat prejudices which lead to racial discrimination.	173 (19)
Convention on the Elimination of All Forms of Discrimination against Women (1979)	• Eliminate discrimination against women in the field of education. • Ensure equality of access to same curricula, qualified teaching staff, and school facilities and equipment of the same quality. • Elimination of stereotyped concept of the roles of men and women by encouraging coeducation. • Reduction of female dropout rates; organization of programmes for those who left school prematurely. • Access to health information, including reproductive health.	185 (21)
Convention concerning Indigenous and Tribal Peoples in Independent Countries [No. 169. Adopted by ILO, 1989]	• Equal opportunities to obtain education. • Education responsive to culture and needs of indigenous peoples. • Educational measures to eliminate prejudices.	18 (5)
Convention on the Rights of the Child (1989)	• Right to free and compulsory primary schooling without any type of discrimination. Access to higher levels of education. • Emphasis on child well-being and development, encouragement of measures to support child care.	193 (3)
International Convention on the Protection of the Rights of All Migrant Workers and Members of their Families (1990)	• Equality of treatment with nationals of the country concerned for access to education. • Facilitation of teaching of mother tongue and culture for the children of migrant workers.	37 (25)
Convention concerning the Prohibition and Immediate Action for the Elimination of the Worst Forms of Child Labour [No. 182. Adopted by ILO, 1999]	Access to free basic education and to vocational training (wherever possible and appropriate) for all children removed from the worst forms of child labour.	165 (160)
Optional Protocol to the Convention on the Rights of the Child on the Involvement of Children in Armed Conflict (2000)	• Limit on voluntary recruitment of children into national armed forces, ban on recruitment of all children into independent armed groups. • Condemnation of the targeting of children and schools during armed conflicts.	117 (117)
Convention on the Rights of Persons with Disabilities (2006)[2]	• No exclusion from free and compulsory primary education, or from secondary education, on the basis of disability. • Assurance of an inclusive education system at all levels and lifelong learning.	2 (2)

1. Total number of ratifications as of August 2007 (ratifications since Dakar in parentheses).
2. Not yet into force. 109 countries and the European Community have signed the Convention and 64 have signed the Optional Protocol.
Five countries have ratified the Convention and three countries have ratified the Optional Protocol.
Sources: ILO (1958, 1989, 1999); OHCHR (1965, 1966*a*, 1966*b*, 1979, 1989, 1990, 2000, 2006); UNESCO (1960); United Nations (1948).

In particular, the Convention on the Rights of the Child constitutes a landmark commitment due to its breadth in terms of the rights that are recognized and to its reach across countries. It reaffirms the right to free and compulsory primary schooling without any type of discrimination, and also emphasizes child well-being and development. This aspect was recently confirmed by the Committee on the Rights of the Child in its General Comment No. 7, which calls attention to governments' obligations to formulate policies aimed specifically at the early childhood phase, considered to range from birth to age 8 (Committee on the Rights of the Child et al., 2006). The right to literacy has also been clearly established (UNESCO, 2005a).

The ratification of international treaties implies that governments have to translate the provisions into national legislation. Some of the conventions listed in Table 1.1 have continued to be ratified since 2000. However, the reality is that political commitments reflected in declarations and legal obligations contained in ratified treaties are both far from being enshrined in the national legal frameworks of many countries, much less enforced when they are.

Achieving EFA in a changing world

The EFA agenda rests on a belief that public policy can radically transform education systems and their relationship to society within a few years, given adequate political will and resources. This belief extends not only to the provision of basic facilities for formal primary schooling, which several developing countries have indeed proven able to dramatically expand over short periods, but also to subtler aspects of the school system such as gender stereotypes and the relationship between teachers and pupils, on which the achievement of Goals 5 and 6, respectively, depends. While the Expanded Commentary on the Dakar Framework states that achieving EFA by 2015 'is a realistic and achievable goal' (UNESCO, 2000a, para. 5), doubts have been expressed concerning the 2015 target; for many countries this would imply, for instance, a speedier transition from elitist to near-universal enrolment in primary education than has ever been observed (Clemens et al., 2004).

In fact, though, there are now new opportunities to speed up the transition to EFA, making the Dakar

Framework more realistic than comparable policy statements made in earlier decades. Few countries still have very low and stagnating enrolment ratios in primary education. Indeed, most developing countries, including those with the largest populations, have either reached relatively high enrolment ratios or are experiencing very steep increases (Wils, 2002). Yet, the changing global context increases the urgency of achieving EFA; and, while national governments and international organizations have indeed put a renewed emphasis on education since 2000, the international architecture planned at Dakar has yet to be fully effective.

Global trends affecting education

The global prospect for achieving EFA is influenced by trends in such diverse and interrelated areas as demography, urbanization, migration, health, and economic and political systems. Changes in these areas, discussed below, have important consequences for government resource allocation (Bloom et al., 2003; Mason, 2006).

A different change has to do with the prominence of EFA among global issues. Its relative priority is understandably, if unacceptably, at risk because of an increased focus since Dakar on other global issues, notably climate change.

Population growth, urbanization and health

The growth rate of the global population (currently 6.7 billion) is declining, reflecting sustained reductions in fertility. However, while the population level in most developed countries remains unchanged, or is even decreasing, four out of five new births occur in developing countries, and the least developed countries[4] stand apart from other developing countries: their average annual rate of population change will be 2.6 times that of the others until mid-century.

People under age 15 account for 42% of the total population in these countries (United Nations, 2007). As a result, the very countries that are furthest from universal school participation at primary and secondary levels, especially in sub-Saharan Africa, will continue to have to enrol increasingly large cohorts over the next few decades. Meanwhile, many other countries that have achieved relatively high enrolment ratios will see their school-age population decline, which

The EFA agenda rests on a belief that public policy can radically transform education systems and their relationship to society within a few years

4. See list of least developed countries in annex, statistical tables, introduction.

CHAPTER 1

(though agriculture remains the largest in sub-Saharan Africa, and South and West Asia), and services now account for about two-thirds of global output (69% in high-income countries, 55% in middle-income countries and 44% in low-income countries) (Primo Braga and Brokhaug, 2005). At the same time, industries in developed countries, faced with surging labour costs or with labour shortages, are relocating in developing countries with less expensive and more plentiful labour, supporting mobility of workers across borders and increasing demand for female labour.

Beyond this, a more knowledge-intensive economy is emerging in many parts of the world, characterized by closer links among science, technological innovation, productivity and countries' competitive advantages. Quality primary education and the development of more complex secondary education systems are crucial, as they can promote higher-order skills, problem-solving, critical thinking, even creativity – which are the foundation for the development of higher education and research.

Women, in particular, stand to benefit from the development of information and communication technology infrastructure, as it appears to reinforce gender equality improvements in both education and employment (Chen, 2004). Although demographic trends noted above have been accompanied by an increase in female labour force participation rates worldwide since the

1980s, improvements in the quality of women's employment has not necessarily followed. Women are more likely than men to work in low-productivity jobs in agriculture and services because they lack education or access to the formal labour market (ILO, 2007).

Democracy and governance: small signs of progress

The democracy gap between countries advancing in political democratization and those where basic political and human rights are consistently violated (Karatnycky, 2002) appears to be somewhat narrowing compared to the 1990s. The number of armed conflicts is on the decline (Project Ploughshares, 2007) and a growing number of countries have acquired a higher level of freedom regarding individual political and civil rights, according to one measure (Figure 1.1). This might help promote greater involvement of civil society in education policy, as the Dakar Framework for Action envisages.[16] At national level, non-violent civic groups are key to creating transitions to democracy and sustaining fledgling democratic reforms (Karatnycky and Ackerman, 2005). At international level, civil society organizations have garnered strength and momentum (Qureshi, 2004), but it is unclear whether they affect decision-making (Cardoso, 2003; Nadoo, 2003).

The higher the democratic accountability, for example as measured by levels of freedom of expression and suffrage rights, the lower the level of corruption (World Bank, 2006a). The World Bank's measurement of governance suggests that, on average, levels of government corruption have not been significantly reduced worldwide in the past few years.[17] Several countries have made significant progress on various dimensions of governance since 1996, however, including Botswana, Ghana, Mozambique, Senegal and the United Republic of Tanzania, as well as Bulgaria and Romania, despite low regional performance in sub-Saharan Africa, Central Asia, and Central and Eastern Europe in 2006.

Improvement of governance, including reduction of corruption, is key to achievement of the EFA goals, which demand considerable political commitment and management capacity. Strengthening and supporting 'fragile states' (Box 1.4) is thus emerging as a key priority on the EFA agenda.

16. See Dakar Framework for Action, para. 8, (iii).

17. Since the late 1990s, the World Bank has published an international comparison of governance and corruption based on several hundred variables from thirty-two sources measuring six dimensions of governance: voice and accountability; political stability and absence of violence; government effectiveness; regulatory quality; rule of law; and control of corruption (World Bank, 2006a).

Figure 1.1: Global political and civil rights, percentage of countries by status, 1990-2006

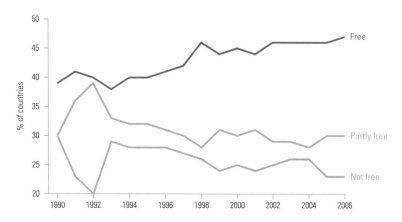

Note: The level of freedom is based on surveys of political rights and civil liberties. The average of these two ratings ranges from 1 (high freedom) to 7 (low freedom); countries with a rating of 1 to 2.5 are considered 'free', 3 to 5 'partly free' and 5.5 to 7 'not free'.
Source: Freedom House (2007).

Box 1.4: The emerging concept of 'fragile states'

International, civil and ethnic conflict, extreme and prolonged economic hardship, weak governance or high levels of inequality may cause state institutions to weaken, fail or collapse. Affected countries could likely benefit from aid but do not generally meet the criteria of policy ownership and partnership required by development agencies. A concept of 'fragile', 'failing' or 'failed' states has been emerging to describe such situations.

An international consensus on a definition of such states has yet to be reached. Often, the concept remains imprecise, especially regarding whether to distinguish between failing economic systems during relatively peaceful times and countries in conflict (Châtaigner and Gaulme, 2005). Empirically, though, the combination of poverty and stagnation substantially increases proneness to civil war (Collier et al., 2003). Save the Children created the 'conflict-affected fragile states' concept to combine these two factors for states with a history of recent armed conflict (Save the Children, 2007b). Recognizing the complexity involved in defining the notion, this Report uses the OECD Development Assistance Committee's list of thirty-five fragile states, shown in Table 1.2. More than half a billion people live in these states (see annex, Statistical Table 1).

Table 1.2: Fragile states, 2005

Sub-Saharan Africa (20)	Angola[1]; Burundi[1,2]; C. A. R.[1]; Chad[1,2]; Comoros[1]; Congo; Côte d'Ivoire[2]; D. R. Congo[1,2]; Eritrea[1]; the Gambia[1]; Guinea[1]; Guinea-Bissau[1]; Liberia[1]; Niger[1]; Nigeria[2]; S. Tome/Principe[1]; Sierra Leone[1]; Somalia[1,2]; Togo[1]; Zimbabwe
Arab States (2)	Djibouti[1]; Sudan[1,2]
Central Asia (2)	Tajikistan; Uzbekistan
East Asia and the Pacific (9)	Cambodia[1]; Kiribati[1]; Lao PDR[1]; Myanmar[1,2]; Papua New Guinea; Solomon Is[1]; Timor-Leste[1]; Tonga; Vanuatu[1]
South and West Asia (1)	Afghanistan[1,2]
Latin America/ Caribbean (1)	Haiti[1,2]

1. Least developed countries.
2. State in armed conflict in 2006.
Note: Thirty of the fragile states are in the bottom two quintiles of the World Bank's Country Policy and Institutions Assessment (CPIA) and five others are unrated by the CPIA. The CPIA is composed of sixteen indicators measuring four categories: economic management, structural policies, policies for social inclusion/equity and public sector management and institutions.
Sources: OECD-DAC (2006c, 2006d, 2007a); Project Ploughshares (2007); World Bank (2007a).

Efforts to increase and harmonize aid

Development aid has been sharply increasing since 2000, even though it has not yet regained its level of the early 1990s. Official development assistance (ODA) from donor countries belonging to the Organisation for Economic Co-operation and Development's Development Assistance Committee (OECD-DAC) has grown by 9% annually since 1999, and the rate of growth was even higher, at 13%, between 2002 and 2005 (Figure 1.2). In 2005, ODA amounted to US$106.4 billion.[18] Several major bilateral donors significantly increased their net ODA disbursements between 2004 and 2005, in particular Germany (+93%), Japan (+81%), the United Kingdom (+51%) and the United States (+51%). However, preliminary data indicate that in 2006, total ODA was 5.1% less than in 2005 (OECD-DAC, 2007b).

Development aid has been sharply increasing since 2000

Figure 1.2: Total official development assistance, net disbursements, 1992–2005

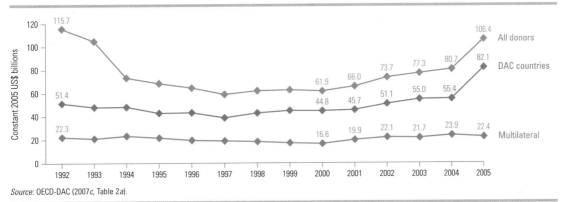

Source: OECD-DAC (2007c, Table 2a).

18. Non-DAC donor countries disbursed about US$1.5 billion, the Middle Eastern Funds disbursed US$2.5 billion and all other official bilateral donors disbursed probably less than US$3 billion.

CHAPTER 1

> If debt relief and humanitarian aid are excluded, aid to Africa has barely increased since 2004

The share of total ODA received by low-income countries increased between 1999 and 2004 from 39% to 46%. However, between 2004 and 2005, the increase in total ODA disbursements mainly benefited middle-income countries. The shift in focus to middle-income countries is mostly due to large contributions to Iraq, to which 20% of total ODA was allocated in 2005. Aid to Iraq has also changed the regional distribution of total ODA disbursements significantly, with the Arab States becoming the second-largest regional recipient, after sub-Saharan Africa (Figure 1.3).

Between 1999 and 2004, debt relief increased rapidly from 5% to 22% of total ODA. The increase has been particularly pronounced since 2002. Between 2004 and 2005, debt relief increased by US$18.5 billion out of a total increase in ODA of US$21 billion, heavily dominated by the Paris Club[19] settlements with Iraq in 2004 and Nigeria in 2005. The growing amount of debt relief is a positive development for low-income countries, as it allows governments to use the savings for programmes, including education. However, it does raise the issue of the sustainability of the increase in total ODA for donors. Since debt relief is likely to diminish in the immediate future as the stock of remaining debt decreases significantly, donors will need to expand other types of aid if they are to meet their pledges.

During the Gleneagles Summit of 2005, the G8 countries made substantial commitments to increase aid through a variety of means, including traditional development assistance and debt relief.

They announced an increase in ODA, compared with 2004, of around US$50 billion a year for all developing countries by 2010, including US$25 billion a year for Africa (Table 1.3). While sub-Saharan Africa is still the largest recipient of total ODA, however, the challenge is significant for donors. Most of the increase in ODA in 2004 was primarily due to debt relief. If debt relief and humanitarian aid are excluded, aid to Africa has barely increased since 2004. Donors will have to accelerate their plans to scale up aid to Africa if they are to maintain the credibility of their promises to double aid to the continent by 2010 (OECD, 2007a).

In addition to renewed attention and commitments about the volume of aid, there is a shift to trying to make aid more effective. Donors are attempting to better harmonize their aid with each other and with developing countries' priorities, sectoral budget support is increasingly popular and there is greater attention to governance issues in developing countries.

To summarize, global developments since Dakar have made achievement of the EFA goals by 2015 more likely than was imagined in 2000 in many regions: demography implies that school-age cohorts are declining in many countries or will soon do so, while sustained economic growth, the reduction in conflict, the rise of civil society and the availability of more development aid increase the feasibility of ambitious education policies. However, these favourable factors are much weaker in the regions and countries that are furthest from the EFA goals. For instance, sub-Saharan Africa still faces increasing school-age cohorts over the next few decades, its economic growth generally remains much lower than that of Asia and promises of increased aid are fragile.

Besides these changes in the context in which education systems function, the years since Dakar have witnessed changes in education policy.

Trends in education research and policy

The previous section discussed the changing context of EFA outside education. In addition, EFA since 2000 has been affected by developments within education: research findings that particularly underline the importance of quality; legal actions to enforce the right to education, including an increase

Figure 1.3: Regional distribution of total official development assistance, 1999–2000 and 2004–2005

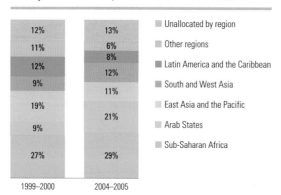

1999–2000	2004–2005	
12%	13%	Unallocated by region
11%	6%	Other regions
12%	8%	Latin America and the Caribbean
9%	12%	South and West Asia
19%	11%	East Asia and the Pacific
9%	21%	Arab States
27%	29%	Sub-Saharan Africa

Note: 'Other regions' category includes North America and Western Europe, Central Asia and Central and Eastern Europe.
Source: OECD-DAC (2007c).

19. The Paris Club is an informal group of official creditors whose role is to find coordinated and sustainable solutions to the payment difficulties experienced by debtor nations (Paris Club, 2007).

in the number of countries with compulsory education laws; growing attention to basic education (though not universal agreement on what the term 'basic' means); a major and growing emphasis on education quality, which has become the principal issue in education for almost all countries, developing or developed; and development in the international architecture for EFA, notably the emergence of the Fast Track Initiative. Yet, by and large, developments in education fall short of what was envisaged at Dakar.

Renewed research evidence on the benefits of education

Research continues to confirm the broad benefits of extending education systems to more people and for longer periods, but points to the need for complementary policies in other social programmes (Hannum and Buchmann, 2004):

- Cognitive neuroscience (see Abadzi (2006) and OECD (2007b) for introductions) shows that early childhood is a critical period for the acquisition of certain cognitive skills and reinforces the need for adequate stimulation of young children. This strengthens the case for early childhood care and education programmes – the special theme of the 2007 *Global Monitoring Report* (UNESCO, 2006a; also see Young and Richardson, 2007).

- Synergies between education and nutrition and health policies are emerging. Better-fed and healthier children are more likely to enrol, develop and learn in school. In addition, schools offer a favourable context for nutrition and health intervention. An experiment in Kenya showed that deworming could have a dramatic impact on health and education outcomes at very low cost (Miguel and Kremer, 2004). Midday meals are more costly and difficult to organize, but their benefits also include the socialization experience they represent (Vermeersch, 2003).

- Development economists have shown that more educated and literate adults/parents have healthier lives, reduced fertility and less disease-prone children with more nutritious diets (Duflo and Breierova, 2002; Schultz, 2002). Cross-cultural studies in Mexico, Nepal, Venezuela and Zambia (LeVine et al., 1991, 2001, 2004) establish how education transforms women's aspirations, skills and models of learning, with positive implications for their children.

Table 1.3: The Gleneagles aid commitments, 2005

	Commitments	Reference to Africa
Canada	• Double international assistance from 2001 to 2010	• Assistance to Africa doubling from 2003/04 to 2008/09
European Union	• Collective target for ODA to reach 0.56% of GNI by 2010 and 0.70% by 2015 • Increase ODA from €34.5 billion in 2004 to €67 billion in 2010	• At least 50% of the increase should go to sub-Saharan Africa
France	• Target for ODA to reach 0.50% of GNI by 2007 and 0.70% by 2012	• Allocate two-thirds of commitments to Africa
Germany	• Target for ODA to reach 0.51% of GNI by 2010 and 0.70% by 2015	
Italy	• Target for ODA to reach 0.51% of GNI by 2010 and 0.70% by 2015	
Japan	• Increase ODA by $10 billion in aggregate between 2005 and 2010	• Double ODA to Africa between 2005 and 2008
Russian Federation		• Cancelled and committed to cancel US$11.3 billion worth of debt owed by African countries, including US$2.2 billion of debt relief to the HIPC Initiative
United Kingdom	• Target for ODA to reach 0.70% of GNI by 2013	• Double bilateral spending in Africa between 2003/04 and 2007/08
United States		• Double aid to sub-Saharan Africa between 2004 and 2010

Source: Group of 8 (2005, Annex 2).

- While individual outcomes such as health and income benefit from increased years of schooling completed, education expansion does not necessarily translate into reduced inequality. Sociological research has consistently shown that expanding educational access and participation only rarely reduces the relative advantage of elite children over those from less privileged backgrounds (Hannum and Buchmann, 2004; Walters, 2000). Children from ethnic and cultural minorities are typically the last to benefit from the creation and expansion of new schools, as has been observed in Nepal (Stash and Hannum, 2001) and China (Hannum, 2002). Similarly, reducing gender disparities in education is a necessary, but insufficient, condition for gender equality. In many countries where enrolment parity has been reached, inequality in women's employment persists, for instance in the Republic of Korea (Cameron et al., 2001), and in Israel and South Africa (Mickelson et al., 2001). Supplementary policies, such as promoting non-discrimination in the labour market, are required if the potential equalizing benefits of education expansion are to materialize.

Education expansion does not necessarily translate into reduced inequality

■ Research has consistently shown that more educated people tend to be more civically and politically engaged and more likely to vote (see Dee (2004) and Milligan et al. (2003) on electoral participation in the United States and the United Kingdom). Paradoxically, though, while education levels have been rising in OECD countries, voter participation has been declining in many of them (OECD, 2007c). More broadly, the relationship between education expansion and democratization remains uncertain (Bratton et al. (1999) about Zambia); there are indications that the expansion of higher education may have a stronger impact than the expansion of basic education.

Recent social science research highlights the likelihood that the benefits of education result not only from the number of years in school, but also from acquiring basic literacy and numeracy skills. The quality of education may even be more beneficial than its quantity (Hanushek and Wößmann, 2007):

Enforcing the right to education implies a commitment to mobilize the necessary resources

■ Much cross-national research has shown the significant positive impact of the quantity of primary and secondary education (measured as enrolment ratios or average years of schooling) on aggregate economic growth (Chabbott and Ramirez, 2000; Topel, 1999). Nevertheless, differences in models, data sources and estimation procedures have resulted in some inconsistent findings (Krueger and Lindahl, 2001). Recent studies have examined the economic impact of the *quality* of education (using aggregate pupil test scores, mainly in mathematics and language), not just quantitative expansion; some studies find that measures of quality have a stronger association with economic growth than measures of quantity (Hanushek and Kimko, 2000; Hanushek and Wößmann, 2007; Ramirez et al., 2006; Temple, 2001). If this is borne out, it has major implications for education policy design, as the expected benefits of education are unlikely to materialize if expansion of school systems is not accompanied by improvement in the functioning of schools.

Supporting the right to education

The right to education requires not only constitutional guarantees and legislation, as discussed above, but also legal enforcement. Similarly, legal actions can lead to improved legislation and constitutions.

A landmark ruling by the Supreme Court in India in 1993 led to mobilization by civil society calling for effective guarantees of the right to education. The court ruled that the right to education up to age 14 provided by the Constitution was a fundamental right, enforceable by the courts, and that parents whose children lacked access to government schools could sue the government. A 2002 law amended the Constitution to this effect, guaranteeing free and compulsory education for children aged 6 to 14 (Aradhya and Kashyap, 2006).

The International Bill of Human Rights and the Convention on the Rights of the Child commit ratifying governments to guarantee the right to free, compulsory primary education. By 2005, 95% of 203 countries had passed compulsory education laws, 23 of them since Dakar (Table 1.4). The duration of compulsory education varies. Twenty-two of the countries that had compulsory education in place at the time of Dakar have since decreased its duration, while twenty have increased it. When countries lack the financial resources to pay for and enforce compulsory education laws, some decide to reduce the gap between policy intentions and realities. In 2005, the duration of compulsory education ranged from five years (in Bangladesh, Equatorial Guinea, the Islamic Republic of Iran, the Lao People's Democratic Republic, Myanmar, Nepal and Pakistan) to twelve or more years in a range of countries including Antigua and Barbuda, Azerbaijan, Belgium, Germany, the Netherlands, Palau, Poland, and Saint Kitts and Nevis. (annex, Statistical tables 4).

Many countries provide no constitutional guarantee of *free* primary education, and even those that nominally do so may have policies in effect contradicting this principle. Thirty-eight out of 173 countries recently reporting, i.e. roughly one in five, do not constitutionally guarantee free and compulsory primary education, and the proportion rises to one in three if North America and Western Europe are excluded (Tomasevski, 2006).[20] A survey conducted among education task team leaders at the World Bank revealed that out of 93 countries, only 16 had no school charges of any type for primary education (Bentaouet-Kattan, 2006).

Enforcing the right to education implies a commitment to mobilize the necessary resources (Singh, 2007). A few countries have opted to secure resources by introducing funding provisions in

20. For the United States, Tomasevski (2006) takes into account state constitutions instead of the federal one. In the United Kingdom, conventions, statutes and the common law establish the right to education and guarantee free primary education.

national legislation. For example, Mexico's 2003 Law of Education allocates 8% of GDP to public education (Singh, 2007). Brazil and Indonesia have constitutionally defined allocations. The 1988 Constitution of Brazil earmarked 18% of national tax revenue, and 25% of that collected by states and municipalities, to education. Amendments in 1996 and 2006 established a fund to guarantee minimum levels of spending per pupil in basic education in all states and municipalities. The 2006 amendment allocated 20% of total state tax revenue to this fund, which redistributes resources among subnational governments in proportion to the number of pupils in basic education – including pre-primary school – to achieve the established minimums per pupil. That legislation also included provisions for funding school quality improvements, required a minimum to be established for teacher pay and provided for an allocation from the education fund for teacher salaries (Brazil Federal Senate, 2007). The Constitution of Indonesia was amended in 2002 to mandate spending for education corresponding to 20% of the country's central and regional budgets. A year later, the Education Law excluded salaries from this provision, thereby increasing the portion for discretionary expenses. However, public education spending in Indonesia is significantly lower than the Constitution stipulates (World Bank, 2007e).

Basic education as a central policy concern

Since Dakar, basic education has gained considerable currency in international organizations and among national education authorities, continuing a trend started in the 1970s and confirmed in Jomtien. While the International Standard Classification of Education (ISCED) considers primary and lower secondary education to be the first two stages of basic education (UNESCO, 1997), in the Dakar Framework the term refers to all programmes providing for basic learning needs – for example, pre-primary and primary education as well as youth and adult programmes, including literacy and equivalency education. In this context, basic education is a synonym for the broad EFA agenda. Similarly, for the OECD-DAC Secretariat basic education encompasses early childhood education, primary education and basic life skills for youths and adults, including literacy.

More and more countries, especially in the developing world, are using the term 'basic education' in official documents. At the end of

Table 1.4: Changes in compulsory education laws since Dakar (to 2005)

Compulsory education law passed after 2000	Change in duration of compulsory education	
	Extended since 2000	Reduced since 2000
Aruba, Bahrain, Bhutan, Brunei Darussalam, Burundi, Ethiopia, the Gambia, Lesotho, Malawi, Maldives, Mauritania, Mozambique, Nepal, Oman, Pakistan, Papua New Guinea, Qatar, Saudi Arabia, Singapore, Swaziland, Timor-Leste, Vanuatu, Zambia	Belarus, Bulgaria, Djibouti, Dominican Republic, The former Yugoslav Republic of Macedonia, Georgia, Ghana, Kiribati, Mauritius, Montserrat, Nauru, Nicaragua, Niger, Palau, Thailand, Ukraine, United Arab Emirates, United States, Uzbekistan, Venezuela	Albania, Cameroon, Côte d'Ivoire, Democratic People's Republic of Korea, Egypt, Guinea, Haiti, Jamaica, Kyrgyzstan, Lao People's Democratic Republic, Morocco, Namibia, Nigeria, Romania, Rwanda, Sao Tome and Principe, Serbia and Montenegro, Somalia, Sudan, Suriname, Tajikistan, Tuvalu

Sources: Annex, Statistical Table 4; UNESCO (2003b).

the 1970s, 14% of national education systems employed the term; by the 1990s, 38% did so. Between 2000 and 2006, almost two-thirds (63%) of the 182 countries with data referred to some segment of their education system as basic education. In most instances the term is meant to capture a country's commitment to the universalization of a cycle beyond primary education. Duration varies: in 48% of the countries, basic education consists of nine years of schooling; in about a third it consists of ten years (20%) or eight years (11%). In the remaining countries it consists of either seven or fewer years or eleven or more years (UNESCO-IBE, 2007d).

An analysis of 113 national definitions of basic education in relation to the formal education system shows that, in two-thirds of the countries, the term follows the ISCED and covers primary and lower secondary education (Table 1.5). In the remaining third, the term is equivalent to primary education only or to primary plus some pre-primary or secondary education.

Addressing the issue of school quality

Since Dakar there has been increasing interest in, and discussion of, education quality among policy-makers, donors and international organizations:

■ Important high-level meetings involving education ministers (and, sometimes, finance ministers) have focused extensively on education quality issues (e.g. International Conference on Education, Geneva, 2004; Intergovernmental Meeting of the Regional Education Project for Latin America and the Caribbean, Buenos Aires, 2007).

Since Dakar there has been increasing interest in education quality

Table 1.5: National definitions of basic education

Basic education definitions (number of countries)		Countries
Primary education only	(8)	Cape Verde, Ethiopia, Guinea-Bissau, Haiti, Maldives, Mozambique, Nicaragua, Portugal
Primary education plus at least one year of pre-primary education	(17)	Albania, Bhutan, Botswana, Brazil, Burkina Faso, Burundi, Cameroon, Democratic Republic of the Congo, Djibouti, Ecuador, Guinea, Macao (China), Mexico, the Niger, Panama, Tunisia, Zimbabwe
Primary education plus lower secondary and at least one year of upper secondary education	(7)	Argentina, Brazil, Republic of Korea, Oman, Philippines, Slovenia, Saint Lucia
Primary education plus some pre-primary and lower secondary and some upper secondary education	(5)	China, Kenya, Myanmar, Peru, Thailand
Primary and lower secondary education	(76)	Remaining countries which use the term basic education

Source: UNESCO-IBE (2007d).

The number of national and international assessments of learning outcomes has risen significantly

- An influential recent report recommends that countries and development partners emphasize learning outcomes as well as school access to improve the economic and social gains from investment in primary education (World Bank Independent Evaluation Group, 2006b).

- The Fast Track Initiative (FTI) plans to incorporate quality measures such as the monitoring of learning outcomes as additional criteria in the endorsement of FTI country plans (FTI technical meetings, Moscow, 2006; Cairo, 2006; Bonn, 2007).

- Several new UNESCO initiatives focus on education quality topics: teacher training and development in sub-Saharan Africa and learning processes (UNESCO, 2007a, 2007b).

- In 2006 international organizations and NGOs participated in a Global Action Week, highlighting quality issues such as teacher supply and pre- and in-service training.

- The number of national and international assessments of learning outcomes has risen significantly (see Chapter 2).

Increased attention to quality does not necessarily imply that quality is improving, but does indicate that it is increasingly recognized as of critical importance, a view supported by new research as discussed above. To be sure, the increased attention to quality issues in diverse policy forums mainly means the incorporation of quality themes in official statements, intentions and plans. This Report examines whether, to what extent and by which effective means there have been actual improvements in education quality since Dakar (see Chapters 2 and 3).

The international architecture for EFA since Dakar

Despite the disappointments during the 1990s, the 2000 World Education Forum envisaged a multilevel international architecture for EFA, building on existing mechanisms: 'In order to realize the six goals presented in this Framework for Action, broad-based and participatory mechanisms at international, regional and national levels are essential. The functions of these mechanisms will include, to varying degrees, advocacy, resource mobilization, monitoring, and knowledge generation and sharing' (UNESCO, 2000a, Commentary, para. 78).

In its Strategies 11 and 12, the Dakar Framework called for:

- systematic monitoring of progress towards EFA goals and strategies at the national, regional and international levels;

- national EFA forums and plans, committing the international community to support these plans;

- regional and subregional efforts to support national efforts;

- continuance of UNESCO's mandate to coordinate EFA partners and maintain their collaborative momentum, with its role, in addition to placing 'the outcomes and priorities of Dakar at the heart of' its education programme, to include convening annual high-level meetings by a small, flexible group of government, civil society and development agency leaders 'to serve as a lever for political commitment and technical and financial resource mobilization';

■ concrete new financial commitments by national governments, bilateral and multilateral donors (such as the World Bank and regional development banks), civil society and foundations (UNESCO, 2000a, Commentary, paras. 75-82).

A range of initiatives has emerged, concerned with particular elements of the Dakar Framework and reflecting the influence of the MDGs. Indeed, there have been many more initiatives associated with EFA since Dakar than in the decade between Jomtien and Dakar. Some focus on specific targets and objectives (e.g. the FTI for universal primary education, the UN Literacy Decade and UNESCO's Literacy Initiative for Empowerment, the UN Girls' Education Initiative for Gender Parity and Equality, various EFA Flagships such as the Inter-Agency Network for Education in Emergencies) or on particular processes (such as education sector planning and campaigns for greater accountability). The effectiveness of these initiatives varies considerably; it would be good for example, if the UN Literacy Decade were to have as much impact as does the FTI.

In addition, broader global efforts often include and benefit basic education; examples are initiatives to increase and improve the quality of aid (as noted above), to address the challenges of HIV/AIDS, to lessen conflict and to promote peace. The FTI, in particular, is increasingly becoming an effective vehicle for donor coordination and has facilitated constructive debate about what constitutes a credible education sector plan deserving donor support.

Relatively few initiatives, however, are directed towards achieving the full range of goals elaborated at Jomtien and reaffirmed at Dakar. Since 2002, the *EFA Global Monitoring Report* has published an annual accounting of progress towards EFA. The EFA High-Level Group and its Working Group on EFA have met annually. The former issues a communiqué, and later a report drawing in part on the monitoring report findings. The Working Group also issues a report. (From 2007 on, the sequencing has been changed, with the Working Group meeting in November to consider the soon-to-be-published

EFA Global Monitoring Report as preparation for the December High-Level Group.) UNESCO has tried three times to develop a global strategy to guide EFA partners' work: the Global Initiative towards Education for All: A Framework for Mutual Understanding (2001), the International Strategy to Put the Dakar Framework for Action into Operation (2002) and the Global Action Plan to improve support to countries in achieving the EFA goals (2007). The latest plan is very general, although the High-Level Group, meeting in Cairo in 2006, broadly approved it and suggested it should now be applied at country level. EFA has also figured on the G8 agenda, particularly at Kananaskis in 2003 and Gleneagles in 2005, but the focus has largely been limited to universal primary education and the FTI, and has not fully encompassed the broad EFA agenda.

Particular initiatives have had more success than the broad EFA agenda largely because bodies such as the World Bank, forums such as the G8 and projects such as the FTI and UNAIDS have carried much more weight politically than anything UNESCO has been able to facilitate thus far, 'despite or perhaps in part because of the fact that UNESCO has a universal membership' (Packer, 2007, p. 24). It is also much easier to focus on a limited goal such as universal primary education than on the broader, but more important, set of goals as a whole. Nonetheless, it is unfortunate that there is still no all-embracing global architecture for EFA, despite the wishes of the convenors of Jomtien and Dakar and despite UNESCO's three attempts since Dakar.

The lack of a global approach (in the sense of encompassing all EFA goals for all countries) has had a particularly worrying consequence: extraordinarily limited attention has been paid to strengthening national capacity. Little significant new thinking has been done about comprehensive strategies for building capacity in the education sector; government budgets allocate relatively little to professional development and organizational reform; and much aid to education remains in the form of technical assistance (see Chapter 4). Capacity-building still seems not to be considered of overriding importance, yet countries need much stronger capacity to deal with the political economy of reforms and with technical constraints on implementation.[21] Aid agencies also need to be sure of their technical capacity as they move towards a higher proportion of aid in the form of budget support.

Extraordinarily limited attention has been paid to strengthening national capacity

21. See Fredriksen (2005) for a discussion of this issue in the context of Africa.

The 2008 *EFA Global Monitoring Report*

The 2008 *EFA Global Monitoring Report* provides a systematic reassessment of the EFA movement at mid-term

Part of the new architecture is greater reliance on the *EFA Global Monitoring Report*. Published annually since 2002, it increasingly serves as a basis for the meeting of the High-Level Group. The Report is prepared by an independent team based at UNESCO headquarters and mostly funded by bilateral donors, the number of which has increased over the years from two to eleven (Canada, Denmark, France, Germany, Ireland, Israel, the Netherlands, Norway, Sweden, Switzerland and the United Kingdom), and UNESCO.

Previous Reports

Since its first edition, *Education for All: Is the World on Track?*, the Report has monitored progress towards the EFA goals annually. In its second through fifth editions, the Report also highlighted a special theme corresponding to one of the six goals; thus, as most of the goals have now been covered.[22]

The 2003/4 Report, *Gender and Education for All: The Leap to Equality*, stressed the urgency of going beyond the purely numerical concept of gender parity and envisaging gender equality, as EFA goal 5 requires. This implies that girls and boys are offered the same chances to go to school and enjoy teaching methods, curricula and academic orientation unaffected by gender bias; and more broadly, it means equal learning achievement and subsequent life opportunities for similar qualifications and experience.

The 2005 Report, *Education for All: The Quality Imperative*, highlighted the fact that many developing countries face a double challenge of increasing enrolment while improving the functioning of schools. The Report advocated policies designed to produce steady investment in the teaching profession (in terms of numbers and training); guarantee 850 to 1,000 hours of learning per year for all primary pupils; improve acquisition of reading skills; renew pedagogy, emphasizing structured teaching, i.e. a combination of direct instruction, guided practice and independent learning in a child-friendly environment; increase the availability of textbooks and other learning materials and of facilities (clean water, sanitation, access for disabled students); and promote autonomous leadership at the school level.

The 2006 Report, *Literacy for Life*, questioned the continued neglect of literacy in education policies and advocated a three-pronged strategy designed to meet the fourth EFA goal: expanding primary and lower secondary education and improving their quality; scaling up youth and adult literacy programmes by increasing their financing and situating them within education policy (the Report noted that programmes should be based on learner demand and motivations, which requires adequate curricula and learning materials, as well as attention to language issues: the use of mother tongues should be encouraged, with a later transition to regional and official languages); and developing rich literate environments, including language policies, book publishing, media, and access to information and reading materials.

The 2007 Report, *Strong Foundations: Early Childhood Care and Education*, emphasized that ECCE is a right recognized by the Convention on the Rights of the Child, and that participation in ECCE programmes improves the well-being and learning capacities of young children. Despite this, the Report showed, ECCE is relatively neglected by national governments and donor agencies; programmes often have insufficient, untrained and poorly remunerated staff; and enrolment of the poor and disadvantaged is generally low. The Report advocated a holistic approach to ECCE programmes, combining interventions on nutrition, health, care and education, and building on traditional childcare practices, respecting children's linguistic and cultural backgrounds. Programmes should include children with special needs and challenge gender stereotypes. Quality programmes need to be reasonably staffed and equipped, and provide a smooth transition to primary schooling.

Assessing the EFA movement at mid-term

Roughly half the time allotted at the World Education Forum to realize the Dakar Framework has passed, and data pertaining to the school year ending in 2005 are now available, allowing an examination of whether countries have achieved gender parity in primary and secondary education, the first part of goal 5. The 2008 *EFA Global Monitoring Report* thus provides a systematic reassessment of the EFA movement at mid-term, asking questions such as:

22. The exceptions are goal 2 (universal primary education), which has received considerable attention in all Reports, and goal 3 (learning and life-skills programmes for youth and adults), for which the information currently available is insufficient for systematic monitoring of initiatives towards meeting it.

■ Which regions and countries have made the most progress towards the EFA goals since 2000? Do they include sub-Saharan Africa, South Asia, the Arab States, the least developed countries and countries in conflict, undergoing reconstruction or otherwise fragile? Which ones still face the greatest challenges? Has the education situation actually worsened in some countries?

■ Have inequities in participation in education both across and within countries been reduced?

■ How do trends observed since Dakar compare to those observed during the 1990s, i.e. is there any sign of acceleration in the realization of EFA?

■ Has progress been made relative to all the Dakar goals, i.e. has the traditional overemphasis on formal primary schooling (goal 2) been balanced by greater attention to the needs of young children (goal 1) and youth and adults (goals 3 and 4)?

■ Has education policy evolved so as to better take into account the functioning of schools and relationships between teachers and learners, leading to less gender inequality (goal 5) and better quality of both educational processes and learning outcomes (goal 6)?

■ In particular, how many countries achieved gender parity by 2005 in key education indicators such as enrolment ratios at primary and secondary level?

■ What are the key policy initiatives taken in the early 2000s that have proved effective in promoting education for all? Do these policies correspond to the Dakar strategies?

■ Has education policy addressed the special areas of concern identified at Dakar (impact of the HIV/AIDS pandemic on education systems, lack of early childhood education opportunities, school health, education of girls and women, adult literacy, provision of education in situations of crisis and emergency)?

■ Have national governments increased the financial resources available for education and has education expenditure become more efficient?

■ Have donors allocated a larger share of their aid to basic education and to the countries where the challenges are greatest? Has the international community delivered on its pledge to provide assistance to countries committed to the EFA agenda?

■ Is EFA being realized? If trends since Dakar continue, will it be achieved by 2015, later, or not in the foreseeable future?

This Report seeks answers to these questions using the latest data from the UNESCO Institute for Statistics, supplemented with other sources such as censuses and household surveys, along with more qualitative evidence for the less quantifiable goals. In particular, whenever possible it analyses trends observed between 1999 and 2005 (post-Dakar) in comparison with those observed between 1991 and 1999 (pre-Dakar) and it provides projections with reference to the 2015 target year. The EFA Development Index, introduced in previous editions of the Report, is updated. A variety of research papers and relevant policy documents, such as national EFA plans and education sector strategies, are used to analyse national education policies. The international community's financial commitment is examined through the database on development aid to education maintained by the OECD-DAC Secretariat.

Outline of the 2008 Report

The 2008 Report is organized as follows. Chapter 2, *The six goals: how far have we come?*, provides a largely statistical assessment of progress made towards each EFA goal since Dakar. Chapter 3, *Countries on the move*, reviews education policy initiatives taken since Dakar by country governments towards the realization of EFA. Chapter 4, *Progress in financing Education for All*, examines national and international financing of education. Chapter 5, *The way forward*, concludes the Report by examining prospects for the realization of EFA by 2015 and by proposing the elements of a policy agenda. ■

Is Education for All being realized?

Several generations at a literacy class in China.

© XINHUA-CHINE NOUVELLE/GAMMA

At school in Syria.

© Giacomo Pirozzi/PANOS

Learning to read Braille in Botswana.

© Giacomo Pirozzi/PANOS

Chapter 2

The six goals: how far have we come?

The EFA movement has sought to satisfy basic learning needs through public policies aimed at providing universal access to primary education of good quality and developing new learning opportunities for young children as well as for youth and adults. Today, midway between the World Education Forum held in Dakar in 2000 and the target date of 2015, where do we stand?

Overview and main findings —— 32

Early childhood care
and education: still not
comprehensive ——————————— 34

Universal primary education:
nearer but not close ——————— 41

Secondary education
and beyond also contribute
to EFA ———————————————— 56

Are the learning needs
of young people and adults
being met? ——————————————— 59

Literacy and literate
environments: essential
yet elusive ————————————— 62

Quality: the continuing
challenge —————————————— 66

Gender parity and equality:
not there yet ———————————— 79

Overall Education for All
achievement —————————————— 91

Taking stock ——————————— 95

Overview and main findings

This chapter provides a systematic assessment of progress towards EFA since Dakar, comparing the latest round of data compiled by the UNESCO Institute for Statistics (UIS), which pertain to the school year ending in 2005, with corresponding 1999 figures. It focuses on the regions and countries that will face the greatest challenges in achieving the goals by 2015 and draws attention as well to inequities within countries – to the unmet educational needs of the disadvantaged areas and populations that typically receive the fewest resources.

The world has made significant progress towards EFA since Dakar, but the progress has been uneven. Despite the commitments at the World Education Forum, some regions and countries have lagged behind and some goals have received insufficient attention. In particular, most countries failed to eliminate gender disparities in primary *and* secondary education by 2005. It is also clear that pervasive imbalances in the development of many education systems create and reinforce disparities, which must be redressed if children, youth and adults are to benefit equally from the opportunities that education provides.

What are the principal developments since 2000 in relation to each of the six goals?

Goal 1: *Expanding and improving comprehensive early childhood care and education, especially for the most vulnerable and disadvantaged children*

■ Immunization campaigns and improved access to basic health facilities have led to a significant decline in child mortality.

■ However, the comprehensive care and education of children below age 3 remains a neglected area and one difficult to monitor for want of adequate data.

■ Meanwhile, the supply of pre-primary education to children aged 3 and above has improved, but remains very uneven. Many developing countries still have limited or non-existent pre-primary education systems; where they exist at all, too often they combine very low enrolment ratios with insufficient numbers of teachers (and even fewer trained teachers), resulting in high pupil/teacher ratios (PTRs). On a more positive note, some of these countries, located in sub-Saharan Africa, and South and West Asia, have registered sharp enrolment increases.

■ Children who are enrolled at the pre-primary level are more likely to come from more affluent households while enrolment of the poor remains low – yet it is the poor who stand to gain relatively the most from early childhood programmes.

Goal 2: *Ensuring that by 2015 all children, particularly girls, children in difficult circumstances and those belonging to ethnic minorities, have access to and complete, free and compulsory primary education of good quality*

■ Access to and participation in primary education have sharply increased since Dakar, and the number of out-of-school children correspondingly dropped from 96 million to 72 million between 1999 and 2005. Most regions are close to reaching universal primary education (UPE). In the three regions that are not – the Arab States, sub-Saharan Africa, and South and West Asia – substantial increases in enrolment ratios have taken place in many countries.

■ However, progression through the primary grades and school completion remain important concerns in those three regions, in Latin America and the Caribbean and in many countries in East Asia and the Pacific.

■ Attention is required to those fragile states, and to those countries in or emerging from conflict, for which no data are available but where the situation of primary education is bound to be worse.

■ Inequalities remain within countries: between regions, provinces or states; between urban and rural areas; between rich and poor households; and between ethnic groups. Recent evidence points to lower participation and completion rates for children living in slums or belonging to poor families living in non-slum areas. Many countries with relatively high primary enrolment ratios need still to address equity issues.

Goal 3: *Ensuring that the learning needs of all young people and adults are met through equitable access to appropriate learning and life-skills programmes*

■ The expansion of formal education beyond the primary level has been the most common strategy to address the learning needs of youth: between 1999 and 2005, the global gross enrolment ratio (GER) in secondary education increased from 60% to 66%.

■ However, many young people and adults acquire skills through purely informal means, or through a great variety of non-formal literacy, equivalency, life-skills and livelihood programmes. The learning needs of young people and adults remain woefully undocumented, preventing monitoring at global or even national level and hampering policy implementation. Goal 3 has been particularly neglected, in part because of the difficulty of defining and monitoring it.

Goal 4: *Achieving a 50 per cent improvement in levels of adult literacy by 2015, especially fo women, and equitable access to basic and continuing education for all adults*

■ Adult literacy remains a global issue: 774 million adults (of whom 64% are women) still lack basic literacy and numeracy skills. East Asia, South and West Asia and sub-Saharan Africa are home to the vast majority of the one in five adults worldwide who are denied the right to literacy.

■ Except in China and a few other countries, there has been little progress during the past decade in reducing the large number of illiterate adults.

Goal 5: *Eliminating gender disparities in primary and secondary education by 2005, and achieving gender equality in education by 2015, with a focus on ensuring girls' full and equal access to and achievement in basic education of good quality*

■ The goal of eliminating gender disparities in both primary *and* secondary education by 2005 was missed in a great majority of countries. Only 59 countries, about one-third of the 181 countries for which data are available, had achieved the gender parity goal, very few of them since 1999. Gender disparities persist in many countries, particularly at the upper levels: while 63% of countries with data had managed to eliminate gender disparities in primary education, only 37% had done so at the secondary level.

Access to and participation in primary education have sharply increased since Dakar

CHAPTER 2

Gender equality has been relatively neglected

- Girls' access to primary and secondary schools, while improving, remains a major issue in countries where overall participation levels are still low. In countries with higher participation levels (developed countries, Latin America and especially the Caribbean, the Pacific), boys' underparticipation in secondary education is a growing problem.

- Gender *equality* has been relatively neglected. Physical violence mainly affects boys; verbal and sexual violence, combined with insecure environments and inadequate sanitation, disproportionately affects girls. Some countries have few female teachers; in many others male and female teachers receive insufficient training in gender issues, which hampers their potential as effective role models. Gender-biased teacher attitudes, perceptions and expectations are common, and boys often dominate classroom time and space. In many instances, textbooks reinforce the gender-specific roles of men and women, and in some cases different subjects are taught to girls and boys. Boys' and girls' levels of achievement are converging, but fields of study and occupational choices continue to be clustered by gender.

Goal 6: *Improving all aspects of the quality of education and ensuring excellence of all so that recognized and measurable learning outcomes are achieved by all, especially in literacy, numeracy and essential life skills*

- International and regional assessments and a growing number of national assessments conducted since 1999 show that relatively poor learning outcomes in language and mathematics, as well as other subjects, still characterize many countries worldwide. The need to improve these outcomes, especially their uneven distribution within countries, remains a salient challenge in all countries.

- On average, more than 60% of countries allocate fewer than 800 yearly hours of instruction in grades 1–6, even though recent research confirms positive correlations between instructional time and learning outcomes.

- Many developing countries, especially in Africa and Asia, and in conflict-affected areas, have crowded classrooms, poor school infrastructure and inadequate learning environments.

- Acute shortages of teachers are common, especially in sub-Saharan Africa, and South and West Asia, and even greater shortages of *trained* teachers in some countries hinder quality teaching and learning.

The following seven sections monitor the EFA goals in greater detail, and describe trends in secondary and tertiary education. A final section examines overall progress towards the Dakar agenda in light of the EFA Development Index (EDI), and identifies the regions and countries still facing the greatest challenges. A clear theme that emerges from this chapter is the dual importance of equity and quality. Achieving equity is a key to increased access and participation, and is also the principal reason for expanding early childhood, adult literacy and non-formal programmes. Improving quality, a concern of countries everywhere, may well be the defining global educational challenge of the early 21st century.

Early childhood care and education: still not comprehensive

Goal 1: *Expanding and improving comprehensive early childhood care and education, especially for the most vulnerable and disadvantaged children*

The 2007 *EFA Global Monitoring Report* highlighted the compelling case for more and better-designed early childhood care and education (ECCE) programmes. Because of the critical nature of early childhood as regards physical and mental development, ECCE programmes help reduce existing and future disadvantages faced by many children, through addressing their nutritional, health and educational needs. ECCE participation reduces the prevalence of undernutrition and stunting, improves cognitive development and contributes to increased school participation, completion and achievement. ECCE becomes the guarantor of children's rights and can open the way to all the EFA goals.

The care and protection of children below age 3 are neglected

Official ECCE programmes targeting children under age 3 are usually of a custodial nature and develop alongside increasing female employment (see annex, Statistical Table 3A). They are found in only 53% of the world's countries, located mostly in North America and Western Europe, Central Asia, and Latin America and the Caribbean. While ministries in charge of health or child welfare see basic health services as within their purview, the organization of broader care and education for very young children is often considered a responsibility of families or private providers, the latter meeting the needs mostly of more affluent middle class and urban families. Few countries have established national frameworks for the financing, coordination and supervision of ECCE programmes for very young children. Often, there is neither a clear lead ministry or agency for ECCE policy, nor a developed national policy with goals, regulations, quality standards and funding commitments. Data on ECCE programmes for very young children are correspondingly sparse (UNESCO, 2006a).

Child well-being is improving nonetheless, through immunization and better health services

There has been noticeable improvement in child well-being over the past decade, as measured by the under-5 mortality rate (see glossary), which captures the cumulative effects of poor care and protection up to the fifth year of life (see annex, Statistical Table 3A). The rate declined worldwide from 92‰ to 78‰ between 1995 and 2005; it fell by more than 25% in the Arab States (to 55‰), East Asia and the Pacific (to 37‰), and Latin America and the Caribbean (to 30‰). At country level, significant improvement occurred, with the rate declining by one-third in twenty-one countries.[1] The few countries where the under-5 mortality rate increased were southern African ones severely affected by the HIV/AIDS pandemic: Botswana, South Africa, Swaziland and Zimbabwe (UNAIDS, 2006). Sub-Saharan Africa, as the region with the highest child mortality rate in 2005 (163‰), still faces the greatest challenge.

Worldwide, around 10 million children below age 5 died in 2005, almost all in developing countries (UNICEF, 2006). Most of these deaths could have been prevented through improved basic health services and child nutrition programmes. Immunization campaigns continue to boost children's basic health worldwide, preventing 1.4 million deaths of children under age 5 in 2003 alone (UNICEF, 2005c). But children in some parts of the world are not inoculated against preventable diseases such as tuberculosis; diphtheria, pertussis (whooping cough) and tetanus (target of the DPT

vaccine); polio; and hepatitis B (see annex, Statistical Table 3A). Meanwhile, undernutrition and malnutrition affect one out of four children under age 5 in developing countries, and 30% of children suffer from stunting worldwide. Children thus affected are more vulnerable to illness and socio-emotional developmental setbacks, and less likely to enrol in school, complete primary schooling and reach high achievement levels (UNESCO, 2006a).

Uneven advances in ECCE provision for age 3 and up

Governments are more active in the provision and supervision of ECCE programmes for children from age 3 to primary school age. In most countries, the ministry in charge of education oversees the national provision of pre-primary education (ISCED level 0).[2] Only thirty countries have compulsory attendance laws at this level, which tend moreover to reflect policy intentions rather than educational realities (UNESCO, 2006a). The duration of pre-primary education varies significantly: it is one year in fourteen countries, two years in fifty-nine, three years in ninety-nine and four years in thirty-one (see annex, Statistical Table 3B).

The number of children enrolled in pre-primary schools worldwide increased by 20 million between 1999 and 2005, to 132 million, mostly because of gains in South and West Asia (by 67%), sub-Saharan Africa (61%) and, to a lesser extent, Latin America and the Caribbean (Table 2.1). Enrolments decreased in East Asia and the Pacific, reflecting in particular the shrinking of the relevant age population in China. The global pre-primary gross enrolment ratio (GER) (see glossary) correspondingly increased from 33% to 40%. The largest GER gains were made in the Pacific, and South and West Asia (fifteen percentage points each) and the Caribbean (twelve percentage points), which already had the second highest GER in 1999. The 20% increase in the GER in Central and Eastern Europe confirmed the recovery from the 1990s decline. GERs in the Arab States and sub-Saharan Africa remained below 20%, despite a 43% rise in the latter.

Overall, as Map 2.1 shows, participation in pre-primary education is highest in developed and transition countries, which account for eighteen of the forty-one countries with GERs 90% or higher in 2005. It is also high in Latin America and the Caribbean, and in East Asia and the Pacific.

Participation in pre-primary education is highest in developed and transition countries

1. Algeria, Argentina, Bahamas, Bangladesh, Cape Verde, Chile, Croatia, Cuba, Ecuador, Egypt, Indonesia, the Islamic Republic of Iran, Maldives, Mexico, Morocco, Norway, the Philippines, the Republic of Korea, the Syrian Arab Republic, the United Republic of Tanzania and Vanuatu.

2. The International Standard Classification of Education (ISCED) is a system that enables the compilation and presentation of comparable indicators and statistics of education internationally. See glossary for ISCED level definitions.

Table 2.1: Pre-primary enrolment and gross enrolment ratios by region, 1999 and 2005

	Total enrolment			Gross enrolment ratios		
	School year ending in		Change between 1999 and 2005	School year ending in		Change between 1999 and 2005
	1999	2005		1999	2005	
	(millions)	(millions)	(%)	(%)	(%)	(%)
World	112.3	132.0	17.6	33	40	19.3
Developing countries	79.9	99.2	24.2	28	34	24.2
Developed countries	25.4	25.6	1.1	73	78	6.1
Countries in transition	7.1	7.2	1.7	46	60	29.7
Sub-Saharan Africa	5.1	8.3	60.9	10	14	43.1
Arab States	2.4	2.9	18.2	15	17	11.8
Central Asia	1.5	1.5	2.2	22	28	23.2
East Asia and the Pacific	37.0	35.8	-3.4	40	43	7.4
East Asia	36.6	35.3	-3.7	40	43	7.1
Pacific	0.4	0.5	25.6	57	72	26.2
South and West Asia	21.4	35.7	66.6	22	37	66.4
Latin America and the Caribbean	16.4	19.1	16.7	56	62	11.0
Caribbean	0.7	0.8	18.2	71	83	16.9
Latin America	15.7	18.3	16.6	55	61	10.8
North America and Western Europe	19.1	19.5	1.8	76	79	4.3
Central and Eastern Europe	9.3	9.3	0.3	49	59	20.2

Note: Changes are computed using non-rounded figures.
Source: Annex, Statistical Table 3B.

Increases in pre-primary enrolment often followed considerable increases in the number of schools

It remains very low in many sub-Saharan African countries and in some of the Arab States: the two regions account for almost three-quarters of the fifty countries with GERs below 30%.

Figure 2.1 shows changes in pre-primary GERs since Dakar, focusing on countries in which the GER was below 90% in 2005. GERs have improved substantially since 1999 in some countries with low or moderate levels of participation in sub-Saharan Africa (Cameroon, Ghana, Lesotho, Namibia and South Africa), the Arab States (Bahrain and Qatar), East Asia and the Pacific (Papua New Guinea and Viet Nam), and South and West Asia (India and the Islamic Republic of Iran). Countries of the former Soviet Union, particularly Georgia, Kazakhstan, the Republic of Moldova and the Russian Federation, continued the recovery begun in the late 1990s. Little progress is recorded for more than a dozen sub-Saharan African countries and several Arab States with limited or non-existent pre-primary education (GERs below 30%), though some of those countries saw their GERs double or treble from a very low base (Burundi, the Congo, Eritrea, Madagascar and Senegal).

Increases in pre-primary enrolment often followed considerable increases in the number of schools

(e.g. 106% in the Congo, 173% in Senegal). In Eritrea, the upward GER trend stemmed from the implementation of a government policy quadrupling the number of child care centres during the period under review. In Ghana, the GER increase from 40% to 56% in 2006 is explained by the introduction of free kindergartens in public schools in 2005, with schools receiving a grant for every child enrolled.

GERs decreased in a few countries, including Bangladesh, the Gambia, Kuwait, Morocco, the Palestinian Autonomous Territories, Thailand, Uganda and several Caribbean and Pacific island states. In other cases, such as Chile, Costa Rica, Guatemala and the Marshall Islands, lower 2005 GERs are due to changes in the age groups to which enrolment ratios refer.

The private sector's role in pre-primary education

Private institutions account for a larger proportion of total pre-primary enrolment in developing countries than in developed or transition countries, with a median value of 47% compared with 8% in developed and 1% in transition countries. The private sector is nearly the sole provider of pre-primary education in five Arab States (Bahrain,

Map 2.1: Pre-primary gross enrolment ratios, 2005

1. TFYR Macedonia
2. Albania
3. Montenegro
4. Serbia
5. Bosnia/Herzeg.
6. Croatia
7. Slovenia
8. Hungary
9. Austria
10. Czech Rep.
11. Slovakia
12. Rep. Moldova
13. Romania
14. Bulgaria

Less than 30%

30% – 49%

50% – 89%

90% or more

No data

Note: See source table for detailed country notes.
Source: Annex, Statistical Table 3B.

The boundaries and names shown and the designations used on this map
do not imply official endorsement or acceptance by UNESCO.
Based on United Nations map.

Jordan, Morocco, Oman and the Palestinian
Autonomous Territories) as well as in Belize,
Bhutan, Ethiopia, Fiji, the Gambia, Indonesia,
Lesotho, Namibia, New Zealand, Uganda and some
small Caribbean island states. In China, enrolment
in private institutions accounted for 31% of total
enrolment in 2005. Compared with 1999, the share
of private enrolment increased slightly (generally
by less than five percentage points) in roughly
one-third of the 126 countries with available data,
remained almost unchanged in another third and
decreased in the remaining third.

Gender and income disparities in pre-primary education

Gender disparities in pre-primary education are
less marked than at other levels of education,
probably because children at this level tend to come
from more affluent groups, where gender biases
are less pronounced than among the poor. The
gender parity index (GPI) – the ratio between the
female and male GER – is close to, or exceeds, 0.90
in all regions in 2005, and 105 of the 169 countries
with available data are at gender parity, including 23
more countries than in 1999 (see annex, Statistical
Table 3B). High disparities against girls (GPI below

Gender disparities
in pre-primary
education are less
marked than at
other levels
of education

Table 2.2: Pupil/teacher ratios in pre-primary education by region, 1999 and 2005

	Pupil/teacher ratios		
	School year ending in		Change between 1999 and 2005
	1999	2005	(%)
World	21	22	4.1
Developing countries	27	28	5.4
Developed countries	17	15	-11.6
Countries in transition	7	8	6.1
Sub-Saharan Africa	29	31	8.1
Arab States	21	20	-3.7
Central Asia	10	11	5.4
East Asia and the Pacific	26	25	-3.5
East Asia	26	25	-3.5
Pacific	16	17	7.3
South and West Asia	36	40	13.5
Latin America and the Caribbean	22	21	-2.4
Caribbean	31	31	0.4
Latin America	22	21	-2.5
North America and Western Europe	17	15	-15.9
Central and Eastern Europe	8	9	6.9

Notes: Weighted averages. Based on headcounts of pupils and teachers.
Source: Annex, Statistical Table 10A.

Figure 2.2: Comparison of pupil/teacher ratios with ratios of pupils to trained teachers in pre-primary education, 2005

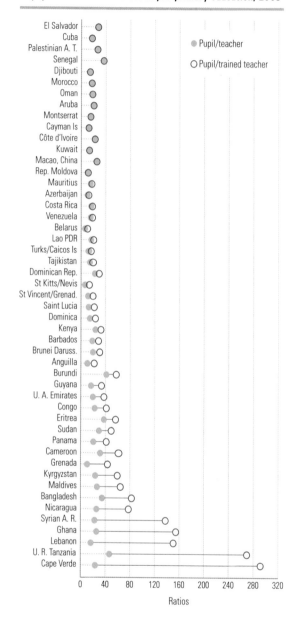

Notes: Countries are listed in ascending order of the difference between the PTRs and the pupil/trained-teacher ratios. See source table for detailed country notes. Only countries with data on pupil/trained-teacher ratios are included.
Sources: Annex, Statistical Table 10A; UIS database.

The teacher shortages observed in many countries are compounded by low percentages of trained teachers

are likely therefore to experience worse teaching and learning conditions (UIS database).

The teacher shortages observed in many countries are compounded by low percentages of trained teachers. Across the fifty countries with data, the percentage of trained teachers ranges from less than 25% in Cape Verde, Ghana, Lebanon, the Syrian Arab Republic and the United Republic of Tanzania to higher than 95% in eighteen countries, most of them Arab States or Caribbean island states (see annex, Statistical Table 10A). Ratios of pupils to trained teachers can be much higher than overall PTRs, as Figure 2.2 shows: e.g. above 100:1 in Cape Verde, Ghana, Lebanon and the Syrian Arab Republic, even though the highest PTR in these countries is 25:1. In countries including Burundi, Cameroon, the Congo, Eritrea and Sudan, the pupil/trained-teacher ratio reveals a shortage of trained teachers not captured by the PTR and percentage of trained teachers.

The availability of trained teachers changed little between 1999 and 2005. Ghana and the Syrian Arab Republic are exceptions, where shortages of trained teachers worsened. The policy on free kindergarten in Ghanaian public schools was accompanied by a rise in the pupil/trained-teacher

ratio to 155:1, from an already high 103:1. In the Syrian Arab Republic, the ratio increased by 400% from 27:1 to 137:1. Shortages in both countries resulted from increases in enrolments and teacher numbers associated with decreases in the absolute number and share of trained teachers (see annex, Statistical Table 10A), a clear example of a quantity/quality trade-off.

Universal primary education: nearer but not close

Goal 2: *Ensuring that by 2015 all children, particularly girls, children in difficult circumstances and those belonging to ethnic minorities, have access to and complete, free and compulsory primary education of good quality*

Access to schooling: different regional trends

The number of new entrants into primary education worldwide grew by 4%, from 130 million to 135 million, between 1999 and 2005 (Table 2.3), but as a result of opposite regional trends. Large increases in sub-Saharan Africa, South and West Asia and, to a lesser extent, the Arab States brought 11 million more pupils into school systems, many of them outside the official school entrance age (Box 2.1). By contrast, decreases in the population of school-entrance age in regions with high and relatively stable gross intake rates (GIRs; see glossary), such as East Asia and the Pacific (particularly China), Central Asia, and North America and Western Europe, reduced the number of new pupils by 5 million.

The 40% increase in the number of new entrants in sub-Saharan Africa is a key achievement, further reflected in country-level GIR changes (Figure 2.3). Policy measures to facilitate access to education for the most disadvantaged (e.g. abolition of school fees in the early 2000s) explain to a great extent the improvements in access in countries such as Madagascar, the United Republic of Tanzania and Zambia. Gains are also reported in Burkina Faso, Cameroon, Chad, the Congo, the Democratic Republic of the Congo, Ethiopia, Ghana, Guinea, Mali, the Niger and Senegal in sub-Saharan Africa, and in Egypt, Djibouti and Yemen. Some of these countries (e.g. Burkina Faso, Guinea, Senegal) may approach universal enrolment in grade 1 by 2009 or 2010, a condition for attaining universal primary completion by 2015. On the other hand, the levels and trends in access to school point to the difficulty of achieving UPE in a number of countries with GIRs below 70%, mainly in sub-Saharan Africa (Central African Republic, Comoros, the Congo, Côte d'Ivoire, the Democratic Republic of the Congo, Eritrea, Mali and the Niger) as well as Djibouti and Sudan. In most of these countries, the goal is particularly challenging as economic conditions are dire[5] and demographic pressure is significant. Declines in GIRs were observed in Eritrea, Jordan, the Maldives, Oman, the Palestinian Autonomous Territories, Viet Nam and some small Pacific island states.

The 40% increase in the number of new entrants in sub-Saharan Africa is a key achievement

Table 2.3: New entrants into grade 1 and gross intake rates by region, 1999 and 2005

	New entrants			Gross intake rates		
	School year ending in 1999	School year ending in 2005	Change between 1999 and 2005	School year ending in 1999	School year ending in 2005	Change between 1999 and 2005
	(millions)	(millions)	(%)	(%)	(%)	(percentage points)
World	129.9	134.9	3.9	106	112	6.7
Developing countries	113.4	120.2	6.0	106	114	7.3
Developed countries	12.3	11.5	-6.4	101	101	-0.7
Countries in transition	4.2	3.2	-23.2	94	100	6.1
Sub-Saharan Africa	16.4	22.9	39.9	90	113	22.4
Arab States	6.3	7.0	11.6	90	97	6.7
Central Asia	1.8	1.5	-15.9	101	104	3.7
East Asia and the Pacific	37.0	32.6	-11.8	102	100	-2.6
East Asia	36.5	32.1	-12.1	102	100	-2.7
Pacific	0.6	0.6	2.9	102	106	3.8
South and West Asia	40.5	44.3	9.4	119	130	11.2
Latin America and the Caribbean	13.2	13.2	0.3	119	119	-0.1
Caribbean	0.6	0.5	-3.2	164	161	-3.0
Latin America	12.6	12.7	0.4	118	118	0.0
North America and Western Europe	9.2	8.8	-4.3	102	102	-0.7
Central and Eastern Europe	5.4	4.5	-18.2	94	96	2.6

Note: Change computed using non-rounded figures.
Source: Annex, Statistical Table 4.

5. All except the Congo, Côte d'Ivoire and Djibouti had GNPs per capita of less than US$2 per day in 2004 (see annex, Statistical Table 1).

Figure 2.3: Gross intake rates to primary education in countries with GIRs below 95% in 1999, 2005 or both

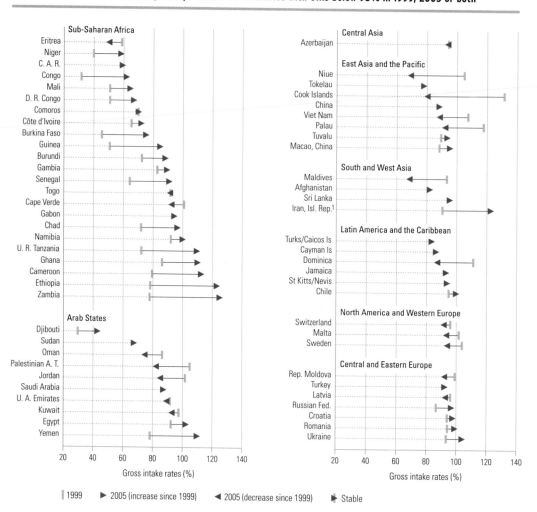

Demographic pressure will remain a challenge for the next decade

Note: See source table for detailed country notes.
1. The apparent increase in the Islamic Republic of Iran is due to the recent inclusion of literacy programmes for adults in primary enrolment statistics.
Source: Annex, Statistical Table 4.

Participation in primary education: increasing but still far from universal

The World Education Forum at Dakar marked a turning point in the expansion of primary education, with the pace of progress quickening in comparison with the previous decade (UNESCO-BREDA, 2007). Global primary school enrolment rose from 647 million to 688 million (6.4%) between 1999 and 2005, with increases especially marked in sub-Saharan Africa (by 29 million, 36%), and South and West Asia (35 million, 22%), regions in which the pace significantly accelerated in the post-Dakar period compared with 1991–99 (Table 2.4). These two regions, along with the Arab States, may be moving towards the higher enrolment ratios

observed elsewhere in the world. However, demographic pressure will remain a challenge for the next decade, when the primary school age population is expected to grow at a sustained pace, particularly in sub-Saharan Africa (with projected growth of 22%) and, to a lesser extent, the Arab States (13%).[6] In many other regions enrolment has been stable or decreased, a trend linked to reduction of the size of the school-age population.[7]

A country's distance from UPE appears most clearly in terms of the net enrolment ratio (NER), the share of children of official primary school age who are actually enrolled in primary schools (see glossary). North America and Western

6. Between 2005 and 2015 growth rates are expected either to exceed 3% per year (the Congo, the Democratic Republic of the Congo and the Niger) or to be just below this rate (e.g. Mali).

7. The GER decrease in Latin America, from 121% to 118%, reflects more a normalization of pupil age, since the NER increased during the same period from 93% to 95%.

Box 2.1: What is the age of children entering school?

Some children enter school earlier than the official school-entrance age. Others enter one or more years later, either for economic reasons or because schools are too far from home for young children to reach them, or even because they keep attending pre-primary schools. Reducing under-age and over-age school entrance matters; over-age children, in particular, are more likely to repeat grades and eventually drop out. High proportions of over-age children are found in many sub-Saharan African countries and,

to a lesser extent, in the Arab States, East Asia and the Pacific, and Latin America and the Caribbean. Over-age enrolment is also common in post-conflict situations, as in Timor-Leste. Under-age enrolment is frequent in countries as diverse as Burkina Faso, Indonesia, Mali, Montserrat, Nicaragua, South Africa and the United Arab Emirates. Figure 2.4 shows that GIRs may overestimate actual levels of access to schooling, as their value can exceed 100% even if not all children of official school-entrance age are enrolled.

Figure 2.4: Distribution of new entrants into primary education relative to official age, 2005

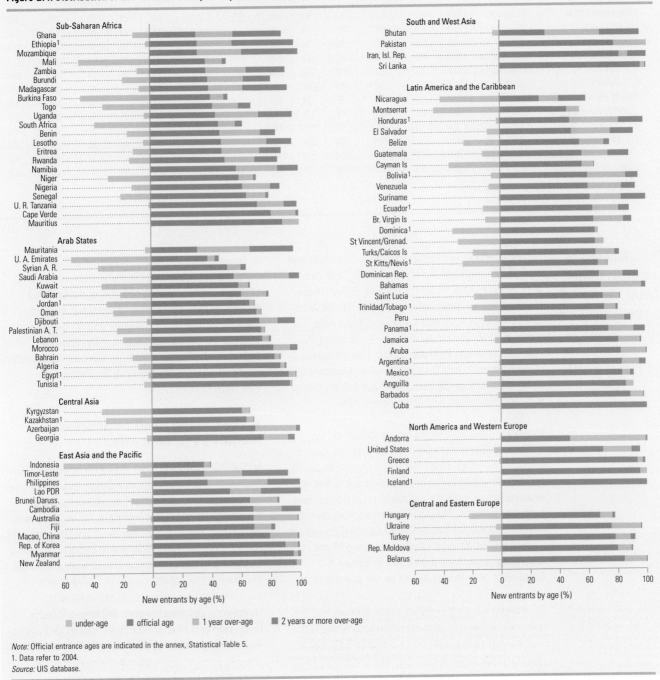

Note: Official entrance ages are indicated in the annex, Statistical Table 5.

1. Data refer to 2004.

Source: UIS database.

Table 2.4: Primary enrolment by region, 1991, 1999 and 2005

	Total enrolment					Gross enrolment ratios					Net enrolment ratios				
	School year ending in			Change between 1991 and 1999	Change between 1999 and 2005	School year ending in			Change between 1991 and 1999	Change between 1999 and 2005	School year ending in			Change between 1991 and 1999	Change between 1999 and 2005
	1991	1999	2005			1991	1999	2005			1991	1999	2005		
	(millions)			(% per year)[1]		(%)	(%)	(%)	(percentage points per year)		(%)	(%)	(%)	(percentage points per year)	
World	598.2	646.7	688.3	1.0	1.0	99	100	107	0.2	1.1	81	83	87	0.2	0.6
Developing countries	507.9	560.5	607.5	1.2	1.4	98	100	108	0.3	1.3	79	81	86	0.3	0.7
Developed countries	72.6	70.4	67.0	-0.4	-0.8	102	102	102	0.0	-0.1	96	97	96	0.0	-0.2
Countries in transition	17.7	15.8	13.7	-1.4	-2.3	97	100	111	0.4	1.8	89	85	90	-0.5	0.8
Sub-Saharan Africa	63.2	80.8	109.7	3.1	5.2	72	80	97	0.9	2.7	54	57	70	0.4	2.1
Arab States	30.5	35.4	39.3	1.9	1.8	83	90	95	0.9	0.8	73	79	83	0.7	0.7
Central Asia	5.4	6.9	6.2	3.1	-1.7	90	99	101	1.1	0.4	84	88	90	0.5	0.3
East Asia and the Pacific	206.9	217.6	197.2	0.6	-1.6	117	112	110	-0.6	-0.3	96	95	94	-0.1	-0.3
East Asia	204.2	214.3	193.7	0.6	-1.7	117	112	111	-0.6	-0.3	96	96	94	0.0	-0.3
Pacific	2.7	3.3	3.5	2.7	1.0	98	94	98	-0.6	0.7	91	87	90	-0.5	0.5
South and West Asia	135.4	157.5	192.7	1.9	3.4	92	94	113	0.2	3.1	72	77	86	0.6	1.4
Latin America/Caribbean	75.4	70.2	69.1	-0.9	-0.3	104	121	118	2.2	-0.5	86	92	94	0.8	0.3
Caribbean	1.4	2.5	2.4	7.1	-0.5	71	115	117	5.5	0.3	52	77	77	3.1	0.1
Latin America	74.0	67.7	66.7	-1.1	-0.3	104	121	118	2.1	-0.6	87	93	95	0.8	0.3
N. America/W. Europe	50.1	52.9	51.6	0.7	-0.4	104	103	102	-0.1	-0.2	96	97	95	0.0	-0.2
Central/Eastern Europe	31.3	25.5	22.5	-2.5	-2.1	98	100	103	0.2	0.6	90	90	91	-0.1	0.2

1. Average annual growth rate based on compound growth.
Sources: Annex, Statistical Table 5; UIS database.

Progress in enrolment since Dakar has rarely been uniform across all subnational divisions within countries

Europe, Central and Eastern Europe, East Asia and the Pacific, and Latin America and the Caribbean are closest to UPE with NERs above 90% in more than half the countries of each region. In the Arab States, Central Asia, and South and West Asia, average NERs are below 90%, the lows being in Djibouti (33%) and Pakistan (68%). The situation remains most critical in sub–Saharan Africa, where more than 60% of the countries have values below 80% and more than one-third below 70%.

Most countries with NERs below 95% in either 1999 or 2005 registered increases over the period (Figure 2.5), which may reflect the impact of public policies designed to facilitate enrolment of the most disadvantaged, such as the abolition of school fees in Benin, Lesotho, Madagascar, Mozambique, the United Republic of Tanzania and Zambia, as well as Cambodia and Yemen. Ethiopia, Guinea, Morocco and Nepal also made significant progress.[8] Enrolment growth was driven by the private sector

in some countries. The percentage of pupils enrolled in private institutions increased in some of the countries mentioned above, particularly Mali (by fifteen percentage points) but also, to a lesser extent, Benin, Guinea and Mauritania. Meanwhile, NERs declined in a few countries, including the Palestinian Autonomous Territories, South Africa, the United Arab Emirates and Viet Nam.[9]

A continuing need to address inequities in education

Geographic disparities and stark contrasts

Progress in enrolment since Dakar has rarely been uniform across all subnational divisions within countries. In Nepal, for example, NERs are above 95% in the Western and Far Western Development Regions but below 60% in some districts of the Eastern and Central regions. In Guinea almost all children in the capital region of Conakry are enrolled, but in outlying districts in Labé or Nzérékoré enrolment ratios fall below 50% (Sherman and Poirier, 2007). Achieving UPE, by definition, implies addressing such inequities.

8. Changes in the structure of education systems at least partly explain NER growth. Thus, the high increase in Ethiopia has to be analysed in relation to a decrease in the duration of primary schooling from six years to four, while the steep rise in Mozambique is all the more impressive considering that the duration of primary education was extended from five years to seven. Other countries that changed the duration of primary schooling were Kenya and the United Arab Emirates (one year less) and Egypt, Kuwait and Lebanon (one year more).

9. In Viet Nam, however, this trend is likely to reverse since a policy to abolish school fees was adopted in 2004.

Figure 2.5: Change in primary net enrolment ratios between 1999 and 2005 in countries with NERs of 95% or lower in both years[1]

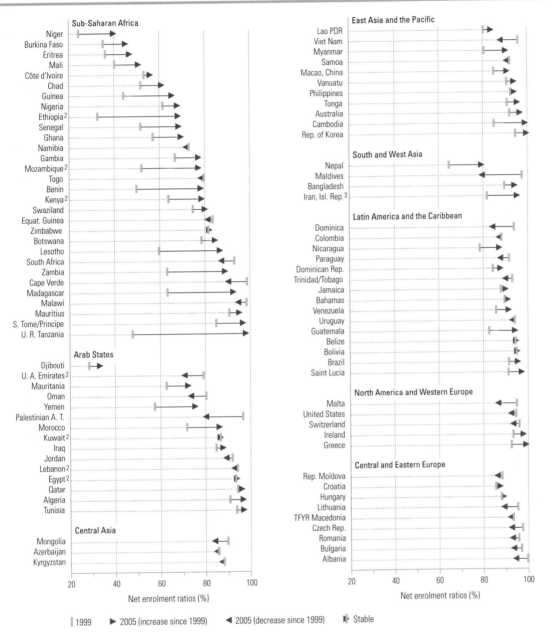

Geographic disparities tend to be lowest in countries that are nearest to universal enrolment

Net enrolment ratios (%)

| | 1999 ▶ 2005 (increase since 1999) ◀ 2005 (decrease since 1999) ▮ Stable

Note: See source table for detailed country notes.
1. The NER exceeded 95% in both years in thirty-two countries: sixteen in Western Europe, nine in Latin America and the Caribbean, three in East Asia and the Pacific, three in Central and Eastern Europe and one in the Arab States.
2. Change in duration of primary education between 1999 and 2005.
3. Increase due to the recent inclusion of literacy programmes in enrolment statistics.
Source: Annex, Statistical Table 5.

10. The 'restricted range' measures the absolute difference between the lower and upper means in the distribution of subnational enrolment ratios in a country. The lower mean is calculated as the unweighted mean of those ratios falling below the country's median; the upper mean is the unweighted mean of those falling above the median. In Guinea's thirty-eight districts, for example, NERs vary from 40% to 99%; the lower mean is 43.2 and the upper mean is 71.4. Thus, the restricted range is 28.2 (71.4 minus 43.2). See Sherman and Poirier (2007) for further details.

To capture the scale of geographic disparities in primary education, countries can be compared using a disparity index called the 'restricted range' (Sherman and Poirier, 2007).[10] Values of the disparity index vary from 2.8 (low disparity) in China to 48.3 (high disparity) in Ethiopia in the pre-Dakar period, and from 1.6 in China to 69.7 in Nigeria in the post-Dakar period. Figure 2.6 presents the index for forty-five countries, sorted by the country-level NER. In principle, disparities tend to be lowest in countries that are nearest to universal enrolment (e.g. Argentina, Brazil, Indonesia, Mexico, Peru)

In most countries net attendance rates in urban areas were found to be higher than those in rural areas

Figure 2.6: Subnational geographic disparities in net enrolment ratios, pre- and post-Dakar[1]

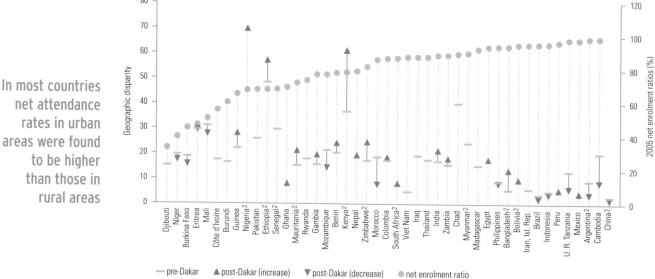

Notes: Countries are in ascending order of 2005 NER. Disparity is measured using the difference between the lower mean and upper mean of regional enrolment ratios in each country. For methodological issues, see source.
1. 'Pre-Dakar' refers to 1996–2000 and 'post-Dakar' to 2001–2006.
2. GERs were used to calculate the geographic disparity measure when NERs were not available for both years, except in Bangladesh and Zimbabwe, where GERs were used only for the post-Dakar period.
Source: Sherman and Poirier (2007).

and highest in those that are farthest from it (e.g. Eritrea, Ethiopia, Guinea, Mali, Nigeria, Senegal). However, stark contrasts can exist between countries with similar NERs. For example, while Ethiopia, Ghana, Mauritania, Nigeria, Pakistan and Senegal all have national NERs of about 70%, their values on the disparity index vary from more than 55 in Nigeria and Ethiopia (high disparity) to less than 22 in Mauritania and even down to 8 in Ghana.[11]

Among the twenty-five countries for which data are available, Argentina, Burkina Faso, Cambodia, Mali, Morocco, Mozambique, the United Republic of Tanzania and, to a lesser extent, Brazil, China, Indonesia and the Niger all reduced geographic disparity over time (Figure 2.6). By contrast, in Bangladesh, Benin, Colombia, Ethiopia, the Gambia, Guinea, India, Kenya, Mauritania, Zambia and Zimbabwe, subnational disparities grew. In Eritrea, the Philippines and Senegal, there was little change.

There is no clear association between the changing level of the NER and geographic disparities. NER increases have led to reduced geographic disparities in Brazil, Burkina Faso, Cambodia, Indonesia, Mali, Morocco, Mozambique, Niger and

the United Republic of Tanzania,[12] but to greater disparities in Bangladesh, Benin, Ethiopia, the Gambia, Guinea, India, Kenya, Mauritania and Zambia (Table 2.5).

Other disparities: rural children, slum children, poor children and those with disabilities fare worst

Households in rural, remote or scattered communities, or those located great distances from urban population centres, tend to be poorer and more socially marginalized than other groups, with less access to good-quality basic education. Recent cross-national compilations of net attendance rates (NAR) from more than 100 household surveys in forty-six countries throw new light on rural/urban disparities (Education Policy and Data Center, 2007c; López et al., 2007). In thirty-two of the forty countries with the relevant survey data, net attendance rates in urban areas were found to be higher than those in rural areas, the rural/urban ratio being below 0.97. In seven other countries the rural and urban attendance rates were nearly at parity (between 0.98 and 1.02) and in Bangladesh the rural rate was higher than the urban one.[13] The extent of rural/urban disparity varies by country, from highly unequal instances such as

11. The relatively high disparity index for Ethiopia and Nigeria is partly due to regional enrolment figures being based on GERs, not NERs; see Figure 2.6 notes.

12. Of special note are Cambodia, Morocco, Mozambique and the United Republic of Tanzania, where NER levels increased by more than fifteen percentage points while the disparity index declined by more than seven points.

13. This is mainly due to the greater prevalence of over-age primary and secondary school attendance in rural areas. In Bangladesh, rural attendance rates were higher than the urban rates starting from age 10, which reflects the spread of alternative schools programmes, such as BRAC, to under-privileged children, especially girls.

Table 2.5: Changes in country-level enrolment ratios and in educational geographic disparity, pre- to post-Dakar

Change in national NERs, 1999 to 2005	Change in subnational geographic disparity, pre- to post-Dakar		
	Reduced geographic disparity	Little or no change	Greater geographic disparity
Increase			
	Brazil	Eritrea	Bangladesh[1]
	Burkina Faso	Philippines	Benin
	Cambodia	Senegal[1]	Ethiopia[1]
	Indonesia		Gambia
	Mali		Guinea
	Morocco		India
	Mozambique		Kenya[1]
	Niger		Mauritania[1]
	U. R. Tanzania		Zambia
Little or no change			
	Argentina[1]		Zimbabwe[1]
	China[1]		
Decrease			
			Colombia

1. GERs were used to calculate the geographic disparity measure when NERs were not available for both years; in Bangladesh and Zimbabwe GERs were used only for the post-Dakar period.
Sources: Annex, Statistical Table 5; Sherman and Poirier (2007); UIS database.

Burkina Faso (0.33), Ethiopia (0.43), Chad (0.54) and Haiti (0.66) to near parity in Brazil, Egypt and Paraguay.

A comparison of attendance figures from household surveys conducted in the 1990s and the 2000s indicates that in twenty-four of the thirty-nine countries with the data, rural/urban disparity in net attendance rates has decreased by more than 1% per year (Figure 2.7), most rapidly in Benin, Ethiopia, Guinea, Mali, Morocco, Senegal and the United Republic of Tanzania. By contrast, in Bolivia, Haiti, Kenya and Namibia the rural/urban ratio worsened over time, either because rural attendance rates rose more slowly than urban rates, or because rural attendance rates declined while urban rates increased (the case of Namibia). In the remaining eleven countries there was little change in rural/urban disparities.

Slums

Not all children who grow up in cities benefit from an 'urban advantage' in education (UN-HABITAT, 2006). In many contexts, the educational participation and completion rates of children living in slums, or belonging to poor families living in non-slum urban areas, are considerably lower than

Figure 2.7: Average annual change in the rural/urban ratio of net attendance rates for thirty-nine countries

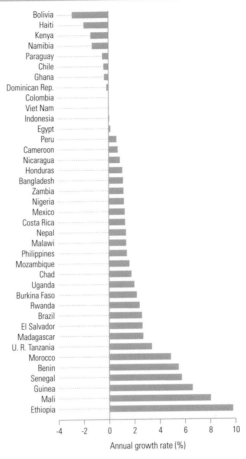

Note: Changes in national rural/urban ratios are expressed as average annual compound growth rates.
Sources: Education Policy and Data Center (2007c); López et al. (2007).

those of other urban children. This is particularly the case in many African cities, where primary school enrolments are increasing. In eastern and southern Africa, for example, the most significant progress in school enrolment in the late 1990s occurred in rural areas, leaving many poor urban families behind. UN-HABITAT analyses of urban survey data found that NERs in the United Republic of Tanzania increased in both rural and non-slum urban areas, but decreased in slum areas. Similar developments have been reported in Zambia and Zimbabwe, as well as in Brazil and Guatemala.

Household poverty

Poverty significantly reduces the likelihood of school participation (Smits et al., 2007). In many countries, children from poor households, whether urban or rural, attend school less than children

Poverty significantly reduces the likelihood of school participation

Education for All Global Monitoring Report 2008

from more affluent homes. In nine of twenty countries with household survey data (Burkina Faso, Cameroon, Ethiopia, Ghana, Kenya, Malawi, Mozambique, the Philippines and Viet Nam) there is a strong negative correlation, -0.4 or above, between household poverty and the primary school attendance rate in both rural and urban regions (Figure 2.8). In Chad, Madagascar, Morocco, Nigeria, Peru and the United Republic of Tanzania the association is strong in rural regions but not in urban ones. In Bangladesh, Egypt, Indonesia, Rwanda and Senegal, however, the association is weak in rural regions – and sometimes also in urban ones.

Ethnicity

In some countries, ethnicity remains an important barrier to education. A recent analysis comparing rates of primary and secondary educational attainment[14] among young adults in ten Latin American countries revealed significant disparities between indigenous and non-indigenous populations at the primary level in six of them (Bolivia, Ecuador, Guatemala, Nicaragua, Panama and Paraguay) and small differences in the remaining four: Brazil, Chile, Cuba and Peru.

> In some countries, ethnicity remains an important barrier to education

In Guatemala, Nicaragua and Panama, where the gaps were most marked, the primary educational attainment rates among young indigenous adults were twenty to thirty percentage points lower than for non-indigenous adults. In fact, less than half of indigenous 15- to 19-year-olds attained primary education.

At the secondary level, significant ethnicity-based disparities exist in all countries, except in Cuba where the disparity is limited to the upper secondary level. Overall, disparities between indigenous and non-indigenous populations were more marked than those between males and females or between areas of residence (UNESCO-OREALC, 2007).

Disabled children

Disabled children are much less likely to attend school than others. Table 2.6 shows the proportions of children aged 6–11 with and without physical disabilities who were not attending school, in seven countries for various years. On average across these countries, a disabled child is half as likely to be in school as a child without disability.

There are, however, considerable differences among countries, with relatively small variations in Mozambique and Mongolia, and a large variation in Indonesia. In a set of three more recent studies, for Malawi, Zambia and Zimbabwe, the chances of a disabled child not being in school are two to three times greater than for a child who is not disabled (Eide and Loeb, 2006; Eide et al., 2003; Loeb and Eide, 2004).

Figure 2.8: Strength and direction of the association between the prevalence of poor households and primary net attendance rates, post-Dakar period

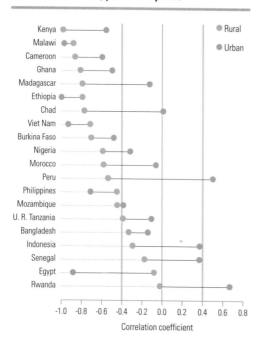

Source: Education Policy and Data Center (2007c).

Table 2.6: Percentages of children with and without disabilities not attending school in seven countries (various years)

Country, year of survey	With disabilities (%)	Without disabilities (%)	Difference (percentage points)
Indonesia, 2003	70.8	11.5	59.3
Cambodia, 2000	62.2	33.2	29.0
Jamaica, 1998	29.4	0.6	28.8
Burundi, 2000	85.4	62.8	22.6
Romania, 1996	42.3	20.8	21.5
Mongolia, 2000	59.0	42.0	17.0
Mozambique, 1996	65.8	50.2	15.0

Note: The data are taken from household surveys that use different definitions of disability.
Source: Filmer (2005).

14. Rates of primary educational attainment were estimated for 15- to 19-year-olds, based on the ISCED definitions.

Which of these educational deficits are most salient? Recent evidence from Latin America and the Caribbean compares the range of educational disparities by gender, ethnicity, residence, and degree of economic inequality and poverty (UNESCO-OREALC, 2007). At the primary level the median disparity index is greatest along the economic dimensions, followed by residence, ethnicity and gender. At the lower secondary level the median disparity index is greater than at the primary level, but the relative importance of the different dimensions remains the same. Moreover, in many countries these dimensions overlap – for example, indigenous populations living in poorer households in rural communities.

A sharp drop since Dakar in the number of out-of-school children

The total number of primary-school-age children not in primary or secondary school in 2005 worldwide was around 72 million, a sharp drop from 96 million in 1999 (Table 2.7). The number of out-of-school children fell most dramatically in South and West Asia (from 31 million to 17 million), and sub-Saharan Africa (42 million to 33 million). Thus, for these two regions combined, the number of children not in school fell from 74 million to 50 million over six years, but they still account for 24% and 45%, respectively, of all out-of-school

children. The share of girls among out-of-school children fell slightly between 1999 and 2005, from 59% to 57%. A marked contrast emerges here: in sub-Saharan Africa girls accounted for only 54% of out-of-school children in 2005, compared with South and West Asia at 66%, and the Arab States at 60%. In regions with very high enrolment ratios, such as Latin America, and North America and Western Europe, non-enrolment has different causes and boys comprise a majority of out-of-school children.

The decrease in the number of out-of-school children has accelerated in recent years: it fell by 5.2 million (5%) between 1999 and 2002, but by 19.2 million (21%) between 2002 and 2005 (Table 2.8).

A global momentum has developed. Much now depends on a few countries: India, Nigeria and Pakistan account for 27% of the world's out-of-

The decrease in the number of out-of-school children has accelerated in recent years

Table 2.8: Estimated number of out-of-school children worldwide, 1999 to 2005 (thousands)

1999	2000	2001	2002	2003	2004	2005
96 459	92 998	90 524	91 295	84 977	74 503	72 124

Sources: 1999 and 2005 from annex, Statistical Table 5; other years from UIS database.

Table 2.7: Estimated number of out-of-school children by region, 1999 and 2005

	1999			2005		
	Total (000)	% by region	% female	Total (000)	% by region	% female
World	96 459	100.0	58.7	72 124	100.0	56.8
Developing countries	92 534	95.9	59.1	68 825	95.4	57.3
Developed countries	1 886	2.0	49.0	2 270	3.1	44.7
Countries in transition	2 039	2.1	51.0	1 029	1.4	49.4
Sub-Saharan Africa	42 423	44.0	53.2	32 774	45.4	54.3
Arab States	7 720	8.0	59.4	6 122	8.5	59.7
Central Asia	490	0.5	52.0	381	0.5	51.7
East Asia and the Pacific	6 824	7.1	50.5	9 524	13.2	52.0
East Asia	6 377	6.6	50.5	9 189	12.7	51.9
Pacific	447	0.5	49.9	335	0.5	55.5
South and West Asia	31 434	32.6	69.0	17 092	23.7	66.3
Latin America and the Caribbean	3 595	3.7	54.3	2 433	3.4	49.0
Caribbean	435	0.5	51.5	449	0.6	52.8
Latin America	3 160	3.3	54.7	1 983	2.7	48.1
North America and Western Europe	1 465	1.5	49.1	1 898	2.6	44.6
Central and Eastern Europe	2 508	2.6	56.7	1 901	2.6	53.1

Source: Annex, Statistical Table 5.

CHAPTER 2

15. Afghanistan, Angola, Burundi, Cambodia, the Central African Republic, Chad, the Comoros, the Congo, Côte d'Ivoire, the Democratic Republic of the Congo, Djibouti, Eritrea, the Gambia, Guinea, Guinea-Bissau, Haiti, Kiribati, the Lao People's Democratic Republic, Liberia, Myanmar, the Niger, Nigeria, Papua New Guinea, Sao Tome and Principe, Sierra Leone, Solomon Islands, Somalia, Sudan, Tajikistan, Timor-Leste, Togo, Tonga, Uzbekistan, Vanuatu and Zimbabwe (OECD, 2006c).

school children; including the other seven countries with more than 1 million out-of-school children (Côte d'Ivoire, Burkina Faso, Ethiopia, Kenya, Mali, the Niger and Viet Nam) raises the proportion to 40% (Map 2.2; Table 2.9). Moreover, the thirty-five 'fragile states' identified by the OECD[15] accounted for roughly 37% of all out-of-school children in 2005. Providing places in primary schools for these children will be particularly problematic. It is difficult to evaluate the situation in China, the most populous country in the world (Box 2.2).

Analyses of the age at which children begin school and the age range in each grade suggest that across all developing countries around 32% of those children of primary school age who are counted as being out of school may eventually enrol as late entrants and that a further 16% had initially enrolled but then left before reaching the 'official' age of completion (Bruneforth, 2007). In other words, more than half of out-of-school children have never been in school and may never enrol without additional incentives. The distribution of out-of-school children by educational experience varies by region, as Figure 2.9 shows.

Map 2.2: Primary education NER and out-of-school children, 2005

Note: See source table for detailed country notes.
Source: Annex, Statistical Table 5.

The boundaries and names shown and the designations used on this map do not imply official endorsement or acceptance by UNESCO.

Based on United Nations map.

Table 2.9: Number of out-of-school children in selected countries,[1] 1999, 2002 and 2005

	Number of out-of-school children (000)		
	1999	2002	2005
Nigeria	7 189	6 707	6 584
India	…	…	6 395
Pakistan	…	7 972	6 303
Ethiopia	4 962	…	2 666
U. R. Tanzania	3 405	1 950	132
Kenya	1 834	1 868	1 123
Iran, Isl. Rep.	1 666	1 076	307
Mozambique	1 602	1 572	872
Niger	1 393	1 381	1 371
Yemen	1 334	…	861
Ghana	1 330	1 307	990
Côte d'Ivoire	1 254	1 144	1 223
Burkina Faso	1 205	1 264	1 202
Bangladesh	1 121	…	399
Morocco	1 114	557	525
Mali	1 113	1 089	1 113
Myanmar	1 051	1 009	487
Nepal	1 046	…	702
Brazil	1 032	934	482
Philippines	854	745	647
Senegal	808	846	518
Madagascar	785	765	188
Zambia	760	737	228
Saudi Arabia	…	760	793
Guinea	709	…	501
Chad	636	…	594
Turkey	…	623	905
Iraq	603	…	552
Benin	585	…	270
Viet Nam	393	634	1 007
South Africa	171	446	569

Note: Estimates labelled 2002 and 2005 are for the closest available year.

1. Countries listed had more than 500,000 out-of-school children in 1999 or 2005. The list is not necessarily complete, since many countries do not provide sufficient information for detailed calculations. The necessary data are available for 101 countries for 1999 and for 122 countries for 2005. Countries with insufficient data include Afghanistan, Angola, Cameroon, the Democratic Republic of the Congo, Papua New Guinea, Serbia and Montenegro, Sierra Leone, Somalia, Sudan, Turkmenistan and Uganda, most of which are fragile states.

Source: Annex, Statistical Table 5.

Box 2.2: China: population data issues pose a UPE monitoring challenge

China has the world's second largest population of primary-school-age children, but there is no internationally agreed figure for its primary NER; indeed, there is a large gap between the NER as calculated at the national level and that at the international level, mainly due to disputed population data. While there is much debate among education experts concerning the quality of the enrolment data, the accuracy of the population projections typically receives much less attention.

The size of China's primary-school-age population has been the subject of discussions within the country as well as among international data users such as the UIS and the United Nations Population Division (UNPD). The Chinese Ministry of Education creates its own population estimates and projections, which are used to calculate enrolment indicators and which are not necessarily the same as either those produced by the national statistical office or those from the UNPD. According to the Ministry of Education, the 2005 primary-school-age population was 90 million; UNPD projections indicate about 100 million. Given the magnitude of this gap, the UIS has suspended publication of the NER for China pending further review of the population data.

The UIS, in co-operation with the Chinese national authorities, has initiated discussions with the national agencies involved in producing population data, as well as with the UNPD, in order to develop a better understanding of the differing population estimates. The findings should help produce an internationally accepted measure of net enrolment in the near future.

Figure 2.9: Distribution of out-of-school children by educational experience and region, 2005

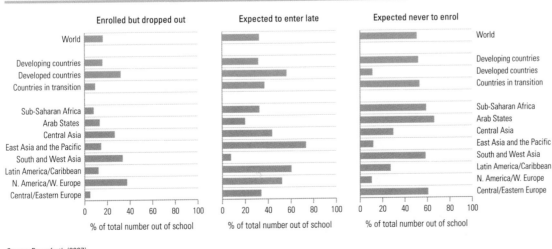

Source: Bruneforth (2007).

High levels of repetition are considered an indication of low quality of education

Overall, children are more likely to be out of school if they are from poor households, live in a rural area and/or have a mother with no schooling. Being a girl accentuates the probability of not being in school for each of these categories (UNESCO, 2006a).

Primary school progression and completion

Grade repetition: a persistent problem

Grade repetition, seen by some educators as a remedy for slow learners, is criticized by others: advocates of automatic promotion cite studies showing that repetition does not necessarily

translate into better learning outcomes. In general, countries seek to reduce grade repetition not only for pedagogical reasons, but also because they consider it a waste of resources, as school places occupied by repeaters reduce the supply of school places for new entrants. High levels of repetition are also considered an indication of low quality of education, as they point to poor mastering of the curriculum by pupils; and pupils may drop out of school rather than repeat grades. (Box 2.3 discusses the relationship between grade repetition and dropout behaviour in Guatemala.) Thus, some countries officially apply a policy of automatic promotion, which is no panacea either without strong measures to support low achievers.[16]

Box 2.3: Repetition and dropout in Guatemala

Repetition and dropout are considered the two components of 'wastage' in education, although many argue that years spent by pupils repeating grades are not necessarily wasted. In most developing regions, countries with the highest levels of dropout are also often those where repetition rates are highest. Both repetition and dropout affect different categories of the population unevenly. In Guatemala children repeat grades and drop out more in rural than in urban areas (Figure 2.10). Both repetition and dropout are highest in grade 1, perhaps as a result of scarce coverage and low quality of pre-primary education. The trend in dropout reveals the role of natural disasters, which particularly affect the most disadvantaged segments of the population, living mostly in rural areas.

Dropout decreased from 1992 to 1997, but the trend reversed abruptly in 1998 with Hurricane Mitch, when dropout rose by 0.8 percentage points in urban areas – and by 6.8 percentage points in rural areas.

An analysis of school survival in relation to income category, urban vs. rural residence, gender and ethnicity found the most significant disparities to be by socio-economic category and residence. For instance, children from families belonging to the 20% of the population with the highest income are 42% more likely to reach grade 6 than their peers belonging to the 20% of the population with the lowest income. The gap in the survival rate to grade 6 between urban and rural children is of the same order.

Figure 2.10: Repetition and dropout in primary education by grade and area of residence, Guatemala, 2005

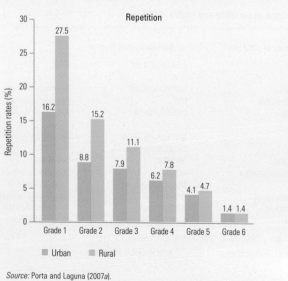

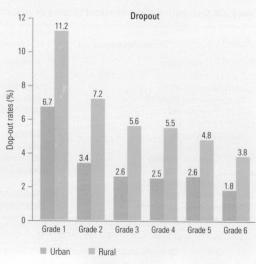

Source: Porta and Laguna (2007a).

16. Countries applying automatic promotion include the Seychelles and Zimbabwe in sub-Saharan Africa; Malaysia and the Pacific island states of Kiribati, Marshall Islands, Niue, Tokelau and Tuvalu; the Caribbean countries of Barbados, Bermuda, and St Kitts and Nevis; and Denmark, the Netherlands and Norway in Western Europe. In addition, the percentage of repeaters is reported to be nil or negligible in the Bahamas, Iceland, Papua New Guinea, the Republic of Korea, the United Kingdom and Uzbekistan.

Repetition rates are highest in sub-Saharan Africa, where the median level of repeaters is 15%, followed by Latin America and the Caribbean, and South and West Asia at 5% each (see annex, Statistical Table 6). In about three in ten countries in sub-Saharan Africa, 20% of primary-school pupils are repeaters. Countries in this group include Cameroon, Chad, Comoros, the Congo, Equatorial Guinea, Malawi, Sao Tome and Principe, and Togo, as well as Burundi, the Central African Republic and Gabon with repetition of 30% or more. The situation is less dramatic in other regions; repeaters represent 20% of pupils in Brazil, Suriname and Nepal. Among developed countries the level of repetition reaches 10% only in Portugal.

In most regions the repetition rate is highest in grade 1, and might be reduced if more children attended ECCE programmes preparing them for the transition to formal primary schooling. After grade 1, repetition rates are highest in the last grade, due to examinations formally marking the completion of primary school. Grade 1 repeaters are particularly numerous in Latin America and the Caribbean (e.g. Brazil, 27%; Guatemala, 24%), but rates are also relatively high in some Asian countries (Cambodia, 24%; the Lao People's Democratic Republic, 34%; Nepal, 37%) and in sub-Saharan Africa (above 20% in Chad, Eritrea, Lesotho, Malawi, Sao Tome and Principe, and Togo, and above 30% in Burundi, Comoros and Gabon). In Burundi, fully 44% of pupils repeat the last primary grade. In the Arab States the highest grade 1 repetition rate is 16%, in Morocco, while Djibouti, Mauritania and Algeria have the highest repetition rates in the last grade, from 15% to 22% (see annex, Statistical Table 6).

Between 1999 and 2005 repetition decreased in two-thirds of the countries with the relevant data, and increased or remained unchanged in the other third. In some cases, targeted measures facilitated the reduction. In Mozambique, a new basic education curriculum (grades 1 to 7) was introduced in 2004 to improve internal efficiency and reduce repetition; the incidence of repetition declined from 24% in 1999 to 10% in 2005. Other countries are gradually adopting policies of automatic promotion, such as Ethiopia, where repetition registered a decline from 11.4% in 1999 to 7% in 2006, a trend particularly pronounced for girls. The implementation of a semi-automatic promotion policy in Madagascar reduced the incidence of repetition from 28% in 1999 to 18% in 2005.

School survival: not guaranteed in many countries

A necessary pre-condition for reaching UPE is to have all children of school admission age entering school. While policies adopted since Dakar have brought about major progress in access to schooling, school systems have not always been able to retain the large flow of new entrants, making achievement of universal primary enrolment and completion difficult. Figure 2.11 shows the relationship across countries between gross intake rates and survival rates to the last grade. Countries with high gross intake rates into primary education and high school survival rates are clustered towards the upper right; they are mostly middle income countries in East Asia and the Pacific, and Latin America and the Caribbean. Developed and transition countries concentrate towards values of 100% for both GIR and survival rates. Countries with low intake and low survival (e.g. Burundi, Chad, the Congo, Gabon, the Niger, the Turks and Caicos Islands) are towards the lower left. Countries reporting high intake but low survival (e.g. Benin, Madagascar, Malawi, Mauritania, Mozambique, Nicaragua, Rwanda, Uganda) are concentrated towards the lower right. Finally, countries with low access to education and relatively high levels of school retention (e.g. Mali, Eritrea, Oman, Sudan) are grouped towards the upper left. Excessively high GIRs do not necessarily mean a positive situation; they often point to high proportions of over-age children, which indicate poor school efficiency. Some countries have high intake due to the introduction of free primary education, but experience a negative side-effect in terms of low survival. In Uganda, for example, which introduced free primary schooling in the 1990s, only 25% of primary school pupils reached the last grade in 2004.

Globally, the rate of survival to the last grade of primary education is below 87% in half the countries with available data for 2004 (Map 2.3 and annex, Statistical Table 7). Median values are lowest in sub-Saharan Africa (63%), followed by South and West Asia (79%). At the other end of the spectrum, Central and Eastern Europe, and North America and Western Europe both have median values above 98%. Medians above 90% are found in the Arab States (94%) and Central Asia (97%). The survival rate to the last grade is particularly low in Benin, Chad, Madagascar, Malawi, Mauritania, Mozambique, Rwanda and Uganda, where fewer than half of pupils reach the last grade.

In Uganda, only 25% of primary school pupils reached the last grade in 2004

CHAPTER 2

Figure 2.11: Situation of countries in terms of access to schooling and survival

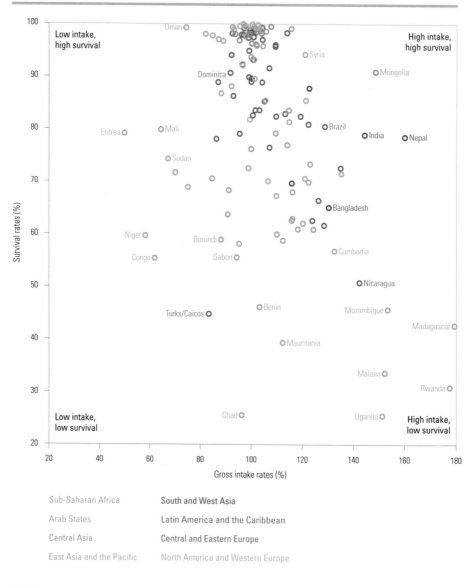

Note: Gross intake rates are for 2005, survival rates for 2004.
Sources: Annex, Statistical Tables 4 and 7.

Survival to the last grade of primary education improved between 1999 and 2004 in most countries for which data are available. Progress has been particularly significant in Colombia, the Dominican Republic, Guatemala, India, Mali, Mozambique, Nepal and South Africa. The situation appears to have deteriorated in Cameroon, Chad, Eritrea, Madagascar, Mauritania and Yemen. In most of the latter group, the deterioration in survival is associated with improvement in NERs (see annex, Statistical Tables 5 and 7). Chad, Eritrea, Madagascar,

Mauritania and Yemen, for example, have found it difficult to expand enrolment and still retain pupils until the end of primary. Countries that have successfully increased both enrolment ratios and survival rates include Cambodia, Ethiopia, Guatemala, Mali, Mozambique and Nepal.

Not all pupils who reach the last grade of primary education complete it. Cohort completion rates[17] are lower than survival rates, quite significantly in some cases, as Figure 2.12 shows for the countries with data for both indicators. The most pronounced

17. The cohort completion rate, a proxy measure of school completion, focuses on children who have access to school, measuring how many successfully complete it. It is computed as the product of the percentage of graduates from primary school (number of graduates as a percentage of enrolment in the last grade) and the survival rate to the last grade.

Map 2.3: Survival rates to the last grade of primary education, 2004

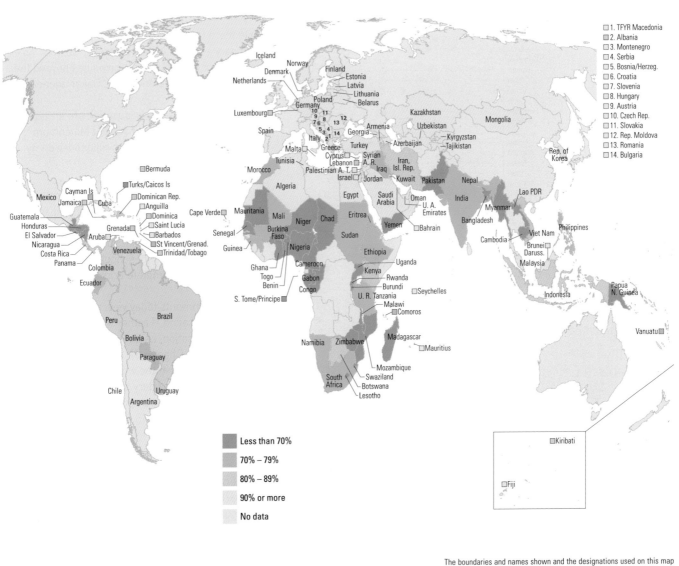

1. TFYR Macedonia
2. Albania
3. Montenegro
4. Serbia
5. Bosnia/Herzeg.
6. Croatia
7. Slovenia
8. Hungary
9. Austria
10. Czech Rep.
11. Slovakia
12. Rep. Moldova
13. Romania
14. Bulgaria

Less than 70%

70% – 79%

80% – 89%

90% or more

No data

Note: See source table for detailed country notes.
Source: Annex, Statistical Table 7.

The boundaries and names shown and the designations used on this map do not imply official endorsement or acceptance by UNESCO.
Based on United Nations map.

gaps (above twenty percentage points) are in Burundi, Brunei Darussalam, Grenada, Nepal, Niger, Pakistan and Senegal.

Why are children dropping out school?

The reasons for dropout are multiple and complex, with the relative incidence of particular factors influenced by countries' situations and the level of educational development. Unsafe, overcrowded and poorly equipped schools with inadequately trained teachers contribute to student dropout. Even the best-equipped schools in many developing countries may not be able to keep students from dropping out where economic hardship or poverty is the cause. The ultimate decision to leave school happens when personal, financial, home or employment problems coincide with children's lack of confidence in the school's ability to give them adequate support. This suggests that schools have the potential to act as powerful support mechanisms for students, enabling them to handle external difficulties without dropping out (Bella and Mputu, 2004; Davies, 1999).

Economic hardship or poverty can cause school dropout

CHAPTER 2

Demand for
and participation
in secondary
education are
growing as more
countries
progress
towards UPE

Figure 2.12: Survival rates to last grade and cohort completion rates, 2004

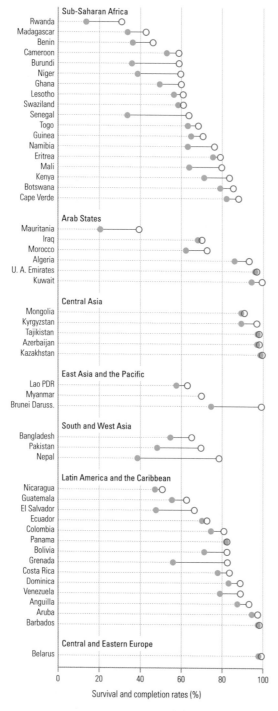

Survival and completion rates (%)

● Cohort completion rate   ○ Survival to last grade

Source: Annex, Statistical Table 7.

18. Basic education as used here covers primary education (first stage) and lower secondary education (second stage).

19. Between 1991 and 1999 the global number of secondary-school students rose from 315 million to 439 million, an increase of 39%. Overall, then, the worldwide growth in secondary education has slowed somewhat since Dakar.

Secondary education and beyond also contribute to EFA

While there is no Dakar goal pertaining to secondary and tertiary education per se, the expansion of educational opportunities beyond the primary level does belong to the Dakar agenda:

■ Secondary and tertiary education are an explicit part of the Education for All and Millennium Development Goals concerning gender parity and equality.

■ The expansion of primary education creates demand for post-primary education; expansion is also dependent on secondary and tertiary education for an adequate supply of teachers and on sufficient secondary school places to increase the incentive to complete primary school.

■ Most governments today view the universalization of basic education,[18] rather than simply of primary education, as an important policy objective (see Chapter 1). In addition, three out of four countries in the world, accounting for 80% of children of secondary school age, include lower secondary in compulsory education (UNESCO-UNEVOC/UIS, 2006).

■ As labour markets increasingly demand higher levels of skills, training and knowledge, access to secondary and tertiary education provides an important avenue for meeting the learning needs of young people and adults (EFA goal 3).

■ The children of parents who have participated in secondary or tertiary education are more likely to attend ECCE, have higher learning outcomes and complete primary schooling.

Secondary education is expanding and diversifying

Demand for and participation in secondary education are growing as more countries progress towards UPE. In 2005, some 512 million students were enrolled in secondary schools worldwide, an increase of more than 73 million (17%) since 1999.[19] This increase was driven by rises in sub-Saharan Africa (by 55%), South and West Asia (25%), the Arab States (25%) and East Asia (21%). Meanwhile, Central and Eastern Europe, Central Asia, the Pacific, and North America and Western Europe, the regions with the highest enrolment ratios in secondary education, now have more secondary- than primary-school students.[20] The nature of secondary education is itself also changing rapidly as access expands (Box 2.4).

Worldwide, participation rates in secondary education have increased significantly since the early 1990s: the average secondary GER was 52% in 1991, 60% in 1999 and 66% in 2005 (Table 2.10). The average secondary NER increased from 53% in 1999 to 59% in 2005. Participation rates in secondary education increased in all regions, except Central Asia in 1991–99, a period of widespread 'educational deterioration' (Silova et al., 2007).

Regional disparities in participation rates at secondary level in 2005 are similar to those at primary level, albeit more pronounced. Countries in North America and Western Europe have almost achieved universal secondary education, with GERs above 100% on average and NERs exceeding 90%. Relatively high secondary NERs (over 80%) are found in Central and Eastern Europe and in Central Asia. Two-thirds or more of secondary-school-age young people are enrolled in secondary schools in Latin America and in East Asia and the Pacific.

Average secondary NERs are lower in the remaining regions, especially sub-Saharan Africa (25%).

Between 1991 and 2005, secondary GERs increased in 127 of the 147 countries with data (see annex, Statistical Table 12). Twenty-one countries experienced significant increases in their secondary GERs (more than thirty percentage points), including Australia, Brazil and Kuwait with rises of more than fifty percentage points.[21] Sixty countries (of 127 with data) experienced more rapid growth in the post-Dakar period than in the pre-Dakar period. Benin, Cambodia, Cameroon, Djibouti, Ethiopia, Guinea, Mozambique, the Syrian Arab Republic and Uganda have had average annual increases above 10% since 1999. For the sixty-seven countries that have experienced slower growth in the secondary GER since Dakar, the median annual growth rate was less than 1% per year.

Lower and upper secondary education: distinct stages

Most countries distinguish between two stages of secondary education (UNESCO, 1997). Lower secondary education (ISCED level 2), often compulsory, seeks to maintain and deepen the

Two-thirds or more of secondary-school-age young people are enrolled in secondary schools in Latin America and in East Asia and the Pacific

---

Box 2.4: Diversification of secondary education reflects changing interests and social needs

As countries have expanded access to secondary education, they have also reorganized the structure and composition of secondary-level programmes of study. These changes go beyond distinctions between lower and upper secondary education, on the one hand, and between academic and technical/vocational enrolment, on the other. Recent analyses (Benavot, 2006; World Bank, 2005d) indicate that:

- Teacher-training programmes, which were prominent in secondary education in the 1960s and 1980s, are today found in only about 10% to 15% of countries. This reflects the upgrading and 'professionalization' of teacher- training programmes, which are increasingly delivered in post-secondary institutions (UNESCO-IBE, 2007b).

- Programmes devoted to religious or theological training were once relatively prominent; today only 6% of countries, mainly Arab States, offer such programmes.

- Only 14% of countries have specialized programmes in the fine arts or sports. In many cases such programmes have either been eliminated or integrated into academic secondary schooling.

- In academic secondary education, few countries today provide a distinctive programme in classical or semi-classical education (e.g. Latin, Greek). More prevalent are comprehensive or general tracks, on the one hand, and specialized tracks, on the other, especially those in mathematics and sciences and in the humanities and the social sciences.

- Especially in OECD countries, some secondary school graduates enrol in post-secondary, non- tertiary programmes (ISCED level 4) that prepare them for specific jobs or occupations in the labour market. Such programmes, which typically last less than two years, have low enrolment levels (see annex, Statistical Table 8). ISCED 4 enrolments are relatively higher in very few countries – mainly Caribbean states having no tertiary institutions, but also Ireland, Kazakhstan and Seychelles.

The expansion of secondary education is thus resulting in greater programmatic and curricular diversification. Countries are redefining the ways in which secondary education addresses increasingly diverse pupil interests and societal needs.

---

20. Changing cohort sizes, due to differential fertility rates, is an important factor in this shift.

21. The other eighteen countries are Belize, Botswana, Cape Verde, Costa Rica, El Salvador, Honduras, Macao (China), Mauritius, New Zealand, Oman, Paraguay, Portugal, Samoa, Saudi Arabia, Thailand, Tunisia, Venezuela and Viet Nam.

Table 2.10: Enrolment ratios in secondary education by region, 1991, 1999 and 2005

	Gross enrolment ratios (%)			Net enrolment ratios (%)	
	School year ending in			School year ending in	
	1991	1999	2005	1999	2005
World	52	60	66	53	59
Developing countries	42	53	60	46	53
Developed countries	93	100	102	89	92
Countries in transition	95	91	91	84	82
Sub-Saharan Africa	22	24	32	19	26
Arab States	51	60	68	52	58
Central Asia	98	86	90	81	84
East Asia and the Pacific	50	64	74	61	70
East Asia	50	64	73	61	70
Pacific	66	107	105	68	69
South and West Asia	41	46	53	40	46
Latin America and the Caribbean	51	80	88	59	68
Caribbean	43	54	58	45	42
Latin America	51	81	89	59	69
North America and Western Europe	94	101	102	89	92
Central and Eastern Europe	81	87	89	80	81

Sources: UIS database; annex, Statistical Table 8.

TVET programmes and enrolments are considerably more prominent at the upper secondary level than lower secondary

educational aims of primary schooling. In some countries it is provided in the same institutions and taught by the same teachers as primary education; in others it is institutionally distinct from primary education and shares more in common with upper secondary education (UIS, 2005). The onset of upper secondary education (ISCED level 3) typically marks the end of compulsory schooling, consists of diverse structures, tracks and programmes, and features a more specialized teaching staff.

Worldwide in 2005, the GER in lower secondary was 79%, much higher than the ratio of 53% in upper secondary (Table 2.11). Differing participation rates between the two levels were especially prominent in East Asia and the Pacific, Latin America and the Caribbean, and the Arab States. By contrast, in North America and Western Europe and in Central and Eastern Europe participation is very similar throughout all of secondary education.

Expanded access to basic education

Of the 203 countries and territories covered in the statistical annex, 192 reported having laws or statutes making education compulsory (see annex, Statistical Table 4). In about three-quarters of them, compulsory education includes lower secondary, which implies an official intention to universalize participation in basic education (see Chapter 1).

In all developed countries, in all countries in transition and in 80% of countries in Latin America and the Caribbean[22] and in East Asia and the Pacific, lower secondary education is indeed compulsory and participation levels are high: GERs were above 90% in 2005. In 75% of the Arab States, lower secondary education is now compulsory but average participation levels, while increasing, are far from universal at 81%. In South and West Asia and in sub-Saharan Africa, where lower secondary education is compulsory in less than 40% of countries, participation levels are considerably lower (66% and 38%, respectively).

Technical and vocational education: an alternative stream within secondary education

Secondary education often includes technical and vocational education and training (TVET) as well as general or academically oriented programmes. In fact, of the more than 512 million students enrolled in secondary schools worldwide in 2005, one in ten was enrolled in secondary-level TVET programmes. The percentage has declined very slightly since 1999 (see annex, Statistical Table 8). The relative share of secondary-level TVET enrolments is highest in the Pacific (32%), Central and Eastern Europe (19%), and North America and Western Europe (15%) and lowest in South and West Asia (2%), the Caribbean (3%), Central Asia (6%) and sub-Saharan Africa (6%).

TVET programmes and enrolments are considerably more prominent at the upper secondary level than lower secondary. Of the 174 countries with available data, 71% report no TVET enrolments in lower secondary education. At the upper secondary level, however, of the 165 countries with available data, 82% report TVET enrolments. In most countries the share of TVET enrolments in upper secondary education was considerably higher than in lower secondary education (UNESCO-UNEVOC/UIS, 2006).

In general, countries' provision of TVET programmes varies greatly in relation to ISCED level, coverage and students' educational options upon programme completion. 'Patterns of provision are strongly related to cultural institutions, colonial history and geographical proximity: Anglophone countries tend to locate TVET programmes in post-secondary, non-tertiary institutions (ISCED 4), which is infrequent in Latin America. In Belgium,

22. The average GER in lower secondary education for Caribbean countries is 75%, considerably lower than the average for Latin America (100%).

ARE WE REACHING THE EDUCATION FOR ALL GOALS?

Are the learning needs of young people and adults being met?

Netherlands and former Dutch colonies, TVET programmes are found at ISCED level 2' (UNESCO-UNEVOC/UIS, 2006). In addition, trained vocational students were once channelled directly into the labour market, but today many graduates of TVET programmes opt to sit for national matriculation exams or enter post-secondary institutions.

Tertiary enrolment: rising worldwide but still very limited

Worldwide, some 138 million students were enrolled in tertiary education in 2005, about 45 million more than in 1999. The vast majority of new places in tertiary institutions were created in large developing countries such as Brazil, China, India and Nigeria, where the combined total of tertiary students rose from 47 million in 1999 to 80 million in 2005 (see annex, Statistical Table 9). Participation rates in higher education were on the rise between 1999 and 2005 in about 90% of the 119 countries for which data are available. Increases of more than ten percentage points were observed in more than forty countries, mostly developed and middle income countries and those in transition. However, large increases of more than twenty-five percentage points were also recorded in several developing countries, including Cuba and the Republic of Korea.

Despite the continuing expansion of tertiary education worldwide since 1999, a relatively small share of the relevant age group has access to this level. The world tertiary GER was around 24% in 2005, but participation varies substantially by region, from 5% in sub-Saharan Africa to 70% in North America and Western Europe (Table 2.12).

Are the learning needs of young people and adults being met?

Goal 3: *Ensuring that the learning needs of all young people and adults are met through equitable access to appropriate learning and life-skills programmes*

The main strategy used for meeting the learning needs of young people and adults has been to expand formal secondary and tertiary education, as analysed above. However, skill acquisition through informal means and in non-formal settings is common, especially among school leavers and

Table 2.11: GERs in lower and upper secondary education by region, 1999 and 2005

	Gross enrolment ratios (%)			
	Lower secondary		Upper secondary	
	School year ending in		School year ending in	
	1999	2005	1999	2005
World	72	79	47	53
Developing countries	66	75	38	46
Developed countries	102	104	98	99
Countries in transition	92	91	87	89
Sub-Saharan Africa	28	38	19	24
Arab States	73	81	46	55
Central Asia	90	95	77	76
East Asia and the Pacific	80	93	46	55
East Asia	80	93	45	54
Pacific	89	89	139	132
South and West Asia	59	66	34	41
Latin America and the Caribbean	95	100	62	73
Caribbean	67	75	40	43
Latin America	96	101	63	74
North America and Western Europe	103	105	98	99
Central and Eastern Europe	92	91	81	87

Source: Annex, Statistical Table 8.

Table 2.12: Tertiary gross enrolment ratios by region, 1999 and 2005

	Gross enrolment ratios (%)	
	School year ending in	
	1999	2005
World	18.3	24.3
Developing countries	12.4	16.8
Developed countries	50.5	66.1
Countries in transition	37.5	56.5
Sub-Saharan Africa	4.4	5.1
Arab States	21.7	21.4
Central Asia	20.1	26.5
East Asia and the Pacific	15.6	23.8
East Asia	15.2	23.4
Pacific	41.3	50.3
South and West Asia	9.2	10.5
Latin America and the Caribbean	20.2	29.2
Caribbean	4.8	6.5
Latin America	20.6	30.0
North America and Western Europe	54.8	70.1
Central and Eastern Europe	36.0	57.0

Source: Annex, Statistical Table 9.

disadvantaged groups. It can be facilitated by the implementation of non-formal education programmes supplementing the formal school system, which 'may cover education programmes to impart adult literacy, basic education for out-of-school children, life skills, work skills and general culture' (UNESCO, 1997). Policy initiatives relevant to the EFA goal remain difficult to monitor, however (Box 2.5).

Provision of non-formal education: responding to diverse circumstances

Non-formal education programmes are extremely diverse and may differ in terms of objectives, target groups, content, pedagogy and scale. Providers are also very diverse. At least seventeen different ministries and national bodies are involved in Bangladesh, the same number in India and at least

nine each in Brazil, Egypt, Indonesia, Namibia and Thailand, not to mention non-government organizations (NGOs) and local communities with small-scale programmes about which few data are readily available.

Large-scale literacy programmes, often extending to life skills (health, civic rights), livelihoods (income generation, farming) and/or equivalency education, and supported by international NGOs and bilateral and multilateral agencies, are common, especially in poor countries including Afghanistan, Ethiopia, Nepal and Senegal.

Equivalency or 'second chance' programmes are a commonly used strategy to provide learning opportunities for young people. Countries including Brazil, Cambodia, Egypt, India, Indonesia, Mexico, the Philippines, Thailand and Viet Nam have pursued a combination of several 'levels' of equivalency programmes, including equivalencies to primary, secondary and sometimes tertiary education. Literacy programmes may also be linked to these structures. India's National Institute of Open Schooling is among the largest distance learning systems in the world. It has 249 centres for 'basic education', 917 vocational study centres and 1,805 academic study centres.

Other national programmes focus on skill development in the informal economy, as in China, Egypt, Ghana, South Africa and Viet Nam. These programmes are typically managed not by ministries of education but by those in charge of economic development and employment. India's Ministry of Labour and Employment, for example, recently developed a new framework for skills development targeted at out-of-school youth and informal sector workers. Programmes focusing on rural development are found and run in cooperation with ministries of agriculture in Brazil, Burkina Faso, China, Ethiopia, India, Nepal, the Philippines and Thailand. China had trained more than 500,000 people by 2005 through its national 'Training Young Farmers for the 21st Century' programme, launched in 1999 (Yonggong and He, 2006).

Non-formal education programmes are often linked with community development. In Thailand, 8,057 community learning centres had been established in 7,232 subdistricts by 2006. They provide a wide range of structured learning activities determined by community needs.

Box 2.5: EFA goal 3: the hardest to define and monitor

The third EFA goal is to ensure 'that the learning needs of all young people and adults are met through equitable access to appropriate learning and life-skills programmes'. The Expanded Commentary to the Dakar Framework for Action elaborates: 'All young people should be given the opportunity for ongoing education. For those who drop out of school or complete school without acquiring the literacy, numeracy and life skills they need, there must be a range of options for continuing their learning. Such opportunities should be both meaningful and relevant to their environment and needs, help them to become active agents in shaping their future and develop useful work-related skills' (UNESCO, 2000a, para. 36). Goal 4 makes similar statements in relation to adult education. These statements suggest that the 'learning needs' of young people and adults are not just about 'basic competencies' but refer to a broader conception of learning that is 'life-wide' and 'life-long' (Hoppers, 2007).

Monitoring the third EFA goal continues to be a major challenge:

● It gives no quantitative target for what should be achieved.

● There is a lack of a common understanding of which learning activities are included.

● Very few comparable and international indicators are available to indicate the extent to which young people's and adults' learning needs are being met.

The 2007 EFA Global Monitoring Report provided an initial conceptualization of EFA goal 3 by suggesting a special focus on non-formal education. However, given the diverse and often fragmented nature of non-formal education programmes, an array of quantitative and qualitative tools is needed to monitor them. The present Report draws on work conducted with a number of non-formal education experts to prepare thirty country profiles compiling qualitative data on the provision of non-formal education.*

* These country profiles are accessible on the Report website (www.efareport.unesco.org).

ARE WE REACHING THE EDUCATION FOR ALL GOALS?

Are the learning needs of young people and adults being met?

Community learning centre activities in Bangladesh, China, Indonesia and the Philippines include literacy classes, continuing education and skills training as the most frequently provided programmes (UNESCO-Bangkok, 2007b).

For some, non-formal education offers an alternative path

While few national data on enrolment in non-formal education exist, information can be obtained from household surveys such as the second Multiple Indicator Cluster Surveys (MICS2), carried out in 2000. In twenty-eight of the sixty-five surveyed countries, respondents were asked if their highest educational attainment level was obtained through a 'non-standard curriculum' (such as religious education outside the formal education system) or non-formal education (such as literacy). Figure 2.13 compares the responses of youth and adults.[23] In twenty of these twenty-eight countries, the proportions are under 1%. In the remaining countries (Burundi, Chad, Côte d'Ivoire, the Gambia, Guinea-Bissau, Myanmar, the Niger and Senegal), the proportions exceed 1%, rising as high as 20% among youth and 31% among adults in Burundi. Myanmar is another example of a country where the gap in the proportion of youth and adults with the highest educational attainment level reached in non-formal education was striking (4% and 18 %, respectively).

Within countries, the following patterns emerge:

■ Among both adults and youth, more men than women reached their highest level of educational attainment in a non-standard curriculum, with particularly large disparities in Chad (eight percentage points) and the Niger (twelve).

■ Highest educational attainment in non-standard curricula is more widespread in rural than in urban areas in Burundi, Chad, the Gambia, the Niger and Senegal.

■ In each country except Guinea-Bissau, respondents from households in the lowest wealth quintile are more likely to declare having reached their highest educational attainment in a non-standard curriculum: 9% of respondents in that quintile do so in Myanmar, ranging up to as high as 22% in Burundi (Education Policy and Data Center, 2007b).

Figure 2.13: Proportion of youth and adults whose reported highest educational attainment level was achieved in non-formal education, 2000

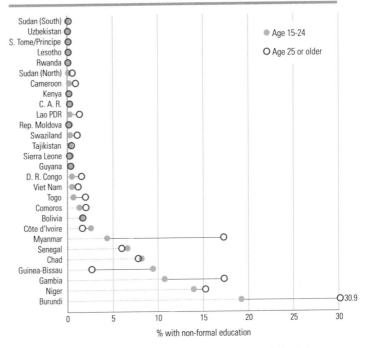

Note: Refers to respondents with highest educational attainment level in non-standard curriculum.
Source: Education Policy and Data Center (2007b).

Data from other sources confirm the limited access of youth and adults to continuing or non-formal education opportunities. A recent study based on data from household surveys and censuses for seventeen countries in Latin America shows that less than 10% of young adults (aged 20 to 39) who have not completed upper secondary education attend some kind of educational programmes.[24] Attendance rates were relatively higher in Brazil, Costa Rica and the Dominican Republic and lower in Chile, Colombia and Peru (UNESCO-OREALC, 2007).

Needed: improved monitoring of non-formal education

The EFA agenda calls for a comprehensive approach to learning in which non-formal education is an essential and integrated part. While a great variety of structured learning activities for youth and adults take place outside formal education systems, the extent to which this supply corresponds to demand is largely unknown. Improved monitoring of the supply and demand for non-formal education is urgently needed at the national and international levels.

23. The share of respondents who participated in non-formal education is bound to be larger, as the surveys identify only respondents who reached their highest attainment level in a non-standard curriculum.

24. This is an imprecise measure based on small absolute numbers. More important, the definition of attendance is not necessarily precise and may not be comparable across cases. However, the indicator remains useful as a rough measure of educational opportunities available to young people who have not completed their formal studies.

8
0
0
2

Education for All Global Monitoring Report

Literacy and literate environments: essential yet elusive

Goal 4: *Achieving a 50 per cent improvement in levels of adult literacy by 2015, especially for women, and equitable access to basic and continuing education for all adults*

25. Literacy assessment based on this definition generally suggests a dichotomy between 'literate' and 'illiterate'; the real picture is more that of a continuum of proficiency or competence.

26. Using these literacy data periods makes it difficult to compare the pre- and post-Dakar situations, but nonetheless gives some indication of changes.

Literacy is a fundamental human right and a basic tool for making informed decisions and participating fully in the development of society. As such, it is a foundation for achieving EFA and reducing poverty (UNESCO, 2005a). Yet, it remains a major challenge. During the most recent period (1995–2004), about 774 million adults worldwide were not literate (see annex, Statistical Table 2A). This figure is based on conventional cross-country data drawn from censuses or household surveys that rely on self-assessments, third-party reporting or educational attainment proxies. Usually in censuses, respondents are asked if they can 'read and write, with understanding, a simple statement of their everyday life', in the words of UNESCO's traditional definition of literacy.[25] The growing availability of data that rely on direct assessments of literacy skills, such as those from a recent survey in Kenya (Box 2.6), suggests that the scale of the literacy challenge may be even greater. Conventional literacy data tend in fact to overestimate literacy levels and should be interpreted with caution.

Adult literacy: still a global challenge

Keeping this data caveat in mind, it appears that the global number of adults who were not literate declined by 90 million between the 1985–1994 and 1995–2004 periods,[26] mainly due to trends in East

---

Box 2.6: Direct literacy assessment: the Kenya National Adult Literacy Survey

Many countries are developing new methodologies based on direct assessments in order to improve the quality of literacy data and related policy-making. In 2006, Kenya carried out an extensive survey of literacy and numeracy in over 15,000 households, the Kenya National Adult Literacy Survey (Kenya National Bureau of Statistics, 2007).* Multi-level scales were developed to assess the extent to which adults had attained 'minimum' or 'desired' levels of literacy and numeracy. The survey was offered in English, Kiswahili and eighteen other local languages (70% of respondents chose either English or Kiswahili).

The Kenyan survey demonstrates in two ways that conventional data relying on self-assessment tend to overstate actual literacy and numeracy levels. First, its estimate of the adult literacy rate is 62% (men 64%, women 59%), much lower than the MICS 2000 result of 74% (men 78%, women 70%). Second, within the survey, self-assessment yields higher literacy levels than direct tests (Table 2.13).

Other key findings from the survey:

● Direct assessment shows Kenyan adults have a stronger mastery of numeracy than literacy (minimum mastery level), with rates of 65% and 62%, respectively, for men and women combined. Only 30% of Kenyan adults attained the higher 'desired' levels of literacy.

● Literacy and numeracy rates vary significantly by geographic district and by age. Among Kenyans aged 15 to

Table 2.13: Comparison of self-assessment and direct assessment of adult literacy[1] by gender, 2006

Assessment type		Women (%)	Men (%)
Literacy			
Self	Report being able to read	72	79
	Report being able to write	71	79
Direct	Minimal mastery of literacy	59	64
	'Desired' mastery of literacy	27	32
Numeracy			
Self	Report being able to compute	77	83
Direct	Minimal mastery of numeracy	61	68
	'Desired' mastery of numeracy	56	63

1. Age 15 or older.
Source: Kenya National Bureau of Statistics (2007).

29 the literacy rate is above 65% and the numeracy rate above 69%; among those aged 55 or above, the respective rates are less than 37% and 41%.

● The schooling 'turning point' with respect to literacy is around grades 4 and 5: literacy rates are under 20% among adults who complete four or fewer grades, but over 65% for those who complete five or more.

● Many survey respondents either had never attended adult literacy programmes or had dropped out; the main reasons given were lack of nearby centres or instructors.

* It was independently conducted by a national team, drawing in part on the methodology developed by the UIS Literacy Assessment and Monitoring Programme.

Asia, particularly China. Nevertheless, this region and those of South and West Asia, and sub-Saharan Africa still concentrate the vast majority of adults denied the right to literacy (Table 2.14).

The global adult literacy rate rose from 76% to 82% (Table 2.15) between the periods 1985-1994 and 1995-2004. The increase was more marked among developing countries, where the average rate rose from 68% to 77%. Adult literacy levels improved in most regions, with the largest increases occurring in the Arab States and in South and West Asia, each up by twelve percentage points. However, increased literacy rates were not always reflected in declines in the number of illiterate adults: the latter rose in sub-Saharan Africa and the Arab States, partly due to continuing high population growth. Adult literacy rates remained well below the world average in South and West Asia and in sub-Saharan Africa (about 60%), as well as in the Arab States and the Caribbean (about 70%).

Progress towards the adult literacy target was also recorded at country level, with increases of more than fifteen percentage points in literacy rates in Algeria, Burundi, Cape Verde, Egypt, the Islamic Republic of Iran, Kuwait, Malawi, Nepal and Yemen

Table 2.14: Estimated number of adult illiterates[1] by region, 1985–1994 and 1995–2004

	1985–1994[2]		1995–2004[2]		Change between 1985–1994 and 2000–2004
	Total (millions)	% female	Total (millions)	% female	(%)
World	864.0	63	774.0	64	-10.4
Developing countries	851.3	63	764.4	64	-10.2
Developed countries	9.3	65	8.2	62	-11.9
Countries in transition	3.4	85	1.3	76	-61.4
Sub-Saharan Africa	131.0	61	150.3	62	14.8
Arab States	55.1	63	56.9	67	3.2
Central Asia	0.6	77	0.4	72	-39.7
East Asia and the Pacific	227.6	69	125.6	70	-44.8
East Asia	226.3	69	124.0	71	-45.2
Pacific	1.3	56	1.6	57	21.7
South and West Asia	394.1	61	387.8	63	-1.6
Latin America/Caribbean	36.6	55	38.2	55	4.4
Caribbean	2.4	52	2.9	52	22.7
Latin America	34.2	56	35.3	55	3.2
N. America/W. Europe	6.4	63	5.8	61	-9.4
Central/Eastern Europe	12.5	78	8.9	79	-28.8

1. Age 15 or older.
2. Data are for the most recent year available during the period specified.
See introduction to statistical tables in annex for broader explanations of national literacy definitions, assessment methods, sources and years of data.
Source: Annex, Statistical Table 2A.

Table 2.15: Estimated adult literacy rates[1] by region, 1985–1994 and 1995–2004

	Literacy rates								Percentage change between 1985–1994 and 1995–2004			
	1985–1994[2]				1995–2004[2]				Total	Male	Female	GPI (F/M)
	Total (%)	Male (%)	Female (%)	GPI (F/M)	Total (%)	Male (%)	Female (%)	GPI (F/M)				
World	76	83	70	0.85	82	87	77	0.89	7.9	5.8	10.4	4.6
Developing countries	68	77	59	0.77	77	84	70	0.84	13.1	9.0	18.7	9.2
Developed countries	99	99	98	0.99	99	99	99	1.00	0.2	0.1	0.3	0.2
Countries in transition	98	99	97	0.98	99	100	99	0.99	1.1	0.2	1.8	1.6
Sub-Saharan Africa	54	63	45	0.71	59	69	50	0.76	10.1	8.6	12.2	6.5
Arab States	58	70	46	0.66	70	81	60	0.74	21.0	15.6	29.5	12.0
Central Asia	99	99	98	0.99	99	100	99	0.99	0.6	0.2	1.0	0.8
East Asia and the Pacific	82	89	75	0.84	92	95	88	0.93	11.3	6.4	17.2	10.1
East Asia	82	89	75	0.84	92	95	88	0.93	11.5	6.5	17.5	10.3
Pacific	94	94	93	0.99	93	94	93	0.98	-0.2	-0.1	-0.3	-0.2
South and West Asia	48	60	34	0.57	60	71	47	0.67	25.3	18.3	39.5	17.9
Latin America and the Caribbean	88	89	87	0.98	90	91	89	0.98	2.6	2.2	3.0	0.8
Caribbean	71	71	71	1.00	71	71	71	1.00	-0.2	-0.2	-0.2	0.0
Latin America	88	89	87	0.98	90	91	90	0.98	2.7	2.3	3.1	0.8
North America and Western Europe	99	99	99	0.99	99	99	99	1.00	0.2	0.1	0.2	0.1
Central and Eastern Europe	96	98	94	0.96	97	99	96	0.97	1.4	0.7	2.1	1.4

1. Age 15 or older.
2. Data are for the most recent year available during the period specified. See introduction to statistical tables in annex for broader explanations of national literacy definitions, assessment methods, sources and years of data.
Sources: Annex, Statistical Tables 2A and 12.

CHAPTER 2

(see Statistical Table 2A). Despite the overall positive trend, very low adult literacy rates, below 50%, still characterize several countries, including Mali, Burkina Faso, Chad, Afghanistan, the Niger, Guinea, Benin, Sierra Leone, Ethiopia, Mozambique, Senegal, Bangladesh, Central African Republic, Nepal, Côte d'Ivoire and Pakistan (Map 2.4).[27]

Clearly, improving global trends in adult literacy will depend on continuing reductions in illiteracy in these countries and, most importantly, on reducing the number of adult illiterates in some

of the most populous developing countries. More than three-quarters of the world's 774 million adult illiterates live in only fifteen countries, including eight high population countries: Bangladesh, Brazil, China, Egypt, India, Indonesia, Nigeria and Pakistan. India alone has nearly 35% of the world total. In most of these fifteen countries, adult literacy rates have improved compared with the 1985-1994 period, although continuing population growth translates into increases in absolute numbers of illiterates in countries including Bangladesh, Ethiopia and Morocco (see annex, Statistical Table 2A).

27. In order of adult literacy rate, from lowest (Mali, 19.0%) to highest (Pakistan, 49.9%).

Map 2.4: Adult literacy rates and number of illiterates,[1] 1995–2004[2]

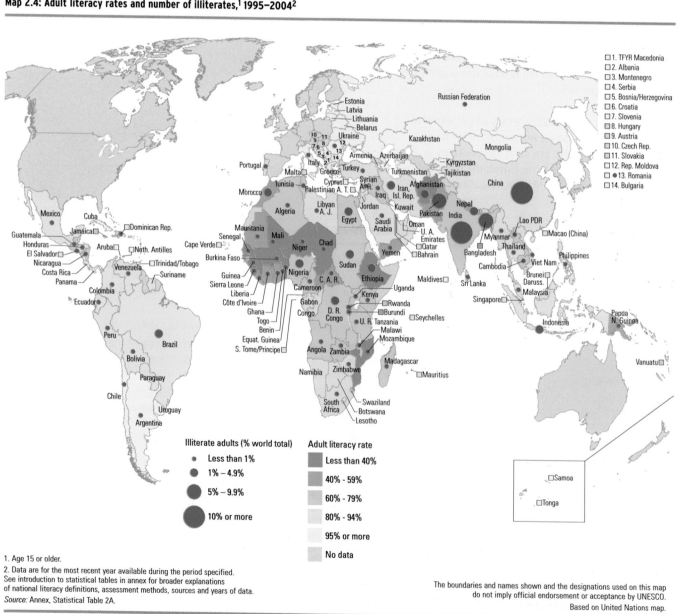

1. Age 15 or older.
2. Data are for the most recent year available during the period specified. See introduction to statistical tables in annex for broader explanations of national literacy definitions, assessment methods, sources and years of data.
Source: Annex, Statistical Table 2A.

The boundaries and names shown and the designations used on this map do not imply official endorsement or acceptance by UNESCO.
Based on United Nations map.

The case of China is worth emphasizing. The substantial increase in the average adult literacy rate among developing countries since 1985–1994 (Table 2.15) is mainly due to a substantial reduction in numbers of adult illiterates in China (by 98 million) and a corresponding increase of thirteen percentage points in the national literacy rate, from 78% to 91%. These results stem largely from increased primary school participation, highly targeted adult literacy programmes (targeted both geographically and to the 15–40 age group) and the dramatic development of literate environments (Ross et al., 2005).

Youth literacy: reflecting increased participation in school

Literacy rates for the 15–24 age group tend to be higher than adult literacy rates in all regions (see annex, Statistical Table 2A), reflecting growing access to and participation in formal schooling in younger generations. Between the periods 1985–1994 and 1995–2004, youth literacy improved more rapidly than adult literacy in all regions, and especially in the Arab States and East Asia. In nearly all regions, the increase in youth literacy rates was accompanied by a reduction in the number of illiterates. Exceptions to this trend are found in the Caribbean and the Pacific island states, where youth literacy rates fell slightly, and in Central Asia, and North America and Western Europe, where the rates were almost unchanged. Although youth literacy rates increased in sub-Saharan Africa by 9%, the region counted 5 million additional young illiterates due to persisting high population growth and low school completion rates.

Disparities in adult literacy: the gender and poverty links

Women's literacy is of crucial importance in addressing wider issues of gender inequality. Yet, worldwide, women still accounted for 64% of adults who were not literate in 1995–2004, a share virtually unchanged from the 63% recorded during 1985–1994 (Table 2.14). The average global GPI in adult literacy was 0.89 in the most recent period. Gender disparities in adult literacy are particularly marked in South and West Asia (GPI of 0.67), the Arab States (0.74) and sub-Saharan Africa (0.76). However, the situation had improved substantially in these regions since 1985–1994. Changes in the GPI were not noticeable in other regions (Table 2.15).

Striking gender disparities in adult literacy remain in some countries (see annex, Statistical Table 2A). In 21 out of 133 countries with literacy data for 1995–2004, literacy rates for females were less than two-thirds of those for males. Most of these countries were in sub-Saharan Africa; two were in the Arab States and four in South and West Asia.[28] On the other hand, some cases of gender disparities favouring women were observed, e.g. in Jamaica (GPI of 1.16) and Lesotho (1.23) – a trend growing elsewhere in the world, particularly among younger cohorts; examples include Botswana, El Salvador, Honduras, Liberia, Malta and Nicaragua.

Besides gender, key factors or correlates of illiteracy include poverty, place of residence and certain individual characteristics. Overall, illiteracy rates are highest in the countries with the greatest poverty. The link between poverty and illiteracy is also observed at household level, with the literacy rates of the poorest households substantially lower than those of the wealthiest. More generally, for various social, cultural or political reasons, certain population groups – such as migrants, indigenous people, ethnic minorities and those with disabilities – find themselves excluded from mainstream society, which often results in reduced access to formal education and literacy programmes (UNESCO, 2005a).

Understanding and monitoring literate environments

Previous editions of the Report have highlighted the literate environment as an enabling context for the acquisition and enhancement of literacy skills. Effective literate environments typically contain written materials (newspapers, books and posters), electronic and broadcast media (radios and TVs) and information and communications technology (fixed and mobile phones, computers and Internet access), which encourage literacy acquisition, a reading culture, improved literacy retention and access to information. Literate environments can be found in both public and private spheres, including home, school, workplace, local community and the nation as a whole. Measuring and monitoring literate environments is a challenge; in the absence of any systematic data, this section can only underline their importance and discuss briefly how they might be monitored.[29]

Illiteracy rates are highest in the countries with the greatest poverty

28. The countries are Angola, Benin, Burkina Faso, the Central African Republic, Chad, Côte d'Ivoire, the Democratic Republic of the Congo, Ethiopia, Guinea, Mali, Mozambique, the Niger, Senegal, Sierra Leone and Togo in sub-Saharan Africa; Morocco and Yemen in the Arab States; and Afghanistan, India, Nepal and Pakistan in South and West Asia.

29. Additional ideas for conceptualizing and monitoring literate environments emerged during an ad hoc consultation conducted by the Global Monitoring Report Team with several experts in this area (see Benavot, 2007).

School-based learning environments are critical

For young children in school, access to and use of reading materials in languages they understand are critical in acquiring basic literacy skills. Numerous international and national learning assessments have demonstrated that the availability of books and other printed materials in school classrooms and libraries is associated with higher student performance in the language arts (Heyneman, 2006; Mullis et al., 2003). Thus, measures of the availability and use of textbooks, written materials and Internet-based information are important indicators of school-based literate environments.

Workplace environments can strengthen literacy skills

The International Adult Literacy Survey (IALS) developed workplace-based reading and writing indices for the variety and frequency of workers' reading, writing or mathematics activities (OECD and Statistics Canada, 2000). IALS concluded that labour force participation, formal employment training and informal uses of literacy at work were significantly associated with higher literacy proficiency, but were less important than other variables such as educational attainment. Literate environments in the workplace mainly reflect work-related tasks and organizational priorities rather than workers' cultural interests and demands; nevertheless, they provide an important enabling context for developing and strengthening literacy skills.

Household and community environments emphasize applied knowledge

Literacy as practised at home and in communities typically differs from that valued by schools or the workplace. Literacy as a socially organized practice 'is not simply knowing how to read and write a particular script but applying this knowledge for specific purposes in specific contexts of use' (Scribner and Cole, 1981, p. 236). Ethnographies of literacy provide considerable evidence of the diverse practical purposes to which literacy skills are put: to address government officials, complete forms, read prices, pay bills, keep records, find jobs, read religious texts, learn about family histories, take or administer medicine, extract information from newspapers, protect against sexually transmitted diseases, and buy and sell goods and services (Hull and Schultz, 2001).

Surveys of working adults in OECD countries provide information on participation in literacy-promoting

activities at home (reading newspapers and books, using public libraries, watching television, getting access to printed materials via the Internet). In Africa, the SACMEQ (Southern and Eastern Africa Consortium for Monitoring Educational Quality) survey compiled data on printed materials (books and magazines) and broadcast media (TVs and radios) in students' homes. Special household surveys focusing on literacy, such as those conducted in Cambodia, Kenya and the Lao People's Democratic Republic, provide information on the literacy resources in households (books, pamphlets and other reading materials) and communities (community learning centres and literacy programmes) that characterize literate environments at subnational level.[30] In short, surveys provide information on the extent to which local contexts encourage or discourage diverse literacy skills.

National measures of the literate environment

At country level, aggregate indicators of literate environments are often compiled, including reported cross-national data, standardized by population, on the circulation of daily and non-daily newspapers, the publication of book titles, the number of library volumes and users, and indicators such as the percentage of households with TVs and radios (UNESCO, 2005a).[31] Recent cross-national surveys have also included information on the availability and quantity of other periodicals (e.g. community and on-line newspapers), personal computers per capita and numbers of Internet users.

Quality: the continuing challenge

Goal 6: *Improving all aspects of the quality of education and ensuring excellence of all so that recognized and measurable learning outcomes are achieved by all, especially in literacy, numeracy and essential life skills*[32]

Quality is at the heart of education. Indeed, while countries and international organizations have long committed themselves to universalizing primary education, improving and sustaining the quality of basic education is equally important. Good-quality teaching and learning environments assure effective learning outcomes (UNESCO, 2000a).

30. See Kenya National Bureau of Statistics (2007) and Lao People's Democratic Republic Ministry of Education (2001).

31. These data can also be found in the longer version of this year's statistical tables that is posted on the Report website (see annex, Statistical Table 2B).

32. In addition, the Expanded Commentary on the Dakar Framework for Action (UNESCO, 2000a, para. 32) stressed that access to basic education of good quality is a fundamental right: 'No one should be denied the opportunity to complete good quality primary education because it is unaffordable.' Improvements in the quality of education require well-trained teachers and active learning techniques; adequate facilities and instructional materials; clearly defined, well-taught and accurately assessed curricular knowledge and skills; and a healthy, safe, gender-sensitive environment that makes full use of local language proficiencies.

Learning outcomes should be monitored

Student learning assessments can be used to evaluate the strengths and weaknesses of an education system and to compare pupil achievements and competencies across schools, regions or systems.[33] International assessments of educational achievement, which began in the 1960s, have markedly increased in visibility and country coverage (Degenhart, 1990; Keeves, 1995; Postlethwaite, 2004).[34]

Comparative tests of achievement are incomplete proxies of what and how much students actually learn in school. They tend to focus on curricular areas such as language and mathematics rather than subjects such as history, geography, arts or moral education, even though the latter encompass important aims of education. They assess knowledge levels but rarely examine student values, attitudes and other non-cognitive skills. Moreover, comparing achievement scores across studies or countries and over time can be problematic due to differences in, for example, test instruments, age groups or sampled populations.[35]

International and regional assessments reveal pervasive low achievement

Key conclusions from international and regional student assessments point to low learning outcomes in much of the world:

■ The PIRLS 2001 assessment found that in many countries, including Argentina, Colombia, the Islamic Republic of Iran, Kuwait, Morocco and Turkey, over 40% of grade 4 pupils read at or below the lowest level (Mullis et al., 2003). The PISA 2003 reading assessment found that 20% or more of 15-year-olds in Austria, Germany, Greece, Hungary, Italy, Luxembourg, Portugal, Spain and Turkey performed at or below the lowest proficiency level.

■ Achievement levels are lower in developing than in developed countries. For example, in TIMSS 2003, 20% to 90% of grade 8 students in low- and middle-income countries did not reach the lowest benchmark level (UNESCO, 2005a). In PISA 2003, 34% to 63% of 15-year-olds who performed at or below proficiency level 1 in reading were in low- and middle-income countries, including Brazil, Indonesia, Mexico, the Russian Federation and Thailand.

■ Pupils from more privileged socio-economic backgrounds (in terms of parents' education, occupational status or household wealth) and those with access to books consistently perform better than those from poorer backgrounds or with limited access to reading materials.

■ Learning disparities in reading, mathematics and science among 15-year-olds are also related to immigrant status, language spoken at home and family structure such as two-parent or non-two-parent households (Hampden-Thompson and Johnson, 2006; OECD, 2006).

■ Behavioural problems among pupils (and teachers) – arriving late and absenteeism, for example – often correlate with poor performance.

■ African and Latin American assessments, notably SACMEQ and LLECE, find strong disparities in favour of urban students, reflecting both higher household incomes and better school provision in urban areas (UNESCO, 2000b).

International and regional assessments also highlight school-based factors affecting student achievement (UNESCO, 2005a):

■ The amount of time students are present in school affects their performance.

■ The time actually spent learning specific subjects, either in school or through homework, positively affects performance, especially in language, mathematics and science.

International and regional student assessments point to low learning outcomes in much of the world

---

33. Learning assessments include international assessments of student achievement or basic skills; national monitoring of subject-specific achievements; standards-based assessments according to grade or age; school-based assessments of pupil progress based on tests, performance or portfolios; and external public examinations at major system transition points, such as from primary to secondary education.

34. Since Dakar, the International Association for the Evaluation of Educational Achievement (IEA) has conducted major comparative studies in reading (Progress in International Reading Literacy Study: PIRLS), mathematics and science (Trends in International Mathematics and Science Study: TIMSS), civic education (Civic Education Study) and pre-primary education (Pre-Primary Project). In addition, there have been three rounds of the OECD-sponsored Programme for International Student Assessment (PISA). The IEA studies concentrate on monitoring curricular provisions and subject-specific achievements of students according to grade or age; PISA focuses on cross-cutting skills and competencies among 15-year-olds in reading, mathematics and science. These assessments mainly concern high-income countries and a growing number of middle- and low-income countries. Regional assessments conducted in developing countries include the Laboratorio Latinamericano de Evaluación de la Calidad de la Educación (LLECE), the Programme d'analyse des systèmes éducatifs de la CONFEMEN (PASEC) and SACMEQ (mentioned earlier).

35. Analysts have begun to make such comparisons (e.g. Crouch and Fasih, 2004; Hanushek, 2004; Pritchett, 2004), but there are questions about the validity of this approach.

■ In many developing countries, the inadequacy of physical and material resources in schools adversely affects pupil achievement. For example, many SACMEQ countries report limited availability of basic instructional resources, as well as poor school infrastructure.[36]

■ Increased availability and use of textbooks improve student learning and can counteract socio-economic disadvantage, particularly in low-income settings.

Differences in average pupil learning achievement between schools and classes are considerable, even after statistically controlling for individual characteristics. They underscore the extent to which strong learning outcomes depend on the availability, use and management of school-based resources (UNESCO-BREDA, 2007).

All these assessments further point to inequalities in learning outcomes within countries. The wider the distribution of student achievement scores around a given mean, the lower the level of equity in education (Scheerens and Visscher, 2004). Recent analyses of pupil achievement in Central and Eastern Europe indicate salient national differences in education equity following the education reforms of the 1990s (Box 2.7).

National assessments also confirm the quality challenge

More and more countries are carrying out national learning assessments that provide country-wide and school-specific information about learning outcomes according to nationally defined standards.[37] Overall, 81% of developed countries, 50% of developing countries and 17% of countries in transition conducted at least one national learning

> All these assessments further point to inequalities in learning outcomes within countries

---

Box 2.7: Education quality and equity in Central and Eastern Europe: new evidence

Equality of educational opportunity was a core principle of the socialist states in Central and Eastern Europe. Little has been known, however, about the impact of education reforms in the 1990s on access and learning outcomes among pupils from various socio-economic groups. The UIS initiated a collaborative project with research teams from Bulgaria, the Czech Republic, Estonia, Hungary, Latvia, Romania, Serbia and Slovakia to address these issues and explore ways to improve student outcomes and reduce inequality.

Using 2003 TIMSS and PISA data, the teams constructed socio-economic gradients or 'learning bars' to reflect the relationship between socio-economic status and learning achievement. These were compared by classroom, school, district and/or region. Among other findings, the project showed that:

● Significant regional disparity in learning achievement existed in all eight countries. For example, in Latvia, 15-year-olds attending schools in Riga and other urban areas scored much higher in reading literacy, on average, than their counterparts in rural areas. In Romania, eighth grade students in urban areas had better scores than their counterparts in rural schools in biology, chemistry, physics and life sciences.

● Differentiation among schools or programmes was an important source of disparity in achievement. In the Czech Republic, where there is little programme differentiation among primary schools, only about

20% of the variation in reading and mathematics performance of fourth graders was at school level. By grade 8, however, school-level variation had more than doubled, and by grade 10 it was close to 60%. In Hungary, students attending academic schools performed better on mathematical literacy tests than those attending vocational schools, who in turn scored higher than students in vocational training programmes.

● Most achievement gaps between regions and between different types of schools or programmes were associated with student socio-economic status. Although Latvian eighth graders in urban schools had higher average mathematics scores than their rural counterparts, the differences largely disappeared once students' family background characteristics at individual and school level were isolated. In Hungary, once the socio-economic composition of schools was considered, the gap in mathematical literacy scores between academic and vocational secondary tracks largely disappeared.

These findings highlight the many challenges facing industrialized countries in reaching quality learning outcomes for all students. They underscore the role that school organization and classroom practices can play in raising overall achievement levels and reducing socio-economic gaps in learning achievement.

Sources: Bankov et al. (2006); Baucal et al. (2006); Geske et al. (2006); Horn et al. (2006); Istrate et al. (2006); Mere et al. (2006); Straková et al. (2006); Zelmanova et al. (2006).

---

36. Countries participating in SACMEQ I (1995–1999) were Kenya, Malawi, Mauritius, Namibia, the United Republic of Tanzania (Zanzibar), Zambia and Zimbabwe. SACMEQ II (2000–2003) countries were Botswana, Kenya, Lesotho, Malawi, Mauritius, Mozambique, Namibia, Seychelles, South Africa, Swaziland, Uganda, the United Republic of Tanzania (Mainland and Zanzibar) and Zambia.

37. The annex section National learning assessments by region and country provides a global overview of national assessment and evaluation activities, although it makes no attempt to evaluate the scientific rigour or technical soundness of the assessments listed. For further details see Benavot and Tanner (2007) and Encinas-Martin (2006).

assessment between 2000 and 2006; the respective figures in the five years before Dakar (1995 to 1999) were 58%, 28% and 0%. The prevalence of national assessments has increased especially in East Asia and the Pacific, the Arab States, South and West Asia, and Central and Eastern Europe (Figure 2.14).

Key findings about national assessments include:

■ *Grade levels:* Assessments focus more on grades 4–6 than grades 1–3 or 7–9. In 2000–2006, for example, eighty-four countries conducted at least one assessment of learning outcomes in grades 4–6; fifty-five countries did so in grades 1–3 and fifty-four countries in grades 7–9.

■ *Type:* National assessments are predominantly curriculum-based and subject-oriented, in contrast to the international assessments of cross-curricular knowledge, skills or competencies (e.g. PISA).

■ *Subject areas:* Almost all the countries that conducted national assessments in 2000–2006 assessed learning outcomes in (the official) language (93%) and mathematics (92%). About half of the countries (51%) assessed learning outcomes in science, almost two-fifths (38%) in the social sciences, 21% in foreign languages and 20% in other areas, including art, physical education, problem-solving, life skills, visual literacy, colouring, cognitive behaviour and music. Assessments of science and the social sciences are more prevalent in Latin America and the Caribbean, and South and West Asia. Assessments of foreign languages are more common in South and West Asia, North America and Western Europe, and the Arab States.

■ *Fragile states:* While half of all developing countries conducted national learning assessments between 2000 and 2006, only fifteen of the thirty-five countries that the OECD categorizes as fragile states, or 43%, did so; nearly half of those were in East Asia and the Pacific.

Despite differences in assessment methods and scales, sample designs and methodological rigour, national assessments almost uniformly call on education authorities to find ways to improve student knowledge levels and competencies:

Figure 2.14: Percentage of countries in each region that carried out at least one national assessment between 1995–1999 and 2000–2006[1]

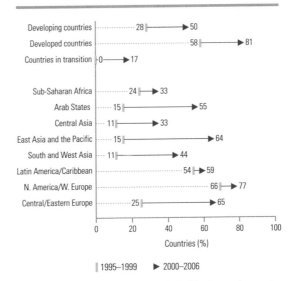

1. The exact dates of the national assessments in the following countries are not known, but it was possible to determine whether the learning assessment occurred before or after 2000: Algeria, Australia, Bulgaria, Fiji, Kiribati, Saint Kitts and Nevis, Samoa, Saudi Arabia, Solomon Islands, Swaziland, Tonga, Tuvalu and Vanuatu.
Source: Annex, National learning assessments.

■ Since 1999 Uganda has carried out five assessments to determine overall achievement levels in grades 3 and 6 in English literacy and numeracy. While fewer than half of pupils reached defined competency levels in English literacy, achievement levels have improved over time. By contrast, achievement levels in numeracy have fluctuated or declined (Table 2.16). A 2006 government report accounted for these findings by noting the impact of government policies to increase the supply and use of English textbooks and the need for better-trained mathematics teachers.

National assessments call on education authorities to find ways to improve student knowledge levels and competencies

Table 2.16: Percentage of grade 3 and 6 pupils in Uganda reaching defined competency levels, by subject, 1999 to 2006

	English literacy (% of pupils)					Numeracy (% of pupils)				
	1999	2003	2004	2005	2006	1999	2003	2004	2005	2006
Grade 3	18	34	...	38	46	39	43	...	41	43
Grade 6	13	20	28	30	34	42	21	38	33	31

Note: The percentage of pupils rated 'proficient' is compared.
Source: Uganda National Examinations Board (2006).

CHAPTER 2

In Haiti girls scored higher than boys in all areas

- In 2006, Morocco's Ministry of National Education assessed grade 6 student achievement in Arabic, French, mathematics and science, using a sample of seven 'strong performing' urban schools and ninety-six schools targeted for intervention. The assessment found overall performance to be 'weak' in terms of the percentages of pupils attaining predetermined 'minimum' or higher 'mastery' levels: 36% achieved the minimum level in Arabic, 18% in French and 43% in mathematics, while in science, where they performed best, 65% achieved the minimum level; achievement rates for mastery levels were 7% in Arabic,1% in French, 11% in mathematics and 20% in science (Hddigui, 2007a).

- In 2004/05, Haiti's Ministry of Education assessed student knowledge in mathematics, French and Creole in grades 1, 3 and 5 to establish baseline levels before implementation of a national school improvement plan. The ministry's report characterized grade 5 students' overall achievement as 'weak', with only 44% meeting expectations (Desse, 2005). Fifth-graders' scores in mathematics were considered 'extremely weak' and in Creole 'not too bad'. The report noted that girls scored higher than boys in all areas, public school students scored higher than private school students and students repeating the year scored lower than new students.

- Hungary, which has participated in over sixteen international assessments in recent decades, began regular assessment of student achievement in grades 4 and 8 in 1986. In 2001, it adopted a new national assessment of basic competencies in reading comprehension and mathematics. Three assessments between 2003 and 2006 showed a slight worsening of mathematics achievement and a slight improvement in reading achievement in grade 6. Large percentages of students performed at or below the lowest proficiency level (level 1) in both: almost 50% in mathematics and 20% in reading. Figure 2.15 reports results from the 2006 assessment in grades 6 and 8 and illustrates the distribution of student scores by competency and residence.

Are learning outcomes improving?

It is possible to assess changes in student achievements over time using findings from national assessments.[38] Table 2.17 reports the percentage change in mean achievement, mainly in language and mathematics, between earlier assessments and the most recent ones in sixteen countries. In Belize, Colombia, El Salvador, Ethiopia, Mexico, Senegal, South Africa and Uganda, for example, the trends in average achievement are generally upwards, with some fluctuation by subject area. In Brazil, Chile and Peru, mean achievement levels are relatively stable. In Honduras, Morocco,

38. Over time, comparability of test scores may be reduced due to changes in student cohort composition, sampling designs, test instruments and other factors.

Figure 2.15: Distribution of student performance in Hungary, by residence, 2006

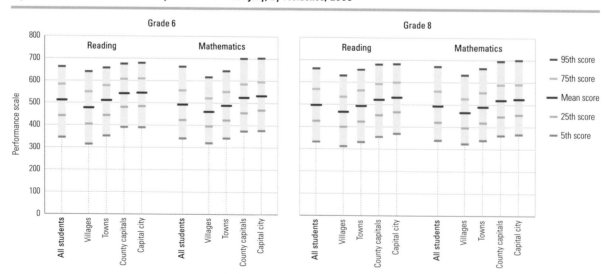

Note: Settlement type in Hungary is not directly related to number of inhabitants, although in general villages are smaller than towns. In addition to the capital city and the eighteen county capitals, there are about 240 towns and 2,900 villages. The towns have from 1,000 to 60,000 inhabitants and the villages up to 12,000.
Source: Balázsi (2007).

Table 2.17: Changes in learning outcomes based on national assessments, various years

	Grade	Initial year	Most recent year	Subject	Percentage change in achievement level since initial year		
					Increase (more than 5%)	Little or no change (between -5% and +5%)	Decrease (more than 5%)
Sub-Saharan Africa							
Ethiopia	4	2000	2004	Basic Reading		1	
				Env. Science	8		
				Mathematics	7		
				English		-3	
Niger	1	2000	2005	French	20		
				Mathematics			-13
	3	2000	2005	French	18		
				Mathematics	16		
	6	2000	2005	French			-7
				Mathematics			-28
Senegal	3	1996	2002	French	15		
				Mathematics	26		
South Africa	3	2000	2003	Literacy	7		
				Numeracy	44		
Arab States							
Morocco	4	1995	2001	Mathematics			-30
				Arabic			-55
	6	2001	2006	French	23		
				Mathematics	11		
				Arabic	44		
East Asia and the Pacific							
Thailand	3	2003	2005	Science		0	
				Mathematics			-7
	6	2001	2004	Thai Language			-19
				Mathematics			-6
				English			-25
	6	2003	2005	Science		-1	
Latin America and the Caribbean							
Belize	6	2000	2004	Language	10		
				Mathematics	30		
				Science	36		
Brazil	4	1999	2005	Language		1	
				Mathematics		1	
Chile	4	2002	2005	Language		-2	
				Mathematics		0	
Colombia	5	2003	2005	Language		3	
				Mathematics	9		
Costa Rica	6	1999	2000	Language		-3	
				Mathematics			-13
El Salvador	6	2003	2005	Language	24		
				Mathematics	15		
Honduras	6	1997	2004	Language			-38
				Mathematics	60		
Mexico	6	2000	2005	Language	5		
				Mathematics		4	
Peru	6	1998	2004	Language		-2	
				Mathematics		2	

Notes: The actual achievement levels compared in each country over time are based on different scales. In Belize, Brazil, Chile, Colombia, Ethiopia, Mexico, Morocco, the Niger, Peru, South Africa and Thailand, the comparison is between mean achievement scores. In El Salvador, the percentage of students achieving the upper performance level is compared, whereas in Honduras, the comparison is between the percentage of students performing at an 'acceptable' level.

Sources: Belize (Mason and Longsworth, 2005); Ethiopia (Academy for Educational Development and USAID Ethiopia, 2001, 2004); Latin America (Murillo, 2007); Morocco (Hddigui, 2007a); Niger (Fomba, 2006; Georges, 2000); Senegal (Ngom, 2007); South Africa (USAID South Africa, 2006); Thailand (Institute for the Promotion of Teaching Science and Technology, 2005).

8
0
0
2

Education for All Global Monitoring Report

the Niger and Thailand, the trends are mixed (varying by grade level), and Costa Rica had a negative trend.

National assessments also provide evidence of disparities by place of residence (Figure 2.16) and gender (see gender equality section below). In most of the eleven countries for which data are available, rural children achieve lower levels in language and mathematics than urban children. This pattern obtains in Belize, El Salvador, Guatemala, Honduras, the Niger, Peru and Uganda and, to a lesser extent, in Mexico and Paraguay. The exceptions are Argentina (although the assessment only included public schools) and Colombia, in which achievement disparities between rural and urban students are relatively small.

What constitutes a good learning environment?

Ample instructional time based on actual, not official hours

Several international agencies and reports have recommended that primary schools operate for between 850 to 1,000 hours per year, or for about 200 days assuming a five-day school week (Lockheed and Verspoor, 1991; World Bank, 2004*a*; see also UNESCO, 2004*b*). Countries vary in the number of days they require schools to operate; typically, the range is between 175 and 210 days per year. The number of hours per school day also varies. Countries using double- or triple-shift school days reduce the yearly instructional time.

Recent data for 125 countries indicate that official intended yearly instructional time increases with grade level (Figure 2.17).[39] Worldwide, countries require an average of 700 annual hours of instruction in grades 1 and 2 and nearly 750 hours in grade 3. By grade 6 the average is 810 hours. Overall, students are expected to receive an accumulated total of almost 4,600 hours of instruction in grades 1 to 6. Regionally, countries in North America and Western Europe require the highest median number of instructional hours over the first six years of schooling (835 hours), followed by East Asia and the Pacific (802 hours), Latin America and the Caribbean (795 hours), and the Arab States (789 hours). The lowest medians are recorded in Central and Eastern Europe (654 hours), and Central Asia (665 hours), while sub-Saharan Africa, and South and West Asia are close to the global median.

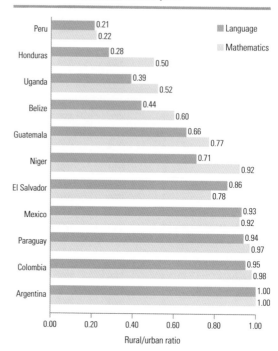

Figure 2.16: Rural-urban disparities in language and mathematics achievement in grade 5 or 6 based on national assessments, various years

	Language	Mathematics
Peru	0.21	0.22
Honduras	0.28	0.50
Uganda	0.39	0.52
Belize	0.44	0.60
Guatemala	0.66	0.77
Niger	0.71	0.92
El Salvador	0.86	0.78
Mexico	0.93	0.92
Paraguay	0.94	0.97
Colombia	0.95	0.98
Argentina	1.00	1.00

Rural/urban ratio

Sources: Belize (Mason and Longsworth, 2005); Latin America (Murillo, 2007); Niger (Fomba, 2006; Georges, 2000); Uganda (Uganda National Examinations Board, 2006).

Official *intended* instructional time should not be confused with the actual number of instructional hours children receive. In several Arab States actual learning time is estimated to be 30% less, on average, than intended instructional time (Abadzi, 2006). In many countries whole school days are lost due to teacher absenteeism, in-service teacher training, strikes, armed conflict, targeted violent attacks and the use of schools as polling stations, military bases or examination sites (Abadzi, 2007; Benavot and Gad, 2004; Bonnet, 2007; O'Malley, 2007; UNESCO-IBE, 2007*b*). The PASEC and SACMEQ surveys report that many African schools cannot conform to the official school year due to teacher turnover and late teacher postings (Bonnet, 2007). Schools that start the school year a month late, end the school year a month early and have higher student absenteeism can end up with as many as 200 to 300 fewer hours of instructional time than those that respect the official calendar (UNESCO-BREDA, 2007). The significant loss of instructional time and inefficient use of classroom time are indications of poor education quality, with detrimental effects on learning outcomes.

Worldwide average annual instruction time in grade 6 is 810 hours

39. Cross-national data on annual intended instructional time – that is, the number of yearly hours that schools are expected to devote to teaching and learning, in accordance with official curricular guidelines – are based on official curricular timetables, which prescribe the subjects to be taught at each grade level, along with the number of weekly 'periods' or instructional 'hours' to be allocated to each subject area (Benavot, 2004; UNESCO-IBE, 2007*c*).

Figure 2.17: Median yearly instructional time in grades 1–6, based on total number of intended hours, by region

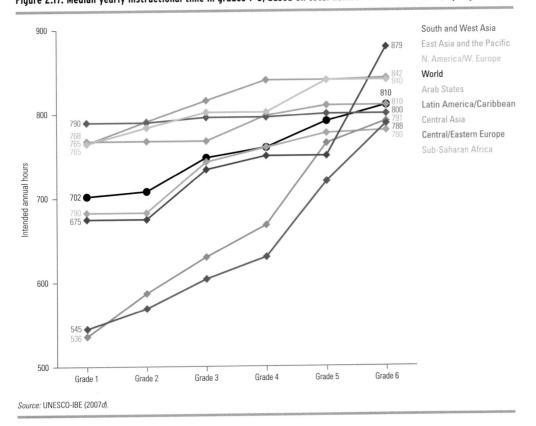

Source: UNESCO-IBE (2007*d*).

In many developing countries, the availability of textbooks and other reading materials is severely limited

Sufficient textbooks and learning materials

Pupil access to textbooks is an important factor in what and how much they learn. In many developing countries, the availability of textbooks and other reading materials is severely limited:

■ The SACMEQ survey found that over half the grade 6 pupils in Kenya, Malawi, Mozambique, Uganda, the United Republic of Tanzania and Zambia reported learning in classrooms that did not have a single book (UNESCO, 2005*a*). Few schools provided a bookshelf or reading corner as part of an enabling literate environment (see the discussion above on literacy and literate environments).

■ In these and other African countries, between 25% and 40% of teachers reported that they did not possess a book or guide in the subjects they taught (Bonnet, 2007).

■ Earlier studies found that in Bolivia, Brazil, Chile, Colombia, Ecuador, Panama, Peru and Venezuela, only about one-third of primary-school pupils had access to textbooks (Montagnes, 2001).

■ The pupil/textbook ratio is a significant measure of education quality. Many classrooms in developing countries, especially in poor and rural areas, possess only one textbook, typically kept by the teacher. Students spend most of their time copying textbook content from blackboards to notebooks, which they are expected to memorize. In Liberia, for example, the government recently estimated this ratio at 27:1 in public primary schools, 20:1 in private schools and 15:1 in mission schools (Liberia Ministry of Education, 2007). These conditions are clearly inadequate for proper learning.

The pedagogical difference between one textbook per classroom and one textbook per student should not be underestimated (Heyneman, 2006).

Comparative research has found that students, especially from poorer households, do better on standardized tests when textbooks are present in the classroom (Fuller and Clarke, 1994; Heyneman and Jamison, 1980; Lockheed and Hanushek, 1988). Textbook provision can reduce achievement disparities between urban and rural students (Jamison et al., 1981). These findings have led several international agencies, particularly the World Bank, to increase financial support for textbook development and distribution in many developing countries (Heyneman, 2006). Investments in textbook production, however, have often been one-shot, short-term projects that have done little to sustain local publishing capacity over the long term (Limage, 2005).

Secure, uncrowded and well-maintained schools

Retention and learning are hampered when pupils attend school in dilapidated or overcrowded buildings, in noisy or unsafe environments, or, especially, in classrooms that are inadequately supplied or poorly lit and ventilated (Watkins, 2000). Girls and boys alike need access to clean water and latrines or other sanitary facilities at school (US Fund for UNICEF, 2007). In low-income countries the poor quality of education facilities is a long-standing problem. In conflict-ridden countries or areas hit by natural disaster, damage to the education infrastructure may be acute, if often transitory.

Overall, systematic cross-national data about the physical state of schools and classrooms are unavailable. Nonetheless, some idea of the severity of this problem in Africa can be indicated (Bonnet, 2007):

- In the SACMEQ countries, 47% of school buildings were reported to need major repairs or complete rebuilding; only 13% were listed in 'good' condition. The percentage of school buildings needing at least some major repair was highest in Uganda (78%) and Lesotho (67%) and lowest in Mauritius (18%) and Seychelles (38%).

- Overcrowded classrooms where students cannot sit comfortably – i.e. where some lack a chair or bench to sit on (or the seating holds more pupils than intended) and a desk or table to write on – were found to be common in Africa. Countries and territories with relatively large proportions of overcrowded classrooms included Chad, Guinea, Malawi and Zanzibar (the United Republic of Tanzania). Since class sizes tend to be larger in the lower grades of primary school, fewer children sit 'comfortably' in the second year than in the fifth.

- At least 90% of classrooms in most SACMEQ and PASEQ countries had a blackboard and chalk; exceptions were Chad, Mauritania, Uganda and Zambia. The availability of maps, dictionaries, wall charts, bookshelves and geometrical instruments such as rulers and compasses also varied greatly within and across countries.

Schools in conflict-affected countries suffer disproportionately. In Iraq, for example, more than 2,700 schools were looted, damaged or burned in 2003 and require considerable rehabilitation (UNESCO-IBE, 2007a). In Tajikistan the civil war of the early 1990s left 20% of schools destroyed or severely damaged (Silova et al., 2007). Education infrastructure was substantially damaged in Bosnia and Herzegovina, Burundi, Kosovo, Mozambique and Timor-Leste (World Bank, 2005i). In post-Soviet Central Asia, education infrastructure seriously deteriorated; many schools fell into disrepair and equipment became outdated (UNICEF, 2001).

The re-emergence of conflict in Liberia in 2001–2003 wrought further damage and destruction on school infrastructure: an estimated 23% of all primary schools were destroyed, while 18% suffered major damage (Liberia Ministry of Education, 2007). In Afghanistan, the burning and bombing of schools and the killing of teachers and students severely affected education provision in some provinces. In 2006, Afghanistan's president stated that 100,000 children who had gone to school in 2003/04 were no longer attending (O'Malley, 2007).

More and better teachers still needed

Teacher shortages in many countries

The quantity, quality and distribution of the teaching workforce are critical factors for reaching the EFA goals, in particular as regards assuring access to and completion of primary education for all children (goal 2) and meeting their learning needs (goal 6) (ILO, 2006b; UNESCO, 2000a, 2004b). This section examines the extent to which countries face shortages of teachers, especially trained teachers, and the extent of disparities in the distribution of the teaching workforce.[40] The main focus is on primary school teachers, though issues pertaining to secondary school teachers are noted.[41]

Girls and boys alike need access to clean water and latrines or other sanitary facilities at school

40. The gender composition of the workforce is discussed in the section on gender equality.

41. The pre-primary teaching workforce is discussed earlier in this chapter in relation to goal 1.

Worldwide, primary education systems employed about 27 million teachers in 2005, more than one-third in East Asia, where 28% of the world's primary pupils are enrolled (Table 2.18).

Between 1999 and 2005 the total number of primary school teachers in the world increased by 5%, or about 1.3 million teachers. Overall, teacher numbers have grown slightly less rapidly than enrolments (which increased by 6%; see annex, Statistical Table 5). Sub-Saharan Africa, and South and West Asia added about half a million teachers each, the effort being relatively greater for the former region (with a 25% increase) than for the latter (14%). In Central and Eastern Europe, Central Asia and East Asia, declines in staff correspond to declines in enrolments. In secondary education, the total number of teachers increased in all regions except Central and Eastern Europe, and more rapidly than in primary education.

The pupil/teacher ratio measures the level of the total supply of teachers a country provides in relation to the size of the pupil population.[42] Generally, high PTRs (i.e. above 40:1)[43] suggest that countries have too few teachers, that teachers are likely overstretched and that the quality of teaching and learning suffers. In 2005, the worldwide weighted average primary PTR was 25:1, with the average for developing countries being higher than that for countries in transition or developed countries (Table 2.19). Twenty-four of 176 countries with data have PTRs above 40:1; most (twenty) are in sub-Saharan Africa, where the highest ratio is that of the Congo (83:1). Other countries in the region with PTRs above 60:1 are Chad, Ethiopia, Mozambique and Rwanda (see annex, Statistical Table 10A).[44] The remaining four countries with very high ratios are Afghanistan (83:1), Bangladesh, Cambodia and Mauritania. About 20% of the countries with data have ratios below 15:1; most are in North America and Western Europe but a few are in other regions.

Table 2.18: Total teaching staff in primary and secondary education by region, 1999 and 2005

	Primary			Secondary		
	Total		Change between 1999 and 2005 (%)	Total		Change between 1999 and 2005 (%)
	(000)			(000)		
	School year ending in			School year ending in		
	1999	2005		1999	2005	
World	25 724	27 048	5.1	24 296	28 457	17.1
Developing countries	20 426	21 713	6.3	15 111	19 049	26.1
Developed countries	4 483	4 598	2.6	6 296	6 564	4.2
Countries in transition	815	738	-9.5	2 888	2 844	-1.5
Sub-Saharan Africa	1 964	2 461	25.3	871	1 171	34.4
Arab States	1 554	1 802	16.0	1 387	1 711	23.3
Central Asia	322	290	-9.9	972	1 069	10.0
East Asia and the Pacific	10 094	9 734	-3.6	7 704	9 116	18.3
East Asia	9 934	9 554	-3.8	7 476	8 867	18.6
Pacific	160	180	12.7	228	249	9.3
South and West Asia	4 301	4 889	13.7	2 956	4 142	40.1
Latin America/Caribbean	2 684	2 971	10.7	2 746	3 436	25.1
Caribbean	104	111	6.8	53	66	25.1
Latin America	2 580	2 861	10.9	2 693	3 370	25.1
N. America/W. Europe	3 443	3 653	6.1	4 487	4 807	7.1
Central/Eastern Europe	1 363	1 247	-8.5	3 172	3 005	-5.3

Sources: Annex, Statistical Tables 10A and 10B.

Worldwide, average PTRs have remained about the same since Dakar, after a slight decrease during the 1990s. PTRs increased in developing countries, particularly in sub-Saharan Africa (by 8.2% between 1999 and 2005) and in South and West Asia (by 7.6%), the two regions in which enrolments grew the most but in which teacher numbers did not keep pace. In the remaining regions, PTRs improved (declined) in the context of declining enrolments except in the Arab States and the Pacific, where the ratios declined slightly even as enrolments increased.

Primary PTRs declined slightly *before* Dakar, at an average annual rate of 0.5%, but increased *after* Dakar, albeit very slightly (0.2%), primarily because of trends in two regions: in South and West Asia, the average PTR declined before Dakar at an average annual rate of 2.4% but increased by an average of 1.3% a year after Dakar; in sub-Saharan Africa, the PTR increased before and after Dakar with the post-Dakar average annual rate being 1.4%, compared with 1.5% in the 1990s. HIV/AIDS has been a complicating factor, especially in the latter region (Box 2.8), together with a decline in teacher salaries relative to other comparable professions (Moon, 2007; UNESCO-BREDA, 2007).[45]

Worldwide, average pupil/teacher ratios have remained about the same since Dakar

42. As has already been noted, the PTR only roughly approximates class size and cannot necessarily be considered an equivalent to it. Among other factors, the ratio takes into account the total number of teachers (including, for instance, distance education teachers). Data for a limited group of countries show that primary PTRs are generally lower than actual class size (UIS database; Bonnet, 2007).

43. Previous editions of this Report use 40:1 as a benchmark, as do recent cross-national projections of teacher needs by UIS (2006c).

44. In Rwanda, projections of the number of student teachers to be trained in teacher-training colleges and colleges of education suggest that recruiting and retaining sufficient teachers of good quality will remain a challenge for at least five more years. To meet the need for teachers, Rwanda is relaxing qualification requirements somewhat (Woods, 2007b).

45. Teacher migration, particularly that of trained teachers, is also a complicating factor in a few countries such as Jamaica and South Africa (Morgan et al., 2006).

Table 2.19: Pupil/teacher ratios in primary and secondary education by region, 1991, 1999 and 2005

	Primary					Secondary		
	School year ending in			Change between		School year ending in		Change between 1999 and 2005
				1991 and 1999	1999 and 2005			
	1991	1999	2005	(average % per year)		1999	2005	(average % per year)
World	26	25	25	-0.5	0.2	18	18	-0.1
Developing countries	29	27	28	-0.6	0.3	21	21	-0.3
Developed countries	17	16	15	-0.7	-1.2	13	13	-0.6
Countries in transition	22	19	19	-1.4	-0.7	11	10	-1.8
Sub-Saharan Africa	37	41	45	1.5	1.4	25	28	2.6
Arab States	25	23	22	-0.9	-0.7	16	17	0.2
Central Asia	21	21	21	-0.1	0.0	10	10	0.0
East Asia and the Pacific	23	22	20	-1.0	-1.0	17	18	0.3
East Asia	23	22	20	-1.0	-1.0	17	18	0.3
Pacific	18	21	19	1.6	-0.9	15	14	-0.5
South and West Asia	45	37	39	-2.4	1.3	33	29	-1.8
Latin America and the Caribbean	25	26	23	0.8	-1.9	19	17	-2.0
Caribbean	25	24	22	-0.6	-1.6	22	19	-1.9
Latin America	25	26	23	0.9	-1.9	19	17	-2.0
North America and Western Europe	16	15	14	-0.4	-1.3	14	13	-0.5
Central and Eastern Europe	21	19	18	-1.4	-0.6	12	12	-1.2

Notes: Weighted averages. Based on headcounts of pupils and teachers.
Sources: Annex, Statistical Tables 10A, 10B and 13.

In Lesotho and Malawi, about a third of all teacher departures are due to terminal illness, most of it presumably HIV-related

Box 2.8: Teachers, HIV/AIDS and absenteeism

In sub-Saharan Africa, deaths and resignations due to HIV/AIDS constitute an important cause of teacher attrition. In Lesotho and Malawi, about a third of all teacher departures are due to terminal illness, most of it presumably HIV-related. In Mozambique, in-service deaths increased by about 72% between 2000 and 2004; the HIV infection rate among teachers was about 15% in 2002 and may reach 17% by 2015. In the United Republic of Tanzania, 42% of teacher deaths between 2000 and 2002 were reported to be HIV/AIDS-related. The highest numbers of deaths occurred among the most experienced teachers, aged between 41 and 50.

In addition to its impact on the supply of teachers, HIV/AIDS is a cause of teacher absenteeism, a major concern in developing countries, with serious consequences for instructional time and student achievement. Teacher absenteeism due to the teacher's own illness or to the care of sick relatives may range from 0.1% to more than 3% of overall teacher years, according to estimates for Eritrea, Kenya, Mozambique, the United Republic of Tanzania and Zambia. Other estimates show that infected teachers are likely to be absent and unable to teach for a total of 260 days before dying of HIV/AIDS. In Zambia a 5% increase in teacher absenteeism between 2001 and 2002 reduced grade 5 student achievement in English and Mathematics by 4% to 8%.

Teacher absenteeism can be a pervasive phenomenon even in countries with low prevalence of HIV/AIDS. A study on Brazil (Pernanbuco State), Ghana, Morocco and Tunisia showed that instructional time losses due to teacher absenteeism ranged from twelve to forty-three days per year, or between 6% and 22% of official intended instructional time.

Sources: Abadzi (2007); Beckmann and Rai (2004); Das et al. (2005); Jukes and Desai (2005); Phamotse et al. (2006); Nilsson (2003); Smith et al. (2006); UNESCO-BREDA (2007).

At the country level, primary PTRs declined between 1999 and 2005 in 103 (73%) of the 141 countries with data, and increased in the rest (see annex, Statistical Table 10A). Many of the improvements (declines) occurred in countries that already had relatively low PTRs.

Several country trends are notable (see annex, Statistical Table 10A):

- Only two countries with PTRs above the 40:1 benchmark in 1999 had managed by 2005 to dramatically reduce their ratios to below the benchmark: Equatorial Guinea, from 57:1 to 32:1, and Bhutan, from 42:1 to 31:1.[46]

- In Afghanistan, the PTR increase was so large (130%) that it moved the country from a 36:1 ratio in 1999 to 83:1 in 2005. The total teacher workforce rose by 96% but this near doubling was not enough to meet the need generated by a 350% rise in enrolments, including the influx of girls previously excluded from school (UNESCO, 2005a).

- The Congo, Ethiopia, Madagascar, Rwanda and the United Republic of Tanzania had ratios above 40:1 at the time of Dakar and have since experienced increases.[47]

- Benin, Cambodia and Ethiopia still have ratios above 40:1 but have improved since Dakar. Cambodia and Ethiopia, particularly the latter, had high annual rates of increase before Dakar; though the ratios have continued to increase, the pace has slowed since 1999. Benin has reversed the trend: its PTR started to decline after 1999, having previously increased.

National averages often hide large in-country disparities in the distribution of teachers, for example between public and private schools and by geographic area. PTRs tend to be much higher in public than in private schools, pointing to teacher shortages in public schools; according to the UIS database this is the case in Benin, Burundi, Cambodia, Djibouti, Eritrea, Madagascar, Mali, Mauritania, Mozambique, Senegal, Uganda and the United Republic of Tanzania. Geographic variations are particularly wide in India, Nepal, Nigeria and Sierra Leone (Sherman and Poirier, 2007).

Trained teachers: the most acute shortages

There are serious teacher shortages in some countries, and shortages of trained teachers (see glossary for definition of trained teachers) that are even more acute.[48] The median percentage of trained primary-school teachers was about 80% or above in Central Asia, Latin America and the Caribbean, and sub-Saharan Africa in 2005, and reached 100% in the Arab States (see annex, Statistical Table 10A). In South and West Asia, the corresponding median was only 64%. Among the eighty-nine countries with 2005 data, the median percentage of trained primary teachers ranged from 14% in Lebanon[49] to about 100% in twenty-five of the countries. Of the fourty-three countries with data for both 1999 and 2005, about 50% registered increases in the percentage of trained teachers.

Although useful for studying the composition of the teacher workforce, the percentage of trained teachers does not show the availability of trained teachers relative to the country's pupil population. For this, the pupil/trained-teacher ratio is a more accurate indicator. Compared with the PTR, it can reveal shortages of trained teachers even in countries with no serious shortage of total teachers.

Figure 2.18 shows exceedingly high pupil/trained-teacher ratios (above 100:1) in Afghanistan, Chad, Madagascar, Mozambique and Nepal, and high ones (above 40:1) in twenty-two other countries, more than half of them in sub-Saharan Africa. Seen in this light, the sharp decline in this ratio in Namibia is remarkable. By 2005, more than 90% of primary teachers had the required training, up from 29% in 1999. As a result, the pupil/trained-teacher ratio declined from 109:1 to 33:1. There was a dramatic increase (60%) in the absolute numbers of trained

National averages often hide large in-country disparities in the distribution of teachers

---

46. Gabon, Nigeria, Togo and Zimbabwe had PTRs of 40:1, and small decreases have enabled them to move to ratios below 40:1, though all are still above 35:1.

47. In the United Republic of Tanzania, the sharpest increase in PTR is observed in 2002, the year after the country abolished school fees and enrolments grew by 23% (between 2001 and 2002), while total staff increased by only 6%.

48. The percentage of trained teachers does not take into account country variations in the level and duration of the minimum organized training required to become a primary-school teacher. Between 15% and 30% of the countries with data train teachers at secondary level, and in a very few countries in sub-Saharan Africa teachers are trained in lower secondary (UIS, 2006c; UNESCO-IBE, 2007b). Regardless of level, the median duration of teacher training is at least one year shorter in developing countries than in developed (three years) or transition countries (four years). Combining the minimum years of schooling required to enter teacher training and the duration of teacher training, teachers in developing countries have at least two years less of schooling (usually fourteen in total) than teachers in developed countries. In sub-Saharan Africa, the median is thirteen years, the lowest for any region.

49. In Lebanon, the low percentage of trained primary-school teachers is apparently due to the use of a definition of trained teacher that differs from that used by UIS.

CHAPTER 2

Figure 2.18: Ratio of pupils to trained teachers in primary education, 1999 and 2005

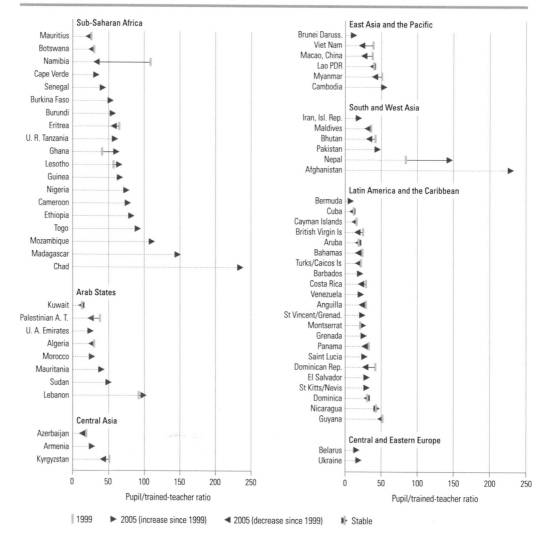

In ten countries
of sub-Saharan
Africa, contract
teachers account
for 50% of
all teachers

| | 1999 ▶ 2005 (increase since 1999) ◀ 2005 (decrease since 1999) ◀▶ Stable

Note: Within regions, countries are listed in ascending order of the pupil/trained-teacher ratio in 2005. Countries with no data for 2005 have been excluded.
Source: UIS database.

teachers between 2000 and 2001, followed by sustained increases of about 15% annually between 2001 and 2005. This significant improvement was due to a policy of upgrading teacher qualifications and replacing untrained teachers with trained ones; the total number of staff increased by only 9% between 1999 and 2005.

Contract teachers: filling a need, but less trained and experienced

Hiring more teachers puts strains on education budgets. Many programmes have been introduced to reduce costs; central to each is the intention to hire new teachers (often with less training and experience) on contracts that are less costly

than the salaries received by government or civil-servant teachers.

Table 2.20 shows data for thirteen francophone countries in sub-Saharan Africa that use contract teachers widely.[50] In ten of these countries, contract teachers accounted for nearly or more than 50% of all teachers. In Cameroon, Chad, the Congo and Madagascar, non-civil-servant teachers are mostly community teachers, although in Chad and Madagascar some under contract are subsidized by the government (Bonnet, 2007; Mingat, 2004). In Guinea, the Niger, Senegal and Togo, the vast majority of non-civil-servant teachers are government teachers hired under contract.

50. Contract teachers are also referred as para-teachers, community or volunteer teachers and *docentes idóneos o empíricos.* Cambodia, India, Kenya and Nicaragua have made extensive use of contract teachers but no recent data are available (Duthilleul, 2005).

Table 2.20: Contract and civil-servant or government teachers in thirteen francophone countries of sub-Saharan Africa

Country	Year	National data			Sample data (PASEC)			
		Contract teachers as a percentage of all teachers			Teachers with no training or with less than 1 month of training (%)		Mean experience (years)	
		Government contract	Community contract	All contracts	Civil servants	Contract	Civil servants	Contract
Benin	2004	24	26	49				
Burkina Faso	2002	24	12	36				
Cameroon	2002	20	45	65				
Chad	2003		61	61	0	79	10	6
Congo	2003	4	54	58				
Côte d'Ivoire	2001		13	13				
Guinea	2004	59		59	1	0	11	4
Madagascar	2004		54	54				
Mali[1]	2004			69	0	14	20	4
Mauritania[2]	2003				6	67	9	7
Niger[1]	2003	50	4	54	4	38	11	2
Senegal	2003	42	15	57				
Togo	2001	31	35	65	31	82	16	6

1. Sample data (PASEC) are for 2002.
2. Sample data (PASEC) for Mauritania show that about 6% of 443 teachers sampled are contract teachers.
Sources: National data come from: Benin (Benin Ministry of Primary and Secondary Education, 2004, p. 4); Burkina Faso, Cameroon, Congo, Côte d'Ivoire, Madagascar, Niger, Senegal and Togo (Mingat, 2004, p. 19); Chad (Organisation Internationale de la Francophonie et al., 2006, p. 49); Guinea (World Bank Development Research Group, 2006, p. 70); Mali (Mali Ministry of Education et al., 2006, p. 112). Sample data (PASEC) come from Bonnet (2007).

Except in Guinea, contract teachers are more likely than civil-servant teachers to have either no training or less than one month of training (Table 2.20). In the Niger, nearly half the contract teachers recruited after 1998 received training similar to that of regular teachers (one to two years), while a third have completed only the required minimum training (forty-five days) (Bonnet, 2007). On average contract teachers are less experienced than civil-servant ones.

Contract teacher salaries tend to be one-quarter to one-half of the amount paid to permanent teachers. In Benin, a contract teacher costs US$705 a year, a community teacher US$300 and a civil service teacher US$3,011. In the Niger, where only contract teachers are being recruited, their starting salary is half that of regular teachers (World Bank, 2004d). In Senegal, contract teachers earn less than a fifth of the salary of civil service teachers (Fyfe, 2006). While the financial advantages of hiring teachers under contract are clear, the extended use of contract teachers poses a quality issue for pupils and a labour rights issue for teachers (Education International, 2006; Fyfe, 2006; ILO/UNESCO, 2006).[51] Policies to upgrade and professionalize untrained contract teachers are urgently needed if the provision of quality teachers is to be assured for all.

Gender parity and equality: not there yet

Goal 5: *Eliminating gender disparities in primary and secondary education by 2005, and achieving gender equality in education by 2015, with a focus on ensuring girls' full and equal access to and achievement in basic education of good quality*

The gender parity goal has been missed and gender equality remains elusive

Disparities in primary and secondary education have been reduced since 1999, but not eliminated. In 2005, only 59 (about one-third) of 181 countries with data available had achieved gender parity (i.e GPIs ranging from 0.97 to 1.03) in their GERs for both primary and secondary education. Most had already achieved parity by 1999 (the exceptions being the Cook Islands, Paraguay and Qatar), and most are developed countries or countries in transition (fourteen in North America and Western Europe, fifteen in Central and Eastern Europe, five in Central Asia), or countries in Latin America and the Caribbean. Only seven countries in East Asia and the Pacific, and two each in sub-Saharan Africa, the Arab States, and South and West Asia, have achieved the EFA gender parity goal.

Contract teacher salaries tend to be one-quarter to one-half of the amount paid to permanent teachers

51. Chapter 3 discusses contract teacher policies further.

In countries where gender disparities still prevail, they are often greater at higher education levels. About 63% of the countries with data have achieved gender parity at primary level, compared with 37% at secondary and less than 3% at tertiary level. Meanwhile, 12% are close to parity at primary level (GPIs of 0.95, 0.96, 1.04 and 1.05), compared with 10% at secondary and 4% at tertiary (Table 2.21). In many parts of the world school environments remain physically unsafe for both boys and girls; teacher attitudes and practices, curricula and textbooks continue to be gender-biased; and while the academic performances of boys and girls are converging, fields of studies and occupational choices remain clustered by gender.

Gender disparities in primary education: some bright spots

Access: more girls entering school

Gender disparities in primary education stem first and foremost from disparities in enrolment in the first grade (UNESCO, 2005a). The global average weighted GPI of gross intake rates (the ratio of the girls' GIR to the boys' GIR) rose from 0.91 in 1999 to 0.94 by 2005. The GPI was below this level in sub-Saharan Africa (0.92), South and West Asia (0.92), and Latin America and the Caribbean (0.93), and 0.95 or above in all other regions (Figure 2.19). Of the 175 countries for which data are available, 118 (more than two-thirds) had achieved gender

Table 2.21: Distribution of countries according to distance from the gender parity goal in primary, secondary and tertiary education, 2005

	Disparities in favour of boys/men			Parity	Disparities in favour of girls/women			
	Far from the goal: GPI below 0.80	Intermediate position: GPI between 0.80 and 0.94	Close to the goal: GPI between 0.95 and 0.96	Goal achieved: GPI between 0.97 and 1.03	Close to the goal: GPI between 1.04 and 1.05	Intermediate position: GPI between 1.06 and 1.25	Far from the goal: GPI above 1.25	Number of countries in the sample
Primary education								
Sub-Saharan Africa	7	14	5	14				40
Arab States	1	6	2	11				20
Central Asia			1	7				8
East Asia and the Pacific		7	4	18		2	1	32
South and West Asia	2	1	1	3		1		8
Latin America and the Caribbean		4	7	26	2			39
North America and Western Europe			1	22				23
Central and Eastern Europe		1		17				18
Total	10	33	21	118	2	3	1	188
Secondary education								
Sub-Saharan Africa	15	9	2	2	1	4	1	34
Arab States	3	5	2	2	3	5		20
Central Asia		1	1	5		1		8
East Asia and the Pacific	3	4	1	10	3	10		31
South and West Asia	2	3		2		1		8
Latin America and the Caribbean		3		18		17	1	39
North America and Western Europe		1	2	14	2	4		23
Central and Eastern Europe		2	2	14				18
Total	23	28	10	67	9	42	2	181
Tertiary education								
Sub-Saharan Africa	22	1		1	1	3	2	30
Arab States	3	1			1	4	7	16
Central Asia	2	1			1	1	3	8
East Asia and the Pacific	7	1		1	1	3	5	18
South and West Asia	4	1				1	1	7
Latin America and the Caribbean	2		1	2		3	17	25
North America and Western Europe		1				9	12	22
Central and Eastern Europe	1					4	13	18
Total	41	6	1	4	4	28	60	144

Sources: Annex, Statistical Tables 5, 8 and 9A.

parity in intake rates by 2005 (see annex, Statistical Table 4). Overall, gender disparities in access improved between 1999 and 2005, sometimes substantially, particularly in South and West Asia, where the average GPI increased from 0.83 to 0.92.

Progress was particularly noteworthy in Burkina Faso, Djibouti, Ethiopia, Equatorial Guinea, Guinea, India, Nepal, the Niger and Yemen. In Ethiopia and Nepal, the GPI of intake rates increased by more than 30% between 1999 and 2006, from 0.69 to 0.90 and from 0.76 to 1.00, respectively (see annex, Statistical Table 4).

However, significant gender disparities in access continue to affect girls in several countries, with the intake rate for girls less than 80% of that for boys in Afghanistan, the Central African Republic, Chad, the Niger, Pakistan and Yemen. Disparities at the expense of boys exist in a limited number of countries, including the Gambia, Ghana, the Islamic Republic of Iran, Malawi, the Maldives, Sao Tome and Principe, Saudi Arabia, Seychelles, and some Pacific and Caribbean island states, in the last case generally relating to low absolute figures.

School participation of boys and girls: uneven progress

The global GPI of primary GERs rose from 0.92 in 1999 to 0.95 in 2005 (see annex, Statistical Table 5). By region, however, the trend differed: the greatest progress towards gender parity occurred in South and West Asia – the region with the worst situation in 1999, where the GPI increased from 0.82 to 0.93 – followed by sub-Saharan Africa and the Arab States, each with an increase of three percentage points. In all other regions, the average GPI was close to unity both years.

The post-Dakar trend towards gender parity is steeper for South and West Asia and, to a lesser extent, for sub-Saharan Africa, two of the three regions with the widest disparities in 1991. In the Arab States, progress has slowed (Figure 2.20).

Worldwide, 118 countries out of the 188 with data had achieved gender parity in primary education by 2005 (Map 2.5; see annex, Statistical Table 5). Many other countries have made progress towards the reduction of gender disparities since 1999, particularly Benin, Burkina Faso, Chad, Ethiopia, the Gambia and Guinea in sub-Saharan Africa; Djibouti, Morocco and Yemen among the Arab

Figure 2.19: Changes in gender disparities in access to primary schooling, by region, between 1999 and 2005

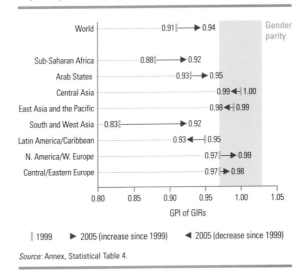

Source: Annex, Statistical Table 4.

Figure 2.20: Gender parity index of primary GERs by region, 1991, 1999 and 2005

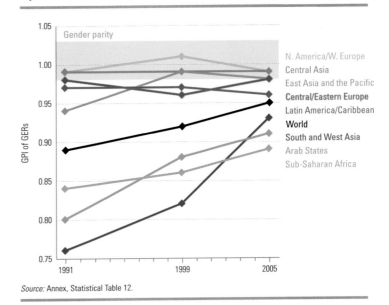

Source: Annex, Statistical Table 12.

States; and Afghanistan, India and Nepal in South and West Asia. The female GER in 2005 was still only 80% of the male GER or less, however, in five sub-Saharan African countries (the Central African Republic, Chad, Côte d'Ivoire, the Democratic Republic of the Congo and the Niger) as well as in Afghanistan, Pakistan and Yemen. Many of these countries are fragile states.

Within countries, gender disparities tend to be wider among poorer people than among the more

CHAPTER 2

Map 2.5: Gender parity index in primary gross enrolment ratios, 2005

1. TFYR Macedonia
2. Albania
3. Montenegro
4. Serbia
5. Bosnia/Herzeg.
6. Croatia
7. Slovenia
8. Hungary
9. Austria
10. Czech Rep.
11. Slovakia
12. Rep. Moldova
13. Romania
14. Bulgaria

No data

Gender parity

0.97 – 1.03

Gender disparity in favour of boys

Less than 0.80

0.80 – 0.94

0.95 – 0.96

Gender disparity in favour of girls

1.04 – 1.05

1.06 or more

Notes: The high disparity in favour of girls in the Islamic Republic of Iran is due to the inclusion in primary enrolment data of literacy programmes for adults, where learners are mostly women. See source table for detailed country notes.
Source: Annex, Statistical Table 5.

The boundaries and names shown and the designations used on this map do not imply official endorsement or acceptance by UNESCO.
Based on United Nations map.

affluent, in rural than in urban areas and, within the latter, in slum than in non-slum areas (UN-HABITAT, 2006). In Latin America and the Caribbean, gender disparities are generally less significant than those relating to socio-economic factors, place of residence, geography and ethnicity (UNESCO-OREALC, 2007).

School progression: girls tend to do better

Once they have access to school, girls tend to do better than boys. The few countries where girls repeat more than boys are mostly in sub-Saharan

Africa (Benin, the Central African Republic, Chad, Côte d'Ivoire, the Democratic Republic of the Congo, Guinea, Mali, the Niger, Nigeria, Togo, Uganda and the United Republic of Tanzania) and the Arab States (Jordan, Mauritania, Oman, Saudi Arabia and Sudan), as well as Turkey. Most of the sub-Saharan African countries are those where disparities in enrolment are markedly in favour of boys. Girls do not repeat more than boys in any country of Latin America and the Caribbean or North America and Western Europe.

In all developed countries and a good number of developing ones, survival rates to the last grade of primary education are virtually the same for boys and girls. Overall, in 2004 the same proportions of girls and boys reached the last grade in seventy countries. In fifty-three countries, however, sizeable differences still exist in school survival, often in favour of girls (Table 2.22). This is particularly the case in Latin America and the Caribbean. In sub-Saharan Africa and the Arab States there is roughly the same number of countries with gender gaps in favour of boys as with gaps in favour of girls.

Gender disparities in secondary education: greater than in primary

Gender disparities are more prevalent and wider in secondary and higher education than at the primary level, but follow more complex patterns. At the secondary level, disparities favouring girls are roughly as frequent (fifty-three countries) as those favouring boys (sixty-one) (see annex, Statistical Table 12). Boys' underachievement in terms of participation and performance is a growing problem (Box 2.9).

The world GPI of the secondary GER was 0.94 in 2005 (Figure 2.21), up from 0.91 in 1999. The pace of reducing gender disparity has been much slower since Dakar than it was between 1991 and 1999, both at a global level and in those regions with the widest disparities in 1991 (the Arab States, East Asia and the Pacific, South and West Asia, and sub-Saharan Africa). Indeed, sub-Saharan Africa moved away from gender parity between 1999 and 2005. This region and South and West Asia combine overall low secondary enrolment with the lowest levels of girls' participation in secondary education at GPIs of 0.83 and 0.79, respectively. Gender disparities are less prevalent in other regions. At 1.08 in Latin America and the Caribbean, the GPI indicates very low participation of boys in secondary education; in eleven countries ninety boys or less are enrolled for every hundred girls.[52] In Suriname, for instance, only seventy-five boys are enrolled in secondary school per hundred girls. Map 2.6 shows the situation at country level.

Overall, the increase in secondary education enrolment discussed above translated into progress towards gender parity in a large majority of

52. The countries are the British Virgin Islands, Colombia, the Dominican Republic, Honduras, Montserrat, Nicaragua, Saint Lucia, Saint Vincent and the Grenadines, Suriname, Uruguay and Venezuela.

Table 2.22: Gender disparities in survival rates to the last grade of primary education, 1999 and 2004

Higher survival for boys (17 countries)			Higher survival for girls (36 countries)		
	GPI			GPI	
	1999	2004		1999	2004
Sub-Saharan Africa			**Sub-Saharan Africa**		
Togo	...	0.83	Nigeria	...	1.04
Chad	0.82	0.85	U. R. Tanzania	...	1.04
Mozambique	0.82	0.87	South Africa	0.96	1.06
Mali	0.93	0.88	Botswana	1.09	1.06
Eritrea	0.95	0.89	Burundi	...	1.07
Benin	...	0.91	Gabon	...	1.07
Malawi	0.88	0.91	Comoros	...	1.07
Guinea	...	0.92	Namibia	1.06	1.07
Senegal	...	0.93	Rwanda	...	1.08
Niger	...	0.96	Ghana	...	1.18
			Swaziland	1.06	1.35
Arab States			**Arab States**		
Iraq	0.92	0.78	Algeria	1.04	1.04
Yemen	...	0.83	Mauritania	...	1.08
Morocco	1.01	0.93	Lebanon	1.07	1.08
Saudi Arabia	...	0.94			
			Central Asia		
			Mongolia	1.06	1.01
			Tajikistan	0.94	1.03
East Asia/Pacific			**East Asia/Pacific**		
Indonesia	...	0.94	Cambodia	0.87	1.05
			Myanmar	...	1.06
			Philippines	...	1.17
			Kiribati	...	1.18
South/West Asia			**South/West Asia**		
India	0.95	0.94	Pakistan	...	1.07
			Bangladesh	1.16	1.07
			Nepal	1.10	1.10
Latin America/Caribbean			**Latin America/Caribbean**		
Guatemala	1.08	0.94	Aruba	0.96	1.04
			Uruguay	...	1.04
			El Salvador	0.99	1.06
			Paraguay	1.06	1.06
			Colombia	1.08	1.07
			Costa Rica	1.04	1.07
			Honduras	...	1.08
			Trinidad/Tobago	...	1.09
			Venezuela	1.09	1.10
			Jamaica	...	1.10
			Nicaragua	1.20	1.11
			Turks/Caicos Is	...	1.13
			N. America/W. Europe		
			Luxembourg	1.11	1.07

Note: The table does not include countries with GPIs between 0.97 and 1.03. See source table for detailed country notes. The countries with the highest disparities in 2004 (GPI below 0.90 or above 1.10) are highlighted.
Source: Annex, Statistical Table 7.

The pace of reducing gender disparity in secondary education has been much slower since Dakar than it was between 1991 and 1999

Box 2.9: Boys' underparticipation in secondary education: background and identity issues

Higher enrolment ratios in secondary education for girls than for boys are increasingly common, especially in OECD and Latin American countries with well-developed education systems, and especially at the upper-secondary level (UNESCO-OREALC, 2007).* Boys are more likely to be low-performing students and to repeat grades, and tend to leave school at a younger age than girls (see annex, Statistical Table 8) (UNESCO, 2006a). More generally, boys are more likely to participate in shorter and less academic secondary programmes not leading to tertiary education, and to leave school early to make a living (OECD, 2001; UNESCO, 2005a).

Socio-economic context, occupational practices and gender identity all appear to play a role in keeping boys away from school. Lesotho, for example, has a tradition of boys herding livestock, which is considered a good way to socialize the male child and make him a responsible member of his family and society (Jha and Kelleher, 2006). Most young male herders come from poor families and are more likely than

girls to drop out of school in order to work and contribute to family income. Poor boys in Chile are four times more likely to drop out of school and enter the workforce than poor girls (UNICEF, 2005a). Conformity to 'masculine' gender identity that clashes with the demands of increasingly women-centred school systems has emerged as another factor in boys' school disaffection and underachievement, for instance in Australia and Jamaica (Jha and Kelleher, 2006).

Boys' underachievement requires policy attention, but should not divert attention from the continuing issue of low access for girls to primary and secondary education in many developing countries.

* Gender disparities at this level reflect an interplay of factors – such as puberty, pregnancy and early marriage, particularly for girls, and household and socio-economic backgrounds – that have a great impact on upper secondary participation and retention (UNESCO, 2006a).

Figure 2.21: Changes in gender disparities in secondary gross enrolment ratios by region, 1991, 1999 and 2005

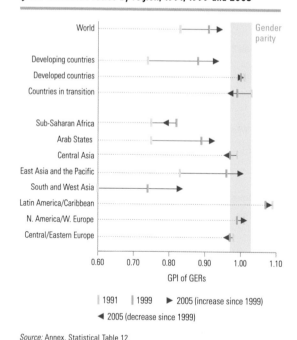

1991 | 1999 | ► 2005 (increase since 1999)
◄ 2005 (decrease since 1999)

Source: Annex, Statistical Table 12.

53. Countries where gender parity was achieved between 1999 and 2005 are Barbados, Belarus, Belize, Bolivia, Chile, the Cook Islands, Cuba, the Czech Republic, Estonia, Greece, Iceland, Latvia, the Netherlands, Paraguay, Peru, Qatar, Seychelles, Sweden and Viet Nam. For Sweden this outcome is the result of the exclusion of adult education from secondary education statistics.

54. Gender parity in tertiary education is not an EFA goal but is included in the Millennium Development Goals.

55. This was the case in Azerbaijan, Botswana, Burkina Faso, Ethiopia, the Islamic Republic of Iran, the Lao People's Democratic Republic, Malawi, Mauritius, Swaziland, Switzerland, Tunisia, Uganda, the United Republic of Tanzania and Yemen. In the Islamic Republic of Iran, Mauritius, the Palestinian Autonomous Territories, Swaziland and Tunisia the tremendous improvement has led to women's overrepresentation in tertiary education.

countries between 1999 and 2005 (see annex, Statistical Table 8). Gender disparities narrowed in two-thirds of the 144 countries with data available for both years, leading in some cases to parity.[53] In countries still far from the gender parity goal, improvement towards gender parity was significant

in Benin, Cambodia, Chad, the Gambia, Guinea, Nepal, Togo, Uganda and Yemen, all with increases in their GPI above 20%.

In tertiary education, gender disparities are the norm

Only Botswana, China, Mexico and Peru had achieved gender parity at the tertiary level by 2005, out of 144 countries with data.[54] Worldwide, many more women than men were enrolled in higher education institutions in 2005: the average GPI was 1.05, a major reversal since 1999 when the tertiary GPI was 0.96, in favour of men (Figure 2.22). In developed countries and countries in transition, the GPI is now close to 1.30, and gender disparities favouring men are now limited to two regions and a subregion: sub-Saharan Africa, where the average GPI worsened between 1999 and 2005 to 0.68; South and West Asia, at 0.74; and East Asia, at 0.92. The expansion of tertiary education between 1999 and 2005 particularly benefited women (see annex, Statistical Table 9A). In countries where gender disparities disadvantaged women, their situation has often improved substantially, with the GPI rising by 20% or above.[55] This positive trend should not obscure the deterioration of women's position in several other countries where their presence was already marginal: gender disparities favouring men increased substantially between 1999 and 2005 in Burundi, the Congo, Djibouti, the Gambia, Nigeria, Viet Nam and, to a lesser extent, Macao (China).

Map 2.6: Gender parity index in secondary gross enrolment ratios, 2005

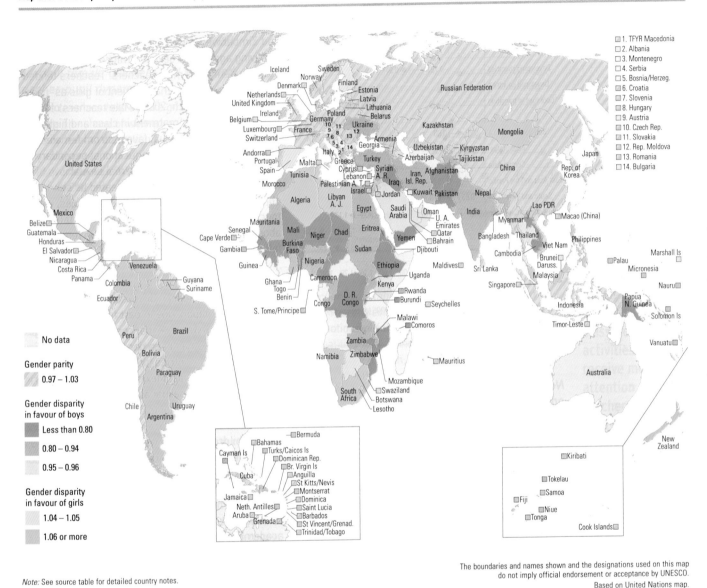

No data

Gender parity

0.97 – 1.03

Gender disparity in favour of boys

Less than 0.80

0.80 – 0.94

0.95 – 0.96

Gender disparity in favour of girls

1.04 – 1.05

1.06 or more

1. TFYR Macedonia
2. Albania
3. Montenegro
4. Serbia
5. Bosnia/Herzeg.
6. Croatia
7. Slovenia
8. Hungary
9. Austria
10. Czech Rep.
11. Slovakia
12. Rep. Moldova
13. Romania
14. Bulgaria

Note: See source table for detailed country notes.
Source: Annex, Statistical Table 12.

The boundaries and names shown and the designations used on this map do not imply official endorsement or acceptance by UNESCO.
Based on United Nations map.

Beyond parity is gender equality, subtler and harder to achieve

Achieving gender equality will require a determined effort to move beyond mere parity by adopting behavioural and other changes that can bring about an enabling environment in which everyone, female and male, thrives (Stromquist, 2007) through:

■ safe and non-discriminatory school environments;

■ the presence of enough female teachers to act as role models, especially in countries with greater disparities in favour of boys, as well as unbiased teacher-based dynamics in the classroom and teacher training in gender issues;

■ unbiased learning content;

■ an absence of significant gender differences in learning outcomes;

■ less gendered choice of subjects in tertiary education.

Education for All Global Monitoring Report

2 0 0 8

How are countries moving towards EFA as a whole since Dakar?

Analysis of changes in the EDI between 1999 and 2005 is possible for only 44 of the 129 countries included in the sample for 2005. The EDI increased in 32 countries – about three-quarters of the 44. While the index rose by 3.4% on average (taking into account both positive and negative changes), progress was substantial in Ethiopia, Guatemala, Lesotho, Mozambique, Nepal and Yemen, where the EDI increased by more than 10% between 1999 and 2005 (Figure 2.26). With the exception of Guatemala, all these countries are in the low EDI category, but they are moving rapidly towards EFA. On the other hand, the EDI declined slightly in the remaining

In general, countries doing well on one EFA goal also tend to do well on the others

Figure 2.26: The EDI in 2005 and change since 1999

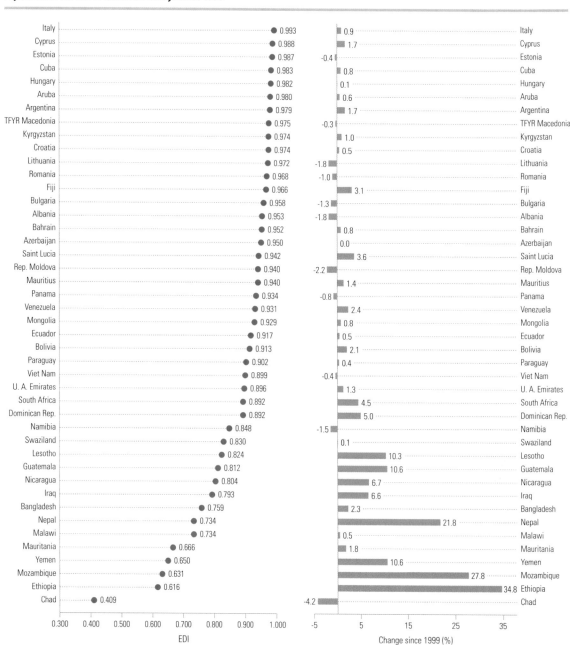

Note: Only countries with EDI values for 1999 and 2005 are included.
Source: Annex, The Education for All Development Index, Table 3.

twelve countries, and decreased by about 2% or more in Albania, Chad, Lithuania and the Republic of Moldova.

In many instances, countries making rapid progress in some indicators did so at the expense of other indicators. Thus, in about two-thirds of the forty-four countries with data for 1999 and 2005, at least one indicator moved in the opposite direction of the others during the period (see annex, The Education for All Development Index, Table A1.3).

Overall, the increase in the total primary NER seems to be the main element responsible for improvement of the EDI between 1999 and 2005, with a mean change (positive and negative) of 6.7% across the forty-four countries, followed by the improvement in gender parity in primary and secondary education, the improvement in adult literacy (3.4%) and the increase in the survival rate to grade 5 (3.1%). The average change in the adult literacy rate was 2.1%.

The increase in the total primary NER was particularly important in most of the countries that experienced significant improvement in the EDI (Ethiopia, Lesotho, Mozambique, Nepal and Yemen). In Ethiopia, the total primary NER more than doubled, from 33% in 1999 to 69% in 2006, while gender parity and school retention also improved, although at a lower pace (by 26% and 19%, respectively).

In most countries that saw low improvement or decline in the EDI, the weak point was the survival rate to grade 5. This was particularly marked in Chad, Malawi and Mauritania; on the other hand, school retention improved substantially in Guatemala, Iraq, Mozambique, Nepal and South Africa. Finally, some countries were able to increase their EDI scores by improving the adult literacy and gender components. This was the case in Yemen, where the EDI increased by 11% even though the survival rate to grade 5 fell considerably.

Taking stock

Uneven and partial though it may be, progress towards EFA has been considerable since 2000, especially among many of the countries farthest from the goals. Fewer children die before age 5 due to improvements in health services and immunization. Access to pre-primary education,

while still out of reach for most children, is expanding. More boys and girls are entering primary school, completing a minimum cycle and making the transition to lower secondary education. Almost two-thirds of countries with data have achieved gender parity at the primary level, though at the secondary level disparities remain pervasive. Gender disparities in learning outcomes have declined. Attention to quality issues – for example, the need for better trained teachers, sufficient learning materials, effective use of instructional time, less absenteeism, better facilities and regular student assessments – is well established.

Despite these overall positive trends, enormous challenges remain, as this chapter illustrates. Many countries lack comprehensive programmes for children under the age of 3, and have done little to increase the number of qualified and trained teachers and caregivers. Access to ECCE among less advantaged children, especially in vulnerable contexts, is very limited, despite the clear benefits. More than 10% of the world's primary school-age children, some 72 million, are still not enrolled. Regular school attendance and progression, weak learning outcomes and low completion rates remain critical issues in many parts of the developing world, especially in fragile states. Educational disparities within countries, disproportionately affecting children from rural, indigenous, poor and/or slum populations, are widespread. Most countries have yet to achieve the gender parity goal. Multiple hurdles to education quality are apparent, including acute teacher shortages, insufficient teacher training, crowded and dilapidated classrooms, and too few textbooks. Many countries inadequately address the learning needs of young people and adults, whose participation in the formal education system has been precarious at best. One adult in five (64% of whom are women) is denied the right to basic literacy and numeracy skills, and little progress has been made on adult literacy.

In short, while particular countries have made considerable progress towards EFA, or towards parts of EFA, for others the pace of educational change is slow. The policies that have worked, and those that are lacking, are the central focus of the next chapter. ■

Progress towards EFA has been considerable since 2000, especially among many of the countries farthest from the goals

Reaching remote
communities: a primary
school in an isolated
Amazon estuary
village, Brazil.

© Dermot Tatlow/PANOS

Chapter 3

Countries on the move

At the 2000 World Education Forum in Dakar, governments were called on to develop and implement policies to achieve the six EFA goals. As guidance, the Dakar Framework for Action set out twelve broad strategies through which governments, supported by civil society organizations, donors and other stakeholders, might achieve or move closer to the goals. Chapter 2 showed a great deal of progress since 2000 in meeting basic learning needs but also significant variation in achievement across countries. This chapter dicusses the ways governments have responded to the goals and strategies in the Dakar Framework.

Monitoring country efforts ___ 98

Developing enabling institutions ___ 100

Comprehensive approaches ___ 107

Expanding equitable access ___ 108

Improving learning ___ 123

Restoring education in difficult circumstances ___ 136

Access and quality are mutually reinforcing ___ 137

Monitoring country efforts

The strategies in the Dakar Framework for Action are summarized in Table 3.1. Those focusing directly on education system development (strategies 2 to 11) provide the starting point for this chapter. (Strategy 1 is discussed in chapter 4 and strategy 12 in chapter 1). Some strategies are very wide-ranging, however – the eighth, for instance, calls for a 'safe, healthy, inclusive and equitably resourced educational environments conducive to excellence in learning' – while others are very focused and specific: the sixth calls for integrating strategies for gender equality, the seventh for education programmes and actions to combat the HIV/AIDS pandemic, the tenth for harnessing information and communication technology (ICT). Moreover, there is overlap, particularly among strategies 2, 3 and 4 as they relate to the role of civil society. Therefore, country experiences in this chapter are organized around three broad policy areas: (i) developing enabling institutions, (ii) expanding equitable access and (iii) improving learning. A final section addresses EFA policy in fragile states, especially those that are or have recently been in conflict.

(i) The Framework for Action underscores the need to develop enabling institutions and calls on governments to develop national action plans, integrate education strategies into broader poverty elimination and development strategies, engage civil society in policy development, and build up participatory and accountable systems of educational governance and management. As part of this environment, it is crucial that national plans and policies encompass the full range of the EFA goals, and not confine themselves to universal primary education (UPE), as is a tendency. The Framework accepts that such enabling institutions may not be present in countries, or regions, where there is social conflict, instability or natural disasters, and highlights the special needs of learners in these situations.

(ii) To ensure the *expansion of equitable access* to basic education for children, youth and adults, the Framework stresses the need to identify and target those who are excluded and to respond flexibly to their requirements. Attention is paid to the need for strategies to: expand early childhood care and education; reduce or eliminate the costs of attending school; address the requirements of particular groups of children including child labourers, those affected by HIV and AIDS, disadvantaged minorities and those in remote communities and urban slums; remove obstacles to access for girls, women, boys and men wherever they exist; be inclusive of children with disabilities; and provide ongoing basic education opportunities for young people and adults.

(iii) To *improve learning* through effective teaching, the Framework emphasizes the need to promote healthy, safe, protective learning environments, improve the effectiveness of teaching and learning, including through ICTs, and mitigate the impact of HIV/AIDS and gender discrimination. Special attention is paid to strategies to improve the status, morale and professionalism of teachers.

Seven years after the World Education Forum, how consistent with the goals and strategies set out in the Framework for Action have governments been in setting and implementing policies for basic learning? The more detailed questions asked in this chapter include the following.

What are countries' experiences of increasing the involvement of civil society organizations (CSOs), delegating powers to lower levels of accountability and placing basic education in a broad context of poverty reduction? What policies and strategies have governments used to increase access of excluded groups to education and with what success? What have been the effects of lowering the costs of schooling for households, including abolishing school tuition fees, and what are the conditions for success? Can effective interventions to improve learning be detected? What emphasis have governments given to professional development for teachers? How have they increased the supply of teachers? What strategies have proved successful in overcoming problems arising from weak governments in fragile states in the provision of education?

To approach these questions, information on the policies and strategies adopted since 2000 by thirty countries,[1] mainly developing, was collected and

1. The countries, in alphabetical order by EFA region, are: Egypt, Morocco, Yemen; Albania, Turkey; Mongolia, Tajikistan; Cambodia, China, Indonesia, the Lao People's Democratic Republic, the Philippines, Viet Nam; Brazil, the Dominican Republic, Guatemala, Mexico, Nicaragua; Bangladesh, India, Pakistan; Burkina Faso, Eritrea, Ethiopia, Mozambique, Nigeria, Rwanda, Senegal, South Africa and the United Republic of Tanzania.

Table 3.1: Summary of strategies in the Expanded Commentary on the Dakar Framework for Action

1. *Mobilize strong national and international political commitment for education for all, develop national action plans and enhance significantly investment in basic education.* This means governments must make firm political commitments and allocate sufficient resources to all components of basic education; funding agencies should also allocate a larger share of their resources, so that no country seriously committed to EFA is thwarted by lack of resources.
2. *Promote EFA policies within a sustainable and well-integrated sector framework clearly linked to poverty elimination and development strategies.* This requires education strategies to complement other sector strategies and be closely linked with civil society. Actions include developing education strategies within broader poverty alleviation measures and developing inclusive education systems that identify, target and respond flexibly to the needs and circumstances of the poorest and most marginalized.
3. *Ensure the engagement and participation of civil society in the formulation, implementation and monitoring of strategies for educational development.* Participation should not be limited to endorsing or financing programmes designed by government but also include mechanisms allowing civil society organizations to contribute to the planning, implementation, monitoring and evaluation of basic education.
4. *Develop responsive, participatory and accountable systems of educational governance and management.* This means better governance in terms of efficiency, accountability, transparency and flexibility, and better management through a move from highly centralized, standardized, command-driven forms to more decentralized, participatory management at lower levels of accountability.
5. *Meet the needs of education systems affected by conflict, natural calamities and instability and conduct educational programmes in ways that promote mutual understanding, peace and tolerance, and that help to prevent violence and conflict.* Capacities of government and civil society should be enhanced so as to rapidly assess education needs, restore learning opportunities and reconstruct destroyed or damaged education systems.
6. *Implement integrated strategies for gender equality in education which recognize the need for changes in attitudes, values and practices.* The content, processes and context of education must be free of gender bias, and encourage and support equality and respect.
7. *Implement as a matter of urgency education programmes and actions to combat the HIV/AIDS pandemic.* Education systems must go through significant changes if they are to survive the impact of HIV/AIDS and counter its spread, especially in response to the impact on teacher supply and student demand.
8. *Create safe, healthy, inclusive and equitably resourced educational environments conducive to excellence in learning, with clearly defined levels of achievement for all.* The quality of learning is necessarily at the heart of EFA. Effective strategies to identify and include the socially, culturally and economically excluded are urgently needed. Learning outcomes must be well defined in both cognitive and non-cognitive domains, and be continually assessed as an integral part of the teaching and learning process.
9. *Enhance the status, morale and professionalism of teachers.* Teachers at all levels of education should be respected and adequately remunerated, have access to training and professional development and support, and be able to participate locally and nationally in actions affecting their professional lives and teaching environments.
10. *Harness new information and communication technologies to help achieve EFA goals.* There is a need to tap the potential of ICTs to enhance data collection and analysis, strengthen management systems, improve access to education by remote and disadvantaged communities, and support teachers' initial and continuing professional development.
11. *Systematically monitor progress towards EFA goals and strategies at the national, regional and international levels.* Robust and reliable education statistics, disaggregated and based on accurate census data, are essential if progress is to be properly measured, experience shared and lessons learned. Ongoing monitoring and evaluation of EFA, with full participation of civil society, should be encouraged.
12. *Build on existing mechanisms to accelerate progress towards education for all.* To realize the six EFA goals, broad-based and participatory mechanisms at international, regional and national level are essential.

Source: UNESCO (2000*a*).

reviewed. The countries were selected according to criteria aimed at providing a diversity of contexts in terms of regional spread, progress in relation to the six EFA goals and the challenges remaining. The experiences recorded in these studies are complemented by those of other countries. Policies and strategies are presented in this chapter according to the three policy areas (see annex table on national policies to advance EFA).

Developing enabling institutions

To ensure the right to a basic education, the Dakar Framework called upon governments to develop responsive, participatory and accountable systems of educational governance and management. Since then, the search for improved institutions better able to deliver education has accelerated and it is now common for education programmes to have a 'good governance' component. The Dakar Framework encouraged governments to (i) develop comprehensive national education plans, linked to national poverty elimination and development strategies, (ii) strengthen the capacity to monitor education progress, (iii) engage civil society in policy-making and monitoring, (iv) improve regulatory frameworks for the provision of education and (v) decentralize educational management. This section explores how governments have responded.

Strong focus on planning

Since 2000, many developing countries have gone through the process of preparing comprehensive national education plans focusing on country-specific issues. As the annex table on national policies shows, most of the thirty countries reviewed now have education plans. For example, Yemen launched its National Basic Education Strategy in 2002, aimed at achieving UPE and improving school quality, with an emphasis on increasing the access and performance of girls (Kefaya, 2007); Albania prepared a National Education Strategy 2004–2015 focusing on improved governance and quality of teaching and learning, higher and more sustainable financing of pre-university education, capacity-building and thedevelopment of vocational and technical education (Albania Ministry of Education and Science, 2005); Mongolia's Master Education Plan (2006–2015) identified among its priorities the needs

of vulnerable children, challenges of herder communities and the increase in internal migration from rural to urban areas (Steiner-Khamsi, 2007); Nicaragua's strategies to meet the EFA goals are contained in the National Education Plan for 2001–2015, which is aligned with the National Development Plan and the Poverty Reduction Strategy Paper (Porta and Laguna, 2007c); and Rwanda introduced its Education Sector Policy in 2003, leading to the formulation of an Education Sector Strategic Plan which includes a financial framework and a commitment to a nine-year cycle of basic education (Woods, 2007b).

Coverage of the EFA goals in education sector plans provides an indication of country priorities. While no international database of key education planning documents exists, the 2006 *EFA Global Monitoring Report* highlighted the status of the EFA goals in thirty-two recently prepared national education sector plans. UPE had the highest priority and was included in all the plans, while EFA goal 3, on the learning needs of young people and adults, was considered in only one-third of them. Just seven plans discussed all six EFA goals (UNESCO-IIEP, 2005).[2] A recent review of twenty-eight education sector plans prepared between 2001 and 2006 and endorsed through the EFA Fast Track Initiative concluded that, overall, plans were based on reasonably sound sector analysis and included well-defined measures to tackle enrolment disparities and education quality in primary education (FTI Secretariat, 2007). Most plans included an analysis of previous achievements and lessons learned, and indicated extensive consultations. A large majority contained clear objectives, key actions, dated targets and performance indicators. However, priority setting across the objectives as well as links between the plans and medium-term budgeting were frequently found to be weak. Less than half the plans included a medium-term financial framework that took all costs into account (FTI Secretariat, 2007). Moreover, too few plans take a comprehensive view of EFA, encompassing ECCE and adult literacy as well as formal schooling for girls and boys.

Education is a cornerstone of many of the Poverty Reduction Strategy Papers (PRSPs) developed in over sixty low-income countries to date. A review of links between education sector plans and PRSPs in eighteen countries[3] found them generally to be strong (Caillods and Hallak, 2004). In a majority of these countries, the PRSPs directly incorporated

Coverage of the EFA goals in education sector plans provides an indication of country priorities

2. The countries involved were Benin, India, Indonesia, Kenya, Paraguay, Sudan and Uzbekistan.

3. Albania, Benin, Bolivia, Burkina Faso, Cambodia, the Gambia, Guinea, Guyana, Honduras, Mauritania, Mozambique, Nicaragua, the Niger, Uganda, the United Republic of Tanzania, Viet Nam, Yemen and Zambia.

education objectives and measures from sector documents. Like the sector plans, the PRSPs systematically covered the levels of the formal education system from primary upwards, while the treatment of ECCE and non-formal education was more mixed. (The *EFA Global Monitoring Report* for 2006 gives extensiv illustrations of similar findings for adult literacy, as does that for 2007 concerning ECCE.) In PRSPs that included skills development, it was most commonly covered in non-education sector programmes aimed at strengthening the capacity of the poor to engage in production and income-generation activities.

Capacity for monitoring of education progress

The Dakar Framework identified improved capacity for monitoring of performance in the education system as fundamental.[4] Experiences in the 1980s and 1990s with developing Education Management Information Systems (EMIS)[5] highlighted the major difficulties in developing sustained institutional support over time and persuading key stakeholders to use the data generated. Since Dakar, many countries have intensified their efforts. For instance, the Philippines began operating its Basic Education Information System in 2002 (Caoli-Rodriguez, 2007); in Morocco the EMIS was strengthened through the National Education and Training Charter in 2000 (Hddigui, 2007*b*); a unified system to monitor education progress is being developed in Yemen (Kefaya, 2007); in Mexico the National Institute for Educational Evaluation was created in 2002 and conducts regular learning assessments (Bracho, 2007); and the monitoring system in Nigeria has been strengthened in recent years and data for local and state government levels are now published annually (Theobald et al., 2007).

A key requirement for improving an EMIS is to understand the demand for data. Previous failures have been related to an overriding emphasis on collecting and publishing data without considering who will use them and for what purposes. An EMIS needs to be closely connected to a special unit or set of key decision-makers who have clearly articulated data needs and the capacities to use the information provided (Cassidy, 2006; Mackay, 2006).

In Latin America, the shift from an emphasis on education access to one combining quality and access has had important implications for educational management. When expanding access to education was the primary objective, the delivery system focused on inputs, such as teachers and school materials. In such a system, individual units were responsible for supplying different inputs and worked relatively separately from each other. In moving towards increased education quality as well as equal access, management systems have had to become more integrated and require more detailed information on inputs, outputs and processes. This requires changes in organizational structures and cultures. The development of an EMIS needs to include strategies to cope with such challenges (Cassidy, 2006).

Management capacity, in general, continues to be a major barrier to education progress in many low-income countries (for example, Burkina Faso: Box 3.1). To address capacity constraints, countries have traditionally invested in training. Well-trained managers and teachers are obviously important for an efficient education system, but there is growing awareness that capacity development also involves changes in organizational and institutional structures (Morgan, 2006). Botswana, Chile and China are examples of countries that have defined agendas for strengthening their public management systems so as to improve performance and the ability to retain competent personnel (OECD-DAC, 2006*a*).

Civil society involvement in EFA planning and monitoring

Until recently, participation of civil society organizations in basic education was limited largely to providing services in areas where governments found it difficult to operate and, in some cases, to engaging local communities in school management. In the lead-up to Dakar, there was a call for greater and wider CSO participation in the

Botswana, China and Chile have defined agendas for strengthening their public management systems

---

4. This section treats national capacity. The *EFA Global Monitoring Report* is responsible for international monitoring as well. At regional level, various arrangements pertain. In sub-Saharan Africa, the Pôle de Dakar, in collaboration with UNESCO-BREDA, has published *Education for All in Africa: Dakar +7 Report*, assessing education trends (UNESCO-BREDA, 2007). In Latin America and the Caribbean, UNESCO's Regional Bureau for education has reviewed and assessed progress towards EFA in the region, with a special focus on education quality (UNESCO/OREALC, 2007). In East Asia and the Pacific, national reports are being collected and integrated into a regional overview; the national reports so far prepared are available at www2.unescobkk.org/education/aims/download/temp/index.html.

5. An EMIS can be defined as 'a system for the collection, integration, processing, maintenance and dissemination of data and information to support decision-making, policy-analysis and formulation, planning, monitoring and management at all levels of an education system. It is a system of people, technology, models, methods, processes, procedures, rules and regulations that function together to provide education leaders, decision-makers and managers at all levels with a comprehensive, integrated set of relevant, reliable, unambiguous and timely data and information to support them in completion of their responsibilities' (Cassidy, 2006).

The concession school programme in Bogota involves contracts with private schools to provide education for low-income learners

Action Aid's Reflect adult literacy method around the world); others have developed effective critical stances on government policies or plans (for example, concerning school fees and girls' education); and there are numerous examples of communities being encouraged and helped to demand accountability from national and local education policy-makers, including through budget-tracking exercises and alternative monitoring and reporting activities (Box 3.4).

Effective oversight of non-state providers

The often crucial role of non-state providers of basic education was pointed out at the World Education Forum and stronger partnerships with governments were encouraged. Chapter 2 demonstrated that in some countries with large increases in primary education enrolment since 1999, including Benin, Guinea, Mali and Mauritania, the role of non-state providers had increased substantially. Others, such as Bangladesh and Pakistan, continued to rely on non-state providers for a large share of places in primary education.

Since governments have an obligation under international treaties to ensure that children, youth and adults receive an adequate education, the Dakar Framework for Action paid attention to regulatory frameworks for the provision of education. In some of the countries with a strong presence of non-state providers, mechanisms have been put in place to improve various kinds of regulations to enhance the advancement towards EFA.

The Indian Government, within the framework of Sarva Shiksha Abhiyan, its plan for UPE, has established a memorandum of understanding with NGOs and the private sector clarifying roles and responsibilities. Over 4,000 non-state providers are reported to participate under the plan, providing education to disadvantaged children (Aga Khan Foundation, 2007).

Partnerships between governments and the non-state sector take various forms, including direct financing, contracting of services and training of teachers. The expansion of such arrangements heightens the need to define roles, responsibilities and expected results. The South African Government's approach to increasing pre-primary

Box 3.4: Scorecards in Latin America

Scorecards are innovative monitoring and advocacy tools, which more and more countries are using to mobilize citizens to demand better education. Since 2001, the Partnership for Education Revitalization in the Americas (PREAL) has published report cards on the state and progress of education in the region, identifying encouraging policy measures to improve schools. As of 2006 it had produced seventeen education report cards and was working on ten others. The aims of the report cards are to provide timely and reliable information on education and to promote transparency and accountability through civil society participation. The report cards have a positive effect on country efforts to improve education in the region. For example, lively national debates are common due to the spread of the reports and governments are encouraged to improve their own reporting to the public. The major challenges have been handling data deficiencies and defining communication priority messages.

Source: Ortega Goodspeed (2006).

enrolment is an example of the state partnering with private schools and local NGOs running early childhood services: the government offers subsidies, monitors quality against national standards and provides a support system to ensure that schools can meet the standards (Rose, 2002).

In some instances the conditions for receiving government finance involve assuring places for disadvantaged children. The concession school programme in Bogota, Colombia, involves contracts with private schools to provide education for low-income learners. After competitive bidding by established, successful private schools, those selected receive public support in the form of new school facilities built in poor areas and funding per child enrolled. They are granted flexibility to contract administrative and teaching staff and to implement their own pedagogical model. In turn, concessionaires have to fulfil conditions related to number of hours of instruction, quality of nutritional provision, minimum teacher and administrator qualifications, availability of educational materials and facility maintenance, as well as guaranteeing not to institute multiple shifts and to carry out evaluation of learning achievements. Above all, they must provide pre-primary and basic education to disadvantaged children and meet performance standards set by the District Secretary of Education, such as surpassing mean test scores in similar schools. Results thus far indicate that the programme is successfully retaining children in school and improving learning outcomes (Barrera-Osorio, 2007).

While there are positive examples, regulations for non-state providers are cumbersome formalities in many countries. Rather than developing a supportive environment for promoting quality and improving access for the underserved, regulations are too often limited to administrative adherence to rules. In addition, since significant costs are often associated with registration and compliance, many schools remain unregistered (Aga Khan Foundation, 2007).

The emphasis generally is on standards for facilities and services that non-state providers must meet in order to register or be recognized, but it can be difficult for new schools to comply immediately with such standards. In Uganda, to start a private school requires a licence that is contingent on criteria such as qualified teachers and suitable infrastructure. Schools are initially licensed for a year, then can be officially registered if they meet curriculum standards. Once registered, schools can apply to hold O-level or A-level exams through the national examinations board (Aga Khan Foundation, 2007).

Once registration standards are met, however, effective oversight of service quality is less frequent. In Bangladesh, to be recognized and receive financial support, non-government schools must meet stringent approval criteria (e.g. land ownership, number and qualifications of teachers, number of classrooms, minimum number of students). A lack of ongoing supervision coupled with a highly decentralized system results nevertheless in quality often being substandard and insufficient provisions are made to ensure that non-government schools are located in underserved areas (Aga Khan Foundation, 2007). In Nigeria, registration of non-government schools involves meeting teacher qualification requirements, but in practice private schools, especially low-budget ones, often rely on underqualified teachers on temporary contracts (Rose, 2006).

Effective oversight is hampered by lack of government capacity for enforcement of regulations and by lack of clarity regarding responsibilities within government. Registering a non-state school in Malawi, for example, involves applying for a licence whose conditions include requirements about land titling, teacher labour contracts, etc. However, a lack of systematic procedures for registration has led to inconsistencies in the way various divisions of the Ministry of Education, Science and Technology grant licences, and many schools open before receiving approval (Lewin and Sayed, 2005). In Bangladesh, provision of education by NGOs is regulated through the NGO Affairs Bureau, which is responsible for auditing and monitoring performance but lacks capacity for these functions. In addition, NGOs that do not receive foreign funding are registered with the Directorate of Social Welfare. In both cases, the Ministry of Education has little involvement with the programmes and, hence, no real knowledge of the number of children involved or the quality of provision (Aga Khan Foundation, 2007).

Chile and South Africa are examples of countries that have introduced incentives for the non-state sector to increase compliance with regulations. Such incentives, entailing financial subsidies and other types of support, are conditional on proof of good quality (Aga Khan Foundation, 2007).

Formal policy dialogue between governments and non-state providers has improved in the past decade, though it is usually dominated by umbrella organizations of registered for-profit providers (Rose, 2006). Where it is well established, ongoing dialogue can enhance regulation as well as enable mutual learning. The Madrasa Early Childhood Programme in East Africa has worked with the governments of Kenya, Uganda and Zanzibar (United Rpublic of Tanzania) as they developed policies for young children. Impact research and twenty years of experience with over 200 communities across the region have been critical to the programme's ability to influence and engage in policy discussions. The programme has also been able to call government officials' attention to practical challenges that community pre-schools face. This has resulted in, for example, small but critical changes that clarified the registration process and made it more transparent (Consultative Group on Early Childhood Care and Development, 2003).

Chile and South Africa are examples of countries that have introduced incentives for the non-state sector to increase compliance with regulations

Decentralization: promises often differ from reality

To promote participation and accountability, the Dakar Framework suggested that countries move towards more decentralized educational management. At the same time, it stressed the need to ensure that decentralization did not lead to increased inequality in the distribution of resources.

Many developing countries have undertaken programmes to decentralize financial, political and administrative responsibilities for education. The nature of these initiatives differs substantially, ranging from attribution of some limited tasks to the regional or provincial level (Burkina Faso, Cambodia, Morocco, Senegal, Turkey) to devolution of broad decision-making responsibility to local government (Indonesia, Pakistan). In many of the poorest countries, although local governments are elected, their powers in relation to the delivery of education remain limited. Recently, with the introduction of block grants, local governments in Ethiopia, Rwanda, Uganda and the United Republic of Tanzania have increased their role in education, often in collaboration with school councils (Tidemand et al., 2007; Watson and Yohannes, 2005; Woods, 2007b).

While legislation may instantly alter the apparent distribution of responsibilities, decentralization is in fact a long, evolutionary process. In countries that undertook major decentralization during the 1990s, including in Eastern Europe and Latin America, the reforms are still being consolidated. The priority given to decentralization may shift with the political direction of the government in power. One recent example is Nicaragua, where the government that took office at the beginning of 2007 immediately abolished the autonomous schools that had been created in one of Latin America's most extensive school-level decentralization programmes. The justification given was that the schools charged fees (Sirias, 2007).

Decentralization holds much promise in making schools responsive to local education needs. In particular, school-based management[7] – the most far-reaching form of decentralization – has received considerable attention in recent years. Guatemala's school-based management programme, PRONADE, is an often-cited reform that has increased community involvement and

school efficiency. It gives community school councils responsibility for key functions such as the hiring, paying and supervision of teachers and the monitoring of student attendance. The aim is to increase enrolment in pre-primary and primary education, notably in poor rural areas, and to give parents a stronger voice in school administration. Evaluations suggest that the councils' increased responsibility has led to better use of teachers and schools, and that the reform had an important role in increasing the net primary enrolment rate from 82% in 1999 to 94% in 2005 (Porta and Laguna, 2007b). Similar programmes in El Salvador, Honduras and Nicaragua have shown that such schools can achieve at least as good results in enrolment expansion and increased completion rates as better resourced traditional schools (Di Gropello, 2006).

While early efforts to promote school-based management aimed at increasing access to schooling and encouraging local participation, the focus in the past decade has turned to its effects on learning. Here the available evidence is mixed. An examination of eighty-three empirical studies on the effects of school-based management on learning outcomes concluded that the outcomes were as likely to be negative as positive (Leithwood and Menzies, 1998).

School-based management policies do not always provide the amount of autonomy initially anticipated. In some cases, extensive regulations regarding curriculum guidelines and central examinations substantially limit schools' powers. South Africa, after apartheid, promoted school autonomy, allowing elected school-site councils (including representatives of school staff, parents and students) to decide on issues such as curriculum and personnel. But in practice, councils often have little influence over the most important decisions, as these have to be made in accordance with detailed guidelines. For example, while schools pay their personnel, salaries are set through national negotiations (Winkler and Gershberg, 2003).

While the clear advice at Dakar was for developing countries to shift from centralized management of the education system to a more decentralized form, with participation at lower levels of accountability, country experiences show that the issues involved are complex. The impact on education access and quality is far from definite.

Guatemala's school-based management programme, PRONADE, has increased community involvement and school efficiency

7. School-based governance, school site management and school self-management are other frequently used terms.

In many systems with centralized traditions, the skills necessary to manage and govern an education system are limited locally. Lack of clarity about new roles and responsibilities is a common problem. In Indonesia, political motives and a drive for democracy led to decentralization of powers to districts in the late 1990s and the 2003 Education Law was intended to clarify responsibilities. Yet many legal and regulatory issues remained vaguely defined, leading to confusion throughout the system. In many cases, district management systems and staff were found to be ill equipped to perform their new responsibilities. The central government meanwhile encountered difficulties in finding its new role within the decentralized system and continued to undertake functions that had been assigned to lower levels, such as construction procurement and teacher management (World Bank, 2004c). A similar situation at the central level is reported in Viet Nam (Henaff et al., 2007).

The Dakar Framework expresses a concern that decentralization should not lead to greater inequality, but this risk remains. An impact evaluation in Ghana found that, while primary school enrolment and quality improved substantially in the country as a whole after decentralization in the 1990s, disparities in school quality between poor and less poor areas widened (World Bank, 2004a). The main reason was reported to be increased reliance on financing from local communities and districts, with the central government unable to contribute much to poorer areas beyond teacher salaries. Decentralization programmes in Argentina and Mexico are also reported to have increased disparities in education quality (Galiani et al., 2005; Skoufias and Shapiro, 2006).

On the whole, there is as yet too little empirical evidence to determine under what conditions decentralization improves education access and learning, and what are the most effective ways of limiting increased inequality. Many countries have been quick to become part of the movement towards decentralization, often encouraged by external influences. But a growing body of evidence points to the challenges involved (Grindle, 2007) and the need for careful analysis of the institutional environment when deciding what levels of government are best suited for which functions in the education system (Bray and Mukundan, 2003).[8]

Comprehensive approaches

Overall, comprehensive education sector planning and monitoring have gained momentum since Dakar. This, despite widespread capacity constraints, has enabled more comprehensive approaches to education, in which access and quality measures may reinforce each other. Without strong institutions, good-quality education is not likely to evolve. Without evidence of quality, children, youth and adults are unlikely to enrol and are more likely to drop out. Without proactive measures to increase access, disadvantaged groups are unlikely to have access to education. These issues are interrelated and addressing one without the others is not sufficient. Mexico's compensatory programmes for the inclusion of disadvantaged groups (Box 3.5) take such a comprehensive approach to education.

Decentralization programmes in Mexico and Argentina have increased disparities in education quality

8. The 2009 *EFA Global Monitoring Report*, whose special theme will be the governance, finance and management of education, will treat these issues in greater depth.

Box 3.5: Compensatory programmes in Mexico

Mexico has a long history of developing compensatory programmes aimed at dispersed rural communities and at migrant and indigenous populations. These have been scaled up since the 1990s and now target the most disadvantaged and lowest-performing schools at all levels of the system, including all primary schools in indigenous communities. The programmes include provision of ECCE and childcare support for parents, support to school management, extension and improvement of primary school infrastructure and equipment, provision of learning materials to each learner, professional development and training for education staff, monetary incentives for teachers to reduce turnover and absenteeism, and a grant and training component to support educational projects developed by parents and community leaders through parents' associations (Bracho, 2007).

These comprehensive interventions have had some success in improving school outcomes. The gap between repetition rates of children in schools supported by the compensatory programmes and of comparable children in other schools was found to have shrunk by six percentage points (Shapiro and Trevino, 2004). They also helped reduce inequalities in learning outcomes, with a 10% annual reduction in the overall test score gap between indigenous and non-indigenous children. For the most disadvantaged children, the gap was reduced by 30% a year. Most of the improvements were in mathematics rather than language. The programmes have also helped reduce children's participation in economic activities and improved school attendance, particularly among 12- to 16-year-olds (Rosati and Rossi, 2007). The longer a school has benefited from the interventions, the greater the reduction in failure and dropout rates (Shapiro and Trevino, 2004). However, evaluations also found that incentives for teachers were not sufficient to prevent them from leaving, adversely affecting learner achievement (Benemérita Universidad Autónoma de Puebla, 2006). The school-based management component (known as AGEs) has had a positive effect on accountability and parental involvement, and Gertler et al. (2006) found that the positive effects on educational outcomes (reduced grade failure, repetition and dropout) of empowering parents' associations persisted even after controlling for participation in the cash transfer programme Progresa-Oportunidades.

Teacher professional development

While much attention is focused on teacher supply, particularly in contexts of teacher shortages, it is also important to improve the skills of practising teachers, update their knowledge and competencies, and increase their motivation (Dembélé, 2005). In-service training is particularly important, both for skill development and to encourage teachers to remain within the profession.

While much is known about the elements of effective small-scale in-service training programmes, very few mass examples exist and it is not known if the same results can be replicated in large-scale programmes (Schwille and Dembélé, 2007; Villegas-Reimers, 2003). Promising small-scale examples include programmes in the Philippines, Pakistan and Romania. The Government of the Philippines is piloting a school-based training programme in science and mathematics that uses an action research approach in which teachers are trained within their schools so that there is immediate application of and feedback on the techniques they have learned. Romania's school-based teacher professional development programme, initiated in 2003 for teachers in rural schools, has resulted in improved learner achievement in grade 8, encouraged underqualified teachers to take upgrading courses, and improved teacher satisfaction and motivation (Zafeirakou, 2007). Pakistan's mentoring programme has resulted

> In the United States, it is estimated that between 40% and 50% of teachers leave within five years of entering the profession

in gains in the confidence and motivation of teachers and teacher mentors (Box 3.12).

Opportunities for professional development and support are important for newly trained teachers. The support they receive in the first few years can have a lasting effect on their practice and may determine how long they remain in the teaching profession (Hedges, 2002). Attrition rates of teachers are high, especially in the early years, in both developed and developing countries. In the United States, it is estimated that between 40% and 50% of teachers leave within five years of entering the profession (Shockley et al., 2006). While effective teacher induction programmes vary in approach, an analysis in developed countries found that they provide opportunities for experienced and newly qualified teachers to learn together in a supportive environment that allows time for collaboration and reflection, and enables a gradual acculturation of new teachers into the profession (Howe, 2006).

Teaching and learning

Effective teaching and learning depend not only on sufficient instructional hours and learning resources, and on trained and motivated teachers but also on classroom practices. There are many aspects to this; of particular importance are a curriculum that is child-centred and focused on outcomes; the use of children's mother tongues,

---

Box 3.12: Cluster-based mentoring in Pakistan

Pakistan developed a cluster-based mentoring programme to deliver school-based training to teachers in selected districts of Sindh and Baluchistan provinces. The programme sought to improve teachers' content knowledge in mathematics, science, social studies and languages; develop skills in teaching across grades and subjects; develop classroom pedagogical practices, especially in multigrade settings; and assist teachers in developing teaching and learning resources using locally available materials. Initial mentoring aimed at practising teachers, who in turn would each become mentors of a cluster of fifteen to twenty-five schools. The training consisted of six weeks at the Institute for Educational Development at Aga Khan University, followed by two weeks in the teachers' own schools and two weeks back at the university. Once trained, the mentors conducted weekly workshops for teachers in their clusters and visited these teachers in their schools,

where they assisted in planning and teaching lessons. The central school of each cluster served as an Open Learning Resource Centre. Between 2004 and 2006, 307 mentor teachers were trained and went on to mentor around 8,000 teachers. It is too early to measure the impact on learning achievement. The mentor teachers report that the mixed-mode training gave them the confidence to deliver training within their clusters. Classroom observations reveal real improvement in school environments, teachers' competencies and teaching skills, pupils' learning and overall school culture. Challenges the programme has encountered include concentrations of large numbers of teachers in some clusters, unavailability of substitutes when the teachers in single-teacher schools attended workshops and a lack of coordination with the broader Education Sector Reform Assistance Programme.

Source: Barett et al. (2007).

at least in the initial years at school; improvement of feedback to policy-makers through national sample system assessments and to students from continuous assessment by teachers; and the use of information and communication technology (ITC).

Towards child-centred and outcome-oriented curricula

Studies of school effectiveness identify the way teachers teach to be of critical importance in any reform designed to improve quality (Scheerens, 2004). The country case studies (see annex, table on national policies) indicate a trend to revise curricula to make classroom interactions more responsive and centred on the child. There is a move way from traditional 'chalk and talk' teaching to more discovery-based learning and a greater emphasis on outcomes that are broader than basic recall of facts and information.

China introduced a new curriculum in 1999, focusing on active learning and providing an integrated curriculum to meet students' diverse needs. It was in place across the country in primary and junior middle schools by 2005 (Zhao and Wenbin, 2007). A comprehensive curriculum reform launched in Turkey in 2003 began in grades 1 to 5 with foundation courses (mathematics, Turkish, life skills, social sciences, science and technology) and is continuing through the higher grades and for more subject areas. To date, curricula for grades 1 to 6 have been developed, piloted and implemented in all schools. An important characteristic of the new curriculum has been a change to the pedagogy, accommodating active learning and different types of assessments (Aydagül, 2007). In Eritrea, the government has introduced an approach that gives as much importance to the process of learning as to content; it integrates subjects as well as providing coherence and continuity; emphasizes English-language competence; and strengthens science and technology. Another common aspect of curriculum reform is to make the content more relevant to the needs of individuals, communities and societies. Morocco's primary curriculum, for instance, has in recent years been enriched by integrating dimensions of environmental and health education (Hddigui, 2007b).

While the introduction of more participatory and inclusive pedagogy is encouraging, it is equally important for teaching to be structured to enable learners to acquire basic skills, such as literacy, in

the early years of schooling (Abadzi, 2006; Kirschner et al., 2006). In addition, in many resource-constrained contexts where there are large classes, few learning resources and inexperienced and underqualified teachers, using a child-centred, outcome-based pedagogy may be difficult. In South Africa, an ambitious reform introduced in 1998 ran into difficulties because teachers were not familiar enough with the theory and practice of such constructivist approaches, and because many schools in the poorest areas did not have photocopiers, libraries, textbooks and reference materials to enable teachers to prepare adequately. These practical problems led to a further round of changes to the curriculum, which remains child-centred and outcome-based but is now being simplified for effective implementation. Given the large class sizes that persist in many countries, it is also important to remember that there are useful teaching methods on the continuum between 'chalk and talk' learning and full exploratory participation by children. This was an important finding of the 2005 Report, which noted the possibilities of a mildly interactive type of structured teaching that involves stopping frequently to make sure pupils have understood (UNESCO, 2004b).

Another important innovation in the curriculum in recent years has been the introduction of HIV/AIDS education, though implementation and impact are mixed (Box 3.13).

Promoting bilingual and multilingual education

Effective teaching and improved learning outcomes are intimately intertwined with issues of language. Successful acquisition and retention of literacy skills depends on how national policies and school practices build on learners' local-language (mother-tongue) proficiencies.[21] While multilingualism is the norm in most countries, public education systems often tend to ignore or downplay the diversity of linguistic realities (UNESCO, 2005a). In Asia, for example, more than 2,000 languages are spoken but fewer than 50 are designated as the medium of instruction in schools (UNESCO-Bangkok, 2007a). As a result, many students – especially from marginalized ethnic or cultural minorities – enter school facing a foreign medium of instruction or a language that differs from the one spoken at home. Multilingual approaches in education, in which language is recognized as an integral part of a student's cultural identity, can thus act as source of inclusion, with important consequences for minority children (UNESCO, 2003a).

It is important for teaching to be structured to enable learners to acquire basic skills, such as literacy, in the early years of schooling

21. The Expanded Commentary on the Dakar Framework of Action (2000: para. 30) also states that an environment that makes full use of local-language proficiencies is intrinsic to quality education.

Box 3.13: HIV/AIDS education

The HIV/AIDS pandemic means that curricula should now include HIV/AIDS education as part of a more concerted focus on life skills. The declaration of the United Nations General Assembly on HIV/AIDS set global targets for 2005 of 90% and for 2010 of 95% of young men and women aged 15 to 24 having access to the information and services necessary to develop the life skills required to reduce their vulnerability to HIV infection. Cambodia and Ethiopia have introduced HIV/AIDS education into their curricula (see annex, table on national policies). Fifty-five out of seventy countries have reported addressing HIV/AIDS in the curriculum at primary level, and sixty-two at secondary level (UNAIDS Interagency Task Team on Education, 2005).

The evidence on implementation and impact is mixed. In a survey of eighteen low-income countries, nearly all had developed an HIV/AIDS curriculum but implementation was limited. In Asia, programmes in Brunei Darussalam, Cambodia, China, Indonesia, Malaysia, Mongolia, Myanmar, Papua New Guinea, the Philippines, Thailand and Viet Nam are restricted to secondary schools and emphasize biological rather than social factors. Conversely, a broad review of studies of school-based HIV/AIDS education in developing countries found that the courses had had a strong impact on increasing relevant knowledge and some impact on behaviour. Similarly, evaluations of the Primary School Action for Better Health programme in Nyanza and Rift Valley provinces in Kenya have demonstrated promising results in changing knowledge, attitudes and behaviour among learners, teachers, and other key family and community leaders.

The introduction of HIV/AIDS education in the curriculum needs to be complemented by the professional development of teachers. However, a survey of teacher training in the eleven Asian countries mentioned above found that instruction on HIV/AIDS tended to be in-service and limited. Among the countries reviewed only Papua New Guinea, Thailand and Viet Nam included HIV/AIDS education in pre-service training.

Sources: Global Campaign for Education (2005); Kirby et al. (2005); Overseas Development Institute (2007); Smith et al. (2003); United Nations (2001b).

While there is a very long way to go in promoting multilingualism and mother-tongue initial instruction in primary education, it is now increasingly accepted and much progress is being made.

- In Cambodia, where Khmer is the national medium of instruction at all levels of education, several minority languages have been introduced as the medium of instruction in pilot projects in the eastern highlands.

- In the Lao People's Democratic Republic, local languages are widely used in oral form in schools in ethnic minority areas.

- In eastern Malaysia, several indigenous groups have been teaching local languages as school subjects since the 1990s, though not as the medium of instruction.

- Uzbekistan, with more than 100 languages, is committed to providing basic education in the seven national languages, including Uzbek. About 10% of all Uzbekistan schools employ the languages of ethnic minorities (Russian, Kazahk, Tajik, Karakalpak, Turkmen and Kyrgyz).

- Zambia launched its Primary Reading Programme in 1998, in which mother tongues are used as a medium of instruction for the first three years of schooling and the more widely used English language is introduced as a subject in the early grades, becoming the medium of instruction by grade 3 or 4. This programme has become a model for other sub-Saharan African countries (Box 3.14).

- A pilot programme of bilingual instruction in Burkina Faso, which by 2006 covered 112 primary schools in 13 regions, had significant positive effects on student retention and achievement: the course has been reduced from six to five years and the pass rate in the national examination in these schools in 2004 was 94%, compared with 74% in all schools.

- In India, where hundred of languages are spoken, twenty-two are listed in the 8th Schedule of the Constitution. India's National Curriculum Framework for School Education, published in 2005, strongly upholds the principle of mother tongue instruction, but the main debate revolves around the choices of regional languages and

In practice, mother tongue education can take different forms: for example, the use of unwritten local languages as transition or auxiliary languages in the early primary grades, to facilitate the acquisition of literacy in a widely used language; the development of written learning materials in local languages; and the teaching of mother tongue languages as a separate curricular subject. Research has consistently shown that children acquire linguistic and cognitive skills more readily in their mother tongue and are then able to transfer these to a widely used, national or regional language (Brock-Utne, 2000; Dutcher, 1997; Geva and Ryan, 1993; Goody and Bennett, 2001; Grin, 2005; Heugh, 2003; Ouane, 2003; Reh, 1981).

English. The state of Andhra Pradesh started the process of introducing instruction in eight tribal languages in 2003, with scripting and analysis of the languages.

Bilingual and multilingual education can have significant benefits for improving education quality and reducing repetition and dropout, but key implementation challenges remain: countries must ensure that there are enough trained teachers proficient in the learners' mother tongue and that learning resources in various languages are widely available.

Improving assessment

As the Framework for Action emphasizes, placing quality at the heart of EFA requires effective strategies to assess knowledge and skills and demonstrate measurable learning outcomes. This has two distinct elements: national systems of assessment, based on sample surveys, to provide information on how the education system as a whole is developing; and classroom-based continuous assessment to enable teachers to provide regular feedback to students to improve their learning and performance. Chapter 2 showed that many countries now undertake regular assessment and participate in international assessments. Between 2000 and 2006, at least fifty-five countries conducted at least one assessment of learning outcomes in grades 1 to 3, eighty-four in grades 4 to 6 and fifty-four in grades 7 to 9. More and more countries are also introducing continuous assessment in the classroom.

In Zambia a national assessment at the end of grade 5 was introduced as part of the 1998–2003 Basic Education Sub-sector Investment Programme. Using the results, the government then organized the distribution of learning materials with priority on the schools where achievement was lowest (Machona and Chilala, 2004). National assessments have also been used to increase incentives for teachers by providing rewards to schools showing demonstrable gains and improvements in learning. In Chile, for example, cash awards are allocated to schools depending on achievement levels of learners on the national assessment tests, and are usually distributed among all professional staff (Benveniste, 2002). However, with assessment systems narrowly tied to rewards and sanctions, there is a risk of introducing negative incentives for schools. It has been reported in South Africa, for instance, that

Box 3.14: Facilitating early literacy in Zambia

Zambia's New Breakthrough to Literacy (NBTL) course, part of the broader Primary Reading Programme, focuses on developing literacy in grade 1 through one of the seven official Zambian languages while simultaneously developing pupils' speaking ability in English. Care is taken to develop written materials in all official languages, where needed. In grade 2, literacy in English is developed through the Step into English course, which uses similar contents, methods and classroom management strategies as NBTL. These courses are intended to prepare learners for the upper primary grades, in which English is the medium of instruction. Pilots began in 1998 and the programme included all primary schools by 2005. Reading levels have improved considerably in both local languages and English (Sampa 2003, Linehan 2004). The Primary Reading Programme and South Africa's Molteno Project, on which it was based, now serve as models in other African countries, including Botswana, Ghana, Malawi, Namibia and Uganda, all of which have accepted the premise that learning through a local language in the early years is easier and more effective and that the acquired literacy skills can be converted to a second language. It remains to be seen whether such programmes can raise language achievement in the longer term in these countries.

Source: Barrett et al. (2007).

learners who are judged to be ill prepared and likely to fail examinations are held back from taking them (South African Democratic Teachers Union, 2003). In Viet Nam, the reporting system on learning achievement and progress in schools, coordinated through the education services at the commune, district and provincial levels to the education ministry, is well organized and provides detailed, comprehensive information. Since all levels have much at stake, it is reported that achievements and learner progress are often exaggerated (Henaff et al., 2007).

Many countries have begun to move towards regular classroom-based continuous assessment (CA) (Kelleghan and Greanley, 2003), including Albania, Brazil, Ethiopia and Morocco (see annex, table on national policies). In Namibia, CA has been introduced at the primary level, with training and support targeted to teachers in both the lower and upper primary phases (du Plessis, 2003). In Malawi, international and local organizations have assisted in developing a model for CA in primary schools, and training teachers and others in its implementation (du Plessis, 2003; Mchazime, 2003).

Not all efforts to use CA in schools have met with success. In Swaziland, it was introduced in 1993 following a recommendation from the National Education Review Commission. Ten years later,

> Many countries have begun to move towards regular classroom-based continuous assessment

Investing in
education in
post-conflict
situations pays
high dividends

While the use of ICT is becoming widespread, in particular among young people, its effective integration into the education system is complex, involving not only technology but also teacher competencies, pedagogy, institutional readiness, curriculum and sustained financial resources. In particular, its effectiveness depends on committed and trained personnel who can use it to maximize teaching and learning. While there has been an increased focus on teachers' ICT training, the recent African survey on ICT initiatives noted that most of such training in the region tends to be one-off and short-term with limited follow-up. To manage ICT in education in a better and more integrated way, many countries have developed ICT policies in recent years (Farrell and Isaacs, forthcoming; Farrell and Wachholz, 2003).

Restoring education in difficult circumstances

The World Education Forum highlighted the need for special support for education systems affected by conflict, natural calamities and instability. These conditions continue to take a heavy toll, denying millions the right to education. Nevertheless, much is being learned about what is effective in restoring affected systems and the importance of aid is increasingly recognized. The thirty-five countries designated as fragile states accounted for 10% of the total developing country population in 2005 but received 14% of aid for basic education. This chapter concludes by providing some examples of effective EFA strategies and policies in fragile states.

Although the number of armed conflicts[24] around the world has been declining (Human Security Centre, 2006), most wars continue to be fought in the developing world, with such adverse consequences for civilians as human rights violations, the spread of disease and the breakdown of social order. The United Nations Security Council recently called for greater protection for civilians, who 'continue to account for the majority of casualties in situations of armed conflict', noting that civilians are often 'deliberately targeted in order to create a climate of fear and to destabilize populations' (UN News Service, 2007). A particularly severe breach of human rights is the recruitment of children by armed groups. In over thirty situations of concern in the world, children are being brutalized, killed, maimed and abducted as part of adult conflicts, and it is

estimated that over 250,000 children continue to be used as child soldiers.[25]

The Inter-Agency Network for Education in Emergencies (INEE), which emerged as a result of the Dakar conference, provides a platform for United Nations and bilateral agencies, NGOs and others to work together for the right to education in emergencies and post-conflict situations. Its handbook on Minimum Standards for Education in Emergencies, Chronic Crises and Early Reconstruction, designed in a consultative process involving over 2,200 individuals from more than 50 countries, has been used in over 60 countries – notably Cambodia, Chad, Guatemala, Nepal, Pakistan and Uganda – to improve the quality of efforts to deliver education services to people affected by crisis.

Education is a significant social investment in preventing a recurrence of conflict. Over the past forty years around half of all civil wars have resulted from post-conflict relapses, 40% of them within the first decade. Investing in education in post-conflict situations pays high dividends, as it gives people confidence in peace by signalling that that the benefits are going to be long term and widespread. A good example of prioritization of education after a conflict is Uganda during the first post-conflict election of the 1990s. In mid-campaign, the ruling party recognized the importance of primary education and announced the abolition of school tuition fees. Enrolment doubled in the following year, signalling a belief that a peaceful future was likely and that education was an important investment for economic growth (Chauvet and Collier, 2007).

A key priority for education in the context of post-conflict recovery is renewing the infrastructure of schools that were destroyed. This is no easy task, as countries in post-conflict situations suffer from shortages not only of teachers but also builders, plumbers and other skilled people required for rebuilding. Alternative forms of schooling can play a role in such a context, as seen in Afghanistan (Box 3.17).

Reintegrating child soldiers is a particularly important priority in post-conflict situations, as disaffected youth often create instability in society and are extremely vulnerable. Using the example of southern Sudan, Box 3.18 shows how their integration into communities and normal life needs to be gradual and flexible.

24. An armed conflict is defined as a political conflict in which armed combat involves the armed forces of at least one state (or one or more armed factions seeking to gain control of all or part of the state), and in which at least 1,000 people have been killed by the fighting during the course of the conflict (Project Ploughshares, 2007).

25. Grave violations have been recorded in Afghanistan, Burundi, Chad, Colombia, Côte d'Ivoire, the Democratic Republic of the Congo, Haiti, Iraq, Israel, Lebanon, Liberia, Myanmar, Nepal, the Palestinian Autonomous Territories, the Philippines, Somalia, Sri Lanka, Sudan and Uganda (Office of the Special Representative of the Secretary-General for Children and Armed Conflict: http://www.un.org/children/conflict/english/conflicts2.html)

Box 3.17: Home-based classrooms in Afghanistan

Since the fall of the Taliban in 2001, Afghanistan has experienced a tumultuous period of post-conflict reconstruction and peace-building. This has included major efforts to rebuild and revitalize a broken education system. Several NGOs have been instrumental in improving access to education, especially for girls, first through the establishment of community-based and home-based schools, and later through mainstreaming of non-formal learners into the formal government system (where it is functioning). In 2004, some 1.3 million girls were enrolled in government primary schools, a major accomplishment given that, in 2001, the number was recorded as zero.

The International Rescue Committee (IRC) operates home-based classrooms in five provinces. Classes are located in teacher's homes or community spaces such as mosques, and run for around three hours a day, six days a week. Teachers are selected and compensated (often in kind) by communities and trained by the IRC, which also provides teaching and learning materials and supervisory support. Among the reasons for the success of this approach are the short travel time and half-day programme, which allow children to continue supporting their families; recruitment of local teachers, often women; the short distance to school and secure and comfortable learning environments, which help attract girls from conservative families; and low learner/teacher ratios. The programme has been vital in restoring hope and optimism to war-torn communities, promoting the re-establishment of formal schools, fostering physical and psychosocial well-being and ensuring that children have genuine opportunities to learn. The IRC's goal is to see that learners are absorbed into government schools once the capacity exists and the organization works for the establishment of these in areas where multiple home-based schools are functioning.

Source: Aga Khan Foundation (2007).

Box 3.18: Education for child soldiers in southern Sudan

A successful education programme for children formerly associated with armed groups is the Miith Akolda Curriculum, developed by CARE during the war in southern Sudan. Several thousand children were evacuated from front-line combat to safer locations in transit camps further south, where a programme was developed within a fortnight. It aimed to disarm and rehabilitate children associated with armed groups and provide a structure for daily activities in the camp. The programme incorporated teaching with many other activities, such as problem-solving, health and hygiene, singing and dancing, using numbers, children's rights, story-telling, sports and physical education, and quiet play. The programme was devised to be flexible, since many children initially were unable to cope with many hours of learning. The time spent in schooling was gradually increased as children became accustomed to life in the camps and learned routine tasks necessary for its running, such as washing, preparing and clearing meals, collecting wood and water, and washing clothes. As a result, the children took responsibility and the security of the routine helped stabilize their lives and allow the slow process of reintegration to take place. What made this programme a success in terms of reintegrating children into their communities was the recognition that children required a combination of activities, enabling them to take on (or continue) their responsibilities, while simultaneously reintegrating them into education.

Sources: Save the Children (2007); UNESCO-IIEP (2004).

While education in post-conflict situations is rightly regarded as a vital social investment, it is also important to recognize that it can contribute to violence, conflict and instability through many causes, including uneven distribution of education and educational opportunities for particular groups, non-recognition of mother tongues in schools, segregated education and negative images conveyed in textbooks. It is important in post-conflict contexts to pay special attention to the curriculum and, in particular, to prioritize peace education programmes so that distrust and hatred between groups is overcome and citizens are equipped with the tools for peaceful conflict resolution. Examples of multicultural education and peace education programmes with conflict resolution elements are found in Bosnia and Herzegovina, in The former Yugoslav Republic of Macedonia and in Romania, where the dynamics of inter-ethnic and intercultural relationships are addressed (Minow, 2002).

Access and quality are mutually reinforcing

This chapter has shown that there are effective measures to increase access to education and to improve education quality. There is no necessary trade-off between these objectives, except occasionally in the very short term when enrolment surges as a result, for example, of removing tuition fees; indeed, the two objectives can be mutually reinforcing if supported with an appropriate institutional environment. Moreover, education systems can be restored after conflicts and other crises, according to principles now well established. Improved access and quality, and more attention to fragile states are key elements of the EFA agenda to 2015 that is developed in the next chapter. ■

Measures to increase access and to improve education quality can be mutually reinforcing

Under her teacher's
eye, a young girl
does her sums in
a multigrade school,
Indonesia.

© ZUMA PRESS/MAXPPP

Chapter 4

Progress in financing Education for All

This chapter reviews the extent to which the components of the 2000 Dakar Framework for Action that deal with the financing of the Education for All agenda and goals are being applied by governments and donor agencies. Central to this part of the Framework was a compact: if developing country governments could demonstrate that they were giving priority to the EFA goals, including through higher expenditure, and that well-developed plans had been elaborated, including through wide consultation, then the donors would provide the additional resources required to implement the plans.

Introduction _____ 140

Changing national financial
commitments to EFA
since Dakar _____ 141

Contribution of external aid
to EFA since Dakar _____ 154

What progress within the
Framework for Action? _____ 172

Introduction

The ultimate responsibility for framing and implementing education policies and plans lies with governments, but for many countries – particularly the poorest, which tend to be furthest away from achieving the EFA goals – progress also relies on support from donors. The Dakar Framework for Action firmly placed governments of low-income countries in the driving seat, urging them to increase the share of public expenditure allocated for all aspects of basic education, and to increase efficiency through improved levels of governance and the wider involvement of non-government bodies. Donors were encouraged to augment government efforts by not only increasing the amount of aid for basic education but also making it available in ways that ensure it is more effective.

Seven years after 164 countries endorsed the Dakar Framework, what is the record of achievement in these areas? Have governments increased their financial priority for education in general and basic education in particular? Are expenditures being made in more efficient ways and with greater accountability and transparency? Have the sources of domestic funding for basic education widened? Are donors allocating a larger share of their aid to basic education and to countries where the challenges are greatest? Is aid being made available in ways that are likely to increase its effectiveness in enabling education systems to move more rapidly towards the EFA goals? Has additional aid flowed to countries where governments can demonstrate that they have given basic education a higher priority and that well-prepared plans have been drawn up with broad societal endorsement? These and other questions arising from the financing sections of the Framework[1] are the focus of this chapter. Not all can be answered with certainty. In some cases the information necessary to compare the current situation with that in 2000 is not available. In others it is too soon to judge initiatives' likely outcomes. Overall, however, sufficient information is available to allow some conclusions to be reached, among them:

■ While a majority of governments, particularly in the least developed countries, and most noticeably in sub-Saharan Africa, have given more financial priority to education, including basic education, many still allocate very low shares of GNP and total government expenditure to it.

Education for All Global Monitoring Report
2008

■ While some governments have reduced the financial burden of schooling on households, others continue to require communities and households to provide too high a share of the cost of schooling, thereby limiting its coverage among the poor.

■ Since 2000 there have been many examples of efforts to reduce waste in the education sector and to increase the accountability and transparency of financial flows, but in most countries this movement has only just begun.

■ Aid for basic education increased systematically between 2000 and 2004, but declined in 2005 and remains inadequate. Too many donors give a higher priority to post-primary education, too high a share of education aid goes to middle income rather than low-income countries and the distribution of aid across low-income countries does not always reflect the needs.

■ Basic education has benefited from the initiatives to increase debt relief for highly indebted poor countries that have been taken since 1999 for bilateral debt and, more recently, for debt to the multilateral institutions. Donor-supported debt relief will now decline, however, and greater increases in sector aid will be required if aid targets are to be met.

■ The call at Dakar for donors to support education sector-wide reforms and programmes has been repeated many times; there is evidence that this has been occurring but the behaviour of donors and the experiences of individual countries vary substantially.

■ Increased aid for basic education does not automatically lead to improved educational outcomes; it may replace existing government expenditure or it may be used ineffectively. However, quantitative studies suggest that the impact of aid is positive, though less than generally expected, and qualitative assessments by donors indicate that some objectives are much easier to reach than others.

■ In some countries governments and donors work well together and have been able to increase financial resources and educational outcomes significantly; in others this has not happened since governments may not be committed to the goals, there is a lack of capacity for developing a credible education plan and/or too few donors provide support. It is these countries – where educational development is low, no strong reform programmes are in place and donor interest is lacking – that are in the greatest danger of not reaching the goals of Dakar.

The chapter has three sections. The first deals with the level and allocation of domestic financial resources from both governments and households for the education sector in general and for basic education, and the second with external aid. The third section assesses government and donor performance explicitly against statements in the Dakar Framework for Action. Each is organized around, but not limited to, statements from the Dakar Framework for Action.

Changing national financial commitments to EFA since Dakar

Public expenditure on education

Among the several sources of finance for EFA, governments are the most important. The Dakar Framework calls for increased shares of national income and total government expenditure to be allocated to education, and within that to basic education. Such increases are also indicative of the political will which is required to trigger additional external aid for basic education. In this subsection the most recent data, mainly for 2005, are used to describe the situation among and within regions and country income groups in terms of public education expenditure, with a particular focus on changes since 1999.

There are considerable limitations to the data. Out of 203 countries and territories for which the UNESCO Institute for Statistics (UIS) attempts to collect information on education, total expenditure as a share of GNP is available for only 127 countries for 1999 and for 125 countries for 2005. Even more limiting, only 107 countries report education expenditure as a share of total government expenditure for 2005, though this is up significantly from eighty countries for 1999. Finally, while the number of countries for which expenditure on primary education as a share of total education expenditure is available has doubled since 1999, the total is only 102; and this measure is available for just forty countries for both 1999 and 2005, about

Among the several sources of finance for EFA, governments are the most important

1. A set of strategies for achieving Education for All formed part of the Expanded Commentary on the Dakar Framework for Action (UNESCO, 2000a).

CHAPTER 4

As countries'
economies grow,
a larger share of
their GNP might
be expected
to be devoted
to education

half of which are developing and transition countries. These serious limitations need to be kept in mind wherever regional performances are discussed.

Education expenditure as a share of GNP: great variation

The share of public education expenditure in GNP varies between regions and among countries within regions (Table 4.1). As a group, in 2005, the countries of North America and Western Europe devoted the highest share (median of 5.7%), followed by Latin America and the Caribbean, and sub-Saharan Africa (5.0% each), Central and Eastern Europe (4.9%), East Asia and the Pacific (4.7%), the Arab States (4.5%), South and West Asia (3.6%) and Central Asia (3.2%). These figures do not tell the whole story, however, since variations between countries in the same region are very large, particularly in East Asia and the Pacific, Latin America and the Caribbean, and sub-Saharan Africa. In each of these regions the share of education expenditure in GNP varies by at least nine percentage points among countries.

Who are the biggest and lowest spenders? Of the 105 countries outside North America and Western Europe for which information is available for 2005:

■ The twenty-six countries in which public expenditure on education was 6% or more of GNP, grouped by region, were Botswana, Cape Verde, Ethiopia, Kenya, Lesotho, Namibia and Swaziland; Djibouti, Morocco, Saudi Arabia and Tunisia; Malaysia; Bolivia and Guyana; and Belarus,

Slovenia and Ukraine, plus nine small island countries of the Pacific and Indian Oceans and the Caribbean. A majority of these twenty-six countries have relatively small populations. Only eight have over 5 million people. Across North America and Western Europe, nine out of twenty countries spent 6% or more.

■ The twenty-four countries in which public expenditure on education was 3% or less of GNP, grouped by region, were Cameroon, Chad, the Congo, the Gambia, Guinea, the Niger and Zambia; Lebanon, Mauritania and the United Arab Emirates; Azerbaijan, Georgia and Kazakhstan; Cambodia, Indonesia, the Lao People's Democratic Republic and the Philippines; Bangladesh and Pakistan; and the Dominican Republic, El Salvador, Guatemala, Peru and Uruguay.

Another way of presenting information on education expenditure as a share of GNP is by income group.[2] The countries for which information is available for 2005 can be grouped into four income categories: low, lower middle, upper middle and high. Table 4.2 presents the median and average shares, and again provides data on country variations within the groups.

Shares tend to increase with income, as the group medians show. Also, the variation among high income countries is much smaller than among low and middle income countries. This pattern suggests

2. The classification of countries by income group used throughout this chapter is that adopted by the OECD-DAC Secretariat (OECD-DAC, 2007a).

Table 4.1: Total public expenditure on education as % of GNP and as % of total government expenditure, selected countries, 2005

	Sub-Saharan Africa	Arab States	Central Asia	East Asia/ Pacific	South/West Asia	Latin America/ Caribbean	N. America/ W. Europe	Centr./East. Europe
Total public expenditure on education as % of GNP								
Median	5.0	4.5	3.2	4.7	3.6	5.0	5.7	4.9
Maximum	11.0	7.6	5.4	10.0	7.5	10.8	8.6	6.5
Minimum	1.8	1.6	2.5	1.0	2.4	1.3	4.3	3.4
Variance	5.1	5.3	1.3	7.2	3.6	5.6	1.5	1.0
Number of countries with data/number of countries in region								
	30/45	*9/20*	*6/9*	*14/33*	*6/9*	*23/41*	*20/26*	*17/20*
Total public expenditure on education as % of total government expenditure								
Median	17.5	25.7	18.0	15.0	14.6	13.4	12.7	12.8
Maximum	29.8	27.6	19.6	25.0	22.8	25.6	17.0	21.1
Minimum	4.0	11.0	13.1	10.7	10.7	7.9	8.5	10.0
Variance	45.1	47.1	11.3	22.4	19.3	17.3	5.3	11.4
Number of countries with data/number of countries in region								
	21/45	*8/20*	*3/9*	*11/33*	*6/9*	*24/41*	*20/26*	*14/20*

Source: Annex, Statistical Table 11.

that, over the long term, as countries' economies grow, a larger share of their GNP might be expected to be devoted to education.

Education expenditure as a share of total government expenditure can measure commitment

The share of education expenditure in GNP is a result of several factors, including governments' ability to collect domestic revenue, which is harder to do in low-income countries. Having a relatively small share of education expenditure in GNP does not necessarily mean education is a low government priority; it may mean the public sector is small. Thus, education's share of total government expenditure is a more direct measure of governments' relative commitment to education, at least as compared to other sectors and areas of expenditure.

Data on the share of education in total government expenditure in 2005 are available for 107 countries, including twenty from North America and Western Europe, and summarized in the lower half of Table 4.1. The relatively few countries in the Arab States region for which data are available tend to devote a significantly higher proportion of total government expenditure to education than do countries in other regions. The region with the next highest median is Central Asia, at 18%, then sub-Saharan Africa at 17.5%.[3] East Asia and the Pacific, Latin America and the Caribbean, and South and West Asia have median shares between 15% and 13%. Again, variations across countries in each of these regions are large. North America and Western Europe, which devotes the highest share of GNP to education, also records the lowest share of total public expenditure (below 13%).

Turning from regions to countries, six of the eight Arab States for which there is information allocated at least 20% of total government expenditure to basic education, as did five of twenty-one sub-Saharan African countries: Botswana, Cape Verde, Kenya, Lesotho and Madagascar. Other countries in the sample achieving this impressive level were the Islamic Republic of Iran, Malaysia, Mexico, the Republic of Moldova and Thailand. Twenty-seven of the eighty-seven countries remaining after omitting North America and Western Europe devoted between 15% and 20%. Seven of these were in sub-Saharan Africa. At the bottom of the range, countries allocating less than 10% of total public expenditure to education were in either sub-

Table 4.2: Total public expenditure on education as % of GNP, by income group, 2005

	High-income countries	Upper-middle-income countries	Lower-middle-income countries	Low-income countries
Total public expenditure on education as % of GNP				
Median	5.5	5.6	4.7	3.9
Maximum	8.5	11.0	9.5	10.8
Minimum	1.6	2.3	1.0	1.8
Variance	5.5	5.7	4.8	4.4
Number of countries with data/number of countries in income group				
	37/54	22/34	27/47	39/68

Source: Annex, Statistical Table 11.

Saharan Africa (Cameroon, the Congo and Equatorial Guinea) or Latin America and the Caribbean (the Dominican Republic, Guatemala, Jamaica, Panama and Uruguay).

Although richer countries tend to spend a greater share of GNP on education, there is little difference across income groups in the share of total expenditure devoted to education. The average (and median) is around 16% to 17% for low-income, lower middle income and upper middle income countries alike. The share in high income countries tends to be lower (13%), largely because allocations for social welfare benefits are larger.

Changes in education expenditure since 1999 are not uniform

How have education expenditure levels changed since 1999? In particular, to what extent have low-income countries increased the share of national income and budgets allocated to education as encouraged in the Dakar Framework? Outside North America and Western Europe, education expenditure as a share of GNP and of total government expenditure is available for both 1999 and 2005 for only eighty-four and forty countries, respectively.

The evidence on the change in education's share of GNP between 1999 and 2005 is mixed (Figure 4.1). In the Arab States, the share increased in four of the six countries for which information is available. The exceptions were Saudi Arabia, which nevertheless allocated a very high 6.7% in 2005, and Mauritania, where the share fell to only 2.4%. The share also increased in seven out of twelve countries in East Asia and the Pacific, and remained high even in those countries where it fell, with the Marshall Islands at 9.5%, Tonga 4.9% and Thailand 4.3%. Across sub-Saharan Africa changes were positive, on the whole. The share of education expenditure

The evidence on the change in education's share of GNP between 1999 and 2005 is mixed

3. It should be noted that the proportion of countries with data available varies by region, and that Central Asia, the Arab States, and East Asia and the Pacific are the regions with the smallest proportions for this indicator.

Figure 4.1: Change in total public expenditure on education as % of GNP between 1999 and 2005 (percentage points)

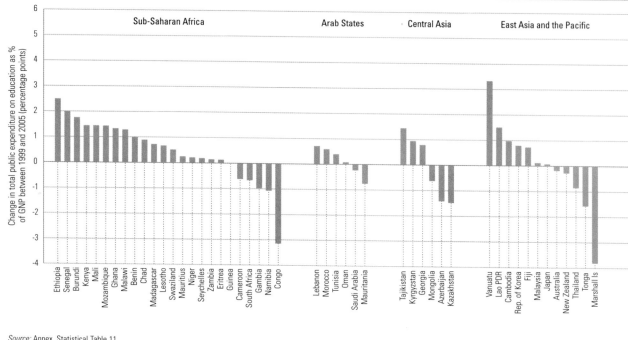

Source: Annex, Statistical Table 11.

in GNP increased in eighteen of the twenty-four countries for which data are available. It fell in Cameroon (to 1.8%), the Gambia (2.1%), the Congo (2.8%), South Africa (5.5%) and Namibia (6.8%), and stayed constant in Guinea (2.1%). In the remaining developing and transition economy regions, the number of countries where the share increased was equal to or just below the number where it decreased.

Countries which increased their share of GNP for education by at least one percentage point between 1999 and 2005 were Barbados, Benin, Burundi, Cambodia, Ethiopia, Ghana, Kenya, the Lao People's Democratic Republic, Malawi, Mali, Mexico, Mozambique, Saint Kitts and Nevis, Saint Vincent and the Grenadines, Senegal, Tajikistan, Ukraine and Vanuatu. Countries in which the share decreased by at least one percentage point and where it was below 3% in 2005 were Azerbaijan, the Congo, the Gambia and Kazakhstan. Again, it needs to be stressed that the data for this comparison are available for only eighty-four countries outside of North America and Western Europe.

For a small number of countries estimates of education expenditure as a share of GNP are also available for 1991 and 1995. Box 4.1 presents these

Box 4.1: The fluctuating nature of education expenditure in sub-Saharan Africa since the Jomtien Conference

Information on education expenditure as a share of GNP between 1991 and 2005 is available for sixteen sub-Saharan African countries. Figure 4.2 presents two sets of data: for the seven countries in which the share of education expenditure in GNP was higher in 2005 than in 1991 and for the nine countries in which the share was lower, though it should be noted that in four of the nine, the share remained above 5% in 2005.

In ten of the sixteen countries, the share of education expenditure in GNP was higher in 1995 than in 1991, implying some post-Jomtien response. However, by 1999 the share was below that of 1995 in, again, ten countries. The post-Dakar response was even more widespread, with thirteen of the sixteen countries having a higher share of expenditure in 2005 than in 1999. Another way of looking at the expenditure data is through rates of growth. Between 1991 and 1995, the median annual growth rate of real expenditure across the sixteen countries was 6%; over the following four years it was just 1%; and between 1999 and 2005 it rose again, to 4%.

Sources: Annex, Statistical Table 11; UIS database.

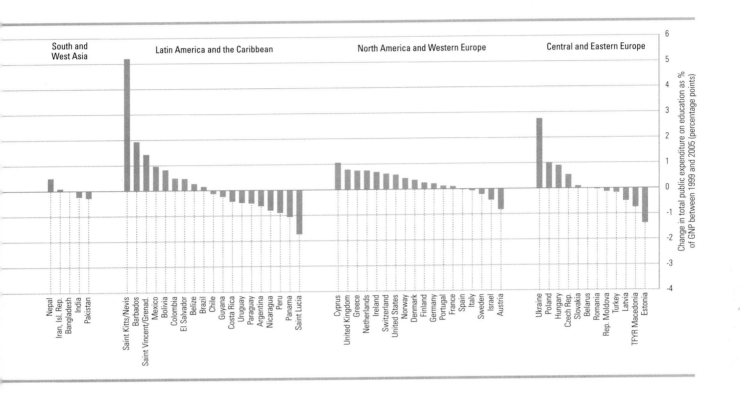

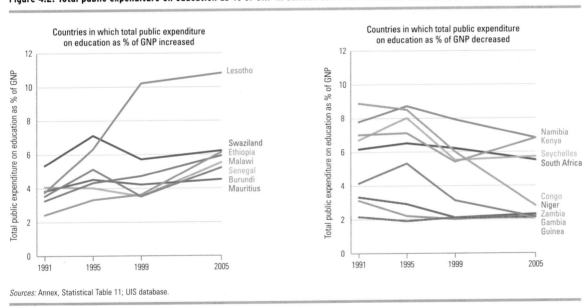

Figure 4.2: Total public expenditure on education as % of GNP in sixteen sub-Saharan African countries, 1991–2005

Countries in which total public expenditure on education as % of GNP increased

Countries in which total public expenditure on education as % of GNP decreased

Sources: Annex, Statistical Table 11; UIS database.

shares together with similar data for 1999 to 2005 for sixteen sub-Saharan African countries. Overall, there is a distinct pattern – an increase in the share in the years immediately following the Jomtien conference of 1990, followed by a reversal, then another surge after Dakar.

On changes in the share of education in total government expenditure, less can be said. Only forty countries outside of North America and Western Europe have provided sufficient information to make comparisons between 1999 and 2005, and fifteen of these are in Latin America and the Caribbean. The data are too limited to support generalizations. However, of the four countries in the Arab States region that provided information – Lebanon, Morocco, Oman and Saudi Arabia – all increased the share of total government expenditure devoted to education. In South and West Asia, the share increased in the Islamic Republic of Iran and Nepal, while it fell in Bangladesh and India. In sub-Saharan Africa, the share increased in Lesotho (to 30%) and fell in Cameroon (9%), the Congo (8%), Mauritius (14%) and South Africa (18%).

Growth in education expenditure: encouraging signs in sub-Saharan Africa and in South and West Asia

A country may be increasing its public expenditure on education substantially but if its rate of overall economic growth is increasing faster, then education expenditure as a share of GNP will be falling. Conversely, in a country that is increasing education expenditure at a low rate, if its rate of economic growth is even lower, the share of GNP for education will increase. To supplement the information on expenditure shares, this subsection looks at rates of growth of education expenditure since 1999.[4] Information is available for 100 countries. Table 4.3 summarizes it by region.

The region with the highest median rate of growth in education expenditure between 1999 and 2005 was Central Asia (8.1%), followed by sub-Saharan Africa (5.5%), Central and Eastern Europe (5.3%), South and West Asia (5.1%), East Asia and the Pacific (4.7%), and the Arab States (4.7%). The lowest rates were for North America and Western Europe (3.2%), and Latin America and the

> The increases in education expenditure in sub-Saharan African countries are encouraging

Caribbean (2.4%). Again, variations by country within each region are very large.

Overall, the increases in education expenditure in sub-Saharan African countries are encouraging. GNP growth in this region has been lower than for any region except North America and Western Europe, and Latin America and the Caribbean, while the growth in education expenditure has been next to the highest. Also, while the countries of South and West Asia have not excelled in terms of increasing education's share in GNP, their rate of growth in education expenditure has been relatively high. It is encouraging that in the two regions where most of the world's out-of-school children live, education expenditure has been increasing rapidly. Of course, this does not apply to all countries in these regions. In the Gambia, Mauritania and Pakistan, for instance, small increases in economic growth were accompanied by even smaller increases in education spending. The Lao People's Democratic Republic provides a good example of the importance of focusing on rates of expenditure growth: while the share of education expenditure in GNP was only 2.5% in 2005, the average growth rate in education spending was 24% a year from 1999.

The distribution of public expenditure on education by level: differences across income level

How do governments distribute their education budgets across the different levels of education? Information for 2004 or 2005 is available for eighty-five countries. Figure 4.3 shows the average shares of expenditure on primary, secondary and tertiary education in the high, upper middle, lower middle and low-income groups.

Table 4.3: Annual compound rates of growth in total real public expenditure on education and GNP, 1999-2005

	Sub-Saharan Africa	Arab States	Central Asia	East Asia/ Pacific	South/West Asia	Latin America/ Caribbean	N. America/ W. Europe	Centr./East. Europe
Total real public expenditure on education, annual rate of growth (%)								
Median	5.5	4.7	8.1	4.7	5.1	2.4	3.2	5.3
Maximum	19.3	8.7	18.9	23.7	8.1	15.6	9.8	17.7
Minimum	-7.3	0.4	2.1	-3.2	2.5	-8.0	-1.0	-4.0
GNP, annual rate of growth (%)								
Median	4.0	4.5	7.5	4.5	4.5	2.7	2.4	4.7
Number of countries with data								
	24	6	6	11	5	18	18	12

Sources: Annex, Statistical Table 11; UIS database.

4. The rates of growth described in this subsection measure changes in education expenditure and GNP expressed in 2004 constant US$. The use of constant prices removes the effects of inflation between 1999 and 2005.

Some clear patterns emerge across the different income groups. Low-income countries, on average, devote almost half their total education expenditure to primary education. This share falls as income rises, to just 25% in high income countries. The average share for secondary education is lowest in low-income countries (28%) and broadly similar in the other three income groups (between 34% and 40%). There is little variation in the average share for tertiary education for the three low and middle income groups (16% to 20%); the share is somewhat higher (22%) for high income countries. Turning to the distribution of expenditure among the education levels within each group, in high income countries and, to a lesser extent, in upper middle income countries, secondary education receives the highest priority. In lower middle income countries, the average share for secondary is slightly below that for primary, while in low-income countries the primary share is much higher than that of secondary education. As the pressure to expand secondary school enrolment intensifies in today's low income countries, so will the competition with primary education for increases in the education budget.

Once again, among countries in each income group there are significant differences. In the low-income group the share of primary education in total public expenditure on education varies from 17% in the Republic of Moldova to 71% in Burkina Faso. Among lower middle income countries the range is from 9% in Belarus to 65% in the Dominican Republic. The variation is less for high income countries. Tertiary education's share in total expenditure also varies substantially. Among low-income countries, Mauritania devotes 5% of its total expenditure on education to tertiary while in Eritrea the share reaches 48%. The distribution across education levels partly reflects the distribution of pupils, but the heterogeneity also indicates the extent to which countries vary in the way they use private and public sources to finance the different levels of education.

The greater emphasis on primary education in low-income countries has an interesting effect on expenditure as a share of GNP. While sixteen countries in sub-Saharan Africa spend more than 1.8% of GNP on primary education, no country except Iceland in North America or Western Europe spends above this share. This is another indication of the efforts many poor countries are making to move towards the EFA goals.

Figure 4.3: Average shares of public current expenditure on education by level, by income group, 2005

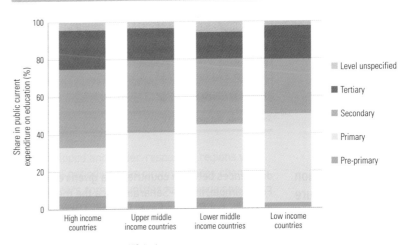

Sources: Annex, Statistical Table 11; UIS database.

Information on changes in the share of total public education expenditure going to primary education between 1999 and 2005 is limited to twenty-six countries, leaving aside North America and Western Europe. The share remained constant in one of these, increased in nine and fell in sixteen. However, the annual rate of growth of real expenditure was negative in only three of the sixteen: Argentina (-1.5%), Saint Lucia (-5.2%) and the Congo (-11.8%). The highest growth rates were in Burundi (15.0%), Bolivia (9.7%), Morocco (8.6%), Bangladesh (7.5%) and Nepal (7.3%). Overall, expenditure on primary education grew in most of the countries in this relatively small group, but at a lower rate than expenditure on other levels. As a result, the share of total education expenditure for primary education decreased in several countries.

Public expenditure per primary school pupil: big differences within regions

Average annual public expenditure on each primary school pupil varies enormously across countries. Since, typically, between 85% and 95% of the expenditure is for teacher salaries, and since much of the variation in these salaries reflects differences in per capita income, little can be learned from a straightforward comparison of expenditure per pupil by country. As a result, the common approach to comparing this 'unit cost' among countries is to present it as a share of each country's per capita GNP. Table 4.4 summarizes the 2005 data for 107 countries. The differences among regions are relatively small. Of greater interest are the

The share of primary education in total public expenditure on education varies from 17% in the Republic of Moldova to 71% in Burkina Faso

Figure 4.4: Relative proportions of public, household and other private expenditure on education institutions

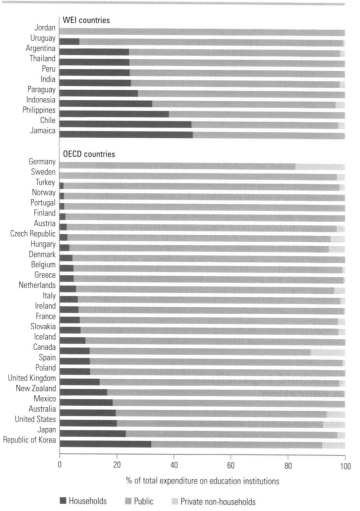

% of total expenditure on education institutions

■ Households ■ Public ■ Private non-households

Note: Data correspond to the financial year ending in 2003, except for Canada, Jordan and Uruguay (2002), Chile, New Zealand and Peru (2004) and Thailand (2005).
Source: UIS (2006a), Table 2.b.i.

7. Expenditure on education institutions includes payments for instruction and provision of education goods by institutions, capital expenditure and rent, provision of ancillary services, and research and development activities (UIS, 2006a).

8. Direct public funding of private schools represents almost 40% of total public expenditure on primary and secondary education in Chile (UIS, 2006a). In addition to receiving vouchers, government-supported private schools are allowed to charge tuition fees.

mainly pay for public and private non-tertiary institutions. In Chile, by contrast, a considerable proportion of expenditure on tertiary education is paid for by households, while public funding covers most of the cost of primary and secondary education through vouchers, even for private institutions (UIS, 2006a).[8] At the other end of the spectrum, Jordan and Uruguay rely heavily on public financing for all levels, with average government participation in total funding that is above even the OECD mean.

In general, governments in developing countries tend to fund a much greater share of primary and secondary education than of tertiary. Exceptions are India, Jamaica and Thailand, where public sources cover over two-thirds of total financing for tertiary. It is worth noting, though, from an EFA perspective, that households still contribute around 20% of total expenditure at these levels.

Overall reliance on public sources to finance education is greater in OECD countries, with their larger tax base, than in WEI countries. In Denmark, Finland, Norway, Portugal, Sweden and Turkey, public funding provides over 95% of total expenditure, and in twenty-two of the twenty-eight OECD countries covered, public funding for all non-tertiary education is at least 90% of the total.

Another way of assessing the extent of household participation in the financing of education is to compare the amounts spent per public school pupil by households and by the government. This comparison is shown for primary schools in eight countries in Figure 4.5. While in most of these cases governments cover the majority of the direct cost of educating a child, households contribute up to one-quarter of the total.

Tuition fees in public primary schools are common, as are other types of private costs

Many countries tolerate the collection of fees and charges in public primary schools despite constitutional provisions guaranteeing free primary education. Indeed, most children enrolled in public primary schools face some type of charges.

Table 4.6 provides examples of the prevalence of several categories of household expenditure for public primary schooling in nine countries. A large percentage of households pay tuition and examination charges in some countries: above 80% in Guatemala and Panama, around 70% in

one-quarter of total expenditure on education institutions.[7] In Chile and Jamaica the household share exceeds 40%, and there is evidence that it has been rising in Argentina, Chile, India, Jamaica and Thailand. The share of private spending is reported to have increased sevenfold in India between 1998 and 2003, to 27%, and by 4.5 times in Thailand between 2000 and 2005, to 24.5%. The combined share of household and other private sources in Jamaica, already 38% in 2000, grew to 47% in three years (UIS, 2006a; UIS/OECD, 2003).

Funding arrangements for the different levels of education vary by country. In Jamaica, households

Nicaragua and 73% of students in Zambia. In addition, other types of costs, such as buying school supplies, are widespread. School uniforms represent 60% of average household education expenditure on public primary schooling in Tajikistan (Tajikistan Goscomstat and World Bank, 2003) and 44% in Timor-Leste (Timor-Leste National Statistics Directorate and World Bank, 2001). The mean annual cost of uniforms in Mozambique was more than three times the cost of fees paid per child enrolled in the lower grades of primary schooling (before fees were abolished), and the cost of textbooks was twice that of fees (World Bank, 2005g). Household surveys conducted in Nigeria, Uganda and Zambia reveal that transport and food are the biggest costs of attending primary school (Nigeria National Population Commission and ORC Macro, 2004; Uganda Bureau of Statistics and ORC Macro, 2001; Zambia Central Statistics Office and ORC Macro, 2003).

Private tutoring is another household expense, found most commonly at secondary level, but increasingly at primary level too, including in Albania, Azerbaijan, Bangladesh, Cambodia, Egypt, Japan, Kenya, Poland, the Republic of Korea and Viet Nam (Bray, 2006; Dang, 2006; Education Support Program, 2006; Kim, 2007). Private tutoring raises serious concerns about equity, as both the amount and the quality tend to be positively associated with household income (Bray, 2006).

Figure 4.5: Mean annual public and household current expenditure per pupil in public primary schools

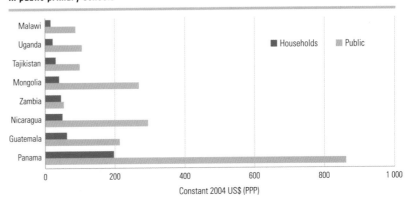

Sources: Annex, Statistical Table 11; Guatemala Government and World Bank (2000); Malawi National Statistics Office and ORC Macro (2003); Mongolia National Statistical Office (2004); Nicaragua National Statistics and Census Institute and World Bank (2001); Panama Government and World Bank (2003); Tajikistan Goscomstat and World Bank (2003); Uganda Bureau of Statistics and ORC Macro (2001); Zambia Central Statistics Office and ORC Macro (2003).

School-related costs may constitute a large share of household spending, especially for the poorest

Household and school surveys indicate that financial contributions to schools, and related expenditures, can represent a large fraction of household expenses (Table 4.7). In Panama, for instance, 7.7% of household total annual expenditure is spent on education while in Nicaragua and Tajikistan the share is 5.5%. Before primary school fees were abolished in

Table 4.6: Household expenditure on public primary schooling, by type of expenditure

	Tuition, exam fees[a]	Uniforms	Textbooks[b]	School supplies	Tutoring	PTA, other	Transport, meals, lodging[c]
% of households							
Guatemala (2000)	82.2	45.7	37.2	95.0	…	…	3.4
Nicaragua (2001)	69.3	78.9	52.1	90.9	…	…	51.1
Panama (2003)	88.1	89.2	60.4	96.2	…	74.0	25.4
Tajikistan (2003)	23.7	92.9	89.4	96.5	0.2	73.5	15.8
Timor-Leste (2001)	33.7	64.4	3.8	95.8	0.9	5.7	5.5
% of students							
Malawi (2001)	3.1	69.0	82.5	…	3.8	56.5	34.2
Nigeria (2003)	47.7	89.1	99.3	…	33.5	71.8	64.2
Uganda (2000)	19.0	78.5	97.5	…	5.0	56.7	20.0
Zambia (2001)	73.0	81.0	98.0	…	12.0	67.0	24.0

Notes: The table shows only the main categories of education expenditure, for illustrative purposes, and should not be considered exhaustive.
a) Exam fees are the larger of the two categories for Malawi, Nigeria, Uganda and Zambia.
b) The column shows exam fees for Nigeria and Uganda.
c) Meals only for Malawi, Nigeria, Uganda and Zambia.
(…) indicates that data are not available.
Sources: Guatemala Government and World Bank (2000); Malawi National Statistics Office and ORC Macro (2003); Nicaragua National Statistics and Census Institute and World Bank (2001); Nigeria National Population Commission and ORC Macro (2004); Panama Government and World Bank (2003); Tajikistan Goscomstat and World Bank (2003); Timor-Leste National Statistics Directorate and World Bank (2001); Uganda Bureau of Statistics and ORC Macro (2001); Zambia Central Statistics Office and ORC Macro (2003).

The financial effort required to continue beyond primary education is often much larger than for the primary cycle

Uganda and Zambia about one-third of households' discretionary spending was for education goods and services, the same share as in Bangladesh (Boyle et al., 2002). For poor households the burden can be particularly heavy. For instance, the household expenditure per primary school pupil in Tajikistan as a share of per capita household expenditure is twice as high for the poorest fifth of households as for the richest fifth.

The financial effort required to continue beyond primary education is often much larger than for the primary cycle. Indian households surveyed in 2001 in selected districts were spending twice the amount per child in upper primary government schools as in primary schools (Jha and Jhingran, 2005). Fees paid by households in the Democratic Republic of Congo for each child enrolled in public primary schools represent up to 14% of average per capita income (varying by region), increasing up to 42% in public secondary schools (World Bank, 2005c). And in Mozambique, before the elimination of school fees, average total household expenditure per child enrolled in the upper grades of basic education was almost three times that for the lower grades, while expenditure on lower secondary could be nine times that for primary education (World Bank, 2005g). Again, the burden is heaviest for the poorest households. The share of a secondary student's expenses in per capita household

expenditure was roughly twice as high in the poorest households as in the richest in Guatemala, Nicaragua, Tajikistan and Timor-Leste (Table 4.7)

School costs are a barrier to school access

While some households can cover the expenses that are associated with school attendance, many poor households cannot. In addition, for such households the perceived benefits of schooling may not be sufficient to justify the expenditure. 'Lack of money', 'economic problems', 'need to work' and 'family can't afford school expenses' are the main reasons cited in several studies of why children do not attend school; see, for example, Bangladesh, Nepal, Uganda and Zambia (Boyle et al., 2002); Yemen (Guarcello et al., 2006b); and Albania, Kazakhstan, Latvia, Mongolia, Slovakia and Tajikistan (Education Support Program, 2007). In Uganda before the elimination of school fees, 71% of children surveyed cited cost of attendance as the main reason for having dropped out of primary school (Deininger, 2003). Fees are cited as a major obstacle to school enrolment in China and Indonesia (Bentaouet-Kattan, 2006).

Amplifying the effects of direct and indirect costs of schooling, many households tend to invest less in children for whom the value of schooling is perceived to be less important, or when cultural

Table 4.7: Education expenditure as a share of household expenditure, selected countries

	Education expenditure as a share of total annual household expenditure								
	All education levels			Primary			Lower secondary		
	Total	Poorest 20%	Richest 20%	Total	Poorest 20%	Richest 20%	Total	Poorest 20%	Richest 20%
Guatemala (2000)	5.1	2.2	8.2	2.5	1.8	3.9	7.6	5.8	7.6
Nicaragua (2001)	5.5	3.8	7.5	2.6	2.7	3.1	4.5	5.6	4.2
Panama (2003)	7.7	5.5	9.3	4.0	2.8	6.6	5.2	4.4	6.9
Tajikistan (2003)	5.5	6.3	6.0	2.8	3.6	2.3	3.4	4.3	3.2
Timor-Leste (2001)	1.5	1.5	1.5	1.0	1.1	0.6	1.5	2.5	1.2

	Education expenditure per pupil as a share of annual household expenditure per capita								
	All education levels			Primary			Lower secondary		
	Total	Poorest 20%	Richest 20%	Total	Poorest 20%	Richest 20%	Total	Poorest 20%	Richest 20%
Guatemala (2000)	13.5	8.4	18.5	9.3	7.3	14.0	31.1	47.7	26.5
Nicaragua (2001)	13.7	11.3	17.5	9.0	9.1	11.1	18.7	34.7	15.0
Panama (2003)	18.9	15.6	20.4	15.2	11.5	24.1	22.9	28.2	25.5
Tajikistan (2003)	16.4	21.0	15.2	13.9	19.4	10.4	15.0	20.5	12.5
Timor-Leste (2001)	4.2	4.6	3.7	3.3	3.8	2.1	7.7	14.2	5.4

Sources: Guatemala Government and World Bank (2000); Nicaragua National Statistics and Census Institute and World Bank (2001); Panama Government and World Bank (2003); Tajikistan Goscomstat and World Bank (2003); Timor-Leste National Statistics Directorate and World Bank (2001).

norms support differing treatments of children in the same household. When there are preferences it is usually girls who are at a disadvantage (Boyle et al., 2002; Drèze and Kingdon, 2001; Emerson and Souza, 2002) and older children (Ejrnæs and Pörtner, 2004; Souza and Emerson, 2002). Direct and indirect costs of schooling in a context of poverty, as well as social and cultural norms, require many households to make tough decisions on which, if any, of their children to send to school and for how long.

Reducing the burden on households but adding to the strain on public resources

Since Dakar, two initiatives for increasing the participation of disadvantaged children have been expanded: abolition of school fees matched by compensatory payments to schools, and cash transfers to targeted households whose children enrol. Both aim to expand access, but can have significant implications for public expenditure.

Since 2000 fourteen countries have eliminated tuition fees for primary school.[9] Governments have had to deal with two financial consequences of this policy: the replacement of revenue lost by the schools and the increased costs resulting from higher enrolment. One of the most common strategies followed by governments to compensate schools has been the allocation of capitation grants directly to them. Kenya, after abolishing school fees in 2003, based the level of its capitation grants on an assessment of the minimum requirements for school functioning and the availability of learning materials. Yearly allocations per student, amounting to the equivalent of US$14, were transferred to accounts managed directly by the schools. In 2003/04 the grants represented 12.5% of the government's total recurrent budget for primary education. Much of the funding was provided through the World Bank and the UK Department for International Development (World Bank and Government of Kenya, 2005). Initial problems in countries adopting capitation grants include allocations below the amounts previously collected from fees, or below agreed amounts, and grants received too late in the school year or not by all schools (Bentaouet-Kattan, 2006).

The second impact of school fee abolition on government finances stems from the intended increase in enrolment and the resulting need to fund additional teachers, classrooms and learning materials. In Malawi, even though additional resources were made available for these purposes, the surge in enrolment resulted in a decline in per-pupil spending (School Fee Abolition Initiative, forthcoming). By contrast, before fees were abolished in the United Republic of Tanzania, the expected consequences for teacher recruitment, deployment and training, as well as for classrooms and learning materials, were fully assessed and integrated into the donor-supported Primary Education Development Plan. Donors have also funded at least part of the additional expenditure resulting from fee abolition in Ghana, Kenya, Mozambique and Uganda. In addition, savings from debt relief through the Enhanced Heavily Indebted Poor Countries (HIPC) Initiative played a supportive role in Ghana and Uganda (Bentaouet-Kattan, 2006; School Fee Abolition Initiative, forthcoming).

As noted earlier, even when school fees are eliminated, families face costs for textbooks, supplies, uniforms and transport. In addition, schooling deprives households of children's paid or unpaid work in or out of the home. In an effort to offset such costs, some governments transfer money directly to households in return for their children's enrolment. These programmes are mainly directed at relatively marginalized populations and are often part of larger poverty reduction efforts referred to generally as conditional cash transfer (CCT) programmes. Evidence presented in Chapter 3 showed that CCTs can be successful, but there is a question of their financial sustainability, particularly when scaled up, and of their appropriateness in countries with weak institutions.

Bolsa Família, in Brazil, is the largest CCT programme in the developing world. It covers about 46 million people, including more than 16 million children receiving the education transfer, and accounts for 0.4% of GDP (*The Economist*, 2007). In 2005 the Mexican poverty alleviation programme Progresa-Oportunidades covered 5 million families. The transfer linked to school attendance was 47% of the total outlay (Levy, 2006). Colombia's expenditure in Familias en Acción for 2001–2004 amounted on average to 0.3% of GDP (Reimers et al., 2006).

The financial importance of the CCT programmes for education in these middle income countries can be seen more clearly when the cost is compared to total government education

Some governments transfer money directly to households in return for their children's enrolment

9. The countries are listed on page 112, note 10, in Chapter 3.

Conditional cash transfer programmes have been effective in increasing access

expenditure. For instance, the cost of the education component of Progresa-Oportunidades in 2006 was equal to 4.6% of Mexico's federal education budget, or 17% of the non-salary portion. In Colombia the cost was equivalent to an even larger proportion of public education expenditure, reaching 10.3% in 2002. Such high shares, however, are not universal. The cost of the education component of the Programa de Asignación Familiar (Family Allowance Programme) in Honduras over 2000–2003 was equal to 1.4% of public education spending.

What would the expansion of such programmes cost? Morley and Coady (2003) estimated the cost of expanding CCT programmes at a minimal level to the very poor across eighteen Latin American countries to be US$1.0 billion a year, while extending them to all children of primary school age below the poverty line would raise the cost to US$2.4 billion a year. Pearson and Alviar (2007) estimate that turning Kenya's programme for orphaned and vulnerable children into a full-scale national programme would cost US$44 million a year. Extending the Malawi Social Cash Transfer Scheme, which is in a pilot stage, to the 250,000 very poor eligible households (10% of all households) would raise the annual costs over a hundredfold, to US$42 million from US$0.4 million now, and represent 2% of the country's 2005 GDP.

CCT programmes have been effective in increasing access to schooling in several middle income Latin American countries. For this approach to be extended to poorer countries would require careful targeting and very stringent administrative procedures, including through the local community, to assure transparency and minimize fraud.

Contribution of external aid to EFA since Dakar

Changing levels, distribution and sources

The third major source of financing EFA comes from official development assistance (ODA). The Dakar meeting in 2000 was essentially initiated by donors and international organizations as a way of reinvigorating the movement towards universal primary education and the other aspects of basic education that had developed at Jomtien in 1990 but had slowed during the following decade.

Among other objectives, the Dakar meeting was intended to galvanize donors into giving increased financial support.

Trends in total aid: positive and a small shift towards low-income countries

The overall trend in total ODA has been positive since 1999, the year preceding the adoption of the Dakar Framework for Action. Net disbursements[10] increased by 9% a year between 1999 and 2005, reaching US$106 billion in 2005.[11] However, preliminary data indicate that in 2006, total ODA was down by 5.1% (OECD-DAC, 2007b). Total ODA commitments have also increased rapidly since 1999, averaging 8% a year to reach US$123 billion in 2005. The distribution of ODA across income groups has changed to the advantage of the 68 countries categorised by the OECD-DAC Secretariat as low-income countries, which received 46% of total ODA commitments in 2005, compared with 42% in 1999. While sub-Saharan Africa is still the main recipient of total ODA, the past few years have been characterized by a significant shift towards countries in the Arab States region.

Out of the US$123 billion in total aid commitments in 2005, US$70 billion, or 58%, was allocated to sectors. While sectoral aid was still the largest category of total ODA in 2005, donors have significantly changed the way they distribute aid since 2001, with debt relief increasing at a faster rate than direct support to sectors. Between 1999 and 2005, the share of debt relief in total ODA grew from 5% to 22%. In 2005, debt relief accounted for US$18.5 billion of the total increase in ODA of US$21 billion since 2004.

Trends in aid to education: after the rise, a fall

The growing importance of budget support, either for a specific sector or for general use, has added to the complexity of calculating the total amount of aid to the education sector and to basic education. Box 4.2 describes the procedures used.

In the years immediately following the adoption of the Dakar Framework, total ODA commitments for education rose rapidly, reaching US$10.7 billion in 2004, compared with US$6.5 billion in 2000 – an increase of 65% in real terms. However, in 2005, allocations fell by over US$2 billion (Figure 4.7), taking commitments to education back to their 2002 level. This fall occured even though total ODA continued to increase. Turning to basic education, total aid increased at an even higher rate between

10. Net disbursements represent the actual international transfer of financial resources and, by extension, the resources available in recipient countries. Commitments, by contrast, represent a firm obligation undertaken by an official donor to provide specified assistance to a recipient country. Commitments are recorded in the full amount of expected transfer for the year in which they are made, irrespective of the time required for the completion of disbursements. For more details, see the introduction to the aid tables in the annex.

11. All data in this section are in 2005 constant US$.

Box 4.2: Assessing total contributions to the education sector

The Secretariat of the OECD Development Assistance Committee (DAC) distinguishes three main levels of education: basic, secondary and post-secondary. Aid to basic education is divided into early childhood education, primary education and basic life skills for youths and adults, including literacy.

In addition to direct allocations to education, the sector receives aid as part of the growing levels of general budget support. Total aid for basic education also includes some of the education sector aid that is not specified as going to a particular education level. Since the 2006 Report it has been assumed that one-fifth of general budget support is allocated to education, and that half of this goes to basic education. It has also been assumed that half of 'level unspecified' aid for education is allocated for basic education. Hence:

- Total aid to education = direct aid to education + 20% of general budget support.

- Total aid to basic education = direct aid to basic education + 10% of general budget support + 50% of 'level unspecified' aid to education.

Figure 4.6 shows the components of total aid to education and to basic education for all recipient countries and for those defined by the OECD-DAC Secretariat as low income countries.

Figure 4.6: Components of total aid commitments to education and to basic education, 1999–2000 and 2004–2005

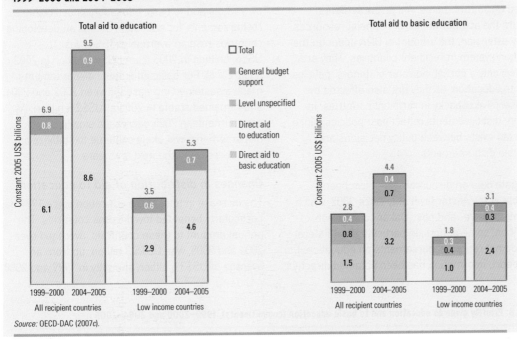

Source: OECD-DAC (2007c).

> The recent decrease in aid for education is at odds with donors' statements of support

2000 and 2004, by 90%, from US$2.7 billion to US$5.1 billion. In 2005, however, basic education commitments also suffered a significant fall, to US$3.7 billion. The increases to 2004 and the severe decrease in 2005 are the two main features of the trend in aid for education since Dakar. The decrease is at odds with the positive statements made by donors over the past two years about their intentions to increase support to education significantly.

Table 4.8 shows that education's share of total ODA decreased slightly, from 9.6% to 8.5%, between 1999–2000 and 2004–2005,[12] due to the increasing share of debt relief in total ODA. The share of education in the part of aid that goes to sectors, however, remained stable at almost 13% across all developing countries, while the share of basic education increased from 5.1% to 5.8%. For the fifty least developed countries, the education sector overall gained slightly and basic education even

12. Two-year averages are used to dampen the effect of the volatility of aid commitments at the sector level.

Figure 4.7: Total aid commitments to education and to basic education, 1999–2005

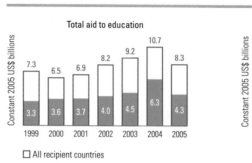

Source: OECD-DAC (2007c).

Donors' policies on aid to education are also affected by the absorptive capacity in recipient countries

more so. In these countries, education's share in total sector aid is around 16% and almost three-fifths is for basic education.

The discussion of aid for education so far has focused on commitments. Aid disbursements measure the actual transfer of financial resources and, by extension, the amount of ODA spent on the education system in recipient countries. They are, however, only a partial indicator of donors' policies on aid to education, as they are also affected by the absorptive capacity in recipient countries. In addition, disbursements reflect past policies, since a time lag exists between policy decisions and actual aid disbursements.

Aggregate data on disbursements have been available at the sector level only since 2002, which prevents any pre- and post-Dakar comparison. In addition, some donors, in particular multilateral ones, do not report disbursements on education. For this Report, information has been obtained directly

from the World Bank's International Development Association (IDA) and the European Commission. When combining these figures on disbursements with those from bilateral donors, it is encouraging to see a rapid increase in disbursements to education as a whole and to basic education since 2002. Disbursements for education across all developing countries rose an average of 15% a year to US$6.7 billion in 2005 from US$4.4 billion in 2002 (Figure 4.8). For basic education, disbursements made a sustained increase between 2002 and 2004, and remained stable in 2005 at US$2.8 billion. As commitments in 2005 decreased significantly, disbursements will likely continue to stabilize or even decrease in the next few years.

Changes in distribution of aid to education

The increase in total aid to education since 1999 has particularly benefited low-income countries. The annual amount to these countries, averaged over 2004 and 2005, was US$5.3 billion, up from an average of US$3.5 billion annually in 1999 and 2000,

Table 4.8: Priority given to education and to basic education (commitments), 1999–2000 and 2004–2005

	Share of education in total ODA (%)			Share of education in sector-allocable ODA (%)			Basic education as a share of total aid to education (%)		
	1999–2000 annual average	2004–2005 annual average	Change 1999–2005 (percentage points)	1999–2000 annual average	2004–2005 annual average	Change 1999–2005 (percentage points)	1999–2000 annual average	2004–2005 annual average	Change 1999–2005 (percentage points)
All low income countries	11.2	10.1	-1.1	14.2	14.9	0.7	51.1	59.1	8.0
Of which least developed countries	10.8	11.2	0.4	14.0	16.0	2.0	51.7	58.6	6.9
All developing countries	9.6	8.5	-1.1	12.8	12.7	-0.1	39.9	45.9	6.0

Source: OECD-DAC (2007c).

Figure 4.8: Aid to education and to basic education (disbursements), 2002–2005

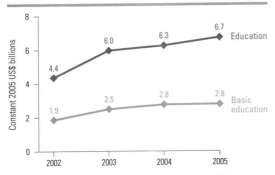

Notes: Italy and Finland did not provide data on disbursements for 2005. Multilateral donors do not report disbursements to the DAC Secretariat, but data on aid to education disbursed by the European Commission and IDA were made available. The IDA data, unlike those of the European Commission, include an allocation from budget support.
Sources: OECD-DAC (2007c); unofficial data provided by the European Commission and IDA.

Figure 4.9: Distribution of total aid to education and to basic education by income group (commitments), 1999–2005

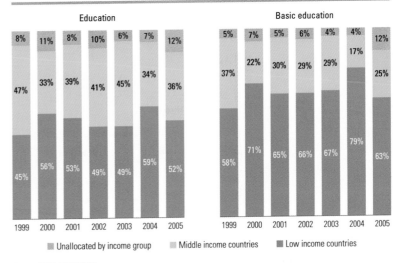

Source: OECD-DAC (2007c).

Figure 4.10: Distribution of total aid to education and to basic education by region (commitments), 1999–2005

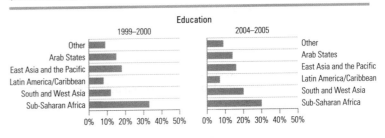

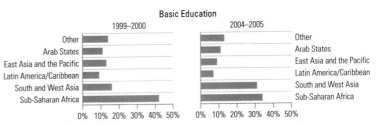

Note: 'Other' regions are North America and Western Europe, Central Asia and Central and Eastern Europe.
Source: OECD-DAC (2007c).

and the share of total aid to education in these countries increased from 50% to 56% (Figure 4.9). The change in distribution was even more favourable to the least developed countries, which received US$3.5 billion in 2005, up from US$2.0 billion in 1999 (see annex, Aid Table 4). The trend in aid towards low income countries was particularly pronounced in the allocation to basic education. In 2004 and 2005, these countries received US$3.1 billion annually, up from US$1.8 billion annually in 1999 and 2000, and equal to almost three-quarters of the total (Figure 4.7).

In addition to the increased focus on low-income countries, the regional distribution of aid to education has changed since 2000. While sub-Saharan African countries continue to receive the largest amount for education in general, and for basic education, the shares for South and West Asia have increased significantly – from 12% to 20% for education and from 16% to 31% for basic education (Figure 4.10).

Thirty-five countries have been described by the OECD as 'fragile states'. In 2005, these countries received 12% of all aid for education and 14% of aid for basic education – shares similar to those in 1999. The aggregate population of these countries is 10% of the total population of all developing countries.

The discussion above suggests that more aid to basic education has been distributed to the poorest countries as a group. However, this does not necessarily mean that it was targeted to the neediest among them. Assessing whether the

distribution of aid to education is efficient in this regard is far from straightforward, but two simple comparisons would suggest it is not. Figure 4.11 shows there is no strong relationship between amounts of aid to basic education per school-age child and education needs as measured by the share of out-of-school children in the school-age population. Some countries, among them Bolivia, Mongolia and Nicaragua, received relatively high

8
0
0
2

Education for All Global Monitoring Report

Figure 4.11: Aid commitments to basic education and out-of-school children, 2005

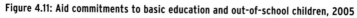

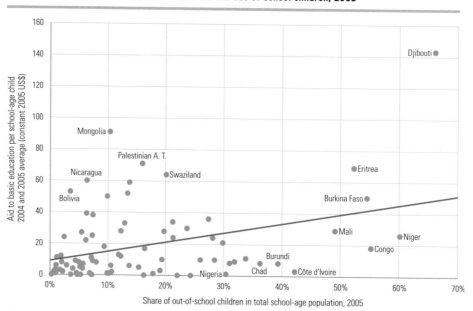

Sources: Annex, Statistical Table 5; annex, Aid Table 4.

Aid to basic
education is not
always targeted
to the neediest
countries

Figure 4.12: Aid commitments to basic education and income per capita, 2005

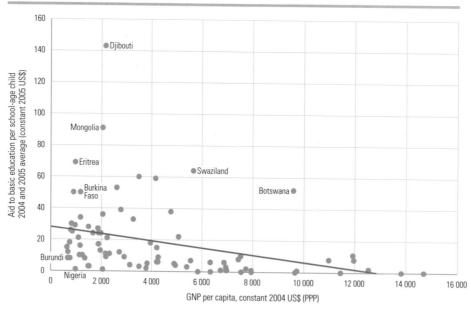

Sources: Annex, Statistical Table 1; annex, Aid Table 4.

amounts of aid for basic education per child while
the share of out-of-school children was relatively
low. Conversely, some countries with a high
proportion of out-of-school children received
relatively low amounts of aid to basic education per
child; most are in sub-Saharan Africa, including

Burundi, Chad, the Congo, Côte d'Ivoire, Mali and
the Niger. Figure 4.12 complements this information
by linking aid for basic education to income per
capita. Again, some countries with a relatively high
level of income per capita receive relatively large
amounts of aid for basic education (Botswana,

Swaziland) while some poor countries receive relatively low amounts (Burundi, Nigeria). These simple comparisons suggest that the allocation of aid to basic education is not strongly related to the share of out-of-school children in the school-age population or to the level of income per capita.

A recent study of the behaviour of some individual donors concluded that while IDA and the United Kingdom tend to allocate their aid to basic education based on education needs and poverty, others – including France, Germany, the United States and the European Commission – are more likely to be influenced by strategic and political factors (Caillaud, 2007). Allocations are also likely to be influenced by considerations of a recipient country's absorptive capacity.

Turning to the individual recipient countries, in 2004 and 2005 four South and West Asian countries (Afghanistan, Bangladesh, India and Pakistan) received 17% of all aid to education while five sub-Saharan African countries (Burkina Faso, Mozambique, Senegal, Uganda and the United Republic of Tanzania) received 10% of the total (see annex, Aid Table 4, for more details). The predominance of South and West Asian countries in aid to basic education is even more striking (Table 4.9). All four of the largest recipients are in this region, with India alone receiving 11% of all aid to basic education in 2004–2005, a similar share to that received in 1999–2000. Afghanistan, Bangladesh and Pakistan increased their share of total aid to basic education substantially. In sub-Saharan Africa, however, several countries

> The allocation of aid to basic education is not strongly related to the share of out-of-school children

Table 4.9: Changes in aid to basic education in the main recipient countries (commitments), 1999–2005

	Total aid to basic education (constant 2005 US$ millions)			Share in total aid to basic education (%)			Basic education as a share of total aid to education (%)		
	1999–2000 annual average	2004–2005 annual average	Annual change 1999–2005 (%)	1999–2000 annual average	2004–2005 annual average	Change 1999–2005 (percentage points)	1999–2000 annual average	2004–2005 annual average	Change 1999–2005 (percentage points)
India	284	482	8	10.3	11.0	0.7	63.7	86.4	22.7
Bangladesh	79	398	26	2.9	9.1	6.2	61.3	64.5	3.2
Pakistan	9	169	52	0.3	3.9	3.6	34.7	61.4	26.7
Afghanistan	2	162	93	0.1	3.7	3.6	22.0	76.0	54.0
Mozambique	81	129	7	2.9	2.9	0.0	53.9	64.9	11.0
Iraq	1	126	114	0.0	2.9	2.9	7.6	80.1	72.5
Zambia	90	116	4	3.3	2.7	-0.6	67.0	77.6	10.6
Burkina Faso	35	111	18	1.3	2.5	1.2	52.7	70.8	18.1
Yemen	48	110	12	1.7	2.5	0.8	75.3	93.2	17.9
Nepal	47	100	12	1.7	2.3	0.6	83.0	91.9	8.9
Viet Nam	35	95	15	1.3	2.2	0.9	18.7	36.7	18.0
Uganda	89	95	1	3.2	2.2	-1.0	60.4	58.4	-2.0
U. R. Tanzania	41	87	11	1.5	2.0	0.5	51.0	37.1	-13.9
Indonesia	121	78	-6	4.4	1.8	-2.6	40.3	39.6	-0.7
Bolivia	29	72	14	1.1	1.6	0.5	73.3	68.6	-4.7
Ghana	86	70	-3	3.1	1.6	-1.5	72.2	47.4	-24.8
Nicaragua	60	51	-2	2.2	1.2	-1.0	81.2	60.5	-20.7
Senegal	75	44	-7	2.7	1.0	-1.7	53.9	22.9	-31.0
Philippines	63	44	-5	2.3	1.0	-1.3	35.7	63.8	28.1
Malawi	94	36	-13	3.4	0.8	-2.6	69.0	53.6	-15.4
Papua New Guinea	48	31	-6	1.7	0.7	-1.0	52.5	74.6	22.1
Morocco	62	21	-14	2.2	0.5	-1.8	24.4	7.8	-16.6
Turkey	81	19	-19	2.9	0.4	-2.5	37.8	14.2	-23.6
Low income countries	1 770	3 147	9	64.2	72.0	7.8	51.1	59.1	8.0
Of which least developed countries	*1 054*	*2 067*	*10*	*38.2*	*47.3*	*9.1*	*52.0*	*59.0*	*7.0*
All developing countries	2 756	4 373	7	100.0	100.0	–	40.0	46.0	6.0

Note: Countries listed were among the 15 main recipients in 1999–2000 and/or in 2004–2005.

Source: OECD-DAC (2007*a*).

France was
the largest
contributor to
the education
sector during
2004–2005,
committing
US$1.5 billion
a year

have seen their share decrease by about two percentage points. This is the case for Ghana, Malawi and Senegal. A positive trend in relation to achievement of the EFA goals is that the share of basic education in total aid to education in each of the top ten recipient countries has increased, averaging 76% in 2004–2005. In these countries, the increase in aid to basic education has resulted more from a higher priority given to this level than from the global increase of aid to education.

The data presented so far do not show the major year-on-year variations that occur in aid commitments. For instance, very large commitments for basic education were made to several of the ten largest recipients in 2004, including to some of the world's most populous countries. Bangladesh, for one, received commitments of US$700 million for basic education in 2004 and India received US$950 million (see annex, Aid Table 4). This pattern was not repeated in 2005.

Changing donor strategies for education

Donor strategies for education in general, and for basic education, vary. As was highlighted in Table 4.8, for all donors combined, the priority given to education remained mostly stable over 1999–2005. However, individual donors behaved differently, as Table 4.10 shows. Among multilateral donors, IDA and the European Commission have been the largest contributors to education. IDA's commitments amounted to an average of US$1.4 billion annually in 2004 and 2005, which was 72% above the level in 1999. The reason was more an increased level of total IDA aid than a higher priority for education. European Commission contributions averaged US$0.8 billion annually in 2004 and 2005. This was equal to only 8% of all sector grants, a lower share than almost all other multilateral and bilateral donors, and represented a decrease in the share compared to 1999.

The importance accorded to education within total aid varies among bilateral donors. France was the largest contributor to the education sector during 2004–2005, committing US$1.5 billion a year, which was 40% of its total aid to sectors. The next largest donors were Japan, at US$1 billion, and the United States, with US$670 million. These levels of aid represent a relatively small share of their total aid. Japan allocates only 12% of its sector aid to education (up from just 5% in 1999), and the United States less than 4%.

The distribution of aid across levels of education is also crucial. Aid to basic education is divided into early childhood education, primary education and basic life skills for youths and adults, including literacy. As previous Reports have pointed out, within basic education, pre-primary education receives low levels of aid. In 2004, nineteen of the twenty-two donors responding to a request for information reported allocating to pre-primary less than 10% of the amount they made available for the primary level, and a majority allocated less than 2% (UNESCO, 2006a). As a share of total aid to education, the majority allocated less than 0.5%. Data on aid to literacy programmes are also difficult to collect, but it is clear that most donors have given them very little priority (UNESCO, 2005a).

On average, multilateral donors allocated 53% of their total aid to education to the basic level in 2004–2005, compared with 43% for the bilateral donors. However, the bilateral share did represent an eight percentage point increase compared with 1999–2000. These averages hide wide variations. IDA allocated 61% of its education aid to basic education and the European Commission 46% in 2004–2005. The Fast Track Initiative Catalytic Fund allocated all of its aid to basic education. Donors had committed a total of US$570 million to the fund by 2006 and pledged to commit a further US$360 million by the end of 2007. As of the end of June 2007, US$130 million had been disbursed to eighteen countries.

Bilateral donors differ widely in how they view basic education. Canada, Denmark, Finland, Ireland, the Netherlands, New Zealand, Norway, the United Kingdom and the United States clearly make basic education a top priority and allocate more than half of their education aid to it. Other donors allocate less than one-third of total education aid to basic education. This group includes France, Germany and Japan – countries that subsidize large numbers of foreign students in their universities and therefore allocate a large part of their education aid to the post-secondary level (Figure 4.13).

Finally, among some of the largest contributors to education, there was a dramatic reduction in aid to basic education in 2005. The United Kingdom and IDA, in particular, decreased commitments for aid to basic education by 70% and 80%, respectively (see annex, Aid Table 2). The donors that reduced

Table 4.10: Aid commitments to education and to basic education by donor, 2004–2005 average and change since 1999

	Total aid to education		Total aid to education as % of total sector ODA		Total aid to basic education		Basic education as % of total aid to education	
	2004–2005 annual average (constant 2005 US$ millions)	Annual change 1999–2005 (%)	2004–2005 annual average	Change since 1999–2000 (percentage points)	2004–2005 annual average (constant 2005 US$ millions)	Annual change 1999–2005 (%)	2004–2005 annual average	Change since 1999–2000 (percentage points)
DAC Bilateral donors								
Australia	127	-10.0	12.1	-9.1	57	-1.7	44.5	18.3
Austria	89	-5.2	39.6	5.3	4	-4.7	4.5	0.1
Belgium	155	9.6	19.6	-0.3	35	15.0	22.7	5.7
Canada	223	15.3	14.4	2.3	173	23.9	77.6	27.1
Denmark	137	12.0	9.8	2.6	82	11.7	59.9	-1.0
Finland	66	16.6	15.9	0.8	40	23.0	61.3	16.9
France	1 537	-0.1	39.6	-1.9	279	-3.9	18.1	-4.7
Germany	760	-1.5	16.9	-5.7	146	3.4	19.2	4.8
Greece	30	...	21.4	...	4	...	13.8	...
Ireland	61	23.4	18.5	-8.4	38	27.7	62.6	11.6
Italy	86	8.3	19.6	7.9	39	17.2	45.8	17.3
Japan	1 047	12.5	11.9	6.7	281	4.7	26.8	-14.5
Luxembourg	26	...	23.4	...	12	...	46.1	...
Netherlands	570	13.1	20.4	2.4	375	13.4	65.8	1.0
New Zealand	58	...	35.0	...	31	...	53.6	...
Norway	186	5.2	14.0	0.4	117	5.5	62.7	1.1
Portugal	60	8.9	29.4	13.0	8	-1.6	13.9	-11.6
Spain	155	-6.0	18.7	-2.5	59	-2.4	37.9	7.7
Sweden	129	11.1	8.7	0.4	66	6.8	51.0	-13.8
Switzerland	35	-4.2	4.8	-2.6	16	-3.4	45.0	2.2
United Kingdom	646	6.8	15.8	5.0	540	9.1	83.6	10.0
United States	672	11.2	3.8	-1.1	563	19.4	83.8	29.0
TOTAL DAC bilateral	**6 812**	**4.7**	**12.9**	**-0.7**	**2 944**	**8.4**	**43.2**	**8.3**
Multilateral donors								
AfDF	141	11.3	9.9	-1.0	55	3.1	39.4	-22.8
AsDF	308	16.3	21.6	11.1	78	44.3	25.3	18.4
EC	762	1.2	9.3	-1.5	351	-4.1	46.0	-17.6
FTI	44	...	100.0	...	44	...	100.0	...
IDA	1 355	9.5	15.1	2.5	822	12.5	60.7	9.1
IDB Special Fund	35	36.6	8.6	7.0	15	32.5	41.6	-8.4
UNICEF	64	15.0	14.4	-1.9	63	14.8	98.8	-1.2
TOTAL multilaterals	**2 709**	**7.7**	**12.1**	**1.1**	**1 428**	**7.1**	**52.7**	**-1.8**
TOTAL all donors	**9 520**	**5.5**	**12.7**	**-0.1**	**4 373**	**8.0**	**45.9**	**6.0**

Notes: AfDF = African Development Fund; AsDF = Asian Development Fund; EC = European Commission; FTI = Fast Track Initiative Catalytic Fund; IDA = International Development Association; IDB = Inter-American Development Bank (Special Fund).
Source: OECD-DAC (2007c).

> Bangladesh and India received three-quarters of the United Kingdom's aid to basic education and half of IDA's in 2004

aid the most in 2005 are also those that concentrated their distribution in 2004. For instance, Bangladesh and India received three-quarters of the United Kingdom's aid to basic education and half of IDA's in 2004. Other donors spread their aid more widely. France, the United States and the European Commission each have a core group of countries to which they allocate aid to basic education almost every year, spreading the rest over several countries. The behaviour of a few donors in

delivering large amounts of aid to a few countries in 2004 partly explains the large drop in 2005.

To round off this discussion of aid to education, two additional sources of external financial flows are discussed. The first is non-concessional loans made for education by the World Bank. Though not treated as aid, these loans are substantial, roughly equal to the amount of IDA credits for education, and they have been particularly important sources

teachers' salaries. However, problems of raising the quality of education and of high dropout and repetition rates remain, suggesting a need for continuous focus on process as well as results. Other achievements noted by staff were greater coherence of donor support to education through, for instance, agreements governing pooled funding, increased ownership of programmes by ministries of education and improved audits of fund flow and implementation capacity. A Netherlands government evaluation of SWAps also pointed to gains in the expansion of education systems that have occurred alongside increases in sector-wide programmes, but expressed qualifications: 'When measuring impact, however, it is the quality of the interventions that is important, i.e. institutional development, capacity building and regulation, factors which cannot be improved through funding alone.' (Netherlands Ministry of Foreign Affairs, 2006).

What progress within the Framework for Action?

This final section broadly summarizes progress since 2000 in implementing the financial strategies advocated in the Dakar Framework for Action.

(i) Governments must allocate sufficient resources to all components of basic education. This will require increasing the share of national income and budgets allocated to education, and, within that, to basic education. EFA will need resources from other parts of society.

The picture overall is mixed but with some important areas of progress. Out of 105 countries outside North America and Western Europe, twenty-six spent 6% or more of GNP on education in 2005 while twenty-four spent 3% or less. Sub-Saharan Africa, and Latin America and the Caribbean had the highest median shares, 5.0% each. South and West Asia lagged with 3.6%. Sub-Saharan Africa and the Arab States are the developing-country regions allocating the highest shares of total public expenditure to education.

Between 1999 and 2005, the share of education expenditure in GNP increased in fifty countries outside North America and Western Europe and decreased in thirty-four. Across a sample of twenty-four sub-Saharan African countries the share increased in eighteen.

Almost half of education expenditure in the least developed countries is for primary education, compared with around 34% in middle income countries and 25% in high income countries. Information on the change in public expenditure on primary education between 1999 and 2005 is limited to nineteen developing countries and is very mixed.

Of the components of basic education covered in the EFA goals, primary education receives almost all the available public funding. Adult literacy and early childhood programmes are, largely, neglected.

While many countries do not now charge tuition fees for public primary schools, the overall financing of basic education continues to rely heavily on households, which often pay up to one-quarter of direct costs, plus bearing the indirect costs. These fall proportionately more on the poor and are an obstacle to further expanding access to schooling.

(ii) Resources need to be used with much greater efficiency and integrity. Corruption is a major drain. Civil society needs to be enabled to be part of transparent and accountable budgeting systems.

Many individual governments have installed expenditure tracking systems and other procedures to reduce opportunities for directing financial resources away from schools and other institutions, and to ensure that other resources (such as teachers) are deployed in situations where they will be most efficient and effective. It is not, however, possible to report overall trends in efficiency and integrity of resource use since 2000. There is evidence of governments and civil society organizations working together, often in innovative ways, to improve the transparency and accountability of budgeted expenditure but, again, progress is difficult to measure universally. Surveys reporting public perceptions of high levels of corruption in the education sector are indicative of continuing problems in this area. These issues, and more generally the governance of education systems, will be dealt with in more detail in the 2009 Report.

(iii) International development agencies need to allocate a larger part of their resources to support primary and other forms of basic education. Challenges are greatest in sub-

The picture overall is mixed but with some important areas of progress

Saharan Africa, South Asia, and among least developed countries and those emerging from conflict. Higher priority should be given to debt relief linked to poverty reduction programmes.

Aid to education increased between 2000 and 2004 by 65% before falling back somewhat in 2005; aid to basic education increased by 90% before a similar fall-back. However, the Framework focuses on education's *share* of aid. Within aid allocated directly to sectors, education's share remained constant at 13% across all developing countries, and increased from 14% to 16% for the least developed countries. The share of education aid going to basic education increased from 40% to 46% across all developing countries, and from 52% to 59% for the least developed countries.

With respect to geographical allocation, sub-Saharan Africa continues to receive the largest share of aid to education and to basic education (30% and 34% respectively in 2004–2005). South and West Asia received a large increase in the share for basic education, from 16% in 1999–2000 to 31% in 2004–2005. The share of aid to basic education targeted to low-income countries increased from around 65% to 71% over the same period.

Debt relief for the thirty countries, potentially forty, that have become or are becoming qualified by preparing a poverty reduction strategy (among other requirements) has been broadened from bilateral debt to incude also debt owed to the IMF, IDA and the African and Inter-American Development Banks.

(iv) Funding agencies should coordinate their efforts around sector-wide reforms and sector policies, and make longer term and more predictable commitments.

Since 2000 the movement to improve the effectiveness of all aid through greater harmonization between donors and alignment between donors and governments has accelerated, and the 2005 Paris Declaration concretized it. One consequence has been the growing support of multiple donors for sector-wide programmes with sectoral budget support, such as for education or basic education. Across least developed countries, the share of total aid for basic education in the form of sectoral support increased from 13% to 35% and is now much higher than the share for individual projects.

The Fast Track Initiative, proposed at Dakar and established in 2002, has taken up seriously the proposal that aid should be coordinated around sector-wide reforms and policies. Plan endorsement by in-country donor staff encourages alignment and harmonization across all sources of aid in addition to that from the FTI's own Catalytic Fund. By end August 2007, education sector plans of thirty-two countries had been endorsed.

As yet, there has been little concrete success in designing longer-term, more predictable aid in general, or for basic education. Potential improvements may exist through the European Commission's consideration of long-term MDG contracts, the United Kingdom's call for ten-year education plans in sub-Saharan African countries and the future development of the FTI Catalytic Fund.

The final part of the Framework dealing with the financing of EFA states that:

(v) No countries seriously committed to Education for All will be thwarted in their achievement of this goal by lack of resources. Keys to releasing resources will be evidence of political commitment and effective consultation with civil society in developing, implementing and monitoring EFA plans.

Global trends in domestic expenditure on education, and changes in both the level and distribution of external aid for basic education, are positive. In each case, though, there are two provisos. The trends are not always very strong, and significant variations exist among countries and, in the case of aid, among donors. In the area of domestic education expenditure, while the data on basic education are too limited to draw any conclusions, measures of total education expenditure have on the whole been increasing, particularly for most countries in sub-Saharan Africa and for low-income countries overall.

The second 'key' to releasing increased aid for EFA is effective consultation with civil society. Although no comprehensive review yet exists, certain patterns are beginning to emerge (Mundy, 2006). There have been dramatic shifts in both government and donor policies towards civil society organizations. Education sector policies in almost every country now call for some form of partnership between government and these organizations.

Global trends in domestic expenditure on education, and changes in both the level and distribution of external aid for basic education, are positive

In addition, in contrast to the 1990s, the notion of partnership refers less to the expansion of a service delivery role and more to the importance of civil society participation in the formulation of national education sector policies. Donor organizations increasingly refer to the role civil society can play in holding governments accountable.

On the other hand, the new call for partnership is not always straightforward. Governments clearly seek ways to manage and sometimes limit civil society participation in policy deliberations and to use organizations to legitimize rather than to influence the content of sector plans. Tensions and challenges arise particularly out of the dual advocacy/service-delivery role now expected from civil society organizations.

The report card for donors is mixed. Overall, aid for basic education has been increasing and has been marginally better targeted to low-income counties. The doubling of aid by some donors is impressive. Yet, in spite of the increase, aid to basic education represents only 6% of sector-allocable aid and one-third of the DAC donors have actually reduced aid to basic education since 1999–2000.

The message from Dakar was that if a government demonstrated commitment to basic education, donors would respond. A country-by-country assessment of the extent to which this has occurred is limited, as the contribution of aid to total expenditure on education in 1999 and 2005 is known for only twenty-one least developed countries. For this group the share of aid in total expenditure in both years was 11%, showing that increases in aid closely kept pace with increases in domestic expenditure. However, it is clear that the situation regarding domestic expenditure on education and the amounts of aid received vary greatly by country.

Some countries and donors have approached the compact made at Dakar within the framework of the FTI. As of August 2007, thirty-two countries had developed education sector plans that local donor representatives had endorsed. Not all low-income countries have adopted this route for attracting more aid; for instance, large countries such as Bangladesh, India and Pakistan have not. However, many countries in sub-Saharan Africa and Central America have joined the FTI. While no causal relationships can be drawn between being an endorsed FTI country and having increased the

Some countries and donors have approached the compact made at Dakar within the framework of the FTI

Figure 4.18: Changes in the share of GNP devoted to education in twenty-one FTI-endorsed countries, 1999–2005

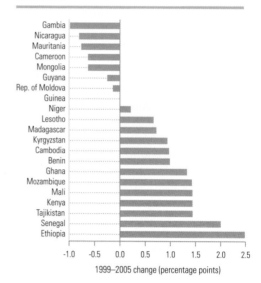

1999–2005 change (percentage points)

Source: Annex, Statistical Table 11.

priority for education sector domestic funding, it is interesting to see what happened to funding for education in these FTI countries between 1999 and 2005. Data are available for twenty-one of the thirty-two countries (Figure 4.18).

The share of education in GNP increased in fourteen of these countries and fell in seven. Of the former group, the increase was equal to 1% of GNP or more in nine countries. Of the seven countries where the share fell, it did so by more than 1% in only one case. However, it is somewhat surprising that the share would fall in any of these countries.

Figure 4.19 compares annual growth rates in domestic expenditure on education in thirty-two low-income countries with annual growth rates in aid to education between 1999 and 2005, to assess whether increased domestic spending has moved broadly in tandem with higher aid growth rates. While there is no necessarily causal effect and there are several outliers, this appears to be the case in most countries, particularly those with endorsed FTI plans, providing some tentative support to the notion that external financial resources, while still very limited, are beginning to move in the direction anticipated at Dakar.

Since 2000 there has been a global acceleration in financial commitments made to EFA by both

Figure 4.19: Annual growth rates of domestic expenditure and aid for education in thirty-two low income countries, 1999–2005

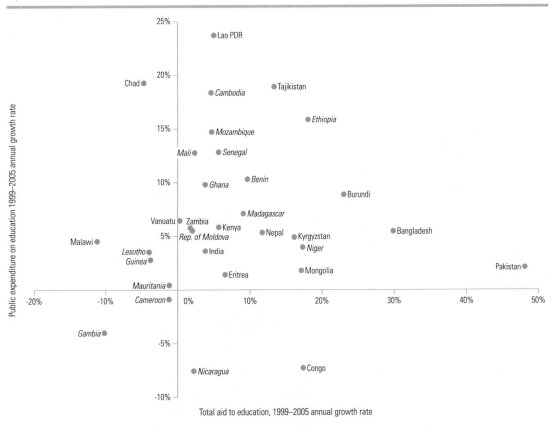

Note: Countries in italics had their plan endorsed by August 2007.
Sources: OECD-DAC (2007c); UIS database.

Many developing countries governments and civil society are becoming increasingly proficient in preparing plans and strategies for achieving education development

national governments and donors, but with a great deal of variation. In some countries, governments and donors have adopted new and more effective ways of working together, though in others the necessary conditions do not yet exist. Nonetheless, many poor countries have shown that it is possible to increase the priority given to education in the allocation of resources and donors have begun to respond in general, if not unanimously. The first third of the period between the Dakar meeting in 2000 and the EFA deadline of 2015, however, may have been the easy part. Many developing country governments, with civil society, are becoming increasingly proficient in preparing plans and strategies for achieving education development, and more capable of implementing them. Yet there are still other countries where governments are not fully functional and the capacity to generate domestic resources and implement policy is low. Governments and donors in both groups face challenges. For the first set of countries the key issue is to respond fully

to remaining financial needs. For the second, it is to ensure that populations are not left further behind. Chapter 5 looks in more detail at these challenges. ■

© Abbie Trayler-Smith/PANOS

Break time in a school
located in a slum area,
Yemen.

Chapter 5

The way forward

As we move beyond the midway point from Dakar to 2015, key questions arise. How can we maintain the recent positive primary school enrolment and completion trends? What about the slower progress towards achieving the goals for early childhood, youth and adults, and quality education for all? What about literacy, the most neglected of the EFA goals? And the missed gender parity goal? With just eight years remaining to achieve EFA, will we make it? What can be done to accelerate the movement, to increase aid and target it better? How can governments and actors at every level sustain the effort to fulfil the Dakar commitments, especially for the most poor, disadvantaged and vulnerable? This concluding chapter addresses these and other questions. It proposes an agenda for the way forward and suggests some of the roles various stakeholders should play if we are to meet our obligations to present and future generations.

CHAPTER 5

Introduction _____ 178

Trends and prospects
for 2015 _____ 178

Financing the EFA goals
to 2015 _____ 185

Towards an agenda _____ 191

Introduction

Chapters 2 to 4 discuss developments relevant to Education for All that have taken place since 2000. This concluding chapter examines education indicators and financing issues to determine if EFA is on track to being realized by 2015. It then proposes the elements of a policy agenda for governments, for civil society organizations and for international agencies and donors to accelerate these trends, focusing on neglected goals and on countries that are lagging behind global progress towards EFA, and taking account of the changes in the global environment since Dakar that are discussed in Chapter 1.

Trends and prospects for 2015

The period from 1999 to 2005, as chapter 2 showed, was one of sharp growth in enrolment at both primary and secondary level, with some reduction in the gender gap and in socio-economic disparities. Especially impressive was performance in countries of sub-Saharan Africa, and South and West Asia, the two regions whose situation was noted at the Dakar World Education Forum as being of particular concern. Yet, a majority of countries missed the gender parity goal fixed for 2005, the poor quality of education is becoming a major issue worldwide and the goals pertaining to young children and to youth and adults have been relatively neglected, particularly as regards adult literacy. This section examines the implications of these trends for the achievement of EFA goals in the near future.

For the three goals that have an explicit quantitative target – goal 2 (universalization of primary education), goal 4 (reduction by half in the level of adult illiteracy) and goal 5 (elimination of gender disparities in primary and secondary education) – relevant education indicators were projected to 2015 and 2025,[1] extrapolating trends observed in each country between the early 1990s and 2005.[2] It is important to note that these are extrapolations of past trends, rather than forecasts: they make no attempt to simulate the impact of education policy alternatives on education indicators and thus may not reflect the impact of recently implemented education policies. What they show is

1. Goal 4 was projected only to 2015.

2. The years vary for each indicator according to data availability.

whether the continuation of ongoing trends is consistent with the achievement by a given country of a given goal by 2015 or 2025.[3] As such, these projections are a useful monitoring tool and provide an early warning of the consequences of maintaining current rates of progress.

Goal 1: early childhood care and education

ECCE is receiving increasing attention, but much remains to be done. Even without projections, it is evident on present trends that participation rates will remain relatively low to 2015:

■ in all developing country regions except Latin America and the Caribbean, and especially in sub-Saharan Africa and the Arab States;

■ among children under 3, for whom there is much less provision than for those aged 3 and over despite increases in pre-primary schooling;

■ among the poor and disadvantaged, who stand to benefit relatively the most from ECCE programmes.

Goal 2: universal primary education

The likelihood that countries will achieve universal primary education (UPE) by 2015 or 2025 was assessed using the total primary net enrolment ratio (TNER), which takes into account children of primary school age enrolled in either primary or secondary school but, of course, does not reflect learning but only enrolment. Table 5.1 shows the most recent situation and prospects for the achievement of this goal by 2015 for the 149 countries having sufficient data. Of these, 63 (42%) had already achieved universal primary enrolment by 2005, with a TNER of 97% and above. These include a large number of OECD countries where compulsory and usually free public education has been long established and rigorously enforced, but also a number of developing countries as diverse as Bangladesh, Cambodia, Egypt, Indonesia and Peru.

Trend projections were run for the remaining 86 countries.[4] Table 5.1 summarizes the results by classifying countries according to how far they were from universal primary enrolment in 2005 (TNER below or above 80% in 2005) and whether they are projected to achieve it by 2015 (projected 2015 TNER below or above 97%):

■ Twenty-eight countries (Quadrant I) have a high chance of achieving universal primary enrolment by 2015, as their 2005 ratio is above 80% and their projected 2015 ratio is above 97%. They include mostly middle income countries of Central and Eastern Europe, and Latin America, but also several low-income sub-Saharan African countries, some Arab States and India.

■ Seventeen countries (Quadrant II) are making rapid progress but have a low chance of achieving the goal by 2015, mainly because they still have a very low TNER (below 80%). They include thirteen sub-Saharan African countries, Pakistan, Saudi Arabia and Yemen. Some of these countries, including Ghana, Kenya, Mozambique and Yemen, have abolished tuition fees in recent years. As the vertical arrow in Table 5.1 indicates, six of the seventeen countries are projected to reach universal primary enrolment by 2025.

■ Thirty-three countries (Quadrant III) are at risk of not achieving universal primary enrolment by 2015 because, while their enrolment ratio was relatively high in 2005, it has progressed very slowly or declined, particularly since 1999. They include several former Soviet republics; some countries severely affected by the HIV/AIDS pandemic (South Africa, Swaziland, Zimbabwe) and by conflict (Iraq, Palestinian Autonomous Territories); and others that have relatively well-developed school systems but have seen their TNER declining over the past few years (Cape Verde, the Dominican Republic, Jordan, Turkey). However, seven of the thirty-three countries are likely to achieve universal primary enrolment by 2025 (horizontal arrow in Table 5.1).

■ Eight countries (Quadrant IV) located in sub-Saharan Africa and the Arab States are at serious risk of not achieving universal primary enrolment by 2015, as they combine low TNERs in 2005 with slow positive or even negative change, particularly between 1999 and 2005. These countries stand in contrast with those of the same regions that have made quick progress since Dakar (Quadrant II), and they deserve specific attention.

To summarize, of the 149 countries for which sufficient information is available:

Forty-one countries are at risk of not achieving universal primary enrolment by 2015

3. The projections of universal primary enrolment and gender parity were run for the *EFA Global Monitoring Report* by the Education Policy and Data Center. See the annex for a discussion of the projection methodology and Education Policy and Data Center (2007a) for the complete results. The projections of adult literacy were run by the UNESCO Institute for Statistics.

4. Countries were included in the projections if at least five observations were available between 1999 and 2005.

CHAPTER 5

Table 5.1: Country prospects for achieving universal primary enrolment by 2015

Goal achieved by 2005
(total NER ≥97%)
63 countries

Algeria, Argentina, Aruba, Australia, Austria, Bahrain, Bangladesh, Barbados, Belgium, Belize, Bermuda, British Virgin Islands, Brunei Darussalam, Cambodia, Canada, Cuba, Cyprus, Denmark, Ecuador, Egypt, Estonia, Fiji, Finland, France, Greece, Iceland, Indonesia, Ireland, Israel, Italy, Japan, Kazakhstan, Kiribati, Luxembourg, Mexico, Montserrat, Netherlands, New Zealand, Norway, Panama, Peru, Poland, Portugal, Qatar, Republic of Korea, Saint Lucia, Samoa, Sao Tome and Principe, Serbia and Montenegro, Seychelles, Slovenia, Spain, Sri Lanka, Sweden, Switzerland, Syrian Arab Republic, Tajikistan, TFYR Macedonia, Timor-Leste, Tonga, Tunisia, United Kingdom, United Republic of Tanzania

		QUADRANT I High chance of achieving the goal by 2015 *(moving towards the goal, with steady progress)* 28 countries	**QUADRANT III** At risk of not achieving the goal by 2015 *(moving away from the goal or progress too slow)* 33 countries	
Distance from 100% total primary NER in 2005	Close or in intermediate position (total NER: 80–96%)	Belarus, Benin, Bolivia, Brazil, Bulgaria, Colombia, El Salvador, Georgia, Guatemala, Hungary, India, Islamic Republic of Iran, Kuwait, Kyrgyzstan, Lebanon, Lesotho, Madagascar, Malawi, Morocco, Myanmar, Nicaragua, Philippines, Romania, Russian Federation, Ukraine, Vanuatu, Venezuela, Zambia *Moving from Quadrant II in 2015 to Quadrant I in 2025* Ethiopia, Gambia, Guinea, Kenya, Mozambique, Yemen	Albania, Anguilla, Armenia, Azerbaijan, Bahamas, Botswana, Cape Verde, Cayman Islands, Croatia, Dominica, Dominican Republic, Equatorial Guinea, Grenada, Iraq, Jamaica, Jordan, Lao People's Democratic Republic, Lithuania, Macao (China), Malaysia, Malta, Mauritius, Mongolia, Palestinian Autonomous Territories, Republic of Moldova, Saint Vincent and the Grenadines, South Africa, Swaziland, Togo, Trinidad and Tobago, Turkey, Viet Nam, Zimbabwe *Moving from Quadrant III in 2015 to Quadrant I in 2025* Botswana, Croatia, Iraq, Lao People's Democratic Republic, Macao (China), Mauritius, Palestinian Autonomous Territories	61
	Far (total NER: <80%)	**QUADRANT II** Low chance of achieving the goal by 2015 *(moving towards the goal, with rapid progress)* 17 countries Burkina Faso, Burundi, Chad, Eritrea, Ethiopia, Gambia, Ghana, Guinea, Kenya, Mali, Mauritania, Mozambique, Niger, Pakistan, Saudi Arabia, Senegal, Yemen	**QUADRANT IV** Serious risk of not achieving the goal by 2015 *(moving away from the goal or progress too slow)* 8 countries Côte d'Ivoire, Djibouti, Maldives, Namibia, Nigeria, Oman, Rwanda, United Arab Emirates	25
Total		45	41	86
		On track	Off track	
		Total primary NER projected for 2015, extrapolating 1991–2005 trends		

Not included in the prospects analysis
(insufficient or no data)
54 countries

Afghanistan, Andorra, Angola, Antigua and Barbuda, Bhutan, Bosnia and Herzegovina, Cameroon, Central African Republic, Chile, China, Comoros, Congo, Cook Islands, Costa Rica, Czech Republic, Democratic People's Republic of Korea, Democratic Republic of the Congo, Gabon, Germany, Guinea-Bissau, Guyana, Haiti, Honduras, Latvia, Liberia, Libyan Arab Jamahiriya, Marshall Islands, Micronesia, Monaco, Nauru, Nepal, Netherlands Antilles, Niue, Palau, Papua New Guinea, Paraguay, Saint Kitts and Nevis, San Marino, Sierra Leone, Singapore, Slovakia, Solomon Islands, Somalia, Sudan, Suriname, Thailand, Tokelau, Turkmenistan, Turks and Caicos Islands, Tuvalu, Uganda, United States, Uruguay, Uzbekistan

- Sixty-three countries had achieved universal primary enrolment by 2005 and twenty-eight will achieve it by 2015.

- Fifty-eight (eleven of them fragile states[5]) will not achieve universal primary enrolment by 2015 if past trends continue.

- Forty-five (seven of them fragile[6]) of the fifty-eight countries will not even achieve universal primary enrolment by 2025 unless recent positive trends accelerate or negative ones are reversed.

Finally, owing to lack of data, projections could not be run for fifty-four countries. Among these are thirteen low-income countries, twelve of them fragile states, that have been identified as having low levels of education development.[7] The challenge of achieving universal primary enrolment is likely to be particularly difficult in these countries.

Goal 3: learning needs of young people and adults

Most countries have yet to seriously address the challenging tasks that EFA goal 3 entails: meeting the diverse learning needs of young people and adults through organized programmes of education, training and the building of basic skills, life skills and livelihood skills. This is of particular concern as the youth and adult populations in sub-Saharan Africa and in South and West Asia will continue to grow in coming decades (UN Population Division, 2007). These are also the two regions with the lowest adult literacy rates and highest numbers of out-of-school children.

Given the understandable pressure to extend the cycle of basic education in schools and to expand secondary education, there is a clear risk of the disparities between formal and non-formal schooling becoming further accentuated in coming years. Most countries, and especially those in sub-Saharan Africa, and South and West Asia, will need to pay much stronger attention to the inclusion of youth and adults in education through literacy, equivalency, life-skills and livelihood-skills programmes, which are frequently provided outside formal education systems.

Goal 4: adult literacy

The likelihood of achieving the adult literacy target by 2015 was assessed for the 127 countries with sufficient data available.[8] Of these, 26 had reached levels close to 'universal literacy' (literacy rates above 97%) by the period 1995–2004, most of them in Central and Eastern Europe or Central Asia. By contrast, no country in sub-Saharan Africa, South and West Asia or the Arab States belongs to this category.

Projections were run for the 101 remaining countries. As adult literacy rates are increasing everywhere, a distinction was made between countries progressing rapidly (fast performers) or slowly (slow performers). A target rate representing the achievement of goal 4 by 2015 was computed, corresponding to a halving of the adult illiteracy rates observed over 1995–2004. The resulting targeted literacy rates were compared with projections of adult literacy rates in 2015. Countries likely to achieve the goal have projected rates equal to or above the targeted rates. Table 5.2 summarizes the results:

- Thirty countries (Quadrant I) stand a high chance of achieving the adult literacy target by 2015 as their literacy rate is already relatively high and continues to increase steadily. They include countries from most EFA regions, but particularly Latin America and the Caribbean, and East Asia and the Pacific. Some developed countries, such as Greece, Malta and Portugal, are also included.

- Eighteen countries (Quadrant II) are moving rapidly towards the target but have a low chance of achieving it, mainly due to low starting positions (adult literacy rates well below 80%). All are in the Arab States, South and West Asia or sub-Saharan Africa.

- Twenty-eight countries (Quadrant III), many of them in East Asia, Latin America and the Caribbean, the Arab States and sub-Saharan Africa, are at risk of not achieving the target. Despite relatively high current literacy rates, they are moving too slowly towards the goal.

- Twenty-five countries (Quadrant IV) are at serious risk of not reaching the adult literacy target by 2015 due to a combination of low and slowly increasing rates. More than two-thirds of these

Most countries have yet to seriously address EFA goal 3

5. Burundi, Chad, Côte d'Ivoire, Djibouti, Eritrea, the Gambia, Guinea, the Lao People's Democratic Republic, the Niger, Nigeria and Zimbabwe.

6. Burundi, Chad, Côte d'Ivoire, Djibouti, Eritrea, the Niger and Nigeria.

7. Afghanistan,* the Central African Republic,* the Comoros,* the Democratic Republic of the Congo,* Guinea-Bissau,* Haiti,* Liberia,* Nepal, Papua New Guinea,* Sierra Leone,* Solomon Islands,* Somalia* and Sudan.* Asterisks indicate fragile states.

8. Internationally comparable figures on adult literacy are based on conventional measures of literacy, such as self-reporting of the ability to read or write, rather than results of actual tests of literacy skills (see Chapter 2, in particular Box 2.6). Australia, Canada, Japan, New Zealand, the United States and many European countries are excluded from the analysis for lack of conventional literacy data, but most of them are close to 'universal literacy'.

Table 5.3: Country prospects for achieving gender parity in primary and secondary education by 2005, 2015 and 2025

(based on past trends, 1991-2005. All countries with GPIs between 0.97 and 1.03 are considered to have achieved parity)

		Gender parity in secondary education				
		Achieved or likely to be achieved in 2005	Likely to be achieved by 2015	Likely to be achieved by 2025	At risk of not being achieved in 2015 or 2025	
Gender parity in primary education	Achieved or likely to be achieved in 2005	Albania, Anguilla, Armenia, Bahamas, Bangladesh, Barbados, Belarus, Belize, Bolivia, Chile, China, Cook Islands, Croatia, Cyprus, Czech Republic, Denmark, Dominica, Ecuador, Estonia, France, Georgia, Germany, Greece, Guyana, Hungary, Iceland, Indonesia, Israel, Italy, Jamaica, Japan, Jordan, Kazakhstan, Kyrgyzstan, Latvia, Lithuania, Malta, Mauritius, Myanmar, Netherlands, Norway, Paraguay, Peru, Poland, Qatar, Republic of Korea, Republic of Moldova, Romania, Russian Federation, Seychelles, Singapore, Slovakia, Slovenia, Sri Lanka, Sweden, TFYR Macedonia, United Kingdom, United States, Uzbekistan **59**	Bahrain, Botswana, Brunei Darussalam, Fiji, Finland, Maldives, Mongolia, Palestinian Autonomous Territories, Saudi Arabia, Spain, Switzerland, Uganda, United Arab Emirates **13**	Nicaragua, Ghana, Lesotho, Venezuela **4**	Argentina, Australia, Austria, Azerbaijan, Belgium, Bermuda, Bulgaria, Colombia, Ireland, Kiribati, Kuwait, Lebanon, Luxembourg, Malawi, Malaysia, Mauritania, Mexico, Namibia, Nauru, Netherlands Antilles, New Zealand, Oman, Panama, Philippines, Rwanda, Samoa, Senegal, Suriname, Trinidad and Tobago, Tunisia, Ukraine, Uruguay, Vanuatu, Zimbabwe **34**	110
	Likely to be achieved in 2015	El Salvador **1**	Saint Lucia, Solomon Islands, Syrian Arab Republic, Turkey **4**	Costa Rica, Guinea **2**	Cambodia, Egypt, India, Nepal, Tajikistan, Thailand, Togo **7**	14
	Likely to be achieved in 2025		Guatemala, Gambia **2**	Burkina Faso **1**	Benin, Democratic Republic of the Congo, Mali, Pakistan, Zambia **5**	8
	At risk of not being achieved in 2015 or 2025	Aruba, Cuba, Saint Kitts and Nevis, Viet Nam **4**	Cayman Islands, Kenya, Macao (China), South Africa **4**	Brazil, Marshall Islands, Portugal, Saint Vincent and the Grenadines **4**	Algeria, British Virgin Islands, Burundi, Cameroon, Cape Verde, Chad, Comoros, Congo, Côte d'Ivoire, Djibouti, Dominican Republic, Eritrea, Ethiopia, Islamic Republic of Iran, Iraq, Lao People's Democratic Republic, Morocco, Mozambique, Niger, Nigeria, Niue, Palau, Papua New Guinea, Sudan, Swaziland, Tokelau, Tonga, Yemen **28**	40
Number of countries		64	23	11	74	172

Not included in the prospects analysis

(insufficient or no data)

31 countries

Afghanistan, Andorra, Angola, Antigua and Barbuda, Bhutan, Bosnia and Herzegovina, Canada, Central African Republic, Democratic People's Republic of Korea, Equatorial Guinea, Gabon, Grenada, Guinea-Bissau, Haiti, Honduras, Liberia, Libyan Arab Jamahiriya, Madagascar, Micronesia, Monaco, Montserrat, San Marino, Sao Tome and Principe, Serbia and Montenegro, Sierra Leone, Somalia, Timor-Leste, Turkmenistan, Turks and Caicos, Tuvalu, United Republic of Tanzania

Notes:

1. In countries whose names are shown in blue, gender disparities at the expense of boys are observed in primary or secondary education.

2. Four countries, among them Cuba, that have achieved gender parity in secondary are at risk of not doing so at primary level, which may seem inconsistent. In the case of Cuba, data available show that while parity was achieved in primary education until 1996, the GPI of GER declined from 0.97 to 0.95 in 2005. This trend in Cuba, along with the situation in the other three countries, requires further investigation.

3. In Australia, enrolment data for upper secondary education include adult education (students over age 25), particularly in pre-vocational/vocational programmes, in which males are in the majority. This explains the high GER (217%) and relatively low GPI (0.90) at this level.

Table 5.4: Primary school teacher needs between 2004 and 2015 by region (millions)

Region	Number of primary school teachers 2004	Additional teachers needed to reach UPE (among 76 countries)	Teachers to fill vacancies due to attrition (6.5%)	Total number of teachers needed
Sub-Saharan Africa	2.4	1.6	2.1	3.8
Arab States	1.8	0.5	1.4	1.8
Central Asia, and Central and Eastern Europe	1.6	0.1	0.8	0.9
East Asia and the Pacific	9.4	0.1	3.9	4.0
South and West Asia	4.4	0.4	3.2	3.6
Latin America and the Caribbean	2.9	0.0	1.6	1.6
North America and Western Europe	3.6	0.1	2.4	2.5
World	26.1	2.7	15.4	18.1

Note: Numbers to fill vacancies are based on a yearly attrition rate set at 6.5% (medium scenario).
Source: UIS (2006c).

2004 and 2015, both to reach UPE and to offset attrition (UIS, 2006c). Overall, the world will need more than 18 million new primary education teachers,[9] compared with its 2004 stock of 26 million (Table 5.4). Sub-Saharan Africa faces the greatest challenge; the teacher stock will have to increase by two-thirds, from 2.4 to 4 million, if UPE is to be reached. Allowing for attrition, which is compounded by the HIV/AIDS pandemic, sub-Saharan Africa will need 3.8 million new primary education teachers by 2015. Challenges are also significant in East Asia and the Pacific, and in South and West Asia, mainly because of attrition. Countries in the Arab States region also need to make a substantial effort by employing 1.8 million new teachers by 2015. In addition, while increasing the number of teachers is important, providing them with adequate training is also key to universal access to and participation in quality education, and the resources needed to hire, retain and train teachers will be significant.

Financing the EFA goals to 2015

Chapter 4 showed that, following a general increase over the first five years after the Jomtien Conference of 1990, the share of national revenue devoted to education fell back in many countries in the late 1990s. In the five years after the World Education Forum in Dakar in 2000, the share increased again in the majority of countries. Maintaining this upward trend through the next decade will need conscious decisions by governments and donors. This section reviews prospects for increasing financial resources from both sources.

Government expenditures

The main funders of programmes aimed at completing the EFA goals are national governments. The degree to which EFA will be financed depends on (a) the growth of total government expenditure, which, in turn, is strongly influenced by the rate of economic growth; and (b) the share of government expenditure allocated to provide for basic learning needs.

There are both opportunities and challenges. Overall, economic growth rates in low-income countries since Dakar have been higher than in the previous decade and are still accelerating. Table 5.5 shows that per capita income across all low-income countries increased by 4% a year between 2001 and 2005, compared with 1.8% between 1991 and 1995 and 2.2% between 1996 and 2000. The estimate for 2006 and 2007 is even higher, averaging 5.6%. Even if government expenditure only rises in line with the growth of per capita

The main funders of EFA programmes are national governments

9. The projections were made on the basis of a pupil/teacher ratio of 40:1 for countries that were above this benchmark. For countries with pupil/teacher ratios below this, the 2004 value was used as the basis.

Table 5.5: Real per capita GDP[a] growth in low-income countries, selected periods (% per year)

	1991–1995	1996–2000	2001–2005	2006*	2007*
World	0.8	2.0	1.5	2.9	2.2
Low-income countries	1.8	2.2	4.0	5.9	5.4
Sub-Saharan Africa	-1.6	1.0	2.4	4.0	4.4
Middle East and North Africa	0.9	2.1	0.4	0.8	-0.6
Europe and Central Asia	-11.3	3.8	6.8	11.5	9.3
East Asia and Pacific	5.4	0.4	3.8	4.7	5.1
South Asia	3.0	3.5	4.7	6.8	5.9
Latin America and Caribbean	-0.3	1.4	0.7	1.8	1.8

a. GDP in constant 2000 US$.
* Projections.
Source: World Bank (2007d).

Table 5.7: Allocation of aid for basic education to the low-income countries most at risk of not achieving UPE, 1999–2000 and 2004–2005

	Year of FTI endorsement	Total aid to basic education				Total aid to basic education per primary school-age child	
		Constant 2005 US$ millions		Country's share in total aid to basic education (%)		Constant 2005 US$ millions	
		1999–2000 annual average	2004–2005 annual average	1999–2000 annual average	2004–2005 annual average	1999–2000 annual average	2004–2005 annual average
Afghanistan	no	2	162	0.1	3.7	0	33
Burkina Faso	2002	35	111	1.3	2.5	17	51
Burundi	pending 2007	2	9	0.1	0.2	2	8
C. A. R.	no	7	6	0.2	0.1	11	9
Chad	pending 2007	11	13	0.4	0.3	8	8
Comoros	no	3	6	0.1	0.1	27	47
Côte d'Ivoire	no	45	8	1.6	0.2	17	3
D. R. Congo	expected 2008	6	48	0.2	1.1	1	5
Eritrea	expected 2008	27	41	1.0	0.9	53	69
Ethiopia	2004	25	70	0.9	1.6	2	8
Gambia	2003	9	5	0.3	0.1	48	25
Ghana	2004	86	70	3.1	1.6	28	21
Guinea	2002	19	17	0.7	0.4	15	11
Guinea-Bissau	pending 2007	5	4	0.2	0.1	26	16
Haiti	pending 2007	18	15	0.6	0.4	14	12
Kenya	2005	39	52	1.4	1.2	6	10
Liberia	2007	1	3	0.0	0.1	3	6
Mali	2006	44	67	1.6	1.5	24	30
Mauritania	2002	11	17	0.4	0.4	25	36
Mozambique	2003	81	129	3.0	2.9	32	34
Nepal	no	47	100	1.7	2.3	15	28
Niger	2002	13	60	0.5	1.4	7	27
Nigeria	expected 2008	40	32	1.5	0.7	2	2
Pakistan	expected 2008	9	169	0.3	3.9	0	9
Papua New Guinea	no	48	31	1.7	0.7	67	33
Rwanda	2006	36	14	1.3	0.3	29	10
Senegal	2006	75	44	2.7	1.0	48	24
Sierra Leone	2007	11	14	0.4	0.3	16	17
Solomon Islands	pending 2007	4	14	0.1	0.3	48	184
Somalia	no	2	8	0.1	0.2	1	6
Sudan	no	5	21	0.2	0.5	1	4
Yemen	2003	48	110	1.8	2.5	15	31
Total		**810**	**1 457**	**29.4**	**33.3**	...	...
All developing countries		**2 756**	**4 373**	**100.0**	**100.0**	**5**	**8**

Note: FTI status as of August 2007.
Sources: Annex, Aid Table 4; FTI Secretariat, 2007.

For many countries, aid to primary education will continue to be needed to sustain and improve the quality of primary schooling

This analysis based on UPE prospects can be usefully complemented by an analysis of progress towards the literacy goal. Among the countries with low primary enrolment that are moving rapidly towards UPE, nine of the fourteen countries for which data are sufficient are doing so in parallel with rapid progress towards the literacy goal. They are low-income countries, mostly in sub-Saharan Africa: Burkina Faso, Chad, Ghana, Guinea, Mali, Mozambique, the Niger, Senegal and Yemen. This

further strengthens the case for continuous support to them. On the other hand, some countries that have achieved UPE (Algeria, Cambodia, Egypt, Tunisia and the United Republic of Tanzania) or will achieve it by 2015 (Guatemala, Madagascar, Nicaragua and Zambia) are at serious risk of not achieving the literacy goal by 2015. For many of these countries, aid to primary education will continue to be needed to sustain and improve the quality of primary schooling. In others, aid for literacy programmes for youth and adults might help accelerate progress towards the literacy goal. These examples underline the need in some countries for better balance in distribution of aid to basic education, among primary education, early childhood programmes and learning programmes for youth and adults.

Chapter 4 showed that the aid policies of bilateral donors reflected diverse motives, not only poverty alleviation in the poorest countries, and that, this being so, the distribution of aid overall or by sector is unlikely to correspond directly to need. Multilateral agencies, such as the World Bank and regional development banks, are more likely to allocate concessional aid according to need. In respect of efforts to increase the likelihood that aid resources allocated outside of bilateral programmes are directed to specified priorities, the growing amount allocated by the FTI through the Catalytic Fund is encouraging but remains limited.

Constraints on increasing aid for basic education

In addition to the overall focus on a relatively small number of countries by the bilateral donors and the limited amounts allocated to the FTI for countries with few donors, there are several other constraints to increasing the global amount of aid to basic education. Many concern countries' capacities to absorb aid effectively and they are of two types. The first, which is of limited applicability to most low-income countries, relates to arguments that increased aid could destabilize the macro-economic environment. The second and more important involves the management of increases in aid and the effectiveness of aid use (Rose, 2007). This concern is greatest for fragile states, including conflict and post-conflict countries, where there may be a general lack of infrastructure and orderly processes and where governments have a limited ability to deliver services. In such cases it is difficult to move large amounts of resources, and innovative financing mechanisms and funding channels need to be developed to provide the basis for further support. It is estimated that 37% of the world's out-of-school children live in fragile states, many of them in conflict and post-conflict settings.

Limits on the ability to make effective use of large amounts of aid, however, are not confined to conflict and post-conflict countries. The World Bank's recent review of its support for primary education since 1990 showed that programmes

aimed at institutional development have had the lowest success rate (World Bank Independent Evaluation Group, 2006b). The implication, however, is that these efforts should be improved, not reduced. As overall enrolment rates rise, the difficulty of achieving further increases by attracting hard-to-reach children intensifies, necessitating more innovative approaches, while interventions to improve quality and learning achievement require even greater management capacity. Appropiate aid for capacity development (not traditional technical assistance) must thus be a very high priority if EFA is to be achieved.

In addition, donors face the same questions as governments when it comes to the relative priority to give basic education within the overall education sector. Evidence favouring arguments for shifting support towards post-primary education is growing. A recent indication is the World Bank's Africa Action Plan, which emphasizes skills development and includes only secondary and tertiary education in the set of monitorable indicators for education. This shift is a further challenge for national and international organizations working to ensure that the basic learning needs of all are met.

Towards an agenda

Enormous strides have been made towards achieving universal enrolment and gender parity at the primary level, and aid has demonstrably supported effective national efforts, as the diverse examples of Burkina Faso, Ethiopia, India, Mozambique, the United Republic of Tanzania, Yemen and Zambia demonstrate. If this momentum is to be maintained and even accelerated, if it is to be complemented by progress towards the other EFA goals of quality, literacy, early childhood and the learning needs of youth and adults, and if it is to be extended to all countries, action is needed by all stakeholders at the global level and by national governments, civil society and donors at the country level.

Global priorities

All stakeholders need to ensure that:

1) *EFA remains a priority on the global agenda* in the face of emerging global issues such as climate change and public health. It is critical to keep up broad advocacy for EFA and to show that

As overall enrolment rates rise, the difficulty of attracting hard-to-reach children intensifies, necessitating more innovative approaches

it can also contribute in important ways to these other dominant issues.

2) *EFA as a whole is the focus and not just UPE.* Since the MDGs include only UPE and gender parity, and since primary enrolment has so far been the area of greatest success, there is a danger of focusing exclusively on this one goal.

3) *Policy and implementation emphasize five key factors – inclusion , literacy, quality, capacity development and finance.*

a) *Inclusion* means encompassing: the marginalized and disadvantaged, whether they be poor, rural and urban slum residents, ethnic and linguistic minorities, or the disabled; all age groups, from early childhood (ECCE) to adults (especially literacy); and girls and women, particularly as the 2005 gender parity goal has been missed. It is essential not to write this goal off but rather to achieve it on a new timetable.

b) *Literacy* is, of course, part of inclusion, but must be singled out separately as it is the most neglected goal and the world suffers the shame of having about one in five adults still not literate, despite the notable example of China.

c) *Quality* is now receiving increasing priority but remains a major challenge everywhere, especially in low-income countries.

d) *Capacity development*, increasingly the obstacle to achieving the full, challenging EFA agenda, is especially an issue as attention turns from broad system expansion alone to encompass inclusion, literacy and quality.

e) *Finance* is a key element when governments face the need to increase national expenditure on EFA as well as on secondary and higher education, and when aid for basic education in low-income countries must be raised to at least US$11 billion a year to achieve EFA.

4) *More focus is put on sub-Saharan Africa and on fragile states*, the region and group of countries least likely to achieve the goals by 2015 or even 2025 on present trends, though other low-income countries must not be neglected.

5) *The international architecture is made more effective*, encompassing all of EFA and integrating the various partial initiatives, with a focus on the five priorities above.

Also, with many countries extending the concept of basic education beyond primary level, the EFA agenda is moving beyond a strict interpretation of the six goals, as reflected by the increased coverage of secondary education in this Report. While it may not be appropriate to redefine the EFA goals formally, the EFA movement can and should take account of the trend towards an extended vision of basic education in the formal sector.

National governments

National governments must focus on the global priorities, appropriately adjusted to each country's individual circumstances. In effect, this means reaffirming the twelve strategies in the Dakar Framework for Action:

1) *All of EFA* – Governments must take full responsibility for ECCE, quality, adult literacy and the learning needs of youth and adults, as well as for universal primary education. This may not mean delivering all necessary services through the public sector but it certainly means taking public responsibility and assuring adequate financing, as envisaged at Dakar. In particular, it is important for governments to recognize, as Chapter 3 showed, that there is not necessarily a trade-off between access and quality but that the two can be mutually reinforcing.

2) *Inclusion* of the poorest and most marginalized children, youth and adults, by:

a) ensuring that all children, particularly the marginalized and disadvantaged, have access to good ECCE programmes;

b) expanding the physical infrastructure of the basic education system in rural and disadvantaged urban areas, providing mechanisms for teachers to work in these areas and improving their working conditions;

c) eliminating school fees through a well-planned and well-managed process to ensure that schools are adequately prepared to deal with increases in enrolment and reductions in school income;

d) providing financial support such as scholarships, cash or in-kind transfers to households, appropriately targeted;

e) taking measures to alleviate the need for child labour and allowing for flexible schooling, non-formal equivalency courses and bridging courses to provide for the learning needs of working children and youth;

f) sustaining efforts to assure gender parity, including improving girls' access to and retention in primary and secondary education and addressing the emerging boys' issues at secondary level;

g) promoting inclusive education for the disabled, indigenous people and other disadvantaged groups;

h) promoting a great diversity of youth and adult education programmes through legislation, public funding arrangements and policies, such as regulation and oversight of the non-state sector and bridges between non-formal and formal education;

i) developing constructive partnerships between governments and the non-state sector to increase access to quality education.

3) *Literacy* – Governments need to step up their efforts on adult literacy through inclusion and quality in primary and lower secondary school and boldly expanding adequately staffed and funded literacy programmes for youth and adults that harness all the different forms of modern media. Policies should be instituted to promote media and publishing, and to encourage reading in schools, the home and the workplace.

4) *Quality* – Governments must ensure that priority is placed on pupils mastering basic skills and competences, with particular attention to:

a) making sure there are enough trained teachers and deploying them appropriately throughout the country;

b) enhancing the professionalism and motivation of teachers by providing ongoing professional development;

c) creating safe and healthy learning environments by tackling violence, particularly against girls and women, and providing health programmes, including deworming and nutrition;

d) maximizing *quality* school time in which teachers and pupils are actively engaged in learning activities, notably by creating administrative supports for teachers' presence in the classroom, ensuring that children arrive at school ready to learn and embracing multilingualism, particularly recognizing the importance of mother tongue instruction in the first years of school, among other measures;

e) ensuring that curricula are inclusive and relevant, and that they incorporate HIV/AIDS education, among other measures;

f) promoting gender equality through teacher training, gender-sensitive curricula and textbooks, and ensuring that there are female teachers in countries and areas with low enrolment of girls;

g) ensuring that there are sufficient learning resources, especially textbooks, for teachers and students to use.

5) *Capacity development* – In addition to training teachers, governments need to step up their efforts to:

a) improve and make better use of the national assessments that are being introduced in growing numbers;

b) develop management capacity at all levels of government – not just the national level – by paying attention to staff training as well as organizational and institutional structures;

c) improve the timeliness and coverage of the statistics used to formulate policy and monitor progress;

d) coordinate complex multisectoral and multiministry programmes such as ECCE and adult literacy, including with the NGOs that often deliver such programmes;

e) formally engage civil society in EFA policy formulation, implementation and monitoring.

Governments must make sure there are enough trained teachers and deploy them appropriately throughout the country

6) *Finance* – National governments must maintain public spending on EFA and, indeed, increase it where necessary. It is critical to ensure that pressure from other priorities does not reduce EFA spending to the minimum necessary for primary school access. Funding is essential for:

Public spending on EFA must be maintained and increased where necessary

a) inclusion, with unit costs likely to rise for enrolling the most disadvantaged and marginalized (often in remote areas or requiring special attention such as the disabled or linguistic minorities);

b) the expansion of ECCE and literacy, so far neglected both financially and as policy priorities;

c) quality, especially as regards teachers and their training and the provision of sufficient textbooks for both teachers and students;

d) capacity development, including for statistical systems and staff training, which are often underfunded.

Civil society

Civil society organizations (CSOs), a vital component of the compact to achieve EFA, have grown in numbers and influence since Dakar. There is a need for:

a) strong and vibrant CSOs that enable citizens to advocate for change and hold government and the international community to account;

b) consistent, regular and timely engagement between CSOs and national governments in education policy formulation, implementation and monitoring;

c) training in education policy analysis and finance to enable CSOs to take on the challenging role envisaged at Dakar more effectively.

Donors and international agencies

Both bilateral and multilateral agencies urgently need to increase the amount of aid and deploy it differently. Measure should be taken to:

a) immediately reverse the decreases in aid to education and basic education of 2005, and increase aid to basic education in low-income countries to meet the annual external financing need of US$11 billion, as soon as possible and no later than 2010;

b) increase the priority given to basic education compared with other levels, particularly higher education;

c) raise to at least 10% the share of basic education in bilateral sectoral aid and further increase multilateral aid for basic education;

d) within aid to basic education, allocate more to early childhood programmes, literacy, other programmes for youth and adults, and capacity development;

e) improve the geographic distribution of aid to more closely reflect needs, involving a particular focus on sub-Saharan Africa, on fragile states and on increased participation in and support for the FTI Catalytic Fund.

Improving the delivery of aid requires more explicit attention to aligning and harmonizing aid behind country-led education sector plans, as stated in the Paris Declaration. This requires:

a) further aligning all programmes, whatever their financing modalities, with government programmes, including through the FTI process and other sectorwide approaches;

b) making longer-term commitments so that aid for basic education is more predictable and ministers of finance can approve major policy initiatives, such as hiring more teachers, in the knowledge that sustainable financing is in place;

c) working with governments to improve their capacity to absorb larger amounts of aid at all levels of service delivery and improving aid in support of capacity development;

d) reducing the transaction costs governments face in managing multiple aid agency partners, multiple aid missions and multiple reporting requirements.

Increasing the quantity and quality of aid requires joint and integrated efforts of all international partners including major multilateral and bilateral agencies, and in particular UNESCO and the other Dakar convening agencies (UNDP, UNFPA, UNICEF and the World Bank). It is vital that such efforts fully involve developing country governments and civil society.

Will we make it?

The evidence since Dakar is clear – determined national governments have made much progress in all regions, and increased aid aligned to national efforts has demonstrably worked to support this progress. We must maintain this momentum – and accelerate it if all the goals are to be met. Time is short. Only if all stakeholders now embrace and maintain a relentless focus on EFA as a whole, rallying around the key elements of inclusion, literacy, quality, capacity development and finance, will the right to education at every age be fulfilled. ■

The evidence since Dakar is clear: determined national governments have made much progress, supported by aid

© GEORGE OSODI/AP/SIPA

On the way
to school
in Sierra

Annex

The Education for All Development Index

Introduction 198
    Table 1: The EFA Development Index and its components, 2005 202
    Table 2: Countries ranked according to value of EDI and components, 2005 204
    Table 3: Change in EDI and its components between 1999 and 2005 205

Prospects for the achievement of EFA by 2015: methodology 206

National learning assessments by region and country

Introduction 208
    Table 1: Sub-Saharan Africa 209
    Table 2: Arab States 211
    Table 3: East Asia and the Pacific, and South and West Asia 212
    Table 4: Latin America and the Caribbean 214
    Table 5: Central and Eastern Europe and Central Asia 216
    Table 6: Western Europe and North America 218

National policies to advance Education for All in thirty countries

Introduction 221
    Table: Summary of national policies to advance EFA since 2000 in thirty countries ... 222

Statistical tables

Introduction 232
    Table 1: Background statistics 244
    Table 2: Adult and youth literacy 252
    Table 3A: Early childhood care and education (ECCE): care 260
    Table 3B: Early childhood care and education (ECCE): education 268
    Table 4: Access to primary education 276
    Table 5: Participation in primary education 284
    Table 6: Internal efficiency: repetition in primary education 292
    Table 7: Internal efficiency: primary education dropout and completion 300
    Table 8: Participation in secondary education 308
    Table 9A: Participation in tertiary education 316
    Table 9B: Tertiary education: distribution of students by field of study
        and female share in each field 324
    Table 10A: Teaching staff in pre-primary and primary education 332
    Table 10B: Teaching staff in secondary and tertiary education 340
    Table 11: Commitment to education: public spending 348
    Table 12: Trends in basic or proxy indicators to measure EFA goals 1, 2, 3, 4 and 5 ... 356
    Table 13: Trends in basic or proxy indicators to measure EFA goal 6 364

Aid tables

Introduction 373
    Table 1: Bilateral and multilateral ODA 375
    Table 2: Bilateral and multilateral aid to education 376
    Table 3: ODA recipients 378
    Table 4: Recipients of aid to education 382

Glossary 390

References 396

Abbreviations 417

Index 420

The Education for All Development Index

Introduction

While each of the six EFA goals is individually important, it is also useful to have a means of indicating achievement of EFA as a whole. The EFA Development Index (EDI), a composite of relevant indicators, provides one way of doing so, at least for the four most easily quantifiable EFA goals: universal primary education (UPE), adult literacy, the quality of education and gender parity.

The two goals not yet included in the EDI are goals 1 and 3. Neither has a quantitative target for 2015. Goal 1 (early childhood care and education) is multidimensional and covers both the care and education aspects. The indicators currently available on this goal cannot easily be incorporated in the EDI because national data are insufficiently standardized and reliable, and comparable data are not available for most countries (see Chapter 2 and *EFA Global Monitoring Report 2007*). Goal 3 (learning needs of youth and adults) has not yet been sufficiently defined for quantitative measurement (see Chapter 2).

In accordance with the principle of considering each goal to be equally important, one indicator is used as a proxy measure for each of the four EDI components,[1] and each component is assigned equal weight in the overall index. The EDI value for a particular country is thus the arithmetic mean of the observed values for each component. Since the components are all expressed as percentages, the EDI value can vary from 0 to 100% or, when expressed as a ratio, from 0 to 1. The closer a country's EDI value is to the maximum, the greater the extent of its overall EFA achievement and the nearer the country is to the EFA goal as a whole.

Choice of indicators as proxy measures of EDI components

In selecting indicators, relevance has to be balanced with data availability.

Universal primary education

The UPE goal implies both universal access to and universal completion of primary education. However, while both access and participation at this level are relatively easy to measure, there is a lack of consensus on the definition of primary school completion. Therefore, the indicator selected to measure UPE achievement (goal 2) in the EDI is the total primary net enrolment ratio (NER), which reflects the percentage of primary-school-age children who are enrolled in either primary or secondary school. Its value varies from 0 to 100%. A NER of 100% means all eligible children are enrolled in school in a given school year, although not all of them will necessarily complete it.

Adult literacy

The adult literacy rate is used as a proxy to measure progress towards the first part of goal 4.[2] This has its limitations. First, the adult literacy indicator, being a statement about the stock of human capital, is slow to change, and thus it could be argued that it is not a good 'leading indicator' of year-by-year progress. Second, the existing data on literacy are not entirely satisfactory. Most of them are based on 'conventional' non-tested methods that usually overestimate the level of literacy among individuals.[3] New methodologies, based on tests and on the definition of literacy as a continuum of skills, are being developed and applied in some countries to improve the quality of literacy data. Providing a new data series of good quality for even a majority of countries will take many years, however. The literacy rates now used are the best currently available internationally.

---

1. The EDI's gender component is itself a composite index.

---

2. The first part of goal 4 is: 'Achieving a 50 per cent improvement in levels of adult literacy by 2015, especially for women'. To enable progress towards this target to be monitored for all countries, whatever their current adult literacy level, it was decided as of the 2006 *EFA Global Monitoring Report* to interpret it in terms of a reduction in the adult illiteracy rate.

3. In most countries, particularly developing countries, current literacy data are derived from methods of self-declaration or third-party reporting (e.g. a household head responding on behalf of other household members) used in censuses or household surveys. In other cases, particularly as regards developed countries, they are based on education attainment proxies. Neither method is based on any test and both are subject to bias (overestimation of literacy), which affects the quality and accuracy of literacy data.

Quality of education

There is considerable debate about the concept of quality and how it should be measured. Several proxy indicators are generally used to measure quality of education, among them measures of students' learning outcomes, which are widely used for this purpose, particularly among countries at similar levels of development. However, measures of learning achievement are incomplete, as they do not include values, capacities and other non-cognitive skills that are also important aims of education (UNESCO, 2004b, pp. 43-4). They also tell nothing about the cognitive value added by schooling (as opposed to home background) or the distribution of ability among children enrolled in school.[4] Despite these drawbacks, learning outcomes would likely be the most appropriate single proxy for the average quality of education, but as comparable data are not yet available for a large number of countries, it is not yet possible to use them in the EDI.

Among the feasible proxy indicators available for a large number of countries, the survival rate to grade 5 seems to be the best available for the quality of education component of the EDI.[5] Figure 1 shows that there is

4. Strictly speaking, it would be necessary to compare average levels of cognitive achievement for pupils completing a given school grade across countries with similar levels and distributions of income and with similar levels of NER, so as to account for home background and ability cohort effects.

5. See *EFA Global Monitoring Report* 2003/4, Appendix 2, for background.

a clear positive link between such survival rates and educational achievement in sub-Saharan African countries participating in the second Southern and Eastern African Consortium for Monitoring Educational Quality (SACMEQ II) assessment. The coefficient of correlation (R^2) is around 34%. Education systems capable of retaining a larger proportion of their pupils to grade 5 tend to perform better, on average, on student assessment tests.

The survival rate to grade 5 is associated even more strongly with learning outcomes in lower secondary school. Figure 2 shows a coefficient of correlation of 41% in the results of the third Trends in International Mathematics and Science Study (TIMSS) and up to 80% in the Programme for International Student Assessment (PISA) study.

Another possible proxy indicator for quality is the pupil/teacher ratio (PTR). Among SACMEQ II countries, the association between this indicator and learning outcomes is higher (44%) than for survival rate to grade 5 (34%) – a ten percentage point difference. Many other studies, however, produce much more ambiguous evidence of the relationship between the PTR and learning outcomes (UNESCO, 2004b). In a multivariate context, PTRs are associated with higher learning outcomes in some studies, but not in many others. In addition, the relationship seems to vary by the level of mean test scores. For low levels of test scores, a decrease in the number of pupils per teacher has a positive

Figure 1: Survival rate to grade 5 and learning outcomes at primary level, 2000

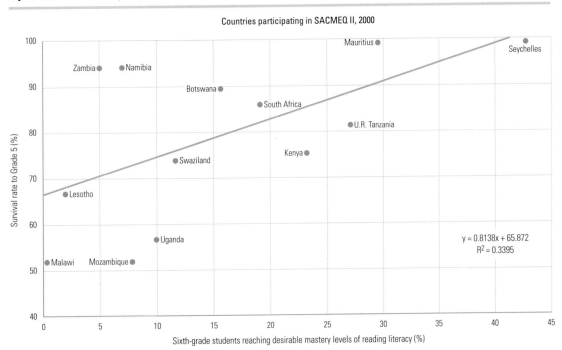

Countries participating in SACMEQ II, 2000

$y = 0.8138x + 65.872$
$R^2 = 0.3395$

Sources: UIS calculation based on SACMEQ II database; UIS database for data on survival rate to grade 5.

ANNEX

Figure 2: Survival rate to grade 5 and learning outcomes at lower secondary level, 2003

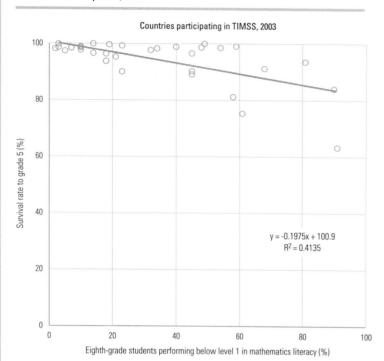

Countries participating in TIMSS, 2003

$y = -0.1975x + 100.9$
$R^2 = 0.4135$

Survival rate to grade 5 (%)

Eighth-grade students performing below level 1 in mathematics literacy (%)

Sources: Mullis et al. (2004); UIS database for data on survival rate to grade 5.

Figure 2 (continued)

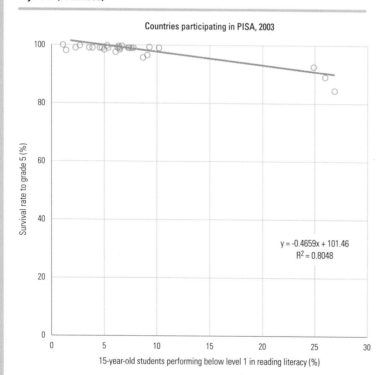

Countries participating in PISA, 2003

$y = -0.4659x + 101.46$
$R^2 = 0.8048$

Survival rate to grade 5 (%)

15-year-old students performing below level 1 in reading literacy (%)

Sources: OECD (2004c); UIS database for data on survival rate to grade 5.

impact on learning outcomes, but for higher levels of test scores, additional teachers, which lead to lower PTRs, have only limited impact. For these reasons, the survival rate was chosen as a safer proxy for learning outcomes and hence for the education quality component of the EDI.[6]

Gender

The fourth EDI component is measured by a composite index, the gender-specific EFA index (GEI). Ideally, the GEI should reflect the whole gender-related EFA goal, which calls for 'eliminating gender disparities in primary and secondary education by 2005, and achieving gender equality in education by 2015, with a focus on ensuring girls' full and equal access to and achievement in basic education of good quality'. There are thus two subgoals: gender parity (achieving equal participation of girls and boys in primary and secondary education) and gender equality (ensuring that educational equality exists between boys and girls).

The first subgoal is measured by the gender parity indexes (GPIs) for the gross enrolment ratios (GERs) at primary and secondary levels. Measuring and monitoring the broader aspects of equality in education is difficult, as the 2003/4 Report demonstrated (UNESCO, 2003b). Essentially, outcome measures, disaggregated by sex, are needed for a range of educational levels. No such measures are available on an internationally comparable basis. As a step in that direction, however, the GEI includes gender parity for adult literacy. Thus, the GEI is calculated as a simple average of three GPIs: for the GER in primary education, for the GER in secondary education and for the adult literacy rate. This means the GEI does not fully reflect the equality aspect of the EFA gender goal.

The GPI, when expressed as the ratio of females to males in enrolment ratios or the literacy rate, can exceed unity when more girls/women than boys/men are enrolled or literate. For the purposes of the index, the F/M formula is inverted to M/F in cases where the GPI is higher than 1. This solves mathematically the problem of including the GEI in the EDI (where all components have a theoretical limit of 1, or 100%) while maintaining the GEI's ability to show gender disparity. Figure 3 shows how 'transformed GPIs' are arrived at to highlight gender disparities that disadvantage males. Once all three GPI values have been calculated and converted into 'transformed GPIs' (from 0 to 1) where needed, the composite GEI is obtained by calculating a simple average of the three GPIs, with each being weighted equally.

6. Another reason is that survival rates, like the other EDI components, but unlike PTRs, range from 0% to 100%. Therefore, the use of the survival rate to grade 5 in the EDI avoids a need to rescale the data.

Figure 4 illustrates the calculation for Lesotho, using data for the school year ending in 2005. The GPIs in primary education, secondary education and adult literacy were 0.998, 1.265 and 1.225, respectively, resulting in a GEI of 0.868.

GEI = 1/3 (primary GPI)
 + 1/3 (transformed secondary GPI)
 + 1/3 (transformed adult literacy GPI)
GEI = 1/3 (0.998) + 1/3 (0.791) + 1/3 (0.816) = 0.868

Calculating the EDI

The EDI is the arithmetic mean of its four components: total primary NER, adult literacy rate, GEI and survival rate to grade 5. As a simple average, the EDI may mask important variations among its components: for example, results for goals on which a country has made less progress can offset its advances on others. Since all the EFA goals are equally important, a synthetic indicator such as the EDI is thus very useful to inform the policy debate on the prominence of all the EFA goals and to highlight the synergy among them.

Figure 5 illustrates the calculation of the EDI, again using Lesotho as an example. The total primary NER, adult literacy rate, value of the GEI and survival rate to grade 5 in 2005 were 0.870, 0.822, 0.868 and 0.733, respectively, resulting in an EDI of 0.824.

EDI = 1/4 (total primary NER)
 + 1/4 (adult literacy rate)
 + 1/4 (GEI)
 + 1/4 (survival rate to grade 5)
EDI = 1/4 (0.870) + 1/4 (0.822) + 1/4 (0.868) + 1/4 (0.733)
 = 0.824

Data sources and country coverage

All data used to calculate the EDI for the school year ending in 2005 are from the statistical tables in this annex and the UNESCO Institute for Statistics (UIS) database, with one exception. Adult literacy data for some OECD countries that did not answer the UIS literacy survey are based on the results of the 2005 European Labour Force Survey.

Only the 129 countries with a complete set of the indicators required to calculate the EDI are included in this analysis (that is four more countries than in the 2007 Report, though). Many countries are thus not included in the EDI, including a number of fragile states. This fact, coupled with the exclusion of goal 1 and 3, means the EDI does not yet provide a fully comprehensive global overview of EFA achievement.

Figure 3: Calculating the 'transformed' secondary education GPI

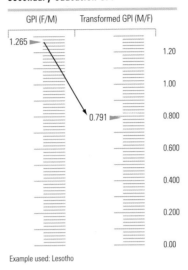

Example used: Lesotho

Figure 4: Calculating the GEI

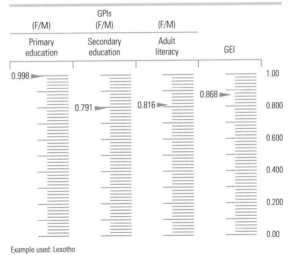

Example used: Lesotho

Figure 5: Calculating the EDI

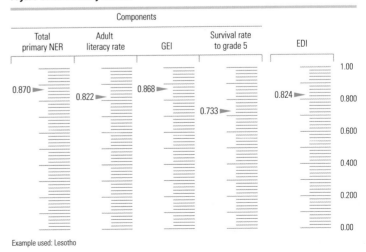

Example used: Lesotho

Table 1: The EFA Development Index and its components, 2005

Ranking according to level of EDI	Countries/Territories	EDI	Total primary NER[1]	Adult literacy rate	Gender-specific EFA index (GEI)	Survival rate to grade 5
High EDI						
1	Norway[2]	0.995	0.981	1.000	0.998	1.000
2	United Kingdom[2]	0.995	1.000	0.998	0.990	0.990
3	Slovenia[3]	0.994	0.998	0.997	0.994	0.989
4	Sweden[2]	0.994	0.986	1.000	0.999	0.990
5	Republic of Korea[4]	0.993	0.996	0.991	0.994	0.991
6	Italy[3]	0.993	0.994	0.988	0.991	0.998
7	Kazakhstan[3]	0.992	0.990	0.996	0.986	0.995
8	Iceland[2]	0.991	0.987	1.000	0.982	0.997
9	France[2]	0.991	0.993	0.987	0.995	0.990
10	Denmark[2]	0.991	0.985	1.000	0.989	0.990
11	Finland[2]	0.990	0.983	1.000	0.983	0.995
12	Netherlands[2]	0.989	0.987	0.987	0.986	0.998
13	Belgium[2]	0.989	0.990	0.990	0.986	0.990
14	Barbados[4]	0.988	0.976	0.993	0.999	0.983
15	Cyprus[3]	0.988	0.997	0.974	0.984	0.996
16	Estonia[3]	0.987	0.974	0.998	0.986	0.988
17	Austria[2]	0.986	0.969	1.000	0.984	0.990
18	Spain[2]	0.986	0.994	0.978	0.971	1.000
19	Switzerland[2]	0.985	0.976	1.000	0.974	0.990
20	Poland[2]	0.983	0.965	0.983	0.992	0.993
21	Greece[3]	0.983	0.991	0.969	0.983	0.990
22	Israel[2]	0.983	0.975	0.971	0.986	0.999
23	Cuba	0.983	0.979	0.998	0.983	0.971
24	Hungary[2]	0.982	0.958	1.000	0.991	0.980
25	Ireland[2]	0.981	0.963	0.994	0.968	0.998
26	Aruba	0.980	0.995	0.973	0.976	0.975
27	Argentina[3]	0.979	0.995	0.974	0.976	0.969
28	Georgia[4]	0.976	0.931	0.998	0.993	0.982
29	TFYR Macedonia[3]	0.975	0.972	0.967	0.980	0.982
30	Kyrgyzstan[3]	0.974	0.946	0.992	0.991	0.969
31	Croatia[3]	0.974	0.931	0.984	0.986	0.996
32	Seychelles	0.974	0.995	0.918	0.991	0.991
33	Czech Republic[2]	0.973	0.922	0.999	0.989	0.984
34	Lithuania[3]	0.972	0.917	0.997	0.996	0.979
35	Tajikistan[3]	0.970	0.974	0.996	0.930	0.980
36	Slovakia[2]	0.970	0.917	0.996	0.991	0.974
37	Chile[3]	0.969	0.941	0.963	0.981	0.990
38	Romania[3]	0.968	0.962	0.975	0.986	0.949
39	Belarus[3]	0.968	0.899	0.997	0.985	0.993
40	Portugal[3]	0.967	0.995	0.938	0.943	0.990
41	Latvia[3]	0.966	0.899	0.998	0.986	0.982
42	Fiji[4]	0.966	0.987	0.929	0.960	0.987
43	Brunei Darussalam	0.965	0.969	0.927	0.967	0.995
44	Luxembourg[2]	0.964	0.965	0.990	0.980	0.920
45	Bahamas[4]	0.964	0.914	0.958	0.991	0.991
46	Bulgaria[3]	0.958	0.947	0.983	0.977	0.923
47	Trinidad and Tobago[3]	0.954	0.948	0.984	0.975	0.910
48	Mexico	0.953	0.998	0.916	0.961	0.938
49	Albania[3]	0.953	0.940	0.989	0.982	0.899
50	Bahrain[3]	0.952	0.983	0.875	0.962	0.989
51	Azerbaijan[3]	0.950	0.846	0.993	0.980	0.981
Medium EDI						
52	Malta[3]	0.949	0.920	0.910	0.975	0.993
53	Armenia[3]	0.949	0.862	0.994	0.975	0.963
54	Uruguay[3]	0.948	0.962	0.976	0.943	0.912
55	Jordan	0.947	0.926	0.911	0.963	0.988
56	Malaysia[3]	0.945	0.954	0.904	0.938	0.984
57	Saint Lucia[4]	0.942	0.979	0.901	0.928	0.960
58	Republic of Moldova[3]	0.940	0.882	0.991	0.982	0.907
59	Mauritius[3]	0.940	0.951	0.866	0.973	0.970
60	Kuwait	0.939	0.865	0.933	0.963	0.994
61	Macao, China	0.938	0.909	0.913	0.935	0.997
62	Indonesia	0.935	0.983	0.904	0.959	0.895
63	Panama[3]	0.934	0.991	0.931	0.963	0.853
64	Venezuela	0.931	0.928	0.930	0.953	0.914
65	Peru	0.931	0.992	0.879	0.954	0.900

Table 1 (continued)

Ranking according to level of EDI	Countries/Territories	EDI	Total primary NER[1]	Adult literacy rate	Gender-specific EFA index (GEI)	Survival rate to grade 5
Medium EDI						
66	Mongolia[3]	0.929	0.880	0.975	0.952	0.909
67	Tonga[3]	0.926	0.981	0.992	0.958	0.772
68	St Vincent/Grenad.[4]	0.926	0.924	0.997	0.901	0.880
69	Palestinian A. T.	0.923	0.840	0.924	0.948	0.981
70	Lebanon[4]	0.921	0.943	0.883	0.923	0.932
71	Ecuador[3]	0.917	0.994	0.923	0.991	0.763
72	Bolivia[3]	0.913	0.965	0.887	0.950	0.848
73	Grenada[4]	0.912	0.865	0.980	0.976	0.826
74	Maldives[3]	0.910	0.797	0.969	0.952	0.921
75	Paraguay[3]	0.902	0.882	0.935	0.978	0.812
76	Brazil[3]	0.901	0.964	0.892	0.943	0.805
77	Turkey	0.901	0.894	0.874	0.866	0.969
78	Colombia	0.899	0.899	0.928	0.961	0.809
79	Viet Nam	0.899	0.878	0.903	0.945	0.868
80	Tunisia	0.896	0.981	0.743	0.889	0.970
81	United Arab Emirates[3]	0.896	0.760	0.887	0.969	0.968
82	Philippines	0.893	0.944	0.926	0.955	0.749
83	South Africa[3]	0.892	0.920	0.866	0.958	0.824
84	Dominican Republic[3]	0.892	0.895	0.892	0.923	0.858
85	Sao Tome and Principe[3]	0.891	0.999	0.875	0.929	0.763
86	Botswana[3]	0.890	0.866	0.813	0.977	0.905
87	Algeria[3]	0.890	0.990	0.737	0.877	0.956
88	Cape Verde[3]	0.890	0.908	0.812	0.913	0.925
89	Jamaica	0.885	0.907	0.799	0.943	0.890
90	Iran, Islamic Republic of	0.883	0.954	0.824	0.877	0.878
91	Egypt	0.883	0.972	0.714	0.859	0.986
92	Oman	0.881	0.777	0.814	0.934	1.000
93	Saudi Arabia	0.881	0.780	0.829	0.943	0.971
94	Myanmar	0.866	0.902	0.899	0.963	0.699
95	El Salvador[3]	0.854	0.948	0.806	0.967	0.694
96	Namibia[3]	0.848	0.716	0.871	0.947	0.861
97	Honduras[3]	0.848	0.937	0.823	0.931	0.700
98	Zimbabwe[3]	0.837	0.825	0.888	0.938	0.697
99	Swaziland	0.830	0.803	0.796	0.956	0.768
100	Kenya	0.824	0.793	0.736	0.939	0.829
101	Lesotho	0.824	0.871	0.822	0.868	0.733
102	Guatemala[3]	0.812	0.956	0.718	0.894	0.680
103	Cambodia	0.807	0.989	0.736	0.871	0.631
104	Nicaragua[3]	0.804	0.937	0.801	0.943	0.535
Low EDI						
105	India[3]	0.797	0.946	0.641	0.811	0.789
106	Iraq	0.793	0.877	0.741	0.750	0.806
107	Bangladesh[3]	0.759	0.976	0.505	0.906	0.651
108	Lao PDR[3]	0.750	0.836	0.714	0.820	0.630
109	Morocco	0.740	0.863	0.523	0.782	0.792
110	Nepal[3]	0.734	0.801	0.539	0.810	0.785
111	Nigeria[3]	0.734	0.696	0.691	0.822	0.726
112	Malawi[3]	0.734	0.952	0.700	0.862	0.421
113	Ghana[3]	0.714	0.704	0.635	0.886	0.633
114	Rwanda	0.688	0.740	0.649	0.904	0.458
115	Togo	0.681	0.809	0.532	0.638	0.746
116	Mauritania[3]	0.666	0.726	0.543	0.858	0.529
117	Burundi	0.665	0.607	0.593	0.792	0.669
118	Senegal	0.651	0.719	0.393	0.763	0.730
119	Yemen[3]	0.650	0.758	0.541	0.570	0.732
120	Pakistan	0.640	0.681	0.499	0.684	0.697
121	Eritrea[4]	0.634	0.477	0.576	0.691	0.791
122	Mozambique[3]	0.631	0.772	0.431	0.696	0.624
123	Ethiopia	0.616	0.695	0.359	0.761	0.733
124	Benin[3]	0.583	0.803	0.390	0.624	0.516
125	Guinea	0.579	0.662	0.295	0.599	0.760
126	Mali[3]	0.559	0.509	0.225	0.635	0.869
127	Burkina Faso	0.531	0.455	0.236	0.678	0.755
128	Niger	0.480	0.399	0.287	0.588	0.648
129	Chad	0.409	0.612	0.257	0.437	0.332

Note: Data in blue indicate that gender disparities are at the expense of boys or men, particularly at secondary level.

1. Total primary NER includes children of primary school age who are enrolled in either primary or secondary schools.

2. The adult literacy rate is a proxy measure based on educational attainment; that is, the proportion of the adult population with at least a complete primary education.

3. Adult literacy rates are UIS annual literacy estimates. The estimates were generated using the UIS Global Age-specific Literacy Projections model.

4. Adult literacy rates are unofficial UIS estimates.

Sources: Annex, Statistical Tables 2, 5 ,7 and 8; UIS database; proxy literacy measure for European countries: European Commission, European Labour Force Survey (2005).

Table 1 (continued)

Country	Name or description of assessment study	Organization/institution(s) responsible for assessment	Target population	Curricular subject(s) assessed	Year(s)
Mauritius	Competency-Based Assessment Pilot Study	MoE	Grade 3	Math, English, French, sci, life skills	Pilot study planned for 2007
			Age 15	Lan, math, ICT, sci	
Mozambique	National Assessment Programme	MoE		Portuguese, math	1997
Namibia	National Learner Baseline Assessment	MoE; Florida State University and Harvard University (USA)	Grades 4, 7	English, math, reading, listening comp (regionally)	1994
Niger	Évaluation Nationale	MoE, SEDEP	Grades 2, 4, 6	Lan, math, sci	2000
	Évaluation du niveau d'acquisition en français, en mathématiques et en sciences des élèves des écoles traditionnelles du cycle de base 1	Division de l'évaluation du suivi des acquis, MoE; World Bank	Grades 2, 4, 6	Lan, math, sci	2005
Nigeria	National Assessment of Learning Achievements	Federal Government; UNICEF; UNESCO	Grade 4	Numeracy, literacy, life skills	1997
	Follow Up Assessment	Universal Basic Education Commission	Grade 5	English, math	2001
	National Assessment of the Universal Basic Education Programme		Grades 4–6	English, math, sci, soc sci	2003
Seychelles	National Test	MoE	Grade 6	English, French, math, sci, Seychellois Creole	Yearly since 2002
Senegal	Système national d'évaluation des rendements scolaires (SNERS I&II)	INEADE	Grades 3, 4, 6	Lan, math	1996, 2002
	SNERS III		Grade 9	Lan, math, sci (life, earth and physical)	2006
South Africa	Assessment of Learning Achievement	MoE	Junior and senior secondary	English, math, social studies, integrated sci	2003
	Monitoring Education Quality	HSRC	Grade 9	English, math, sci	Yearly since 1996
	Learner Assessment Results	HSRC; District Development Support Programme; USAID	Grade 3	Reading	2003
	Systematic Evaluation Study	MoE; HSRC	Grade 6	Lan, math, sci	2005
	Analysis of the Impact on Pupil Performance of the District Development Support Programme	MoE; USAID	Grade 3	Literacy, numeracy	2000, 2001, 2003
Swaziland	…	Exams Council of Swaziland	Grades 4, 7, 10	…	Post-Dakar period[1]
Uganda	National Assessment of Progress in Education	Uganda National Examinations Board	Grades 3, 6	Literacy, numeracy	2005
			Grades 3, 6	English literacy, local lan literacy, numeracy	2006
Zambia	Reading Levels and Bilingual Literacy in Primary Schools	DFID	Grades 3–6	Lan, English	1998
	Primary Reading Programme	ADEA	Grades 1–6	Reading, writing	1999, 2002
	National Exam	MoE; USAID	Grade 5	Lan, math, English	1999, 2001, 2003

1. The exact year of the assessment is uncertain, but the evidence would appear to indicate that it took place sometime after the 2000 World Education Forum in Dakar.
… Information not available.

Table 2: Arab States

Country	Name or description of assessment study	Organization/institution(s) responsible for assessment	Target population	Curricular subject(s) assessed	Year(s)
Algeria	Programme national d'évaluation du rendement du système éducatif algérien	MoE	Grades 3, 6, 9, 1S	Arabic, French, math	Post-Dakar period[1]
Djibouti	Évaluation du niveau de qualité et du rendement cognitive	Centre de Recherche, d'Information et de Production de l'Éducation Nationale	Primary, lower secondary	French, Arabic, math	1991, 1992, 1997–2000
Egypt	Global evaluation	MoE	Grades 1–3	All school subjects	2005, 2006
Jordan	National test	MoE; DFID	Grade 10	Arabic, English, math, sci, social sci	Yearly since 2000
Kuwait	Multilevel Analysis Approach for Determining 8th Grade Mathematics Achievement in the State of Kuwait	Kuwait University; Kuwait Society for the Advancement of Arab Children; Arab Fund for Economic and Social Development	Grade 8	Math	2006
Lebanon	Évaluation des acquis d'apprentissage	Centre de Recherche et de Développement Pédagogiques	Grade 4	Arabic, French, math, sci, transversal competencies	1994, 1995
	Mesure des acquis d'apprentissage		Grade 4 complementary	Arabic, French, math, sci, *savoir-être*	1995, 1996
Mauritania	Analyse empirique des programmes de l'enseignement fondamental en Mauritanie	Institut Pédagogique National	Grades 3–6	Mother tongue, second lan, math, *étude du milieu*	1999
	Évaluation de l'enseignement fondamental en Mauritanie		Grades 4, 6		2001
	Évaluation de la 2e année fondamentale (AF)		Grade 2	Mother tongue, second lan, math	2001–2002
	Analyse de la couverture de programme en classe de 5e AF en Mauritanie		Grade 5	Mother tongue, second lan, math, *étude du milieu*	2003–2004
	L'évaluation de la couverture des programmes des disciplines scientifiques en 5e C et D		Secondary (5th year, tracks C and D)	Sci (physics, chemistry), math	2004
	Évaluation de l'effet de la formation continue en Multigrade		Grade 5	Mother tongue, second lan, math	2006–2007
Morocco	Diagnostic et appui aux apprentissages	MoE	Grades 3, 5, 8	Arabic, French, math	2000
	Évaluations des pré-acquis	MoE; UNICEF	Grades 4, 6	Arabic, French, math, life skills	2001
	Évaluation des acquis des élèves	MoE; EU	Grade 6	Arabic, French, math, life skills	2006
Oman	Evaluation of Basic Education Cycle One	MoE; Canedcom International (Canada)	Grade 4	Arabic, English, sci, math	2003–2004
Qatar	Comprehensive Educational Assessment and School Surveys	Evaluation Institute	Grades 4–11	Arabic, English, math, sci	Yearly since 2004
Saudi Arabia	Diagnostic Test in the Public Evaluation System	MoE	Grades 1–3	Arabic, math	Post-Dakar period[1]
United Arab Emirates	National Assessment of Student Achievement and Progress	Australian Council for Educational Research	Grades 5, 7	Literacy, numeracy	2005

1. The exact year of the assessment is uncertain, but the evidence would appear to indicate that it took place sometime after the 2000 World Education Forum in Dakar.

Table 3: East Asia and the Pacific, and South and West Asia

Country	Name or description of assessment study	Organization/institution(s) responsible for assessment	Target population	Curricular subject(s) assessed	Year(s)
Australia	National Basic Skills Test (New South Wales only)	New South Wales Department of Education and Training	Grades 3, 5	Literacy, numeracy	Pre- and post-Dakar period
	Adaptation of National Basic Skills Test (South Australia only)	Department of Education and Children's Services	Grades 3, 5	Literacy, numeracy	
	State learning assessments	State MoEs	Grades 3, 5, 7	State-specific subjects	
Bangladesh	Assessment of the Achievement of Pupils Completing Grade 4	MoE, National Curriculum and Textbook Board	Grade 4	Bangla, English, math, sci, soc sci	2000
	National Assessment	MoE	Grades 3, 5	Bangla, math, sci, soc sci, env sci	2001
	Intensive District Approach to Education for All (IDEAL)		Grades 1, 5	Bangla, English, math, sci, soc sci	2004
Cambodia	Learning Assessment System	MoE; World Bank	Grade 3	Khmer, math	2006
			Grade 6	Khmer, math	Planned for 2007
			Grade 9	Khmer, math	Planned for 2008
Cook Islands	Standardized National Diagnostic Testing	MoE	Grades 4, 6	English, CI Maori and math	Yearly from 2000 to 2006
Fiji	National Assessment	MoE; SPBEA	Grades 4, 6	Literacy, numeracy	Post-Dakar period[1]
India	Baseline Assessment Survey	NCERT	Grades 1, 3, 4, 5, 7, 8 (variable)	Lan, math, env sci (variable)	1994, 2002, 2003, 2004
	Mid-term Assessment Survey		Grades 1, 3, 4	Lan, math	1997
	Terminal Assessment Survey		Grades 1, 3, 4	Lan, math	2001
Indonesia	Assessment of Students Learning Achievement	Educational National Standard Board	Grade 3 (primary) and senior (secondary)	Indonesian, English, math	Yearly since 2005
Japan	National Assessment of Learning Outcomes	NIER	Grades 5, 9, 12 (variable)	Japanese, English, math, sci, soc sci, geography, history, civics	2002, 2003, 2004
	National Assessment of Student Performance	MoE; NIER	Grades 6, 9	Japanese, math	2007
Kiribati*	National Assessment	MoE; SPBEA	Grades 4, 6	Literacy, numeracy	Post-Dakar period[1]
Lao PDR	National Literacy Survey	MoE; UNESCO; UNICEF	Age 6 and above	Reading, writing, numeracy, visual literacy	2000
	Assessment of Student Learning Outcomes	MoE, National Research Institute for Educational Science	Grade 5		2006
Malaysia	Primary School Achievement Test	MoE, Malaysian Examination Syndicate	Grade 6	Malay, English, math, sci, Chinese, Tamil	Yearly since 1987
Maldives	Sample testing	MoE, Supervision and Quality Improvement Section; World Bank	...	Math, Dhivehi, English	2002–2003
Myanmar	Learning Achievement Study	MoE; UNICEF	Grades 3, 5	Lan, math, sci	2005, 2006
New Zealand	National Education Monitoring Project	New Zealand Council for Educational Research; University of Otago Educational Assessment Research Unit	Grades 4, 8 (not including Maori medium schools)	Art, sci, graphs, tables, maps	1995, 1999, 2003 (4 year cycles)
				Reading and speaking, technology, music	1996, 2000, 2004 (4 year cycles)
				Math, information skills, social studies	1997, 2001, 2005 (4 year cycles)
				Listening and viewing, health, physical education	1998, 2002, 2006 (4 year cycles)

Table 3 (continued)

Country	Name or description of assessment study	Organization/institution(s) responsible for assessment	Target population	Curricular subject(s) assessed	Year(s)
			Grade 8 (Maori medium schools)	Sci, art, graphs, tables, maps	1999, 2003 (4 year cycles)
				Music, technology, reading and speaking,	2000, 2004 (4 year cycles)
				Writing, listening, viewing, health, physical education	2002, 2006 (4 year cycles)
Pakistan	National Achievement Test	MoE, National Education Assessment System	Grades 4, 8 and teachers (variable)	Lan, math, sci, social studies	2005, 2006
	Quality of Education	Academy of Educational Planning and Management	Grade 4	Sindhi, Urdu, math	2000
	Learning Levels and Gaps in Pakistan (Punjab Province)	LEAPS	Grade 3	Urdu, math, English	2004
Philippines	National Achievement Test	MoE, National Education Testing and Research Centre	Grades 4, 6 and year 2 secondary	English, Filipino, sci, social studies, math	2005, 2006
	Reading Test in English and Filipino for Elementary Level		Grade 3	Reading comprehension	2005, 2006
	Philippine Informal Reading Inventory	MoE	Grades 1–6	Reading	2004, 2005
Republic of Korea	National Assessment of Educational Assessment	Korean Institute of Curriculum and Evaluation	Grades 6, 9, 10	Math, social studies	1998–2000
			Grades 6, 9, 10	Korean, math, sci, social studies and English	2001–2002
			Grades 6, 9, 10	Korean, math, sci, social studies and English	2003, 2006
Samoa	National Assessment	MoE; SPBEA	Grades 4, 6	Literacy and numeracy	Post-Dakar period[1]
Singapore	Core Research Program	Centre for Research in Pedagogy and Practice	Pre-school to secondary	Lan, math, sci, ICT	2003
Solomon Islands	National Assessment	MoE; SPBEA	Grades 4, 6	Literacy, numeracy	Post-Dakar period[1]
Thailand	Effectiveness study (pilot schools)	IPST	Grades 3, 6, 9	Sci, math	2003–2004, 2006
	Nationwide Assessment		Grades 3, 6, 9	Sci, math	2005
	National Achievement Study	National Institute of Education Testing Service	Grades 6, 9, 12	Thai, math, English, sci (only 2003)	Yearly since 2001
Tonga	National Assessment	MoE; SPBEA	Grade 4	Literacy, numeracy	Post-Dakar period[1]
Tuvalu	National Assessment	MoE; SPBEA	Grades 4, 6	Literacy, numeracy	Post-Dakar period[1]
Vanuatu	National Assessment	MoE; SPBEA	Grades 4, 6	Literacy, numeracy	Post-Dakar period[1]
Viet Nam	Reading and Mathematics Assessment Study	MoE; World Bank	Grade 5	Reading, math	2001

1. The exact year of the assessment is uncertain, but the evidence would appear to indicate that it took place sometime after the 2000 World Education Forum in Dakar.

* Information for this country should be treated with caution, as it has not been confirmed by national experts.

··· Information not available.

Table 4: Latin America and the Caribbean

Country	Name or description of assessment study	Organization/institution(s) responsible for assessment	Target population	Curricular subject(s) assessed	Year(s)
Anguilla*	Test of Standards	MoE	Grades 3, 5, 6	Lan, math	Since 1992
Argentina	Operativo Nacional de Evaluación	MoE, Dirección Nacional de Información y Evaluación de la Calidad Educativa	Grades 3, 6/7, 9 (primary or basic), 5/6 (secondary) (variable)	Lan, math, sci, soc sci (variable)	Yearly from 1993 to 2000 and 2002 to 2003, then every 2 years
Bahamas	Grade Level Assessment Test	Testing and Evaluation Section, MoE	Grade 3	English, lan, math	Since 1984
			Grade 6	English lan, math, sci, social studies	
Belize	Belize Junior Achievement Test	Assessment and Evaluation Unit, MoE	Grade 3	Lan, math	Yearly since 2000
	Primary School Examination		Grade 6	English, math, sci	Yearly since 2000
Bolivia	Sistema de Medición y Evaluación de la Calidad de la Educación	MoE	Grades 1, 3, 6, 8 (primary), 4 (secondary)	Lan, math	Yearly from 1996 to 2000
Brazil	National System of Evaluation of Basic Education	MoE, INEP	Grades 1, 3, 4, 5, 7, 8, 11 (variable)	Lan, math, sci, soc sci (variable)	1990–2005 (variable)
	National Secondary Education Examination	INEP	Last year of primary	Problem solving	Yearly from 1998 to 2006
Chile	Prueba de Evaluación del Rendimiento Escolar	MoE; Universidad Católica	Grades 4, 8	Lan, math, sci, soc sci	1982, 1983, 1984
	Sistema de Medición de Calidad de la Educación	MoE	Grades 4, 8 and year 2 secondary (variable)	Lan, math, sci, soc sci, behaviour (variable)	Yearly from 1988 to 2006
Colombia	Medición y Evaluación de Aprendizajes	MoE, ICFES	Grades 3, 5, 7, 9	Lan, math	Yearly from 1991 to 1994
	Pruebas Evaluación de la Educación Básica – SABER	MoE	Grades 3, 5, 7, 9 (variable)	Lan, math, sci	Yearly from 1997 to 2005
	Exámenes de Estado	MoE, ICFES	Grade 11	Lan, math, sci, soc sci	Yearly from 1980 to 2006
Costa Rica	Pruebas de Conocimientos	MoE; Universidad de Costa Rica	Grades 3, 5, 7, 9 (variable)	Lan, math, sci, soc sci	Yearly from 1986 to 1997
	Pruebas de conclusión y acreditación de la educación básica	MoE	Cicles I, II, III (basic education)	Lan, math, sci, soc sci	Yearly from 1996 to 2005
	Pruebas Nacionales de Bachillerato		Secondary school		Yearly from 1988 to 2006
Cuba	Pruebas de Aprendizaje	MoE, Sistema de Evaluación de la Calidad de la Educación, Instituto de Ciencias Pedagógicas	Grades 3, 4, 6, 9, 12	Lan, math	1975, 1996, 1997, 1998, 2000, 2002
Dominican Republic	Sistema de Pruebas Nacionales	MoE; IADB; World Bank	Grades 8 (primary) and 4 (secondary)	Lan, math, sci, soc sci	Yearly from 1991 to 2003
Ecuador	Pruebas APRENDO	MoE; World Bank; Universidad Católica	Grades 3, 7, 10	Lan, math	Yearly from 1996 to 2000
El Salvador	Sistema Nacional de Evaluación	MoE; World Bank; USAID	Pre-school, grades 1–6, 9, and year 2 secondary (variable)	Lan, math, sci, soc sci, health education	Yearly from 1993 to 2001
	Pruebas de Aprendizaje y Aptitudes para Egresados de Educación Media	MoE	Grades 2, 3 (secondary) and technical education	Lan, math, sci, soc sci	Yearly from 1997 to 2004
	Evaluación censal de logros de aprendizaje en educación básica	MoE, Dirección Nacional de Monitoreo y Evaluación	Grades 3, 6, 9	Lan, math	2005
	Logros de aprendizaje de educación básica en El Salvador	MoE	Grade 1	Lan, math	2005–2006
Guatemala	Sistema Nacional de Medición del Logro Académico	MoE; World Bank; Universidad del Valle de Guatemala	Grades 3, 7, and years 2, 5 secondary (variable)	Lan, math, sci, soc sci (variable)	Yearly from 1992 to 1996
	Programa Nacional de Evaluación del Rendimiento Escolar		Grades 1, 3, 6	Lan, math	1998, 1999, 2000, 2004
	Dirección General de Educación Bilingüe Intercultural	MoE; IADB	Grades 1, 3	Lan, math	2003
	Programa Nacional de Evaluación del Rendimiento Escolar	MoE	Grade 6 and year 6 secondary	Lan, math	2005

Education for All Global Monitoring Report 2008

Table 4 (continued)

Country	Name or description of assessment study	Organization/institution(s) responsible for assessment	Target population	Curricular subject(s) assessed	Year(s)
Guyana	National Grade Two Assessment	MoE; National Centre for Educational Resource Development	Grade 2	Math, English, reading	Yearly since 2001
	National Grade Six Assessment	MoE	Grade 6	Math, English, social studies, sci	2007
	National Grade Nine Examination		Grade 9	Math, English, social studies, sci	Post-Dakar period[1]
Haiti	Évaluation des acquis scolaires (as part of PARQE)	MoE; EU	Grades 1, 3, 5	Creole, French, math	2004–2005
Honduras	Proyecto de Eficiencia de la Educación Primaria	MoE	Grades 1–5	Lan, math, sci, soc sci	1990–1994
	Evaluaciones Nacionales del Rendimiento Académico	Unidad de Medición de Calidad Educativa	Grades 3–6 (variable)	Lan, math, sci (variable)	1997–2000, 2002, 2004
Jamaica	Grade One Readiness Inventory	MoE	Grade 1 (pre-entry)	Numeracy, literacy, colouring skills, visual comprehension	Since 1999
	Grade Three Diagnostic Test		Grade 3	Lan, math	
	Grade Four Literacy Test		Grade 4	Literacy	
	Grade Six Achievement Test		Grade 6	Math, lan, arts, social studies, sci, writing	
Mexico	Sistema Nacional de Evaluación Educativa de la Educación Primaria	MoE	Grades 3, 4, 5, 6	Lan, math, sci, soc sci	Yearly from 1996 to 2000
	Estándares Nacionales	MoE, INEE	Grades 2, 4, 5, 6	Lan, math	Yearly from 1997 to 2004
	Aprovechamiento Escolar – Carrera Magistral		Grades 3–6 and years 1–3 secondary	Lan, math, sci, soc sci, foreign lan	Yearly from 1994 to 2006
	Instrumento para el Diagnóstico de Alumnos de Nuevo Ingreso Secundaria	MoE	Grade 6	Reading, verbal and numerical reasoning	Yearly from 1995 to 2006
	Exámenes de la Calidad y el Logro Educativos		Grades 3, 6 and year 3 secondary	Spanish, math	2006
	Evaluación Nacional del Logro Académico en Centros Escolares		Grades 3–6 and year 3 secondary	Spanish, math	2007
Nicaragua	Evaluación del Currículo Transformado	MoE	Grades 4, 5 and year 3 secondary	Lan, math	1996, 1997
	Sistema Nacional de Evaluación de la Educación Básica y Media	USAID; UNESCO	Grades 3, 6	Lan, math	2002
Panama	Programa de Pruebas de Diagnóstico	MoE; various agencies	Grades 3, 6 primary and 6 secondary	Lan, math	1985, 1986, 1987, 1988, 1992
	Coordinación Educativa y Cultural Centroamericana (CECE)		Years 1–6 secondary	Lan, math	1995
	Sistema Nacional de Evaluación de la Calidad de la Educación	MoE; CECE	Grades 3, 6, 9	Lan, math, sci, soc sci (variable)	1999, 2000, 2001
Paraguay	Sistema Nacional de Evaluación del Proceso Educativo	MoE; IADB	Grades 3, 6, 9, 12	Lan, math, sci, soc sci (variable)	Yearly from 1996 to 2001
Peru	Evaluaciones Nacionales de la Unidad de Medición de la Calidad	MoE	Grades 2, 4, 6 (primary) and 3–5 (secondary) (variable)	Lan, math, sci, soc sci, citizenship (variable)	1996, 1998, 2001, 2004
Saint Kitts and Nevis*	Test of Standards	MoE	Grades 3–6	Lan, math, sci, social studies	Probably post-Dakar period
Uruguay	Evaluaciones Nacionales de la Unidad de Medición de Resultados Educativos	Administración Nacional de Educación Publica	Pre-school, grades 1–4, 6 (variable)	Lan, math, sci, soc sci, behaviour, cognitive and affective development (variable)	1996, 1998, 1999, 2001, 2002, 2006
Venezuela	Sistema Nacional de Medición y Evaluación del Aprendizaje	MoE; World Bank; Univ. Católica; Centro Nacional para el Mejoramiento de la Enseñanza en Ciencia	Grade 6	Lan, math	1998

1. The exact year of the assessment is uncertain, but the evidence would appear to indicate that it took place sometime after the 2000 World Education Forum in Dakar.

* Information for this country should be treated with caution, as it has not been confirmed by national experts.

Education for All Global Monitoring Report

8
0
0
2

Summary of national policies to advance EFA since 2000 in thirty countries

Country	Institutional environment	Measures to expand access	Measures to improve learning
Arab States			
EGYPT **Main achievements** • Increased pre-primary GER by 54%. • Maintained high NER in primary education amid demographic pressures. • Achieved large increase in adult literacy rate. **Main challenges** • Further improving low pre-primary coverage. • Redressing regional and income disparities in access to primary education. • Continuing to reduce the large number of illiterates, especially women.	• 2006 General Framework for Education Policies: eight strategic approaches, including decentralization, national standards, school-based reform and strengthened partnerships with civil society, private sector and local government. • Establishment of a Strategic Planning Unit, to improve and decentralize planning and management, with similar decentralized units at governorate level. • Movement towards school-based management, including school-development planning and standards-based self-assessment. • 2005 ministerial decree mandating establishment of Boards of Trustees, Parents and Teachers in each school, which can collect and spend local contributions.	• Improved coordination among government agencies, e.g. recent establishment of Early Childhood Coordination Committee with broad representation. • Construction of pre-primary classrooms to increase access in disadvantaged areas. • School construction, targeting rural and poorest governorates in Upper Egypt with low levels of girls' enrolment. • Several successful initiatives to increase girls' access: one-classroom schools, community schools, small schools, girl-friendly schools, other programmes targeting marginalized girls. Children with disabilities: teacher training in special needs, integration into community schools.	• Standards-based curriculum for grades 1 to 12. • Professional development programmes for teachers using ICT (e.g. digital education enhancement project). • Development of different types of contracts with adult education teachers.
MOROCCO **Main achievements** • Increased by 20% primary education NER and decreased by 53% the number of out-of-school children while reducing subnational disparities. • Reduced gender disparity in primary education. • Increased adult literacy rate. **Main challenges** • Continuing to reduce the large numbers of out-of-school children and illiterate youth and adults.	• 2005 National Human Development Initiative to tackle exclusion and seek intersectoral synergies. • Public sector management reform, which has established monitoring, capacity-building in the civil service and movement towards decentralization and community-level management. • 2000–2009 National Education and Training Charter promoting universal basic schooling, higher-quality teaching, improved governance and girls' education. • Reform of education and training system, decentralizing services and creating public regional academies with independent decision-making and management authority. • Strengthened monitoring and evaluation. • Establishment of participatory school management committees, with planning and special financing opportunities at individual school level.	**ECCE and basic education** • Expanded school infrastructure with priority to disadvantaged areas and groups, particularly rural areas and girls (e.g. integrating pre-primary classes into primary schools, latrines for girls). • Incentives for girls' enrolment: conditional food aid in rural areas, boarding facilities, boarding grants. • Integration classes for slightly to moderately disabled pupils and access facilities. **Youth and adults** • Four literacy programmes, differing in terms of populations targeted and operators running them in collaboration with the central government agency for literacy and NFE. • NFE programmes since late 1990s, focused on out-of-school children, including street and working children.	• Revised curricula, more responsive to local circumstances, in both the formal and non-formal sectors. Improved production and distribution of textbooks and teacher guides to disadvantaged regions and groups. Decentralized responsibilities for equipment procurement and distribution. • Teams in regional academies to prepare and introduce regional and local curricula. Berber language teaching in primary school, particularly in Berber regions. • Project to expand use of ICT in teaching, focusing mainly on educational equipment, training and content. • To cope with growing enrolment, regional recruitment of temporary teachers who are progressively integrated into the public-sector system. • Measures to encourage and motivate teachers: competitive examinations for internal promotion, improved benefits. • Learning assessment mechanisms: reintroduction of certificates at end of primary education cycle and lower secondary. • Establishment of examination centre to standardize rules for preparing, administering and marking tests, to create test-item banks and analyse results.
YEMEN **Main achievements** • Increased by 31% primary education NER. • Improved gender parity at all levels of education. • Increased adult literacy rate by 17%. **Main challenges** • Improving very low pre-primary GER. • Reducing large number of out-of-school children. • Reversing large fall in survival rate to grade 5.	• 2002 National Basic Education Strategy, which aims for UPE and school quality, with emphasis on girls' access. • Ongoing development of unified monitoring system of the national strategy. • Lack of ECCE in national education policies; weak role of government in the sector. • Priority on girls' and women's education: National Girls' Education Strategy, establishment of girls' education unit in MoE (2006), gender as cross-cutting theme in PRSP. • Capacity-building to identify gaps and design strategies, especially to improve girls' education.	**ECCE** • Work with religious leaders and local communities to change perceptions about early childhood and girls' education. **Basic education** • Increase in coeducational and female-only schools, particularly in rural areas, and reduction of male-only schools. Sustained construction of schools, though not enough to meet enrolment growth. • Waiving of school fees for girls in all grades of primary school and for boys in grades 1 to 3 in 2006.	• Revised curriculum and teaching methods to make schools more 'girl-friendly'. • New ECCE diploma at Sana'a University to increase numbers of qualified teachers. • Increased numbers of female teachers (but greater efforts needed, especially in rural areas).

(Continued)

Country	Institutional environment	Measures to expand access	Measures to improve learning
• Further reducing large number of illiterate youth and adults. • Improving low levels of most indicators, especially for girls and women and in rural areas.			
Central and Eastern Europe			
ALBANIA **Main achievements** • Increased by 13.5% pre-primary GER. **Main challenges** • Reversing decreases in primary education NER and survival rate to grade 5. • Redressing disparities in enrolment and completion of primary education by income groups and geographical location. • Improving learning outcomes from low levels measured in international assessments.	• National Education Strategy 2004–2015, prepared with involvement of civil society. Focus on improved governance, quality of teaching and learning, financing of pre-university education, capacity-building, development of vocational and technical education. National Strategy for Socio-Economic Development makes education one of highest priorities in next ten years, supported by funds from Poverty Reduction Strategy Credit. • Distribution of provision and funding among three government levels; shared responsibility with local governments in funding school operating expenses and maintenance. • Ongoing MoE development of educational planning and policy analysis unit, and management information system, both requiring capacity-building efforts.	**Basic education** • Transfer programmes (cash and in-kind) to stimulate enrolment and completion of basic education of children from poorest households.	• Free textbooks for all basic education pupils. • Restructured Institute of Pedagogical Studies with curriculum and teacher training centres. Application of new curriculum, including assessment standards. • Financial incentives to teach in rural areas. • 2001 establishment of independent National Assessment and Evaluation Centre, in charge of national examinations. Sample-based learning assessments in basic education grades since 2002.
TURKEY **Main achievements** • Increased to 61% pre-primary education GER. **Main challenges** • Further improving continued low coverage of pre-primary education. • Redressing disparities in girls' educational attainments and subnational disparities in availability of infrastructure, learning resources and teachers. • Reducing the large numbers of out-of-school children and of young and adult illiterates.	• Two waves of education reform: after Jomtien, a focus on increasing access; now a focus on improving content and quality in education while expanding access. • National plan of action after Dakar, but lacking any role as a benchmark for evaluating and monitoring progress towards EFA. No specific education sector plan in earlier National Development Plan, though National Development Plan 2007–2013 addresses EFA goals: ECCE, universal coverage and quality of basic education; also priority on girls, students in rural areas and addressing dropout as an important policy objective. • 2003 Law on Public Fiscal Administration and Control: use of public funds linked with development plans and programmes, with emphasis on fiscal transparency and accountability, strategic planning and performance-based budgeting. Preparation of MoE's strategic plan (began in 2006). • Recognition of need to restructure the central administration of education, with 2004 reform plan but very slow implementation. • Partial transfer of responsibility to municipalities for building and maintaining public schools (Law on Municipalities). • Important role of NGOs promoting EFA policies, e.g. through campaigns to expand ECCE ('7 is too late'). • Emergence of civil society monitoring groups to inform public of EFA advances and contribute to the process. First joint report (2005).	**Basic education** • Extension of compulsory basic education from five to eight years in 1997, accompanied by accelerated construction and teacher recruitment, particularly between 1997 and 2002. • Campaign ('100 % Support to Education') to stimulate private sector contributions to education, especially infrastructure investments through tax incentives. • Strategies to increase schooling in dispersed rural areas: busing and free boarding schools, especially since 1997. • Conditional cash transfers targeting regular school attendance in basic education by poorest households. • Major campaign (2003–2005) to increase girls' access ('Let's go to school, girls!'), with intersectoral government coordination.	• 2003 Board of Education launch of comprehensive curriculum reform in all grades of basic education: change of pedagogy, focus on skills, measurements to include process as well as outcomes. Accompanied by new textbooks and teacher guides, in-service teacher training. • Distance-learning approach to meet demand for English language and pre-school teachers since 2000. • New staffing norms to reduce teacher shortages in disadvantaged regions; increased transparency in assignment and promotion mechanisms (use of assessment tests), school-based plans for enhancing teacher professional development. • National assessments of basic education since 1992, with several subject evaluations every three years. Participation in international assessments. • Improved but inadequate efforts on gender sensitivity in textbooks. • Distribution of free textbooks.
Central Asia			
MONGOLIA **Main achievements** • Increased pre-primary education GER. • Moderately increased survival rate to grade 5 and gender parity. **Main challenges** • Reversing the fall of primary education NER.	• Master Education Plan (2006–2015): emphasis on vulnerable children, herder communities and internal migration from rural to urban areas.	**Basic education** • Subsidies for schools favouring disadvantaged regions (Kazakh minority area). • Subsidies and dormitories for children from herder communities. • Pilot programmes for children with special needs.	• Multilingual instruction in schools serving Kazakh minority, but hampered by lack of textbooks.

ANNEX

(Continued)

Country	Institutional environment	Measures to expand access	Measures to improve learning
TAJIKISTAN **Main achievements** ● Moderately increased survival rate to grade 5. Continued to increase primary education NER. ● Increased gender parity. **Main challenges** ● Improving low indicators of school quality.	● Social Economic Development Programme, with strong poverty reduction strategy. ● 2004 Law on Education and government education plan: promotion of participatory governance, higher teacher salaries and better quality of education. ● Monitoring through a database children's well-being.	● Special measures for children in rural areas. ● Special measures for out-of-school children aged 6 to 15. ● Ban on recruitment of pupils for labour in agricultural activities.	● Attempts to change curriculum. ● Improvement to teacher qualifications through in-service programmes. ● Distribution of free textbooks to disadvantaged students.

East Asia and the Pacific

Country	Institutional environment	Measures to expand access	Measures to improve learning
CAMBODIA **Main achievements** ● Increased primary education NER and survival rate to grade 5. **Main challenges** ● Reducing low levels of survival rate to grade 5, gender parity and adult literacy.	● Education Strategic Plans 2000–2005 and 2006–2010, incorporating Dakar EFA goals. ● Move towards sector-wide approach involving much dialogue and negotiation with donors. ● Decentralization, with some funding direct to schools for first time. ● All schools given operational budgets (2001). ● Capacity-building to support decentralization.	**ECCE** ● Emphasis on disadvantaged communities. Pre-school year for 5- to 6-year-olds, home-based and family support programmes for children under 5. **Basic education** ● Construction of schools, especially in remote areas. ● Multigrade approaches to reduce number of 'incomplete schools' in border, remote and ethnic minority areas. ● Multiple shifts in overcrowded schools. ● Advocacy on benefits of girls' education through partnerships with NGOs, CSOs. ● 'Safe boarding places' for girls. **Youth and adults** ● Re-entry classes for joining primary or lower secondary. ● Equivalency courses combining basic education with practical livelihood and life skills. ● NFE for 'hard to reach' groups.	● Improvement of toilets and water access in new and existing schools. ● New curriculum in basic education grades, based on achievement standards and more gender sensitive. ● Inclusion of locally relevant life skills and HIV/AIDS programmes in schools. ● Pilot bilingual education programmes in ethnic minority areas. ● Incentives to recruit teachers locally and attract teachers to rural areas, especially female teachers. ● Continuous in-service training and teacher development through school clusters. ● Automatic grade promotion.
CHINA **Main achievements** ● Increased adult literacy rate. **Main challenges** ● Redressing disparities to the detriment of rural areas in access to primary education and quality.	● Strategic plan aligned with EFA goals. ● Decision on Reform and Development of Basic Education (2001), covering fiscal management, quality, curriculum and teacher education. ● Decision on Further Enhancing Rural Education (2003): policies to redress disparities affecting rural areas. ● Compulsory Education Law (revised 2006), stressing right to a free education without discrimination on the basis of gender, ethnicity, race, wealth or regional status. ● Management training for school principals. ● Public sector management reform, addressing capacity constraints.	**Basic education** ● Expanded school construction and boarding facilities, especially in poor provinces and rural areas. ● Extension of policy to offset schooling costs: 'Two Exemptions One Subsidy', waiving tuition and other charges, with free textbooks, subsidized boarding. ● Reform of subnational funding of basic education, with higher share for poorest regions. ● Educational campaigns encouraging girls' enrolment in poor western provinces. **Youth and adults** ● One example among several: Action to Eliminate Women's Illiteracy (government partnership with All China Women's Federation), combining literacy, agriculture, women's rights.	● New national curriculum, phased in since 1999: active learning, problem-solving, participatory approach, more autonomy for schools in curriculum management; reform of student evaluation system (but lack of funds and teacher training impedes implementation). ● Increased teacher recruitment in rural areas: free education provided graduates commit to three years in rural schools; university internships in rural schools; Master of Education for Rural Schools combining higher-level studies with teaching in rural schools. ● Improvement to teacher qualifications via teacher networks and distance education. ● Distribution of free textbooks to disadvantaged students.
INDONESIA **Main achievements** ● Increased pre-primary education GER. ● Increased adult literacy rate. **Main challenges** ● Reducing large number of out-of-school children. ● Improving survival rate to grade 5 from current low level.	● 2003 EFA National Plan of Action: detailed EFA targets for 2015, integrated into 2005–2009 MoE strategy. Each province has own strategic education plan. ● Decentralized education since 2001; overall strategy of community-based school management. ● National movement for completion of basic education involving parents, communities, teachers, leaders, NGOs.	**ECCE** ● Expanded pre-primary schools in rural areas. **Basic education** ● Multiple shifts in overcrowded schools. ● Pilots to test other approaches to reach poor and remote communities. ● School-community partnerships to support students at risk of dropping out. **Youth and adults** ● Non-formal re-entry and equivalency programmes.	● Outcome-based curriculum. ● Mother tongue in early grades outside Bahasa Indonesia areas. ● Efforts to improve teacher qualifications.

Summary of national policies to advance EFA since 2000 in thirty countries

(Continued)

Country	Institutional environment	Measures to expand access	Measures to improve learning
LAO PEOPLE'S DEMOCRATIC REPUBLIC **Main achievements** ● Reduced number of out-of-school children. ● Increased survival rate to grade 5. **Main challenges** ● Improving low levels of most indicators.	● Law of 2000: free basic education for all. ● Ethnic Minorities Committee under National Assembly. ● Since 2004, strengthened monitoring capacity of MoE.	**Basic education** ● Boarding schools for ethnic minorities. ● Since 2004, community-based school construction initiative. ● Community Grants Programme for poorest. ● Since 1993, inclusive education programme, developing learning materials and training teachers.	● Since 2001, revised textbooks and new teacher guides. ● Multilingual materials and teaching, with Teacher Development Centre coordinating curriculum, textbooks and teacher guides for all teacher training colleges. ● Since 2000, revised pre- and in-service teacher training. ● Upgrading of contract teachers.
PHILIPPINES **Main achievements** ● Close to achieving UPE enrolment. **Main challenges** ● Raising low levels of pre-primary GER and survival to grade 5.	● Governance of Basic Education Act (2001), defining government responsibility for EFA, including non-formal learning centres for out-of-school youth and adults and decentralized school-based management. Complemented in 2005 by Basic Education Sector Reform Agenda. ● Philippine National Action Plan for EFA 2015 Goals (2006): focus on out-of-school youths and adults, universal completion of full cycle of basic education, community involvement. ● Medium-Term Philippine Development Plan 2005–2010: explicit attention to anchoring goals of Philippine basic education in EFA by 2015. ● Public expenditure management system to improve link between planning and budgeting. ● Monitoring system since 2002: quality, access and internal efficiency of basic education.	**ECCE** ● 2000 Early Childhood Care and Development Law, four strategies: strengthening formal pre-school through whole-child development curriculum; targeting disadvantaged children through contracts with non-state sector; assuring ECCE exposure for all incoming grade 1 students; including ECCE in teacher education. **Basic education** ● Mobilization of civil society groups and parents to support school construction and improvements, e.g. Adopt-a-School and Brigada Eskwela programmes. ● Multiple shifts in overcrowded schools (2004). ● Multigrade classes in distant and remote areas. ● Food for School, an in-kind conditional transfer programme for children in pre-school and grade 1 in poorest areas. ● NFE programmes through school-community partnerships (Modified In-School Off-School Approach) to assist children in difficulty during final half of elementary education. **Youth and adults** ● Bureau of Alternative Learning System. Also, two regular NFE programmes: Basic Literacy Programme and Accreditation, offering community-based learning for illiterate youth and adults with focus on life skills; and Equivalency Programme for youth and adults who have dropped out of formal elementary or secondary education. ● Alternative Learning System based on Indigenous Peoples Core Curriculum.	● Flexible curriculum to accommodate cultural diversity. Madrasa Education programme, setting standards and ensuring madrasa 'equivalency'. ● Every Child a Reader (2004) with goal of reading with comprehension by grade 3. ● Goal of one textbook per pupil for core subjects. ● Rainbow Spectrum: deploys teachers to hard to reach areas. ● New teacher education curriculum (2005): more experiential courses. ● Teacher Education Development Programme, including competency standards for teacher performance and school-based training in science and mathematics. ● Move to school-based management, improving quality through participatory school improvement planning, training of principals and school report cards. ● Participations in international learning assessments. ● Comprehensive policy for application of ICT in education, as part of national development policy.
VIET NAM **Main achievements** ● Improved quality indicators. ● Increased literacy levels and gender parity. **Main challenges** ● Decreasing large number of out-of-school children.	● National EFA Action Plan 2003–2015, linked to government's Education Development Strategy 2000–2010. ● Administrative reform and decentralization to provincial and district levels. National targeted programme of funding for poorer provinces and support for provincial EFA planning, guided by national framework. ● Decentralization to provincial and district level of school improvement planning and funding of teaching and learning resources other than textbooks.	● ECCE programmes with emphasis on ethnic minority and poor urban areas. **Basic education** ● Classroom construction and rehabilitation targeting rural and ethnic minority areas. ● Multigrade classes in mountainous ethnic minority areas. ● Multiple shifts in overcrowded schools. ● Primary Education for Disadvantaged Children targeting unreached children in poorest provinces. ● Strong mobilization campaign known as Socialisation of Education, identifying 'compulsory education officers' in each school who follow up on unenrolled children and dropouts. ● 'Equalization programme: evening classes for primary and secondary out-of-school children, using regular primary and secondary teachers and facilities.	● New learner-centred curriculum. ● Pilots of bilingual approaches in ethnic minority areas. ● Better textbook provision, linked to development of private publishing; rental fees replaced by loan programme. ● Teacher incentives for work in remote and ethnic minority regions. ● Comprehensive reporting system on learning achievement and progress in schools.

(Continued)

Country	Institutional environment	Measures to expand access	Measures to improve learning
Latin America and the Caribbean			
BRAZIL **Main achievements** ● Increased by 9% pre-primary education GER. ● Sustained high levels of primary education enrolment while reducing subnational disparities. ● Reduced number of out-of-school children by over 50%. ● Decreased repetition rates and PTRs in primary education. **Main challenges** ● Redressing income and geographical disparities in pre-primary enrolment. ● Further reducing large numbers of out-of-school children and illiterate adults. ● Reversing declines in primary and lower secondary learning achievements as measured by national assessments.	● 1988 Constitution: mandatory and free elementary education, with defined governance responsibilities and minimum levels of federal and subnational funding. National Education Plan (2001), formulated by civil society and government: goals for 2010, promotion of development of subnational plans and ways to reduce social and regional discrepancies in education access and survival. ● Educational Development Plan (2007): focus on basic education, tying federal transfers to improved quality and school performance. ● Civil society involvement: since 2005, All for Education movement, involving NGOs, educators, businesses, with aim of achieving basic education of good quality for all by 2022, the bicentenary of Brazilian independence. ● Promotion of school-based management. Since 1998, support from Fundescola for improvement in school quality by expanding school autonomy, promoting strategic planning and funding school projects. ● Creation of the Secretariat of Continuing Literacy and Diversity (SECAD) in 2004 to promote youth and adult education in an integrated way.	**ECCE** ● Normative framework for ECCE expansion: 1996 National Education Guidelines and Framework Law, making early childhood education the first stage of basic education and giving responsibility to municipalities. 2001 National Education Plan: quality and expansion goals, including for children under age 3. 2006 incorporation of early childhood education in Fundeb/Fundef, fund that redistributes resources for education across regions. **Basic education** ● More schools, including in indigenous areas. ● Fundeb/Fundef (1996): assuring minimum allocation for public basic education, redistributed at subnational level according to number of students and funding needs. ● Conditional cash transfer programme to increase access and retention in primary school among children from disadvantaged households: now integrated with Bolsa Familia; coverage planned for 15- to 17-year-olds. ● Programme for Eradication of Child Labour: providing conditional subsidy for children attending school and not working, plus extracurricular support and after-school activities (Jornada Ampliada); working with families, monitoring compliance with child labour laws. ● Expansion of education to children with disabilities under 1996 framework law. **Youth and adults** ● Accelerated learning programmes. ● National literacy programme funding for initiatives.	● Introduction of continuous progression within cycles in over 10% of schools, to reduce failure and repetition. ● Improvement to teacher qualifications in pre-primary. ● Pilot of performance-based incentives for teachers in one state (2005). ● Learning assessment through sample-based Brazilian Educational System Assessment (SAEB), which compares basic education results over time, and Prova Brasil, providing accountability through school-level data on test scores. ● Promotion of ICT in education through ProInfo, which installs laboratories in schools and creates regional Education Technology Centres for training and support.
DOMINICAN REPUBLIC **Main achievements** ● Continued expansion of primary education. ● Increased survival rate to grade 5. **Main challenges** ● Redressing disparities in access to pre-primary and in retention in primary education. ● Reversing increased repetition rates in primary education.	● For *Plan Decenal* 1993–2002 and General Law of Education 1997, national debate on ways to increase access and improve quality. After evaluation of results (but no national dialogue), Strategic Plan for Dominican Republic Educational Development 2003–2012. ● 2005 Presidential Forum for the Excellence of Education: representatives from schools, parent organizations and business, supporting revitalization and reform of education. ● Limited decentralization, with schools preparing education projects but not taking decisions. Institutionalized parent and community participation, limited to management of school equipment and local fundraising.	**ECCE** ● Initial Education Strengthening Programme to expand and improve pre-primary schooling for 5-year-olds, especially in rural areas. **Basic education** ● Cash transfer programme Solidarity, stimulating demand for basic education. ● Multiphase Programme for Equality in Basic Education, since 2005: to reduce repetition and dropout in poor, urban settings through remedial and accelerated learning. Strengthening Education for Diversity: creating inclusive conditions for children with different educational needs.	● In *Plan Decenal*, curricular reform but no changes in teaching practices. Improvement to teacher qualifications through new curriculum, post-graduate courses, transformation of teacher training schools into higher education institutions. ● Textbook production in several subjects but inefficient distribution. ● Use of ICT in teaching upgrade programme.
GUATEMALA **Main achievements** ● Increased by 14% primary NER. Achieved large fall in out-of-school children, by 69%. ● Improved survival rate to grade 5. ● Decreased by 16% repetition rate. ● Decreased by 18% PTR.	● Guatemala Education Plan 2004–2007; National Education for All Plan 2004–2015; Long-term National Education Plan 2004–2023. ● Emphasis on universalizing education, quality, citizenship, gender equity, recognition of culturally diverse and multilingual nation. ● Civil society participation: Vision for Education, involving fifty-two leaders of social sectors and their recommendations to expand and improve education.	**ECCE** ● Community Pre-school Education Readiness Centres: preparing children aged 6 and over from various ethnic groups to enter primary school. **Basic education** ● Grant programmes to increase enrolment among disadvantaged children, including girls, and child labourers.	● School meals, primarily in rural areas. ● Let's Pass First Grade, to improve promotion rates at beginning of primary. ● Free textbooks and materials. ● Teacher training and phased implementation of pupil-centred primary school curriculum, with focus on capacities, skills and knowledge by grade.

Summary of national policies to advance EFA since 2000 in thirty countries

(Continued)

Country	Institutional environment	Measures to expand access	Measures to improve learning
Main challenges • Tackling persistent disparities in school access and retention, in youth and adult literacy and in learning outcomes to the detriment of women, indigenous peoples and rural and lower-income households. • Further improving the still low survival rate to grade 5. • Addressing school infrastructure vulnerability to recurrent natural phenomena.	• National System of Education indicators to monitor plan goals. • MoE measures to increase accountability, including school reports. • Social audits of MoE programmes, carried out by civil society. • Continuing movement towards school-based management, aimed in particular at increasing access and quality in rural areas.	**Youth and adults** • National Literacy Committee: literacy and post-literacy programmes in Spanish and seventeen Maya languages, in partnership with government and NGOs.	• Consolidation of national evaluation system, with tests in Spanish and mathematics since 1998. and recent participation in regional assessments. • Use of ICT in teaching upgrade programme.
MEXICO **Main achievements** • Accelerated pre-primary coverage, reaching GER of 93% in 2005. • Maintained high NER and survival rate to grade 5. **Main challenges** • Removing disparities in completion of basic education and in youth and adult literacy, affecting in particular indigenous population. • Eliminating socio-economic disparities in student performance levels measured by national assessments, and improving low performance levels at the end of basic education.	• 2001 law for compulsory pre-primary education from age 3. • Transfer of education management to state and local governments in 1993, though design and implementation of curriculum are centralized.	**ECCE** • Phased implementation of compulsory education law together with school construction. **Basic education** • Oportunidades-Progresa, conditional cash transfer programme to increase access and retention in primary and secondary education among disadvantaged children; since 1997 in rural areas, 2001 in urban areas. Other grants to students at risk of dropping out. • National Education Promotion Council (CONAFE) to reduce disparities in access and learning in pre-primary and basic education in rural and indigenous communities.	• *Enciclomedia*: digitizes fifth and sixth grade textbooks to familiarize students with new technology and help teachers improve their teaching. • National reading programme: creates classroom libraries so primary school pupils can improve reading and comprehension skills. • Strengthened bilingual and intercultural education: teacher recruitment and textbook publishing in indigenous languages. • Quality Schools Programme (2001): better schools in disadvantaged urban areas through school-based management projects. • *Carrera Magisterial* ('teaching career'), performance-based incentive programme. • Since 2002, National Institute for Educational Evaluation, national education indicators and learning assessments. Participation in international assessments. • Promotion of ICTs in education: Red Escolar, which installs multimedia laboratories in schools and teacher training institutes, connected to Internet and to Edusat satellite.
NICARAGUA **Main achievements** • Increased by 31% pre-primary school GER. • Increased by 14% primary education NER. • Increased survival rate to grade 5. **Main challenges** • Addressing subnational economic disparities in access to primary school and in retention. • Reducing high repetition rates. • Increasing survival to grade 5 from very low level. • Improving low level of learning achievements in national assessments.	• National Education Plan 2001–2015 and MoE Joint Work Plan 2005–2008, aligned with the National Development Plan aimed at meeting EFA goals Main areas: relevance and quality; extended supply and demand for education; better governance. • First General Law on Education (2006): rights and responsibilities of individuals, society and the state regarding education. Decentralized education management to municipal governments from 2004 to 2007. • Participation of local governments and civil society in formulation of municipal educational plans.	**ECCE** • Expanded community pre-school education centres, located mainly in rural and urban areas of extreme poverty, mostly with teachers lacking formal qualifications. **Basic education** • Grants to reduce school costs for very poor households, especially in rural areas; e.g. Social Protection Network, providing conditional cash transfers to increase enrolment and retention in primary school. • School meal programmes in disadvantaged areas to reduce dropout. • Children with disabilities: endorsement of inclusive education, but disregarded in practice.	• Measures to address early school failure: elimination of automatic promotion, introduction of educational upgrading programme for grades 1 and 2. • Pilot of new curriculum based on competencies. • Efforts by MoE to keep parents informed about school performance; use of national assessment results to address weaknesses (e.g. academic guides, management training for principals).

(Continued)

Country	Institutional environment	Measures to expand access	Measures to improve learning
South and West Asia			
BANGLADESH **Main achievements** ● Close to universal enrolment in primary education. **Main challenges** ● Increasing levels of most other indicators, which remain low.	● Aims of Primary Education Development Programme II (PEDPII, 2002): improve quality and access to primary education, improve management and capacity. ● Policy environment: characterized by high level of donor support and involvement. ● Strict requirements for registration of non-state providers of education, but lack of ongoing supervision and fragmented distribution of oversight responsibilities among government agencies.	**Basic education** ● More schools and classrooms under PEDPII. ● Stipend programme for primary education since 2002. ● Reaching Out of School Projects (2002), which complements PEDPII by enrolling half a million out-of-school children in primary education. ● Stipend programme to increase girls' participation in secondary education.	● School meals at primary level. ● Move towards child-centred education. ● Education for Indigenous Children, operated by BRAC. ● NGO efforts to improve quality: e.g. PLAN Community Learning for children from disadvantaged communities.
INDIA **Main achievements** ● High level of primary education NER. ● Significantly improved adult literacy and gender parity. **Main challenges** ● Providing primary education to socially marginalized minority groups. ● Reducing dropout rate in primary education. ● Improving quality of learning.	● Constitutional amendment (2002) making education for ages 6 to 14 a fundamental right for all. ● National Child Rights Commission (2006). ● Ongoing work to enact a 'right to education' law. ● Memoranda of understanding with non-state providers clarifying responsibilities in service delivery to disadvantaged populations.	**Basic education** ● Since 1975, much expanded Integrated Child Development Scheme covering nutrition, health and pre-school education nationwide. ● Small schools (one teacher/one classroom) to increase access. ● Backward Region Grant Fund to reduce disparities in poorest regions. ● Incentives to increase demand and reduce cost for the poor, particularly girls: midday meals, school uniforms, free textbooks. ● National Programme for Education of Girls at Elementary Level. ● Residential schools for girls. **Youth and adults** ● Programmes such as Jan Shikshan Sansthan, offering vocational training for 14- to 25-year-olds, and Women's Training Centres.	● New National Curriculum Framework (2005): child centred cooperative learning; revised syllabuses and textbooks. ● Assessment of student learning through government (NCERT: National Council of Educational Research and Training) and non-government organizations (Pratham); in Karnataka, state School Quality Assessment Organization. ● Decentralized countrywide on-site support to teachers through Block- and Cluster-level Resource Centres. NCERT: framework for school quality indicators in preparation, for assessing and grading schools. ● Support for principle of mother tongue. In Andhra Pradesh, instruction in eight tribal languages since 2003. ● Distribution of free textbooks to disadvantaged students. ● Promotion of ICTs in education: SchoolsNet, supports creation of schools networks to enhance teaching and learning through collaboration and information sharing.
PAKISTAN **Main achievements** ● Improved primary education NER, literacy and gender parity. **Main challenges** ● Raising low levels of most indicators.	● National Education Plan (2000–2010), National Action Plan for EFA (2001–2015), and short- and medium-term plans. ● Decentralization: responsibility for policy formulation at federal level, with provinces responsible for delivery and teacher training. ● Monitoring a priority; national Education Census.	● Stipend and voucher programmes for girls in secondary education. ● Many NGO non-formal programmes for working children and others: Community School for Gypsy Children, Community Based School Programmes for Girls, Zindagi Trust programmes.	● Twana Pakistan: school nutrition programme for 5- to 12-year-olds. ● Planned new curriculum with focus on integrated national curriculum framework. ● 2002 madrasa reform: introduction of secular subjects into curriculum. ● Gender-sensitive textbooks. ● Examination system emphasizing rote learning. ● 2007 pilot of National Education Assessment System for grades 4, 8. ● Increased use of contract teachers. ● Donor and NGO efforts to improve teacher training: AED Pakistan Teacher Education and Professional Development Programme to upgrade mathematics, science, English-language skills.
Sub-Saharan Africa			
BURKINA FASO **Main achievements** ● Increased by 29% primary education NER while improving gender parity. ● Increased survival rate to grade 5 to 76%. **Main challenges** ● Improving low levels of most indicators.	● 2000 PRSP: focus on primary and non-formal basic education. Ten-year basic education development plan (PDDEB, 2002). ● Civil society involvement in PDDEB through national education coalition. ● Harmonization of donor support to PDDEB. ● Joint Review Missions to improve PDDEB monitoring. ● Centralized public administration, but with 2004 Code for Territorial Communities and 2006 municipal elections marking a new phase in decentralization strategy.	**Basic education** ● High priority on school infrastructure, with 37% increase in number of primary school classrooms since 2001. ● Resources targeted to 20 least-educated provinces and to monitoring. ● Gender equity: waiver of fees for girls in the first year of primary school. ● Literacy: Fund for Literacy and Non-Formal Education.	● Expansion of school canteens in rural areas. ● 2006 convention on school health care and nutrition. ● Expansion of bilingual schools. ● 47% increase in teacher numbers since 2001.

Summary of national policies to advance EFA since 2000 in thirty countries

(Continued)

Country	Institutional environment	Measures to expand access	Measures to improve learning
ERITREA **Main achievements** ● Doubled pre-primary GER. ● Increased by 31% primary NER. **Main challenges** ● Raising still-low levels of most indicators.	● Education Sector Development Programme 2003/4–2007/8: consultation with local stakeholders to improve access, equity and quality, promote science and technology and diversify education. Pivotal in achieving education goals in 2004 Interim PRSP. Consistent with sector reforms in National Economic Policy Framework and Programme. ● Decentralization policy since 1996, though planning, coordination and decision-making remain centralized in practice.	**ECCE** ● Introduction of national policy to support two years of ECCE for each child. ● Establishment, within the framework of 2001–2005 ECCE programme, of ECCE centres, accompanied by increase in number of teachers. **Basic education** ● Design of low-cost but durable school facilities to cut costs. ● Focus on increasing girls' and disadvantaged groups' access, including incentives for girls. New gender education policy and strategy: five-year National Gender Action Plan to create enabling environment. ● Rehabilitation and vocational training for street children. ● Boarding and hostel facilities for disadvantaged ethnic minorities and nomadic groups. ● Mai-Nefhi Teacher Training Institute: reserved for teacher trainees from marginalized, ethnic minority and nomadic groups.	● National Education Policy, road map for reform. New curriculum based on outcomes and interactive, learner-centred approach. Assessment as formative tool. ● Incorporation of HIV/AIDS awareness into basic education curriculum. ● Textbook Production Unit: production of low-cost textbooks, including in 8 Eritrean languages, distributed at 1:1 ratio. ● New curriculum for adult literacy. ● National adult literacy programme, since 1998/99: Bana Radio, operated by MoE, broadcasting literacy lessons in four local languages.
ETHIOPIA **Main achievements** ● Substantially increased primary NER by 106%. ● Significantly improved gender parity at primary level. ● Increased survival rate to grade 5. **Main challenges** ● Improving low level of pre-primary coverage. ● Reducing large numbers of out-of-school children and illiterate youth and adults. ● Addressing regional disparities.	● Since 1994 Education and Training Policy, strong commitment to EFA, especially UPE by 2015. Three subsequent Education Sector Development Programmes (ESDPs): focus on expanding equitable access to primary and vocational education, restructuring education system and improving quality. Linked to government poverty reduction strategy. ● A range of donors supporting education. Regular dialogue and joint sector reviews with government to develop ESDPs. ● Non-state provision: gradual expansion, with better dialogue between NGOs, and government regulation of non-state provision through registration, but concern about quality of teacher training. ● Regular collection of education data by most districts and regions, but weak analysis.	● ESDP 3: affirmative actions for females, pastoral and agro-pastoral groups and those with special needs. Some specific approaches for pastoralist children: mobile schools, boarding hostels. ● Strategies to promote girls' enrolment: community sensitization campaigns, improving safety by accompanying girls to school, reducing distance travelled, improving toilets and sanitation. ● For out-of-school children: alternative basic education, providing link to upper primary; but coverage still low. ● 2006 MoE special needs education strategy.	● Continuous assessment and automatic promotion for grades 1 to 3. ● Teacher reforms with focus on pre- and in-service training. Quotas encouraging more female teachers in rural schools and more women in education management. ● Leadership and Management Programme: nationwide initiative to upgrade skills of primary and secondary school principals. ● Distribution of free textbooks to disadvantaged students. ● Establishment of a Master's programme in Adult Education and Lifelong Learning in 2007.
MOZAMBIQUE **Main achievements** ● Increased by 48% primary NER and improved gender parity. ● Improved by 44% survival rate to grade 5. **Main challenges** ● Extending pre-primary coverage from low level. ● Further expanding primary enrolment, in particular for girls. ● Improving low levels of youth and adult literacy.	● Education Sector Strategic Plan II (2005–2009): based on National Education Policy (1995) as well as ESSP I. Continued commitment to EFA and MDGs. ● Broader strategy of public sector reform, emphasizing decentralisation, improved management, strengthened capacity at all levels. ● Directorate for Adult and Non-Formal Education within MoE, with provincial and district-level representation.	● 2005 abolition of school fees. ● New strategy for adult and non-formal education, based on research and stakeholder consultation. ● Expansion of adult literacy classes.	● New curriculum for primary education: mother tongue instruction in early grades, transition later to national language (also in in-service teacher training). ● Increase in female recruits in pre-service teacher training institutions. ● HIV/AIDS training for teachers and managers. ● Increased management and training for school principals. ● Direct Support to Schools, providing direct grants for learning materials and supplies.

Table 1 (continued)

Country or territory	Total population (000) 2005	Average annual growth rate (%) total population 2005-2010	Average annual growth rate (%) age 0-4 population 2005-2010	Life expectancy at birth (years) 2005-2010 Total	Male	Female	Total fertility rate (children per woman) 2005-2010	HIV prevalence rate (%) in adults (15-49) 2005 Total	% of women among people (age 15+) living with HIV 2005	Orphans due to AIDS (000) 2005
Comoros	798	2.6	1.1	65	63	67	4.3	<0.1	…	…
Congo	3 999	2.9	3.1	54	52	55	6.3	5.3	61	110
Côte d'Ivoire	18 154	1.7	0.7	46	46	47	4.5	7.1	59	450
D. R. Congo	57 549	3.1	3.4	45	44	46	6.7	3.2	58	680
Equatorial Guinea	504	2.2	2.6	42	41	42	5.9	3.2	59	5
Eritrea	4 401	3.1	2.2	56	54	58	5.0	2.4	58	36
Ethiopia	77 431	2.3	1.6	49	48	49	5.4	…	…	…
Gabon	1 384	1.6	0.0	53	53	54	3.5	7.9	59	20
Gambia	1 517	2.3	0.7	58	56	59	4.2	2.4	58	4
Ghana	22 113	1.9	0.6	58	58	59	3.8	2.3	60	170
Guinea	9 402	2.2	1.5	54	54	54	5.5	1.5	68	28
Guinea-Bissau	1 586	2.9	3.1	45	44	47	7.1	3.8	59	11
Kenya	34 256	2.6	3.0	50	51	49	5.0	6.1	62	1 100
Lesotho	1 795	-0.3	-0.6	34	34	34	3.3	23.2	60	97
Liberia	3 283	2.9	3.1	43	42	43	6.8	…	…	…
Madagascar	18 606	2.6	1.4	56	55	57	4.9	0.5	28	13
Malawi	12 884	2.2	1.1	41	42	41	5.7	14.1	59	550
Mali	13 518	2.9	2.5	49	49	50	6.6	1.7	60	94
Mauritius	1 245	0.8	-0.3	73	70	76	1.9	0.6	…	…
Mozambique	19 792	1.8	0.8	42	42	42	5.1	16.1	60	510
Namibia	2 031	1.0	-0.6	46	47	45	3.5	19.6	62	85
Niger	13 957	3.3	2.5	45	45	45	7.5	1.1	59	46
Nigeria	131 530	2.1	1.1	44	44	44	5.3	3.9	62	930
Rwanda	9 038	2.3	2.3	45	43	46	5.2	3.1	57	210
Sao Tome and Principe	157	2.2	1.0	64	63	65	3.6	…	…	…
Senegal	11 658	2.3	1.2	57	56	58	4.5	0.9	59	25
Seychelles	81	0.9	…	…	…	…	…	…	…	…
Sierra Leone	5 525	2.1	2.0	42	41	43	6.5	1.6	60	31
Somalia	8 228	3.1	2.2	49	48	50	6.0	0.9	58	23
South Africa	47 432	0.2	-1.0	44	44	44	2.6	18.8	58	1 200
Swaziland	1 032	-0.4	-0.9	30	31	29	3.5	33.4	57	63
Togo	6 145	2.5	1.4	56	54	57	4.8	3.2	61	88
Uganda	28 816	3.6	4.0	52	51	53	7.1	6.7	58	1 000
United Republic of Tanzania	38 329	1.4	0.1	64	62	67	3.3	6.5	55	710
Zambia	11 668	1.7	1.1	39	40	39	5.2	17.0	57	1 100
Zimbabwe	13 010	0.6	0.1	37	38	36	3.2	20.1	59	1 100

	Sum	Weighted average						Weighted average		
World	6 450 253	1.1	0.5	68	66	70	2.5	1.0	48	15 200
Countries in transition	277 567	0.0	0.3	66	61	72	2.2	…	…	…
Developed countries	1 007 223	0.4	-0.1	75	73	78	1.6	…	…	…
Developing countries	5 165 463	1.3	0.6	67	65	69	2.8	…	…	…
Arab States	312 085	2.0	1.1	69	67	70	3.3	…	…	…
Central and Eastern Europe	403 681	0.0	-0.4	69	65	74	1.5	…	…	…
Central Asia	76 570	0.9	0.5	67	62	70	2.2	…	…	…
East Asia and the Pacific	2 102 740	0.7	-0.1	72	70	75	1.9	…	…	…
East Asia	2 069 561	0.7	-0.1	72	70	74	1.9	…	…	…
Pacific	33 178	1.3	0.5	75	73	77	2.4	…	…	…
Latin America/Caribbean	556 309	1.3	-0.1	73	70	76	2.4	…	…	…
Caribbean	15 589	1.0	0.2	…	…	…	…	…	…	…
Latin America	540 720	1.3	-0.1	73	70	77	2.4	…	…	…
N. America/W. Europe	735 606	0.5	0.1	79	76	82	1.7	…	…	…
South and West Asia	1 552 874	1.5	0.4	65	64	66	2.9	…	…	…
Sub-Saharan Africa	710 389	2.2	1.7	47	46	47	5.2	…	…	…

1. United Nations Population Division statistics, 2004 revision, medium variant, UN Population Division (2005).
2. UNAIDS (2006).
3. World Bank (2007f).
4. UNDP (2006).
5. Data are for the most recent year available during the period specified. For more details see UNDP (2006).

2008 — Education for All Global Monitoring Report

GNP, AID AND POVERTY							INEQUALITY IN INCOME OR EXPENDITURE[4]				
GNP per capita[3]				Net aid per capita (US$)[4]	Population living on less than US$1 per day[4] (%)	Population living on less than US$2 per day[4] (%)	Share of income or expenditure %		Inequality measure		
Current US$		PPP US$					Poorest 20%	Richest 20%	Richest 20% to poorest 20%[6]	Gini index[7]	
1998	2005	1998	2005	2004	1990-2004[5]	1990-2004[5]	1996-2004[5]	1996-2004[5]	1996-2004[5]	1996-2004[5]	Country or territory
410	650	1 640	1 980	31.5	...	...	...	...	...	...	Comoros
530	950	670	980	29.9	...	...	...	...	...	...	Congo
780	870	1 510	1 570	8.6	14.8	48.8	5.2	50.7	9.7	44.6	Côte d'Ivoire
110	120	710	680	32.5	...	...	...	...	...	...	D. R. Congo
1 060	...	3 570	...	60.3	...	...	...	...	...	...	Equatorial Guinea
220	170	1 070	1 100	61.3	...	...	...	...	...	...	Eritrea
100	160	600	1 050	24.1	23.0	77.8	9.1	39.4	4.3	30.0	Ethiopia
3 870	5 010	5 570	6 280	27.7	...	...	...	...	...	...	Gabon
320	290	1 500	1 860	42.5	59.3	82.9	4.8	53.4	11.2	50.2	Gambia
380	450	1 760	2 450	62.7	44.8	78.5	5.6	46.6	8.4	40.8	Ghana
520	420	1 810	2 280	30.3	...	...	6.4	47.2	7.3	40.3	Guinea
140	180	660	790	49.5	...	...	5.2	53.4	10.3	47.0	Guinea-Bissau
360	540	990	1 230	19.0	22.8	58.3	6.0	49.1	8.2	42.5	Kenya
690	950	2 640	4 080	56.8	36.4	56.1	1.5	66.5	44.2	63.2	Lesotho
110	130	...	...	...	...	...	...	...	...	...	Liberia
260	290	760	910	68.2	61.0	85.1	4.9	53.5	11.0	47.5	Madagascar
220	160	560	650	37.8	41.7	76.1	4.9	56.1	11.6	50.3	Malawi
250	380	720	990	43.2	72.3	90.6	4.6	56.2	12.2	50.5	Mali
3 760	5 250	8 610	12 700	30.8	...	...	...	...	...	...	Mauritius
200	310	760	1 160	63.2	37.8	78.4	6.5	46.5	7.2	39.6	Mozambique
2 050	2 990	5 890	7 690	89.1	34.9	55.8	1.4	78.7	56.1	74.3	Namibia
200	240	780	780	39.7	60.6	85.8	2.6	53.3	20.7	50.5	Niger
260	560	760	990	4.5	70.8	92.4	5.0	49.2	9.7	43.7	Nigeria
250	230	980	1 190	52.6	51.7	83.7	9.7	39.1	4.0	28.9	Rwanda
270	440	...	2 090	218.5	...	...	...	...	...	...	Sao Tome and Principe
510	700	1 330	1 760	92.4	22.3	63.0	6.4	48.2	7.5	41.3	Senegal
7 320	8 180	...	15 250	129.4	...	...	...	...	...	...	Seychelles
150	220	470	780	67.4	...	74.5	1.1	63.4	57.6	62.9	Sierra Leone
...	...	...	...	...	...	...	...	...	...	...	Somalia
3 290	4 770	8 820	10 880	13.1	10.7	34.1	3.5	62.2	17.9	57.8	South Africa
1 400	2 280	4 340	4 870	112.7	...	...	2.7	64.4	23.8	60.9	Swaziland
350	350	1 580	1 480	10.3	...	...	...	...	...	...	Togo
290	280	1 110	1 430	41.7	...	...	5.9	49.7	8.4	43.0	Uganda
230	340	470	740	46.4	57.8	89.9	7.3	42.4	5.8	34.6	United Republic of Tanzania
330	500	700	960	94.2	75.8	94.1	6.1	48.8	8.0	42.1	Zambia
560	350	2 640	1 950	14.4	56.1	83.0	4.6	55.7	12.0	50.1	Zimbabwe
Weighted average							Weighted average				
...	7 011	...	9 489	11.7	...	...	...	...	...	...	World
...	...	...	...	...	...	...	...	...	...	...	Countries in transition
...	...	...	...	...	...	...	...	...	...	...	Developed countries
...	...	...	...	10.5	...	...	...	...	...	...	Developing countries
...	...	...	...	35.9	...	...	...	...	...	...	Arab States
...	...	...	...	...	...	...	...	...	...	...	Central and Eastern Europe
...	...	...	...	...	...	...	...	...	...	...	Central Asia
...	1 630	...	6 060	3.3	...	...	...	...	...	...	East Asia and the Pacific
...	...	...	...	...	...	...	...	...	...	...	East Asia
...	...	...	...	...	...	...	...	...	...	...	Pacific
...	4 045	...	8 129	10.3	...	...	...	...	...	...	Latin America/Caribbean
...	...	...	...	...	...	...	...	...	...	...	Caribbean
...	...	...	...	...	...	...	...	...	...	...	Latin America
...	...	...	...	...	...	...	...	...	...	...	N. America/W. Europe
...	...	...	...	...	...	...	...	...	...	...	South and West Asia
...	746	...	1 913	33.0	...	...	...	...	...	...	Sub-Saharan Africa

6. Data show the ratio of income or expenditure share of the richest group to that of the poorest.
7. A value of 0 represents perfect equality, and a value of 100 perfect inequality.

Table 2
Adult and youth literacy

Country or territory	ADULT LITERACY RATE (15 and over) (%)									ADULT ILLITERATES (15 and over)					
	1985-1994[1]			1995-2004[1]			Projected 2015			1985-1994[1]		1995-2004[1]		Projected 2015	
	Total	Male	Female	Total	Male	Female	Total	Male	Female	Total (000)	% Female	Total (000)	% Female	Total (000)	% Female
Arab States															
Algeria	50*	63*	36*	70*	80*	60*	81	88	74	6 573	64*	6 423	66*	5 389	68
Bahrain	84*	89*	77*	87*	89*	84*	92	93	90	56	56*	66	49*	56	49
Djibouti	...	...	...	...	...	...	...	...	...	...	...	...	...	...	...
Egypt	44*	57*	31*	71*	83*	59*	77	86	68	16 541	62*	14 210	71*	13 961	70
Iraq	...	...	...	74*	84*	64*	81	88	74	...	...	3 707	69*	4 371	67
Jordan	...	...	...	91*	95*	87*	96	98	93	...	...	312	71*	210	77
Kuwait	74*	78*	69*	93*	94*	91*	96	96	95	276	48*	139	49*	114	48
Lebanon	...	...	...	...	...	...	...	...	...	...	...	...	...	...	...
Libyan Arab Jamahiriya	75	87	61	84	93	75	90	96	83	716	73	633	77	497	81
Mauritania	...	...	...	51*	60*	43*	61	67	55	...	...	732	60*	911	58
Morocco	42*	55*	29*	52*	66*	40*	63	75	51	9 676	62*	10 106	65*	9 602	67
Oman	...	...	...	81*	87*	74*	89	93	84	...	...	300	57*	244	62
Palestinian A. T.	...	...	...	92*	97*	88*	95	98	93	...	...	148	78*	134	76
Qatar	76*	77*	72*	89*	89*	89*	93	93	93	68	30*	67	29*	54	31
Saudi Arabia	71*	80*	57*	83*	88*	76*	89	92	85	2 962	59*	2 595	60*	2 255	62
Sudan[2]	...	...	...	61*	71*	52*	71	79	63	...	...	7 557	63*	8 143	64
Syrian Arab Republic	...	...	...	81*	88*	74*	87	92	82	...	...	2 248	68*	2 068	70
Tunisia	...	...	...	74*	83*	65*	83	90	76	...	...	1 878	68*	1 469	71
United Arab Emirates	79	80	79	89	89	88	94	94	92	339	29	377	29	289	35
Yemen	37*	57*	17*	54	73	35	70	84	55	4 579	65*	4 974	70	4 903	74
Central and Eastern Europe															
Albania	...	...	...	99*	99*	98*	99	99	99	...	...	28	69*	18	58
Belarus	98*	99*	97*	100*	100*	99*	100	100	100	167	87*	33	77*	15	49
Bosnia and Herzegovina	...	...	...	97*	99*	94*	97	99	96	...	...	106	86*	90	85
Bulgaria	...	...	...	98*	99*	98*	98	98	98	...	...	121	66*	116	58
Croatia	97*	99*	95*	98*	99*	97*	99	100	99	120	82*	69	83*	31	74
Czech Republic	...	...	...	...	...	...	...	...	...	...	...	...	...	...	...
Estonia	100*	100*	100*	100*	100*	100*	100	100	100	3	79*	3	57*	2	46
Hungary	...	...	...	...	...	...	...	...	...	...	...	...	...	...	...
Latvia	99*	100*	99*	100*	100*	100*	100	100	100	12	80*	5	64*	4	50
Lithuania	98*	99*	98*	100*	100*	100*	100	100	100	44	76*	10	54*	8	50
Poland	...	...	...	...	...	...	...	...	...	...	...	...	...	...	...
Republic of Moldova	96*	99*	94*	99	100	99	100	100	100	114	82*	32	79	13	63
Romania	97*	99*	95*	97*	98*	96*	98	98	98	589	78*	491	71*	397	58
Russian Federation	98*	99*	97*	99*	100*	99*	100	100	100	2 288	88*	676	75*	390	61
Serbia and Montenegro[2]	92*	97*	88*	96*	99*	94*	99	99	98	606	81*	246	85*	120	75
Slovakia	...	...	...	...	...	...	...	...	...	...	...	...	...	...	...
Slovenia	100*	100*	99*	100	100	100	100	100	100	7	60*	6	56	5	54
TFYR Macedonia	94*	97*	91*	96*	98*	94*	98	99	97	87	77*	62	77*	36	73
Turkey	79*	90*	69*	87*	95*	80*	92	97	86	7 639	75*	6 389	81*	5 201	83
Ukraine	...	...	...	99*	100*	99*	100	100	100	...	...	229	80*	79	58
Central Asia															
Armenia	99*	99*	98*	99*	100*	99*	100	100	100	31	77*	14	76*	8	62
Azerbaijan	...	...	...	99*	99*	98*	100	100	100	...	...	67	79*	24	76
Georgia	...	...	...	...	...	...	...	...	...	...	...	...	...	...	...
Kazakhstan	98*	99*	96*	100*	100*	99*	100	100	100	276	82*	53	77*	32	65
Kyrgyzstan	...	...	...	99*	99*	98*	99	100	99	...	...	41	74*	22	56
Mongolia	...	...	...	98*	98*	98*	96	94	98	...	...	36	56*	87	31
Tajikistan	98*	99*	97*	99*	100*	99*	100	100	100	68	74*	19	71*	11	62
Turkmenistan	...	...	...	99*	99*	98*	100	100	100	...	...	31	73*	12	61
Uzbekistan	...	...	...	...	...	...	...	...	...	...	...	...	...	...	...
East Asia and the Pacific															
Australia	...	...	...	...	...	...	...	...	...	...	...	...	...	...	...
Brunei Darussalam	88*	92*	82*	93*	95*	90*	94	93	95	21	67*	17	65*	21	40
Cambodia	...	...	...	74*	85*	64*	81	88	74	...	...	2 262	73*	2 182	71
China	78*	87*	68*	91*	95*	87*	96	98	93	185 405	70*	87 019	73*	50 200	75
Cook Islands	...	...	...	...	...	...	...	...	...	...	...	...	...	...	...
DPR Korea	...	...	...	...	...	...	...	...	...	...	...	...	...	...	...

YOUTH LITERACY RATE (15-24) (%)									YOUTH ILLITERATES (15-24)						Country or territory
1985-1994[1]			1995-2004[1]			Projected 2015			1985-1994[1]		1995-2004[1]		Projected 2015		
Total	Male	Female	Total	Male	Female	Total	Male	Female	Total (000)	% Female	Total (000)	% Female	Total (000)	% Female	
															Arab States
74*	86*	62*	90*	94*	86*	95	95	95	1 215	73*	705	69*	319	48	Algeria
97*	97*	97*	97*	97*	97*	100	100	100	3	53*	3	43*	0.1	46	Bahrain
...	...	...	...	...	...	...	...	...	...	...	...	...	...	...	Djibouti
63*	71*	54*	85*	90*	79*	91	92	90	3 506	61*	2 382	67*	1 447	55	Egypt
...	...	...	85*	89*	80*	84	87	82	...	...	765	63*	1 159	57	Iraq
...	...	...	99*	99*	99*	100	100	100	...	...	12	47*	4	53	Jordan
87*	91*	84*	100*	100*	100*	100	100	100	37	62*	1	38*	0.05	37	Kuwait
...	...	...	...	...	...	...	...	...	...	...	...	...	...	...	Lebanon
95	99	91	98	100	96	100	100	100	52	89	26	88	0.7	67	Libyan Arab Jamahiriya
...	...	...	61*	68*	55*	71	73	70	...	...	199	58*	219	53	Mauritania
58*	71*	46*	70*	81*	60*	83	89	78	2 287	65*	1 888	67*	1 041	66	Morocco
...	...	...	97*	98*	97*	99	100	99	...	...	14	59*	3	64	Oman
...	...	...	99*	99*	99*	99	99	100	...	...	7	57*	6	36	Palestinian A. T.
90*	89*	91*	96*	95*	98*	99	99	99	6	31*	4	24*	1.01	62	Qatar
88*	94*	81*	96*	97*	95*	99	99	98	374	74*	183	62*	83	76	Saudi Arabia
...	...	...	77*	85*	71*	82	85	78	...	...	1 468	64*	1 622	59	Sudan[2]
...	...	...	92*	95*	90*	96	97	95	...	...	325	64*	165	60	Syrian Arab Republic
...	...	...	94*	96*	92*	98	98	97	...	...	118	67*	39	57	Tunisia
94	95	91	97	98	95	99	100	98	23	55	22	56	7	81	United Arab Emirates
60*	83*	35*	75	91	59	90	97	83	1 072	78*	1 074	81	580	87	Yemen
															Central and Eastern Europe
...	...	...	99*	99*	99*	99	99	99	...	...	3	46*	4	41	Albania
100*	100*	100*	100*	100*	100*	100	100	100	3	43*	3	40*	2	34	Belarus
...	...	...	100*	100*	100*	100	100	100	...	...	1	38*	0.46	49	Bosnia and Herzegovina
...	...	...	98*	98*	98*	96	96	96	...	...	20	52*	28	47	Bulgaria
100*	100*	100*	100*	100*	100*	100	100	100	2	53*	2	48*	2	44	Croatia
...	...	...	...	...	...	...	...	...	...	...	...	...	...	...	Czech Republic
100*	100*	100*	100*	100*	100*	100	100	100	0.3	35*	0.5	40*	0.27	36	Estonia
...	...	...	...	...	...	...	...	...	...	...	...	...	...	...	Hungary
100*	100*	100*	100*	100*	100*	100	100	100	0.8	40*	0.8	43*	0.8	41	Latvia
100*	100*	100*	100*	100*	100*	100	100	100	2	44*	1	43*	0.8	50	Lithuania
...	...	...	...	...	...	...	...	...	...	...	...	...	...	...	Poland
100*	100*	100*	100	100	100	100	100	100	2	48*	2	49	2	49	Republic of Moldova
99*	99*	99*	98*	98*	98*	96	96	97	35	53*	77	49*	86	42	Romania
100*	100*	100*	100*	100*	100*	100	100	100	55	44*	67	41*	53	36	Russian Federation
99*	99*	98*	99*	99*	99*	99	99	99	22	64*	7	52*	10	48	Serbia and Montenegro[2]
...	...	...	...	...	...	...	...	...	...	...	...	...	...	...	Slovakia
100*	100*	100*	100	100	100	100	100	100	0.7	44*	0.4	39	0.3	30	Slovenia
99*	99*	99*	99*	99*	98*	99	99	98	4	62*	4	59*	4	52	TFYR Macedonia
93*	97*	88*	96*	98*	93*	97	98	95	866	76*	583	77*	480	74	Turkey
...	...	...	100*	100*	100*	100	100	100	...	...	14	42*	12	39	Ukraine
															Central Asia
100*	100*	100*	100*	100*	100*	100	100	100	0.5	49*	1	37*	1.3	33	Armenia
...	...	...	100*	100*	100*	100	100	100	...	...	2	43*	0.6	18	Azerbaijan
...	...	...	...	...	...	...	...	...	...	...	...	...	...	...	Georgia
100*	100*	100*	100*	100*	100*	100	100	100	8	44*	4	40*	5	36	Kazakhstan
...	...	...	100*	100*	100*	99	99	100	...	...	3	42*	6	31	Kyrgyzstan
...	...	...	98*	97*	98*	91	86	95	...	...	12	34*	49	24	Mongolia
100*	100*	100*	100*	100*	100*	100	100	100	3	56*	2	49*	2	44	Tajikistan
...	...	...	100*	100*	100*	100	100	100	...	...	2	49*	2	33	Turkmenistan
...	...	...	...	...	...	...	...	...	...	...	...	...	...	...	Uzbekistan
															East Asia and the Pacific
...	...	...	...	...	...	...	...	...	...	...	...	...	...	...	Australia
98*	98*	98*	99*	99*	99*	99	98	99	0.9	49*	0.7	49*	1.01	27	Brunei Darussalam
...	...	...	83*	88*	79*	91	93	89	...	...	543	63*	295	59	Cambodia
94*	97*	91*	99*	99*	99*	100	100	100	14 355	73*	2 260	63*	902	51	China
...	...	...	...	...	...	...	...	...	...	...	...	...	...	...	Cook Islands
...	...	...	...	...	...	...	...	...	...	...	...	...	...	...	DPR Korea

Table 2 (continued)

Country or territory	ADULT LITERACY RATE (15 and over) (%)									ADULT ILLITERATES (15 and over)					
	1985-1994[1]			1995-2004[1]			Projected 2015			1985-1994[1]		1995-2004[1]		Projected 2015	
	Total	Male	Female	Total	Male	Female	Total	Male	Female	Total (000)	% Female	Total (000)	% Female	Total (000)	% Female
Saint Kitts and Nevis	...	...	...	...	...	...	...	...	...	...	...	...	...	...	...
Saint Lucia	...	...	...	...	...	...	...	...	...	...	...	...	...	...	...
St Vincent/Grenad.	...	...	...	...	...	...	...	...	...	...	...	...	...	...	...
Suriname	...	...	...	90*	92*	87*	93	95	92	...	...	32	62*	23	62
Trinidad and Tobago	97	98	96	98	99	98	99	99	99	25	69	17	68	10	62
Turks and Caicos Islands	...	...	...	...	...	...	...	...	...	...	...	...	...	...	...
Uruguay	95*	95*	96*	97*	96*	97*	98	98	99	102	46*	78	44*	52	39
Venezuela	90*	91*	89*	93*	93*	93*	96	95	96	1242	54*	1166	52*	973	47
North America and Western Europe															
Andorra	...	...	...	...	...	...	...	...	...	...	...	...	...	...	...
Austria	...	...	...	...	...	...	...	...	...	...	...	...	...	...	...
Belgium	...	...	...	...	...	...	...	...	...	...	...	...	...	...	...
Canada	...	...	...	...	...	...	...	...	...	...	...	...	...	...	...
Cyprus	94*	98*	91*	97*	99*	95*	99	99	98	26	81*	18	79*	9	75
Denmark	...	...	...	...	...	...	...	...	...	...	...	...	...	...	...
Finland	...	...	...	...	...	...	...	...	...	...	...	...	...	...	...
France	...	...	...	...	...	...	...	...	...	...	...	...	...	...	...
Germany	...	...	...	...	...	...	...	...	...	...	...	...	...	...	...
Greece	93*	96*	89*	96*	98*	94*	98	99	97	615	74*	375	73*	192	66
Iceland	...	...	...	...	...	...	...	...	...	...	...	...	...	...	...
Ireland	...	...	...	...	...	...	...	...	...	...	...	...	...	...	...
Israel	...	...	...	...	...	...	...	...	...	...	...	...	...	...	...
Italy	...	...	...	98*	99*	98*	99	99	99	...	...	785	64*	366	61
Luxembourg	...	...	...	...	...	...	...	...	...	...	...	...	...	...	...
Malta	...	...	...	88*	86*	89*	93	91	95	...	...	36	45*	24	37
Monaco	...	...	...	...	...	...	...	...	...	...	...	...	...	...	...
Netherlands	...	...	...	...	...	...	...	...	...	...	...	...	...	...	...
Norway	...	...	...	...	...	...	...	...	...	...	...	...	...	...	...
Portugal	88*	92*	85*	94	96	92	97	98	96	965	67*	542	68	270	67
San Marino	...	...	...	...	...	...	...	...	...	...	...	...	...	...	...
Spain	96*	98*	95*	...	...	...	...	...	...	1124	73*	...	...	...	...
Sweden	...	...	...	...	...	...	...	...	...	...	...	...	...	...	...
Switzerland	...	...	...	...	...	...	...	...	...	...	...	...	...	...	...
United Kingdom	...	...	...	...	...	...	...	...	...	...	...	...	...	...	...
United States	...	...	...	...	...	...	...	...	...	...	...	...	...	...	...
South and West Asia															
Afghanistan	...	...	...	28*	43*	13*	36	52	19	...	...	9048	59*	14585	61
Bangladesh	35*	44*	26*	47*	54*	41*	61	65	58	40818	56*	43394	55*	44680	53
Bhutan	...	...	...	...	...	...	...	...	...	...	...	...	...	...	...
India[2]	48*	62*	34*	61*	73*	48*	71	80	62	285690	62*	268426	65*	259234	65
Iran, Islamic Republic of	66*	74*	56*	82*	88*	77*	89	93	85	11125	62*	8693	65*	6572	69
Maldives	96*	96*	96*	96*	96*	96*	98	97	98	5	47*	6	47*	6	46
Nepal	33*	49*	17*	49*	63*	35*	66	77	56	7619	63*	7661	65*	7344	67
Pakistan	...	...	...	50*	64*	35*	59	71	47	...	...	48597	63*	51925	63
Sri Lanka[2]	...	...	...	91*	92*	89*	93	94	92	...	...	1380	57*	1257	55
Sub-Saharan Africa															
Angola	...	...	...	67*	83*	54*	70	81	60	...	...	2401	74*	3403	69
Benin	27*	40*	17*	35*	48*	23*	47	59	36	2129	59*	2718	60*	3434	61
Botswana	69*	65*	71*	81*	80*	82*	87	87	87	256	47*	206	50*	143	51
Burkina Faso	14*	20*	8*	24*	31*	17*	32	37	26	3996	54*	5310	55*	6576	54
Burundi	37*	48*	28*	59*	67*	52*	68	69	67	1938	61*	1373	62*	1825	53
Cameroon	...	...	...	68*	77*	60*	...	...	...	...	...	2764	64*	...	...
Cape Verde	63*	75*	53*	81	88	76	89	93	86	70	70*	56	70	45	68
Central African Republic	34*	48*	20*	49*	65*	33*	56	69	44	1084	63*	1107	67*	1218	66
Chad	12	...	...	26*	41*	13*	38	54	22	3132	...	3206	61*	4166	64
Comoros	...	...	...	...	...	...	...	...	...	...	...	...	...	...	...
Congo	74	83	65	85	91	79	93	96	90	398	68	315	70	210	72
Côte d'Ivoire	34*	44*	23*	49*	61*	39*	67	75	60	4145	55*	4733	59*	4355	60
D. R. Congo	...	...	...	67*	81*	54*	67	76	58	...	...	8901	71*	13353	64

2008
Education for All Global Monitoring Report

CHILD WELL-BEING[2]					PROVISION FOR UNDER-3s		WOMEN'S EMPLOYMENT AND MATERNITY LEAVE		
1-year-old children immunized against (%)									
Tuberculosis	Diphtheria Pertussis Tetanus	Polio	Measles	Hepatitis B	Official programmes targeting children	Youngest age group targeted in programmes	Female labour force participation rate, age 15 and above[4]	Duration of paid maternity leave[5]	
Corresponding vaccines:									
BCG	DPT3	Polio3	Measles	HepB3	under age 3	(years)	(%)	(weeks)	
2005	2005	2005	2005	2005	2005	c. 2005	2003	2005-2007[3]	Country or territory
									Arab States
98	88	88	83	83	…	…	34	14	Algeria
…	98	98	99	98	Yes	0-2	29	…	Bahrain
52	71	71	65	…	…	…	53	…	Djibouti
98	98	98	98	98	Yes	2-3	21	13	Egypt
93	81	87	90	81	…	…	20	…	Iraq
89	95	95	95	95	Yes	0-3	26	…	Jordan
…	99	99	99	99	No	•	45	…	Kuwait
…	92	92	96	88	Yes	0-2	30	…	Lebanon
99	98	98	97	97	…	…	28	12	Libyan Arab Jamahiriya
87	71	71	61	42	…	…	54	14	Mauritania
95	98	98	97	96	No	•	27	14	Morocco
98	99	99	98	99	No	•	20	…	Oman
99	99	99	99	99	Yes	0-4	…	…	Palestinian A. T.
99	97	98	99	97	…	…	36	…	Qatar
96	96	96	96	96	…	…	17	10	Saudi Arabia
57	59	59	60	52	Yes	0-6	23	0	Sudan
99	99	99	98	99	Yes	0-2	37	…	Syrian Arab Republic
…	98	98	96	97	No	•	27	4	Tunisia
98	94	94	92	92	No	•	36	…	United Arab Emirates
66	86	87	76	86	No	•	29	0	Yemen
									Central and Eastern Europe
98	98	97	97	98	No	•	50	52	Albania
99	99	98	99	99	…	…	53	18	Belarus
95	93	95	90	93	Yes	0-3	55	…	Bosnia and Herzegovina
98	96	97	96	96	No	•	45	19	Bulgaria
98	96	96	96	99	…	…	45	58	Croatia
99	97	96	97	99	No	•	51	28	Czech Republic
99	96	96	96	95	Yes	1-6	53	20	Estonia
99	99	99	99	…	Yes	0-2	43	24	Hungary
99	99	99	95	98	No	•	51	16	Latvia
99	94	93	97	95	No	•	53	18	Lithuania
94	99	99	98	98	…	…	48	16	Poland
97	98	98	97	99	…	…	57	18	Republic of Moldova
98	97	97	97	98	No	•	49	17	Romania
97	98	98	99	97	…	…	54	20	Russian Federation
98	98	98	96	65	…	…	47	52	Serbia and Montenegro
98	99	99	98	99	…	…	53	28	Slovakia
…	96	96	94	…	Yes	1-3	50	15	Slovenia
99	98	98	96	96	No	•	43	…	TFYR Macedonia
89	90	90	91	85	Yes	0-2	27	12	Turkey
96	96	95	96	97	Yes	0-3	51	18	Ukraine
									Central Asia
94	90	92	94	91	Yes	2	50	16	Armenia
98	93	97	98	96	Yes	0-2	60	18	Azerbaijan
95	84	84	92	74	Yes	0-2	57	8	Georgia
69	98	99	99	94	Yes	1-6	64	18	Kazakhstan
96	98	98	99	97	Yes	1-3	55	18	Kyrgyzstan
99	99	99	99	98	Yes	2-3	54	…	Mongolia
98	81	84	84	81	No	•	49	…	Tajikistan
99	99	99	99	99	Yes	0-2	61	16	Turkmenistan
93	99	99	99	99	Yes	2-3	56	18	Uzbekistan
									East Asia and the Pacific
…	92	92	94	94	Yes	1-4	55	52	Australia [6]
96	99	99	97	99	…	…	44	…	Brunei Darussalam
87	82	82	79	…	Yes	0-6	74	…	Cambodia

Table 3A (continued)

Country or territory	CHILD SURVIVAL[1]		CHILD WELL-BEING[2]						
				% of children under age 5 suffering from:			% of children who are:		
	Infant mortality rate (‰)	Under-5 mortality rate (‰)	Infants with low birth weight (%)	Underweight moderate and severe	Wasting moderate and severe	Stunting moderate and severe	Exclusively breastfed (<6 months)	Breastfed with complementary food (6-9 months)	Still breastfeeding (20-23 months)
	2005-2010	2005-2010	1998-2005[3]	1996-2005[3]	1996-2005[3]	1996-2005[3]	1996-2005[3]	1996-2005[3]	1996-2005[3]
China	31	36	4	8	…	14	51	32	15
Cook Islands	…	…	3	…	…	…	19	…	…
DPR Korea	41	53	7	23	7	37	65	31	37
Fiji	20	24	10	…	…	…	47	…	…
Indonesia	34	41	9	28	…	…	40	75	59
Japan	3	4	8	…	…	…	…	…	…
Kiribati	…	…	5	…	…	…	80	…	…
Lao People's Democratic Republic	80	126	14	40	15	42	23	10	47
Macao, China	7	8	…	…	…	…	…	…	…
Malaysia	9	11	9	11	…	…	29	…	12
Marshall Islands	…	…	12	…	…	…	63	…	…
Micronesia (Federated States of)	34	42	18	…	…	…	60	…	…
Myanmar	66	98	15	32	9	32	15	66	67
Nauru	…	…	…	…	…	…	…	…	…
New Zealand	5	6	6	…	…	…	…	…	…
Niue	…	…	0	…	…	…	…	…	…
Palau	…	…	9	…	…	…	59	…	…
Papua New Guinea	64	87	11	…	…	…	59	74	66
Philippines	23	28	20	28	6	30	34	58	32
Republic of Korea	4	5	4	…	…	…	…	…	…
Samoa	22	27	4	…	…	…	…	…	…
Singapore	3	4	8	3	2	2	…	…	…
Solomon Islands[7]	31	52	13	…	…	…	65	…	…
Thailand	17	21	9	18	5	13	4	71	27
Timor-Leste	81	114	12	46	12	49	31	82	35
Tokelau	…	…	…	…	…	…	…	…	…
Tonga	19	22	0	…	…	…	62	…	…
Tuvalu	…	…	5	…	…	…	…	…	…
Vanuatu	28	34	6	…	…	…	50	…	…
Viet Nam	25	32	9	27	8	31	15	…	26
Latin America and the Caribbean									
Anguilla	…	…	…	…	…	…	…	…	…
Antigua and Barbuda	…	…	8	…	…	…	…	…	…
Argentina	13	16	8	4	1	4	…	…	…
Aruba	…	…	…	…	…	…	…	…	…
Bahamas	11	14	7	…	…	…	…	…	…
Barbados	10	11	11	…	…	…	…	…	…
Belize	29	39	6	…	…	…	24	54	23
Bermuda	…	…	…	…	…	…	…	…	…
Bolivia	46	61	7	8	1	27	54	74	46
Brazil	24	30	8	6	2	11	…	30	17
British Virgin Islands	…	…	…	…	…	…	…	…	…
Cayman Islands	…	…	…	…	…	…	…	…	…
Chile	7	9	6	1	0	1	63	47	…
Colombia	22	28	9	7	1	12	47	65	32
Costa Rica	10	11	7	5	2	6	35	47	12
Cuba	5	6	5	4	2	5	41	42	9
Dominica	…	…	11	…	…	…	…	…	…
Dominican Republic	30	43	11	5	2	9	10	41	16
Ecuador	21	26	16	12	…	26	35	70	25
El Salvador	22	29	7	10	1	19	24	76	43
Grenada	…	…	8	…	…	…	39	…	…
Guatemala	30	42	12	23	2	49	51	67	47
Guyana	43	59	13	14	11	11	11	42	31
Haiti	57	100	21	17	5	23	24	73	30
Honduras	28	43	14	17	1	29	35	61	34
Jamaica	14	20	10	4	4	3	…	…	…
Mexico	17	20	8	8	2	18	…	…	…
Montserrat	…	…	…	…	…	…	…	…	…
Netherlands Antilles	12	13	…	…	…	…	…	…	…

Tuberculosis	Diphtheria Pertussis Tetanus	Polio	Measles	Hepatitis B	Official programmes targeting children under age 3	Youngest age group targeted in programmes (years)	Female labour force participation rate, age 15 and above[4] (%)	Duration of paid maternity leave[5] (weeks)	Country or territory
BCG	DPT3	Polio3	Measles	HepB3					
2005	2005	2005	2005	2005	2005	c. 2005	2003	2005-2007[3]	
86	87	87	86	84	Yes	0-3	70	13	China
99	99	99	99	99	…	…	…	…	Cook Islands
94	79	97	96	92	Yes	0-3	51	…	DPR Korea
90	75	80	70	75	No	•	50	…	Fiji
82	70	70	72	70	Yes	0-6	51	0	Indonesia
…	99	97	99	…	Yes	0-6	49	14	Japan
94	62	61	56	67	No	•	…	…	Kiribati
65	49	50	41	49	Yes	0-2	54	12	Lao People's Democratic Republic
…	…	…	…	…	No	•	54	…	Macao, China
99	90	90	90	90	Yes	0-3	45	0	Malaysia
93	77	88	86	89	…	…	…	0	Marshall Islands
70	94	94	96	91	…	…	…	…	Micronesia (Federated States of)
76	73	73	72	62	…	…	68	12	Myanmar
90	80	80	80	80	…	…	…	…	Nauru
…	89	89	82	87	Yes	0-5	59	14	New Zealand
97	85	86	99	86	…	…	…	…	Niue
…	98	98	98	98	…	…	…	…	Palau
73	61	50	60	63	No	•	72	…	Papua New Guinea
91	79	80	80	44	No	•	52	9	Philippines
97	96	96	99	99	Yes	0-5	49	12	Republic of Korea
86	64	73	57	60	…	…	40	…	Samoa
98	96	96	96	96	Yes	2-6	50	12	Singapore
84	80	75	72	72	No	•	55	0	Solomon Islands[7]
91	90	91	91	90	Yes	0-5	65	13	Thailand
99	97	98	96	53	…	…	54	…	Timor-Leste
96	82	80	70	…	…	…	…	…	Tokelau
99	99	99	99	99	…	…	46	…	Tonga
99	93	99	62	79	…	…	…	…	Tuvalu
65	66	56	70	56	…	…	79	12	Vanuatu
95	95	94	95	94	Yes	0-2	72	17	Viet Nam
									Latin America and the Caribbean
…	…	…	…	…	…	…	…	…	Anguilla
…	99	98	99	99	…	…	…	13	Antigua and Barbuda
99	92	92	99	87	Yes	0-5	52	13	Argentina
…	…	…	…	…	…	…	…	…	Aruba
…	93	93	85	93	…	…	64	13	Bahamas
…	92	91	93	92	Yes	0-2	65	12	Barbados
96	96	96	95	97	…	…	42	14	Belize
…	…	…	…	…	…	…	…	4	Bermuda
93	81	79	64	81	Yes	0-4	63	13	Bolivia
99	96	98	99	92	Yes	0-3	57	17	Brazil
…	…	…	…	…	Yes	0-3	54	13	British Virgin Islands
…	…	…	…	…	…	…	…	…	Cayman Islands
95	91	92	90	…	Yes	0-2	37	18	Chile
87	87	87	89	87	Yes	0-5	60	12	Colombia
88	91	91	89	90	Yes	0-3	42	17	Costa Rica
99	99	99	98	99	Yes	1-6	43	18	Cuba
98	98	98	98	…	…	…	…	12	Dominica
99	77	73	99	77	…	…	44	12	Dominican Republic
99	94	93	93	94	Yes	0-4	54	12	Ecuador
84	89	89	99	89	Yes	0-3	47	12	El Salvador
…	99	99	99	99	Yes	0-2	…	12	Grenada
96	81	81	77	27	Yes	0-6	33	12	Guatemala
96	93	93	92	93	No	•	43	13	Guyana
71	43	43	54	…	Yes	0-3	55	…	Haiti
91	91	91	92	91	Yes	0-3	44	12	Honduras
95	88	83	84	87	No	•	57	8	Jamaica
99	98	98	96	98	Yes	0-3	39	12	Mexico
…	…	…	…	…	…	…	…	…	Montserrat
…	…	…	…	…	…	…	50	…	Netherlands Antilles

263

Table 3A (continued)

| Country or territory | CHILD SURVIVAL[1] | | CHILD WELL-BEING[2] | | | | | | |
| | Infant mortality rate (‰) 2005-2010 | Under-5 mortality rate (‰) 2005-2010 | Infants with low birth weight (%) 1998-2005[3] | % of children under age 5 suffering from: | | | % of children who are: | | |
				Underweight moderate and severe 1996-2005[3]	Wasting moderate and severe 1996-2005[3]	Stunting moderate and severe 1996-2005[3]	Exclusively breastfed (<6 months) 1996-2005[3]	Breastfed with complementary food (6-9 months) 1996-2005[3]	Still breastfeeding (20-23 months) 1996-2005[3]
Nicaragua	26	35	12	10	2	20	31	68	39
Panama	18	24	10	8	1	18	25	38	21
Paraguay	34	41	9	5	1	14	22	60	...
Peru	29	45	11	8	1	24	64	81	41
Saint Kitts and Nevis	...	...	9	...	...	...	56	...	...
Saint Lucia	14	18	10	...	...	...	...	...	...
Saint Vincent and the Grenadines	22	26	10	...	...	...	...	...	...
Suriname	22	27	13	13	7	10	9	25	11
Trinidad and Tobago	13	18	23	6	4	4	2	19	10
Turks and Caicos Islands	...	...	...	...	...	...	...	...	...
Uruguay	12	14	8	5	1	8	...	...	...
Venezuela	16	26	9	5	4	13	7	50	31
North America and Western Europe									
Andorra	...	...	...	...	...	...	...	...	...
Austria	4	5	7	...	...	...	...	...	...
Belgium	4	6	8	...	...	...	...	...	...
Canada	5	6	6	...	...	...	...	...	...
Cyprus	6	7	...	...	...	...	...	...	...
Denmark	5	6	5	...	...	...	...	...	...
Finland	4	5	4	...	...	...	...	...	...
France	4	5	7	...	...	...	...	...	...
Germany	4	5	7	...	...	...	...	...	...
Greece	6	7	8	...	...	...	...	...	...
Iceland	3	4	4	...	...	...	...	...	...
Ireland	5	6	6	...	...	...	...	...	...
Israel	5	6	8	...	...	...	...	...	...
Italy	5	6	6	...	...	...	...	...	...
Luxembourg	5	6	8	...	...	...	...	...	...
Malta	7	8	6	...	...	...	...	...	...
Monaco	...	...	...	...	...	...	...	...	...
Netherlands	4	6	...	...	...	...	...	...	...
Norway	3	4	5	...	...	...	...	...	...
Portugal	5	7	8	...	...	...	...	...	...
San Marino	...	...	...	...	...	...	...	...	...
Spain	4	6	6	...	...	...	...	...	...
Sweden	3	4	4	...	...	...	...	...	...
Switzerland	4	5	6	...	...	...	...	...	...
United Kingdom	5	6	8	...	...	...	...	...	...
United States[7]	6	8	8	2	6	1	...	...	...
South and West Asia									
Afghanistan	142	237	...	39	7	54	...	29	54
Bangladesh	50	65	36	48	13	43	36	69	90
Bhutan	48	70	15	19	3	40	...	...	...
India	60	86	30	47	16	46	37	44	66
Iran, Islamic Republic of	27	32	7	11	5	15	44	...	0
Maldives	34	42	22	30	13	25	10	85	...
Nepal	55	73	21	48	10	51	68	66	92
Pakistan	71	100	19	38	13	37	16	31	56
Sri Lanka	14	16	22	29	14	14	53	...	73
Sub-Saharan Africa									
Angola	130	230	12	31	6	45	11	77	37
Benin	98	147	16	23	8	31	38	66	62
Botswana	43	98	10	13	5	23	34	57	11
Burkina Faso	116	186	19	38	19	39	19	38	81
Burundi	99	173	16	45	8	57	62	46	85
Cameroon	91	156	13	18	5	32	24	79	29
Cape Verde	25	29	13	...	...	...	57	64	13
Central African Republic	93	167	14	24	9	39	17	77	53

CHILD WELL-BEING[2]					PROVISION FOR UNDER-3s		WOMEN'S EMPLOYMENT AND MATERNITY LEAVE		
1-year-old children immunized against (%)									
Tuberculosis	Diphtheria Pertussis Tetanus	Polio	Measles	Hepatitis B	Official programmes targeting children	Youngest age group targeted in programmes	Female labour force participation rate, age 15 and above[4]	Duration of paid maternity leave[5]	
		Corresponding vaccines:							
BCG	DPT3	Polio3	Measles	HepB3	under age 3	(years)	(%)	(weeks)	
2005	2005	2005	2005	2005	2005	c. 2005	2003	2005-2007[3]	Country or territory
...	86	87	96	86	Yes	0-3	36	12	Nicaragua
99	85	86	99	85	Yes	2-4	47	14	Panama
78	75	74	90	75	Yes	0-4	64	9	Paraguay
93	84	80	80	84	Yes	0-5	58	13	Peru
99	99	99	99	99	...	...	...	13	Saint Kitts and Nevis
99	95	95	94	95	Yes	0-2	52	12	Saint Lucia
95	99	93	97	99	...	...	52	13	Saint Vincent and the Grenadines
...	83	84	91	83	...	...	35	...	Suriname
98	95	97	93	95	Yes	0-5	49	13	Trinidad and Tobago
...	...	...	...	...	Yes	2	...	...	Turks and Caicos Islands
99	96	96	95	96	Yes	0-3	55	12	Uruguay
95	87	81	76	88	Yes	0-2	53	24	Venezuela
North America and Western Europe									
...	98	98	94	79	Yes	0-3	...	16	Andorra
...	86	86	75	86	Yes	1-3	50	16	Austria
...	97	97	88	78	Yes	1-3	43	15	Belgium
...	94	89	94	...	Yes	0-6	61	17	Canada
...	98	98	86	88	Yes	0-5	54	16	Cyprus
...	93	93	95	...	Yes	0-2	60	18	Denmark
98	97	97	97	...	Yes	0-6	57	18	Finland
84	98	98	87	29	Yes	0-3	48	16	France
...	90	94	93	84	Yes	0-2	50	14	Germany
88	88	87	88	88	Yes	0-3	41	17	Greece
...	95	95	90	...	Yes	0-6	70	13	Iceland
93	90	90	84	...	Yes	0-5	49	26	Ireland
61	95	93	95	95	Yes	0-4	49	12	Israel
...	96	97	87	96	Yes	0-2	37	21	Italy
...	99	99	95	95	No	...	44	16	Luxembourg
...	92	94	86	78	...	...	30	14	Malta
90	99	99	99	99	...	...	...	16	Monaco
94	98	98	96	...	Yes	0-3	55	16	Netherlands
...	91	91	90	...	Yes	0-5	62	9	Norway
89	93	93	93	94	Yes	0-3	55	17	Portugal
...	95	95	94	95	...	...	...	72	San Marino
...	96	96	97	96	Yes	0-3	44	16	Spain
16	99	99	94	...	Yes	1-6	60	15	Sweden
...	93	95	82	...	Yes	0-5	59	16	Switzerland
...	91	91	82	...	Yes	1-3	55	26	United Kingdom
...	96	92	93	92	Yes	0-4	59	12	United States[7]
South and West Asia									
73	76	76	64	...	...	...	38	12	Afghanistan
99	88	88	81	62	No	•	55	12	Bangladesh
99	95	95	93	95	No	•	39	...	Bhutan
75	59	58	58	8	Yes	0-6	35	12	India
99	95	95	94	94	Yes	0-6	35	16	Iran, Islamic Republic of
99	98	98	97	98	Yes	0-3	40	...	Maldives
87	75	78	74	41	No	•	51	7	Nepal
82	72	77	78	73	Yes	0-6	32	12	Pakistan
99	99	99	99	99	...	...	35	12	Sri Lanka
Sub-Saharan Africa									
61	47	46	45	...	...	...	74	...	Angola
99	93	93	85	92	Yes	2-5	54	14	Benin
99	97	97	90	85	Yes	0-4	48	12	Botswana
99	96	94	84	...	...	...	77	14	Burkina Faso
84	74	64	75	74	...	...	91	12	Burundi
77	80	79	68	79	Yes	1-6	52	14	Cameroon
78	73	72	65	69	...	...	34	6	Cape Verde
70	40	40	35	...	Yes	2-5	71	14	Central African Republic

Table 3A (continued)

Country or territory	CHILD SURVIVAL[1]		CHILD WELL-BEING[2]						
	Infant mortality rate (‰)	Under-5 mortality rate (‰)	% of children under age 5 suffering from:				% of children who are:		
			Infants with low birth weight (%)	Underweight moderate and severe	Wasting moderate and severe	Stunting moderate and severe	Exclusively breastfed (<6 months)	Breastfed with complementary food (6-9 months)	Still breastfeeding (20-23 months)
	2005-2010	2005-2010	1998-2005[3]	1996-2005[3]	1996-2005[3]	1996-2005[3]	1996-2005[3]	1996-2005[3]	1996-2005[3]
Chad	111	195	22	37	14	41	2	77	65
Comoros	48	63	25	25	8	44	21	34	45
Congo	68	102	…	15	7	26	19	78	21
Côte d'Ivoire	114	183	17	17	7	21	5	73	38
Democratic Rep. of the Congo	112	197	12	31	13	38	24	79	52
Equatorial Guinea	94	170	13	19	7	39	24	…	…
Eritrea	57	81	14	40	13	38	52	43	62
Ethiopia	91	157	15	38	11	47	49	54	86
Gabon	51	88	14	12	3	21	6	62	9
Gambia	68	111	17	17	8	19	26	37	54
Ghana	56	91	16	22	7	30	53	62	67
Guinea	97	147	16	26	9	35	27	41	71
Guinea-Bissau	111	194	22	25	10	30	37	36	67
Kenya	63	107	10	20	6	30	13	84	57
Lesotho	59	113	13	20	4	38	36	79	60
Liberia	132	209	…	26	6	39	35	70	45
Madagascar	71	118	17	42	13	48	67	78	64
Malawi	103	167	16	22	5	48	53	78	80
Mali	126	206	23	33	11	38	25	32	69
Mauritius	14	16	14	15	14	10	21	…	…
Mozambique	91	163	15	24	4	41	30	80	65
Namibia	37	71	14	24	9	24	19	57	37
Niger	145	248	13	40	14	40	1	56	61
Nigeria	108	189	14	29	9	38	17	64	34
Rwanda	112	191	9	23	4	45	90	69	77
Sao Tome and Principe	78	104	20	13	4	29	56	53	42
Senegal	77	121	18	17	8	16	34	61	42
Seychelles	…	…	…	…	…	…	…	…	…
Sierra Leone	160	278	23	27	10	34	4	51	53
Somalia	113	187	…	26	17	23	9	13	8
South Africa	39	73	15	12	3	25	7	46	…
Swaziland	64	135	9	10	1	30	24	60	25
Togo	87	127	18	25	12	22	18	65	65
Uganda	77	128	12	23	4	39	63	75	50
United Republic of Tanzania	85	110	10	22	3	38	41	91	55
Zambia	88	161	12	20	6	50	40	87	58
Zimbabwe	59	113	11	17	5	26	33	90	35

	Weighted average			Weighted average			Weighted average		
World	52	78	15	25	9	30	36	52	46
Countries in transition	31	39	9	5	3	14	22	47	28
Developed countries	6	7	7	–	moderate	moderate	–	–	–
Developing countries	57	86	16	27	10	31	36	52	46
Arab States	42	55	15	16	8	24	30	59	24
Central and Eastern Europe	21	25	…	…	…	…	…	…	…
Central Asia	61	75	…	…	…	…	…	…	…
East Asia and the Pacific	30	37	7	15	–	19	43	43	27
East Asia	30	37	…	…	…	…	…	…	…
Pacific	31	43	…	…	…	…	…	…	…
Latin America and the Caribbean	22	30	9	7	2	15	–	49	26
Caribbean	…	…	…	…	…	…	…	…	…
Latin America	22	29	…	…	…	…	…	…	…
N. America/W. Europe	6	7	…	…	…	…	…	…	…
South and West Asia	62	89	…	…	…	…	…	…	…
Sub-Saharan Africa	96	163	14	28	9	37	30	67	55

1. United Nations Population Division statistics, 2004 revision, medium variant, UN Population Division (2005).
2. UNICEF (2006).
3. Data are for the most recent year available during the period specified.

4. Employed plus unemployed women as a share of the working age population, including women with a job but temporarily not at work (e.g. on maternity leave), home employment for the production of goods and services for own household consumption, and domestic and personal services produced by employing paid domestic staff. Data exclude women occupied solely in domestic duties in their own households (ILO, 2006a).

CHILD WELL-BEING[2]					PROVISION FOR UNDER-3s		WOMEN'S EMPLOYMENT AND MATERNITY LEAVE		
1-year-old children immunized against (%)					Official programmes targeting children	Youngest age group targeted in programmes	Female labour force participation rate, age 15 and above[4]	Duration of paid maternity leave[5]	
Tuberculosis	Diphtheria Pertussis Tetanus	Polio	Measles	Hepatitis B					
Corresponding vaccines:					under age 3	(years)	(%)	(weeks)	
BCG	DPT3	Polio3	Measles	HepB3					Country or territory
2005	2005	2005	2005	2005	2005	c. 2005	2003	2005-2007[3]	
40	20	36	23	...	...	...	65	14	Chad
90	80	85	80	80	...	...	58	...	Comoros
...	65	65	56	...	...	...	61	15	Congo
...	56	56	51	56	...	...	39	14	Côte d'Ivoire
84	73	73	70	...	...	...	61	14	Democratic Rep. of the Congo
73	33	39	51	...	...	...	50	12	Equatorial Guinea
91	83	83	84	83	Yes	0-6	59	...	Eritrea
67	69	66	59	...	No	·	71	6	Ethiopia
89	38	31	55	55	...	...	61	14	Gabon
89	88	90	84	88	...	...	59	...	Gambia
99	84	85	83	84	Yes	0-2	71	0	Ghana
90	69	70	59	...	Yes	0-3	79	...	Guinea
80	80	80	80	...	...	...	62	...	Guinea-Bissau
85	76	70	69	76	...	...	69	8	Kenya
96	83	80	85	83	No	·	47	...	Lesotho
82	87	77	94	...	Yes	2-6	55	...	Liberia
72	61	63	59	61	Yes	0-3	79	14	Madagascar
...	93	94	82	93	...	...	85	0	Malawi
82	85	84	86	85	Yes	0-3	72	14	Mali
99	97	97	98	97	Yes	0-2	41	12	Mauritius
87	72	70	77	72	...	...	85	...	Mozambique
95	86	86	73	...	Yes	0-1	47	...	Namibia
93	89	89	83	...	Yes	2-6	71	14	Niger
48	25	39	35	...	Yes	0-3	46	12	Nigeria
91	95	95	89	95	...	...	81	8	Rwanda
98	97	97	88	96	...	...	30	9	Sao Tome and Principe
92	84	84	74	84	Yes	0-5	57	14	Senegal
99	99	99	99	99	Yes	0-3	...	10	Seychelles
...	64	64	67	...	No	·	56	0	Sierra Leone
50	35	35	35	...	...	...	59	...	Somalia
97	94	94	82	94	Yes	0-5	47	26	South Africa
84	71	71	60	71	Yes	0-6	31	...	Swaziland
70	55	55	48	...	...	...	51	14	Togo
92	84	83	86	84	...	...	80	...	Uganda
...	...	...	...	...	...	...	86	12	United Republic of Tanzania
94	80	80	84	80	Yes	0-6	66	0	Zambia
98	...	90	85	90	...	...	63	13	Zimbabwe

Weighted average							Median		
83	78	78	77	55	...	...	52	14	World
93	95	95	96	92	...	...	56	18	Countries in transition
–	96	94	92	64	...	...	50	16	Developed countries
83	75	76	75	54	...	...	52	12	Developing countries
89	89	90	89	88	...	...	29	...	Arab States
...	...	...	...	...	...	...	51	19	Central and Eastern Europe
...	...	...	...	...	...	...	56	18	Central Asia
87	84	84	84	78	...	...	54	...	East Asia and the Pacific
...	...	...	...	...	...	...	56	12	East Asia
...	...	...	...	...	...	...	55	...	Pacific
96	91	91	92	85	...	...	52	13	Latin America and the Caribbean
...	...	...	...	...	...	...	52	13	Caribbean
...	...	...	...	...	...	...	47	12	Latin America
...	...	...	...	...	...	...	54	16	N. America/W. Europe
...	...	...	...	...	...	...	38	12	South and West Asia
76	66	68	65	37	...	...	61	13	Sub-Saharan Africa

5. Refers to paid employment-protected leave duration for employed women around the time of childbirth.
6. Maternity leave duration refers to unpaid parental leave, as no specific maternity leave policy exists (except for special medical cases).

7. Maternity leave duration refers to unpaid maternity leave.
Sources: (Women's maternity leave status) US Social Security Administration (2005, 2006*a*, 2006*b*, 2007); OECD Family Database.

Table 3B
Early childhood care and education (ECCE): education

	Country or territory	Age group 2005	ENROLMENT IN PRE-PRIMARY EDUCATION				Enrolment in private institutions as % of total enrolment		GROSS ENROLMENT RATIO (GER) IN PRE-PRIMARY EDUCATION (%)			
			School year ending in				School year ending in		School year ending in			
			1999		2005		1999	2005	1999			
			Total (000)	% F	Total (000)	% F			Total	Male	Female	GPI (F/M)
	Arab States											
1	Algeria	4-5	36	49	71	48	.	–	3	3	3	1.00
2	Bahrain	3-5	14	48	18	48	100	99	35	36	34	0.95
3	Djibouti	4-5	0.2	60	0.5	51	100	84	0.4	0.3	0.5	1.50
4	Egypt	4-5	328	48	542	48	54	31	11	11	10	0.95
5	Iraq	4-5	68	48	93	49	.	.	5	5	5	0.98
6	Jordan	4-5	74	46	92	47	100	95z	29	30	27	0.91
7	Kuwait	4-5	57	49	65	50	24	37	79	78	80	1.02
8	Lebanon	3-5	143	48	151	48	78	77	67	68	66	0.97
9	Libyan Arab Jamahiriya	4-5	10	48	18	49	.	15y	5	5	5	0.97
10	Mauritania	3-5	...	...	5	...	...	78	...	...	...	...
11	Morocco	4-5	805	34	691	39	100	100	62	81	43	0.52
12	Oman	4-5	7	45	10	47	100	100	6	6	6	0.88
13	Palestinian Autonomous Territories	4-5	77	48	73	48	100	100	40	41	39	0.96
14	Qatar	3-5	8	48	14	48	100	94	25	26	25	0.97
15	Saudi Arabia	3-5	...	...	188	48	...	45	...	...	...	...
16	Sudan	4-5	366	...	498	49	90	71	20	...	...	...
17	Syrian Arab Republic	3-5	108	46	150	47	67	74	8	9	8	0.90
18	Tunisia	3-5	78	47	109y	48y	88	...	14	14	13	0.95
19	United Arab Emirates	4-5	64	48	83	48	68	75	63	64	62	0.97
20	Yemen	3-5	12	45	18	45	37	49	0.7	0.8	0.6	0.86
	Central and Eastern Europe											
21	Albania	3-5	82	50	80z	48z	.	5z	44	42	45	1.07
22	Belarus	3-5	263	47*	269	48	–	5	80	82*	77*	0.95*
23	Bosnia and Herzegovina	3-5	...	...	...	...	...	...	...	...	...	...
24	Bulgaria	3-6	219	48	203	48	0.1	0.3	69	69	68	0.99
25	Croatia	3-6	81	48	87y	48y	5	8y	40	40	39	0.98
26	Czech Republic	3-5	312	50	288	48	2	1	94	91	97	1.06
27	Estonia	3-6	55	48	53	49	0.7	2	90	90	89	0.99
28	Hungary	3-6	376	48	326	48	3	5	80	80	79	0.98
29	Latvia	3-6	58	48	63	48	1	3	53	54	52	0.95
30	Lithuania	3-6	94	48	87	48	0.3	0.1	51	51	50	0.97
31	Poland	3-6	958	49	832	49	3	8	50	50	50	1.01
32	Republic of Moldova[1,2]	3-6	103	48	99	48	...	0.7	46	47	45	0.96
33	Romania	3-6	625	49	645	49	0.6	1	63	63	64	1.02
34	Russian Federation	3-6	4 225	47	4 423	47	7	1	67	69	65	0.94
35	Serbia and Montenegro[1]	3-6	166	48	...	...	.	...	44	44	44	0.99
36	Slovakia	3-5	169	...	153	48	0.4	1	83	...	...	...
37	Slovenia	3-5	59	46	42	48	1	1	75	79	72	0.91
38	TFYR Macedonia	3-6	33	49	33	49	.	.	28	28	28	1.01
39	Turkey	3-5	261	47	435	48	6	4	6	6	6	0.94
40	Ukraine	3-5	1 103	48	996	48	0.04	3	48	49	48	0.98
	Central Asia											
41	Armenia	3-6	57	...	46	50	–	1	26	...	...	...
42	Azerbaijan	3-5	111	46	108	48	–	0.1	22	23	21	0.89
43	Georgia	3-5	74	48	75	51	0.1	–	38	37	38	1.01
44	Kazakhstan	3-6	165	48	288	48	10	5	15	16	15	0.95
45	Kyrgyzstan	3-6	48	43	53	49	1	1	10	11	9	0.80
46	Mongolia	3-6	74	54	83	52	4	1	25	23	28	1.21
47	Tajikistan	3-6	56	42	62	47	.	.	8	9	7	0.76
48	Turkmenistan	3-6	...	...	...	...	...	...	...	...	...	...
49	Uzbekistan	3-6	...	...	615z	47z	...	.z	...	...	...	...
	East Asia and the Pacific											
50	Australia	4-4	...	...	263	49	...	66	...	...	...	...
51	Brunei Darussalam	3-5	11	49	12	49	66	65	51	50	52	1.04
52	Cambodia	3-5	58	50	95	51	22	24	6	6	6	1.03
53	China	4-6	24 030	46	21 790	45	...	31	38	39	37	0.97
54	Cook Islands[1]	4-4	0.4	47	0.5z	50z	25	22z	86	87	85	0.98

GROSS ENROLMENT RATIO (GER) IN PRE-PRIMARY EDUCATION (%) School year ending in 2005				NET ENROLMENT RATIO (NER) IN PRE-PRIMARY EDUCATION (%) School year ending in 2005				GROSS ENROLMENT RATIO (GER) IN PRE-PRIMARY AND OTHER ECCE PROGRAMMES (%) School year ending in 2005				NEW ENTRANTS TO THE FIRST GRADE OF PRIMARY EDUCATION WITH ECCE EXPERIENCE (%) School year ending in 2005			
Total	Male	Female	GPI (F/M)	Total	Male	Female	GPI (F/M)	Total	Male	Female	GPI (F/M)	Total	Male	Female	
														Arab States	
6	6	6	0.96	6	6	6	0.96	...	...	...	...	3	3	3	1
47	48	46	0.97	46	46	45	0.97	49	50	49	0.97	80	80	79	2
1	1	1	1.06	0.8	0.7	0.9	1.25	1	1	1	1.06	...	...	...	3
16	17	16	0.94	*15*	*16*	*15*	*0.94*	16	17	16	0.94	...	...	...	4
6	*6*	*6*	*1.00*	*6*	*6*	*6*	*1.00*	*6*	*6*	*6*	*1.00*	...	...	...	5
31	32	30	0.93	28	29	27	0.94	31	32	30	0.93	49z	...	...	6
73	72	74	1.03	57	56	58	1.03	73	72	74	1.03	77	76	78	7
74	75	73	0.98	72	72	71	0.98	74	75	73	0.98	94	94	94	8
8	**8**	**8**	**1.00**	**7**	**7**	**7**	**0.99**	...	...	...	...	...	...	...	9
2	...	...	...	...	...	...	...	...	...	...	...	25z	25z	24z	10
54	65	42	0.65	47	57	37	0.66	54	65	42	0.65	...	...	...	11
8	**8**	**8**	**0.94**	**7**	**7**	**7**	**0.95**	**8**	**8**	**8**	**0.94**	...	...	...	12
30	31	29	0.96	23	24	23	0.95	30	31	29	0.96	...	...	...	13
36	37	36	0.96	35	36	33	0.92	36	37	36	0.96	...	...	...	14
10	10	10	0.95	9	10	9	0.95	10	10	10	0.95	...	...	...	15
25	25	25	1.00	*25*	*25*	*25*	*1.00*	25	25	25	1.00	49z	52z	44z	16
10	11	10	0.91	10	11	10	0.91	10	11	10	0.91	12	12	12	17
22ʸ	*22ʸ*	*22ʸ*	*0.99ʸ*	*22ʸ*	*22ʸ*	*22ʸ*	*0.99*	*22ʸ*	*22ʸ*	*22ʸ*	*0.99ʸ*	...	...	...	18
64	65	64	0.98	46	46	45	0.98	64	65	64	0.98	79	79	79	19
0.9	1	0.8	0.85	*0.5ʸ*	*0.5ʸ*	*0.5ʸ*	*0.94ʸ*	...	...	...	...	...	...	...	20
														Central and Eastern Europe	
49z	49z	49z	1.00z	47z	47z	47z	1.00z	49z	49z	49z	1.00z	...	...	...	21
105	106	104	0.98	92	92	91	0.99	123	124	121	0.98	...	...	...	22
...	...	...	...	...	...	...	...	...	...	...	...	...	...	...	23
79	79	79	0.99	75	76	75	0.99	79	79	79	0.99	...	...	...	24
47ʸ	47ʸ	46ʸ	0.98ʸ	46ʸ	46ʸ	45ʸ	0.97ʸ	53ʸ	54ʸ	53ʸ	0.98ʸ	98*,ʸ	98*,ʸ	98*,ʸ	25
109	111	107	0.96	*98*	*100*	*97*	*0.97*	109	111	107	0.96	...	...	...	26
111	111	111	1.00	88	88	88	1.01	111	111	111	1.00	...	...	...	27
83	84	82	0.98	82	82	81	0.98	83	84	82	0.98	...	...	...	28
84	85	84	0.99	82	82	82	1.00	84	85	84	0.99	...	...	...	29
68	69	66	0.97	66	67	65	0.98	...	...	...	...	...	...	...	30
54	54	54	1.00	53	53	53	1.01	54	54	54	1.00	...	...	...	31
62	63	61	0.97	60	61	59	0.97	62	63	61	0.97	...	...	...	32
75	75	76	1.02	74	74	75	1.02	75	75	76	1.02	...	...	...	33
84	86	81	0.94	67z	...	...	...	84	86	81	0.94	...	...	...	34
...	...	...	...	...	...	...	...	...	...	...	...	...	...	...	35
95	96	93	0.97	*86*	*87*	*84*	*0.96*	95	96	93	0.97	...	...	...	36
79	81	78	0.96	78	79	76	0.97	79	81	78	0.96	...	...	...	37
33	33	34	1.03	32	31	32	1.02	...	...	...	...	...	...	...	38
10	10	10	0.95	10	10	10	0.95	10	10	10	0.95	...	...	...	39
86	87	84	0.96	44	45	44	0.97	86	87	84	0.96	...	...	...	40
														Central Asia	
33	30	35	1.16	...	...	...	...	33	30	35	1.16	...	...	...	41
29	29	29	1.02	21	20	21	1.04	30	29	30	1.02	7	7	7	42
51	48	54	1.13	43	41	46	1.13	51	48	54	1.13	2z	2z	2z	43
34	34	33	0.97	33	33	33	0.97	34	34	33	0.97	...	...	...	44
13	13	13	1.00	10	10	10	1.00	13	13	13	1.00	15	16	15	45
40	38	42	1.12	35	...	...	...	52	48	55	1.14	...	...	...	46
9	10	9	0.91	7	7	7	0.93	...	...	...	...	...	...	...	47
...	...	...	...	...	...	...	...	...	...	...	...	...	...	...	48
28z	*29z*	*27z*	*0.93z*	21ʸ	...	...	...	...	...	...	...	...	...	...	49
														East Asia and the Pacific	
104	104	104	1.00	62	62	62	1.00	104	104	104	1.00	...	...	...	50
52	52	52	1.01	47	47	48	1.01	52	52	52	1.01	100	*100*	*100*	51
9	9	10	1.08	9	8	9	1.09	9	9	10	1.08	15	15	16	52
40	**42**	**38**	**0.91**	...	...	...	...	**40**	**42**	**38**	**0.91**	...	...	...	53
91z	*87z*	*97z*	*1.11z*	...	...	...	...	*91z*	*87z*	*97z*	*1.11z*	...	...	...	54

Table 3B (continued)

	Country or territory	Age group 2005	ENROLMENT IN PRE-PRIMARY EDUCATION — School year ending in 1999 Total (000)	1999 % F	2005 Total (000)	2005 % F	Enrolment in private institutions as % of total enrolment — School year ending in 1999	2005	GROSS ENROLMENT RATIO (GER) IN PRE-PRIMARY EDUCATION (%) — School year ending in 1999 Total	Male	Female	GPI (F/M)
171	Democratic Rep. of the Congo	3-5	...	...	71ʸ	50ʸ	...	84ʸ	...	...	...	...
172	Equatorial Guinea	3-6	17	51	25	45	37	49	31	31	32	1.04
173	Eritrea	5-6	12	47	31	50	97	48	6	6	5	0.88
174	Ethiopia	4-6	90	49	**158**	**48**	100	100	1	1	1	0.97
175	Gabon	3-5	...	...	...	...	...	...	...	...	...	...
176	Gambia	3-6	29	47	30ᶻ	50ᶻ	...	100ᶻ	20	21	19	0.91
177	Ghana	3-5	667	49	**996**	**50**	33	34	40	40	40	1.02
178	Guinea	3-6	...	...	76	49	...	91ᶻ	...	...	...	...
179	Guinea-Bissau	4-6	4	51	...	...	62	...	3	3	3	1.05
180	Kenya	3-5	1 188	50	1 643	49	10	31	44	44	44	1.00
181	Lesotho	3-5	33	52	45	51	100	100	23	23	24	1.08
182	Liberia	3-5	112	42	...	...	39	...	41	47	35	0.74
183	Madagascar	3-5	50	51	171ᶻ	...	93	90ʸ	3	3	3	1.02
184	Malawi	3-5	...	...	...	...	...	...	...	...	...	...
185	Mali	3-6	21	51	46	49	...	...	1	1	1	1.09
186	Mauritius	3-4	42	50	37	49	85	83	100	99	101	1.02
187	Mozambique	3-5	...	...	...	...	...	...	...	...	...	...
188	Namibia	3-5	35	53	48ᶻ	52ᶻ	100	100ᶻ	19	18	21	1.16
189	Niger	4-6	12	50	20	50	33	32	1	1	1	1.05
190	Nigeria	3-5	...	...	1 860	49	...	...	...	...	...	...
191	Rwanda	4-6	...	...	...	...	...	...	...	...	...	...
192	Sao Tome and Principe	3-6	4	51	5	51	–	–	27	26	28	1.09
193	Senegal	4-6	24	50	79	52	68	68	3	3	3	1.00
194	Seychelles[1]	4-5	3	49	3	51	5	5ʸ	109	107	111	1.04
195	Sierra Leone	3-5	...	...	...	...	...	...	...	...	...	...
196	Somalia	3-5	...	...	...	...	...	...	...	...	...	...
197	South Africa	6-6	207	50	387ᶻ	50ᶻ	26	7ᶻ	20	20	20	1.01
198	Swaziland	3-5	...	...	15ᶻ	49ᶻ	...	–ᶻ	...	...	...	...
199	Togo	3-5	11	50	13ᶻ	50ᶻ	53	59ᶻ	2	2	2	0.99
200	Uganda	4-5	66	50	30	50	100	100	4	4	4	1.00
201	United Republic of Tanzania	5-6	...	...	**669**	**50**	...	2	...	...	...	...
202	Zambia	3-6	...	...	...	...	...	...	...	...	...	...
203	Zimbabwe	3-5	439	51	448ʸ	...	...	...	41	40	41	1.03

			Sum	% F	Sum	% F	Median		Weighted average			
I	World	...	112 289	48	132 010	48	29	32	33	34	33	0.96
II	Countries in transition	...	7 070	47	7 187	47	0.04	1	46	48	45	0.94
III	Developed countries	...	25 367	49	25 636	48	8	8	73	74	73	0.99
IV	Developing countries	...	79 851	47	99 188	48	47	47	28	28	27	0.95
V	Arab States	...	2 441	43	2 885	46	83	75	15	17	13	0.77
VI	Central and Eastern Europe	...	9 292	48	9 322	48	0.7	2	49	50	48	0.97
VII	Central Asia	...	1 450	47	1 483	48	0.1	0.5	22	23	22	0.92
VIII	East Asia and the Pacific	...	37 027	47	35 775	47	48	45	40	41	40	0.98
IX	East Asia	...	36 611	47	35 252	47	57	58	40	41	40	0.98
X	Pacific	...	416	49	523	48	...	20	57	57	57	1.00
XI	Latin America and the Caribbean	...	16 392	49	19 126	49	29	41	56	55	56	1.01
XII	Caribbean	...	672	50	794	51	88	79	71	69	72	1.04
XIII	Latin America	...	15 720	49	18 332	49	23	21	55	55	56	1.01
XIV	North America and Western Europe	...	19 133	48	19 476	48	26	19	76	76	75	0.98
XV	South and West Asia	...	21 425	46	35 689	49	...	46	22	23	21	0.91
XVI	Sub-Saharan Africa	...	5 129	49	8 256	49	53	49	10	10	9	0.98

1. National population data were used to calculate enrolment ratios.
2. Enrolment and population data exclude Transnistria.
3. For the first time, data include French overseas departments and territories (DOM-TOM).
4. Enrolment ratios were not calculated due to lack of United Nations population data by age.

5. The decline in enrolment is essentially due to a reclassification of programmes. From 2004, it was decided to include children categorized as age '4 rising 5' (those who are under 5 but over 4.5) in primary education enrolment rather than pre-primary enrolment even if they started the school year at the latter level. Such children typically (though not always) start primary school reception classes in the second or third term of the school year.

GROSS ENROLMENT RATIO (GER) IN PRE-PRIMARY EDUCATION (%) School year ending in 2005				NET ENROLMENT RATIO (NER) IN PRE-PRIMARY EDUCATION (%) School year ending in 2005				GROSS ENROLMENT RATIO (GER) IN PRE-PRIMARY AND OTHER ECCE PROGRAMMES (%) School year ending in 2005				NEW ENTRANTS TO THE FIRST GRADE OF PRIMARY EDUCATION WITH ECCE EXPERIENCE (%) School year ending in 2005			
Total	Male	Female	GPI (F/M)	Total	Male	Female	GPI (F/M)	Total	Male	Female	GPI (F/M)	Total	Male	Female	
1[y]	1[y]	1[y]	1.01[y]	1[y]	1[y]	1[y]	1.01[y]	...	...	...	...	...	...	...	171
41	45	37	0.83	39[y]	...	...	...	41	45	37	0.83	70	67	72	172
12	12	12	1.02	8	8	9	1.01	16	16	17	1.03	...	...	...	173
2	**2**	**2**	**0.94**	...	...	...	...	**2**	**2**	**2**	**0.94**	...	...	...	174
...	...	...	...	...	...	...	...	...	...	...	...	...	...	...	175
18[z]	18[z]	19[z]	1.03[z]	...	...	...	...	...	...	...	...	...	...	...	176
56	**55**	**57**	**1.05**	**36**	**35**	**37**	**1.05**	**65**	**63**	**68**	**1.09**	...	...	...	177
7	7	7	1.02	6	6	6	1.02	7	7	7	1.02	17	17	18	178
...	...	...	...	...	...	...	...	...	...	...	...	...	...	...	179
52	52	52	0.99	29	28	29	1.02	52	52	52	0.99	...	...	...	180
34	33	35	1.06	27	26	28	1.07	34	33	35	1.06	...	...	...	181
...	...	...	...	...	...	...	...	...	...	...	...	...	...	...	182
10[z]	...	...	...	10[z]	...	...	...	10[z]	...	...	...	...	...	...	183
...	...	...	...	...	...	...	...	...	...	...	...	...	...	...	184
3	3	3	1.01	...	...	...	...	3	3	3	1.01	7	6	7	185
95	95	96	1.01	85	85	86	1.01	95	95	96	1.01	100	100	100	186
...	...	...	...	...	...	...	...	...	...	...	...	...	...	...	187
29[z]	27[z]	30[z]	1.12[z]	...	...	...	...	...	...	...	...	.[z]	.[z]	.[z]	188
1	1	1	1.05	0.9	0.9	0.9	1.05	1	1	1	1.05	19[y]	19[y]	19[y]	189
15	15	15	0.99	11[z]	11[z]	11[z]	0.97[z]	...	...	...	...	...	...	...	190
...	...	...	...	...	...	...	...	...	...	...	...	...	...	...	191
32	31	33	1.06	32	31	33	1.06	44	43	45	1.05	...	...	...	192
8	7	8	1.11	4	4	5	1.11	...	...	...	...	4[z]	4[z]	5[z]	193
109	110	109	0.98	96	97	95	0.99	109	110	109	0.98	100[y]	100[y]	100[y]	194
...	...	...	...	...	...	...	...	...	...	...	...	...	...	...	195
...	...	...	...	...	...	...	...	...	...	...	...	...	...	...	196
37[z]	37[z]	38[z]	1.03[z]	16[y]	16[y]	16[y]	1.02[y]	57[z]	56[z]	58[z]	1.03[z]	...	...	...	197
18[z]	18[z]	18[z]	0.99[z]	12[z]	12[z]	12[z]	0.99[z]	18[z]	18[z]	18[z]	0.99[z]	...	...	...	198
2[z]	2[z]	2[z]	0.98[z]	2[z]	2[z]	2[z]	0.98[z]	2[z]	2[z]	2[z]	0.98[z]	...	...	...	199
1	1	1	1.01	0.9	0.9	0.9	1.01	...	...	...	...	...	...	...	200
30	**29**	**30**	**1.03**	29	29	29	1.02	...	...	...	...	...	...	...	201
...	...	...	...	...	...	...	...	...	...	...	...	21	20	22	202
43[y]	...	...	...	...	...	...	...	43[y]	...	...	...	...	...	...	203

Weighted average				Median				Median				Median			
40	40	39	0.97	...	...	...	...	...	...	...	...	...	...	...	I
60	62	58	0.94	...	...	...	...	...	...	...	...	...	...	...	II
78	79	77	0.98	...	...	...	...	...	...	...	...	...	...	...	III
34	35	34	0.97	...	...	...	...	...	...	...	...	...	...	...	IV
17	18	16	0.88	...	...	...	...	...	...	...	...	...	...	...	V
59	60	57	0.96	...	...	...	...	...	...	...	...	...	...	...	VI
28	28	27	0.95	...	...	...	...	...	...	...	...	...	...	...	VII
43	44	42	0.95	...	...	...	...	...	...	...	...	...	...	...	VIII
43	44	42	0.95	...	...	...	...	...	...	...	...	...	...	...	IX
72	73	72	1.00	...	...	...	...	...	...	...	...	...	...	...	X
62	62	62	1.00	...	...	...	...	...	...	...	...	...	...	...	XI
83	80	85	1.06	...	...	...	...	...	...	...	...	...	...	...	XII
61	61	61	0.99	...	...	...	...	...	...	...	...	...	...	...	XIII
79	80	78	0.97	...	...	...	...	...	...	...	...	...	...	...	XIV
37	37	37	1.00	...	...	...	...	...	...	...	...	...	...	...	XV
14	14	13	0.97	...	...	...	...	...	...	...	...	...	...	...	XVI

6. Enrolment ratios were not calculated due to inconsistencies between enrolment and the United Nations population data.

Data in italic are UIS estimates.
Data in bold are for the school year ending in 2006.

(z) Data are for the school year ending in 2004.
(y) Data are for the school year ending in 2003.
(*) National estimates.

Table 4
Access to primary education

Country or territory	Compulsory education (age group)	Legal guarantees of free education[1]	New entrants (000) School year ending in 1999	New entrants (000) School year ending in 2005	GIR 1999 Total	GIR 1999 Male	GIR 1999 Female	GIR 1999 GPI (F/M)	GIR 2005 Total	GIR 2005 Male	GIR 2005 Female	GIR 2005 GPI (F/M)
Arab States												
Algeria[2]	6-16	Yes	745	598	101	102	100	0.98	101	102	99	0.97
Bahrain	6-15	Yes	13	14	101	99	103	1.04	104	104	104	1.00
Djibouti	6-15	No	6	9	30	34	25	0.74	43	45	40	0.89
Egypt[3]	6-13	Yes	1451	1659	92	94	90	0.96	102	104	100	0.96
Iraq	6-11	Yes	709	844	102	109	95	0.88	107	110	103	0.94
Jordan[2]	6-16	Yes	126	127	102	101	102	1.00	85	85	85	1.01
Kuwait[2]	6-14	Yes	35	40	97	97	98	1.01	93	93	92	0.99
Lebanon[2, 3]	6-12	Yes	71	72	102	106	98	0.92	101	102	100	0.98
Libyan Arab Jamahiriya[2]	6-15	Yes	…	…	…	…	…	…	…	…	…	…
Mauritania[3]	6-14	Yes	…	97	…	…	…	…	112	112	113	1.01
Morocco	6-14	Yes	731	628	112	115	109	0.94	99	101	97	0.96
Oman	6-15	Yes	52	**44**	86	86	86	1.00	**74**	**74**	**75**	**1.01**
Palestinian A. T.	6-15	…	95	95	105	104	106	1.01	82	82	82	0.99
Qatar[3]	6-14	Yes	11	12	111	112	109	0.98	106	106	105	0.99
Saudi Arabia	6-11	Yes	…	536	…	…	…	…	87	85	89	1.05
Sudan[3]	6-13	Yes	…	642	…	…	…	…	67	72	62	0.86
Syrian Arab Republic[2]	6-12	Yes	466	561	107	110	103	0.94	121	123	119	0.97
Tunisia	6-16	Yes	204	165	101	101	100	1.00	100	99	101	1.01
United Arab Emirates[3]	6-15	Yes	47	56	91	93	90	0.97	89	89	89	1.00
Yemen[3]	6-14	Yes	440	691[z]	78	91	65	0.71	110[z]	122[z]	97[z]	0.80[z]
Central and Eastern Europe												
Albania[3]	6-13	Yes	67	56[z]	102	103	102	0.99	99[z]	99[z]	99[z]	0.99[z]
Belarus[3]	6-16	Yes	173	89	131	132	130	0.99	104	105	103	0.98
Bosnia and Herzegovina[3]	…	Yes	…	…	…	…	…	…	…	…	…	…
Bulgaria[2, 3]	7-16	Yes	93	63	101	102	100	0.98	96	98	95	0.98
Croatia[3]	7-15	Yes	50	49[y]	94	95	93	0.98	98[y]	99[y]	97[y]	0.98[y]
Czech Republic	6-15	Yes	124	90	101	102	100	0.98	102	102	102	1.00
Estonia	7-15	Yes	18	12	100	100	99	0.98	101	102	99	0.97
Hungary	7-16	Yes	127	100	102	104	100	0.97	96	97	95	0.98
Latvia[3]	7-15	Yes	32	18	96	96	96	0.99	93	93	93	1.00
Lithuania[2]	7-16	Yes	54	36	105	105	104	0.99	97	97	96	0.99
Poland[2, 4]	7-18	Yes	535	404	101	101	100	0.99	97	97	97	1.00
Republic of Moldova[3, 5, 6]	6-16	Yes	62	41	99	99	99	1.00	92	93	91	0.98
Romania[3]	7-14	Yes	269	217	94	94	94	0.99	99	100	98	0.99
Russian Federation[3]	6-15	Yes	1659	1271	86	…	…	…	97	98	96	0.98
Serbia and Montenegro[3, 5]	7-14	Yes	…	…	…	…	…	…	…	…	…	…
Slovakia[2]	6-16	Yes	75	57	102	102	101	0.99	99	99	98	0.99
Slovenia[2]	6-15	Yes	21	18	99	99	99	0.99	99	101	98	0.97
TFYR Macedonia[2, 3]	7-15	Yes	32	26	102	102	102	1.00	99	99	99	1.00
Turkey[3]	6-14	Yes	…	1340	…	…	…	…	92	94	90	0.96
Ukraine[3]	6-17	Yes	623	426*	93	94	93	0.99	104*	104*	104*	1.00*
Central Asia												
Armenia[3]	7-15	Yes	…	41	…	…	…	…	100	98	102	1.04
Azerbaijan[3]	6-17	Yes	175	126	94	94	95	1.01	94	94	93	0.99
Georgia[3]	6-14	Yes	74	54	99	99	100	1.02	104	103	105	1.02
Kazakhstan	7-17	Yes	…	239	…	…	…	…	108	108	107	0.99
Kyrgyzstan[3]	7-15	Yes	120*	102	99*	99*	100*	1.02*	95	97	94	0.97
Mongolia[3]	7-16	Yes	70	77	111	111	111	1.00	149	148	149	1.00
Tajikistan[3]	7-15	Yes	177	167	99	102	97	0.95	99	101	97	0.96
Turkmenistan[3]	7-15	Yes	…	…	…	…	…	…	…	…	…	…
Uzbekistan[3]	7-16	Yes	…	596[z]	…	…	…	…	102[z]	102[z]	102[z]	1.00[z]
East Asia and the Pacific												
Australia	5-15	Yes	…	269	…	…	…	…	105	105	105	0.99
Brunei Darussalam	5-16	No	8	7	107	107	106	0.99	102	103	100	0.97
Cambodia[3]	…	Yes	404	436	117	120	114	0.95	133	137	128	0.94
China[3, 7]	6-14	Yes	…	**16764**	…	…	…	…	**88**	**90**	**87**	**0.97**

NET INTAKE RATE (NIR) IN PRIMARY EDUCATION (%)								SCHOOL LIFE EXPECTANCY (expected number of years of formal schooling from primary to tertiary education)						
School year ending in								School year ending in						
1999				2005				1999			2005			
Total	Male	Female	GPI (F/M)	Total	Male	Female	GPI (F/M)	Total	Male	Female	Total	Male	Female	Country or territory
														Arab States
77	79	76	0.97	88	89	86	0.96	...	...	...	13	13	13	Algeria[2]
86	83	88	1.06	86	86	86	1.00	13	13	14	14	14	15	Bahrain
22	25	19	0.75	30	33	28	0.85	3	4	3	4	5	4	Djibouti
...	...	...	...	92z	92z	91z	0.99z	12	...	...	13	...	...	Egypt[3]
79	83	75	0.90	82	85	79	0.92	8	9	7	10	11	8	Iraq
68	67	69	1.02	60z	60z	60z	1.00z	...	...	...	13	13	13	Jordan[2]
62	63	61	0.97	54	54	55	1.02	14	13	14	13	12	13	Kuwait[2]
75	77	74	0.95	75	77	74	0.97	13	13	13	14	14	15	Lebanon[2,3]
...	...	...	...	...	...	...	...	...	...	...	16y	16y	17y	Libyan Arab Jamahiriya[2]
...	...	...	...	35	35	34	0.98	7	...	...	8	8	7	Mauritania[3]
51	53	49	0.93	81	83	79	0.95	8	9	7	10	11	9	Morocco
70	69	70	1.01	53	52	53	1.01	...	...	...	11	11	11	Oman
...	...	...	...	61	62	60	0.96	12	12	12	13	13	14	Palestinian A. T.
...	...	...	...	...	...	...	...	13	12	14	13	13	14	Qatar[3]
...	...	...	...	48	47	49	1.04	...	...	...	13	13	13	Saudi Arabia
...	...	...	...	...	...	...	...	5	...	...	...	...	...	Sudan[3]
60	61	60	0.98	62	62	61	0.98	...	...	...	...	...	...	Syrian Arab Republic[2]
...	...	...	...	88z	88z	89z	1.02z	13	13	13	14	14	14	Tunisia
48	48	47	0.99	34	34	33	0.98	11	11	12	10y	10y	11y	United Arab Emirates[3]
26	31	21	0.68	...	...	...	...	8	10	5	9	11	7	Yemen[3]
														Central and Eastern Europe
...	...	...	...	...	...	...	...	11	11	11	11z	11z	12z	Albania[3]
76	77	76	0.99	88*	88*	87*	0.98*	14	13	14	15	14	15	Belarus[3]
...	...	...	...	...	...	...	...	...	...	...	...	...	...	Bosnia and Herzegovina[3]
...	...	...	...	...	...	...	...	13	13	13	13	13	13	Bulgaria[2,3]
68	69	66	0.97	71y	73y	70y	0.95y	12	12	12	13y	13y	13y	Croatia[3]
...	...	...	...	...	...	...	...	13	13	14	15	15	15	Czech Republic
...	...	...	...	...	...	...	...	14	14	15	16	15	17	Estonia
...	...	...	...	65	67	63	0.94	14	14	14	15	15	16	Hungary
...	...	...	...	...	...	...	...	14	13	14	16	14	17	Latvia[3]
...	...	...	...	...	...	...	...	14	14	15	16	15	17	Lithuania[2]
...	...	...	...	...	...	...	...	15	14	15	15	15	16	Poland[2,4]
...	...	...	...	73	74	72	0.98	11	11	12	12	11	12	Republic of Moldova[3,5,6]
...	...	...	...	...	...	...	...	12	12	12	14	13	14	Romania[3]
...	...	...	...	...	...	...	...	...	...	...	14	13	14	Russian Federation[3]
...	...	...	...	...	...	...	...	13*	13*	13*	...	...	...	Serbia and Montenegro[3,5]
...	...	...	...	...	...	...	...	13	13	13	14	14	15	Slovakia[2]
...	...	...	...	...	...	...	...	15	14	15	17	16	18	Slovenia[2]
...	...	...	...	...	...	...	...	12	12	12	12	12	12	TFYR Macedonia[2,3]
...	...	...	...	72	73	71	0.97	...	...	...	11	12	10	Turkey[3]
66	...	...	...	78*	78*	78*	1.00*	13	12	13	14	14	14	Ukraine[3]
														Central Asia
...	...	...	...	75y	73y	77y	1.05y	...	...	...	11	11	11	Armenia[3]
...	...	...	...	65	66	64	0.96	10	10	10	11	11	11	Azerbaijan[3]
69	68	69	1.02	90z	90z	90z	1.00z	12	12	12	12	12	13	Georgia[3]
...	...	...	...	67z	69z	65z	0.95z	12	12	12	15	15	16	Kazakhstan
58*	59*	58*	0.99*	58	59	56	0.95	12	11	12	12	12	13	Kyrgyzstan[3]
83	83	82	1.00	75	74	76	1.03	9	8	10	12	12	13	Mongolia[3]
93	95	90	0.95	...	...	...	...	10	11	9	11	12	10	Tajikistan[3]
...	...	...	...	...	...	...	...	...	...	...	...	...	...	Turkmenistan[3]
...	...	...	...	85y	85y	85y	1.0y	...	...	...	11z	12z	11z	Uzbekistan[3]
														East Asia and the Pacific
...	...	...	...	71	69	74	1.08	20	20	20	20	20	20	Australia
...	...	...	...	67	68	65	0.96	14	13	14	14	14	14	Brunei Darussalam
69	70	68	0.97	89	89	90	1.01	...	...	...	10z	11z	9z	Cambodia[3]
...	...	...	...	...	...	...	...	...	...	...	11	11	11	China[3,7]

Table 4 (continued)

Country or territory	Compulsory education (age group)	Legal guarantees of free education[1]	New entrants (000) School year ending in 1999	New entrants (000) School year ending in 2005	GIR 1999 Total	GIR 1999 Male	GIR 1999 Female	GIR 1999 GPI (F/M)	GIR 2005 Total	GIR 2005 Male	GIR 2005 Female	GIR 2005 GPI (F/M)
Panama[3]	6-11	Yes	69	73	112	113	111	0.99	110	110	109	0.98
Paraguay[3]	6-14	Yes	*179*	164[z]	*122*	*125*	*120*	*0.96*	107[z]	108[z]	106[z]	0.98[z]
Peru[3]	6-16	Yes	676	633	111	111	111	1.00	105	104	106	1.01
Saint Kitts and Nevis[5]	5-16	No	...	0.9	...	...	...	...	94	91	97	1.07
Saint Lucia	5-16	No	*4*	3	*98*	*99*	*96*	*0.97*	109	109	109	1.00
St Vincent/Grenad.	5-15	No	...	*2*	...	...	...	...	95	101	90	0.88
Suriname[3]	6-11	Yes	...	10	...	...	...	...	102	102	103	1.01
Trinidad and Tobago[2, 3]	5-12	Yes	20	17*	98	99	97	0.98	101*	104*	99*	0.96*
Turks and Caicos Islands	4-16	...	*0.3*	0.4	...	...	...	...	83	83	84	1.01
Uruguay[3]	6-15	Yes	60	56[z]	107	107	107	1.00	100[z]	101[z]	99[z]	0.99[z]
Venezuela[3]	6-15	Yes	537	550	98	99	97	0.98	100	101	98	0.97
North America and Western Europe												
Andorra[2, 5]	6-16	...	...	0.8	...	...	...	...	100	97	103	1.06
Austria[2, 4]	6-15	Yes	100	*89*[z]	106	107	104	0.98	*105*[z]	*105*[z]	*105*[z]	*1.00*[z]
Belgium[4]	6-18	Yes	...	*120*[z]	...	...	...	...	*103*[z]	*103*[z]	*104*[z]	*1.01*[z]
Canada	6-16	Yes	...	...	...	...	...	...	...	...	...	...
Cyprus[2, 5]	6-15	Yes	...	9	...	...	...	...	101	100	102	1.01
Denmark	7-16	Yes	66	67	100	100	100	1.00	96	96	97	1.00
Finland	7-16	Yes	65	59	100	101	100	1.00	98	98	98	1.00
France[8]	6-16	Yes	736	...	102	*103*	*101*	*0.98*	...	...	...	...
Germany	6-18	Yes	869	824	100	101	100	1.00	103	103	103	0.99
Greece[2]	6-15	Yes	113	105	106	107	105	0.98	99	99	99	1.00
Iceland	6-16	Yes	4	4[z]	99	101	97	0.96	95[z]	98[z]	93[z]	0.95[z]
Ireland	6-15	Yes	51	*58*	99	100	98	0.98	*103*	*103*	*103*	*0.99*
Israel[3]	5-15	Yes	...	122	...	...	...	...	97	95	99	1.04
Italy[2]	6-16	Yes	558	546	100	101	99	0.99	103	103	102	0.98
Luxembourg	6-15	Yes	5	6	97	...	...	...	99	97	102	1.04
Malta[2]	5-16	Yes	5	4	102	102	101	0.99	93	94	92	0.99
Monaco[2, 9]	6-16	No	...	0.4[z]	...	...	...	...	...	...	...	...
Netherlands[2, 4]	6-17	Yes	199	197[z]	100	101	99	0.99	100[z]	100[z]	99[z]	0.99[z]
Norway	6-16	Yes	61	59	99	100	99	0.98	97	96	97	1.01
Portugal[2]	6-15	Yes	...	116	...	...	...	...	104	104	105	1.01
San Marino[2, 9]	6-16	No	...	0.3[z]	...	...	...	...	...	...	...	...
Spain	6-16	Yes	*403*	397	*106*	*106*	*105*	*0.99*	100	101	100	0.99
Sweden	7-16	Yes	127	*93*	104	105	103	0.98	*94*	*94*	*93*	*0.99*
Switzerland	7-15	Yes	82	75	96	94	98	1.04	91	89	94	1.05
United Kingdom	5-16	Yes	...	...	...	...	...	...	...	...	...	...
United States	6-17	No	4 235	*4 052*	102	105	100	0.95	*101*	*103*	*100*	*0.98*
South and West Asia												
Afghanistan[3]	7-12	Yes	...	742	...	...	...	...	82	96	67	0.70
Bangladesh[3]	6-10	Yes	4 005	4 318[z]	121	122	119	0.98	130[z]	129[z]	131[z]	1.02[z]
Bhutan[3, 10]	6-16	Yes	12	14	...	...	...	...	...	...	...	...
India[3]	6-14	Yes	29 639	34 110	127	138	115	0.83	144	149	140	0.94
Iran, Islamic Republic of[3]	6-10	Yes	1 563	1 407	90	91	90	0.99	123	107	139	1.29
Maldives	6-12	No	8	6	93	93	94	1.01	68	66	71	1.07
Nepal[3]	6-10	Yes	879	**1 155***	132	149	113	0.76	**160***	**160***	**160***	**1.00***
Pakistan	5-9	No	...	4 618	...	...	...	...	116	128	103	0.81
Sri Lanka[2]	5-14	No	...	*309*[z]	...	...	...	...	95[z]	...	...	...
Sub-Saharan Africa												
Angola[2]	6-14	No	...	...	...	...	...	...	...	...	...	...
Benin	6-11	No	...	252	...	...	...	...	103	109	97	0.89
Botswana	6-15	No	50	47	111	112	110	0.99	*105*	*108*	*102*	*0.94*
Burkina Faso	6-16	No	154	295	45	53	38	0.72	75	81	69	0.85
Burundi	7-12	No	*146*	185	*72*	*79*	*65*	*0.83*	88	92	84	0.92
Cameroon	6-11	No	*335*	496*	*79*	*87*	*71*	*0.81*	112*	120*	104*	0.87*
Cape Verde[2]	6-16	No	*13*	12	*101*	*102*	*100*	*0.98*	92	94	90	0.96
Central African Republic	6-15	No	...	69	...	...	...	...	59	69	50	0.72
Chad[2, 3]	6-14	Yes	175	287	72	84	59	0.70	96	112	81	0.72

Education for All Global Monitoring Report 2 0 0 8

NET INTAKE RATE (NIR) IN PRIMARY EDUCATION (%)								SCHOOL LIFE EXPECTANCY (expected number of years of formal schooling from primary to tertiary education)						
School year ending in								School year ending in						
1999				2005				1999			2005			Country or territory
Total	Male	Female	GPI (F/M)	Total	Male	Female	GPI (F/M)	Total	Male	Female	Total	Male	Female	
84	84	84	1.00	88z	87z	89z	1.02z	13	12	13	13	13	14	Panama [3]
...	...	...	...	...	...	...	...	11	11	11	12z	11z	12z	Paraguay [3]
79	79	80	1.00	76	75	76	1.01	...	...	...	13	13	13	Peru [3]
...	...	...	...	66z	66z	67z	1.00z	...	...	...	12	12	13	Saint Kitts and Nevis [5]
69	69	68	0.99	76	77	76	1.00	...	...	...	13	12	13	Saint Lucia
...	...	...	...	62	66	58	0.88	...	...	...	12	12	12	St Vincent/Grenad.
...	...	...	...	63	58	68	1.18	...	...	...	...	...	...	Suriname [3]
69	69	70	1.01	68*,z	68*,z	68*,z	1.00*,z	12	12	12	12	12	12	Trinidad and Tobago [2,3]
...	...	...	...	54	57	51	0.90	...	...	...	11	11	12	Turks and Caicos Islands
...	...	...	...	...	...	...	...	14	13	15	15z	14z	16z	Uruguay [3]
60	60	61	1.01	60	60	60	1.01	...	...	...	12z	...	...	Venezuela [3]
														North America and Western Europe
...	...	...	...	47	48	46	0.97	...	...	...	11	11	11	Andorra [2,5]
...	...	...	...	...	...	...	...	15	15	15	16	15	16	Austria [2,4]
...	...	...	...	...	...	...	...	18	17	18	16	16	16	Belgium [4]
...	...	...	...	...	...	...	...	...	...	...	16z	16z	17z	Canada
...	...	...	...	...	...	...	...	13	12	13	14	13	14	Cyprus [2,5]
...	...	...	...	72	68	76	1.11	16	16	17	17	16	18	Denmark
...	...	...	...	93	91	95	1.04	17	17	18	17	17	18	Finland
...	...	...	...	...	...	...	...	16	15	16	16	16	17	France [8]
...	...	...	...	...	...	...	...	16	16	16	...	...	...	Germany
97	97	96	0.99	92	92	93	1.01	14	13	14	17	17	17	Greece [2]
98	100	96	0.96	95z	97z	92z	0.95z	17	16	17	18z	17z	19z	Iceland
...	...	...	...	45	42	48	1.1	16	16	17	18	18	18	Ireland
...	...	...	...	...	...	...	...	15	15	15	15	15	16	Israel [3]
...	...	...	...	95y	96y	95y	1.00y	15	15	15	16	16	17	Italy [2]
...	...	...	...	...	...	...	...	13	13	13	14z	13z	14z	Luxembourg
...	...	...	...	...	...	...	...	...	...	...	15	15	15	Malta [2]
...	...	...	...	...	...	...	...	...	...	...	...	...	...	Monaco [2,9]
...	...	...	...	98y	98y	97y	0.98y	17	17	16	17	17	17	Netherlands [2,4]
...	...	...	...	...	...	...	...	17	17	18	18	17	18	Norway
...	...	...	...	...	...	...	...	16	15	16	15	15	16	Portugal [2]
...	...	...	...	...	...	...	...	...	...	...	...	...	...	San Marino [2,9]
...	...	...	...	...	...	...	...	16	16	16	16	16	17	Spain
...	...	...	...	...	...	...	...	19	17	21	16	15	17	Sweden
...	...	...	...	55y	55y	56y	1.01y	15	16	14	15	16	15	Switzerland
...	...	...	...	...	...	...	...	16	16	16	17	16	17	United Kingdom
...	...	...	...	71	70	72	1.03	16	...	...	16	15	17	United States
														South and West Asia
...	...	...	...	...	...	...	...	...	...	...	7z	9z	4z	Afghanistan [3]
79	79	79	1.00	91z	88z	93z	1.06z	9	9	9	9z	9z	9z	Bangladesh [3]
...	...	...	...	...	...	...	...	...	...	...	...	...	...	Bhutan [3,10]
...	...	...	...	...	...	...	...	...	...	...	11	11	10	India [3]
44	44	43	0.97	94	...	...	...	12	12	11	13	13	13	Iran, Islamic Republic of [3]
80	79	80	1.01	...	...	...	...	12	12	12	11z	11z	11z	Maldives
...	...	...	...	...	...	...	...	...	...	...	9y	10y	8y	Nepal [3]
...	...	...	...	90	100	80	0.81	...	...	...	7	7	6	Pakistan
...	...	...	...	92z	...	...	...	...	...	...	...	...	...	Sri Lanka [2]
														Sub-Saharan Africa
...	...	...	...	...	...	...	...	4	4	3	...	...	...	Angola [2]
...	...	...	...	48	51	45	0.89	6	8	5	...	...	...	Benin
22	20	24	1.20	...	...	...	...	11	11	11	12z	12z	12z	Botswana
19	23	16	0.71	30	33	27	0.82	3	4	3	5	5	4	Burkina Faso
...	...	...	...	34	36	33	0.91	...	...	...	6	7	6	Burundi
...	...	...	...	...	...	...	...	8	...	...	11	12	10	Cameroon
65	64	66	1.03	75	75	75	1.00	...	...	...	11	11	11	Cape Verde [2]
...	...	...	...	...	...	...	...	...	...	...	...	...	...	Central African Republic
22	25	18	0.71	...	...	...	...	...	...	...	6	8	4	Chad [2,3]

Table 4 (continued)

Country or territory	Compulsory education (age group)	Legal guarantees of free education[1]	New entrants (000) School year ending in 1999	New entrants (000) School year ending in 2005	GIR 1999 Total	GIR 1999 Male	GIR 1999 Female	GIR 1999 GPI (F/M)	GIR 2005 Total	GIR 2005 Male	GIR 2005 Female	GIR 2005 GPI (F/M)
Comoros[2]	6-14	No	13	*16*	70	76	64	0.84	*70*	*74*	*66*	*0.89*
Congo[3]	6-16	Yes	32	77	32	31	32	1.02	62	62	62	1.00
Côte d'Ivoire	6-15	No	309	354*,y	65	72	58	0.80	72*,y	75*,y	68*,y	0.91*,y
D. R. Congo[3]	6-15	Yes	767	*1 102y*	51	49	52	1.07	*67y*	*72y*	*61y*	*0.84y*
Equatorial Guinea	7-11	Yes	33	15	269	313	225	0.72	105	109	100	0.92
Eritrea	7-13	No	57	62	59	65	52	0.81	50	55	45	0.83
Ethiopia	7-12	No	1 537	**2 775**	78	93	63	0.69	**123**	**129**	**117**	**0.90**
Gabon	6-16	Yes	...	35y	...	...	...	...	94y	94y	94y	1.00y
Gambia[3]	7-16	Yes	28	33y	83	85	80	0.94	89y	86y	92y	1.07y
Ghana[2, 3]	6-15	Yes	469	**627**	86	88	84	0.96	**110**	**107**	**113**	**1.05**
Guinea	6-12	No	119	222	51	55	45	0.82	85	87	81	0.93
Guinea-Bissau[3]	7-12	Yes	*35*	...	*92*	*106*	*79*	*0.74*	...	...	...	...
Kenya	6-13	No	892	*1 113*	103	105	102	0.97	*115*	*117*	*112*	*0.96*
Lesotho	6-12	No	51	55	106	106	107	1.01	124	128	120	0.94
Liberia[2]	6-16	No	50	...	59	72	46	0.63	...	...	...	...
Madagascar[3]	6-14	Yes	495	994	107	108	106	0.98	179	182	176	0.97
Malawi	6-13	No	616	648	177	176	178	1.01	152	147	158	1.08
Mali[3]	7-15	Yes	*171*	266	*51*	*57*	*44*	*0.77*	64	70	59	0.85
Mauritius[3]	5-16	Yes	22	20	98	96	99	1.04	102	102	102	1.00
Mozambique	6-12	No	536	899	102	110	93	0.85	153	159	148	0.93
Namibia[3]	6-15	Yes	54	56	92	90	93	1.03	100	99	101	1.02
Niger[3]	4-16	Yes	133	248	40	46	33	0.71	58	65	51	0.77
Nigeria[3]	6-11	Yes	...	4 431	...	...	...	...	116	124	107	0.87
Rwanda[3]	6-12	Yes	295	*448*	134	136	132	0.97	*177*	*178*	*177*	*1.00*
Sao Tome and Principe	7-12	Yes	4	5	109	110	108	0.98	116	113	119	1.06
Senegal[3]	7-12	Yes	190	291	64	*66*	*63*	*0.96*	91	90	92	1.02
Seychelles[5]	6-15	Yes	2	1	117	116	118	1.02	115	113	118	1.05
Sierra Leone	...	No	...	...	...	...	...	...	...	...	...	...
Somalia	6-13	No	...	...	...	...	...	...	...	...	...	...
South Africa	7-15	No	1 157	1 173z	114	115	112	0.98	114z	117z	111z	0.95z
Swaziland	6-12	Yes	31	33z	100	102	98	0.96	118z	122z	114z	0.94z
Togo	6-15	No	139	161	91	97	86	0.88	91	94	88	0.93
Uganda	...	No	...	1 486	...	...	...	...	151	153	150	0.98
United Republic of Tanzania[3]	7-13	No	714	**1 193**	72	72	72	0.99	**109**	**110**	**108**	**0.98**
Zambia	7-13	No	252	436	78	77	78	1.01	125	126	123	0.98
Zimbabwe	6-12	No	398	417y	110	111	108	0.97	120y	122y	118y	0.97y

			Sum	Sum	Weighted average							
World	...	...	129 884	134 926	106	110	101	0.91	112	115	109	0.94
Countries in transition	...	...	4 232	3 250	94	95	94	0.99	100	101	100	0.99
Developed countries	...	...	12 286	11 497	101	103	100	0.98	101	101	100	0.99
Developing countries	...	...	113 366	120 179	106	112	101	0.90	114	117	110	0.94
Arab States	...	...	6 297	7 026	90	94	87	0.93	97	100	95	0.95
Central and Eastern Europe	...	...	5 445	4 451	94	95	92	0.97	96	97	95	0.98
Central Asia	...	...	1 785	1 500	101	101	100	1.00	104	105	104	0.99
East Asia and the Pacific	...	...	37 021	32 634	102	103	102	0.99	104	105	104	0.99
East Asia	...	...	36 459	32 056	102	103	102	0.99	100	101	98	0.98
Pacific	...	...	562	578	102	103	101	0.98	106	108	104	0.96
Latin America/Caribbean	...	...	13 176	13 215	119	122	116	0.95	119	123	115	0.93
Caribbean	...	...	565	547	164	162	166	1.02	161	159	162	1.02
Latin America	...	...	12 612	12 668	118	121	114	0.95	118	122	113	0.93
N. America/W. Europe	...	...	9 241	8 842	102	104	101	0.97	102	102	101	0.99
South and West Asia	...	...	40 522	44 324	119	130	107	0.83	130	135	125	0.92
Sub-Saharan Africa	...	...	16 397	22 933	90	96	85	0.88	113	118	108	0.92

1. *Source:* Tomasevsky (2006).
2. Information on compulsory education comes from the Reports under the United Nations Human Rights Treaties.
3. Some primary school fees continue to be charged despite the legal guarantee of free education (Bentaouet-Kattan, 2005; Tomasevsky, 2006; World Bank, 2002).
4. No tuition fees are charged but some direct costs have been reported (Bentaouet-Kattan, 2005; Tomasevsky, 2006; World Bank, 2002).
5. National population data were used to calculate enrolment ratios.
6. Enrolment and population data exclude Transnistria.

NET INTAKE RATE (NIR) IN PRIMARY EDUCATION (%)								SCHOOL LIFE EXPECTANCY (expected number of years of formal schooling from primary to tertiary education)						Country or territory
School year ending in								School year ending in						
1999				2005				1999			2005			
Total	Male	Female	GPI (F/M)	Total	Male	Female	GPI (F/M)	Total	Male	Female	Total	Male	Female	
16	18	13	0.70	...	...	...	...	7	7	6	8z	9z	7z	Comoros [2]
...	...	...	...	...	...	...	...	...	...	...	8y	9y	7y	Congo [3]
27	30	24	0.79	27*,y	28*,y	26*,y	0.94*,y	6	7	5	...	...	...	Côte d'Ivoire
23	22	24	1.09	...	...	...	...	4	...	...	...	...	...	D. R. Congo [3]
...	...	...	...	...	...	...	...	...	...	...	...	...	...	Equatorial Guinea
19	20	17	0.89	24	25	23	0.90	5	5	4	6z	7z	5z	Eritrea
20	23	18	0.80	31z	33z	30z	0.92z	4	5	3	6	7	6	Ethiopia
...	...	...	...	...	...	...	...	12	12	12	...	...	...	Gabon
48	49	47	0.96	...	...	...	...	7	8	6	8z	8z	8z	Gambia [3]
29	29	29	1.00	**34**	**33**	**35**	**1.06**	...	...	...	**9**	**9**	**8**	Ghana [2,3]
19	20	18	0.89	36	37	36	0.97	...	...	...	7	9	6	Guinea
...	...	...	...	...	...	...	...	...	...	...	...	...	...	Guinea-Bissau [3]
30	29	31	1.05	42y	41y	43y	1.05y	...	...	...	10z	10z	10z	Kenya
28	27	29	1.06	59	59	60	1.01	9	9	10	11	11	11	Lesotho
...	...	...	...	...	...	...	...	8	10	7	...	...	...	Liberia [2]
...	...	...	...	71	71	71	1.00	6	6	6	...	...	...	Madagascar [3]
...	...	...	...	...	...	...	...	11	12	10	10z	10z	9z	Malawi
...	...	...	...	24	26	21	0.83	4	5	3	6	7	5	Mali [3]
72	71	74	1.03	90	90	91	1.01	12	12	12	14	14	13	Mauritius [3]
18	18	17	0.93	49	49	49	0.99	5	...	...	8	9	7	Mozambique
52	51	54	1.07	57	56	59	1.05	...	...	...	11z	11z	11z	Namibia [3]
25	30	20	0.68	34	39	29	0.75	...	...	...	3	4	3	Niger [3]
...	...	...	...	72z	77z	67z	0.87z	8	8	7	9	10	8	Nigeria [3]
...	...	...	...	91z	90z	92z	1.03z	7	...	...	8	8	8	Rwanda [3]
...	...	...	...	...	...	...	...	...	...	...	10	10	10	Sao Tome and Principe
36	36	35	0.96	58	58	59	1.01	5	...	...	6	...	...	Senegal [3]
75	74	77	1.03	69y	67y	72y	1.06y	14	14	14	13	13	14	Seychelles [5]
...	...	...	...	...	...	...	...	...	...	...	...	...	...	Sierra Leone
...	...	...	...	...	...	...	...	...	...	...	...	...	...	Somalia
43	44	42	0.96	51z	52z	51z	0.98z	13	13	14	13z	13z	13z	South Africa
42	41	44	1.06	50z	49z	51z	1.03z	10	10	10	10z	10z	10z	Swaziland
37	40	35	0.87	38	40	37	0.92	9	11	7	...	...	...	Togo
...	...	...	...	66	66	66	1.01	10	11	9	10z	11z	10z	Uganda
14	13	15	1.16	90	89	90	1.02	5	5	5	...	...	...	United Republic of Tanzania [3]
35	33	36	1.07	47	48	45	0.94	6	7	6	...	...	...	Zambia
...	...	...	...	45y	45y	46y	1.03y	10	...	...	9y	9y	9y	Zimbabwe

Median								Weighted average						
...	...	...	...	69	69	70	1.02	10	10	9	11	11	11	World
...	...	...	...	71	71	71	0.99	12	12	12	13	13	13	Countries in transition
...	...	...	...	...	...	...	...	15	15	16	16	15	16	Developed countries
...	...	...	...	66	66	67	1.00	9	10	9	10	11	10	Developing countries
65	65	65	1.00	61	62	60	0.97	10	11	9	11	11	10	Arab States
...	...	...	...	...	...	...	...	12	12	12	13	13	13	Central and Eastern Europe
...	...	...	...	75	74	76	1.03	11	11	11	12	12	12	Central Asia
...	...	...	...	...	...	...	...	10	11	10	12	12	11	East Asia and the Pacific
...	...	...	...	...	...	...	...	10	11	10	11	12	11	East Asia
...	...	...	...	...	...	...	...	15	14	15	15	15	15	Pacific
...	...	...	...	69	68	71	1.04	13	12	13	13	13	13	Latin America/Caribbean
...	...	...	...	67	67	67	1.00	11	11	11	11	11	11	Caribbean
...	...	...	...	75	75	76	1.00	13	12	13	13	13	13	Latin America
...	...	...	...	...	...	...	...	16	15	16	16	16	17	N. America/W. Europe
...	...	...	...	...	...	...	...	8	9	7	10	10	9	South and West Asia
28	27	29	1.06	48	49	47	0.96	7	7	6	8	9	7	Sub-Saharan Africa

7. Children can enter primary school at age 6 or 7.
8. For the first time, data include French overseas departments and territories (DOM-TOM).
9. Enrolment ratios were not calculated due to lack of United Nations population data by age.
10. Enrolment ratios were not calculated due to inconsistencies between enrolment and the United Nations population data.

Data in italic are UIS estimates.
Data in bold are for the school year ending in 2006.
(z) Data are for the school year ending in 2004.
(y) Data are for the school year ending in 2003.
(*) National estimates.

Table 5
Participation in primary education

Country or territory	Age group 2005	School-age population[1] (000) 2004	ENROLMENT IN PRIMARY EDUCATION — School year ending in 1999 Total (000)	1999 % F	2005 Total (000)	2005 % F	Enrolment in private institutions as % of total enrolment — School year ending in 1999	2005	GROSS ENROLMENT RATIO (GER) IN PRIMARY EDUCATION (%) — School year ending in 1999 Total	Male	Female	GPI (F/M)
Arab States												
1 Algeria	6-11	3 902	4 779	47	4 362	47	.	–	105	110	100	0.91
2 Bahrain	6-11	80	76	49	83	49	19	24	105	105	105	1.01
3 Djibouti	6-11	126	38	41	51	45	9	15	35	40	29	0.71
4 Egypt	6-11	9 487	*8 086*	47	9 564	47	…	7	*101*	*106*	*97*	*0.91*
5 Iraq	6-11	4 499	3 604	44	*4 430*	44	.	.	92	101	83	0.82
6 Jordan	6-11	840	706	49	805	49	29	30	99	99	99	1.00
7 Kuwait	6-10	207	140	49	203	48	32	33	100	99	101	1.01
8 Lebanon	6-11	426	395	48	453	48	66	66	115	117	112	0.95
9 Libyan Arab Jamahiriya	6-11	666	822	48	**710**	**49**	.	3ʸ	114	115	113	0.98
10 Mauritania	6-11	476	346	48	444	50	2	8	87	89	84	0.94
11 Morocco	6-11	3 828	3 462	44	4 023	46	4	7	87	96	78	0.81
12 Oman	6-11	352	316	48	**288**	**49**	5	**5**	91	92	89	0.97
13 Palestinian Autonomous Territories	6-9	437	368	49	387	49	9	9	106	106	107	1.01
14 Qatar	6-11	66	61	48	70	49	37	45	105	107	103	0.96
15 Saudi Arabia	6-11	3 597	…	…	3 264	49	…	7	…	…	…	…
16 Sudan	6-11	5 424	*2 513*	45	3 278	46	2	5	*51*	*55*	*47*	*0.85*
17 Syrian Arab Republic	6-9	1 813	2 738	47	2 252	48	4	4	102	107	98	0.92
18 Tunisia	6-11	1 082	1 443	47	1 184	48	0.7	1	114	117	111	0.95
19 United Arab Emirates	6-10	315	270	48	263	48	44	61	90	91	89	0.97
20 Yemen	6-11	3 634	2 303	35	3 220	42	1	2	73	93	52	0.56
Central and Eastern Europe												
21 Albania	6-9	231	292	48	250ᶻ	48ᶻ	.	4ᶻ	110	111	109	0.98
22 Belarus	6-9	374	632	48	380	48	0.1	0.1	109	110	108	0.98
23 Bosnia and Herzegovina	6-9	185	…	…	…	…	…	…	…	…	…	…
24 Bulgaria	7-10	284	412	48	290	48	0.3	0.4	106	107	104	0.97
25 Croatia	7-10	200	203	49	192ʸ	49ʸ	0.1	0.2ʸ	92	93	92	0.98
26 Czech Republic	6-10	497	655	49	503	48	0.8	1	104	104	103	0.99
27 Estonia	7-12	85	127	48	86	48	1	2	102	104	100	0.97
28 Hungary	7-10	441	503	48	431	48	5	6	102	102	101	0.98
29 Latvia	7-10	92	141	48	84	48	1	1	99	100	98	0.98
30 Lithuania	7-10	166	220	48	158	49	0.4	0.4	103	104	102	0.98
31 Poland	7-12	2 782	3 434	48	2 724	49	…	2	98	99	97	0.98
32 Republic of Moldova[3, 4]	7-10	…	262	49	184	48	.	1	95	95	95	1.00
33 Romania	7-10	907	1 285	49	970	48	.	0.2	105	105	104	0.98
34 Russian Federation[5]	7-9	4 125	6 138	49	5 309	49	0.3	0.5	100	100	99	0.99
35 Serbia and Montenegro[3]	7-10	…	418	49	…	…	.	…	104	105	103	0.99
36 Slovakia	6-9	246	317	49	242	48	4	5	103	103	102	0.99
37 Slovenia	6-10	92	92	48	93	48	0.1	0.1	101	102	100	0.99
38 TFYR Macedonia	7-10	112	130	48	110	48	.	.	101	102	100	0.98
39 Turkey	6-11	8 518	…	…	*7 948*	48	…	2	…	…	…	…
40 Ukraine	6-9	1 821	2 200	49	1 946	49	0.3	0.5	105	106	105	0.99
Central Asia												
41 Armenia	7-9	134	…	…	125	48	…	1	…	…	…	…
42 Azerbaijan	6-9	590	707	49	568	48	–	0.2	94	94	94	1.00
43 Georgia	6-11	360	302	49	337	48	0.5	3	98	98	98	1.00
44 Kazakhstan	7-10	939	1 249	49	1 024	49	0.5	0.7	98	98	98	1.00
45 Kyrgyzstan	7-10	444	470	49	434	49	0.2	0.3	98	98	97	0.99
46 Mongolia	7-11	269	251	50	251	49	0.5	3	98	97	100	1.04
47 Tajikistan	7-10	685	690	48	693	48	.	.	98	101	95	0.95
48 Turkmenistan	7-9	305	…	…	…	…	.	.	…	…	…	…
49 Uzbekistan	7-10	2 374	…	…	2 441ᶻ	49ᶻ	…	.ᶻ	…	…	…	…
East Asia and the Pacific												
50 Australia	5-11	1 863	1 885	49	1 935	49	27	29	98	98	98	1.00
51 Brunei Darussalam	6-11	43	46	47	46	48	36	36	114	115	112	0.97
52 Cambodia	6-11	2 010	2 127	46	2 695	47	2	0.5	99	106	92	0.87
53 China[6]	7-11	99 967	…	…	**108 925**	**47**	…	**4**	…	…	…	…

GROSS ENROLMENT RATIO (GER) IN PRIMARY EDUCATION (%)				NET ENROLMENT RATIO (NER) IN PRIMARY EDUCATION (%)								OUT-OF-SCHOOL CHILDREN[2]				
School year ending in 2005				School year ending in								School year ending in				
				1999				2005				1999		2005		
Total	Male	Female	GPI (F/M)	Total	Male	Female	GPI (F/M)	Total	Male	Female	GPI (F/M)	Total (000)	% F	Total (000)	% F	
												Arab States				
112	116	107	0.93	91	93	89	0.96	97	98	95	0.98	362	61	39	100	1
104	105	104	0.99	96	95	97	1.02	97	97	97	1.00	0.9	7	1.3	48	2
40	44	36	0.82	28	33	24	0.73	33	37	30	0.81	79	53	83	52	3
101	104	97	0.94	*93*	*97*	*90*	*0.93*	*94*	*96*	*91*	*0.95*	*320*	*91*	*269*	*96*	4
98	*108*	*89*	*0.83*	85	91	78	0.85	88	94	81	0.86	603	71	*552*	*76*	5
96	95	96	1.01	92	91	92	1.01	89	88	90	1.02	33	45	62	44	6
98	99	97	0.98	87	86	87	1.01	87	87	86	0.99	10	46	28	50	7
106	108	105	0.97	*94*	*96*	*92*	*0.96*	92	93	92	0.99	*13*	*69*	24	51	8
106	**106**	**105**	**0.99**	...	...	...	...	...	...	...	...	...	...	...	...	9
93	93	94	1.01	63	65	61	0.94	72	72	72	1.00	150	52	130	50	10
105	111	99	0.89	72	77	66	0.86	86	89	83	0.94	1 114	59	525	59	11
82	**81**	**82**	**1.01**	80	80	80	1.00	**73**	**73**	**74**	**1.02**	63	48	**86**	**47**	12
89	89	88	0.99	97	96	97	1.01	80	80	80	0.99	4	26	70	50	13
106	106	106	0.99	94	94	94	1.01	96	96	96	1.00	0.6	46	0.3	–	14
91	91	91	1.00	...	...	...	...	78	77	79	1.03	...	...	793	46	15
60	65	56	0.87	...	...	...	...	...	...	...	...	...	...	...	...	16
124	127	121	0.95	*92*	*95*	*88*	*0.93*	...	...	...	...	*137*	*84*	...	...	17
109	111	108	0.97	94	95	92	0.98	97	97	97	1.01	72	58	22	36	18
83	85	82	0.97	79	79	79	0.99	71	71	70	0.97	56	50	76	52	19
89	101	75	0.74	57	72	42	0.59	*75z*	*87z*	*63z*	*0.73z*	1 334	66	*861z*	*73z*	20
												Central and Eastern Europe				
106z	106z	105z	0.99z	*99*	*100*	*99*	*0.99*	94z	94z	94z	1.00z	*1.6*	*100*	14z	*49z*	21
101	103	100	0.97	...	...	...	...	89	*91*	*88*	0.97	...	...	38	*56*	22
...	...	...	...	...	...	...	...	...	...	...	...	...	...	...	...	23
102	103	101	0.99	97	98	96	0.98	93	93	93	0.99	5	79	15	51	24
94y	95y	94y	0.99y	85	86	85	0.98	87y	88y	87y	0.99y	18	52	14y	51y	25
101	102	100	0.98	*97*	*97*	*97*	*1.00*	*92*	*91*	*93*	*1.02*	*18*	*45*	*39*	*42*	26
100	102	99	0.97	*96*	*96*	*95*	*0.98*	95	95	95	0.99	*0.2*	*86*	2	42	27
98	99	97	0.98	88	88	88	0.99	89	90	88	0.98	15	46	19	50	28
92	94	90	0.96	...	...	...	...	*88*	*86*	*89*	*1.03*	...	...	*9*	*39*	29
95	95	95	1.00	95	96	95	0.99	89	89	89	1.00	4	46	14	45	30
98	98	98	0.99	96	96	96	1.00	96	96	97	1.00	133	48	96	46	31
92	93	92	0.99	*88*	...	...	...	86	86	86	0.99	*24*	...	24	49	32
107	108	106	0.99	96	96	95	0.99	93	93	92	0.99	1.6	100	34	52	33
129	129	128	1.00	...	...	...	...	*92*	*92*	*93*	*1.01*	...	...	*323*	*46*	34
...	...	...	...	...	...	...	...	...	...	...	...	...	...	...	...	35
99	99	98	0.99	...	...	...	...	*92*	*91*	*92*	*1.01*	...	...	*20*	*46*	36
101	102	100	0.99	97	98	97	0.99	98	99	98	0.99	0.5	81	0.2	100	37
98	98	98	1.00	93	94	92	0.98	92	92	92	1.00	1.4	95	3	45	38
93	*96*	*91*	*0.95*	...	...	...	...	89	92	87	0.95	...	...	905	59	39
107	107	107	1.00	...	...	...	...	83	83*	83*	1.00*	...	...	296	49*	40
												Central Asia				
94	92	96	1.04	...	...	...	...	79	77	81	1.05	...	...	18	40	41
96	97	95	0.98	85	85	86	1.01	85	85	84	0.98	110	47	91	50	42
94	93	94	1.01	...	...	...	...	93z	93z	92z	0.99z	...	...	26z	50z	43
109	110	108	0.99	...	...	...	...	91	92	90	0.98	...	...	9	59	44
98	98	97	0.99	88*	89*	87*	0.99*	87	87	86	0.99	28*	50*	24	48	45
93	92	94	1.02	90	88	91	1.04	84	83	85	1.03	20	36	32	42	46
101	103	99	0.96	...	...	...	...	97	99	96	0.96	...	...	18	86	47
...	...	...	...	...	...	...	...	...	...	...	...	...	...	...	...	48
100z	*100z*	*99z*	*0.99z*	...	...	...	...	...	...	...	...	...	...	...	...	49
												East Asia and the Pacific				
104	104	104	0.99	92	92	92	1.01	97	96	97	1.00	154	47	61	45	50
107	108	107	1.00	...	...	...	...	93	93	94	1.01	...	...	1.3	37	51
134	139	129	0.92	*85*	*89*	*81*	*0.91*	99	100	98	0.98	321	63	23	85	52
112	**113**	**111**	**0.98**	...	...	...	...	...	...	...	...	...	...	...	...	53

Table 5 (continued)

	Country or territory	Age group 2005	School-age population[1] (000) 2004	ENROLMENT IN PRIMARY EDUCATION School year ending in 1999 Total (000)	1999 % F	2005 Total (000)	2005 % F	Enrolment in private institutions as % of total enrolment School year ending in 1999	2005	GROSS ENROLMENT RATIO (GER) IN PRIMARY EDUCATION (%) School year ending in 1999 Total	Male	Female	GPI (F/M)
54	Cook Islands[3]	5-10	...	3	46	2[z]	47[z]	15	19[z]	96	99	94	0.95
55	DPR Korea	6-9	1 557	...	...	...	...	...	...	...	...	...	...
56	Fiji	6-11	107	116	48	114	48	...	99	110	111	110	0.99
57	Indonesia	7-12	24 855	...	...	29 150	48	...	17	...	...	...	...
58	Japan	6-11	7 226	7 692	49	7 232	49	0.9	1	101	101	101	1.00
59	Kiribati[3]	6-11	...	14	49	16	49	...	...	104	104	105	1.01
60	Lao People's Democratic Republic	6-10	769	828	45	891	46	2	2	117	126	107	0.85
61	Macao, China	6-11	35	47	47	37	47	95	96	100	102	97	0.96
62	Malaysia	6-11	3 317	3 040	48	3 159[z]	49[z]	6	0.9[z]	100	101	99	0.98
63	Marshall Islands[3]	6-11	...	8	48	8	47	25	24[y]	101	102	100	0.98
64	Micronesia (Federated States of)	6-11	16	...	...	19	48	...	...	...	...	...	...
65	Myanmar	5-9	4 966	4 733	49	4 948	50	.	.	88	88	87	0.99
66	Nauru[3]	6-11	...	...	...	1[z]	47[z]	...	21[y]	...	...	...	...
67	New Zealand	5-10	345	361	49	353	49	2	12	102	102	103	1.01
68	Niue[3]	5-10	...	0.3	46	0.2	51	.	...	99	99	98	1.00
69	Palau[3]	6-10	...	2	47	2	48	18	19	114	118	109	0.93
70	Papua New Guinea	7-12	945	623	45	681[y]	45[y]	2	...	78	81	75	0.93
71	Philippines	6-11	11 634	12 503	49	13 084	49	8	8	113	113	113	1.00
72	Republic of Korea	6-11	3 937	3 845	47	**4 031**	**47**	2	**1**	95	95	96	1.01
73	Samoa	5-10	32	27	48	32	48	16	17	99	99	98	0.98
74	Singapore	6-11	373	300	48	290	48	...	...	83	83	83	1.00
75	Solomon Islands	6-11	75	58	46	73	47	...	...	88	91	85	0.93
76	Thailand	6-11	6 151	6 120	48	**5 844**	**48**	13	**17**	94	97	92	0.95
77	Timor-Leste	6-11	118	...	...	178	47	...	...	...	...	...	...
78	Tokelau[3]	5-10	...	...	...	0.2[z]	57[z]	...	.[y]	...	...	...	...
79	Tonga	5-10	15	17	46	17	47	7	9	112	113	110	0.98
80	Tuvalu[3]	6-11	...	1	48	1[z]	50[z]	...	...	98	97	99	1.02
81	Vanuatu	6-11	33	34	48	39	48	...	...	110	111	109	0.98
82	Viet Nam	6-10	8 225	10 250	47	7 773	47	0.3	0.4	108	112	104	0.93

Latin America and the Caribbean

	Country or territory	Age group 2005	School-age population (000) 2004	1999 Total (000)	1999 % F	2005 Total (000)	2005 % F	1999	2005	1999 Total	Male	Female	GPI (F/M)
83	Anguilla	5-11	...	2	50	1	51	5	11	...	...	...	...
84	Antigua and Barbuda	5-11	...	...	...	...	...	...	...	...	...	...	...
85	Argentina	6-11	4 140	4 821	49	4 686[z]	49[z]	20	21[y]	117	116	117	1.00
86	Aruba[3]	6-11	...	9	49	10	48	83	79	112	114	111	0.98
87	Bahamas	5-10	37	34	49	37	49	...	28	95	96	94	0.98
88	Barbados	5-10	21	25	49	22	49	...	12	108	108	107	0.98
89	Belize	5-10	40	44	48	50	48	...	85	118	120	116	0.97
90	Bermuda[3]	5-10	...	...	...	5	50	...	34	...	...	...	...
91	Bolivia	6-11	1 374	1 445	49	1 542[z]	49[z]	...	20[y]	113	114	112	0.98
92	Brazil	7-10	13 613	20 939	48	18 969[z]	47[z]	8	10[z]	155	159	150	0.94
93	British Virgin Islands[3]	5-11	...	3	49	3	48	13	22	112	113	110	0.97
94	Cayman Islands	5-10	...	3	47	3	48	36	34	...	...	...	...
95	Chile	6-11	1 659	1 805	48	1 721	48	45	51	101	102	99	0.97
96	Colombia	6-10	4 729	5 162	49	5 298	48	20	19	113	113	112	1.00
97	Costa Rica	6-11	495	552	48	542	48	7	6	108	109	107	0.98
98	Cuba	6-11	879	1 074	48	895	48	.	.	106	109	104	0.96
99	Dominica[3]	5-11	...	12	48	9	49	24	30	104	107	102	0.95
100	Dominican Republic	6-11	1 144	1 315	49	1 290	48	14	17	113	114	112	0.98
101	Ecuador	6-11	1 711	1 899	49	2 000	49	21	28	114	114	114	1.00
102	El Salvador	7-12	924	940	48	1 045	48	11	10	111	113	109	0.96
103	Grenada[3]	5-11	...	...	...	16	49	...	76[y]	...	...	...	...
104	Guatemala	7-12	2 060	1 824	46	2 345	48	15	11	101	108	94	0.87
105	Guyana	6-11	88	107	49	117	49	1	2	119	120	118	0.98
106	Haiti	6-11	1 229	...	...	...	...	...	...	...	...	...	...
107	Honduras	6-11	1 123	...	...	1 268	49	...	...	...	...	...	...
108	Jamaica	6-11	345	316	49	326	49	4	8	93	93	93	1.00
109	Mexico	6-11	13 459	14 698	49	14 700	49	7	8	109	110	107	0.97
110	Montserrat[3]	5-11	...	0.4	44	0.5	46	38	34	...	...	...	...
111	Netherlands Antilles	6-11	17	25	48	23[y]	49[y]	74	73[y]	134	139	130	0.94
112	Nicaragua	7-12	845	830	49	945	48	16	15	103	103	103	1.01
113	Panama	6-11	387	393	48	430	48	10	10	108	110	106	0.97

GROSS ENROLMENT RATIO (GER) IN PRIMARY EDUCATION (%)				NET ENROLMENT RATIO (NER) IN PRIMARY EDUCATION (%)								OUT-OF-SCHOOL CHILDREN[2]				
School year ending in 2005				School year ending in								School year ending in				
				1999				2005				1999		2005		
Total	Male	Female	GPI (F/M)	Total	Male	Female	GPI (F/M)	Total	Male	Female	GPI (F/M)	Total (000)	% F	Total (000)	% F	
82[z]	83[z]	81[z]	0.98[z]	85	87	83	0.96	...	...	...	...	0.4	54	...	...	54
...	...	...	...	...	...	...	...	...	...	...	...	...	...	...	...	55
106	107	105	0.98	99	99	99	1.01	96	97	96	0.99	1.1	32	1.4	60	56
117	119	115	0.96	...	...	...	...	96	97	94	0.96	...	...	414	100	57
100	100	100	1.00	100	100	100	1.00	100	100	100	1.00	3	100	12	—	58
112	111	113	1.02	97	96	98	1.01	...	...	...	...	0.1	...	...	...	59
116	123	108	0.88	80	84	77	0.92	84	86	81	0.95	141	58	126	56	60
106	111	102	0.92	85	84	85	1.01	91	92	89	0.96	7	47	3	58	61
96[z]	96[z]	96[z]	1.00[z]	98	99	97	0.98	95[z]	96[z]	95[z]	1.00[z]	67	69	150[z]	50[z]	62
103	105	101	0.96	...	...	...	...	90[y]	90[y]	89[y]	0.99[y]	...	...	0.7[y]	49[y]	63
115	116	113	0.97	...	...	...	...	...	...	...	...	...	...	...	...	64
100	99	101	1.02	80	81	80	0.99	90	89	91	1.02	1 051	50	487	45	65
84[z]	84[z]	83[z]	0.99[z]	...	...	...	...	...	...	...	...	...	...	...	...	66
102	102	102	1.00	99	98	99	1.01	99	99	99	1.00	3.1	22	2	57	67
86	78	97	1.24	99	99	98	1.00	...	...	...	...	0.004	50	...	...	68
104	108	101	0.93	97	99	94	0.94	...	...	...	...	0.05	91	...	...	69
75[y]	80[y]	70[y]	0.88[y]	...	...	...	...	...	...	...	...	...	...	...	...	70
112	113	112	0.99	92	92	92	1.00	94	93	95	1.02	854	48	648	39	71
104	**105**	**104**	**0.99**	94	94	95	1.01	**99**	**100**	**99**	**1.00**	214	43	**9**	82	72
100	100	100	1.00	92	92	91	0.99	90[z]	90[z]	91[z]	1.00[z]	2	50	0.3[z]	—[z]	73
78	78	78	1.00	82	82	82	1.00	...	...	...	...	67	48	...	...	74
97	99	94	0.95	...	...	...	...	63[y]	65[y]	62[y]	0.96[y]	...	...	26[y]	50[y]	75
96	**98**	**94**	**0.96**	...	...	...	...	**88**	**90**	**86**	**0.96**	...	...	**419**	63	76
151	157	145	0.92	...	...	...	...	98	...	...	...	...	...	3	...	77
93[z]	79[z]	107[z]	1.35[z]	...	...	...	...	...	...	...	...	...	...	...	...	78
115	118	112	0.95	91	92	89	0.97	95	97	93	0.96	1.4	55	0.3	100	79
99[z]	95[z]	102[z]	1.07[z]	...	...	...	...	...	...	...	...	...	...	...	...	80
118	120	116	0.97	91	91	90	0.99	94	95	93	0.98	2.8	50	2	56	81
95	98	91	0.94	96	...	...	...	88	...	...	...	393	...	1 007	...	82
Latin America and the Caribbean																
91	89	94	1.06	...	...	...	...	89	86	91	1.06	...	...	0.1	32	83
...	...	...	...	...	...	...	...	...	...	...	...	...	...	...	...	84
113[z]	113[z]	112[z]	0.99[z]	99*	99*	99*	1.00*	99[z]	99[z]	98[z]	0.99[z]	10*	52*	22[z]	86[z]	85
114	116	112	0.97	98	97	98	1.01	99	99	100	1.00	0.2	39	0.04	32	86
101	101	101	1.00	89	90	89	0.99	91	90	92	1.03	4	50	3	41	87
108	108	108	1.00	97	97	97	0.99	98	98	98	1.00	0.7	55	0.5	48	88
127	130	125	0.96	94	94	94	1.00	94	93	96	1.03	2	48	1.0	2	89
102	100	103	1.03	...	...	...	...	98	...	...	...	...	...	0.1	...	90
113[z]	113[z]	113[z]	1.00[z]	95	95	95	1.00	95[z]	94[z]	96[z]	1.01[z]	52	51	47[z]	40[z]	91
140[z]	146[z]	135[z]	0.93[z]	91	...	...	...	95[z]	95[z]	95[z]	1.00[z]	1 032	...	482[z]	47[z]	92
111	113	108	0.96	96	95	97	1.02	95	96	95	0.99	0.04	42	0.06	53	93
90	95	84	0.89	...	...	...	...	81	86	77	0.90	...	...	0.6	65	94
104	106	101	0.96	...	...	...	...	90	90	89	0.98	...	...	97	54	95
112	113	111	0.98	88	88	89	1.01	87	87	87	1.00	431	46	479	48	96
110	110	109	0.99	...	...	...	...	...	...	...	...	...	...	...	...	97
102	104	99	0.95	98	98	98	1.00	97	98	96	0.98	4	...	19	72	98
92	93	92	0.99	94	95	93	0.98	84	83	85	1.02	0.4	61	1.2	45	99
113	115	110	0.95	84	84	85	1.01	88	87	88	1.01	167	46	120	44	100
117	117	117	1.00	97	97	98	1.01	98[z]	97[z]	98[z]	1.01[z]	17	16	11[z]	—[z]	101
113	115	111	0.96	...	...	...	...	93	93	93	1.00	...	...	48	45	102
93	94	91	0.96	...	...	...	...	84	84	83	0.99	...	...	2	49	103
114	118	109	0.92	82	86	79	0.91	94	96	92	0.95	292	61	90	75	104
132	133	131	0.98	...	...	...	...	...	...	...	...	...	...	...	...	105
...	...	...	...	...	...	...	...	...	...	...	...	...	...	...	...	106
113	113	113	1.00	...	...	...	...	91	90	92	1.02	...	...	70	39	107
95	95	94	1.00	88	88	88	1.00	90	90	90	1.00	38	49	32	48	108
109	110	108	0.98	98	98	97	1.00	98	98	98	1.00	25	38	30	46	109
116	115	119	1.04	...	...	...	...	96	...	...	...	...	...	0.01	...	110
126[y]	127[y]	124[y]	0.98[y]	...	...	...	...	...	...	...	...	...	...	...	...	111
112	113	110	0.97	78	78	79	1.01	87	88	86	0.98	145	47	53	50	112
111	113	109	0.97	96	96	96	0.99	98	99	98	0.99	11	53	4	64	113

Table 5 (continued)

	Country or territory	Age group 2005	School-age population[1] (000) 2004	ENROLMENT IN PRIMARY EDUCATION				Enrolment in private institutions as % of total enrolment		GROSS ENROLMENT RATIO (GER) IN PRIMARY EDUCATION (%)			
				School year ending in				School year ending in		School year ending in			
				1999		2005		1999	2005	1999			
				Total (000)	% F	Total (000)	% F			Total	Male	Female	GPI (F/M)
114	Paraguay	6-11	904	*951*	*48*	931[z]	48[z]	*15*	16[z]	*113*	*115*	*111*	*0.96*
115	Peru	6-11	3 626	4 350	49	4 077	49	13	16	123	123	122	0.99
116	Saint Kitts and Nevis[3]	5-11	...	...	...	6	50	...	17	...	...	...	...
117	Saint Lucia	5-11	22	26	49	24	49	*2*	3	103	104	102	0.98
118	Saint Vincent and the Grenadines	5-11	16	...	...	18	47	...	3	...	...	...	...
119	Suriname	6-11	55	...	...	66	48	...	47	...	...	...	...
120	Trinidad and Tobago	5-11	129	172	49	130*	49*	*72*	70	102	102	101	0.99
121	Turks and Caicos Islands	6-11	...	2	49	2	51	18	30	...	...	...	...
122	Uruguay	6-11	337	366	49	366[z]	48[z]	...	13[z]	112	113	111	0.99
123	Venezuela	6-11	3 289	3 261	49	3 449	48	15	14	100	101	99	0.98
	North America and Western Europe												
124	Andorra[3]	6-11	...	...	...	4	47	...	2	...	...	...	...
125	Austria	6-9	342	389	48	363	49	4	5	102	103	102	0.99
126	Belgium	6-11	711	763	49	739	49	55	55	104	104	103	0.99
127	Canada	6-11	2 366	2 429	49	...	...	6	...	98	98	99	1.00
128	Cyprus[3]	6-11	...	64	48	61	49	4	6	97	98	97	1.00
129	Denmark	7-12	420	372	49	414	49	11	12	102	102	102	1.00
130	Finland	7-12	384	383	49	382	49	1	1	99	99	99	1.00
131	France[7]	6-10	3 623	3 944	49	4 015	48	15	15	107	107	106	0.99
132	Germany	6-9	3 272	3 767	49	3 306	49	2	3	106	106	105	0.99
133	Greece	6-11	644	646	48	650	48	7	7	94	94	95	1.00
134	Iceland	6-12	31	30	48	31[z]	48[z]	1	1[z]	99	100	98	0.98
135	Ireland	4-11	424	457	49	454	49	0.9	1	103	104	103	0.99
136	Israel	6-11	719	722	49	785	49	...	–	112	113	112	0.99
137	Italy	6-10	2 712	2 876	48	2 771	48	7	7	103	103	102	0.99
138	Luxembourg	6-11	35	31	49	35	49	7	7	100	99	100	1.01
139	Malta	5-10	30	35	49	29	47	36	37	106	106	106	1.01
140	Monaco[8]	6-10	...	2	50	2[z]	...	31	26[z]	...	...	...	...
141	Netherlands	6-11	1 192	1 268	48	1 278	48	68	69[z]	108	109	107	0.98
142	Norway	6-12	438	412	49	430	49	1	2	100	100	100	1.00
143	Portugal	6-11	658	815	48	753	48	9	11	124	127	121	0.96
144	San Marino[8]	6-10	...	...	...	1[z]	...	...	.[z]	...	...	...	...
145	Spain	6-11	2 333	2 580	48	2 485	48	33	33	107	108	106	0.98
146	Sweden	7-12	681	763	49	658	48	3	7	110	108	111	1.03
147	Switzerland	7-12	516	530	49	524	49	3	4	104	104	104	0.99
148	United Kingdom	5-10	4 343	4 661	49	4 635	49	5	5	102	102	102	1.01
149	United States	6-11	24 694	24 938	49	24 455	49	12	10	101	100	103	1.03
	South and West Asia												
150	Afghanistan	7-12	4 992	957	7	4 319	36	...	...	25	46	4	0.08
151	Bangladesh	6-10	16 526	17 622	49	17 953[z]	50[z]	37	42[z]	110	110	109	0.99
152	Bhutan[9]	6-12	...	81	46	99	49	2	2	...	...	...	...
153	India	6-10	117 416	110 986	43	*146 375*	*47*	...	17.0[y]	97	107	87	0.82
154	Iran, Islamic Republic of	6-10	6 600	8 667	47	7 307	54	...	5	96	98	93	0.95
155	Maldives	6-12	62	74	49	58	48	3	1	130	130	131	1.01
156	Nepal	5-9	3 557	3 588	42	**4 503**	**47**	...	15	114	128	98	0.77
157	Pakistan	5-9	19 764	...	...	17 258	42	...	36	...	...	...	...
158	Sri Lanka	5-9	1 634	...	...	*1 612.3*[z]	...	...	2.0[y]	...	...	...	...
	Sub-Saharan Africa												
159	Angola	6-9	1 846	*1 057*	*46*	...	...	*5*	...	*64*	*69*	*59*	*0.86*
160	Benin	6-11	1 370	872	39	1 318	44	7	12	74	89	59	0.67
161	Botswana	6-12	312	322	50	331	49	5	5[z]	102	101	102	1.00
162	Burkina Faso	7-12	2 204	816	40	1 271	44	11	14	44	52	36	0.70
163	Burundi	7-12	1 221	*702*	*44*	1 037	46	*0.8*	1	*61*	*68*	*54*	*0.80*
164	Cameroon	6-11	2 571	2 134	45	3 001*	46*	28	24*	89	98	80	0.82
165	Cape Verde	6-11	77	92	49	83	49	–	–	119	122	116	0.96
166	Central African Republic	6-11	662	...	...	*368*	*40*			...	...	...	...
167	Chad	6-11	1 639	840	37	1 262	40	25	31	64	81	47	0.58
168	Comoros	6-11	125	83	45	*107*	*46*	12	*10*	76	82	69	0.85
169	Congo	6-11	681	276	49	597	48	10	27	50	51	48	0.95

GROSS ENROLMENT RATIO (GER) IN PRIMARY EDUCATION (%)				NET ENROLMENT RATIO (NER) IN PRIMARY EDUCATION (%)								OUT-OF-SCHOOL CHILDREN[2]				
School year ending in 2005				School year ending in 1999				2005				School year ending in 1999		2005		
Total	Male	Female	GPI (F/M)	Total	Male	Female	GPI (F/M)	Total	Male	Female	GPI (F/M)	Total (000)	% F	Total (000)	% F	
104z	106z	103z	0.97z	92	91	92	1.00	88z	87z	88z	1.00z	68	48	106z	48z	114
112	113	112	1.00	98	98	98	1.00	96	96	97	1.00	2	100	30	33	115
99	96	102	1.06	...	...	...	...	93	91	96	1.06	...	...	0.3	19	116
109	110	107	0.97	91	91	91	0.99	97	98	96	0.98	2	50	0.5	70	117
111	117	105	0.90	...	...	...	...	90	92	88	0.95	...	...	1.2	61	118
120	120	120	1.00	...	...	...	...	94	93	96	1.04	...	...	2.4	22	119
100*	102*	99*	0.97*	93	93	93	1.00	90*	90*	90*	1.00*	5	47	7*	48*	120
90	88	92	1.04	...	...	...	...	78	75	81	1.07	...	...	0.5	42	121
109z	110z	108z	0.98z	94	94	94	1.00	93z	92z	93z	1.01z	8	42	13z	43z	122
105	106	104	0.98	86	85	86	1.01	91	91	92	1.01	423	47	236	45	123

North America and Western Europe

GER Total	Male	Female	GPI	NER99 Total	Male	Female	GPI	NER05 Total	Male	Female	GPI	OOS99 Total	% F	OOS05 Total	% F	
87	89	85	0.95	...	...	...	...	80	81	79	0.97	10	38	0.8	51	124
106	106	106	1.00	97	97	98	1.01	97	96	98	1.02	...	...	...	...	125
104	104	103	0.99	99	99	99	1.00	99	99	99	1.00	8	53	7	44	126
...	...	...	...	98	98	99	1.00	...	...	...	...	41	43	...	...	127
101	101	101	1.00	95	95	95	1.00	99	99	99	1.00	1.3	49	0.2	37	128
98	98	99	1.00	97	97	97	1.00	95	95	96	1.01	8	41	17	40	129
99	100	99	0.99	99	99	98	1.00	98	98	98	1.00	5	58	6	45	130
111	111	110	0.99	99	99	99	1.00	99	...	...	...	9	34	26	...	131
101	101	101	1.00	...	...	...	...	...	...	...	...	...	...	...	...	132
101	101	101	1.00	92	92	93	1.01	99	99	99	1.00	31	44	6	53	133
99z	101z	98z	0.97z	99	100	98	0.98	99z	100z	97z	0.97z	0.3	100	0.4z	100z	134
107	108	106	0.99	93	93	93	1.01	98	98	98	1.00	31	46	10	47	135
109	109	110	1.01	98	98	98	1.00	97	97	98	1.01	15	51	18	41	136
102	103	102	0.99	99	99	98	0.99	99	99	98	0.99	9	100	16	75	137
100	100	100	1.00	96	95	97	1.02	95	95	95	1.01	0.9	31	1.2	43	138
98	101	95	0.94	95	94	96	1.02	86	88	84	0.95	2	41	2.4	25	139
...	...	...	...	...	...	...	...	...	...	...	...	...	...	...	...	140
107	108	106	0.98	99	100	99	0.99	99	99	98	0.99	6	99	16	72	141
98	98	98	1.00	100	100	100	1.00	98	98	98	1.00	0.8	67	8	49	142
114	117	112	0.96	...	...	...	...	98	98	98	1.00	...	...	3	35	143
...	...	...	...	...	...	...	...	...	...	...	...	...	...	...	...	144
106	108	105	0.98	99	...	...	...	99	100	99	0.99	13	...	15	83	145
97	97	97	1.00	100	100	99	0.99	96	96	96	1.00	2	100	25.2	49	146
102	102	101	0.99	96	96	95	0.99	93	93	93	0.99	2	46	12	45	147
107	107	107	1.00	100	99	100	1.01	99	99	99	1.00	20	2	0.9	95	148
99	99	99	0.99	94	94	94	1.00	92	91	93	1.01	1 154	46	1 558	44	149

South and West Asia

GER Total	Male	Female	GPI	NER99 Total	Male	Female	GPI	NER05 Total	Male	Female	GPI	OOS99 Total	% F	OOS05 Total	% F	
87	108	64	0.59	...	...	...	...	...	...	...	...	...	...	...	...	150
109z	107z	111z	1.03z	89*	90*	89*	1.00*	94*,z	93*,z	96*,z	1.03*,z	1 121*	48*	399*,z	15*,z	151
...	...	...	...	...	...	...	...	...	...	...	...	...	...	...	...	152
125	129	120	0.93	...	...	...	...	89	92	85	0.93	...	...	6 395	81	153
111	100	122	1.22	82	83	80	0.97	95	91	100	1.10	1 666	52	307	–	154
94	95	93	0.98	97	97	98	1.01	79	79	79	1.00	1.3	42	13	48	155
126	129	123	0.95	65*	72*	57*	0.79*	79z	84z	74z	0.87z	1 046*	60*	702z	62z	156
87	99	75	0.76	...	...	...	...	68	77	59	0.76	...	...	6 303	63	157
98z	...	...	...	...	...	...	...	97z	...	...	...	...	...	47z	...	158

Sub-Saharan Africa

GER Total	Male	Female	GPI	NER99 Total	Male	Female	GPI	NER05 Total	Male	Female	GPI	OOS99 Total	% F	OOS05 Total	% F	
...	...	...	...	...	...	...	...	...	...	...	...	...	...	...	...	159
96	107	85	0.80	50*	59*	40*	0.68*	78	86	70	0.81	585*	59*	270	72	160
106	107	105	0.98	78	77	80	1.04	85	85	84	1.00	63	45	42	48	161
58	64	51	0.80	35	41	29	0.69	45	50	40	0.79	1 205	54	1 202	54	162
85	91	78	0.86	...	...	...	...	60	63	58	0.91	...	...	480	54	163
117*	126*	107*	0.85*	...	...	...	...	...	...	...	...	...	...	...	...	164
108	111	105	0.95	99	99	98	0.98	90	91	89	0.98	0.8	90	7	53	165
56	67	44	0.66	...	...	...	...	...	...	...	...	...	...	...	...	166
77	92	62	0.67	52	64	40	0.62	61y	72y	50y	0.69y	636	63	594y	65y	167
85	91	80	0.88	49	54	45	0.85	...	...	...	...	53	54	...	...	168
88	91	84	0.92	...	...	...	...	44	39	48	1.20	...	...	376	46	169

Table 5 (continued)

	Country or territory	Age group 2005	School-age population[1] (000) 2004	ENROLMENT IN PRIMARY EDUCATION — School year ending in 1999 Total (000)	1999 % F	2005 Total (000)	2005 % F	Enrolment in private institutions as % of total enrolment — School year ending in 1999	2005	GROSS ENROLMENT RATIO (GER) IN PRIMARY EDUCATION (%) — School year ending in 1999 Total	Male	Female	GPI (F/M)
170	Côte d'Ivoire	6-11	2 902	1 911	43	2 046*,ʸ	44*,ʸ	12	11ʸ	70	80	60	0.74
171	Democratic Rep. of the Congo	6-11	9 568	4 022	47	5 590ʸ	44ʸ	19	11ʸ	48	51	46	0.90
172	Equatorial Guinea	7-11	66	75	…	76	49	33	30	132	…	…	…
173	Eritrea	7-11	589	262	45	378	44	11	8	57	62	51	0.82
174	Ethiopia	7-10	8 589	4 368	38	**8 779**	**47**	…	4	59	72	45	0.62
175	Gabon	6-11	218	265	50	281ᶻ	49ᶻ	17	29ᶻ	132	132	132	1.00
176	Gambia	7-12	220	150	46	175ᶻ	51ᶻ	3	3ᶻ	80	86	74	0.85
177	Ghana	6-11	3 315	2 377	47	**3 131**	**48**	13	**15**	76	79	72	0.92
178	Guinea	7-12	1 483	727	38	1 207	44	15	21ᶻ	57	68	45	0.65
179	Guinea-Bissau	7-12	256	145	40	…	…	19	…	70	84	56	0.67
180	Kenya	6-11	5 417	4 782	49	6 076	49	…	4	93	94	92	0.97
181	Lesotho	6-12	321	365	52	422	50	…	0.3	105	101	110	1.08
182	Liberia	6-11	556	396	42	…	…	38	…	85	97	72	0.74
183	Madagascar	6-10	2 598	2 012	49	3 598	49	22	19	94	95	92	0.97
184	Malawi	6-11	2 345	2 582	49	2 868	50	…	0.9	139	143	136	0.95
185	Mali	7-12	2 267	959	41	1 506	43	22	37	51	59	43	0.72
186	Mauritius	5-10	121	133	49	124	49	24	25	105	105	106	1.00
187	Mozambique	6-12	3 834	2 302	43	3 943	46	…	2	69	79	59	0.74
188	Namibia	6-12	407	383	50	404	50	4	5	104	103	105	1.02
189	Niger	7-12	2 280	530	39	1 064	41	4	4	29	34	23	0.68
190	Nigeria[10]	6-11	21 645	17 907	44	22 267	45	4	…	93	102	83	0.82
191	Rwanda	7-12	1 436	1 289	50	1 724	51	…	0.8ᶻ	99	100	98	0.98
192	Sao Tome and Principe	7-12	23	24	49	30	49	–	–	106	108	105	0.98
193	Senegal	7-12	1 842	1 034	46	1 444	49	12	12	61	66	57	0.86
194	Seychelles[3]	6-11	…	10	49	9	48	5	5ᶻ	116	117	116	0.99
195	Sierra Leone	6-11	833	…	…	…	…	…	…	…	…	…	…
196	Somalia	6-12	1 464	…	…	…	…	…	…	…	…	…	…
197	South Africa	7-13	7 176	7 935	49	7 444ᶻ	49ᶻ	2	2ᶻ	114	116	113	0.98
198	Swaziland	6-12	200	213	49	218ᶻ	48ᶻ	–	–ᶻ	100	102	98	0.95
199	Togo	6-11	995	954	43	997	46	36	42	112	127	96	0.75
200	Uganda	6-12	6 086	6 288	47	7 224	50	…	9	126	132	120	0.92
201	United Republic of Tanzania	7-13	7 113	4 190	50	**7 960**	**49**	0.2	**1**	64	64	64	1.00
202	Zambia	7-13	2 308	1 556	48	2 565	48	…	3	75	78	72	0.92
203	Zimbabwe	6-12	2 406	2 460	49	2 362ʸ	49ʸ	88	87ʸ	98	100	97	0.97

			Sum	Sum	% F	Sum	% F	Median		Weighted average			
I	World	…	641 643	646 731	47	688 285	47	7	8	100	104	96	0.92
II	Countries in transition	…	12 349	15 834	49	13 739	49	0.2	0.5	100	101	100	0.99
III	Developed countries	…	65 995	70 444	49	67 022	49	3	4	102	102	103	1.00
IV	Developing countries	…	563 298	560 453	46	607 524	47	11	11	100	105	95	0.91
V	Arab States	…	41 256	35 402	46	39 345	47	4	7	90	96	84	0.88
VI	Central and Eastern Europe	…	21 739	25 489	48	22 460	48	0.3	0.8	100	102	98	0.96
VII	Central Asia	…	6 099	6 853	49	6 172	49	0.3	0.5	99	99	98	0.99
VIII	East Asia and the Pacific	…	178 639	217 564	48	197 224	48	7	14	112	112	111	0.99
IX	East Asia	…	175 065	214 276	48	193 727	48	2	2	112	113	112	0.99
X	Pacific	…	3 573	3 287	48	3 498	48	15	19	94	94	93	0.99
XI	Latin America and the Caribbean	…	58 754	70 206	48	69 072	48	15	17	121	123	119	0.97
XII	Caribbean	…	2 057	2 500	49	2 419	49	21	30	115	117	113	0.97
XIII	Latin America	…	56 697	67 705	48	66 652	48	15	15	121	123	119	0.97
XIV	North America and Western Europe	…	50 635	52 882	49	51 649	49	7	7	103	102	103	1.01
XV	South and West Asia	…	170 927	157 510	44	192 700	47	…	10	94	103	85	0.82
XVI	Sub-Saharan Africa	…	113 594	80 825	46	109 663	47	11	8	80	86	74	0.86

1. Data are for 2004 except for countries with a calendar school year, in which case data are for 2005.
2. Data reflect the actual number of children not enrolled at all, derived from the age-specific enrolment ratios of primary school age children, which measures the proportion of those who are enrolled either in primary or in secondary schools (total primary NER).
3. National population data were used to calculate enrolment ratios.
4. Enrolment and population data exclude Transnistria.

5. In countries where two or more education structures exist, indicators were calculated on the basis of the most common or widespread structure. In the Russian Federation this is three grades of primary education starting at age 7. However, a four-grade structure also exists, in which about one-third of primary pupils are enrolled. Gross enrolment ratios may be overestimated.
6. Children enter primary school at age 6 or 7. Since 7 is the most common entrance age, enrolment ratios were calculated using the 7-11 age group for population.

GROSS ENROLMENT RATIO (GER) IN PRIMARY EDUCATION (%) School year ending in 2005				NET ENROLMENT RATIO (NER) IN PRIMARY EDUCATION (%) School year ending in 1999				School year ending in 2005				OUT-OF-SCHOOL CHILDREN[2] School year ending in 1999		2005		
Total	Male	Female	GPI (F/M)	Total	Male	Female	GPI (F/M)	Total	Male	Female	GPI (F/M)	Total (000)	% F	Total (000)	% F	
72*,y	80*,y	63*,y	0.79*,y	53	61	46	0.75	56*,y	62*,y	50*,y	0.80*,y	1 254	58	1 223*,y	58*,y	170
62y	69y	54y	0.78y	...	...	...	...	...	...	...	...	...	...	...	...	171
114	117	111	0.95	83	...	...	...	81y	85y	77y	0.90y	9	...	10y	63y	172
64	71	57	0.81	36	39	34	0.86	47	51	43	0.86	293	52	308	53	173
100	107	94	0.88	33	38	28	0.74	68	71	66	0.93	4 962	54	2 666	54	174
130z	130z	129z	0.99z	...	...	...	...	...	...	...	...	...	...	...	...	175
81z	79z	84z	1.06z	67	71	62	0.88	77y	77y	77y	0.99y	61	57	47y	50y	176
94	94	93	0.98	57	58	56	0.96	69	69	70	1.01	1 330	50	990	48	177
81	88	74	0.84	44	51	36	0.71	66	70	61	0.87	709	55	501	56	178
...	...	...	...	45	53	37	0.71	...	...	...	...	114	57	...	...	179
112	114	110	0.96	64	63	64	1.01	79	78	79	1.01	1 834	49	1 123	49	180
132	132	131	1.00	60	56	63	1.13	87	84	89	1.06	139	45	41	40	181
...	...	...	...	41	47	36	0.77	...	...	...	...	271	55	...	...	182
138	141	136	0.96	63	63	63	1.01	92	93	92	1.00	785	50	188	50	183
122	121	124	1.02	98	99	97	0.98	95	92	97	1.05	23	100	113	27	184
66	74	59	0.80	40	46	34	0.73	51	56	45	0.81	1 113	54	1 113	55	185
102	102	102	1.00	91	90	91	1.01	95	94	96	1.02	12	47	6	42	186
103	111	94	0.85	52	58	46	0.80	77	81	74	0.91	1 602	56	872	58	187
99	99	100	1.01	73	70	76	1.08	72	69	74	1.07	100	44	116	45	188
47	54	39	0.73	24	29	20	0.68	40	46	33	0.73	1 393	52	1 371	54	189
103	111	95	0.86	61	67	56	0.84	68	72	64	0.88	7 189	56	6 583.6	56	190
120	119	121	1.02	...	...	...	...	74	72	75	1.04	...	...	373	47	191
134	135	132	0.98	85	85	84	0.99	97	97	96	0.99	3	50	0.03	100	192
78	80	77	0.97	52	55	48	0.88	69	70	67	0.97	808	53	518	52	193
116	115	116	1.01	...	...	...	...	99z	99z	100z	1.01z	...	...	0.04z	—z	194
...	...	...	...	...	...	...	...	...	...	...	...	...	...	...	...	195
...	...	...	...	...	...	...	...	...	...	...	...	...	...	...	...	196
104z	106z	102z	0.96z	93	92	94	1.02	87z	87z	87z	1.00z	171	19	569z	44z	197
107z	111z	104z	0.93z	75	74	75	1.02	80z	79z	80z	1.01z	53	48	40z	48z	198
100	108	92	0.85	79	89	70	0.79	78	84	72	0.86	148	81	190	67	199
119	119	119	1.00	...	...	...	...	...	...	...	...	...	...	...	...	200
110	112	109	0.97	48	47	49	1.04	98	99	97	0.99	3 405	49	132	68	201
111	114	108	0.95	63	64	62	0.96	89	89	89	1.00	760	51	228	48	202
96y	97y	95y	0.98y	81	81	82	1.01	82y	81y	82y	1.01y	449	49	429y	48y	203
Weighted average				Weighted average				Weighted average				Sum	% F	Sum	% F	
107	110	104	0.95	83	86	80	0.93	87	88	85	0.96	96 459	59	72 124	57	I
111	112	111	0.99	85	85	84	0.99	90	90	89	1.00	2 039	51	1 029	49	II
102	102	101	0.99	97	97	97	1.00	96	95	96	1.01	1 886	49	2 270	45	III
108	111	104	0.94	81	85	78	0.92	86	88	83	0.95	92 534	59	68 825	57	IV
95	100	91	0.91	79	83	75	0.90	83	86	80	0.93	7 720	59	6 122	60	V
103	105	102	0.98	90	91	88	0.97	91	91	90	0.98	2 508	57	1 901	53	VI
101	102	101	0.99	88	88	88	0.99	90	90	89	0.99	490	52	381	52	VII
110	111	109	0.98	95	96	95	1.00	94	94	93	0.99	6 824	50	9 524	52	VIII
111	112	110	0.98	96	96	95	1.00	94	94	93	0.99	6 377	51	9 189	52	IX
98	100	96	0.96	87	88	87	0.99	90	92	89	0.97	447	50	335	55	X
118	120	115	0.96	92	93	91	0.98	94	94	94	1.00	3 595	54	2 433	49	XI
117	118	116	0.98	77	78	75	0.96	77	79	76	0.96	435	51	449	53	XII
118	120	115	0.96	93	93	92	0.98	95	95	95	1.00	3 160	55	1 983	48	XIII
102	102	102	0.99	97	97	96	1.00	95	95	96	1.01	1 465	49	1 898	45	XIV
113	116	109	0.93	77	84	70	0.83	86	89	82	0.92	31 434	69	17 092	66	XV
97	102	91	0.89	57	60	54	0.90	70	73	67	0.92	42 423	53	32 774	54	XVI

7. For the first time, data include French overseas departments and territories (DOM-TOM).
8. Enrolment ratios were not calculated due to lack of United Nations population data by age.
9. Enrolment ratios were not calculated due to inconsistencies between enrolment and the United Nations population data.
10. Due to the continuing discrepancy in enrolment by single age, the net enrolment ratio in primary education is estimated using the age distribution of the 2004 DHS data.

Data in italic are UIS estimates.
Data in bold are for the school year ending in 2006.
(z) Data are for the school year ending in 2004.
(y) Data are for the school year ending in 2003.
(*) National estimates.

Table 6
Internal efficiency: repetition in primary education

		REPETITION RATES BY GRADE IN PRIMARY EDUCATION (%)											
		School year ending in 2004											
	Duration[1] of primary education	Grade 1			Grade 2			Grade 3			Grade 4		
Country or territory	2005	Total	Male	Female	Total	Male	Female	Total	Male	Female	Total	Male	Female
Arab States													
Algeria	6	11.2	12.9	9.3	7.2	8.7	5.6	8.6	10.8	6.2	10.8	13.5	7.7
Bahrain	6	3.0	2.4	3.5	3.2	3.7	2.6	3.4	4.0	2.8	2.5	3.2	1.8
Djibouti	6	2.9	2.8	3.0	...	...	...	7.2	6.9	7.5	6.5	6.3	6.6
Egypt	6	*0.1*	...	...	*2.0*	...	...	*2.7*	...	...	*4.0*	...	...
Iraq	6	*9.2*	*10.3*	*7.9*	*7.7*	*8.7*	*6.5*	*6.4*	*7.4*	*5.2*	*7.2*	*8.5*	*5.5*
Jordan	6	0.3	0.3	0.4	0.3	0.2	0.3	0.2	0.2	0.3	1.2	1.1	1.4
Kuwait	5	3.1	3.2	3.0	1.8	2.0	1.6	2.7	3.1	2.3	2.4	3.1	1.6
Lebanon	6	5.8	7.0	4.6	6.7	7.9	5.3	6.7	8.3	5.0	17.9	20.2	15.3
Libyan Arab Jamahiriya	6	...	...	...	...	...	...	...	...	...	...	...	...
Mauritania	6	9.6	9.4	9.9	8.6	8.5	8.7	9.6	9.4	9.8	10.8	10.5	11.2
Morocco	6	16.0	17.2	14.6	13.9	15.6	11.8	14.3	16.5	11.6	11.3	13.9	8.3
Oman	6	**0.3**	**0.3**	**0.2**	**0.1**	**0.1**	**0.0**	**0.1**	**0.1**	**0.1**	**0.03**	**0.03**	**0.04**
Palestinian A. T.	4	0.0	0.0	0.0	0.0	0.0	0.0	0.4	0.4	0.4	2.2	2.4	2.1
Qatar	6	*4.5*y	*4.3*y	*4.8*y	...	...	...	...	...	...	...	...	...
Saudi Arabia	6	9.2	9.3	9.0	5.0	5.8	4.2	6.5	5.9	7.1	5.3	4.1	6.4
Sudan	6	1.4	1.1	1.8	1.6	1.4	1.9	1.8	1.6	2.1	2.1	1.7	2.5
Syrian Arab Republic	4	11.6	12.3	10.8	8.3	9.5	7.0	5.2	5.9	4.4	4.0	4.5	3.4
Tunisia	6	0.9	1.1	0.8	10.2	11.7	8.6	2.9	3.6	2.3	13.3	16.1	10.1
United Arab Emirates	5	2.6	2.5	2.6	1.7	1.8	1.7	1.6	1.9	1.3	1.9	2.6	1.0
Yemen	6	*3.6*y	*3.7*y	*3.4*y	*4.1*y	*4.2*y	*3.9*y	*4.9*y	*5.2*y	*4.4*y	*5.5*y	*6.1*y	*4.4*y
Central and Eastern Europe													
Albania	4	3.2y	3.7y	2.7y	2.1y	2.5y	1.6y	1.5y	1.9y	1.1y	1.7y	2.0y	1.4y
Belarus	4	0.2	0.2*	0.2*	0.02	0.02*	0.02*	0.01	0.0*	0.0*	0.01	0.01*	0.01*
Bosnia and Herzegovina	4	...	...	...	...	...	...	...	...	...	...	...	...
Bulgaria	4	0.8	0.9	0.7	2.9	3.4	2.4	2.1	2.4	1.7	2.8	3.1	2.4
Croatia	4	0.9x	1.0x	0.8x	0.3x	0.3x	0.2x	0.2x	0.2x	0.1x	0.1x	0.1x	0.1x
Czech Republic	5	1.5	1.7	1.2	1.0	1.2	0.8	0.9	1.1	0.7	0.9	1.1	0.7
Estonia	6	1.1	1.3	0.9	0.7	1.0	0.4	0.9	1.2	0.6	1.1	1.4	0.7
Hungary	4	4.3	5.0	3.5	1.6	2.0	1.3	1.2	1.4	0.9	1.2	1.5	0.9
Latvia	4	5.4	6.8	3.8	1.9	2.6	1.2	1.9	2.7	1.1	2.3	3.3	1.2
Lithuania	4	1.3	1.6	1.0	0.4	0.6	0.3	0.4	0.5	0.2	0.5	0.8	0.2
Poland	6	0.7	...	...	0.3	...	...	0.4	...	...	0.9	...	...
Republic of Moldova	4	0.5	0.6	0.4	0.2	0.2	0.1	0.1	0.2	0.1	0.1	0.2	0.1
Romania	4	3.9	4.4	3.4	1.7	2.1	1.3	1.3	1.6	1.0	1.4	1.8	1.1
Russian Federation	3	1.7	...	...	...	...	...	...	...	...	.	.	.
Serbia and Montenegro	4	...	...	...	...	...	...	...	...	...	...	...	...
Slovakia	4	4.8	5.2	4.5	2.2	2.4	2.0	1.6	1.7	1.4	1.6	1.7	1.5
Slovenia	5	0.4	0.4	0.3	...	...	...	...	...	...	...	...	...
TFYR Macedonia	4	0.3	0.3	0.2	0.2	0.2	0.2	0.1	0.1	0.1	0.2	0.2	0.1
Turkey	6	4.3	4.6	3.9	2.0	2.0	2.0	2.0	1.7	2.2	2.3	1.8	2.7
Ukraine	4	...	...	...	...	...	...	...	...	...	...	...	...
Central Asia													
Armenia	3	—x	—x	—x	0.2x	0.2x	0.1x	0.2x	0.2x	0.2x	.	.	.
Azerbaijan	4	0.3	0.4	0.3	0.3	0.3	0.3	0.2	0.2	0.2	0.3	0.2	0.3
Georgia	6	0.2y	0.2y	0.2y	0.2y	0.2y	0.2y	...	...	...	...	...	...
Kazakhstan	4	0.0	0.1	0.0	0.2	0.2	0.1	0.1	0.1	0.1	0.1	0.1	0.0
Kyrgyzstan	4	0.1	0.1	0.1	0.1	0.1	0.1	0.1	0.1	0.0	0.1	0.1	0.0
Mongolia	5	1.3y	1.4y	1.2y	0.5y	0.6y	0.5y	0.3y	0.3y	0.2y	0.2y	0.2y	0.2y
Tajikistan	4	0.2	*0.2*	*0.2*	0.2	*0.2*	*0.2*	0.2	*0.2*	*0.2*	0.3	*0.3*	*0.3*
Turkmenistan	3	...	...	...	...	...	...	...	...	...	.	.	.
Uzbekistan	4	—y	—y	—y	—y	—y	—y	—y	—y	—y	—y	—y	—y
East Asia and the Pacific													
Australia	7	...	...	...	...	...	...	...	...	...	...	...	...
Brunei Darussalam	6	0.6	0.7	0.4	0.8	1.0	0.6	1.0	1.4	0.5	1.7	2.6	0.7
Cambodia	6	23.9	24.8	22.9	16.3	17.6	14.7	13.3	14.9	11.5	9.3	10.7	7.7
China	5	*1.3*	*1.4*	*1.2*	...	...	...	...	...	...	...	...	...
Cook Islands	6	...	...	...	...	...	...	...	...	...	...	...	...

REPETITION RATES BY GRADE IN PRIMARY EDUCATION (%)						REPEATERS, ALL GRADES (%)						
School year ending in 2004						School year ending in						
Grade 5			Grade 6			1999			2005			
Total	Male	Female	Total	Male	Female	Total	Male	Female	Total	Male	Female	Country or territory
												Arab States
11.2	14.1	7.8	15.2	18.2	11.8	11.9	14.6	8.7	11.2	13.6	8.4	Algeria
2.8	3.5	2.1	1.9	3.1	0.8	3.8	4.6	3.1	2.8	3.3	2.3	Bahrain
6.3	6.2	6.3	21.8	21.1	22.9	16.6	16.9	16.1	9.2	9.3	9.1	Djibouti
3.8	...	...	...	...	...	6.0	7.1	4.6	2.2	2.7	1.5	Egypt
13.1	15.2	10.2	4.2	4.4	3.8	10.0	10.7	9.2	8.0	9.1	6.5	Iraq
1.8	1.7	1.8	1.9	1.8	1.9	0.7	0.7	0.7	0.9	0.9	1.0	Jordan
...	...	...	...	...	...	3.3	3.4	3.1	1.9	2.2	1.7	Kuwait
11.8	13.5	10.0	10.6	11.7	9.4	9.1	10.5	7.7	10.1	11.7	8.4	Lebanon
...	...	...	...	...	...	...	...	...	...	...	...	Libyan Arab Jamahiriya
11.5	11.0	12.0	15.4	14.7	16.2	...	...	...	10.1	9.9	10.3	Mauritania
9.5	11.8	6.7	9.1	11.2	6.5	12.4	14.1	10.2	12.7	14.7	10.4	Morocco
1.4	**0.9**	**1.9**	**1.3**	**0.8**	**1.9**	8.0	9.5	6.4	**0.6**	**0.4**	**0.8**	Oman
...	...	...	...	...	...	2.1	2.2	2.0	0.7	0.7	0.7	Palestinian A. T.
...	...	...	...	...	...	2.7	3.5	1.9	2.7	3.7	1.7	Qatar
2.9	2.9	2.9	1.1	1.1	1.1	...	...	...	5.1	4.9	5.2	Saudi Arabia
1.8	1.5	2.2	1.9	1.5	2.4	11.3	10.9	11.8	1.7	1.4	2.1	Sudan
.	.	.	.	.	.	6.5	7.2	5.6	7.3	8.1	6.4	Syrian Arab Republic
11.2	13.4	8.8	7.5	9.1	5.8	18.3	20.0	16.4	8.5	10.2	6.6	Tunisia
1.8	2.4	1.1	.	.	.	3.5	4.4	2.5	1.9	2.2	1.5	United Arab Emirates
5.5y	6.1y	4.4y	4.5y	5.1y	3.3y	10.6	11.7*	8.7*	4.3z	4.8z	3.7z	Yemen
												Central and Eastern Europe
.	.	.	.	.	.	3.9	4.6	3.2	2.1z	2.6z	1.7z	Albania
.	.	.	.	.	.	0.5	0.5	0.5	0.1	0.1*	0.1*	Belarus
.	.	.	.	.	.	...	...	...	...	...	...	Bosnia and Herzegovina
.	.	.	.	.	.	3.2	3.7	2.7	2.3	2.7	2.0	Bulgaria
.	.	.	.	.	.	0.4	0.5	0.3	0.4y	0.4y	0.3y	Croatia
0.8	1.0	0.6	.	.	.	1.2	1.5	1.0	1.1	1.3	0.9	Czech Republic
1.6	2.6	0.5	2.7	4.0	1.3	2.5	3.5	1.4	1.6	2.3	0.8	Estonia
.	.	.	.	.	.	2.2	2.1	2.2	2.1	2.5	1.7	Hungary
.	.	.	.	.	.	2.1	2.7	1.3	3.0	4.1	1.9	Latvia
.	.	.	.	.	.	0.9	1.3	0.5	0.7	0.9	0.5	Lithuania
1.0	...	...	0.6	...	...	1.2	...	...	0.7	1.1	0.3	Poland
.	.	.	.	.	.	0.9	0.9	0.9	0.3	0.3	0.2	Republic of Moldova
.	.	.	.	.	.	3.4	4.1	2.6	2.3	2.7	1.8	Romania
.	.	.	.	.	.	1.2	...	...	...	...	...	Russian Federation
.	.	.	.	.	.	...	...	...	...	...	...	Serbia and Montenegro
.	.	.	.	.	.	2.3	2.6	2.0	2.6	2.9	2.4	Slovakia
.	.	.	.	.	.	1.0	1.3	0.7	0.5	0.6	0.4	Slovenia
.	.	.	.	.	.	0.0	0.1	0.0	0.2	0.2	0.2	TFYR Macedonia
2.3	1.7	2.9	5.4	5.0	5.8	...	...	...	3.0	2.8	3.2	Turkey
.	.	.	.	.	.	0.8	...	...	0.1	...	...	Ukraine
												Central Asia
.	.	.	.	.	.	...	...	...	0.2	0.2	0.1	Armenia
.	.	.	.	.	.	0.4	0.4	0.4	0.3	0.3	0.3	Azerbaijan
.	.	.	.	.	.	0.3	0.5	0.2	0.3	0.4	0.2	Georgia
...	...	...	...	...	...	0.3	...	...	0.1	0.2	0.1	Kazakhstan
...	...	...	...	...	...	0.3	0.4	0.2	0.1	0.1	0.1	Kyrgyzstan
...	...	...	...	...	...	0.9	1.0	0.8	0.4	0.5	0.4	Mongolia
...	...	...	...	...	...	0.5	0.5	0.6	0.2	0.2	0.2	Tajikistan
...	...	...	...	.	...	...	...	...	...	...	...	Turkmenistan
...	...	...	...	...	...	...	...	...	-z	-z	-z	Uzbekistan
												East Asia and the Pacific
...	...	...	...	...	...	...	...	...	...	...	...	Australia
1.5	2.1	0.8	7.4	9.4	5.0	.	.	.	2.3	3.0	1.4	Brunei Darussalam
5.9	7.1	4.7	2.6	3.0	2.2	24.6	25.4	23.5	13.8	15.1	12.4	Cambodia
...	...	...	...	...	...	...	...	...	**0.3**	**0.3**	**0.2**	China
...	...	...	...	...	...	2.6	...	...	...	...	...	Cook Islands

Table 6 (continued)

Country or territory	Duration[1] of primary education	REPETITION RATES BY GRADE IN PRIMARY EDUCATION (%)											
		School year ending in 2004											
		Grade 1			Grade 2			Grade 3			Grade 4		
	2005	Total	Male	Female	Total	Male	Female	Total	Male	Female	Total	Male	Female
Saint Kitts and Nevis	7	.	.	.	.	.	.	.	.	.	.	.	.
Saint Lucia	7	6.7	7.2	6.0	2.1	2.2	1.9	1.2	1.6	0.8	1.0	0.8	1.3
St Vincent/Grenad.	7	5.0	6.3	3.7	…	…	…	…	…	…	…	…	…
Suriname	6	…	…	…	…	…	…	…	…	…	…	…	…
Trinidad and Tobago	7	10.8*	12.8*	8.6*	3.5*	2.7*	4.3*	4.1*	5.1*	3.0*	4.1*	4.9*	3.2*
Turks and Caicos Islands	6	0.9ʸ	1.8ʸ	−ʸ	…	…	…	…	…	…	…	…	…
Uruguay	6	14.8ʸ	17.1ʸ	12.3ʸ	9.4ʸ	10.8ʸ	8.0ʸ	7.1ʸ	8.5ʸ	5.6ʸ	5.6ʸ	6.9ʸ	4.4ʸ
Venezuela	6	10.9	12.8	8.8	8.4	10.2	6.5	8.1	10.1	6.0	5.9	7.4	4.3
North America and Western Europe													
Andorra	6	…	…	…	…	…	…	…	…	…	…	…	…
Austria	4	…	…	…	…	…	…	…	…	…	…	…	…
Belgium	6	…	…	…	…	…	…	…	…	…	…	…	…
Canada	6	…	…	…	…	…	…	…	…	…	…	…	…
Cyprus	6	1.3	1.5	1.2	0.1	0.1	0.1	0.01	−	0.0	0.01	−	0.02
Denmark	6	.	.	.	.	.	.	.	.	.	.	.	.
Finland	6	0.9	1.2	0.5	0.9	1.2	0.6	0.3	0.4	0.3	0.2	0.3	0.1
France	5	…	…	…	…	…	…	…	…	…	…	…	…
Germany	4	1.4	1.5	1.3	1.9	1.9	1.8	1.4	1.5	1.3	0.8	0.9	0.7
Greece	6	1.6	1.8	1.3	0.6	0.7	0.5	0.3	0.4	0.3	0.3	0.4	0.3
Iceland	7	−ʸ	−ʸ	−ʸ	−ʸ	−ʸ	−ʸ	−ʸ	−ʸ	−ʸ	−ʸ	−ʸ	−ʸ
Ireland	8	2.5ʸ	2.8ʸ	2.1ʸ	1.6ʸ	1.8ʸ	1.3ʸ	0.9ʸ	1.0ʸ	0.8ʸ	0.6ʸ	0.6ʸ	0.5ʸ
Israel	6	2.3	3.3	1.3	1.0	1.4	0.6	1.2	1.7	0.6	1.2	1.6	0.7
Italy	5	0.4	0.5	0.2	0.2	0.3	0.2	0.2	0.2	0.1	0.1	0.2	0.1
Luxembourg	6	4.5	4.8	4.2	5.4	5.7	5.1	6.1	6.7	5.5	…	…	…
Malta	6	0.8	0.8	0.8	0.8	0.9	0.6	…	…	…	…	…	…
Monaco	5	−ʸ	…	…	−ʸ	…	…	−ʸ	…	…	−ʸ	…	…
Netherlands	6	.ʸ	.ʸ	.ʸ	.ʸ	.ʸ	.ʸ	.ʸ	.ʸ	.ʸ	.ʸ	.ʸ	.ʸ
Norway	7	.	.	.	.	.	.	.	.	.	.	.	.
Portugal	6	−	−	−	…	…	…	…	…	…	…	…	…
San Marino	5	…	…	…	…	…	…	…	…	…	…	…	…
Spain	6	−	−	−	3.4	3.9	2.9	−	−	−	3.8	4.4	3.2
Sweden	6	…	…	…	…	…	…	…	…	…	…	…	…
Switzerland	6	…	…	…	…	…	…	…	…	…	…	…	…
United Kingdom	6	…	…	…	…	…	…	…	…	…	…	…	…
United States	6	…	…	…	…	…	…	…	…	…	…	…	…
South and West Asia													
Afghanistan	6	…	…	…	…	…	…	…	…	…	…	…	…
Bangladesh	5	7.1ʸ	6.8ʸ	7.4ʸ	6.7ʸ	6.6ʸ	6.7ʸ	9.2ʸ	9.4ʸ	8.9ʸ	7.7ʸ	8.2ʸ	7.3ʸ
Bhutan	7	…	…	…	…	…	…	…	…	…	…	…	…
India	5	4.0	3.9	4.0	2.9	2.9	2.9	4.1	4.1	4.2	…	…	…
Iran, Islamic Republic of	5	4.1	…	…	…	…	…	…	…	…	…	…	…
Maldives	7	0.6	0.9	0.2	0.4	0.4	0.3	0.6	0.6	0.5	0.8	1.0	0.7
Nepal	5	**37.0**	**36.8**	**37.3**	**19.3**	**18.5**	**20.1**	**15.0**	**15.0**	**15.1**	**15.9**	**15.9**	**16.0**
Pakistan	5	3.7	4.0	3.2	3.0	3.2	2.8	2.8	2.9	2.6	2.8	2.9	2.6
Sri Lanka	5	…	…	…	…	…	…	…	…	…	…	…	…
Sub-Saharan Africa													
Angola	4	…	…	…	…	…	…	…	…	…	…	…	…
Benin	6	7.5	7.6	7.3	14.6	14.6	14.7	18.4	17.9	18.9	21.3	20.5	22.3
Botswana	7	7.6	7.5	7.7	…	…	…	…	…	…	…	…	…
Burkina Faso	6	6.4	6.7	6.1	10.0	10.1	9.8	12.7	13.0	12.2	13.8	13.9	13.7
Burundi	6	30.8	30.8	30.8	30.6	30.7	30.6	29.0	28.8	29.4	28.0	27.7	28.3
Cameroon	6	29.8	30.5	28.9	…	…	…	…	…	…	…	…	…
Cape Verde	6	1.5	…	…	24.9	…	…	11.4	…	…	20.2	…	…
Central African Republic	6	27.2	27.3	27.2	…	…	…	…	…	…	…	…	…
Chad	6	23.2	22.8	23.7	21.9	21.2	22.7	21.5	19.5	24.7	21.3	20.3	22.8
Comoros	6	33.3	35.0	31.2	28.9	27.5	30.4	28.5	30.4	26.2	24.1	26.0	21.9
Congo	6	27.7	…	…	…	…	…	…	…	…	…	…	…
Côte d'Ivoire	6	13.3ˣ	14.0ˣ	12.5ˣ	…	…	…	…	…	…	…	…	…
Democratic Rep. of the Congo	6	18.5ˣ	18.8ˣ	18.1ˣ	…	…	…	…	…	…	…	…	…
Equatorial Guinea	5	35.3ˣ	30.6ˣ	40.2ˣ	…	…	…	…	…	…	…	…	…

Grade 5 Total	Male	Female	Grade 6 Total	Male	Female	1999 Total	Male	Female	2005 Total	Male	Female	Country or territory
.	.	.	.	.	.	.	.	.	.	.	.	Saint Kitts and Nevis
1.5	1.7	1.4	1.4	1.2	1.5	*2.4*	*2.8*	*2.0*	2.7	2.9	2.6	Saint Lucia
...	...	...	...	...	...	...	...	...	4.1	5.0	3.0	St Vincent/Grenad.
...	...	...	...	...	...	...	...	...	20.3	22.3	18.1	Suriname
4.2*	5.0*	3.3*	5.2*	6.5*	4.0*	4.7	4.9	4.4	5.2*	6.0*	4.4*	Trinidad and Tobago
...	...	...	...	...	...	...	...	...	2.9	3.2	2.6	Turks and Caicos Islands
4.2y	5.3y	3.0y	2.1y	2.5y	1.7y	7.9	9.3	6.5	7.5z	8.8z	6.0z	Uruguay
4.1	5.2	3.0	1.8	2.2	1.3	*7.0*	*8.5*	*5.5*	6.8	8.3	5.1	Venezuela
												North America and Western Europe
...	...	...	...	...	...	...	...	...	–z	–z	–z	Andorra
.	.	.	.	.	.	1.5	1.8	1.3	...	...	...	Austria
...	...	...	...	...	...	...	...	...	...	...	...	Belgium
...	...	...	...	...	...	...	...	...	...	...	...	Canada
0.03	0.05	–	0.0	0.0	0.0	0.4	0.5	0.3	0.2	0.3	0.2	Cyprus
.	.	.	.	.	.	.	.	.	.	.	.	Denmark
0.2	0.3	0.1	0.2	0.3	0.1	0.4	0.6	0.3	0.5	0.6	0.3	Finland
...	...	...	.	.	.	*4.2*	*4.2*	*4.2*	...	...	...	France
.	.	.	.	.	.	1.7	1.9	1.5	1.4	1.5	1.3	Germany
0.3	0.3	0.3	0.3	0.3	0.3	–	–	–	0.6	0.7	0.5	Greece
–y	–y	–y	–y	–y	–y	–	–	–	–z	–z	–z	Iceland
0.7y	0.6y	0.7y	0.6y	0.6y	0.6y	1.8	2.1	1.6	*0.9*	*0.9*	*0.8*	Ireland
1.4	1.9	0.9	1.1	1.5	0.7	...	...	...	1.6	2.2	1.0	Israel
0.3	0.3	0.2	.	.	.	0.4	0.5	0.3	0.2	0.3	0.2	Italy
...	...	...	...	...	...	...	...	...	4.4	4.9	3.9	Luxembourg
...	...	...	...	...	...	2.1	2.4	1.8	2.6	2.9	2.2	Malta
–y	...	...	.	.	.	–	–	–	–z	...	...	Monaco
.y	.y	.y	.y	.y	.y	.	.	.	.z	.z	.z	Netherlands
.	.	.	.	.	.	.	.	.	.	.	.	Norway
...	...	...	...	...	...	...	...	...	*10.2*	...	...	Portugal
...	...	...	.	.	.	...	...	...	–z	...	...	San Marino
–	–	–	5.8	6.9	4.7	...	...	...	2.3	2.6	1.9	Spain
...	...	...	...	...	...	...	...	...	...	...	...	Sweden
...	...	...	...	...	...	1.8	1.9	1.6	1.6	1.8	1.5	Switzerland
...	...	...	...	...	...	–	–	–	–	–	–	United Kingdom
...	...	...	...	...	...	...	...	...	...	...	...	United States
												South and West Asia
...	...	...	...	...	...	...	...	...	...	...	...	Afghanistan
5.1y	5.5y	4.7y	.	.	.	6.5	6.8	6.2	7.0z	7.2z	6.9z	Bangladesh
...	...	...	...	...	...	12.1	12.5	11.7	9.6	10.4	8.8	Bhutan
...	...	...	.	.	.	4.0	4.0	4.1	*3.4*	*3.4*	*3.4*	India
...	...	...	...	...	...	...	...	...	2.0	2.8	1.4	Iran, Islamic Republic of
1.6	2.3	0.9	...	...	...	*8.4*	*7.6*	*9.2*	5.2	5.8	4.5	Maldives
12.0	**11.8**	**12.3**	.	.	.	22.9	22.2	23.8	**20.6**	**20.8**	**20.4**	Nepal
4.0	4.5	3.2	.	.	.	...	...	...	3.1	3.3	2.7	Pakistan
...	...	...	.	.	.	...	...	...	...	...	...	Sri Lanka
												Sub-Saharan Africa
...	...	...	.	.	.	*29.0*	*29.0*	*29.0*	...	...	...	Angola
21.9	20.6	23.7	24.6	23.6	26.3	...	...	...	16.8	16.7	16.9	Benin
...	...	...	...	...	...	3.3	3.9	2.7	*4.8*	*5.2*	*4.3*	Botswana
14.7	14.0	15.7	31.2	30.3	32.3	17.7	17.5	18.0	11.9	12.1	11.7	Burkina Faso
38.6	37.1	40.7	43.7	41.8	46.1	*20.3*	*20.3*	*20.4*	30.4	30.4	30.4	Burundi
...	...	...	21.8	22.5	20.9	*26.7*	*26.8*	*26.5*	25.8*	26.2*	25.3*	Cameroon
10.0	...	...	15.4	...	...	*11.6*	*12.8*	*10.3*	15.4	18.0	12.7	Cape Verde
...	...	...	36.6	37.7	34.5	...	...	...	*30.5*	*30.3*	*30.8*	Central African Republic
22.6	21.1	25.1	23.2	22.9	23.9	25.9	25.7	26.3	22.5	21.8	23.5	Chad
22.7	*23.6*	*21.7*	*26.2*	*27.9*	*24.3*	26.0	26.4	25.5	27.1	28.2	25.9	Comoros
...	...	...	...	...	...	39.1	40.0	38.2	23.9	24.7	23.1	Congo
...	...	...	...	...	...	*23.7*	*22.8*	*24.9*	17.6*,y	17.5*,y	17.7*,y	Côte d'Ivoire
...	...	...	11.8x	11.3x	12.4x	...	...	...	*16.3y*	*16.0y*	*16.7y*	Democratic Rep. of the Congo
29.9x	31.4x	28.3x	.	.	.	11.8	9.3	14.9	25.6	25.5	25.6	Equatorial Guinea

Table 6 (continued)

Education for All Global Monitoring Report 2 0 0 8

Country or territory	Duration[1] of primary education 2005	Grade 1 Total	Grade 1 Male	Grade 1 Female	Grade 2 Total	Grade 2 Male	Grade 2 Female	Grade 3 Total	Grade 3 Male	Grade 3 Female	Grade 4 Total	Grade 4 Male	Grade 4 Female
Eritrea	5	20.5	20.7	20.2	12.1	12.3	11.8	10.8	10.7	10.8	11.2	11.4	10.9
Ethiopia	4	*5.9*	*6.4*	*5.3*	…	…	…	…	…	…	…	…	…
Gabon	6	*48.1[x]*	*49.1[x]*	*47.0[x]*	*33.2[x]*	*33.7[x]*	*32.6[x]*	*37.0[x]*	*38.3[x]*	*35.6[x]*	*24.8[x]*	*25.1[x]*	*24.5[x]*
Gambia	6	*7.1[x]*	*7.5[x]*	*6.7[x]*	…	…	…	…	…	…	…	…	…
Ghana	6	9.7	10.1	9.3	…	…	…	…	…	…	…	…	…
Guinea	6	2.8	2.8	2.8	11.6	11.1	12.2	4.5	4.1	4.9	12.3	11.6	13.2
Guinea-Bissau	6	…	…	…	…	…	…	…	…	…	…	…	…
Kenya	6	*6.2*	*6.4*	*5.9*	*5.8*	*6.0*	*5.6*	*6.1*	*6.4*	*5.8*	*6.2*	*6.5*	*5.9*
Lesotho	7	28.3	…	…	14.5	…	…	21.1	…	…	19.9	…	…
Liberia	6	…	…	…	…	…	…	…	…	…	…	…	…
Madagascar	5	12.3	12.6	12.1	27.8	29.1	26.4	29.7	30.7	28.8	9.4	9.6	9.2
Malawi	6	24.7	25.7	23.8	20.9	20.5	21.2	21.7	22.7	20.8	16.6	17.0	16.1
Mali	6	13.3	13.2	13.5	13.0	12.7	13.3	19.1	18.9	19.4	22.7	21.9	23.8
Mauritius	6	.	.	.	.	.	.	.	.	.	.	.	.
Mozambique	7	7.8	8.0	7.6	17.2	17.5	16.9	7.4	7.5	7.2	16.6	16.4	16.8
Namibia	7	16.1	18.3	13.8	13.5	16.0	11.0	12.0	14.4	9.6	14.1	16.9	11.3
Niger	6	0.6	0.6	0.6	3.5	3.4	3.6	4.5	4.2	4.9	6.2	5.9	6.6
Nigeria	6	1.2	1.3	1.2	…	…	…	…	…	…	…	…	…
Rwanda	6	*19.1*	*19.2*	*18.9*	…	…	…	…	…	…	…	…	…
Sao Tome and Principe	6	29.2	30.0	28.3	25.7	27.2	23.9	23.6	25.5	21.5	17.0	17.3	16.7
Senegal	6	8.1	8.2	8.0	10.3	10.3	10.2	11.0	11.1	11.0	12.2	12.0	12.3
Seychelles	6	.[y]	.[y]	.[y]	.[y]	.[y]	.[y]	.[y]	.[y]	.[y]	.[y]	.[y]	.[y]
Sierra Leone	6	…	…	…	…	…	…	…	…	…	…	…	…
Somalia	7	…	…	…	…	…	…	…	…	…	…	…	…
South Africa	7	10.2[y]	10.7[y]	9.6[y]	8.0[y]	8.6[y]	7.4[y]	9.1[y]	9.8[y]	8.3[y]	9.5[y]	9.9[y]	8.9[y]
Swaziland	7	19.9[y]	22.5[y]	17.0[y]	…	…	…	…	…	…	…	…	…
Togo	6	27.8	28.1	27.5	23.5	23.6	23.3	25.0	24.6	25.5	21.0	20.2	21.8
Uganda	7	12.3	11.1	13.6	*12.2*	*12.5*	*11.9*	*14.3*	*15.2*	*13.4*	*13.2*	*13.2*	*13.2*
United Republic of Tanzania	7	**9.2**	**9.1**	**9.2**	**5.3**	**5.4**	**5.3**	**4.4**	**4.3**	**4.5**	**9.4**	**9.0**	**9.8**
Zambia	7	5.8	5.7	5.9	…	…	…	…	…	…	…	…	…
Zimbabwe	7	.[x]	.[x]	.[x]	.[x]	.[x]	.[x]	.[x]	.[x]	.[x]	.[x]	.[x]	.[x]
World[2]	…	3.9	5.1	2.6	2.2	2.5	1.8	2.0	1.7	2.2	1.9	2.6	1.2
Countries in transition	…	0.3	0.3	0.3	0.2	0.2	0.1	0.1	0.2	0.1	0.0	0.1	0.0
Developed countries	…	0.8	1.0	0.6	0.7	0.9	0.5	0.4	0.5	0.2	0.6	0.7	0.4
Developing countries	…	5.9	6.4	5.3	4.7	8.4	5.7	4.5	4.8	4.2	4.3	5.2	3.3
Arab States	…	3.1	3.2	3.0	4.1	4.2	3.9	4.2	4.6	3.6	4.6	…	…
Central and Eastern Europe	…	1.3	1.6	1.0	1.0	1.2	0.8	0.9	1.2	0.6	1.5	1.8	1.3
Central Asia	…	0.1	0.2	0.1	0.2	0.2	0.1	0.2	0.2	0.2	0.1	0.1	0.0
East Asia and the Pacific	…	0.6	0.6	0.6	0.0	0.0	0.0	0.0	0.0	0.0	0.0	0.0	0.0
East Asia	…	2.4	2.8	2.0	2.6	3.2	1.8	1.8	1.8	1.8	1.6	1.9	0.8
Pacific	…	.	.	.	–	–	–	–	–	–	–	–	–
Latin America/Caribbean	…	7.3	8.2	6.3	4.2	…	…	4.3	5.3	3.3	6.3	7.5	4.9
Caribbean	…	4.6	5.9	3.2	1.7	…	…	0.8	1.3	0.4	0.4	0.3	0.7
Latin America	…	10.1	11.6	8.4	7.7	8.9	6.5	6.6	7.8	5.2	4.8	5.9	3.6
N. America/W. Europe	…	0.6	0.6	0.5	0.6	0.7	0.5	0.1	0.1	0.1	0.1	0.2	0.1
South and West Asia	…	4.0	…	…	3.0	3.2	2.9	4.1	4.1	4.2	…	…	…
Sub-Saharan Africa	…	12.3	11.9	12.8	13.3	14.3	12.2	15.6	16.7	14.5	18.4	19.4	17.6

Table header: **REPETITION RATES BY GRADE IN PRIMARY EDUCATION (%)** — School year ending in 2004

1. Duration in this table is defined according to ISCED97 and may differ from that reported nationally.
2. All values shown are medians.
Data in italic are UIS estimates.
Data in bold are for the school year ending in 2005 for repetition rates by grade, and the school year ending in 2006 for percentage of repeaters (all grades).

(z) Data are for the school year ending in 2004.
(y) Data are for the school year ending in 2003.
(x) Data are for the school year ending in 2002.
(·) National estimates.

REPETITION RATES BY GRADE IN PRIMARY EDUCATION (%)						REPEATERS, ALL GRADES (%)						
School year ending in 2004						School year ending in						
Grade 5			Grade 6			1999			2005			
Total	Male	Female	Total	Male	Female	Total	Male	Female	Total	Male	Female	Country or territory
5.7	6.1	5.1	.	.	.	19.4	18.2	20.8	12.9	13.0	12.7	Eritrea
.	.	.	.	.	.	11.4	10.7	12.5	**7.0**	**7.6**	**6.3**	Ethiopia
27.7ˣ	27.4ˣ	28.0ˣ	19.3ˣ	18.9ˣ	19.6ˣ	...	...	...	34.4ʸ	35.1ʸ	33.7ʸ	Gabon
...	...	...	...	...	...	12.2	12.1	12.3	9.7ʸ	10.2ʸ	9.2ʸ	Gambia
...	...	...	...	...	...	4.2	4.3	4.1	5.8	6.0	5.7	Ghana
4.4	4.0	4.9	23.0	21.5	25.2	26.2	25.5	27.4	8.7	8.4	9.0	Guinea
...	...	...	...	...	...	24.0	23.6	24.5	...	...	...	Guinea-Bissau
5.9	...	...	5.5	...	...	...	...	...	5.8	6.0	5.6	Kenya
15.3	...	...	13.4	...	...	20.3	22.9	17.9	19.0	20.9	17.0	Lesotho
...	...	...	...	...	...	...	...	...	...	...	...	Liberia
26.1	26.0	26.1	.	.	.	28.3	29.2	27.4	18.3	18.8	17.7	Madagascar
15.1	15.4	14.8	12.3	12.5	12.1	14.4	14.4	14.4	20.2	20.6	19.7	Malawi
28.8	27.7	30.2	29.8	28.8	31.4	17.4	17.2	17.7	18.6	18.4	18.9	Mali
.	.	.	21.8	24.1	19.4	3.8	4.1	3.5	4.8	5.4	4.2	Mauritius
16.3	16.1	16.8	2.8	3.2	2.3	23.8	23.2	24.7	10.4	10.6	10.2	Mozambique
21.6	25.2	18.0	13.0	14.3	11.7	12.3	13.9	10.7	15.1	17.4	12.9	Namibia
9.1	8.8	9.7	21.2	20.1	22.8	12.2	12.4	11.8	5.3	5.2	5.5	Niger
...	...	...	1.9	1.9	1.9	...	...	...	2.9	2.4	3.0	Nigeria
...	...	...	17.9	17.5	18.3	29.1	29.2	29.0	18.8	18.7	18.9	Rwanda
16.7	17.2	16.2	28.9	29.4	28.3	30.7	32.6	28.7	23.5	24.5	22.4	Sao Tome and Principe
13.6	13.1	14.1	23.8	23.1	24.7	14.4	14.5	14.2	11.9	11.9	11.8	Senegal
.ʸ	.ʸ	.ʸ	.ʸ	.ʸ	.ʸ	.	.	.	.	.	.	Seychelles
...	...	...	...	...	...	...	...	...	...	...	...	Sierra Leone
...	...	...	...	...	...	...	...	...	...	...	...	Somalia
7.3ʸ	7.8ʸ	6.7ʸ	5.8ʸ	5.7ʸ	5.8ʸ	10.4	11.6	9.2	8.0ᶻ	8.4ᶻ	7.5ᶻ	South Africa
...	...	...	...	...	...	17.1	19.5	14.5	16.2ᶻ	18.5ᶻ	13.6ᶻ	Swaziland
21.9	21.3	22.7	16.6	15.7	17.7	31.2	30.9	31.6	22.9	22.6	23.3	Togo
13.8	13.7	13.9	13.2	11.9	14.5	...	...	...	13.1	13.0	13.3	Uganda
0.2	**0.2**	**0.2**	**0.0**	**0.0**	**0.0**	3.2	3.1	3.2	**4.9**	**4.8**	**5.0**	United Republic of Tanzania
...	...	...	...	...	...	6.1	6.4	5.8	6.3	6.6	6.1	Zambia
.ˣ	.ˣ	.ˣ	.ˣ	.ˣ	.ˣ	.	.	.	.ʸ	.ʸ	.ʸ	Zimbabwe
1.5	...	...	.	.	.	3.8	4.2	3.4	3.1	3.7	2.3	World [2]
.	.	.	.	.	.	0.5	0.5	0.5	0.2	0.2	0.1	Countries in transition
–	–	–	.	.	.	1.2	...	...	0.7	1.0	0.4	Developed countries
3.3	4.1	2.4	1.5	1.7	1.1	6.6	7.6	5.5	5.8	6.0	5.7	Developing countries
4.7	...	...	4.2	4.4	3.3	8.0	9.5	6.4	4.3	4.8	3.7	Arab States
.	.	.	.	.	.	1.2	...	...	1.1	1.3	0.9	Central and Eastern Europe
...	...	...	.	.	.	0.4	0.5	0.3	0.3	0.3	0.2	Central Asia
0.0	0.0	0.0	.	.	.	1.3	1.4	1.3	0.6	0.7	0.5	East Asia and the Pacific
1.0	1.5	0.6	0.0	0.0	0.0	2.7	2.9	2.5	2.2	2.9	1.6	East Asia
–	–	–	–	–	–	1.8	2.0	1.5	2.2	2.9	1.6	Pacific
2.7	3.3	2.2	1.4	1.2	1.5	4.7	5.1	4.2	5.2	6.0	4.4	Latin America/Caribbean
0.7	...	...	0.8	0.9	0.6	3.1	3.6	2.5	3.4	4.1	2.6	Caribbean
3.3	4.1	2.4	1.5	1.7	1.4	6.5	7.5	5.3	6.7	7.9	5.4	Latin America
.	.	.	.	.	.	0.4	0.5	0.3	0.3	0.4	0.3	N. America/W. Europe
...	...	...	.	.	.	8.4	7.6	9.2	5.2	5.8	4.5	South and West Asia
14.9	14.7	15.3	14.4	...	...	17.4	17.5	17.7	15.3	16.3	13.1	Sub-Saharan Africa

Table 7
Internal efficiency: primary education dropout and completion

Country or territory	Duration[1] of primary education 2005	Grade 1			Grade 2			Grade 3			Grade 4			Grade 5		
		Total	Male	Female	Total	Male	Female	Total	Male	Female	Total	Male	Female	Total	Male	Female
Arab States																
Algeria	6	0.8	1.3	0.3	1.0	1.5	0.4	0.5	0.3	0.8	1.7	2.1	1.2	2.2	2.5	1.9
Bahrain	6	–	–	–	–	–	–	0.0	–	0.4	0.2	–	0.5	0.1	–	0.2
Djibouti	6	...	...	...	...	...	...	3.2	2.0	4.7	2.9	5.0	0.3	–	–	
Egypt	6	0.2[y]	0.3[y]	0.1[y]	0.4[y]	0.5[y]	0.4[y]	0.3[y]	0.3[y]	0.2[y]	0.4[y]	0.5[y]	0.3[y]	...	...	...
Iraq	6	11.1	9.1	13.4	1.4	–	3.7	1.1	–	2.9	5.2	3.2	7.8	11.2	8.8	14.6
Jordan	6	0.7[y]	1.2[y]	0.3[y]	–[y]	–[y]	–[y]	–[y]	–[y]	–[y]	0.9[y]	0.3[y]	1.5[y]	1.0[y]	0.8[y]	1.2[y]
Kuwait	5	–	–	–	...	...	...	...	...	...	...	...	...	...	...	...
Lebanon	6	1.5	1.7	1.2	0.6	0.6	0.5	0.7	1.1	0.3	3.3	4.4	2.0	3.4	4.6	2.1
Libyan Arab Jamahiriya	6	...	...	...	...	...	...	...	...	...	...	...	...			
Mauritania	6	5.8	6.8	4.7	12.4	13.3	11.5	16.3	17.0	15.7	18.1	18.4	17.8	22.6	22.8	22.3
Morocco	6	6.0	5.5	6.5	2.9	2.5	3.4	4.7	4.1	5.5	5.8	4.8	6.9	7.6	6.7	8.6
Oman	6	**0.2**	**0.3**	**0.1**	–	–	–	–	–	–	–	–	–	**1.9**	**1.2**	**2.6**
Palestinian A. T.	4	0.9	0.9	0.9	–	–	–	1.2	1.2	1.4	...	...	...	.	.	.
Qatar	6	...	...	...	...	...	...	...	...	...	...	...	...			
Saudi Arabia	6	0.5	–	2.3	0.3	–	2.9	0.4	1.0	–	–	–	–	2.1	2.8	1.3
Sudan	6	6.1	6.7	5.3	6.3	5.6	7.1	4.9	4.8	5.0	5.7	6.6	4.6	5.5	5.8	5.0
Syrian Arab Republic	4	3.5	4.0	3.0	0.7	0.7	0.7	1.0	1.1	0.9	...	...	...	.	.	.
Tunisia	6	–	–	–	0.9	0.9	0.9	0.3	0.3	0.2	1.6	1.7	1.5	3.1	3.5	2.6
United Arab Emirates	5	3.9	3.9	3.9	–	–	–	–	–	–	0.2	0.2	0.2	...	...	...
Yemen	6	11.3[y]	10.2[y]	12.7[y]	5.2[y]	4.1[y]	6.6[y]	4.9[y]	3.3[y]	7.2[y]	7.2[y]	5.4[y]	10.1[y]	7.6[y]	6.6[y]	9.4[y]
Central and Eastern Europe																
Albania	4	3.5[y]	4.1[y]	2.8[y]	3.4[y]	3.8[y]	3.1[y]	3.3[y]	3.5[y]	3.0[y]	...	...	...	.	.	.
Belarus	4	–	–[*]	–[*]	0.3	0.2[*]	0.4[*]	0.1	–[*]	0.4[*]	...	...	...	.	.	.
Bosnia and Herzegovina	4	...	...	...	...	...	...	...	...	...	...	...	...	.	.	.
Bulgaria	4	3.2	4.0	2.3	2.8	2.7	2.8	1.8	2.0	1.7	...	...	...	.	.	.
Croatia	4	–[x]	–[x]	–[x]	–[x]	–[x]	–[x]	–[x]	–[x]	–[x]	...	...	...	.	.	.
Czech Republic	5	1.0	1.1	0.9	0.2	0.2	0.3	0.1	0.2	0.0	0.2	0.2	0.1	...	...	...
Estonia	6	0.5	1.0	–	0.2	0.0	0.3	0.2	0.3	0.0	0.4	0.1	0.7	0.0	–	0.2
Hungary	4	1.7	2.0	1.5	0.2	0.3	0.0	–	–	–	...	...	...	.	.	.
Latvia	4	1.0	0.7	1.3	0.3	0.2	0.3	0.5	0.4	0.6	...	...	...	.	.	.
Lithuania	4	1.0	1.1	0.9	0.6	0.9	0.4	0.5	0.4	0.5	...	...	...	.	.	.
Poland	6	0.4	...	...	0.0	...	...	0.1	...	...	0.2			0.1		
Republic of Moldova	4	6.6	6.8	6.3	1.5	1.0	2.1	1.4	1.9	0.9	...	...	...	.	.	.
Romania	4	2.5	2.8	2.2	1.3	1.4	1.1	1.2	1.2	1.2	...	...	...	.	.	.
Russian Federation	3	...	...	...	...	...	...	...	...	...	...	...	...	.	.	.
Serbia and Montenegro	4	...	...	...	...	...	...	...	...	...	...	...	...	.	.	.
Slovakia	4	2.0	2.4	1.5	0.2	0.3	0.1	0.3	0.3	0.3	...	...	...	.	.	.
Slovenia	5	0.6[x]	0.7[x]	0.4[x]	0.1[x]	0.3[x]	–[x]	0.4[x]	0.5[x]	0.3[x]	...	...	...	.	.	.
TFYR Macedonia	4	1.0	1.5	0.5	0.1	0.0	0.3	0.6	0.8	0.5	...	...	...	.	.	.
Turkey	6	0.1	0.5	–	0.8	0.7	0.9	1.0	0.9	1.2	1.1	0.6	1.6	2.9	1.9	3.9
Ukraine	4	...	...	...	...	...	...	...	...	...	...	...	...	.	.	.
Central Asia																
Armenia	3	2.6[x]	2.7[x]	2.4[x]	1.2[x]	1.1[x]	1.2[x]	...	...	...	...	...	...	.	.	.
Azerbaijan	4	0.5	1.1	–	0.9	0.9	0.9	0.5	0.1	1.0	...	...	...	.	.	.
Georgia	6	0.3[x]	–[x]	1.1[x]	0.6[x]	0.9[x]	0.3[x]	1.0[x]	0.3[x]	1.6[x]	.	.	.	.	.	.
Kazakhstan	4	–	–	–	0.4	0.4	0.4	0.1	0.2	0.0	...	...	...	.	.	.
Kyrgyzstan	4	1.2	1.8	0.6	1.1	0.7	1.5	0.9	0.8	0.9	...	...	...	.	.	.
Mongolia	5	5.6[y]	5.5[y]	5.7[y]	2.0[y]	1.9[y]	2.0[y]	1.7[y]	2.2[y]	1.2[y]	...	...	...	.	.	.
Tajikistan	4	0.3	0.5	0.1	0.7	1.0	0.4	1.0	1.8	0.2	...	...	...	.	.	.
Turkmenistan	3	...	...	...	...	...	...	...	...	...	...	...	...	.	.	.
Uzbekistan	4	1.2[x]	0.1[x]	2.3[x]	2.4[x]	3.1[x]	1.6[x]	0.4[x]	0.4[x]	0.4[x]	...	...	...	.	.	.
East Asia and the Pacific																
Australia	7	...	...	...	...	...	...	...	...	...	...	...	...	...	...	...
Brunei Darussalam	6	0.4	0.6	0.2	–	–	–	–	–	–	–	–	–	1.2	0.7	1.7
Cambodia	6	10.1	10.3	9.9	9.1	9.7	8.4	8.5	9.0	8.0	8.6	8.6	8.5	9.3	9.0	9.5
China	5	...	...	...	...	...	...	...	...	...	...	...	...	...	...	...

PRIMARY EDUCATION COMPLETION

SURVIVAL RATE TO GRADE 5 (%)						SURVIVAL RATE TO LAST GRADE (%)						PRIMARY COHORT COMPLETION RATE (%)			Country or territory
School year ending in						School year ending in						School year ending in			
1999			2004			1999			2004			2004			
Total	Male	Female	Total	Male	Female	Total	Male	Female	Total	Male	Female	Total	Male	Female	
															Arab States
95	94	96	96	94	97	91	90	93	93	91	95	86	84	88	Algeria
97	97	98	99	100	98	92	91	93	99	100	97	…	…	…	Bahrain
77	71	85	…	…	…	…	…	…	…	…	…	…	…	…	Djibouti
99	99	99	99[y]	98[y]	99[y]	99	99	99	99[y]	98[y]	99[y]	68	75	60	Egypt
66	67	63	81	87	73	49	51	47	70	78	61	68	75	60	Iraq
98	98	97	99[y]	99[y]	99[y]	97	97	97	98[y]	98[y]	98[y]				Jordan
…	…	…	…	…	…	94	93	95	99	100	99	94[y]	94[y]	95[y]	Kuwait
91	88	95	93	91	96	91	88	95	90	86	93	…	…	…	Lebanon
…	…	…	…	…	…	…	…	…	…	…	…	…	…	…	Libyan Arab Jamahiriya
68	70	66	53	51	55	61	…	…	39	38	41	21	21	20	Mauritania
82	82	82	79	81	77	75	75	76	73	75	70	62	66	58	Morocco
94	94	94	**100**	**100**	**100**	92	92	92	**99**	**100**	**99**	…	…	…	Oman
…	…	…	…	…	…	99	100	99	98	99	97	…	…	…	Palestinian A. T.
…	…	…	…	…	…	…	…	…	…	…	…	…	…	…	Qatar
…	…	…	…	…	…	…	…	…	97	100	94	…	…	…	Saudi Arabia
84	81	88	79	78	79	77	74	81	74	73	75	…	…	…	Sudan
92	92	91	…	…	…	87	87	87	94	94	95	…	…	…	Syrian Arab Republic
92	91	93	97	97	97	87	86	88	94	93	95	…	…	…	Tunisia
92	93	92	97	96	97	90	90	89	97	96	97	96	96	96	United Arab Emirates
87	…	…	73[y]	78[y]	67[y]	80	…	…	67[y]	72[y]	60[y]	…	…	…	Yemen
															Central and Eastern Europe
…	…	…	…	…	…	92	90	95	90[y]	89[y]	91[y]	…	…	…	Albania
…	…	…	…	…	…	99	99	99	99	100*	98*	98	97*	99*	Belarus
…	…	…	…	…	…	…	…	…	…	…	…	…	…	…	Bosnia and Herzegovina
…	…	…	…	…	…	93	93	93	92	91	93	…	…	…	Bulgaria
…	…	…	…	…	…	100	99	100	100[x]	99[x]	100[x]	…	…	…	Croatia
98	98	99	98	98	99	98	98	99	98	98	99	…	…	…	Czech Republic
99	99	99	99	98	99	99	98	99	99	99	99	…	…	…	Estonia
…	…	…	…	…	…	97	96	98	98	98	98	…	…	…	Hungary
…	…	…	…	…	…	97	97	97	98	99	98	…	…	…	Latvia
…	…	…	…	…	…	99	99	100	98	98	98	…	…	…	Lithuania
99	…	…	99	…	…	98	…	…	99	…	…	…	…	…	Poland
…	…	…	…	…	…	95	…	…	91	90	91	…	…	…	Republic of Moldova
…	…	…	…	…	…	96	95	96	95	94	95	…	…	…	Romania
…	…	…	…	…	…	…	…	…	…	…	…	…	…	…	Russian Federation
…	…	…	…	…	…	…	…	…	…	…	…	…	…	…	Serbia and Montenegro
…	…	…	…	…	…	97	96	98	97	97	98	…	…	…	Slovakia
…	…	…	…	…	…	…	…	…	99[x]	98[x]	99[x]	…	…	…	Slovenia
…	…	…	…	…	…	97	96	99	98	98	99	…	…	…	TFYR Macedonia
…	…	…	97	97	97	…	…	…	94	95	93	…	…	…	Turkey
…	…	…	…	…	…	97	…	…	…	…	…	…	…	…	Ukraine
															Central Asia
…	…	…	…	…	…	…	…	…	96[x]	96[x]	96[x]	…	…	…	Armenia
…	…	…	…	…	…	97	96	98	98	98	98	97	…	…	Azerbaijan
…	…	…	…	…	…	99	99	100	98[x]	99[x]	97[x]	…	…	…	Georgia
…	…	…	…	…	…	…	…	…	99	99	100	99	99	99	Kazakhstan
…	…	…	…	…	…	95*	95*	94*	97	97	97	89	85	94	Kyrgyzstan
…	…	…	…	…	…	87	85	90	91[y]	91[y]	91[y]	89	85	94	Mongolia
…	…	…	…	…	…	97	100	94	98	97	99	97	96	99	Tajikistan
…	…	…	…	…	…	…	…	…	…	…	…	…	…	…	Turkmenistan
…	…	…	…	…	…	…	…	…	96[x]	96[x]	96[x]	…	…	…	Uzbekistan
															East Asia and the Pacific
…	…	…	…	…	…	…	…	…	…	…	…	…	…	…	Australia
92	92	92	100	99	100	92	91	94	99	99	99	75	70	80	Brunei Darussalam
56	58	54	63	62	65	49	52	45	57	56	58	…	…	…	Cambodia
…	…	…	…	…	…	…	…	…	…	…	…	…	…	…	China

ANNEX

Table 7 (continued)

DROPOUT RATES BY GRADE IN PRIMARY EDUCATION (%)

School year ending in 2004

Country or territory	Duration[1] of primary education 2005	Grade 1 Total	Male	Female	Grade 2 Total	Male	Female	Grade 3 Total	Male	Female	Grade 4 Total	Male	Female	Grade 5 Total	Male	Female
Cook Islands	6	...	...	...	...	...	...	...	...	...	...	...	...	...	...	...
DPR Korea	4	...	...	...	...	...	...	...	...	...	...	...	...	.	.	.
Fiji	6	2.1y	2.3y	2.0y	0.5y	0.3y	0.6y	–y	–y	–y	–y	–y	–y	3.3y	3.3y	3.2y
Indonesia	6	–	–	–	6.3	5.2	7.4	1.6	1.5	1.7	3.5	3.2	3.8	4.4	4.2	4.6
Japan	6	...	...	...	...	...	...	...	...	...	...	...	...	...	...	...
Kiribati	6	12.0y	11.4y	12.5y	2.9y	4.2y	1.6y	0.8y	1.6y	0.1y	3.3y	8.7y	–y	0.6y	1.5y	–y
Lao PDR	5	13.0	12.9	13.0	6.5	6.4	6.7	6.8	6.3	7.5	6.4	5.7	7.3	...	...	...
Macao, China	6	–x	–x	–x	–x	–x	–x	–x	–x	–x	–x	–x	–x	...	...	...
Malaysia	6	1.7x	1.7x	1.6x	–x	–x	–x	–x	–x	–x	0.3x	0.1x	0.5x	0.7x	0.7x	0.7x
Marshall Islands	6	...	...	...	...	...	...	...	...	...	...	...	...	...	...	...
Micronesia	6	...	...	...	...	...	...	...	...	...	...	...	...	...	...	...
Myanmar	5	13.7	13.8	13.6	5.5	5.5	5.6	7.2	8.5	5.8	7.5	8.8	6.1	...	...	...
Nauru	6	9.7x	7.7x	12.1x	...	...	...	...	...	...	...	...	...	...	...	...
New Zealand	6	...	...	...	...	...	...	...	...	...	...	...	...	...	...	...
Niue	6	...	...	...	...	...	...	...	...	...	...	...	...	...	...	...
Palau	5	–	–	–	...	...	...	...	...	...	...	...	...	...	...	...
Papua New Guinea	6	7.2x	6.8x	7.8x	13.7x	13.1x	14.3x	9.4x	9.8x	9.0x	6.5x	6.9x	6.0x	14.2x	14.0x	14.4x
Philippines	6	14.4	16.1	12.5	4.6	5.5	3.6	3.7	4.8	2.5	3.6	4.9	2.3	4.5	6.0	2.9
Republic of Korea	6	–	–	–	**0.3**	**0.3**	**0.2**	**0.4**	**0.3**	**0.4**	**0.4**	**0.4**	**0.4**	**0.4**	**0.4**	**0.4**
Samoa	6	4.8x	...	...	...	...	...	...	...	...	...	...	...	...	...	...
Singapore	6	...	...	...	...	...	...	...	...	...	...	...	...	...	...	...
Solomon Islands	6	...	...	...	...	...	...	...	...	...	...	...	...	...	...	...
Thailand	6	...	...	...	...	...	...	...	...	...	...	...	...	...	...	...
Timor-Leste	6	...	...	...	...	...	...	...	...	...	...	...	...	...	...	...
Tokelau	6	...	...	...	...	...	...	...	...	...	...	...	...	...	...	...
Tonga	6	10.3y	12.7y	7.5y	7.2y	10.5y	3.3y	5.0y	6.4y	3.6y	2.4y	–y	7.1y	...	...	...
Tuvalu	6	...	...	...	...	...	...	...	...	...	...	...	...	...	...	...
Vanuatu	6	7.6	...	...	3.9	...	...	6.7	...	...	3.4	...	...	8.5	...	...
Viet Nam	5	5.5x	5.3x	5.8x	0.9x	1.6x	0.05x	8.2x	7.5x	9.0x	–x	–x	–x	...	...	...
Latin America and the Caribbean																
Anguilla	7	1.0	3.2	–	–	–	–	0.9	–	1.9	1.0	0.9	1.3	–	...	...
Antigua and Barbuda	7	...	...	...	...	...	...	...	...	...	...	...	...	...	...	...
Argentina	6	2.1y	2.3y	1.9y	0.1y	0.2y	0.1y	–y	–y	–y	0.6y	0.9y	0.3y	1.2y	1.7y	0.7y
Aruba	6	2.1	1.8	2.4	0.1	–	1.0	0.7	1.7	–	–	–	–	–	–	–
Bahamas	6	1.5	1.7	1.3	–	...	...	–	...	...	–	...	...	–	...	...
Barbados	6	–	–	–	–	–	–	0.3	1.5	–	0.3	0.9	–	–	–	–
Belize	6	–y	–y	–y	...	...	...	...	...	...	...	...	...	...	...	...
Bermuda	6	2.0	...	...	0.4	...	...	3.1	...	...	1.6	...	...	4.5	...	...
Bolivia	6	7.9y	8.2y	7.7y	1.6y	1.5y	1.6y	3.8y	3.6y	4.0y	2.6y	2.4y	2.8y	2.7y	1.7y	3.8y
Brazil	4	8.4y	...	...	2.0y	...	...	5.5y	...	...	...	.	.			
British Virgin Islands	7	–	...	...	5.2	...	...	...	...	...	...	...	...	...	...	...
Cayman Islands	6	5.6	4.9	6.3	5.7	1.9	9.9	6.6	7.8	5.4	6.4	9.8	2.0	–	...	...
Chile	6	0.4y	0.4y	0.5y	1.3y	1.5y	1.1y	–y	–y	–y	–y	–y	–y	0.5y	0.7y	0.3y
Colombia	5	11.5	12.4	10.6	2.2	2.9	1.4	3.1	3.6	2.5	2.4	3.0	1.8	...	...	...
Costa Rica	6	5.2	5.9	4.5	1.0	1.3	0.6	1.0	1.6	0.4	5.4	6.5	4.2	3.3	3.2	3.4
Cuba	6	1.6	1.8	1.3	1.3	1.6	0.9	0.0	0.0	–	0.0	0.2	–	0.1	0.2	0.1
Dominica	7	2.2	1.7	2.7	1.5	–	3.5	2.3	3.6	0.9	1.2	0.6	1.9	5.3	7.6	2.7
Dominican Republic	6	0.2	...	...	5.6	...	...	4.2	...	...	3.4	...	...	3.1	...	...
Ecuador	6	12.9y	13.0y	12.8y	2.9y	3.1y	2.7y	3.7y	4.0y	3.4y	5.5y	6.1y	4.9y	4.8y	4.3y	5.3y
El Salvador	6	14.8	15.7	13.7	8.8	9.2	8.3	2.1	3.0	1.0	5.6	5.5	5.7	4.2	3.7	4.7
Grenada	7	13.4x	13.3x	13.4x	1.2x	4.0x	–x	5.9x	10.1x	1.6x	1.1x	1.1x	1.1x	–x	...	...
Guatemala	6	9.4	9.1	9.7	6.2	5.7	6.8	7.3	6.5	8.2	8.1	7.4	8.9	7.6	7.2	8.1
Guyana	6	7.4	7.8	7.1	...	...	...	...	...	...	...	...	...	...	...	...
Haiti	6	...	...	...	...	...	...	...	...	...	...	...	...	...	...	...
Honduras	6	8.8	9.0	8.5	4.7	6.0	3.3	7.5	6.3	8.7	9.5	12.0	6.9	11.6	11.3	12.0
Jamaica	6	0.8x	1.3x	0.3x	1.1x	1.0x	1.3x	–x	–x	–x	9.3x	12.2x	6.0x	3.1x	4.3x	1.8x
Mexico	6	1.9	2.0	1.7	1.1	1.2	1.0	1.7	1.8	1.6	1.3	1.4	1.1	2.3	2.5	2.0
Montserrat	7	1.4	...	...	12.5	...	...	...	...	...	...	...	...	...	...	...
Netherlands Antilles	6	–x	...	...	...	...	...	...	...	...	...	...	...	...	...	...
Nicaragua	6	17.7	18.2	17.3	10.4	11.7	9.0	8.9	9.8	8.0	13.5	13.9	13.0	4.9	5.2	4.6
Panama	6	5.1	4.9	5.4	3.4	3.6	3.3	2.6	2.8	2.5	3.2	3.3	3.0	3.3	3.3	3.3

PRIMARY EDUCATION COMPLETION

SURVIVAL RATE TO GRADE 5 (%)						SURVIVAL RATE TO LAST GRADE (%)						PRIMARY COHORT COMPLETION RATE (%)			
School year ending in						School year ending in						School year ending in			
1999			2004			1999			2004			2004			
Total	Male	Female	Total	Male	Female	Total	Male	Female	Total	Male	Female	Total	Male	Female	Country or territory
...	...	...	...	...	...	...	...	...	...	...	...	...	...	...	Cook Islands
...	...	...	...	...	...	...	...	...	...	...	...	...	...	...	DPR Korea
87	89	86	99[y]	100[y]	97[y]	82	82	82	96[y]	97[y]	95[y]	...	...	...	Fiji
...	...	...	89	92	87	...	...	...	85	88	83	...	...	...	Indonesia
...	...	...	...	...	...	...	...	...	...	...	...	...	...	...	Japan
...	...	...	82[y]	76[y]	88[y]	...	...	...	81[y]	75[y]	89[y]	...	...	...	Kiribati
54	55	54	63	64	62	54	55	54	63	64	62	58	58	57	Lao PDR
...	...	...	100[x]	99[x]	100[x]	...	...	...	...	...	...	...	...	...	Macao, China
...	...	...	98[x]	99[x]	98[x]	...	...	...	98[x]	98[x]	97[x]	...	...	...	Malaysia
...	...	...	...	...	...	...	...	...	...	...	...	...	...	...	Marshall Islands
...	...	...	...	...	...	...	...	...	...	...	...	...	...	...	Micronesia
...	...	...	70	68	72	...	...	...	70	68	72	70	...	...	Myanmar
...	...	...	...	...	...	...	...	...	...	...	...	...	...	...	Nauru
...	...	...	...	...	...	...	...	...	...	...	...	...	...	...	New Zealand
...	...	...	...	...	...	...	...	...	...	...	...	...	...	...	Niue
...	...	...	...	...	...	...	...	...	...	...	...	...	...	...	Palau
65	67	62	68[x]	68[x]	68[x]	57	60	54	58[x]	59[x]	58[x]	...	...	...	Papua New Guinea
...	...	...	75	71	80	...	...	...	72	66	77	...	...	...	Philippines
100	100	100	**99**	**99**	**99**	100	100	100	**99**	**99**	**99**	...	...	...	Republic of Korea
94	91*	96*	...	...	...	92	91*	94*	...	...	...	...	...	...	Samoa
...	...	...	...	...	...	...	...	...	...	...	...	...	...	...	Singapore
...	...	...	...	...	...	...	...	...	...	...	...	...	...	...	Solomon Islands
...	...	...	...	...	...	...	...	...	...	...	...	...	...	...	Thailand
...	...	...	...	...	...	...	...	...	...	...	...	...	...	...	Timor-Leste
...	...	...	...	...	...	...	...	...	...	...	...	...	...	...	Tokelau
...	...	...	77[y]	75[y]	80[y]	...	...	...	...	...	...	...	...	...	Tonga
...	...	...	...	...	...	...	...	...	...	...	...	...	...	...	Tuvalu
72	72	72	78	...	...	69	67	71	71	...	...	...	...	...	Vanuatu
83	80	86	87[x]	87[x]	86[x]	83	80	86	87[x]	87[x]	86[x]	...	...	...	Viet Nam
															Latin America and the Caribbean
...	...	...	97	94	100	...	...	...	93	...	...	88	...	...	Anguilla
...	...	...	...	...	...	...	...	...	...	...	...	...	...	...	Antigua and Barbuda
90	90	90	97[y]	96[y]	98[y]	89	88	89	96[y]	94[y]	97[y]	...	...	...	Argentina
97	97	96	...	...	...	97	99	95	98	96	99	95	93	97	Aruba
...	...	...	99	...	...	...	...	...	...	...	...	...	...	...	Bahamas
93	95	92	...	...	...	94	95	93	98	...	...	98	...	...	Barbados
78	76	79	...	...	...	77	77	76	...	...	...	...	...	...	Belize
...	...	...	93	...	...	...	...	...	89	...	...	...	...	...	Bermuda
82	83	81	85[y]	85[y]	85[y]	80	82	77	82[y]	83[y]	81[y]	71[x]	72[x]	71[x]	Bolivia
...	...	...	...	...	...	...	...	...	80[y]	...	...	...	...	...	Brazil
...	...	...	...	...	...	...	...	...	...	...	...	...	...	...	British Virgin Islands
...	...	...	78	77	78	...	...	...	78	...	...	...	...	...	Cayman Islands
100	100	100	99[y]	99[y]	99[y]	100	99	100	98[y]	98[y]	98[y]	...	...	...	Chile
67	64	69	81	78	84	67	64	69	81	78	84	75	73	77	Colombia
91	90	93	87	84	90	88	86	89	84	81	87	78	75	81	Costa Rica
94	94	94	97	96	98	93	92	93	97	96	98	...	...	...	Cuba
91	...	...	93	94	91	...	...	...	89	...	...	83[y]	83[y]	83[y]	Dominica
75	71	79	86	...	...	71	66	75	83	...	...	...	...	...	Dominican Republic
77	77	77	76[y]	75[y]	77[y]	75	74	75	73[y]	72[y]	73[y]	70[y]	70[y]	71[y]	Ecuador
65	64	66	69	67	72	62	63	62	66	65	68	48	46	50	El Salvador
...	...	...	...	...	...	...	...	...	83[x]	...	...	56[x]	...	...	Grenada
56	55	58	68	70	66	52	50	54	63	64	61	55[x]	58[x]	53[x]	Guatemala
95	...	...	...	...	...	93	...	...	...	...	...	...	...	...	Guyana
...	...	...	...	...	...	...	...	...	...	...	...	...	...	...	Haiti
...	...	...	70	67	73	...	...	...	62	59	64	...	...	...	Honduras
...	...	...	89[x]	86[x]	92[x]	...	...	...	86[x]	82[x]	91[x]	...	...	...	Jamaica
89	88	90	94	93	94	87	86	88	92	91	92	...	...	...	Mexico
...	...	...	...	...	...	...	...	...	...	...	...	...	...	...	Montserrat
84	80	88	...	...	...	84	78	91	...	...	...	...	...	...	Netherlands Antilles
48	44	53	54	51	56	46	42	50	51	48	54	47	44	51	Nicaragua
92	92	92	85	85	86	90	90	91	82	82	83	82	81	83	Panama

Table 7 (continued)

Country or territory	Duration[1] of primary education 2005	DROPOUT RATES BY GRADE IN PRIMARY EDUCATION (%) School year ending in 2004														
		Grade 1			Grade 2			Grade 3			Grade 4			Grade 5		
		Total	Male	Female	Total	Male	Female	Total	Male	Female	Total	Male	Female	Total	Male	Female
Paraguay	6	6.2ʸ	6.7ʸ	5.7ʸ	3.5ʸ	3.9ʸ	3.0ʸ	3.8ʸ	4.0ʸ	3.6ʸ	4.9ʸ	5.5ʸ	4.3ʸ	5.7ʸ	6.0ʸ	5.4ʸ
Peru	6	3.0	3.2	2.8	2.4	2.4	2.4	1.9	1.8	2.1	2.0	1.7	2.4	4.9	4.6	5.1
Saint Kitts and Nevis	7	6.2	11.1	0.9	3.0	5.9	–	…	…	…	…	…	…	…	…	…
Saint Lucia	7	1.5	1.8	1.1	1.1	–	2.3	0.2	0.1	0.3	1.2	1.8	0.6	2.0	3.3	0.7
St Vincent/Grenad.	7	1.0ˣ	…	…	3.0ˣ	…	…	3.5ˣ	…	…	4.2ˣ	…	…	4.2ˣ	…	…
Suriname	6	…	…	…	…	…	…	…	…	…	…	…	…	…	…	…
Trinidad and Tobago	7	–*	–*	–*	3.8*	5.1*	2.4*	3.9*	4.7*	3.1*	1.6*	1.4*	1.9*	4.1*	4.3*	3.8*
Turks and Caicos Islands	6	23.4ˣ	30.2ˣ	17.9ˣ	20.2ˣ	10.8ˣ	27.8ˣ	8.5ˣ	9.4ˣ	7.5ˣ	12.9ˣ	20.1ˣ	2.9ˣ	2.2ˣ	–ˣ	6.5ˣ
Uruguay	6	4.5ʸ	5.2ʸ	3.8ʸ	0.9ʸ	1.2ʸ	0.6ʸ	1.1ʸ	1.1ʸ	1.1ʸ	1.5ʸ	1.8ʸ	1.1ʸ	1.7ʸ	1.9ʸ	1.4ʸ
Venezuela	6	2.6	3.3	1.8	1.4	2.4	0.4	1.5	2.1	0.9	2.6	3.4	1.7	2.5	3.2	1.8
North America and Western Europe																
Andorra	6	…	…	…	…	…	…	…	…	…	…	…	…	…	…	…
Austria	4	…	…	…	…	…	…	…	…	…	…	…	…	.	.	.
Belgium	6	…	…	…	…	…	…	…	…	…	…	…	…	…	…	…
Canada	6	…	…	…	…	…	…	…	…	…	…	…	…	…	…	…
Cyprus	6	–	–	–	–	–	–	–	–	–	–	–	–	–	–	–
Denmark	6	1.0	0.8	1.3	4.8	4.8	4.9	1.6	1.6	1.6	–	–	–	1.4	1.5	1.3
Finland	6	0.0	0.3	–	–	–	–	–	–	–	–	–	–	–	–	–
France	5	…	…		…			…			…			…		
Germany	4	–	–	–	0.5	0.6	0.3	0.4	0.4	0.3	…	…	…	.	.	.
Greece	6	1.2	1.5	1.0	0.2	0.4	0.0	–	–	–	–	–	–	–	–	–
Iceland	7	–ˣ	–ˣ	–ˣ	0.3ˣ	0.9ˣ	–ˣ	–ˣ	–ˣ	–ˣ	–ˣ	–ˣ	–ˣ	–ˣ	–ˣ	–ˣ
Ireland	8	–ʸ	–ʸ	–ʸ	–ʸ	–ʸ	–ʸ	–ʸ	–ʸ	–ʸ	–ʸ	–ʸ	–ʸ	–ʸ	–ʸ	–ʸ
Israel	6	–	–	–	–	–	–	–	–	–	–	–	–	0.2	0.3	0.1
Italy	5	–	–	–	–	–	–	–	–	–	–	–	–	…	…	…
Luxembourg	6	2.3ˣ	2.0ˣ	2.7ˣ	0.8ˣ	0.9ˣ	0.6ˣ	1.8ˣ	3.6ˣ	–ˣ	2.8ˣ	1.8ˣ	3.8ˣ	10.6ˣ	12.5ˣ	8.7ˣ
Malta	6	0.9ˣ	0.5ˣ	1.2ˣ	–ˣ	–ˣ	–ˣ	–ˣ	–ˣ	–ˣ	0.3ˣ	0.8ˣ	–ˣ	0.3ˣ	0.2ˣ	0.4ˣ
Monaco	5	…	…	…	…	…	…	…	…	…	…	…	…	…	…	…
Netherlands	6	–ˣ	–ˣ	–ˣ	–ˣ	–ˣ	–ˣ	–ˣ	–ˣ	–ˣ	–ˣ	–ˣ	–ˣ	1.9ˣ	1.3ˣ	2.6ˣ
Norway	7	…	…	…	…	…	…	…	…	…	…	…	…	–	–	–
Portugal	6	…	…	…	…	…	…	…	…	…	…	…	…	…	…	…
San Marino	5	…	…	…	…	…	…	…	…	…	…	…	…	…	…	…
Spain	6	–	–	–	–	–	–	–	–	–	–	–	–	–	–	–
Sweden	6	…	…	…	…	…	…	…	…	…	…	…	…	…	…	…
Switzerland	6	…	…	…	…	…	…	…	…	…	…	…	…	…	…	…
United Kingdom	6	…	…	…	…	…	…	…	…	…	…	…	…	…	…	…
United States	6	…	…	…	…	…	…	…	…	…	…	…	…	…	…	…
South and West Asia																
Afghanistan	6	…	…	…	…	…	…	…	…	…	…	…	…	…	…	…
Bangladesh	5	14.6ʸ	17.6ʸ	11.2ʸ	9.9ʸ	11.4ʸ	8.3ʸ	5.8ʸ	5.2ʸ	6.4ʸ	7.2ʸ	5.5ʸ	8.9ʸ			
Bhutan	7	…	…	…	…	…	…	…	…	…	…	…	…	…	…	…
India	5	14.4ʸ	14.0ʸ	14.9ʸ	4.4ʸ	3.6ʸ	5.2ʸ	4.4ʸ	4.0ʸ	4.9ʸ	–ʸ	–ʸ	–ʸ			
Iran, Islamic Republic of	5	–	…	…	…	…	…	…	…	…	…	…	…			
Maldives	7	–	–	–	0.7	–	2.3	8.2	13.7	1.7	–	–	–	0.1	1.1	–
Nepal	5	**10.8**	**12.2***	**9.3***	**0.3**	**1.1***	**–***	**1.3**	**1.5***	**1.0***	**2.1**	**2.8***	**1.4***			
Pakistan	5	15.3	15.4	15.1	4.7	6.1	2.5	3.8	4.7	2.5	9.2	9.1	9.4	…	…	…
Sri Lanka	5	…	…	…	…	…	…	…	…	…	…	…	…			
Sub-Saharan Africa																
Angola	4	…	…	…	…	…	…	…	…	…	…	…	…			
Benin	6	18.3	18.0	18.7	11.3	11.0	11.7	10.6	10.6	10.7	11.5	10.4	13.0	8.1	7.5	8.9
Botswana	7	4.7ʸ	5.2ʸ	4.2ʸ	1.3ʸ	1.8ʸ	0.8ʸ	3.5ʸ	3.8ʸ	3.2ʸ	–ʸ	–ʸ	–ʸ	1.8ʸ	2.3ʸ	1.3ʸ
Burkina Faso	6	9.6	8.5	10.8	3.4	3.5	3.2	6.2	6.7	5.6	5.1	5.8	4.1	7.4	8.1	6.6
Burundi	6	10.0	9.5	10.4	5.0	5.3	4.6	5.8	6.4	5.1	4.3	4.9	3.7	5.2	6.4	3.7
Cameroon	6	17.3ˣ	17.9ˣ	16.6ˣ	2.3ˣ	0.4ˣ	4.5ˣ	3.1ˣ	3.8ˣ	2.4ˣ	5.2ˣ	4.9ˣ	5.5ˣ	4.8ˣ	4.0ˣ	5.8ˣ
Cape Verde	6	–	…	…	1.6			1.7			4.1			4.2		
Central African Republic	6	21.4ʸ	19.4ʸ	24.3ʸ	…	…	…	…	…	…	…	…	…	…	…	…
Chad	6	20.0	18.9	21.6	12.2	11.2	13.5	22.4	25.3	17.8	19.7	18.3	21.9	17.6	15.9	20.3
Comoros	6	1.4	1.7	1.2	2.2	2.3	2.2	3.2	4.1	2.3	7.0	6.1	8.2	7.4	8.8	5.9
Congo	6	6.3ˣ	5.8ˣ	6.8ˣ	1.2ˣ	1.4ˣ	0.9ˣ	9.6ˣ	9.9ˣ	9.3ˣ	8.2ˣ	8.6ˣ	7.7ˣ	10.9ˣ	9.9ˣ	11.9ˣ

PRIMARY EDUCATION COMPLETION

SURVIVAL RATE TO GRADE 5 (%)						SURVIVAL RATE TO LAST GRADE (%)						PRIMARY COHORT COMPLETION RATE (%)			Country or territory
School year ending in						School year ending in						School year ending in			
1999			2004			1999			2004			2004			
Total	Male	Female	Total	Male	Female	Total	Male	Female	Total	Male	Female	Total	Male	Female	
78	76	80	81ʸ	79ʸ	83ʸ	73	71	76	76ʸ	74ʸ	79ʸ	...	...	...	Paraguay
87	88	87	90	90	90	83	84	82	85	86	85	...	...	...	Peru
...	...	...	...	...	...	...	...	...	...	...	...	...	...	...	Saint Kitts and Nevis
90	...	...	...	...	...	...	...	...	96	95	97	...	...	...	Saint Lucia
...	...	...	88ˣ	...	...	...	...	...	79ˣ	...	...	...	...	...	St Vincent/Grenad.
...	...	...	...	...	...	...	...	...	...	...	...	...	...	...	Suriname
...	...	...	91*	90*	92*	...	...	...	84*	80*	87*	...	...	...	Trinidad and Tobago
...	...	...	46ˣ	42ˣ	51ˣ	...	...	...	45ˣ	43ˣ	48ˣ	...	...	...	Turks and Caicos Islands
...	...	...	91ʸ	90ʸ	93ʸ	...	...	...	90ʸ	88ʸ	91ʸ	...	...	...	Uruguay
91	88	94	91	88	95	88	84	92	89	85	93	79ˣ	76ˣ	82ˣ	Venezuela
															North America and Western Europe
...	...	...	...	...	...	...	...	...	...	...	...	...	...	...	Andorra
...	...	...	...	...	...	...	...	...	...	...	...	...	...	...	Austria
...	...	...	...	...	...	...	...	...	...	...	...	...	...	...	Belgium
...	...	...	...	...	...	...	...	...	...	...	...	...	...	...	Canada
96	95	97	...	...	...	96	95	97	100	100	99	...	...	...	Cyprus
100	100	100	93	93	93	100	100	100	92	92	92	...	...	...	Denmark
100	100	100	...	...	...	100	100	100	99	99	100	...	...	...	Finland
98	98	97	...	...	...	98	98	97	...	...	...	...	...	...	France
...	...	...	...	...	...	99	99	100	99	99	100	...	...	...	Germany
...	...	...	99	98	100	...	...	...	99	98	100	...	...	...	Greece
100	100	100	100ˣ	100ˣ	99ˣ	100	...	...	100ˣ	99ˣ	100ˣ	...	...	...	Iceland
95	94	97	100ʸ	100ʸ	100ʸ	...	...	...	...	...	...	...	...	...	Ireland
...	...	...	...	...	...	...	...	...	100	100	100	...	...	...	Israel
97	...	...	100	100	100	97	...	...	100	100	100	...	...	...	Italy
96	93	100	92ˣ	91ˣ	93ˣ	89	84	94	82ˣ	79ˣ	85ˣ	...	...	...	Luxembourg
99	100	99	99ˣ	99ˣ	100ˣ	99	...	...	99ˣ	99ˣ	100ˣ	...	...	...	Malta
...	...	...	...	...	...	...	...	...	...	...	...	...	...	...	Monaco
100	100	100	100ˣ	100ˣ	100ˣ	100	100	100	98ˣ	99ˣ	98ˣ	...	...	...	Netherlands
100	100	100	100	100	100	100	100	100	100	100	100	...	...	...	Norway
...	...	...	...	...	...	...	...	...	...	...	...	...	...	...	Portugal
...	...	...	...	...	...	...	...	...	...	...	...	...	...	...	San Marino
...	...	...	100	100	100	...	...	...	100	100	100	...	...	...	Spain
...	...	...	...	...	...	...	...	...	...	...	...	...	...	...	Sweden
...	...	...	...	...	...	...	...	...	...	...	...	...	...	...	Switzerland
...	...	...	...	...	...	...	...	...	...	...	...	...	...	...	United Kingdom
...	...	...	...	...	...	...	...	...	...	...	...	...	...	...	United States
															South and West Asia
...	...	...	...	...	...	...	...	...	...	...	...	...	...	...	Afghanistan
65	60	70	65ʸ	63ʸ	67ʸ	65	60	70	65ʸ	63ʸ	67ʸ	55ʸ	52ʸ	58ʸ	Bangladesh
90	89	92	...	...	...	81	78	86	...	...	...	...	...	...	Bhutan
62	63	60	79ʸ	81ʸ	76ʸ	62	63	60	79ʸ	81ʸ	76ʸ	...	...	...	India
...	...	...	88ˣ	88ˣ	87ˣ	...	...	...	88ˣ	88ˣ	87ˣ	...	...	...	Iran, Islamic Republic of
...	...	...	92	89	96	...	...	...	...	...	...	...	...	...	Maldives
58	56	61	**79**	**75**	**83**	58	56	61	**79**	**75**	**83**	39	35	43	Nepal
...	...	...	70	68	72	...	...	...	70	68	72	48	47	51	Pakistan
...	...	...	...	...	...	...	...	...	...	...	...	...	...	...	Sri Lanka
															Sub-Saharan Africa
...	...	...	...	...	...	...	...	...	...	...	...	...	...	...	Angola
...	...	...	52	53	50	...	...	...	46	48	44	36	38	34	Benin
...	...	...	90ʸ	89ʸ	92ʸ	82	79	86	85ʸ	83ʸ	88ʸ	79ʸ	...	...	Botswana
87	84	89	76	75	76	61	59	63	69	68	70	...	...	...	Burkina Faso
68	67	70	67	66	68	...	...	...	59	57	61	36	38	32	Burundi
...	...	...	64ˣ	64ˣ	63ˣ	78	...	...	59ˣ	60ˣ	58ˣ	53ˣ	...	...	Cameroon
81	...	...	93	...	...	...	...	...	88	...	...	82	...	...	Cape Verde
...	...	...	...	...	...	...	...	...	...	...	...	...	...	...	Central African Republic
55	58	50	33	34	32	47	50	41	26	27	23	...	...	...	Chad
...	...	...	80	79	81	...	...	...	72	69	74	...	...	...	Comoros
...	...	...	66ˣ	65ˣ	67ˣ	...	...	...	55ˣ	55ˣ	55ˣ	...	...	...	Congo

Table 7 (continued)

DROPOUT RATES BY GRADE IN PRIMARY EDUCATION (%)

School year ending in 2004

Country or territory	Duration[1] of primary education 2005	Grade 1			Grade 2			Grade 3			Grade 4			Grade 5		
		Total	Male	Female	Total	Male	Female	Total	Male	Female	Total	Male	Female	Total	Male	Female
Côte d'Ivoire	6	...	...	...	...	...	...	...	...	...	...	...	...	...	...	...
Democratic Rep. of the Congo	6	...	...	...	...	...	...	...	...	...	...	...	...	...	...	...
Equatorial Guinea	5	...	...	...	...	...	...	...	...	...	...	...	...	...	...	...
Eritrea	5	6.7	6.3	7.2	3.6	2.6	4.9	3.5	2.3	5.0	5.4	3.6	7.7	...	...	...
Ethiopia	4	15.5	15.5	15.6	6.4	7.0	5.7	4.5	5.2	3.8						
Gabon	6	3.6x	3.6x	3.6x	—x	—x	—x	6.7x	6.4x	7.0x	9.0x	8.9x	9.1x	12.5x	13.2x	11.8x
Gambia	6	...	...	...	...	...	...	...	...	...	...	...	...	...	...	...
Ghana	6	10.4x	9.5x	11.4x	11.3x	14.9x	7.3x	8.0x	7.4x	8.6x	10.8x	10.3x	11.3x	5.0x	10.1x	—x
Guinea	6	1.1	—	2.4	6.4	5.4	7.7	7.6	7.4	7.9	8.7	8.8	8.6	6.8	6.1	7.8
Guinea-Bissau	6	...	...	...	...	...	...	...	...	...	...	...	...	...	...	...
Kenya	6	9.1	9.9	8.3	5.9	6.6	5.1	—	—	—	4.0	4.2	3.8	—	...	...
Lesotho	7	—	...	...	12.9	...	...	4.2	...	...	6.8	...	...	9.5	...	...
Liberia	6	...	...	...	...	...	...	...	...	...	...	...	...	...	...	...
Madagascar	5	27.1	27.1	27.0	7.6	7.7	7.6	9.9	9.6	10.2	17.4	17.3	17.6	...	...	...
Malawi	6	23.2	21.3	24.9	7.4	7.7	7.1	15.7	14.8	16.5	13.2	13.1	13.3	16.9	16.2	17.6
Mali	6	3.6	3.5	3.8	0.7	—	1.5	3.2	2.2	4.6	3.6	3.0	4.5	5.4	4.1	7.2
Mauritius	6	0.7	0.7	0.7	0.2	0.1	0.4	1.0	0.9	1.0	1.1	1.3	0.9	1.2	1.6	0.7
Mozambique	7	12.6	11.4	13.8	8.3	7.3	9.4	8.1	7.3	8.9	10.0	8.5	12.0	15.8	15.2	16.6
Namibia	7	6.3	6.9	5.7	1.6	1.8	1.4	2.0	2.3	1.8	2.4	2.8	2.1	5.1	6.0	4.1
Niger	6	6.2	6.3	6.1	17.4	16.7	18.2	8.6	8.0	9.7	6.8	7.0	6.7	7.2	7.1	7.5
Nigeria	6	8.7y	9.1y	8.3y	2.7y	3.0y	2.3y	7.1y	7.4y	6.7y	11.1y	12.0y	9.9y	13.5y	13.3y	13.7y
Rwanda	6	21.0y	21.4y	20.5y	11.7y	11.7y	11.7y	10.8y	13.4y	8.3y	12.4y	13.8y	11.0y	24.9y	23.9y	25.9y
Sao Tome and Principe	6	2.5	2.3	2.8	3.1	2.8	3.5	3.0	2.6	3.4	11.0	12.1	9.8	8.8	7.6	9.8
Senegal	6	11.7	10.8	12.6	6.4	5.8	6.9	6.3	6.1	6.5	2.7	2.5	2.8	11.0	10.2	11.9
Seychelles	6	—x	—x	—x	—x	—x	—x	0.4x	0.4x	0.4x	0.6x	1.5x	—x	—x	—x	—x
Sierra Leone	6	...	...	...	...	...	...	...	...	...	...	...	...	...	...	...
Somalia	7	...	...	...	...	...	...	...	...	...	...	...	...	...	...	...
South Africa	7	10.0y	10.6y	9.4y	2.9y	3.1y	2.7y	1.7y	1.1y	2.3y	2.2y	2.7y	1.6y	2.6y	2.9y	2.2y
Swaziland	7	6.1x	6.5x	5.7x	3.3x	5.3x	1.0x	5.1x	4.5x	5.9x	6.3x	6.7x	5.8x	8.1x	15.1x	0.1x
Togo	6	6.5	6.0	7.1	2.5	1.7	3.5	6.0	5.2	7.0	5.5	4.1	7.3	6.0	4.0	8.7
Uganda	7	31.6	32.8	30.5	3.9	4.7	3.0	7.1	4.5	9.6	11.4	11.7	11.1	15.2	14.4	16.0
United Republic of Tanzania	7	**1.7**	**1.6**	**1.8**	**1.8**	**1.2**	**2.4**	**2.1**	**3.3**	**0.8**	**8.9**	**9.8**	**7.9**	**2.0**	**2.3**	**1.6**
Zambia	7	—	—	—	...	...	...	...	...	...	...	...	...	...	...	...
Zimbabwe	7	15.3x	15.6x	14.9x	11.1x	11.8x	10.4x	6.0x	6.4x	5.5x	1.7x	2.1x	1.2x	2.3x	2.0x	2.7x
World[2]	...	2.2	1.7	2.7	1.4	0.9	2.2	1.7	1.1	2.3	2.6	2.4	2.8	1.9	1.3	2.6
Countries in transition	...	0.5	0.5	0.6	0.9	0.9	0.9	0.7	0.4	0.6	...	...	...	.	.	.
Developed countries	...	0.9	0.8	1.1	0.2	0.3	0.0	0.2	0.3	0.0	...	...	...	.	.	.
Developing countries	...	5.2	5.4	4.9	2.4	2.4	2.4	3.2	2.2	4.6	3.4	...	...	3.3	3.3	3.3
Arab States	...	0.9	1.3	1.2	0.6	0.5	0.5	0.6	0.7	0.6	1.7	2.1	1.5	2.2	2.8	2.1
Central and Eastern Europe	...	1.0	1.1	0.9	0.3	0.2	0.3	0.4	0.5	0.4	...	...	...	.	.	.
Central Asia	...	0.8	0.8	0.8	1.0	1.0	1.1	0.9	0.4	0.9	...	...	...	.	.	.
East Asia and the Pacific	...	6.4	6.0	6.8	...	...	...	...	...	...	...	...	...	...	...	...
East Asia	...	3.6	3.5	3.7	2.7	3.4	1.91	2.6	3.1	2.1	1.9	1.8	1.4	...	...	...
Pacific	...	...	...	...	...	...	...	...	...	...	...	...	...	...	...	...
Latin America/Caribbean	...	2.4	2.5	2.3	2.0	...	...	2.5	3.2	1.7	2.4	3.0	1.8	2.9	3.0	2.8
Caribbean	...	1.5	1.8	1.1	1.3	2.0	1.7	2.3	3.6	0.9	1.2	1.8	0.6	2.1	1.7	3.6
Latin America	...	5.2	5.9	4.5	2.2	2.9	1.4	2.6	2.8	2.5	2.9	2.9	2.9	3.2	...	...
N. America/W. Europe	...	—	—	—	—	—	—	—	—	—	—	—	—	—	—	—
South and West Asia	...	12.6	13.1	12.1	4.4	3.6	5.2	4.4	4.7	2.5	2.1	2.8	1.4	...	...	...
Sub-Saharan Africa	...	7.7	7.7	7.8	3.5	3.1	4.0	5.9	6.4	5.3	6.8	...	...	7.2	7.1	7.5

1. Duration in this table is defined according to ISCED97 and may differ from that reported nationally.
2. All values shown are medians.
Data in italic are UIS estimates.
Data in bold are for the school year ending in 2005.

(y) Data are for the school year ending in 2003.
(x) Data are for the school year ending in 2002.
(*) National estimates.

PRIMARY EDUCATION COMPLETION

SURVIVAL RATE TO GRADE 5 (%)						SURVIVAL RATE TO LAST GRADE (%)						PRIMARY COHORT COMPLETION RATE (%)			Country or territory
School year ending in						School year ending in						School year ending in			
1999			2004			1999			2004			2004			
Total	Male	Female	Total	Male	Female	Total	Male	Female	Total	Male	Female	Total	Male	Female	
69	73	65	...	...	...	62	67	56	...	...	...	...	...	...	Côte d'Ivoire
...	...	...	...	...	...	...	...	...	...	...	...	...	...	...	Democratic Rep. of the Congo
...	...	...	...	...	...	...	...	...	...	...	...	...	...	...	Equatorial Guinea
95	97	93	79	83	74	95	97	93	79	83	74	76ʸ	82ʸ	68ʸ	Eritrea
...	...	...	...	...	...	62	61	63	73	72	75	...	...	...	Ethiopia
...	...	...	69ˣ	68ˣ	71ˣ	...	...	...	56ˣ	54ˣ	57ˣ	...	...	...	Gabon
...	...	...	...	...	...	...	...	...	...	...	...	...	...	...	Gambia
...	...	...	63ˣ	62ˣ	65ˣ	...	...	...	60ˣ	55ˣ	65ˣ	49ˣ	46ˣ	53ˣ	Ghana
...	...	...	76	78	73	...	...	...	71	73	67	65ʸ	69ʸ	59ʸ	Guinea
...	...	...	...	...	...	...	...	...	...	...	...	...	...	...	Guinea-Bissau
...	...	...	83	81	85	...	...	...	84	...	...	71	...	...	Kenya
74	67	80	73	...	...	58	50	66	61	...	...	56	...	...	Lesotho
...	...	...	...	...	...	...	...	...	...	...	...	...	...	...	Liberia
51	51	52	43	43	43	51	51	52	43	43	43	34	...	...	Madagascar
49	55	43	42	44	41	37	39	34	34	35	32	...	...	...	Malawi
78	79	77	87	90	83	66	67	63	80	84	74	64	69	57	Mali
99	100	99	97	97	97	99	100	99	96	95	96	...	...	...	Mauritius
43	47	37	62	66	58	28	31	25	46	49	42	...	...	...	Mozambique
92	92	93	86	84	88	82	79	84	76	73	79	63ʸ	59ʸ	67ʸ	Namibia
...	...	...	65	66	64	...	...	...	60	61	58	39	40	36	Niger
...	...	...	73ʸ	71ʸ	75ʸ	...	...	...	63ʸ	61ʸ	64ʸ	...	...	...	Nigeria
45	...	...	46ʸ	43ʸ	49ʸ	30	...	...	31ʸ	30ʸ	32ʸ	13ʸ	15ʸ	12ʸ	Rwanda
...	...	...	76	76	77	...	...	...	68	68	68	...	...	...	Sao Tome and Principe
...	...	...	73	75	71	...	...	...	64	66	62	34	36	31	Senegal
99	98	100	...	...	...	99	99	100	99ˣ	98ˣ	100ˣ	...	...	...	Seychelles
...	...	...	...	...	...	...	...	...	...	...	...	...	...	...	Sierra Leone
...	...	...	...	...	...	...	...	...	...	...	...	...	...	...	Somalia
65	65	64	82ʸ	82ʸ	83ʸ	57	59	56	77ʸ	75ʸ	79ʸ	...	...	...	South Africa
80	72	88	77ˣ	74ˣ	80ˣ	64	62	66	61ˣ	53ˣ	71ˣ	58ˣ	50ˣ	69ˣ	Swaziland
...	...	...	75	79	70	...	...	...	68	74	62	63	70	55	Togo
...	...	...	49	49	49	...	...	...	25	26	25	...	...	...	Uganda
...	...	...	85	84	86	...	...	...	79	78	81	...	...	...	United Republic of Tanzania
81	83	78	...	...	...	66	70	62	...	...	...	...	...	...	Zambia
...	...	...	70ˣ	68ˣ	71ˣ	...	...	...	62ˣ	62ˣ	63ˣ	...	...	...	Zimbabwe
...	...	...	...	...	...	...	...	...	87	87	86	...	...	...	World[2]
...	...	...	...	...	...	97	...	...	98	97	97	...	...	...	Countries in transition
...	...	...	...	...	...	98	...	...	98	98	99	...	...	...	Developed countries
...	...	...	81	...	...	...	...	...	79	78	81	...	...	...	Developing countries
92	92	91	96	94	97	90	89	92	94	94	95	...	...	...	Arab States
...	...	...	...	...	...	97	97	97	98	98	98	...	...	...	Central and Eastern Europe
...	...	...	...	...	...	97	96	94	97	97	97	...	...	...	Central Asia
...	...	...	...	...	...	...	...	...	...	...	...	...	...	...	East Asia and the Pacific
...	...	...	88	90	87	...	...	...	85	87	83	...	...	...	East Asia
...	...	...	...	...	...	...	...	...	...	...	...	...	...	...	Pacific
89	88	90	87	84	90	84	78	91	84	80	87	...	...	...	Latin America/Caribbean
...	...	...	...	...	...	...	...	...	88	...	...	...	...	...	Caribbean
85	85	84	86	...	...	81	83	80	82	83	81	...	...	...	Latin America
...	...	...	...	...	...	...	...	...	99	99	100	...	...	...	N. America/W. Europe
...	...	...	79	78	80	...	...	...	79	75	76	...	...	...	South and West Asia
...	...	...	73	...	...	62	67	56	63	64	63	...	...	...	Sub-Saharan Africa

Table 8
Participation in secondary education[1]

	Country or territory	TRANSITION FROM PRIMARY TO SECONDARY GENERAL EDUCATION [%] School year ending in 2004			Age group 2005	School-age population[2] (000) 2004	ENROLMENT IN SECONDARY EDUCATION Total enrolment School year ending in 1999		2005		Enrolment in private institutions as % of total enrolment School year ending in 2005	Enrolment in technical and vocational education School year ending in 2005	
		Total	Male	Female			Total (000)	% F	Total (000)	% F		Total (000)	% F
	Arab States												
1	Algeria	79.5	76.2	83.2	12-17	4 522	...	...	*3 756*	51	–	464	39
2	Bahrain	97.1	95.3	98.9	12-17	73	59	51	72	50	16	16	39
3	Djibouti	71.4	74.4	67.3	12-18	126	16	42	30	40	23	2	46
4	Egypt	*76.9*	*72.4*	*82.0*	12-17	9 562	*7 671*	*47*	8 177	47	4	2 244	45
5	Iraq	*70.2*	*72.9*	*66.4*	12-17	3 918	1 105	38	*1 751*	*39*	.	*140*	*32*
6	Jordan	96.7	96.3	97.2	12-17	716	579	49	626	49	17ᶻ	31	35
7	Kuwait	94.5	92.7	96.5	11-17	262	*235*	*49*	249	50	28ᶻ	15	36
8	Lebanon	85.6	83.2	88.2	12-17	407	372	52	362	52	53	49	41
9	Libyan Arab Jamahiriya	...	...	...	12-17	713	...	...	**727**	**54**	3ʸ	...	...
10	Mauritania	45.9	48.3	43.4	12-18	452	*63*	*42*	93	46	13	3	38
11	Morocco	78.2	78.5	77.9	12-17	3 926	1 470	43	*1 952*	*45*	5	*118*	*39*
12	Oman	98.4	98.7	98.1	12-17	336	229	49	**299**	**48**	1	.	.
13	Palestinian A. T.	99.9	100.0	99.7	10-17	691	444	50	686	50	4	6	31
14	Qatar	*94.7*	*90.9*	*98.8*	12-17	56	44	50	56	49	32	0.5	.
15	Saudi Arabia	95.0	93.1	97.0	12-17	3 121	...	...	2 732	48	8	86	9
16	Sudan	89.5	87.9	91.5	12-16	4 001	*965*	...	1 370	48	10	18	28
17	Syrian Arab Republic	94.6	94.1	95.0	10-17	3 536	1 030	47	2 389	47	4	122	43
18	Tunisia	88.1	86.1	90.2	12-18	1 478	1 059	49	1 239	51	5	103	39
19	United Arab Emirates	97.5	96.7	98.4	11-17	446	202	50	285	49	42	1	.
20	Yemen	...	...	...	12-17	3 112	1 042	26	1 455	32	2	10	6
	Central and Eastern Europe												
21	Albania	*99.7ʸ*	*100.0ʸ*	*99.5ʸ*	10-17	506	364	48	397ᶻ	48ᶻ	3ᶻ	24ᶻ	34ᶻ
22	Belarus	99.6	99.2*	100.0*	10-16	973	978	50	928	49	0.1	5	32
23	Bosnia and Herzegovina	...	...	...	10-17	403	...	...	...	...	...	...	...
24	Bulgaria	95.6	95.3	95.9	11-17	665	700	48	686	48	0.9	204	38
25	Croatia	*99.9ˣ*	*99.8ˣ*	*100.0ˣ*	11-18	441	416	49	400ʸ	49ʸ	1ʸ	146ʸ	46ʸ
26	Czech Republic	99.6	99.3	100.0	11-18	1 018	928	50	975	49	7	383	46
27	Estonia	97.2	95.9	98.6	13-18	124	116	50	124	49	2	19	33
28	Hungary	*99.0*	*98.8*	*99.2*	11-18	999	1 007	49	960	49	10	131	38
29	Latvia	97.2	96.7	97.7	11-18	277	255	50	272	49	1	40	38
30	Lithuania	98.7	98.3	99.2	11-18	438	407	49	424	49	0.4	38	36
31	Poland	*99.3*	...	...	13-18	3 466	3 984	49	3 445	49	2	814	37
32	Republic of Moldova[3, 4]	98.6	99.3	97.9	11-17	...	415	50	383	50	1	23	38
33	Romania	98.4	98.4	98.4	11-18	2 451	2 218	49	2 090	49	0.5	693	44
34	Russian Federation	...	...	...	10-16	13 523	...	...	12 433	49	0.5	2 023	37
35	Serbia and Montenegro[3]	...	...	...	11-18	...	814	49	...	...	...	...	...
36	Slovakia	98.3	98.2	98.5	10-18	699	674	50	663	49	8	227	46
37	Slovenia	*99.4ˣ*	*100.0ˣ*	*98.7ˣ*	11-18	182	220	49	181	49	1	62	43
38	TFYR Macedonia	99.6	100.0	99.1	11-18	254	219	48	214	48	0.6	58	43
39	Turkey	91.6	92.8	90.3	12-16	6 741	...	...	*5 076*	*44*	*2*	1 040	37
40	Ukraine	*99.8ʸ*	*100.0ʸ*	*99.7ʸ*	10-16	4 559	5 214	50*	4 043	47	0.4	320	34
	Central Asia												
41	Armenia	*98.8ʸ*	*97.7ʸ*	*100.0ʸ*	10-16	415	...	...	365	50	0.7	3	38
42	Azerbaijan	99.0	99.4	98.6	10-16	1 292	929	49	1 070	48	0.3	3	30
43	Georgia	*98.3ˣ*	*98.1ˣ*	*98.5ˣ*	12-16	381	440	49	315	49	3ᶻ	8	31
44	Kazakhstan	99.9	99.7	100.0	11-17	2 070	1 966	49	2 040	49	0.8	102	34
45	Kyrgyzstan	99.0	98.1	100.0	11-17	835	633	50	721	49	0.7	28	36
46	Mongolia	97.4	96.2	98.7	12-17	369	205	55	339	52	4	20	50
47	Tajikistan	97.6	*98.4*	*96.7*	11-17	1 204	769	46	984	45	.	24	27
48	Turkmenistan	...	...	...	10-16	810	...	...	...	...	...	...	...
49	Uzbekistan	*99.6ˣ*	*100.0ˣ*	*99.2ˣ*	11-17	4 522	...	...	*4 235ᶻ*	*49ᶻ*	.ᶻ	*378ᶻ*	*44ᶻ*
	East Asia and the Pacific												
50	Australia[5]	*99.9ˣ*	*99.9ˣ*	*99.8ˣ*	12-17	1 682	2 491	49	2 491	48	27	1 028	44
51	Brunei Darussalam	89.8	87.5	92.6	12-18	46	34	51	44	49	13	3	41
52	Cambodia	82.2	84.0	80.2	12-17	2 108	*318*	*34*	*632ᶻ*	*40ᶻ*	0.3ʸ	*15ᶻ*	*34ᶻ*

GROSS ENROLMENT RATIO (GER) IN SECONDARY EDUCATION (%)																NET ENROLMENT RATIO (NER) IN SECONDARY EDUCATION (%)				
Lower secondary — School year ending in 2005				Upper secondary — School year ending in 2005				Total secondary — School year ending in 1999				Total secondary — School year ending in 2005				Total secondary — School year ending in 2005				
Total	Male	Female	GPI (F/M)	Total	Male	Female	GPI (F/M)	Total	Male	Female	GPI (F/M)	Total	Male	Female	GPI (F/M)	Total	Male	Female	GPI (F/M)	
Arab States																				
_108_	_111_	_105_	_0.95_	_58_	_49_	_67_	_1.36_	...	...	...	...	_83_	_80_	_86_	_1.07_	_66[z]_	_65[z]_	_68[z]_	_1.05[z]_	1
101	101	101	1.01	96	90	102	1.13	94	91	98	1.08	99	96	102	1.06	90	87	93	1.07	2
29	34	23	0.67	17	21	13	0.63	15	17	12	0.72	24	29	19	0.66	_23_	_27_	_18_	_0.66_	3
96	100	92	0.92	75	78	72	0.93	_81_	_84_	_77_	_0.91_	86	89	82	0.92	_82_	_85_	_79_	_0.92_	4
_57_	_69_	_44_	_0.64_	_31_	_37_	_26_	_0.70_	34	41	26	0.63	_45_	_54_	_35_	_0.66_	38	44	31	0.71	5
93	93	93	1.01	76	74	77	1.04	88	87	89	1.03	87	87	88	1.02	79	77	80	1.04	6
93	94	91	0.97	98	89	107	1.22	_99_	_98_	_99_	_1.02_	95	92	98	1.06	...	...	...	...	7
99	95	103	1.09	78	74	83	1.11	80	76	84	1.10	89	85	93	1.10	...	...	...	...	8
114	**112**	**116**	**1.03**	**97**	**80**	**115**	**1.44**	...	...	...	...	**105**	**96**	**115**	**1.21**	...	...	...	...	9
20	22	19	0.86	21	22	19	0.84	_19_	_22_	_16_	_0.73_	21	22	19	0.85	15	17	14	0.85	10
_65_	_70_	_59_	_0.83_	_35_	_37_	_33_	_0.88_	37	41	33	0.79	_50_	_54_	_46_	_0.85_	_35[y]_	_38[y]_	_32[y]_	_0.86[y]_	11
93	**95**	**91**	**0.95**	**83**	**84**	**82**	**0.97**	75	76	75	0.99	**88**	**90**	**86**	**0.96**	**77**	**77**	**77**	**1.00**	12
106	104	109	1.05	76	70	81	1.16	79	78	81	1.04	99	96	102	1.07	95	92	98	1.06	13
102	104	99	0.96	98	98	98	1.00	90	87	93	1.07	100	101	99	0.98	90	91	89	0.98	14
87	88	87	0.99	88	91	84	0.93	71	...	...	...	88	89	86	0.96	66	_63_	_68_	_1.08_	15
46	49	43	0.89	26	26	26	1.00	_26_	...	...	...	34	35	33	0.94	...	...	...	...	16
90	93	86	0.93	32	32	31	0.97	40	42	38	0.91	68	70	65	0.94	62	64	60	0.94	17
105	105	105	0.99	69	62	76	1.22	73	72	73	1.02	84	80	88	1.09	_65[y]_	_62[y]_	_68[y]_	_1.09[y]_	18
70	71	68	0.95	56	51	62	1.22	82	79	86	1.08	64	62	66	1.05	57	56	59	1.06	19
53	69	36	0.52	40	55	25	0.46	41	59	22	0.37	47	62	31	0.49	...	...	...	...	20
Central and Eastern Europe																				
_99[z]_	_100[z]_	_99[z]_	_0.99[z]_	_56[z]_	_59[z]_	_54[z]_	_0.92[z]_	74	76	72	0.95	_78[z]_	_79[z]_	_77[z]_	_0.96[z]_	_74[z]_	_75[z]_	_73[z]_	_0.98[z]_	21
109	111	107	0.96	68	63	73	1.18	83	81	86	1.06	95	95	96	1.01	89	_88_	_89_	1.01	22
...	...	...	...	...	...	...	...	...	...	...	...	...	...	...	...	...	...	...	...	23
88	91	85	0.93	120	122	118	0.97	91	92	90	0.98	103	106	101	0.95	88	89	87	0.97	24
_94[y]_	_95[y]_	_93[y]_	_0.98[y]_	_83[y]_	_81[y]_	_85[y]_	_1.05[y]_	84	84	85	1.02	_88[y]_	_87[y]_	_89[y]_	_1.02[y]_	_85[y]_	_84[y]_	_86[y]_	_1.02[y]_	25
99	99	100	1.01	93	91	94	1.03	83	81	84	1.04	96	95	97	1.02	...	...	...	...	26
111	114	108	0.95	92	88	96	1.09	93	91	95	1.04	101	100	101	1.01	91	90	93	1.02	27
98	99	97	0.99	94	94	94	1.00	94	93	94	1.02	96	96	96	0.99	90	90	90	1.00	28
100	101	98	0.97	96	94	99	1.06	89	87	90	1.04	98	98	98	1.01	...	...	...	...	29
98	99	97	0.98	93	91	95	1.04	96	96	97	1.01	97	97	96	0.99	91	91	91	1.00	30
100	101	99	0.98	99	99	99	1.01	99	100	99	0.99	99	100	99	0.99	93	92	94	1.01	31
88	88	87	1.00	69	65	74	1.14	84	84	85	1.01	82	80	83	1.03	76	75	77	1.03	32
97	98	96	0.98	77	75	78	1.04	79	79	80	1.01	85	85	86	1.01	80	79	82	1.03	33
88	87	88	1.00	100	102	98	0.96	...	...	...	...	92	93	91	0.99	...	...	...	...	34
...	...	...	...	...	...	...	...	92	92	93	1.01	...	...	...	...	...	...	...	...	35
97	98	97	0.99	92	91	94	1.03	85	84	86	1.02	95	94	95	1.01	94	94	95	1.01	36
98	98	97	0.99	101	101	101	1.00	101	100	102	1.02	100	100	99	1.00	82	83	81	0.98	37
94	94	94	1.01	75	77	73	0.94	82	83	81	0.97	84	85	83	0.98	67	72	61	0.85	38
_86_	_93_	_80_	_0.86_	68	76	59	0.78	...	...	...	...	_75_	_83_	_68_	_0.82_	...	...	...	...	39
87	92	83	0.91	92	94	89	0.94	97	96*	98*	1.02*	89	92	85	0.92	79	82*	77*	0.94*	40
Central Asia																				
93	93	94	1.01	76	73	80	1.10	...	...	...	...	88	87	89	1.03	84	83	86	1.03	41
89	90	87	0.97	68	70	67	0.96	76	76	76	1.00	83	84	81	0.96	78	79	76	0.97	42
95	95	94	0.99	66	64	67	1.05	79	80	78	0.98	83	82	83	1.01	_81[z]_	_81[z]_	_81[z]_	_1.00[z]_	43
104	105	104	0.99	86	88	83	0.94	91	91	91	0.99	99	100	97	0.97	92	92	91	0.99	44
90	90	90	1.00	77	76	78	1.03	84	83	84	1.02	86	86	87	1.01	80	80	81	1.01	45
98	94	102	1.09	82	73	91	1.24	58	51	65	1.27	92	86	98	1.13	84	79	90	1.14	46
92	98	87	0.89	54	67	41	0.61	71	79	68	0.86	82	89	74	0.83	80	86	73	0.85	47
...	...	...	...	...	...	...	...	...	...	...	...	...	...	...	...	...	...	...	...	48
_98[z]_	_98[z]_	_97[z]_	_0.99[z]_	_87[z]_	_91[z]_	_83[z]_	_0.91[z]_	...	...	...	...	_95[z]_	_96[z]_	_93[z]_	_0.97[z]_	...	...	...	...	49
East Asia and the Pacific																				
114	114	114	1.00	217	228	205	0.90	154	154	154	1.00	148	152	144	0.95	_86_	_86_	_87_	_1.01_	50
115	118	112	0.95	80	74	86	1.16	85	81	89	1.09	96	94	98	1.04	_87_	_85_	_90_	_1.05_	51
_44[z]_	_50[z]_	_37[z]_	_0.7[z]_	_15[z]_	_20[z]_	_11[z]_	_0.57[z]_	16	21	11	0.53	_29[z]_	_35[z]_	_24[z]_	_0.69[z]_	_24_	_27_	_22_	_0.84_	52

ANNEX

Table 8 (continued)

		TRANSITION FROM PRIMARY TO SECONDARY GENERAL EDUCATION (%)			ENROLMENT IN SECONDARY EDUCATION								
		School year ending in 2004			Age group	School-age population[2] (000)	Total enrolment				Enrolment in private institutions as % of total enrolment	Enrolment in technical and vocational education	
							School year ending in				School year ending in 2005	School year ending in 2005	
							1999		2005				
	Country or territory	Total	Male	Female	2005	2004	Total (000)	% F	Total (000)	% F		Total (000)	% F
53	China	...	...	...	12-17	135 361	77 436	...	**101 195**	**48**	8	15 306	51
54	Cook Islands[3]	...	...	...	11-17	...	2	50	2z	49z	19z	.y	.y
55	DPR Korea	...	...	...	10-15	2 374	...	...	...	...	...	...	...
56	Fiji	98.6	97.3	100.0	12-18	116	98	51	102	50	92	3	28
57	Indonesia	78.5	78.6	78.3	13-18	25 332	...	...	15 993	49	44	2 164	42
58	Japan	...	...	...	12-17	7 596	8 959	49	7 710	49	19	994	43
59	Kiribati[3]	...	...	...	12-17	...	9	53	11	52	...	–	–
60	Lao PDR	78.0	80.1	75.5	11-16	843	240	40	394	42	2	6	37
61	Macao, China	88.0	85.5	90.7	12-17	48	32	51	47	49	94	2	46
62	Malaysia	...	...	...	12-18	3 454	2 177	51	2 584z	52z	5z	148z	42z
63	Marshall Islands[3]	...	...	...	12-17	...	6	50	6	50	34y	.	.
64	Micronesia	...	...	...	12-17	16	...	...	14	49	...	...	...
65	Myanmar	71.7	72.3	71.0	10-15	6 429	2 059	50	2 589	49	–	–	–
66	Nauru[3]	...	...	...	12-17	...	...	...	0.6z	50z	19y	.z	.z
67	New Zealand	...	...	...	11-17	429	437	50	526	50	22	...	...
68	Niue[3]	...	...	...	11-16	...	0.3	54	0.2	...	...	.	.
69	Palau[3]	88.8	89.4	88.1	11-17	...	2	49	2	50	27	.	.
70	Papua New Guinea	76.8x	77.0x	76.5x	13-18	782	144	40	190y	41y	...	17y	27y
71	Philippines	91.8	91.3	92.4	12-15	7 452	5 117	51	6 352	52	20	.	.
72	Republic of Korea	**99.5**	**99.5**	**99.6**	12-17	3 975	4 368	48	**3 786**	**47**	33	503	46
73	Samoa	96.3y	95.3y	97.4y	11-17	30	22	50	24	51	32	.	.
74	Singapore	...	...	...	12-17	383	197	49	242	49	...	28	38
75	Solomon Islands	69.8x	71.4x	67.9x	12-18	76	17	41	22	43	...	.	.
76	Thailand	...	...	...	12-17	6 449	...	...	**4 530**	**51**	15	703	45
77	Timor-Leste	...	...	...	12-17	144	...	...	75	49	...	3	40
78	Tokelau[3]	87.5x	91.7x	82.1x	11-15	...	...	...	0.2z	45z	.y	.z	.z
79	Tonga	80.9	78.4	83.8	11-16	14	15	50	14z	49z	...	1z	32z
80	Tuvalu	...	...	...	12-17	...	...	...	...	...	...	...	...
81	Vanuatu	52.5	50.3	55.0	12-18	34	9	45	14z	45z	...	3z	30z
82	Viet Nam	...	...	...	11-17	13 115	7 401	47	9 939	49	10	467	55
	Latin America and the Caribbean												
83	Anguilla	97.9	100.0	95.8	12-16	...	1	53	1	50	.	0.1	46
84	Antigua and Barbuda	...	...	...	12-16	...	...	...	...	...	...	...	...
85	Argentina	94.6y	93.4y	95.8y	12-17	4 117	3 722	51	3 516z	51z	27y	1 270z	52z
86	Aruba[3]	98.4	96.9	100.0	12-16	...	6	51	7	51	91	1	38
87	Bahamas	98.0	100.0	95.9	11-16	36	27	49	32	50	29	.	.
88	Barbados	99.4	100.0	98.9	11-15	19	22	51	21	49	5	0.1	38
89	Belize	90.1	90.7	89.6	11-16	37	22	54	31	50	74y	3	43
90	Bermuda[3]	98.2	...	...	11-17	...	...	...	5	52	40	.	.
91	Bolivia	90.2y	90.0y	90.4y	12-17	1 241	830	48	1 049y	48y	...	50y	65y
92	Brazil	80.5y	...	...	11-17	23 543	24 983	52	25 128z	52z	12z	718z	47z
93	British Virgin Islands[3]	91.6	93.8	89.4	12-16	...	2	47	2	54	9	0	59
94	Cayman Islands	...	...	...	11-16	...	2	48	3	48	25	.	.
95	Chile	96.7	95.6	98.0	12-17	1 795	1 305	50	1 630	49	52	398	46
96	Colombia	100.0	100.0	100.0	11-16	5 505	3 589	52	4 297	52	24	283	54
97	Costa Rica	96.9	...	...	12-16	438	235	51	347	50	13z	61	51
98	Cuba	98.5	98.3	98.8	12-17	1 001	740	50	937	49	.	269	44
99	Dominica[3]	98.9	99.3	98.4	12-16	...	7	57	7	50	33	0.3	68
100	Dominican Republic	87.6	83.4	91.8	12-17	1 143	611	55	808	54	25	40	60
101	Ecuador	73.4	75.8	71.0	12-17	1 638	904	50	1 000	49	33	224	52
102	El Salvador	92.9	92.8	93.0	13-18	835	406	49	524	50	18	108	53
103	Grenada[3]	...	...	...	12-16	...	...	...	14*	50*	60y	0.7*	46*
104	Guatemala	93.8y	95.0y	92.5y	13-17	1 470	435	45	754	48	74	222	51
105	Guyana	...	...	...	12-16	69	66	50	71	50	2y	7	45
106	Haiti	...	...	...	12-18	1 476	...	...	...	...	...	.z	.z
107	Honduras	...	...	...	12-16	863	...	...	566	55	...	211	55
108	Jamaica	98.6	100.0	97.3	12-16	282	231	50	246	50	6	–	–
109	Mexico	93.7	94.7	92.6	12-17	13 166	8 722	50	10 564	51	15	1 484	57
110	Montserrat[3]	...	...	...	12-16	...	0.3	47	0.3	49	.	.	.
111	Netherlands Antilles	...	...	...	12-17	18	15	54	15y	52y	81y	6y	54y

GROSS ENROLMENT RATIO (GER) IN SECONDARY EDUCATION (%)																NET ENROLMENT RATIO (NER) IN SECONDARY EDUCATION (%)				
Lower secondary				Upper secondary				Total secondary								Total secondary				
School year ending in 2005				School year ending in 2005				School year ending in 1999				School year ending in 2005				School year ending in 2005				
Total	Male	Female	GPI (F/M)	Total	Male	Female	GPI (F/M)	Total	Male	Female	GPI (F/M)	Total	Male	Female	GPI (F/M)	Total	Male	Female	GPI (F/M)	
99	**99**	**99**	**1.00**	**55**	**54**	**56**	**1.03**	62	...	...	...	**76**	**75**	**76**	**1.01**	...	...	...	...	53
85z	88z	81z	0.93z	54z	49z	61z	1.24z	60	58	63	1.08	72z	72z	73z	1.02z	...	...	...	...	54
...	...	...	...	...	...	...	...	...	...	...	...	...	...	...	...	...	...	...	...	55
100	98	102	1.04	70	67	74	1.11	81	77	85	1.11	88	85	91	1.07	83	80	85	1.06	56
77	76	77	1.02	50	51	48	0.95	...	...	...	...	63	63	63	0.99	58	59	58	0.99	57
101	101	101	1.00	102	102	102	1.00	102	101	102	1.01	102	101	102	1.00	100	...	...	...	58
110	106	114	1.07	65	57	73	1.26	84	77	91	1.18	87	82	93	1.13	68	65	71	1.10	59
56	63	50	0.79	37	43	31	0.72	33	39	27	0.69	47	53	40	0.76	38	41	35	0.85	60
117	118	115	0.97	80	75	85	1.13	76	73	78	1.08	97	96	99	1.04	78	75	81	1.08	61
95z	93z	98z	1.05z	60z	53z	67z	1.26z	69	66	73	1.10	76z	72z	81z	1.14z	76z	71z	81z	1.14z	62
105	106	104	0.98	63	60	66	1.10	...	70	74	1.06	76	75	78	1.05	74y	72y	77y	1.06y	63
106	101	110	1.09	75	74	77	1.05	...	...	...	...	85	83	88	1.07	...	...	...	...	64
45	45	44	0.98	31	31	31	1.02	34	34	34	1.00	40	41	40	0.99	37	38	37	0.98	65
...	...	...	...	...	...	...	...	...	...	...	...	48z	46z	50z	1.07z	...	...	...	...	66
108	108	108	1.00	141	132	151	1.14	110	107	113	1.06	123	119	127	1.07	...	...	...	...	67
...	...	...	...	...	...	...	...	98	93	103	1.10	99	104	94	0.91	...	...	...	...	68
118	123	113	0.92	87	77	98	1.28	101	98	105	1.07	101	97	105	1.08	...	...	...	...	69
35y	38y	30y	0.79y	6y	7y	5y	0.70y	22	24	19	0.76	26y	29y	23y	0.79y	...	...	...	...	70
87	84	91	1.09	79	71	87	1.21	76	73	79	1.09	85	81	90	1.12	61	55	66	1.20	71
98	**98**	**99**	**1.00**	**93**	**93**	**93**	**1.00**	100	100	100	1.00	**96**	**95**	**96**	**1.00**	**94**	**94**	**94**	**1.01**	72
100	100	100	1.00	72	65	79	1.20	80	76	84	1.10	80	76	85	1.12	66z	62z	70z	1.14z	73
80	80	79	1.00	25	22	28	1.25	...	66	67	1.02	63	62	64	1.03	...	...	...	...	74
47	50	44	0.88	16	18	13	0.73	24	27	21	0.75	29	32	27	0.83	26y	28y	24y	0.86y	75
87	**87**	**87**	**1.00**	55	51	59	1.15	...	...	...	...	**71**	**69**	**72**	**1.05**	**64**	**62**	**66**	**1.07**	76
71	70	71	1.02	34	34	33	0.96	...	...	...	...	52	52	52	1.00	...	...	...	...	77
...	...	...	...	...	...	...	...	...	...	...	...	101z	107z	94z	0.88z	...	...	...	...	78
93z	95z	91z	0.95z	108z	91z	127z	1.4z	101	96	106	1.11	98z	94z	102z	1.08z	68z	61z	75z	1.23z	79
...	...	...	...	...	...	...	...	...	...	...	...	...	...	...	...	...	...	...	...	80
47z	47z	48z	1.03z	32z	41z	24z	0.58z	30	32	28	0.88	41z	44z	38z	0.86z	39z	42z	36z	0.86z	81
88	90	86	0.95	59	58	60	1.03	62	65	58	0.90	76	77	75	0.97	69	71	68	0.96	82

Latin America and the Caribbean

81	83	79	0.95	98	97	99	1.01	...	...	...	...	87	88	86	0.97	81	83	79	0.96	83
...	...	...	...	...	...	...	...	...	...	...	...	...	...	...	...	...	...	...	...	84
102z	100z	103z	1.03z	70z	66z	74z	1.13z	94	91	97	1.07	86z	83z	89z	1.07z	79z	76z	82z	1.07z	85
116	121	111	0.92	85	79	91	1.16	101	98	103	1.05	97	96	99	1.03	76	75	78	1.05	86
96	97	94	0.96	85	82	87	1.06	115	79	78	0.99	90	90	91	1.00	84	83	85	1.02	87
112	114	111	0.97	114	112	117	1.04	104	101	107	1.05	113	113	113	1.00	96	96	97	1.01	88
97	98	96	0.98	56	52	61	1.18	64	62	67	1.08	84	83	85	1.02	71	71	72	1.01	89
96	93	99	1.06	83	78	88	1.12	...	...	...	...	89	85	93	1.09	...	...	...	...	90
106y	106y	106y	1.01y	79y	81y	77y	0.9y	78	80	75	0.93	88y	90y	87y	0.97y	73z	73z	72z	0.99z	91
114z	112z	117z	1.04z	94z	86z	103z	1.19z	99	94	104	1.11	106z	101z	111z	1.10z	78z	75z	81z	1.08z	92
113	102	123	1.21	91	85	97	1.13	99	103	94	0.91	104	96	113	1.18	88	82	95	1.16	93
114	121	107	0.88	88	89	88	0.98	...	...	...	...	102	106	98	0.92	96	99	92	0.92	94
99	101	98	0.98	86	85	88	1.03	79	78	81	1.04	91	90	91	1.01	...	...	...	...	95
85	82	89	1.08	63	57	68	1.19	71	67	75	1.11	78	74	82	1.11	...	...	...	...	96
95	93	96	1.03	57	53	61	1.16	57	55	60	1.09	79	77	82	1.06	...	...	...	...	97
101	103	99	0.96	87	84	89	1.06	80	78	83	1.06	94	93	94	1.00	87	87	88	1.02	98
125	134	117	0.87	81	73	89	1.22	90	77	104	1.35	107	109	106	0.97	92	92	92	1.00	99
83	78	88	1.14	65	57	72	1.27	55	49	62	1.27	71	64	78	1.21	53	47	59	1.24	100
69	71	68	0.97	52	51	54	1.05	57	56	57	1.03	61	61	61	1.00	52z	52z	53z	1.01z	101
78	78	78	1.00	46	44	48	1.09	51	51	50	0.98	63	62	64	1.03	53	52	54	1.04	102
102	104	100	0.96	97*	89*	104*	1.17*	...	...	...	...	100*	99*	102*	1.03*	79	78	80	1.02	103
56	60	51	0.86	44	44	44	1.01	33	36	31	0.84	51	54	49	0.91	34z	35z	32z	0.92z	104
126	125	127	1.01	66	64	67	1.05	81	81	82	1.02	102	101	103	1.02	...	...	...	...	105
...	...	...	...	...	...	...	...	...	...	...	...	...	...	...	...	...	...	...	...	106
60	56	64	1.14	75	63	87	1.39	...	...	...	...	65	58	73	1.24	...	...	...	...	107
94	94	93	1.00	77	73	81	1.11	88	87	88	1.02	87	86	89	1.03	78	77	80	1.05	108
104	100	108	1.07	55	54	57	1.06	69	68	70	1.02	80	78	83	1.07	65	64	66	1.04	109
123	124	121	0.97	106	91	125	1.38	...	...	...	...	116	111	123	1.10	96z	...	...	...	110
116y	120y	112y	0.94y	71y	63y	79y	1.25y	97	90	104	1.16	87y	83y	90y	1.09y	77y	73y	81y	1.10y	111

311

Table 8 (continued)

| # | Country or territory | TRANSITION FROM PRIMARY TO SECONDARY GENERAL EDUCATION (%) School year ending in 2004 | | | Age group | School-age population[2] (000) | ENROLMENT IN SECONDARY EDUCATION Total enrolment School year ending in | | | | Enrolment in private institutions as % of total enrolment School year ending in 2005 | Enrolment in technical and vocational education School year ending in 2005 | |
		Total	Male	Female	2005	2004	1999 Total (000)	% F	2005 Total (000)	% F		Total (000)	% F
112	Nicaragua	...	...	...	13-17	660	321	54	438	53	27	23	55
113	Panama	64.6	63.7	65.5	12-17	365	230	51	256	51	15	98	49
114	Paraguay	90.3y	90.3y	90.3y	12-17	825	425	50	526z	50z	20z	47z	46z
115	Peru	94.7	95.9	93.5	12-16	2 935	2 278	48	2 691	50	22	279	63
116	Saint Kitts and Nevis[3]	90.4y			12-16	...	...	...	4	51	3	.	.
117	Saint Lucia	70.5	62.7	78.9	12-16	18	12	56	14	54	4	0.8	40
118	St Vincent/Grenad.	81.1	76.3	85.2	12-16	13	...	...	10	55	25	0.4	34
119	Suriname	...	...	...	12-17	53	...	...	46	56	20	22	50
120	Trinidad and Tobago	92.7*	93.6*	91.9*	12-16	120	117	52	97*	50*	24*	0.9	28
121	Turks and Caicos Islands	87.5	83.8	92.0	12-16	1	...	51	2	48	16	0.1	48
122	Uruguay	80.8y	74.6y	87.1y	12-17	326	284	53	339z	53z	11z	52z	45z
123	Venezuela	98.7	98.4	99.0	12-16	2 724	1 439	54	2 028	52	25	78	50
	North America and Western Europe												
124	Andorra[3]	95.5y	95.2y	95.9y	12-17	...	...		4	50	4	0.2	49
125	Austria	...	...	...	10-17	763	748	48	781	48	10	300	44
126	Belgium	...	...	...	12-17	741	1 033	51	815	48	68	329	43
127	Canada	...	...	...	12-17	2 581	...	...	...	...	...	...	...
128	Cyprus[3]	99.7	100.0	99.4	12-17	...	63	49	64	49	13	4	17
129	Denmark	99.7	100.0	99.4	13-18	374	422	50	465	49	13	125	44
130	Finland	99.9	99.9	100.0	13-18	389	480	51	431	50	7	123	46
131	France[6]	...	...	...	11-17	5 211	5 955	49	6 036	49	25	1 595	44
132	Germany	99.1	99.2	99.0	10-18	8 254	8 185	48	8 268	48	8	1 790	43
133	Greece	99.6	99.3	100.0	12-17	702	771	49	716	48	6	137	38
134	Iceland	99.7y	100.0y	99.3y	13-19	30	32	50	33z	50z	4z	7z	41z
135	Ireland	98.8	...	...	12-16	281	346	50	317	51	0.6	51	55
136	Israel	73.4	73.9	72.9	12-17	661	569	49	610	49	–	125	43
137	Italy	99.7	100.0	99.4	11-18	4 534	4 450	49	4 507	48	5	1 669	40
138	Luxembourg	...	...	...	12-18	38	33	50	36	50	18	11	49
139	Malta	93.2	89.7	97.0	11-17	39	...	...	39	49	29	4	33
140	Monaco[7]	...	...	...	11-17	...	3	51	3z	...	23z	0.5z	...
141	Netherlands	98.1y	96.4y	100.0y	12-17	1 190	1 365	48	1 410	48	83z	725	46
142	Norway	99.9	99.9	99.8	13-18	354	378	49	403	49	7	132	44
143	Portugal	...	...	...	12-17	677	848	51	670	51	15	110	42
144	San Marino	...	...	...	11-18	...	...	...	...	...	...	–z	–z
145	Spain	...	...	...	12-17	2 510	3 299	50	3 108	50	28	487	49
146	Sweden	...	...	...	13-18	715	964	55	735	49	10	201	44
147	Switzerland	99.6	99.3	100.0	13-19	608	544	47	575	47	7	180	40
148	United Kingdom	...	...	...	11-17	5 467	5 192	49	5 747	49	30	1 333	49
149	United States	...	...	...	12-17	25 787	22 445	...	24 432	49	9	.	.
	South and West Asia												
150	Afghanistan	...	...	...	13-18	4 011	...	...	651	23	...	9	10
151	Bangladesh	89.3y	86.5y	92.1y	11-17	22 150	9 912	49	10 355z	50z	96z	168z	27z
152	Bhutan[8]	...	...	...	13-18	...	20	44	42	47	8	1	34
153	India	85.1	86.5	83.4	11-17	158 173	67 090	39	92 743	43	42y	772	16
154	Iran, Islamic Republic of	90.3	94.9	85.6	11-17	12 329	9 727	47	9 942	47	8	876	38
155	Maldives	78.2	74.6	82.2	13-17	40	15	51	29z	52z	11z	1z	30z
156	Nepal	76.7y	78.7y	74.3y	10-16	4 499	1 265	40	1 984	45	27	22	22
157	Pakistan	69.0	67.0	72.0	10-16	26 971	...	...	7 245	41	25	154	25
158	Sri Lanka	97.0x	96.4x	97.7x	10-17	2 792	...	...	2 332z	49z	2y	...	...
	Sub-Saharan Africa												
159	Angola	...	...	...	10-16	2 828	300	46	...	...	...	...	...
160	Benin	51.1x	51.1x	51.0x	12-18	1 339	213	31	435	35	25	58	43
161	Botswana	95.1	94.9	95.3	13-17	226	158	51	170z	51z	4y	11z	38z
162	Burkina Faso	46.0	47.3	44.2	13-19	2 104	173	38	295	41	39	22	49
163	Burundi	32.8	35.0	29.9	13-19	1 291	...	...	174	43	12	14	48
164	Cameroon	44.7*	42.6*	47.2*	12-18	2 704	626	45	1 198*	44*	40*	381*	36*
165	Cape Verde	72.8	68.4	77.4	12-17	76	...	...	52	52	–	3	39
166	Central African Republic	...	...	...	12-18	668	...	...	...	...	...	...	...

Education for All Global Monitoring Report 2008

GROSS ENROLMENT RATIO (GER) IN SECONDARY EDUCATION (%)																NET ENROLMENT RATIO (NER) IN SECONDARY EDUCATION (%)				
Lower secondary				Upper secondary				Total secondary								Total secondary				
School year ending in 2005				School year ending in 2005				School year ending in 1999				2005				School year ending in 2005				
Total	Male	Female	GPI (F/M)	Total	Male	Female	GPI (F/M)	Total	Male	Female	GPI (F/M)	Total	Male	Female	GPI (F/M)	Total	Male	Female	GPI (F/M)	
75	72	78	1.08	53	46	60	1.31	*52*	*48*	*57*	*1.19*	66	62	71	1.15	43	40	46	1.15	112
85	84	86	1.03	55	52	59	1.15	67	65	69	1.07	70	68	73	1.07	64	61	67	1.09	113
75ᶻ	75ᶻ	75ᶻ	1.00ᶻ	52ᶻ	51ᶻ	53ᶻ	1.04ᶻ	57	56	58	1.04	64ᶻ	63ᶻ	64ᶻ	1.02ᶻ	…	…	…	…	114
104	102	106	1.04	72	73	71	0.96	83	86	81	0.94	92	91	92	1.01	70	70	69	0.99	115
99	*106*	*92*	*0.87*	*86*	*78*	*94*	*1.20*	…	…	…	…	*94*	*95*	*93*	*0.98*	*86*	*87*	*85*	*0.99*	116
81	74	88	1.18	73	65	82	1.26	72	63	80	1.28	78	71	85	1.21	*68*	*61*	*76*	*1.24*	117
90	83	96	1.16	54	44	64	1.46	…	…	…	…	75	67	83	1.24	*64*	*57*	*71*	*1.23*	118
94	86	104	1.21	73	54	93	1.71	…	…	…	…	87	75	100	1.33	*75*	*63*	*87*	*1.39*	119
82*	81*	83*	1.02*	79*	77*	81*	1.06*	82	78	85	1.08	81*	79*	82*	1.04*	69	68	70	1.03	120
86	*89*	*84*	*0.95*	*85*	*89*	*82*	*0.92*	…	…	…	…	*86*	*89*	*83*	*0.94*	*70*	*72*	*69*	*0.96*	121
110ᶻ	106ᶻ	115ᶻ	1.08ᶻ	100ᶻ	89ᶻ	111ᶻ	1.25ᶻ	92	84	99	1.17	105ᶻ	98ᶻ	113ᶻ	1.16ᶻ	…	…	…	…	122
86	83	89	1.08	57	51	63	1.25	56	51	62	1.23	74	70	79	1.13	63	59	67	1.15	123
																North America and Western Europe				
97	94	100	1.06	70	61	80	1.31	…	…	…	…	88	83	93	1.12	76	73	80	1.10	124
104	105	104	0.99	100	105	96	0.92	99	101	97	0.96	102	105	100	0.95	…	…	…	…	125
116	119	113	0.94	107	108	106	0.98	142	137	147	1.08	110	112	108	0.97	97	97	98	1.01	126
…	…	…	…	…	…	…	…	105	…	…	…	…	…	…	…	…	…	…	…	127
97	97	97	1.00	96	94	98	1.03	93	92	95	1.03	97	96	97	1.02	94	93	95	1.02	128
119	118	121	1.02	130	127	133	1.05	124	121	128	1.06	124	122	126	1.03	92	91	93	1.03	129
101	101	101	1.00	121	116	126	1.09	121	116	126	1.09	111	108	113	1.05	95	95	95	1.01	130
115	116	114	0.98	117	115	118	1.03	110	110	111	1.00	116	116	116	1.00	99	98	100	1.02	131
102	103	102	1.00	96	98	93	0.95	98	99	97	0.98	100	101	99	0.98	…	…	…	…	132
99	101	98	0.97	104	105	104	0.98	90	89	92	1.04	102	103	101	0.98	91	90	92	1.02	133
105ᶻ	105ᶻ	105ᶻ	1.00ᶻ	110ᶻ	108ᶻ	113ᶻ	1.05ᶻ	109	107	112	1.05	108ᶻ	107ᶻ	109ᶻ	1.03ᶻ	88ᶻ	87ᶻ	89ᶻ	1.03ᶻ	134
106	104	108	1.04	123	114	132	1.16	107	104	110	1.06	113	108	118	1.09	88	85	91	1.06	135
77	77	77	1.00	108	109	107	0.99	90	90	90	1.00	92	93	92	0.99	89	89	89	1.01	136
106	107	104	0.97	96	96	96	1.00	92	92	91	0.99	99	100	99	0.99	92	92	93	1.01	137
102	101	103	1.03	88	84	92	1.10	92	91	94	1.03	94	91	97	1.06	82	79	85	1.08	138
104	101	107	1.06	89	91	86	0.94	…	…	…	…	99	98	101	1.03	84	84	83	0.98	139
…	…	…	…	…	…	…	…	…	…	…	…	…	…	…	…	…	…	…	…	140
130	133	127	0.96	107	106	107	1.01	124	127	122	0.96	119	120	117	0.98	87	86	88	1.02	141
102	102	102	1.00	127	126	127	1.01	120	119	121	1.02	114	114	114	1.01	97	97	97	1.01	142
110	108	112	1.03	88	81	96	1.19	106	102	111	1.08	99	94	104	1.10	83	79	87	1.11	143
…	…	…	…	…	…	…	…	…	…	…	…	…	…	…	…	…	…	…	…	144
122	123	122	1.00	127	117	137	1.17	109	106	113	1.07	124	121	127	1.05	98	97	100	1.03	145
104	104	104	1.00	102	101	102	1.01	160	141	180	1.28	103	103	103	1.00	99	99	100	1.01	146
112	111	113	1.01	81	87	74	0.85	96	101	91	0.90	94	98	91	0.93	84	87	81	0.93	147
103	103	102	1.00	107	104	110	1.05	101	101	101	1.00	105	104	107	1.03	95	94	97	1.04	148
102	103	101	0.98	88	86	90	1.05	95	…	…	…	95	94	95	1.02	89	88	90	1.03	149
																South and West Asia				
22	32	11	0.35	10	15	4	0.28	…	…	…	…	16	24	8	0.33	…	…	…	…	150
64ᶻ	61ᶻ	68ᶻ	1.10ᶻ	34ᶻ	35ᶻ	32ᶻ	0.94ᶻ	49	49	49	1.01	47ᶻ	47ᶻ	48ᶻ	1.03ᶻ	44ᶻ	44ᶻ	45ᶻ	1.04ᶻ	151
…	…	…	…	…	…	…	…	…	…	…	…	…	…	…	…	…	…	…	…	152
75	80	68	0.85	46	52	40	0.76	46	54	38	0.69	59	65	52	0.81	…	…	…	…	153
86	90	82	0.91	77	78	75	0.96	77	80	74	0.93	81	83	78	0.94	77	79	75	0.94	154
108ᶻ	98ᶻ	118ᶻ	1.2ᶻ	18ᶻ	21ᶻ	15ᶻ	0.70ᶻ	43	42	45	1.07	*73ᶻ*	*68ᶻ*	*78ᶻ*	*1.14ᶻ*	*63*	*60*	*66*	*1.10*	155
66	**70**	**63**	**0.89**	***24***	***26***	***22***	***0.87***	34	40	28	0.70	***43***	***46***	***40***	***0.89***	…	…	…	…	156
33	38	28	0.73	11	12	10	0.83	…	…	…	…	27	31	23	0.74	*21*	*24*	*18*	*0.74*	157
95ᶻ	*94ᶻ*	*97ᶻ*	*1.04ᶻ*	*70ᶻ*	*72ᶻ*	*69ᶻ*	*0.96ᶻ*	…	…	…	…	*83ᶻ*	*82ᶻ*	*83ᶻ*	*1.00ᶻ*	…	…	…	…	158
																Sub-Saharan Africa				
…	…	…	…	…	…	…	…	*13*	*14*	*12*	*0.83*	…	…	…	…	…	…	…	…	159
41	*51*	*30*	*0.58*	*20*	*27*	*14*	*0.52*	19	26	12	0.47	*33*	*41*	*23*	*0.57*	…	…	…	…	160
87ᶻ	84ᶻ	89ᶻ	1.07ᶻ	58ᶻ	57ᶻ	58ᶻ	1.02ᶻ	71	69	74	1.07	*75ᶻ*	*73ᶻ*	*77ᶻ*	*1.05ᶻ*	*60*	*57*	*62*	*1.09*	161
19	22	16	0.73	7	9	5	0.60	10	13	8	0.61	14	16	12	0.70	11	13	9	0.70	162
17	*20*	*15*	*0.76*	*8*	*9*	*6*	*0.68*	…	…	…	…	*13*	*15*	*11*	*0.74*	…	…	…	…	163
49	*52*	*47*	*0.91*	*37*	*46*	*28*	*0.61*	27	29	24	0.83	44*	49*	39*	0.80*	…	…	…	…	164
90	*87*	*92*	*1.06*	*45*	*43*	*47*	*1.10*	…	…	…	…	68	65	70	1.07	58	55	60	1.09	165
14ʸ	*18ʸ*	*10ʸ*	*0.54ʸ*	…	…	…	…	…	…	…	…	…	…	…	…	…	…	…	…	166

Table 8 (continued)

	Country or territory	TRANSITION FROM PRIMARY TO SECONDARY GENERAL EDUCATION (%) School year ending in 2004			Age group 2005	School-age population[2] (000) 2004	ENROLMENT IN SECONDARY EDUCATION Total enrolment School year ending in 1999		School year ending in 2005		Enrolment in private institutions as % of total enrolment School year ending in 2005	Enrolment in technical and vocational education School year ending in 2005	
		Total	Male	Female			Total (000)	% F	Total (000)	% F		Total (000)	% F
167	Chad	*51.3*	*56.1*	*41.8*	12-18	1 526	123	21	*237*	25	...	3	41
168	Comoros	*63.2*	*70.3*	*55.1*	12-18	123	29	44	*43*	43	41	0.2	7
169	Congo	*58.1*	*58.1*	*58.1*	12-18	629	...	...	*235[z]*	*46[z]*	*22[z]*	*43[z]*	*48[z]*
170	Côte d'Ivoire	...	...	...	12-18	3 078	*592*	35	...	...	...	...	...
171	Democratic Rep. of the Congo	...	...	...	12-17	7 900	1 235	34	*1 655[y]*	*37[y]*	...	*443[y]*	*38[y]*
172	Equatorial Guinea	...	...	...	12-18	78	20	27	...	...	...	...	...
173	Eritrea	88.6	91.0	85.1	12-18	690	115	41	217	37	6	2	36
174	Ethiopia	85.4	85.1	85.9	11-18	14 529	1 859	38	**5 185**	**41**	6	**124**	**50**
175	Gabon	...	...	...	12-18	227	87	46	...	...	...	...	...
176	Gambia	...	...	...	13-18	188	50	39	*85[z]*	*45[z]*	*39[z]*	*0.4[y]*	*82[y]*
177	Ghana	86.8[x]	86.9[x]	86.7[x]	12-17	3 099	1 024	44	**1 409**	**46**	**14**	**31**	**50**
178	Guinea	64.0	67.9	58.0	13-19	1 390	*172*	*26*	*423*	*33*	*10[z]*	8	48
179	Guinea-Bissau	...	...	...	13-17	172	...	...	...	...	...	...	...
180	Kenya	...	...	...	12-17	5 053	1 822	49	*2 464*	49	6	14	46
181	Lesotho	65.9	67.5	64.7	13-17	244	74	57	94	56	2	1	52
182	Liberia	...	...	...	12-17	461	114	39	...	...	...	...	...
183	Madagascar	54.3	55.8	52.9	11-17	2 959	*347*	*49*	...	...	...	...	...
184	Malawi	74.3	76.7	71.7	12-17	1 822	556	41	515	45	15	.	.
185	Mali	57.1	63.0	48.2	13-18	1 827	218	34	430	37	26	42	40
186	Mauritius	64.2	59.5	69.2	11-17	145	104	49	*128*	49	...	*18*	*31*
187	Mozambique	53.2	51.3	55.9	11-17	2 323	103	41	306	41	15	25	30
188	Namibia	*87.4[y]*	*86.1[y]*	*88.6[y]*	13-17	263	116	53	148	53	5	.	.
189	Niger	58.7	62.5	52.8	13-19	2 079	105	38	182	39	11	5	39
190	Nigeria	...	...	...	12-17	18 681	3 845	47	6 398	45	...	−	−
191	Rwanda	...	...	...	13-18	1 432	105	51	*204*	48	44[y]	73	48
192	Sao Tome and Principe	55.9	56.6	55.2	13-17	18	...	...	8	51	−	0.1	18
193	Senegal	*49.1*	*51.7*	*46.2*	13-19	1 903	237	39	406	42	23	5	40
194	Seychelles[3]	94.9[y]	92.5[y]	97.3[y]	12-16	...	8	50	8	48	4[y]	.	.
195	Sierra Leone	...	...	...	12-17	711	...	...	...	...	...	...	...
196	Somalia	...	...	...	13-17	852	...	...	...	...	...	...	...
197	South Africa	89.7[y]	88.5[y]	90.9[y]	14-18	4 932	4 239	53	4 593[z]	52[z]	3[z]	276[z]	40[z]
198	Swaziland	89.6[y]	90.8[y]	88.5[y]	13-17	151	62	50	68[z]	49[z]	−[z]	...	...
199	Togo	66.6	69.5	62.5	12-18	988	232	29	*399*	34	28	22	18
200	Uganda	*37.4*	*37.1*	*37.8*	13-18	4 074	*318*	40	*760*	44	45[z]	32	32
201	United Republic of Tanzania	**46.1**	**47.0**	**45.2**	14-19	5 403	*271*	45	...	...	...	...	...
202	Zambia	55.3	54.1	56.8	14-18	1 445	237	43	*409*	45	4[z]	8	8
203	Zimbabwe	*69.7[x]*	*69.3[x]*	*70.2[x]*	13-18	2 105	835	47	*758[y]*	48[y]	...	.[y]	.[y]

		Median				Sum	Sum	% F	Sum	% F	Median	Sum	% F
I	World	91.8	91.3	92.4	...	775 474	438 570	47	511 936	47	11	51 100	45
II	Countries in transition	99.0	99.3	99.4	...	31 053	32 000	49	28 127	48	0.5	2 943	37
III	Developed countries	99.3	...	...	...	83 730	84 659	49	85 280	49	8	14 738	44
IV	Developing countries	87.5	87.7	87.1	...	660 691	321 911	46	398 529	47	15	33 419	46
V	Arab States	92.0	89.4	93.3	...	41 453	22 682	46	28 275	47	7	3 592	42
VI	Central and Eastern Europe	99.0	98.8	99.2	...	39 033	39 608	48	34 880	48	1	6 626	40
VII	Central Asia	98.9	98.3	99.0	...	11 899	9 688	49	10 679	48	1	593	41
VIII	East Asia and the Pacific	87.5	85.5	83.8	...	218 312	133 794	47	161 333	48	19	19 789	49
IX	East Asia	85.1	84.7	85.4	...	214 965	130 486	47	157 828	48	14	18 661	49
X	Pacific	87.5	89.4	83.8	...	3 347	3 308	49	3 505	48	27	1 127	44
XI	Latin America/Caribbean	93.7	94.7	92.6	...	66 788	52 953	51	58 504	51	22	5 962	53
XII	Caribbean	95.3	96.8	93.8	...	2 187	1 151	50	1 273	50	22	43	48
XIII	Latin America	93.7	94.7	92.6	...	64 601	51 802	51	57 231	51	22	5 919	53
XIV	N. America/W. Europe	99.6	99.3	100.0	...	61 977	60 679	49	63 205	49	10	9 559	44
XV	South and West Asia	85.1	86.5	83.4	...	231 272	97 783	41	121 870	44	18	2 915	23
XVI	Sub-Saharan Africa	63.2	63.0	58.0	...	104 741	21 381	45	33 190	44	12	2 063	40

1. Refers to lower and upper secondary education (ISCED levels 2 and 3).
2. Data are for 2004 except for countries with a calendar school year, in which case data are for 2005.
3. National population data were used to calculate enrolment ratios.

4. Enrolment and population data exclude Transnistria.
5. Enrolment data for upper secondary education include adult education (students over age 25), particularly in pre-vocational/vocational programmes, in which males are in the majority. This explains the high level of GER and the relatively low GPI.
6. For the first time, data include French overseas departments and territories (DOM-TOM).

GROSS ENROLMENT RATIO (GER) IN SECONDARY EDUCATION (%)																				NET ENROLMENT RATIO (NER) IN SECONDARY EDUCATION (%)				
Lower secondary				Upper secondary				Total secondary												Total secondary				
School year ending in 2005				School year ending in 2005				School year ending in												School year ending in 2005				
								1999								2005								
Total	Male	Female	GPI (F/M)	Total	Male	Female	GPI (F/M)	Total	Male	Female	GPI (F/M)	Total	Male	Female	GPI (F/M)					Total	Male	Female	GPI (F/M)	
19	28	10	0.35	10	16	4	0.26	10	16	4	0.26	16	23	8	0.33					11y	16y	5y	0.33y	167
41	47	35	0.75	27	30	24	0.78	25	28	22	0.81	35	40	30	0.76					…	…	…	…	168
50z	53z	47z	0.88z	21z	25z	17z	0.69z	…	…	…	…	39z	42z	35z	0.84z					…	…	…	…	169
…	…	…	…	…	…	…	…	22	28	15	0.54	…	…	…	…					…	…	…	…	170
30y	37y	23y	0.63y	18y	23y	12y	0.54y	18	24	12	0.52	22y	28y	16y	0.58y					…	…	…	…	171
…	…	…	…	…	…	…	…	31	45	17	0.37	…	…	…	…					…	…	…	…	172
44	54	34	0.64	21	27	14	0.52	24	28	19	0.68	31	40	23	0.59					25	30	20	0.67	173
49	**56**	**41**	**0.73**	**19**	**24**	**14**	**0.58**	15	19	12	0.62	**35**	**41**	**28**	**0.69**					**32**	**38**	**26**	**0.70**	174
…	…	…	…	…	…	…	…	45	49	42	0.86	…	…	…	…					…	…	…	…	175
59z	63z	56z	0.90z	33z	39z	27z	0.69z	33	40	26	0.65	47z	51z	42z	0.82z					45z	49z	41z	0.83z	176
65	**68**	**61**	**0.91**	**24**	**27**	**22**	**0.81**	37	41	33	0.80	**45**	**48**	**42**	**0.88**					**38**	**40**	**36**	**0.91**	177
37	48	26	0.54	21	27	14	0.52	15	21	8	0.37	30	39	21	0.53					24	31	17	0.55	178
…	…	…	…	…	…	…	…	…	…	…	…	…	…	…	…					…	…	…	…	179
91	92	91	0.99	28	29	26	0.90	38	39	37	0.96	49	50	48	0.95					42	42	42	1.01	180
48	42	54	1.31	25	23	27	1.15	30	26	35	1.35	39	34	43	1.26					25	19	30	1.56	181
…	…	…	…	…	…	…	…	29	35	23	0.65	…	…	…	…					…	…	…	…	182
28	28	28	0.98	…	…	…	…	14	14	14	0.96	…	…	…	…					…	…	…	…	183
40	43	36	0.85	15	18	13	0.73	37	43	30	0.70	28	31	25	0.81					24	25	22	0.88	184
33	40	26	0.64	13	16	10	0.58	14	18	10	0.54	24	29	18	0.62					…	…	…	…	185
99	98	100	1.02	80	81	78	0.96	76	76	75	0.98	88	89	88	0.99					82	81	82	1.02	186
19	22	15	0.70	4	5	3	0.62	5	6	4	0.69	13	16	11	0.69					7	8	6	0.79	187
72	67	78	1.17	29	28	30	1.07	57	54	61	1.13	56	52	60	1.15					39	33	44	1.34	188
12	14	10	0.69	4	4	3	0.63	6	7	5	0.65	9	10	7	0.68					8	9	6	0.71	189
37	40	34	0.87	31	34	28	0.81	24	25	23	0.91	34	37	31	0.84					27	29	25	0.87	190
18	19	17	0.89	10	11	10	0.89	10	10	10	1.00	14	15	13	0.89					…	…	…	…	191
71	66	75	1.14	27	27	27	0.98	…	…	…	…	44	43	46	1.08					32	30	34	1.11	192
28	31	24	0.78	12	15	10	0.67	15	18	12	0.64	21	24	18	0.75					17	19	15	0.75	193
101	102	100	0.98	112	111	113	1.01	113	111	115	1.04	105	106	105	0.99					97	94	100	1.06	194
…	…	…	…	…	…	…	…	…	…	…	…	…	…	…	…					…	…	…	…	195
…	…	…	…	…	…	…	…	…	…	…	…	…	…	…	…					…	…	…	…	196
97z	94z	99z	1.06z	91z	87z	95z	1.09z	88	82	93	1.13	93z	90z	97z	1.07z					…	…	…	…	197
53z	53z	54z	1.02z	32z	35z	30z	0.84z	45	45	45	1.00	45z	46z	44z	0.97z					33z	31z	35z	1.13z	198
54	69	39	0.57	20	31	10	0.31	28	40	16	0.40	40	54	27	0.51					…	…	…	…	199
22	24	20	0.84	10	12	8	0.68	10	11	8	0.66	19	21	17	0.81					15	16	14	0.90	200
…	…	…	…	…	…	…	…	6	6	5	0.82	…	…	…	…					…	…	…	…	201
44	47	41	0.87	17	20	15	0.73	20	22	17	0.77	28	31	25	0.82					26	29	23	0.80	202
55y	56y	53y	0.95y	27y	29y	25y	0.86y	43	45	40	0.88	36y	38y	35y	0.91y					34y	35y	33y	0.93y	203
Weighted average																				Weighted average				
79	81	76	0.94	53	54	51	0.94	60	63	57	0.91	66	68	64	0.94					59	60	57	0.95	I
91	92	90	0.98	89	92	87	0.95	91	91	91	0.99	91	92	89	0.97					82	83	81	0.98	II
104	105	104	0.99	99	98	100	1.02	100	100	100	1.00	102	102	102	1.00					92	91	93	1.02	III
75	77	72	0.93	46	48	44	0.92	53	56	49	0.88	60	63	58	0.93					53	55	51	0.93	IV
81	86	76	0.89	54	55	53	0.96	60	63	56	0.89	68	71	65	0.92					59	61	58	0.94	V
91	93	90	0.96	87	89	84	0.95	87	89	86	0.97	89	91	87	0.96					81	82	80	0.98	VI
95	97	94	0.98	76	80	73	0.91	86	88	85	0.97	90	92	88	0.96					84	86	83	0.97	VII
93	93	93	1.00	55	54	55	1.01	64	66	63	0.96	74	74	74	1.00					70	70	70	1.00	VIII
93	93	93	1.00	54	53	54	1.01	64	65	62	0.96	73	73	74	1.00					70	70	70	1.00	IX
89	90	89	0.99	132	134	130	0.96	107	106	107	1.01	105	106	103	0.98					69	69	69	1.01	X
100	98	102	1.05	73	68	77	1.13	80	77	83	1.07	88	84	91	1.08					68	66	70	1.07	XI
75	75	75	1.01	43	42	43	1.04	54	53	55	1.03	58	57	59	1.02					42	40	43	1.07	XII
101	99	103	1.05	74	69	79	1.13	81	78	84	1.07	89	85	92	1.08					69	67	71	1.07	XIII
105	106	104	0.99	99	97	100	1.03	101	101	100	0.99	102	102	102	1.01					92	91	92	1.02	XIV
66	70	61	0.86	41	46	36	0.78	46	53	39	0.74	53	57	48	0.83					46	51	42	0.83	XV
38	43	34	0.80	24	27	21	0.78	24	26	21	0.82	32	35	28	0.79					25	28	23	0.82	XVI

7. Enrolment ratios were not calculated due to lack of United Nations population data by age.
8. Enrolment ratios were not calculated due to inconsistencies between enrolment and the United Nations population data.
Data in italic are UIS estimates.
Data in bold are for the school year ending in 2006.

(z) Data are for the school year ending in 2004.
(y) Data are for the school year ending in 2003.
(x) Data are for the school year ending in 2002.
(∗) National estimates.

8
0
0
2

Education for All Global Monitoring Report

Table 9A
Participation in tertiary education

	ENROLMENT IN TERTIARY EDUCATION												
	Total students enrolled				Gross enrolment ratio (GER) (%)							
	School year ending in				School year ending in							
	1999		2005		1999				2005			
Country or territory	Total (000)	% F	Total (000)	% F	Total	Male	Female	GPI (F/M)	Total	Male	Female	GPI (F/M)
Arab States												
Algeria	456	…	755	57	14	…	…	…	20	17	24	1.37
Bahrain	11	60	19	68	21	16	27	1.76	36	22	50	2.23
Djibouti	0.2	51	2	42	0.3	0.3	0.3	1.05	2	3	2	0.73
Egypt	2447	…	2594	…	36	…	…	…	34	…	…	…
Iraq	272	34	425ᶻ	36ᶻ	11	15	8	0.54	15ᶻ	19ᶻ	11ᶻ	0.59ᶻ
Jordan	…	…	218	50	…	…	…	…	39	38	40	1.06
Kuwait	32	68	35	66	23	14	34	2.39	18	11	25	2.19
Lebanon	113	50	166	53	36	36	37	1.04	51	47	54	1.15
Libyan Arab Jamahiriya	308	49	375ʸ	51ʸ	53	53	52	0.98	56ʸ	54ʸ	59ʸ	1.09ʸ
Mauritania	13	…	9	25	5	…	…	…	3	5	2	0.33
Morocco	273	42	367	45	9	10	8	0.74	11	12	10	0.85
Oman	…	…	48	51	…	…	…	…	18	18	19	1.09
Palestinian A. T.	66	46	127	50	25	26	23	0.89	38	37	39	1.04
Qatar	9	72	10	68	25	13	41	3.23	19	10	33	3.45
Saudi Arabia	350	57	604	58	20	17	24	1.38	28	23	34	1.47
Sudan	201	47	…	…	6	6	6	0.92	…	…	…	…
Syrian Arab Republic	…	…	…	…	…	…	…	…	…	…	…	…
Tunisia	157	48	315	57	17	17	17	0.97	30	26	35	1.37
United Arab Emirates	40	67	68ʸ	66ʸ	19	10	31	3.03	22ʸ	12ʸ	39ʸ	3.24ʸ
Yemen	164	21	201	26	10	16	4	0.28	9	14	5	0.37
Central and Eastern Europe												
Albania	39	60	53ᶻ	62ᶻ	16	13	18	1.40	19ᶻ	15ᶻ	23ᶻ	1.57ᶻ
Belarus	387	56	529	57	52	45	59	1.32	62	53	72	1.37
Bosnia and Herzegovina	…	…	…	…	…	…	…	…	…	…	…	…
Bulgaria	270	59	238	52	46	36	56	1.54	44	41	47	1.14
Croatia	96	53	122ʸ	53ʸ	31	28	33	1.16	39ʸ	35ʸ	42ʸ	1.19ʸ
Czech Republic	231	50	336	53	26	26	27	1.03	48	44	52	1.16
Estonia	49	58	68	62	51	42	60	1.42	66	50	82	1.66
Hungary	279	54	436	58	33	30	37	1.24	65	53	78	1.46
Latvia	82	62	131	63	50	38	62	1.64	74	54	96	1.79
Lithuania	107	60	195	60	44	35	53	1.52	76	59	93	1.57
Poland	1399	57	2118	58	44	37	52	1.38	63	53	74	1.41
Republic of Moldova[2, 3]	104	56	119	59	33	29	38	1.30	34	27	41	1.48
Romania	408	51	739	55	22	21	23	1.09	45	40	50	1.26
Russian Federation	…	…	9020	57	…	…	…	…	71	60	82	1.36
Serbia and Montenegro[2]	197	54	…	…	34	31	37	1.19	…	…	…	…
Slovakia	123	52	181	55	26	25	28	1.11	41	36	46	1.29
Slovenia	79	56	112	58	53	45	61	1.36	81	67	96	1.43
TFYR Macedonia	35	55	49	57	22	19	24	1.28	30	25	35	1.38
Turkey	1465	40	2106	42	22	25	17	0.68	31	36	26	0.74
Ukraine	1737	53	2605	54	47	44	51	1.14	69	63	75	1.20
Central Asia												
Armenia	61	54	87	55	24	22	25	1.11	28	25	31	1.22
Azerbaijan	108	39	129	47	15	19	12	0.64	15	16	14	0.90
Georgia	130	52	174	50	36	35	37	1.07	46	45	47	1.04
Kazakhstan	324	53	753	58	25	23	26	1.16	53	44	62	1.42
Kyrgyzstan	131	51	220	55	29	28	30	1.04	41	37	46	1.25
Mongolia	65	65	124	61	26	18	34	1.88	43	33	54	1.62
Tajikistan	76	25	119	26	14	20	7	0.35	17	26	9	0.35
Turkmenistan	…	…	…	…	…	…	…	…	…	…	…	…
Uzbekistan	…	…	408ᶻ	44ᶻ	…	…	…	…	15ᶻ	17ᶻ	14ᶻ	0.80ᶻ
East Asia and the Pacific												
Australia	846	54	1015	54	66	59	72	1.22	72	64	80	1.25
Brunei Darussalam	3.7	66	5	67	12	8	16	1.97	15	10	20	2.02
Cambodia	…	…	57	31	…	…	…	…	3	5	2	0.46
China	6366	…	**23361**	**47**	6	…	…	…	**22**	**22**	**21**	**0.97**
Cook Islands	.	.	.	.	.	.	.	.	.	.	.	.

DISTRIBUTION OF STUDENTS BY ISCED LEVEL (%)						FOREIGN STUDENTS				
Total students			Percentage of females at each level			School year ending in				
School year ending in 1999			School year ending in 2005			1999		2005		
Level 5A	Level 5B	Level 6	Level 5A	Level 5B	Level 6	Total (000)	% F	Total (000)	% F	Country or territory
										Arab States
77	*19*	4	*64*	*30*	44	...	...	5^z	...	Algeria
92	8	0	69	52	30	...	...	0.8	43	Bahrain
69	31	.	39	48	.	–	–	–	–	Djibouti
...	...	...	...	...	...	...	...	...	...	Egypt
78	*17*	5	*39*	*22*	35	...	...	4^z	19^z	Iraq
88	11	1	49	61	28	...	...	21	27	Jordan
98	.	2	66	.	51	...	...	...	...	Kuwait
84	15	1	54	47	35	16	...	14	53	Lebanon
72^y	*26^y*	*2^y*	*52^y*	*50^y*	*38^y*	...	...	...	...	Libyan Arab Jamahiriya
96	4	.	25	13	.	...	...	0.2^z	...	Mauritania
77	17	5	46	45	32	4.2	16	5	29	Morocco
79	*20*	*1*	*54*	*41*	*22*	...	...	...	...	Oman
90	10	.	*50*	*49*	.	3	29	–^z	–^z	Palestinian A. T.
97	*3*	1	*68*	*87*	39	...	...	2	61	Qatar
84	14	2	65	21	40	6	25	13	33	Saudi Arabia
...	...	...	...	...	...	...	...	...	...	Sudan
...	...	...	...	...	...	...	...	...	...	Syrian Arab Republic
...	...	...	...	...	...	2.7^j	...	2.3^z	...	Tunisia
...	...	...	...	...	...	...	...	...	...	United Arab Emirates
...	...	0	...	...	31	...	...	...	...	Yemen
										Central and Eastern Europe
99^z	1^z	./.^{1,z}	62^z	73^z	./.^{1,z}	0.8	27	0.5^z	25^z	Albania
69	30	1	58	55	53	3	...	4	...	Belarus
...	...	...	...	...	...	...	...	...	...	Bosnia and Herzegovina
90	8	2	52	55	50	8	42	9	41	Bulgaria
66^y	34^y	0^y	55^y	50^y	36^y	0.5^j	...	3^y	46^y	Croatia
83	10	7	52	68	37	5	*41*	19	...	Czech Republic
62	36	3	62	62	53	0.8	58	1.1	56	Estonia
93	5	2	58	64	45	9^j	54	14	46	Hungary
86	13	1	64	59	58	2^j	...	1.7	...	Latvia
70	29	1	60	60	57	0.5	22	0.9	48	Lithuania
97	1	2	57	81	48	6^j	48	10	53	Poland
98	–	2	59	–	61	2	...	2.3	35	Republic of Moldova [2,3]
91	6	3	55	56	47	13	40	11	...	Romania
76	*22*	...	58	54	...	41	...	90	...	Russian Federation
...	...	...	...	...	...	1.3	37	...	...	Serbia and Montenegro [2]
92	3	6	56	64	41	...	...	1.6	45	Slovakia
50	49	1	61	55	46	0.7	40	1.1	...	Slovenia
94	6	–	57	50	–	0.3	43	0.3	49	TFYR Macedonia
69	29	1	43	39	40	18^v	28	18	29	Turkey
78	21	1	54	53	52	18	...	23	...	Ukraine
										Central Asia
98	.	2	56	.	36	...	...	4	44	Armenia
99	.	1	47	.	27	1.7	35	2.5	15	Azerbaijan
99	.	1	50	.	65	0.3	...	0.2	...	Georgia
99	.	1	58	.	55	8	...	9	...	Kazakhstan
99	.	1	55	.	62	1.1	*51*	24	61	Kyrgyzstan
94	5	1	62	59	61	0.3	50	0.8	34	Mongolia
99	.	1	26	.	29	5	*25*	1.0	40	Tajikistan
...	...	...	...	...	...	...	...	...	...	Turkmenistan
59^z	*40^z*	*1^z*	*39^z*	*51^z*	*39^z*	...	...	...	...	Uzbekistan
										East Asia and the Pacific
80	16	4	55	52	50	117	49	207	46	Australia
60	39	0	69	64	13	0.07	53	0.2	42	Brunei Darussalam
99	.	*1*	*32*	.	*27*	0.02	25	0.0^z	18^z	Cambodia
...	...	...	...	...	...	...	...	**36**	**45**	China
.	.	.	.	.	.	.	.	.^z	.^z	Cook Islands

Table 9A (continued)

Country or territory	ENROLMENT IN TERTIARY EDUCATION											
	Total students enrolled				Gross enrolment ratio (GER) (%)							
	School year ending in				School year ending in							
	1999		2005		1999				2005			
	Total (000)	% F	Total (000)	% F	Total	Male	Female	GPI (F/M)	Total	Male	Female	GPI (F/M)
DPR Korea	...	...	...	...	...	...	...	...	...	...	...	...
Fiji	...	...	13	53	...	...	...	...	15	14	17	1.20
Indonesia	...	...	3 640	44	...	...	...	...	17	19	15	0.79
Japan	3 941	45	4 038	46	45	49	41	0.85	55	59	52	0.89
Kiribati	.	.	.	.	.	.	.	.	.	.	.	.
Lao People's Democratic Republic	12	32	47	41	2	3	2	0.49	8	9	7	0.72
Macao, China	7	46	23	43	27	31	24	0.77	61	71	52	0.73
Malaysia	473	50	731ᶻ	55ᶻ	23	23	24	1.04	32ᶻ	28ᶻ	36ᶻ	1.31ᶻ
Marshall Islands	...	...	0.9ʸ	56ʸ	...	...	...	...	17ʸ	15ʸ	19ʸ	1.30ʸ
Micronesia (Federated States of)	2	...	...	...	14	...	...	...	...	...	...	...
Myanmar	335	61	...	...	7	5	9	1.60	...	...	...	...
Nauru	.	.	.	.	.	.	.	.	...	...	...	.
New Zealand	167	59	240	59	67	55	79	1.45	82	66	99	1.50
Niue	.	.	.	.	.	.	.	.	.	.	.	.
Palau	...	...	...	...	...	...	...	...	...	...	...	...
Papua New Guinea	10	35	...	...	2	3	1	0.55	...	...	...	...
Philippines	2 209	55	2 403	54	29	25	32	1.26	28	25	31	1.23
Republic of Korea	2 636	35	3 210	37	66	83	47	0.57	91	111	70	0.63
Samoa	1.9	47	...	...	12	11	12	1.04	...	...	...	...
Singapore	...	...	...	...	...	...	...	...	...	...	...	...
Solomon Islands	.	.	.	.	.	.	.	.	.	.	.	.
Thailand	1 814	53	2 339	51	32	30	35	1.16	43	42	44	1.06
Timor-Leste	...	...	...	...	...	...	...	...	...	...	...	...
Tokelau	.	.	.	.	.	.	.	.	...	...	...	...
Tonga	0.4	55	0.7ᶻ	60ᶻ	3	3	4	1.27	6ᶻ	5ᶻ	8ᶻ	1.67ᶻ
Tuvalu	.	.	.	.	.	.	.	.	.	.	.	.
Vanuatu	0.6	...	1.0ᶻ	36ᶻ	4	...	...	...	5ᶻ	6ᶻ	4ᶻ	0.58ᶻ
Viet Nam	810	43	1 355	41	11	12	9	0.76	16	19	13	0.71
Latin America and the Caribbean												
Anguilla	.	.	0.03	76	.	.	.	.	3	2	5	3.11
Antigua and Barbuda	.	.	.ᶻ	.ᶻ	.	.	.	.	.ᶻ	.ᶻ	.ᶻ	.ᶻ
Argentina	1 601	62	2 127ᶻ	58ᶻ	49	37	60	1.63	65ᶻ	54ᶻ	76ᶻ	1.41ᶻ
Aruba²	1.4	54	2.1	60	26	24	28	1.16	34	27*	40	1.49
Bahamas	.	.	.ᶻ	.ᶻ	.	.	.	.	.ᶻ	.ᶻ	.ᶻ	.ᶻ
Barbados	7	69	...	...	33	20	46	2.29	...	...	...	...
Belize	...	...	0.7ᶻ	70ᶻ	...	...	...	...	3ᶻ	2ᶻ	4ᶻ	2.43ᶻ
Bermuda	...	...	...	...	...	...	...	...	...	...	...	...
Bolivia	253	...	346ᶻ	...	33	...	...	...	41ᶻ	...	...	...
Brazil	2 457	56	4 275ᶻ	56ᶻ	14	13	16	1.26	24ᶻ	21ᶻ	27ᶻ	1.32ᶻ
British Virgin Islands²	0.9	70	1.2	69	60	36	86	2.40	75	46	106	2.28
Cayman Islands⁴	0.4	74	...	...	...	...	...	...	...	...	...	...
Chile	451	47	664	48	38	39	36	0.91	48	49	47	0.96
Colombia	878	52	1 224	51	22	21	23	1.11	29	28	31	1.09
Costa Rica	59	53	111	54	16	15	17	1.17	25	23	28	1.26
Cuba	153	53	472	62*	20	18	21	1.18	61	46*	78*	1.72*
Dominica	.	.	.	.	.	.	.	.	.	.	.	.
Dominican Republic	...	...	294ᶻ	61ᶻ	...	...	...	...	33ᶻ	25ᶻ	41ᶻ	1.64ᶻ
Ecuador	...	...	...	...	...	...	...	...	...	...	...	...
El Salvador	118	55	122	55	18	16	19	1.25	19	17	21	1.23
Grenada	.	.	.	.	.	.	.	.	.	.	.	.
Guatemala	...	...	115ʸ	43ʸ	...	...	...	...	10ʸ	11ʸ	8ʸ	0.72ʸ
Guyana	...	...	7	68	...	...	...	...	10	6	13	2.13
Haiti	...	...	...	...	...	...	...	...	...	...	...	...
Honduras	85	56	123ᶻ	59ᶻ	14	12	16	1.29	16ᶻ	13ᶻ	20ᶻ	1.46ᶻ
Jamaica	...	...	46ʸ	70ʸ	...	...	...	...	19ʸ	12ʸ	26ʸ	2.29ʸ
Mexico	1 838	48	2 385	50	18	19	17	0.92	24	24	24	0.99
Montserrat	.	.	.	.	.	.	.	.	.	.	.	.
Netherlands Antilles	2	53	...	...	23	22	25	1.13	...	...	...	...
Nicaragua	...	...	104ʸ	52ʸ	...	...	...	...	18ʸ	17ʸ	19ʸ	1.11ʸ
Panama	109	61	126	61	41	31	50	1.59	44	34	55	1.63
Paraguay	66	57	149ᶻ	57ᶻ	13	11	15	1.38	24ᶻ	21ᶻ	28ᶻ	1.34ᶻ

DISTRIBUTION OF STUDENTS BY ISCED LEVEL (%)						FOREIGN STUDENTS				
Total students			Percentage of females at each level							
School year ending in 1999			School year ending in 2005			School year ending in				
						1999		2005		
Level 5A	Level 5B	Level 6	Level 5A	Level 5B	Level 6	Total (000)	% F	Total (000)	% F	Country or territory
...	...	...	...	...	...	...	...	...	...	DPR Korea
86	12	1	52	63	43	...	...	4z	53z	Fiji
73	26	2	42	49	35	0.3	...	0.4z	...	Indonesia
74	24	2	41	62	29	57	43	126	49	Japan
.	.	.	.	.	.	.	.	.z	.z	Kiribati
45	55	.	42	41	.	0.08	14	0.2	28	Lao People's Democratic Republic
86	13	2	40	62	24	...	...	13	30	Macao, China
54z	45z	1z	58z	52z	38z	4	...	30y	...	Malaysia
14y	86y	.y	57y	56y	.y	...	...	...	...	Marshall Islands
...	...	...	...	...	...	...	...	...	...	Micronesia (Federated States of)
...	...	...	...	...	...	...	...	...	...	Myanmar
.	.	.	.	.	.	.	.	.z	.z	Nauru
73	25	2	59	58	52	7	51	41	50	New Zealand
.	.	.	.	.	.	.	.	.z	.z	Niue
...	...	...	...	...	...	...	...	...	...	Palau
...	...	...	...	...	...	0.3	32	...	...	Papua New Guinea
89	11	0	54	53	61	4	...	5	...	Philippines
61	38	1	37	37	33	3	38	15	47	Republic of Korea
...	...	...	...	...	...	0.1	39	...	...	Samoa
...	...	...	...	...	...	...	...	...	...	Singapore
.	.	.	.	.	.	.	.	.y	.y	Solomon Islands
83	17	0	52	48	54	2j	55	...	...	Thailand
...	...	...	...	...	...	...	...	...	...	Timor-Leste
.	.	.	.	.	.	.	.	.	.	Tokelau
30z	42z	28z	34z	95z	36z	...	...	...	...	Tonga
.	.	.	.	.	.	.	.	.z	.z	Tuvalu
...	...	...	...	...	...	.	.	...	...	Vanuatu
67	30	3	47	29	28	0.5	15	2.1	21	Viet Nam
										Latin America and the Caribbean
52	48	.	71	81	.	.	.	.z	.z	Anguilla
.z	.z	.z	.z	.z	.z	.	.	...	...	Antigua and Barbuda
74z	26z	0z	55z	67z	56z	...	...	...	...	Argentina
30	70	.	73	54	.	...	...	0.04	80	Aruba [2]
.z	.z	.z	.z	.z	.z	...	...	...	...	Bahamas
...	...	...	...	...	...	...	...	...	...	Barbados
100z	.z	.z	70z	.z	.z	...	...	—z	—z	Belize
.	100	.	...	...	...	...	...	...	...	Bermuda
...	...	...	...	...	...	...	...	...	...	Bolivia
94z	4z	3z	57z	35z	56z	...	...	1.2y	...	Brazil
67	33	.	75	56	.	.	.	.z	.z	British Virgin Islands [2]
...	...	...	...	...	.z	...	...	...	...	Cayman Islands [4]
67	33	0	52	40	39	1.5	...	2.0	...	Chile
75	25	0	57	35	41	...	...	...	...	Colombia
85z	13z	1z	56z	43z	58z	...	...	1.6z	...	Costa Rica
99	.	1	62*	.	44	...	...	14	...	Cuba
.	.	.	.	.	.	.	.	.z	.z	Dominica
91z	8z	1z	65z	25z	40z	...	...	...	...	Dominican Republic
...	...	...	...	...	...	...	...	...	...	Ecuador
88	12	0	55	54	13	...	...	0.5	...	El Salvador
.	.	.	.	.	.	...	...	.z	.z	Grenada
95y	5y	.y	42y	66y	.y	...	...	...	...	Guatemala
81	19	.	65	78	.	...	...	0.04	51	Guyana
...	...	...	...	...	...	...	...	...	...	Haiti
91z	9z	0z	58z	67z	33z	...	...	0.8y	35y	Honduras
37y	56y	7y	73y	68y	71y	0.6	...	...	...	Jamaica
96	3	1	51	42	40	2	...	...	...	Mexico
.	.	.	.	.	.	.	.	.z	.z	Montserrat
...	...	...	...	...	...	...	...	...	...	Netherlands Antilles
95y	5y	.y	52y	59y	.y	...	...	...	...	Nicaragua
89	11	0	62	55	57	...	...	...	...	Panama
87z	13z	...	55z	67z	...	...	...	...	...	Paraguay

319

Table 9A (continued)

Country or territory	ENROLMENT IN TERTIARY EDUCATION											
	Total students enrolled				Gross enrolment ratio (GER) (%)							
	School year ending in				School year ending in							
	1999		2005		1999				2005			
	Total (000)	% F	Total (000)	% F	Total	Male	Female	GPI (F/M)	Total	Male	Female	GPI (F/M)
Peru	...	...	908	50	...	...	...	...	33	33	34	1.03
Saint Kitts and Nevis	.	.	.	.	.	.	.	.	.	.	.	.
Saint Lucia	...	...	2.2	74	...	...	...	...	14	7	20	2.80
Saint Vincent and the Grenadines	.	.	.	.	.	.	.	.	.	.	.	.
Suriname	...	...	...	...	...	...	...	...	...	...	...	...
Trinidad and Tobago	7.6	57	*17*	*56*	6	5	7	1.38	*12*	*11*	*14*	*1.27*
Turks and Caicos Islands	.	.	.	.	.	.	.	.	.	.	.	.
Uruguay	*91*	*63*	*103ᶻ*	*66ᶻ*	*34*	*25*	*44*	*1.76*	*41ᶻ*	*27ᶻ*	*55ᶻ*	*2.03ᶻ*
Venezuela	...	...	1 050*,ᶻ		...	...	...	...	41*,ᶻ	...	...	...
North America and Western Europe												
Andorra[2]	...	...	0.3	51	...	...	...	...	8	8	9	1.06
Austria	253	50	244	54	54	52	55	1.04	50	46	55	1.20
Belgium	352	53	390	54	56	52	60	1.15	63	56	70	1.24
Canada	1 221	56	...	...	60	51	69	1.34	...	...	...	...
Cyprus[2]	11	56	20	52	21	19	23	1.25	33	31	35	1.13
Denmark	190	56	232	57	56	48	64	1.33	80	67	94	1.39
Finland	263	54	306	54	82	74	91	1.22	92	83	101	1.21
France[5]	2 012	54	2 187	55	52	47	58	1.24	56	49	64	1.29
Germany	...	...	...	...	...	...	...	...	...	...	...	...
Greece	388	50	647	51	47	45	49	1.11	89	83	95	1.14
Iceland	8	62	*15ᶻ*	*65ᶻ*	40	30	50	1.68	*68ᶻ*	*48ᶻ*	*88ᶻ*	*1.85ᶻ*
Ireland	151	54	187	55	45	41	49	1.20	59	52	67	1.27
Israel	247	58	311	56	48	40	57	1.44	58	50	66	1.34
Italy	1 797	55	2 015	57	47	41	53	1.28	66	56	76	1.36
Luxembourg	2.7	52	*3ᶻ*	*53ᶻ*	11	10	11	1.09	*12ᶻ*	*11ᶻ*	*13ᶻ*	*1.18ᶻ*
Malta	6	51	9	56	20	18	21	1.13	32	27	37	1.36
Monaco	.	.	.	.	.	.	.	.	.	.	.	.
Netherlands	470	49	565	51	50	50	50	1.01	61	58	63	1.08
Norway	187	57	214	60	66	56	78	1.40	80	63	97	1.54
Portugal	357	56	381	56	45	39	51	1.30	56	49	64	1.30
San Marino	...	...	...	...	...	...	...	...	...	...	...	...
Spain	1 787	53	1 809	54	55	50	60	1.18	67	60	74	1.22
Sweden	335	58	427	60	64	53	75	1.41	82	64	100	1.55
Switzerland	156	42	200	46	38	44	31	0.70	47	52	43	0.84
United Kingdom	2 081	53	2 288	57	60	56	64	1.15	60	50	70	1.39
United States	13 769	*56*	17 272	57	73	*63*	*83*	*1.31*	83	69	97	1.40
South and West Asia												
Afghanistan	...	...	*28ᶻ*	*20ᶻ*	...	...	...	...	*1ᶻ*	*2ᶻ*	*0.5ᶻ*	*0.28ᶻ*
Bangladesh	709	32	912	33	6	8	4	0.51	6	8	4	0.53
Bhutan[6]	*1.5*	*36*	...	...	...	...	...	...	...	...	...	...
India	...	...	11 777	40	...	...	...	...	11	13	9	0.70
Iran, Islamic Republic of	1 308	43	2 126	51	19	21	17	0.80	24	23	25	1.09
Maldives			*0.1ᶻ*	*70ᶻ*					*0.2ᶻ*	*0.1ᶻ*	*0.3ᶻ*	*2.37ᶻ*
Nepal	...	...	*147ᶻ*	*28ᶻ*	...	...	...	...	*6ᶻ*	*8ᶻ*	*3ᶻ*	*0.40ᶻ*
Pakistan	...	...	783	45	...	...	...	...	5	5	4	0.88
Sri Lanka	...	...	...	...	...	...	...	...	...	...	...	...
Sub-Saharan Africa												
Angola	8	39	*13ʸ*	*40ʸ*	0.6	0.7	0.5	0.63	*0.8ʸ*	*1.0ʸ*	*0.7ʸ*	*0.66ʸ*
Benin	16	21	...	...	3	4	1	0.26	...	...	...	...
Botswana	5.5	44	11	50	3	3	3	0.79	5	5	5	1.00
Burkina Faso	10	23	28	31	1.0	1.5	0.5	0.30	2	3	1	0.45
Burundi	5	30	*17*	*28*	1	1	1	0.41	*2*	*3*	*1*	*0.38*
Cameroon	67	...	100*	40*	5	...	...	...	6*	7*	5*	0.66*
Cape Verde	0.7	...	4	51	2	...	...	...	7	7	7	1.04
Central African Republic	6	16	6	...	2	3	1	0.18	2	...	...	...
Chad	...	...	*10*	*13*	...	...	...	...	1	2	0	0.14
Comoros	0.6	43	*2ᶻ*	*43ᶻ*	1	1	1	0.75	*2ᶻ*	*3ᶻ*	*2ᶻ*	*0.77ᶻ*
Congo	11	21	*12ʸ*	*16ʸ*	4	6	1	0.26	*4ʸ*	*6ʸ*	*1ʸ*	*0.19ʸ*
Côte d'Ivoire	97	26	...	...	6	10	3	0.36	...	...	...	...

DISTRIBUTION OF STUDENTS BY ISCED LEVEL (%)						FOREIGN STUDENTS				
Total students			Percentage of females at each level			School year ending in				
School year ending in 1999			School year ending in 2005			1999		2005		
Level 5A	Level 5B	Level 6	Level 5A	Level 5B	Level 6	Total (000)	% F	Total (000)	% F	Country or territory
58	42	...	45	57	...	...	...	...	...	Peru
.	.	.	.	.	.	.	.	.z	.z	Saint Kitts and Nevis
75	25	.	80	56	.	...	...	.z	.z	Saint Lucia
.	.	.	.	.	.	.	.	.	.	Saint Vincent and the Grenadines
...	...	...	...	...	...	...	...	...	...	Suriname
51	34	15	60	48	58	1.0	46	1.0z	55z	Trinidad and Tobago
.	.	.	.	.	.	.	.	.z	.z	Turks and Caicos Islands
73z	27z	...	60z	83z	...	0.9	...	...	...	Uruguay
61*,z	...	...	...	...	...	...	...	2z	...	Venezuela
										North America and Western Europe
27	73	.	60	48	.	...	...	0.0y	...	Andorra [2]
83	10	6	53	68	45	30	49	34z	52z	Austria
46	52	2	51	58	40	36	48	21	59	Belgium
...	...	...	...	...	...	40	44	...	...	Canada
21	77	1	76	46	50	2	39	5	...	Cyprus [2]
84	14	2	59	47	45	12	61	10	59	Denmark
93	0	7	54	32	51	5	41	8	45	Finland
72	24	4	55	56	48	131±	...	237	...	France [5]
...	...	...	48	60	...	178	46	205	51	Germany
61	35	3	53	49	43	...	...	16	55	Greece
95z	5z	0z	65z	49z	53z	0.2	72	0.5z	66z	Iceland
67	30	3	58	49	48	7eo	51	13	50	Ireland
80	17	3	57	54	52	...	...	...	...	Israel
97	1	2	57	60	51	23	50	45	57	Italy
60z	40z	1z	54z	52z	52z	1j	...	...	...	Luxembourg
85	14	1	56	57	30	0.3j	53	0.6	57	Malta
.	.	.	.	.	.	.	.	.z	.z	Monaco
99	.	1	51	.	41	14	46	26	55	Netherlands
97	1	2	60	57	43	9	53	13	44	Norway
94	1	5	56	56	56	...	...	17	50	Portugal
...	...	...	...	...	.	...	...	...	...	San Marino
82	14	4	54	51	51	33	51	18	55	Spain
91	4	5	61	50	48	24	45	20	...	Sweden
73	18	8	48	41	39	25	44	26	47	Switzerland
73	23	4	55	66	44	233	47	318	47	United Kingdom
77	21	2	57	60	51	452	42	590	...	United States
										South and West Asia
...	...	...	...	...	...	...	...	...	...	Afghanistan
91	9	0	35	20	28	...	...	0.7	...	Bangladesh
...	...	...	...	...	...	...	...	...	...	Bhutan [6]
100	–	0	39	–	41	...	...	8z	...	India
71	28	1	55	41	25	...	...	2	35	Iran, Islamic Republic of
.z	100z	.z	.z	70z	.z	.	.	–y	–y	Maldives
99z	.z	1z	28z	.z	23z	...	...	...	...	Nepal
97	2	1	46	29	28	...	...	0.4y	...	Pakistan
...	...	...	...	...	...	...	...	–y	–y	Sri Lanka
										Sub-Saharan Africa
100y	.y	–y	40y	.y	–y	...	...	...	...	Angola
...	...	...	...	...	...	...	...	...	...	Benin
94	6	–	52	16	–	...	...	0.7	...	Botswana
...	...	...	...	...	...	...	...	0.9	38	Burkina Faso
33	67	0	25	29	19	0.1	...	...	...	Burundi
...	...	...	...	...	...	...	...	1.6	...	Cameroon
100	.	0	51	.	63	...	...	...	...	Cape Verde
...	...	...	...	...	...	...	...	...	...	Central African Republic
...	...	...	...	...	...	...	...	...	...	Chad
68z	32z	.z	39z	52z	.z	.	.	...	...	Comoros
84y	15y	1y	16y	13y	31y	...	...	0.1z	...	Congo
...	...	...	...	...	...	...	...	...	...	Côte d'Ivoire

Table 9A (continued)

Country or territory	ENROLMENT IN TERTIARY EDUCATION											
	Total students enrolled				Gross enrolment ratio (GER) (%)							
	School year ending in				School year ending in							
	1999		2005		1999				2005			
	Total (000)	% F	Total (000)	% F	Total	Male	Female	GPI (F/M)	Total	Male	Female	GPI (F/M)
Democratic Rep. of the Congo	60	…	…	…	1	…	…	…	…	…	…	…
Equatorial Guinea	…	…	…	…	…	…	…	…	…	…	…	…
Eritrea	4	14	5ᶻ	13ᶻ	1.1	2.0	0.3	0.15	1ᶻ	2ᶻ	0ᶻ	0.15ᶻ
Ethiopia	52	19	191	24	0.9	1.4	0.3	0.23	3	4	1	0.32
Gabon	7.5	36	…	…	7	9	5	0.54	…	…	…	…
Gambia	1.2	23	1.5ᶻ	19ᶻ	1.1	1.7	0.5	0.29	1ᶻ	2ᶻ	0ᶻ	0.23ᶻ
Ghana	…	…	**110**	**34**	…	…	…	…	**5**	**6**	**3**	**0.53**
Guinea	…	…	24	19	…	…	…	…	3	5	1	0.24
Guinea-Bissau	0.5	16	…	…	0.4	0.7	0.1	0.18	…	…	…	…
Kenya	…	…	108ᶻ	37ᶻ	…	…	…	…	3ᶻ	4ᶻ	2ᶻ	0.60ᶻ
Lesotho	4	64	8	57	2	2	3	1.64	3	3	4	1.27
Liberia	21	19	…	…	8	13	3	0.24	…	…	…	…
Madagascar	31	46	45	47	2	2	2	0.84	3	3	2	0.89
Malawi	3.2	28	5ᶻ	35ᶻ	0.3	0.4	0.2	0.38	0.4ᶻ	0.5ᶻ	0.3ᶻ	0.54ᶻ
Mali	19	32	33	31	2	2	1	0.47	3	3	2	0.47
Mauritius	7.6	46	17	55	7	7	6	0.88	17	15	19	1.26
Mozambique	10	…	28	33	0.6	…	…	…	1	2	1	0.49
Namibia	…	…	12ᶻ	53ᶻ	…	…	…	…	6ᶻ	6ᶻ	7ᶻ	1.15ᶻ
Niger	…	…	11	30	…	…	…	…	1	1	1	0.45
Nigeria	699	43	1 290ᶻ	35ᶻ	7	7	6	0.78	10ᶻ	13ᶻ	7ᶻ	0.55ᶻ
Rwanda	6	…	26	39	0.9	…	…	…	3	3	2	0.62
Sao Tome and Principe	.	.	.	.	.	.	.	.	.	.	.	.
Senegal	29	…	59*	…	3	…	…	…	5*	…	…	…
Seychelles	.	.	.	.	.	.	.	.	.	.	.	.
Sierra Leone	…	…	…	…	…	…	…	…	…	…	…	…
Somalia	…	…	…	…	…	…	…	…	…	…	…	…
South Africa	633	54	735	55	14	13	15	1.17	15	14	17	1.22
Swaziland	5	48	6	52	5	5	4	0.86	4	4	5	1.06
Togo	15	17	…	…	3	5	1	0.21	…	…	…	…
Uganda	41	35	88ᶻ	38ᶻ	2	2	1	0.53	3ᶻ	4ᶻ	3ᶻ	0.62ᶻ
United Republic of Tanzania	19	21	51	32	0.6	1.0	0.3	0.27	1	2	1	0.48
Zambia	23	32	…	…	2	3	1	0.46	…	…	…	…
Zimbabwe	43	…	56ʸ	39ʸ	3	…	…	…	4ʸ	5ʸ	3ʸ	0.63ʸ

	Sum	%F	Sum	%F	Weighted average				Weighted average			
World	92 863	48	137 769	50	18	18	18	0.96	24	24	25	1.05
Countries in transition	9 272	54	14 208	56	41	37	45	1.20	56	50	64	1.29
Developed countries	36 365	53	43 411	55	55	50	60	1.19	66	58	74	1.28
Developing countries	47 225	43	80 150	46	11	12	10	0.78	17	18	16	0.91
Arab States	5 165	42	6 783	49	19	22	16	0.74	21	21	21	1.01
Central and Eastern Europe	12 960	53	19 414	55	39	36	43	1.19	57	51	63	1.25
Central Asia	1 279	48	2 060	51	19	20	18	0.92	27	26	28	1.08
East Asia and the Pacific	22 674	42	41 424	47	14	16	12	0.75	24	25	23	0.93
East Asia	21 629	41	40 128	46	13	15	11	0.73	23	24	22	0.92
Pacific	1 045	55	1 296	55	46	41	51	1.24	50	44	57	1.31
Latin America and the Caribbean	10 663	53	15 293	54	21	20	23	1.12	29	27	32	1.17
Caribbean	79	57	105	63	6	5	6	1.33	6	5	8	1.70
Latin America	10 583	53	15 189	54	22	21	23	1.12	30	28	32	1.17
North America and Western Europe	28 230	54	33 412	56	61	55	68	1.23	70	60	80	1.33
South and West Asia	9 758	37	15 842	41	8	9	6	0.63	11	12	9	0.74
Sub-Saharan Africa	2 133	40	3 540	38	4	4	3	0.68	5	6	4	0.62

1. Data are included in ISCED level 5A.
2. National population data were used to calculate enrolment ratios.
3. Enrolment and population data exclude Transnistria.

4. Enrolment ratios were not calculated due to lack of United Nations population data by age.
5. For the first time, data include French overseas departments and territories (DOM-TOM).
6. Enrolment ratios were not calculated due to inconsistencies between enrolment and the United Nations population data.

DISTRIBUTION OF STUDENTS BY ISCED LEVEL (%)						FOREIGN STUDENTS				
Total students			Percentage of females at each level							
School year ending in 1999			School year ending in 2005			School year ending in				
						1999		2005		
Level 5A	Level 5B	Level 6	Level 5A	Level 5B	Level 6	Total (000)	% F	Total (000)	% F	Country or territory
...	...	...	...	...	...	...	...	...	...	Democratic Rep. of the Congo
...	...	...	...	...	...	...	...	...	...	Equatorial Guinea
77z	23z	.z	12z	16z	.	0.1	16	...	...	Eritrea
98	.	2	25	.	9	...	...	...	...	Ethiopia
...	...	...	...	...	...	0.4	...	...	...	Gabon
100z	.z	.z	19z	.z	.z	...	...	—z	—z	Gambia
75	**25**	**0**	**34**	**32**	**17**	...	...	...	...	Ghana
...	...	...	...	...	...	...	...	*0.5*	*27*	Guinea
...	...	...	...	...	...	...	...	...	...	Guinea-Bissau
62z	33z	5z	35z	43z	36z	...	...	...	...	Kenya
51	49	.	58	56	.	1.0	46	0.1y	47y	Lesotho
...	...	...	...	...	...	...	...	...	...	Liberia
79	18	3	48	46	40	1.1	...	1.2	25	Madagascar
100z	.z	.z	35z	.z	.z	...	...	...	...	Malawi
95	*5*	.	*31*	*51*	.	1.2	...	...	...	Mali
51	48	1	51	61	38	...	...	0.08z	53z	Mauritius
100	.	.	33	.	.	...	...	...	...	Mozambique
61z	39z	0.1z	55z	51z	44z	...	...	1.0y	...	Namibia
65	35	...	21	46	...	...	...	*0.2*	*25*	Niger
58z	*41z*	*1z*	*26z*	*46z*	*39z*	...	...	...	...	Nigeria
65	*35*	.	*41*	*35*	.	0.1	...	...	...	Rwanda
.	.	.	.	.	.	.	.	.	.	Sao Tome and Principe
...	...	...	...	...	...	1.3	...	...	...	Senegal
.	.	.	.	.	.	.	.	.	.	Seychelles
...	...	...	...	...	...	...	...	...	...	Sierra Leone
...	...	...	...	...	...	...	...	...	...	Somalia
62	37	1	55	55	41	...	...	50	—	South Africa
100	.	.	52	.	.	0.1	...	...	...	Swaziland
...	...	...	...	...	...	0.5	33	...	...	Togo
62z	36z	2z	41z	35z	37z	...	...	...	...	Uganda
78	*17*	*6*	33	33	*27*	...	...	0.3z	20z	United Republic of Tanzania
...	...	...	...	...	...	...	...	...	...	Zambia
38y	*59y*	...	32y	44y	...	...	...	...	...	Zimbabwe

Median			Median			Sum	%F	Sum	%F	
82	16	2	54	50	39	...	...	...	...	World
98	.	2	55	.	62	...	...	...	...	Countries in transition
83	12	6	56	60	48	...	...	...	...	Developed countries
79	18	3	52	46	31	...	...	...	...	Developing countries
84	14	2	53	45	30	...	...	...	...	Arab States
84	11	4	57	68	51	...	...	...	...	Central and Eastern Europe
99	.	1	53	.	47	...	...	...	...	Central Asia
...	...	...	...	...	...	...	...	...	...	East Asia and the Pacific
73	26	2	42	49	29	...	...	...	...	East Asia
.	.	.	.	.	.	...	...	...	...	Pacific
70	30	...	56	55	...	...	...	...	...	Latin America and the Caribbean
.	.	.	.	.	.	...	...	...	...	Caribbean
88	12	0	56	55	...	...	...	...	...	Latin America
80	17	3	56	56	52	...	...	...	...	North America and Western Europe
94	5	1	37	10	34	...	...	...	...	South and West Asia
71	29	0	35	37	27	...	...	...	...	Sub-Saharan Africa

(eo) Full-time only.
(j) Data refer to ISCED levels 5A and 6 only.
(l) Data refer to ISCED level 5B only.
(v) Data do not include ISCED level 6.

± Partial data.
Data in italic are UIS estimates.
Data in bold are for the school year ending in 2006.

(z) Data are for the school year ending in 2004.
(y) Data are for the school year ending in 2003.
(*) National estimates.

Table 9B. Tertiary education: distribution of students by field of study and female share in each field, school year ending in 2005

Country or territory	Total enrolment (000)	% F	PERCENTAGE DISTRIBUTION BY FIELD OF STUDY Education	Humanities and arts	Social sciences, business and law	Science	Engineering, manufacturing and construction	Agriculture	Health and welfare	Services	Not known or unspecified
Arab States											
Algeria	755	57	1ᶻ	15ᶻ	38ᶻ	8ᶻ	10ᶻ	2ᶻ	7ᶻ	1ᶻ	18ᶻ
Bahrain	19	68	3	9	53	9	8	.	8	3	8
Djibouti	2	42	.	5	31	9	.	.	.	5	50
Egypt	2 594	…	…	…	…	…	…	…	…	…	100ᶻ
Iraq	425	36	20ᶻ	11ᶻ	21ᶻ	5ᶻ	19ᶻ	4ᶻ	8ᶻ	12ᶻ	—ᶻ
Jordan	218	50	20	16	26	11	12	2	11	0.3	3
Kuwait	35	66	26	27	15	11	7	.	5	.	9
Lebanon	166	53	3	18	42	12	12	0.4	9	3	0.4
Libyan Arab Jamahiriya	375ʸ	51ʸ	…	…	…	…	…	…	…	…	…
Mauritania	9	25	4	13	20	6	–	–	–	–	57
Morocco	367	45	2	20	51	17	5	1	4	1	0.0
Oman	48	51	30	8	20	11	9	0.2	3	–	18
Palestinian A. T.	127	50	28ᶻ	14ᶻ	33ᶻ	11ᶻ	7ᶻ	0.4ᶻ	6ᶻ	—ᶻ	0.0ᶻ
Qatar	10	68	13ᶻ	6ᶻ	48ᶻ	14ᶻ	5ᶻ	0.2ᶻ	4ᶻ	—ᶻ	9ᶻ
Saudi Arabia	604	58	24	32	15	14	3	0.4	5	0.1	6
Sudan	…	…	…	…	…	…	…	…	…	…	…
Syrian Arab Republic	…	…	…	…	…	…	…	…	…	…	…
Tunisia	315	57	1	21	31	15	10	3	8	0.5	12
United Arab Emirates	68ʸ	66ʸ	…	…	…	…	…	…	…	…	…
Yemen	201	26	…	…	…	…	…	…	…	…	…
Central and Eastern Europe											
Albania	53ᶻ	62ᶻ	33ʸ	10ʸ	32ʸ	3ʸ	9ʸ	3ʸ	9ʸ	2ʸ	—ʸ
Belarus	529	57	13	5	39	2	25	8	4	3	–
Bosnia and Herzegovina	…	…	…	…	…	…	…	…	…	…	…
Bulgaria	238	52	7	8	42	5	21	2	6	7	0.2
Croatia	122ʸ	53ʸ	5ʸ	10ʸ	35ʸ	7ʸ	17ʸ	4ʸ	8ʸ	15ʸ	—ʸ
Czech Republic	336	53	15	10	28	9	20	4	10	4	0.5
Estonia	68	62	8	11	38	10	12	3	9	9	–
Hungary	436	58	13	8	43	5	12	3	8	8	–
Latvia	131	63	14	7	55	5	9	1	5	4	–
Lithuania	195	60	13	7	41	6	19	2	9	3	–
Poland	2 118	58	13	9	40	8	12	2	4	7	6
Republic of Moldova	119	59	…	…	…	…	…	…	…	…	…
Romania	739	55	2	11	47	5	20	3	6	3	3
Russian Federation	9 020	57	…	…	…	…	…	…	…	…	100ᶻ
Serbia and Montenegro	…	…	…	…	…	…	…	…	…	…	…
Slovakia	181	55	16	6	28	9	17	3	14	7	–
Slovenia	112	58	9	8	44	5	16	3	7	8	–
TFYR Macedonia	49	57	13	11	33	7	18	4	9	4	–
Turkey	2 106	42	12	5	18	7	14	3	5	3	33
Ukraine	2 605	54	9	5	42	4	22	5	5	6	2
Central Asia											
Armenia	87	55	18	4	35	–	7	2	8	2	24
Azerbaijan	129	47	…	…	…	…	…	…	…	…	…
Georgia	174	50	6	33	22	5	18	3	8	3	0.03
Kazakhstan	753	58	…	…	…	…	…	…	…	…	…
Kyrgyzstan	220	55	25	7	40	7	10	1	3	7	–
Mongolia	124	61	10	13	38	7	16	3	8	5	0.4
Tajikistan	119	26	…	…	…	…	…	…	…	…	…
Turkmenistan	…	…	…	…	…	…	…	…	…	…	…
Uzbekistan	408ᶻ	44ᶻ	…	…	…	…	…	…	…	…	…
East Asia and the Pacific											
Australia	1 015	54	9	12	38	12	11	1	15	3	0.04
Brunei Darussalam	5	67	53	10	14	6	4	–	9	–	4
Cambodia	57	31	1ᶻ	14ᶻ	52ᶻ	16ᶻ	2ᶻ	4ᶻ	3ᶻ	5ᶻ	2ᶻ
China	**23 361**	**47**	…	…	…	…	…	…	…	…	**100**
Cook Islands	.	.	…	…	…	…	…	…	…	…	…
DPR Korea	…	…	…	…	…	…	…	…	…	…	…

		PERCENTAGE FEMALE IN EACH FIELD							
Education	Humanities and arts	Social sciences, business and law	Science	Engineering, manufacturing and construction	Agriculture	Health and welfare	Services	Not known or unspecified	Country or territory
									Arab States
70[z]	73[z]	57[z]	54[z]	31[z]	48[z]	57[z]	15[z]	27[z]	Algeria
57	87	68	75	23	.	85	71	74	Bahrain
.	55	53	8	.	.	.	57	38	Djibouti
…	…	…	…	…	…	…	…	…	Egypt
50[z]	38[z]	33[z]	51[z]	19[z]	30[z]	41[z]	37[z]	–[z]	Iraq
77	65	39	38	25	54	46	58	57	Jordan
81	64	69	60	50	.	74	.	38	Kuwait
92	64	54	46	20	52	67	35	72	Lebanon
…	…	…	…	…	…	…	…	…	Libyan Arab Jamahiriya
17	24	26	21	–	–	–	–	25	Mauritania
51	52	46	36	24	30	66	43	36	Morocco
69	*60*	*41*	*53*	*20*	*25*	*67*	*–*	*40*	Oman
64[z]	64[z]	34[z]	50[z]	31[z]	18[z]	57[z]	–[z]	32[z]	Palestinian A. T.
89[z]	73[z]	65[z]	75[z]	16[z]	–[z]	100[z]	–[z]	94[z]	Qatar
71	64	43	60	15	0	44	270	45	Saudi Arabia
…	…	…	…	…	…	…	…	…	Sudan
…	…	…	…	…	…	…	…	…	Syrian Arab Republic
…	…	…	…	…	…	…	…	…	Tunisia
…	…	…	…	…	…	…	…	…	United Arab Emirates
…	…	…	…	…	…	…	…	…	Yemen
									Central and Eastern Europe
77[y]	72[y]	56[y]	63[y]	26[y]	48[y]	65[y]	50[y]	–[y]	Albania
77	75	70	51	29	29	81	38	–	Belarus
…	…	…	…	…	…	…	…	…	Bosnia and Herzegovina
66	60	58	49	32	43	65	47	49	Bulgaria
92[y]	71[y]	65[y]	46[y]	25[y]	43[y]	72[y]	29[y]	–[y]	Croatia
74	63	60	36	21	54	75	38	11	Czech Republic
89	76	65	39	27	52	89	50	–	Estonia
73	66	65	33	19	46	77	58	–	Hungary
86	78	66	30	21	46	87	49	–	Latvia
78	73	68	35	26	47	84	45	–	Lithuania
72	69	62	33	26	55	76	50	71	Poland
…	…	…	…	…	…	…	…	…	Republic of Moldova
77	67	62	56	29	35	65	48	44	Romania
…	…	…	…	…	…	…	…	57[z]	Russian Federation
…	…	…	…	…	…	…	…	…	Serbia and Montenegro
74	56	61	33	28	38	81	40	–	Slovakia
80	73	65	32	24	55	80	45	–	Slovenia
74	68	60	55	32	34	74	38	–	TFYR Macedonia
49	56	46	40	18	36	61	27	44	Turkey
…	…	…	…	…	…	…	…	…	Ukraine
									Central Asia
76	65	51	–	26	25	63	11	59	Armenia
…	…	…	…	…	…	…	…	…	Azerbaijan
61	63	39	69	33	29	75	11	46	Georgia
…	…	…	…	…	…	…	…	…	Kazakhstan
82	61	51	54	29	20	50	19	–	Kyrgyzstan
77	72	65	47	41	60	81	34	67	Mongolia
…	…	…	…	…	…	…	…	…	Tajikistan
…	…	…	…	…	…	…	…	…	Turkmenistan
…	…	…	…	…	…	…	…	…	Uzbekistan
									East Asia and the Pacific
74	64	55	34	21	51	76	53	68	Australia
70	56	63	57	39	–	79	–	76	Brunei Darussalam
26[z]	33[z]	37[z]	14[z]	4[z]	17[z]	36[z]	44[z]	34[z]	Cambodia
…	…	…	…	…	…	…	…	**47**	China
…	…	…	…	…	…	…	…	…	Cook Islands
…	…	…	…	…	…	…	…	…	DPR Korea

Table 9B (continued)

Country or territory	Total enrolment (000)	Total enrolment % F	PERCENTAGE DISTRIBUTION BY FIELD OF STUDY Education	Humanities and arts	Social sciences, business and law	Science	Engineering, manufacturing and construction	Agriculture	Health and welfare	Services	Not known or unspecified
Saint Lucia	2	74	…	…	…	…	…	…	…	…	…
St Vincent/Grenad.	.	.	…	…	…	…	…	…	…	…	…
Suriname	…	…	…	…	…	…	…	…	…	…	…
Trinidad and Tobago	17	56	5[z]	8[z]	27[z]	14[z]	23[z]	4[z]	10[z]	4[z]	5.9[z]
Turks and Caicos Islands	.	.	.[z]	.[z]	.[z]	.[z]	.[z]	.[z]	.[z]	.[z]	.[z]
Uruguay	103[z]	66[z]	…	…	…	…	…	…	…	…	…
Venezuela	1 050*,[z]	…	…	…	…	…	…	…	…	…	…
North America and Western Europe											
Andorra	0.3	51	2	3	53	27	–	–	15	–	–
Austria	244	54	13	14	36	12	12	2	9	2	0.04
Belgium	390	54	13	10	32	6	10	3	17	1	8
Canada	…	…	…	…	…	…	…	…	…	…	…
Cyprus	20	52	10	9	44	13	5	0.1	5	14	1
Denmark	232	57	11	15	30	8	10	1	22	2	–
Finland	306	54	5	14	22	12	26	2	13	5	–
France[1]	2 187	55	…	…	…	…	…	…	…	…	100
Germany	…	…	…	…	…	…	…	…	…	…	…
Greece	647	51	7	12	32	16	16	6	7	5	–
Iceland	15[z]	65[z]	19[z]	15[z]	36[z]	9[z]	7[z]	1[z]	12[z]	2[z]	–[z]
Ireland	187	55	5	17	22	12	10	1	11	4	17
Israel	311	56	16	11	37	10	18	0.5	7	.	1
Italy	2 015	57	7	16	37	8	16	2	12	2	0.3
Luxembourg	3[z]	53[z]	…	…	…	…	…	…	…	…	…
Malta	9	56	16	13	42	6	8	0.8	15	0.2	–
Monaco	.	.	.[z]	.[z]	.[z]	.[z]	.[z]	.[z]	.[z]	.[z]	.[z]
Netherlands	565	51	15	8	40	8	8	2	16	3	2
Norway	214	60	15	11	32	9	7	1	19	4	2
Portugal	381	56	9	9	31	8	22	2	14	5	–
San Marino	…	…	…	…	…	…	…	…	…	…	…
Spain	1 809	54	9	10	32	12	18	2	11	5	0.3
Sweden	427	60	15	13	26	9	16	1	17	2	0.2
Switzerland	200	46	10	13	38	11	13	1	10	4	0.4
United Kingdom	2 288	57	9	17	27	14	8	1	19	1	5
United States	17 272	57	9	11	27	9	7	1	14	5	18
South and West Asia											
Afghanistan	28[z]	20[z]	…	…	…	…	…	…	…	…	…
Bangladesh	912	33	3	24	34	15	5	1	2	0.2	15
Bhutan	…	…	…	…	…	…	…	…	…	…	…
India	9 327	40	1[z]	36[z]	15[z]	16[z]	7[z]	–[z]	2[z]	–[z]	24[z]
Iran, Islamic Republic of	2 126	51	3	13	28	13	27	6	6	2	2
Maldives	0.1[z]	70[z]	100[y]	.[y]	.[y]	.[y]	.[y]	.[y]	.[y]	.[y]	.[y]
Nepal	147[z]	28[z]	…	…	…	…	…	…	…	…	…
Pakistan	783	45	–	23	17	20	4	–	3	–	33
Sri Lanka	…	…	…	…	…	…	…	…	…	…	…
Sub-Saharan Africa											
Angola	13[y]	40[y]	…	…	…	…	…	…	…	…	…
Benin	…	…	…	…	…	…	…	…	…	…	…
Botswana	11	50	21	26	25	12	6	–	–	0.3	11
Burkina Faso	28	31	…	…	…	…	…	…	…	…	…
Burundi	17	28	…	…	…	…	…	…	…	…	…
Cameroon	100*	40*	5*,[z]	17*,[z]	44*,[z]	20*,[z]	3*,[z]	1*,[z]	1*,[z]	–*,[z]	9*,[z]
Cape Verde	4	51	…	…	…	…	…	…	…	…	…
Central African Republic	6	…	…	…	…	…	…	…	…	…	…
Chad	10	13	…	…	…	…	…	…	…	…	…
Comoros	2[z]	43[z]	9[y]	29[y]	38[y]	11[y]	.[y]	.[y]	8[y]	4[y]	.[y]
Congo	12[y]	16[y]	…	…	…	…	…	…	…	…	…
Côte d'Ivoire	…	…	…	…	…	…	…	…	…	…	…
D. R. Congo	…	…	…	…	…	…	…	…	…	…	…
Equatorial Guinea	…	…	…	…	…	…	…	…	…	…	…
Eritrea	5[z]	13[z]	22[z]	2[z]	24[z]	9[z]	28[z]	9[z]	6[z]	–[z]	–[z]

PERCENTAGE FEMALE IN EACH FIELD

Education	Humanities and arts	Social sciences, business and law	Science	Engineering, manufacturing and construction	Agriculture	Health and welfare	Services	Not known or unspecified	Country or territory
...	...	...	...	...	...	...	...	...	Saint Lucia
...	...	...	...	...	...	...	...	...	St Vincent/Grenad.
...	...	...	...	...	...	...	...	...	Suriname
69[z]	78[z]	70[z]	51[z]	21[z]	55[z]	64[z]	66[z]	67[z]	Trinidad and Tobago
.[z]	.[z]	.[z]	.[z]	.[z]	.[z]	.[z]	.[z]	.[z]	Turks and Caicos Islands
...	...	...	...	...	...	...	...	...	Uruguay
...	...	...	...	...	...	...	...	...	Venezuela
									North America and Western Europe
83	80	60	10	–	–	83	–	–	Andorra
75	66	55	34	21	63	68	51	49	Austria
70	58	54	34	21	49	73	50	49	Belgium
...	...	...	...	...	...	...	...	...	Canada
91	76	50	35	13	–	71	40	17	Cyprus
71	63	50	32	33	52	81	22	–	Denmark
80	71	63	41	19	51	84	70		Finland
...	...	...	...	...	...	...	...	55	France[1]
...	...	...	...	...	...	...	...	...	Germany
70	73	55	39	28	44	74	44	–	Greece
85[z]	66[z]	59[z]	35[z]	31[z]	38[z]	85[z]	83[z]	–[z]	Iceland
79	64	57	41	16	43	79	48	55	Ireland
83	64	56	40	27	56	77	.	63	Israel
87	72	57	49	28	44	65	48	64	Italy
...	...	...	...	...	...	...	...	...	Luxembourg
72	57	56	35	28	31	67	33	–	Malta
.[z]	.[z]	.[z]	.[z]	.[z]	.[z]	.[z]	.[z]	.[z]	Monaco
73	55	47	20	13	46	74	51	39	Netherlands
75	62	56	32	24	57	81	49	59	Norway
84	62	60	49	26	55	77	50	–	Portugal
...	...	...	...	...	...	...	...	...	San Marino
78	61	59	35	28	46	75	58	49	Spain
77	63	61	42	28	58	81	58	78	Sweden
70	59	46	28	14	45	68	51	50	Switzerland
74	62	55	36	19	62	79	67	61	United Kingdom
79	58	56	38	16	50	80	53	56	United States
									South and West Asia
...	...	...	...	...	...	...	...	...	Afghanistan
36	41	33	26	15	17	38	33	36	Bangladesh
...	...	...	...	...	...	...	...	...	Bhutan
50[z]	44[z]	37[z]	40[z]	24[z]	–[z]	42[z]	–[z]	32[z]	India
69	71	58	67	21	40	74	50	75	Iran, Islamic Republic of
70[y]	.[y]	.[y]	.[y]	.[y]	.[y]	.[y]	.[y]	.[y]	Maldives
...	...	...	...	...	...	...	...	...	Nepal
–	43	43	43	43	–	43	–	50	Pakistan
...	...	...	...	...	...	...	...	...	Sri Lanka
									Sub-Saharan Africa
...	...	...	...	...	...	...	...	...	Angola
...	...	...	...	...	...	...	...	...	Benin
58	62	56	9	12	–	–	87	53	Botswana
...	...	...	...	...	...	...	...	...	Burkina Faso
...	...	...	...	...	...	...	...	...	Burundi
...	...	...	...	...	...	...	...	...	Cameroon
...	...	...	...	...	...	...	...	...	Cape Verde
...	...	...	...	...	...	...	...	...	Central African Republic
...	...	...	...	...	...	...	...	...	Chad
...	...	...	...	...	...	...	...	...	Comoros
53[y]	36[y]	47[y]	27[y]	.[y]	.[y]	55[y]	57[y]	.[y]	Congo
...	...	...	...	...	...	...	...	...	Côte d'Ivoire
...	...	...	...	...	...	...	...	...	D. R. Congo
...	...	...	...	...	...	...	...	...	Equatorial Guinea
9[z]	41[z]	16[z]	21[z]	10[z]	6[z]	20[z]	–[z]	–[z]	Eritrea

Table 9B (continued)

Country or territory	Total enrolment (000)	% F	PERCENTAGE DISTRIBUTION BY FIELD OF STUDY Education	Humanities and arts	Social sciences, business and law	Science	Engineering, manufacturing and construction	Agriculture	Health and welfare	Services	Not known or unspecified
Ethiopia	191	24	30	3	38	8	9	5	6	0.2	0.3
Gabon	...	...	...	...	...	...	...	...	...	...	...
Gambia	2ᶻ	19ᶻ	4ᶻ	35ᶻ	19ᶻ	21ᶻ	.ᶻ	.ᶻ	15ᶻ	.ᶻ	7ᶻ
Ghana	**110**	**34**	11ᶻ	39ᶻ	12ᶻ	15ᶻ	12ᶻ	4ᶻ	4ᶻ	2ᶻ	1ᶻ
Guinea	24	19	7ᶻ	10ᶻ	25ᶻ	22ᶻ	12ᶻ	5ᶻ	9ᶻ	2ᶻ	8ᶻ
Guinea-Bissau	...	...	...	...	...	...	...	...	...	...	...
Kenya	108ᶻ	37ᶻ	...	...	...	...	...	...	...	...	...
Lesotho	8	57	32	8	33	23	1	1	1.1	–	–
Liberia	...	...	...	...	...	...	...	...	...	...	...
Madagascar	45	47	3	15	51	15	5	3	7	0.3	0.4
Malawi	5ᶻ	35ᶻ	...	...	...	...	...	...	...	...	...
Mali	33	*31*	...	...	...	...	...	...	...	...	...
Mauritius	17	55	21	13	30	8	18	2	0.3	1.0	8.3
Mozambique	28	33	8	11	44	14	10	5	5	3	0.5
Namibia	12ᶻ	53ᶻ	25ʸ	4ʸ	41ʸ	8ʸ	5ʸ	3ʸ	4ʸ	3ʸ	8ʸ
Niger	11	30	...	...	...	...	...	...	...	...	...
Nigeria	1 290ᶻ	35ᶻ	...	...	...	...	...	...	...	...	...
Rwanda	*26*	*39*	...	...	...	...	...	...	...	...	...
Sao Tome and Principe	.	.	.	.	.	.	.	.	.	.	.
Senegal	59*	...	...	...	...	...	...	...	...	...	...
Seychelles	.	.	.	.	.	.	.	.	.	.	.
Sierra Leone	...	...	...	...	...	...	...	...	...	...	...
Somalia	...	...	...	...	...	...	...	...	...	...	...
South Africa	735	55	14	5	51	11	9	2	6	1	–
Swaziland	6	52	24	15	34	5	4	5	12	2	.
Togo	...	...	...	...	...	...	...	...	...	...	...
Uganda	88ᶻ	38ᶻ	32ᶻ	5ᶻ	40ᶻ	3ᶻ	7ᶻ	2ᶻ	4ᶻ	4ᶻ	2ᶻ
United Republic of Tanzania	*51*	*32*	13	7	20	15	9	5	7	2	22
Zambia	...	...	...	...	...	...	...	...	...	...	...
Zimbabwe	*56ʸ*	*39ʸ*	...	...	...	...	...	...	...	...	*100ʸ*

	Sum	% F	Median								
World	137 769	50	12	22	15	11	13	4	5	2	17
Countries in transition	14 208	56	...	...	...	...	...	...	...	...	...
Developed countries	43 411	55	10	13	38	11	13	1	10	4	0.4
Developing countries	80 150	46	...	...	...	...	...	...	...	...	...
Arab States	6 783	49	8	10	34	10	2	0.1	2	–	33
Central and Eastern Europe	19 414	55	13	8	41	7	15	2	6	5	3
Central Asia	2 060	51	...	...	...	...	...	...	...	...	...
East Asia and the Pacific	41 424	47	...	...	...	...	...	...	...	...	...
East Asia	40 128	46	13	10	27	19	21	2	5	3	0.1
Pacific	1 296	55	...	...	...	...	...	...	...	...	...
Latin America/Caribbean	15 293	54	...	...	...	...	...	...	...	...	...
Caribbean	105	63	...	...	...	...	...	...	...	...	...
Latin America	15 189	54	13	3	18	8	9	3	11	3	32
N. America/W. Europe	33 412	56	10	13	38	11	13	1	10	4	0.4
South and West Asia	15 842	41	3	13	28	13	27	6	6	2	2
Sub-Saharan Africa	3 540	38	...	...	...	...	...	...	...	...	...

1. For the first time, data include French overseas departments and territories.
Data in italic are UIS estimates.
Data in bold are for the school year ending in 2006.

(z) Data are for the school year ending in 2004.
(y) Data are for the school year ending in 2003.
(*) National estimates.

PERCENTAGE FEMALE IN EACH FIELD

Education	Humanities and arts	Social sciences, business and law	Science	Engineering, manufacturing and construction	Agriculture	Health and welfare	Services	Not known or unspecified	Country or territory
20	30	29	26	14	22	26	19	18	Ethiopia
…	…	…	…	…	…	…	…	…	Gabon
2[z]	19[z]	14[z]	14[z]	.[z]	.[z]	13[z]	.[z]	68[z]	Gambia
36[z]	37[z]	42[z]	27[z]	8[z]	20[z]	37[z]	22[z]	33[z]	Ghana
2[z]	20[z]	19[z]	16[z]	7[z]	8[z]	26[z]	15[z]	18[z]	Guinea
…	…	…	…	…	…	…	…	…	Guinea-Bissau
…	…	…	…	…	…	…	…	…	Kenya
58	67	56	54	37	61	53	–	–	Lesotho
…	…	…	…	…	…	…	…	…	Liberia
46	56	51	33	18	37	51	51	67	Madagascar
…	…	…	…	…	…	…	…	…	Malawi
…	…	…	…	…	…	…	…	…	Mali
55	67	55	53	28	58	42	32	100	Mauritius
33	36	41	21	10	27	54	21	23	Mozambique
54[y]	58[y]	56[y]	37[y]	18[y]	39[y]	81[y]	64[y]	58[y]	Namibia
…	…	…	…	…	…	…	…	…	Niger
…	…	…	…	…	…	…	…	…	Nigeria
…	…	…	…	…	…	…	…	…	Rwanda
.	.	.	.	.	.	.	.	.	Sao Tome and Principe
.	…	…	…	…	…	…	…	…	Senegal
.	.	.	.	.	.	.	.	.	Seychelles
…	…	…	…	…	…	…	…	…	Sierra Leone
…	…	…	…	…	…	…	…	…	Somalia
71	60	56	44	24	42	68	65	–	South Africa
52	66	50	37	11	27	72	43	.	Swaziland
…	…	…	…	…	…	…	…	…	Togo
39[z]	41[z]	41[z]	24[z]	19[z]	22[z]	40[z]	53[z]	55[z]	Uganda
38	56	41	24	10	26	29	16	32	United Republic of Tanzania
…	…	…	…	…	…	…	…	…	Zambia
…	…	…	…	…	…	…	…	39[y]	Zimbabwe

Median									
71	56	35	30	16	32	63	31	.	World
…	…	…	…	…	…	…	…	…	Countries in transition
75	62	56	32	24	57	81	49	59	Developed countries
…	…	…	…	…	…	…	…	…	Developing countries
69	60	41	53	20	25	67	–	40	Arab States
77	72	56	63	26	48	65	50	–	Central and Eastern Europe
…	…	…	…	…	…	…	…	…	Central Asia
…	…	…	…	…	…	…	…	…	East Asia and the Pacific
62	66	49	36	25	39	71	77	2	East Asia
…	…	…	…	…	…	…	…	…	Pacific
…	…	…	…	…	…	…	…	…	Latin America/Caribbean
…	…	…	…	…	…	…	…	…	Caribbean
72	57	57	38	27	38	59	55	31	Latin America
77	63	61	42	28	58	81	58	78	N. America/W. Europe
50	44	37	40	24	–	42	–	32	South and West Asia
…	…	…	…	…	…	…	…	…	Sub-Saharan Africa

Table 10A
Teaching staff in pre-primary and primary education

	PRE-PRIMARY EDUCATION											
	Teaching staff				Trained teachers (%)[1]						Pupil/teacher ratio[2]	
	School year ending in				School year ending in						School year ending in	
	1999		2005		1999			2005			1999	2005
Country or territory	Total (000)	% F	Total (000)	% F	Total	Male	Female	Total	Male	Female		
Arab States												
Algeria	1	93	2	86	…	…	…	…	…	…	28	29
Bahrain	0.7	100	1	99	18	–	18	…	…	…	21	15
Djibouti	0.01	100	0.03	47	…	…	…	100	100	100	29	14
Egypt	*14*	*99*	23	*99*	…	…	…	…	…	…	*24*	24
Iraq	5	100	*6*	*100*	…	…	…	100[z]	.[z]	100[z]	15	*16*
Jordan	3	100	5	99	…	…	…	…	…	…	22	20
Kuwait	4	100	5	100	100	100	100	100	100	100	15	13
Lebanon	11	95	9	99	…	…	…	11	13	11	13	16
Libyan Arab Jamahiriya	1	100	**2.2**	**97**	…	…	…	…	…	…	8	**8**
Mauritania	…	…	*0.3*	*100*	…	…	…	100[z]	.[z]	100[z]	…	*19*
Morocco	40	40	40	54	…	…	…	100	100	100	20	17
Oman	0.4	100	**0.5**	**100**	93	–	93	**100**	**.**	**100**	20	**18**
Palestinian A. T.	3	100	3	99	…	…	…	100	100	100	29	26
Qatar	*0.4*	*96*	1	100	…	…	…	…	…	…	*21*	17
Saudi Arabia	…	…	…	…	…	…	…	…	…	…	…	…
Sudan	*12*	*84*	17	99	…	…	…	60	60	60	*30*	29
Syrian Arab Republic	5	96	7	98	87	84	87	16	15	16	24	22
Tunisia	4	95	*6*[y]	*95*[y]	…	…	…	…	…	…	20	*19*[y]
United Arab Emirates	3	100	4	100	59	71	59	50	80	50	19	19
Yemen	0.8	93	1.2	97	…	…	…	…	…	…	17	15
Central and Eastern Europe												
Albania	4	100	*4*[z]	*100*[z]	…	…	…	…	…	…	20	*21*[z]
Belarus	53	…	44	99	…	…	…	65	65	65	5	6
Bosnia and Herzegovina	…	…	…	…	…	…	…	…	…	…	…	…
Bulgaria	19	*100*	18	100	…	…	…	…	…	…	11	11
Croatia	6	100	7[y]	100[y]	76	86	76	84[y]	100[y]	84[y]	13	12[y]
Czech Republic	17	*100*	22	100	…	…	…	…	…	…	18	13
Estonia	7	100	7	100	…	…	…	…	…	…	8	7
Hungary	32	100	31	100	…	…	…	…	…	…	12	11
Latvia	7	99	6	100	…	…	…	…	…	…	9	11
Lithuania	13	99	11	99	…	…	…	…	…	…	7	8
Poland	*77*	…	47	97	…	…	…	…	…	…	*12*	18
Republic of Moldova	13	100	10	100	*92*	*.*	*92*	89	.	89	8	10
Romania	37	100	35	100	…	…	…	…	…	…	17	18
Russian Federation	618	…	619	…	…	…	…	94[y]	…	…	7	7
Serbia and Montenegro	12	100	…	…	96	.	96	…	…	…	14	…
Slovakia	16	100	11	100	…	…	…	…	…	…	10	14
Slovenia	3	*99*	2	100	…	…	…	…	…	…	18	18
TFYR Macedonia	3	99	3	99	…	…	…	…	…	…	10	11
Turkey	17	*99*	22	95	…	…	…	…	…	…	15	20
Ukraine	143	100	118	99	…	…	…	…	…	…	8	8
Central Asia												
Armenia	8	…	5	100	…	…	…	56[z]	20[z]	56[z]	7	9
Azerbaijan	12	100	11	100	78	–	78	84	90	84	9	10
Georgia	6	100	8	100	…	…	…	97[y]	.[y]	97[y]	13	10
Kazakhstan	19	…	27	99	…	…	…	…	…	…	9	11
Kyrgyzstan	3	100	2	99	32	–	32	38	39	38	18	23
Mongolia	3	100	3	89	99	75	99	…	…	…	25	24
Tajikistan	5	100	4	100	…	…	…	74	.	74	11	14
Turkmenistan	…	…	…	…	…	…	…	…	…	…	…	…
Uzbekistan	…	…	*64*[z]	*95*[z]	…	…	…	100[y]	100[y]	100[y]	…	*10*[z]
East Asia and the Pacific												
Australia	…	…	…	…	…	…	…	…	…	…	…	…
Brunei Darussalam	0.6*	83*	0.6	96	…	…	…	64	96	63	20*	19
Cambodia	*2*	*99*	4	99	…	…	…	…	…	…	*27*	25
China	875	94	**952**	**98**	…	…	…	…	…	…	27	**23**

PRIMARY EDUCATION

Teaching staff School year ending in				Trained teachers (%)[1] School year ending in						Pupil/teacher ratio[2] School year ending in		Country or territory
1999		2005		1999			2005			1999	2005	
Total (000)	% F	Total (000)	% F	Total	Male	Female	Total	Male	Female			
												Arab States
170	46	171	50	94	92	96	99	98	99	28	25	Algeria
...	...	...	...	...	...	...	...	...	...	...	...	Bahrain
1.0	28	*1.5*	*27*	...	...	...	...	...	...	40	*35*	Djibouti
346	*52*	*373*	*55*	...	...	...	...	...	...	*23*	*26*	Egypt
141	72	*216*	*72*	...	...	...	100z	100z	100z	25	21	Iraq
...	...	*39y*	*64y*	...	...	...	...	...	...	...	*20y*	Jordan
10	73	17	86	100	100	100	100	100	100	13	12	Kuwait
28	82	32	85	15	...	...	14	17	14	14	14	Lebanon
...	...	**148**	**82**	...	...	...	...	...	...	...	**5**	Libyan Arab Jamahiriya
7	26	11	31	...	...	...	100	100	100	47	40	Mauritania
123	39	148	46	...	...	...	100	100	100	28	27	Morocco
12	52	**20**	**65**	100	100	99	**100**	**100**	**100**	25	**14**	Oman
10	54	16	50	100	100	100	100	100	100	38	25	Palestinian A. T.
5	75	6	66	...	...	...	...	...	...	13	11	Qatar
...	...	...	...	...	...	...	...	...	...	...	...	Saudi Arabia
...	...	113	66	...	...	...	58	81	46	...	29	Sudan
110	*65*	...	...	81	...	...	...	...	...	25	...	Syrian Arab Republic
60	50	59	52	...	...	...	...	...	...	24	20	Tunisia
17	73	17	84	...	...	...	60	69	58	16	15	United Arab Emirates
103	*20*	...	...	...	...	...	...	...	...	*22*	...	Yemen
												Central and Eastern Europe
13	*75*	*12z*	*76z*	...	...	...	...	...	...	*23*	*21z*	Albania
32	99	24	99	...	...	...	100	100	100	20	16	Belarus
...	...	...	...	...	...	...	...	...	...	...	...	Bosnia and Herzegovina
23	*91*	18	93	...	...	...	...	...	...	18	16	Bulgaria
11	89	11y	90y	100	100	100	100y	100y	100y	19	18y	Croatia
36	*85*	31	84	...	...	...	...	...	...	18	16	Czech Republic
8	*86*	...	...	...	...	...	...	...	...	16	...	Estonia
47	85	41	96	...	...	...	...	...	...	11	10	Hungary
9	97	7	97	...	...	...	...	...	...	15	12	Latvia
13	98	11	98	...	...	...	...	...	...	17	14	Lithuania
...	...	236	85	...	...	...	...	...	...	...	12	Poland
12	96	10	97	...	...	...	...	...	...	21	18	Republic of Moldova
69	86	57	86	...	...	...	...	...	...	19	17	Romania
349	*98*	*317*	*99*	...	...	...	*99v*	...	...	*18*	*17*	Russian Federation
21	*82*	...	...	*100*	*100*	*100*	...	...	...	*20*	...	Serbia and Montenegro
17	93	14	90	...	...	...	...	...	...	19	18	Slovakia
6	96	6	97	...	...	...	...	...	...	14	15	Slovenia
6	66	6	70	...	...	...	...	...	...	22	19	TFYR Macedonia
...	...	...	...	...	...	...	...	...	...	...	...	Turkey
107	98	104	99	...	...	...	99.7	...	...	20	19	Ukraine
												Central Asia
...	...	6	99	...	...	...	77	22	78	...	21	Armenia
37	83	42	85	100	100	100	100	100	100	19	13	Azerbaijan
17	92	17y	95y	...	...	...	97y	...	...	17	14y	Georgia
...	...	59	98	...	...	...	...	...	...	...	17	Kazakhstan
19	95	18	96	48	49	48	58	58	58	24	24	Kyrgyzstan
8	93	7	94	...	...	...	...	...	...	32	34	Mongolia
31	56	32	63	...	...	...	84z	...	...	22	21	Tajikistan
...	...	...	...	...	...	...	...	...	...	...	...	Turkmenistan
...	...	...	...	...	...	...	...	...	...	...	...	Uzbekistan
												East Asia and the Pacific
105	...	...	...	...	...	...	...	...	...	*18*	...	Australia
3*	66*	5	71	...	...	...	84	90	82	14*	10	Brunei Darussalam
45	*37*	51	41	...	...	...	98	...	...	*48*	53	Cambodia
...	...	**6 116**	**55**	...	...	...	...	...	...	...	**18**	China

Table 10A (continued)

Country or territory	PRE-PRIMARY EDUCATION											
	Teaching staff				Trained teachers (%)[1]						Pupil/teacher ratio[2]	
	School year ending in				School year ending in						School year ending in	
	1999		2005		1999			2005			1999	2005
	Total (000)	% F	Total (000)	% F	Total	Male	Female	Total	Male	Female		
Cook Islands	0.03	100	0.03ʸ	100ʸ	...	...	...	...	...	...	14	18ʸ
DPR Korea	...	...	...	...	...	...	...	...	...	...	...	...
Fiji	...	...	0.4	99	...	...	...	...	...	...	...	21
Indonesia	118	98	182	98	...	...	...	...	...	...	17	16
Japan	96	...	105	98	...	...	...	...	...	...	31	29
Kiribati	...	...	...	...	...	...	...	...	...	...	...	...
Lao People's Democratic Republic	2	100	3	99	86	100	86	82	61	82	18	16
Macao, China	1	100	0.5	99	93	–	93	98	75	98	31	24
Malaysia	21	100	29ᶻ	96ᶻ	...	...	...	...	...	...	27	23ᶻ
Marshall Islands	0.1	...	0.1ʸ	60ʸ	...	...	...	...	...	...	11	12ʸ
Micronesia (Federated States of)	...	...	...	...	...	...	...	...	...	...	...	...
Myanmar	2	...	...	...	...	...	...	...	...	...	22	...
Nauru	...	...	0.04ᶻ	100ᶻ	...	...	...	...	...	...	...	13ᶻ
New Zealand	7	98	7	99	...	...	...	...	...	...	15	15
Niue	0.01	100	...	...	...	...	...	...	...	...	11	...
Palau	...	...	...	...	...	...	...	...	...	...	...	...
Papua New Guinea	2	41	3ʸ	37ʸ	...	...	...	...	...	...	30	35ʸ
Philippines	18	92	24	97	100	...	...	...	...	...	33	34
Republic of Korea	23	100	**27**	**99**	...	...	...	...	...	...	24	**20**
Samoa	...	...	0.1ᶻ	94ᶻ	...	...	...	...	...	...	...	42ᶻ
Singapore	...	...	...	...	...	...	...	...	...	...	...	...
Solomon Islands	...	...	...	...	...	...	...	...	...	...	...	...
Thailand	111	79	**98.8**	**78**	...	...	...	...	...	...	25	**25**
Timor-Leste	...	...	0.2	97	...	...	...	...	...	...	...	29
Tokelau	...	...	0.01ᶻ	100ᶻ	...	...	...	...	...	...	...	14ᶻ
Tonga	0.1	100	...	...	...	...	...	...	...	...	18	...
Tuvalu	...	...	...	...	...	...	...	...	...	...	...	...
Vanuatu	...	...	...	...	...	...	...	...	...	...	...	...
Viet Nam	94	100	156	98	44	.	44	...	...	...	23	18
Latin America and the Caribbean												
Anguilla	0.03	100	0.04	100	38	.	38	49	.	49	18	10
Antigua and Barbuda	...	...	...	...	...	...	...	...	...	...	...	...
Argentina	50	96	53ʸ	97ʸ	...	...	...	...	...	...	24	24ʸ
Aruba	0.1	100	0.1	99	100	–	100	100	100	100	26	20
Bahamas	0.2	97	0.3ʸ	100ʸ	53	50	53	...	...	...	9	11ʸ
Barbados	0.3	93	0.3	95	...	...	...	63	29	65	18	18
Belize	0.2	98	0.3	99	...	...	...	70ᶻ	–ᶻ	70.5ᶻ	19	17
Bermuda	...	...	...	...	...	...	...	...	...	...	...	...
Bolivia	5.0	93	6	92	...	...	...	79ʸ	32ʸ	82ʸ	42	41
Brazil	304	98	369ᶻ	98ᶻ	...	...	...	...	...	...	19	18ᶻ
British Virgin Islands	0.03	100	0.05	100	29	–	29	20ᶻ	.ᶻ	20ᶻ	13	14
Cayman Islands	0.1	96	0.05	100	92	50	94	100	.	100	9	12
Chile	...	...	20	98	...	...	...	...	...	...	...	21
Colombia	59	94	50	96	...	...	...	...	...	...	18	22
Costa Rica	4	97	7	94	92	...	...	88	77*	89*	19	16
Cuba	26	98	27	100	98	–	100	100	.	100	19	17
Dominica	0.1	100	0.2	100	75	.	75	78ᶻ	.	78ᶻ	18	14
Dominican Republic	8	95	9	96	54	59	53	77	71	77	24	22
Ecuador	10	90	13	87	...	...	...	72ᶻ	60ᶻ	73ᶻ	18	17
El Salvador	...	...	9	88	...	...	...	100	100	100	...	27
Grenada	0.2	96	0.3	99	...	...	...	32ʸ	–	33ʸ	18	10
Guatemala	12	...	17	...	...	...	...	...	...	...	26	25
Guyana	2	99	2	99	38	41	38	48	21	49	18	16
Haiti	...	...	...	...	...	...	...	...	...	...	...	...
Honduras	...	...	10	94	...	...	...	64ᶻ	53ᶻ	65ᶻ	...	20
Jamaica	5	...	7	98	...	...	...	...	...	...	25	22
Mexico	150	94	142	96	...	...	...	...	...	...	22	29
Montserrat	0.01	100	0.01	100	100	.	100	100	.	100	12	15
Netherlands Antilles	0.3	99	0.3ʸ	100ʸ	100	100	100	...	...	...	21	19ʸ
Nicaragua	6	97	8	96	32	19	33	33	24	33	26	25
Panama	3	98	4	95	36	35	36	48	7	50	19	20

PRIMARY EDUCATION

Teaching staff				Trained teachers (%)[1]						Pupil/teacher ratio[2]		Country or territory
School year ending in				School year ending in						School year ending in		
1999		2005		1999			2005			1999	2005	
Total (000)	% F	Total (000)	% F	Total	Male	Female	Total	Male	Female			
0.1	86	0.1ʸ	…	…	…	…	…	…	…	18	16ʸ	Cook Islands
…	…	…	…	…	…	…	…	…	…	…	…	DPR Korea
…	…	4	57	…	…	…	…	…	…	…	28	Fiji
…	…	1 428	61	…	…	…	…	…	…	…	20	Indonesia
367	…	383	65	…	…	…	…	…	…	21	19	Japan
0.6	62	0.7	75	…	…	…	…	…	…	25	25	Kiribati
27	43	28	45	76	69	85	83	78	89	31	31	Lao People's Democratic Republic
1.5	87	1.6	89	81	62	84	91	75	93	31	23	Macao, China
143	66	181ᶻ	67ᶻ	…	…	…	…	…	…	21	17ᶻ	Malaysia
0.6	…	0.5ʸ	34ʸ	…	…	…	…	…	…	15	17ʸ	Marshall Islands
…	…	…	…	…	…	…	…	…	…	…	…	Micronesia (Federated States of)
155	73	160	81	60	60	60	76	80	75	31	31	Myanmar
…	…	0.1ᶻ	95ᶻ	…	…	…	…	…	…	…	22ᶻ	Nauru
20	82	22	83	…	…	…	…	…	…	18	16	New Zealand
0.02	100	0.02ᶻ	100ᶻ	…	…	…	…	…	…	16	12ᶻ	Niue
0.1	82	…	…	…	…	…	…	…	…	15	…	Palau
17	39	19ʸ	39ʸ	…	…	…	…	…	…	36	35ʸ	Papua New Guinea
360	87	373	87	100	…	…	…	…	…	35	35	Philippines
124	64	**145**	**75**	…	…	…	…	…	…	31	**28**	Republic of Korea
1.1	71	1.2ᶻ	73ᶻ	…	…	…	…	…	…	24	25ᶻ	Samoa
11	80	12.3	83	…	…	…	…	…	…	27	24	Singapore
3	41	…	…	…	…	…	…	…	…	19	…	Solomon Islands
298	63	***313***	***60***	…	…	…	…	…	…	21	***19***	Thailand
…	…	5	31	…	…	…	…	…	…	…	34	Timor-Leste
…	…	0.04ᶻ	69ᶻ	…	…	…	…	…	…	…	6ᶻ	Tokelau
0.8	67	0.8	63	…	…	…	…	…	…	21	20	Tonga
0.1	…	0.1ᶻ	…	…	…	…	…	…	…	19	19ᶻ	Tuvalu
1.4	49	2.0	54	…	…	…	…	…	…	24	20	Vanuatu
337	78	361	78	78	75	78	93	…	…	30	22	Viet Nam
												Latin America and the Caribbean
0.07	87	0.1	89	76	78	76	68	20	74	22	15	Anguilla
…	…	…	…	…	…	…	…	…	…	…	…	Antigua and Barbuda
221	88	270ʸ	86ʸ	…	…	…	…	…	…	22	17ʸ	Argentina
0.5	78	0.6	81	100	100	100	100	100	100	19	18	Aruba
2	63	2	88	58	57	59	89	90	88	14	16	Bahamas
1	76	1	78	…	…	…	73	78	72	18	15	Barbados
2	64	2	72	…	…	…	51ᶻ	51ᶻ	52ᶻ	24	24	Belize
…	…	0.6	88	…	…	…	100	100	100	…	8	Bermuda
58	61	64ᶻ	61ᶻ	…	…	…	…	…	…	25	24ᶻ	Bolivia
807	93	887ᶻ	90ᶻ	…	…	…	…	…	…	26	21ᶻ	Brazil
0.2	86	0.2	88	72	55	75	87	35	94	18	15	British Virgin Islands
0.2	89	0.3	89	98	96	98	99	100	99	15	13	Cayman Islands
56	77	66	78	…	…	…	…	…	…	32	26	Chile
215	77	187	77	…	…	…	…	…	…	24	28	Colombia
20	80	25	79	93	…	…	97	97*	97*	27	21	Costa Rica
91	79	87	78	100	100	100	100	100	100	12	10	Cuba
0.6	75	0.5	85	64	46	70	60	45	63	20	18	Dominica
…	…	53	76	…	…	…	88	81.3	90.5	…	24	Dominican Republic
71	68	86	70	…	…	…	71ᶻ	71ᶻ	71ᶻ	27	23	Ecuador
…	…	35.3	70	…	…	…	100	100	100	…	30	El Salvador
…	…	0.9	76	…	…	…	67	65	68	…	18	Grenada
48	…	76	…	…	…	…	…	…	…	38	31	Guatemala
4	86	4	86	52	52	52	57	52	58	27	28	Guyana
…	…	…	…	…	…	…	…	…	…	…	…	Haiti
…	…	39	75	…	…	…	87ᶻ	86ᶻ	88ᶻ	…	33	Honduras
…	…	12	89	…	…	…	…	…	…	…	28	Jamaica
540	62	519	66	…	…	…	…	…	…	27	28	Mexico
0.02	84	0.03	100	100	100	100	80	—	80	21	20	Montserrat
1	86	1ʸ	86ʸ	100	100	100	…	…	…	20	20ʸ	Netherlands Antilles
24	83	28	78	79	63	82	77	58	82	34	34	Nicaragua
15	75	18	76	79	86	77	90	92	89	26	24	Panama

Table 10A (continued)

	Teaching staff				Trained teachers (%)[1]						Pupil/teacher ratio[2]	
	School year ending in				School year ending in						School year ending in	
	1999		2005		1999			2005			1999	2005
Country or territory	Total (000)	% F	Total (000)	% F	Total	Male	Female	Total	Male	Female		
Paraguay	...	...	6Y	88Y	...	...	...	...	...	...	...	26Y
Peru	...	...	45	97	...	...	...	...	...	...	...	25
Saint Kitts and Nevis	...	...	0.3	100	...	...	...	46	.	46	...	6
Saint Lucia	0.3	100	0.4	100	...	...	...	56	.	56	13	12
Saint Vincent and the Grenadines	...	...	0.3	100	...	...	...	59	.	59	...	11
Suriname	...	...	0.7	100	...	...	...	...	...	...	...	24
Trinidad and Tobago	2	100	2*	100*	20	–	20	25z	–z	25z	13	14*
Turks and Caicos Islands	0.1	92	0.1	95	61	40	63	76	25	78	13	12
Uruguay	3	98	4z	...	...	...	...	...	...	...	31	27z
Venezuela	...	...	63	94	...	...	...	86	70	87	...	15
North America and Western Europe												
Andorra	...	...	0.2	92	...	...	...	...	...	...	...	14
Austria	14	99	15	99	...	...	...	...	...	...	16	14
Belgium	...	...	29	98	...	...	...	...	...	...	...	14
Canada	30	68	...	...	...	...	...	...	...	...	17	...
Cyprus	1	99	0.9	99	...	...	...	...	...	...	19	18
Denmark	45	92	...	...	...	...	...	...	...	...	6	...
Finland	10	96	11	97	...	...	...	...	...	...	12	12
France	128	78	139z	81z	...	...	...	...	...	...	19	18z
Germany	...	...	190	98	...	...	...	...	...	...	...	12
Greece	9	100	11	99	...	...	...	...	...	...	16	12
Iceland	2	98	2z	97z	...	...	...	...	...	...	5	6z
Ireland	...	...	...	...	...	...	...	...	...	...	...	...
Israel	...	...	11	100	...	...	...	...	...	...	...	34
Italy	119	99	134	100	...	...	...	...	...	...	13	12
Luxembourg	...	...	1.1	98	...	...	...	...	...	...	...	14
Malta	0.9	99	0.7	98	...	...	...	...	...	...	12	12
Monaco	0.1	100	0.05z	100z	...	...	...	...	...	...	18	17z
Netherlands	...	...	...	...	...	...	...	...	...	...	...	...
Norway	...	...	...	...	...	...	...	...	...	...	...	...
Portugal	...	...	17	98	...	...	...	...	...	...	...	15
San Marino	...	...	0.1z	...	...	...	...	...	...	...	...	8z
Spain	68	93	105	89	...	...	...	...	...	...	17	14
Sweden	...	...	33	97	...	...	...	...	...	...	...	10
Switzerland	...	...	11	98	...	...	...	...	...	...	...	15
United Kingdom	...	...	46	97	...	...	...	...	...	...	...	17
United States	327	95	430	91	...	...	...	...	...	...	22	17
South and West Asia												
Afghanistan	...	...	4z	100z	...	...	...	...	...	...	...	7z
Bangladesh	68	33	33z	90z	...	...	...	41z	50z	40z	27	34z
Bhutan	0.01	31	0.02	...	100	100	100	...	...	...	22	23
India	...	...	717	100	...	...	...	...	...	...	...	41
Iran, Islamic Republic of	9	98	19	89	...	...	...	79y	...	...	23	27
Maldives	0.4	90	0.5	95	47	46	47	41	42	41	31	26
Nepal	10	31	12y	41y	–	–	–	–y	–y	–y	24	20y
Pakistan	...	...	86z	45z	...	...	...	...	...	...	...	41z
Sri Lanka	...	...	...	...	...	...	...	...	...	...	...	...
Sub-Saharan Africa												
Angola	...	...	...	...	...	...	...	...	...	...	...	...
Benin	0.6	61	0.6	71	100	100	100	100z	100z	100z	28	43
Botswana	...	...	...	...	...	...	...	...	...	...	...	...
Burkina Faso	...	...	...	...	...	...	...	...	...	...	...	...
Burundi	0.2	99	0.3*	88*	...	...	...	72*	64*	73*	28	41*
Cameroon	4	97	7*	99*	...	...	...	51*	39*	51*	23	31*
Cape Verde	...	...	0.9	100	...	...	...	8	.	8	...	23
Central African Republic	...	...	...	...	...	...	...	...	...	...	...	...
Chad	...	...	0.2	...	...	...	...	...	...	...	...	38
Comoros	0.1	94	...	...	...	...	...	...	...	...	26	...

PRIMARY EDUCATION

Teaching staff				Trained teachers (%)[1]						Pupil/teacher ratio[2]		Country or territory
School year ending in				School year ending in						School year ending in		
1999		2005		1999			2005			1999	2005	
Total (000)	% F	Total (000)	% F	Total	Male	Female	Total	Male	Female			
...	...	34Y	72Y	...	...	...	...	...	...	...	28Y	Paraguay
...	...	177	64	...	...	...	...	...	...	...	23	Peru
...	...	0.4	86	...	...	...	58	67	57	...	18	Saint Kitts and Nevis
1.2	84	1.1	86	...	...	...	80	73	81	22	22	Saint Lucia
...	...	1.0	73	...	...	...	74	68	76	...	18	Saint Vincent and the Grenadines
...	...	3.5	92	...	...	...	...	...	...	...	19	Suriname
8	76	8*	72*	71	74	71	81*,z	72*,z	84*,z	21	17*	Trinidad and Tobago
0.1	92	0.1	89	81	63	82	82	81	83	18	15	Turks and Caicos Islands
18	92	18z	...	...	...	...	...	...	...	20	21z	Uruguay
...	...	184	81	...	...	...	84	70	87	...	19	Venezuela
												North America and Western Europe
...	...	0.4	74	...	...	...	...	...	...	...	11	Andorra
29	89	29	90	...	...	...	...	...	...	13	12	Austria
...	...	64	79	...	...	...	...	...	...	...	11	Belgium
141	68	...	...	...	...	...	...	...	...	17	...	Canada
4	67	3	83	...	...	...	...	...	...	18	18	Cyprus
37	63	...	...	...	...	...	...	...	...	10	...	Denmark
22	71	25	76	...	...	...	...	...	...	17	16	Finland
209	78	203z	81z	...	...	...	...	...	...	19	19z	France
221	82	234	84	...	...	...	...	...	...	17	14	Germany
48	57	59	63	...	...	...	...	...	...	14	11	Greece
3	76	3z	78z	...	...	...	...	...	...	11	11z	Iceland
21	85	25	84	...	...	...	...	...	...	22	18	Ireland
54	...	60	86	...	...	...	...	...	...	13	13	Israel
254	95	264	96	...	...	...	...	...	...	11	10	Italy
...	...	3	71	...	...	...	...	...	...	...	11	Luxembourg
2	87	3	86	...	...	...	...	...	...	20	11	Malta
0.1	87	0.1z	80z	...	...	...	...	...	...	16	14z	Monaco
...	...	133	82	...	...	...	...	...	...	...	10	Netherlands
...	...	41z	73z	...	...	...	...	...	...	...	11z	Norway
...	...	72	82	...	...	...	...	...	...	...	11	Portugal
...	...	0.2z	...	...	...	...	...	...	...	...	6z	San Marino
172	68	181	69	...	...	...	...	...	...	15	14	Spain
62	80	66	81	...	...	...	...	...	...	12	10	Sweden
...	...	41	78	...	...	...	...	...	...	...	13	Switzerland
244	76	265	82	...	...	...	...	...	...	19	17	United Kingdom
1 618	86	1 731	89	...	...	...	...	...	...	15	14	United States
												South and West Asia
26	–	52	34	...	...	...	36	...	...	36	83	Afghanistan
312	33	353z	34z	64	64	64	48z	47z	52z	56	51z	Bangladesh
2	32	3	38	100	100	100	94	93	95	42	31	Bhutan
3 135*	33*	...	...	...	...	...	...	...	...	35*	...	India
327	53	380	61	...	...	...	100	100	100	27	19	Iran, Islamic Republic of
3	60	3	66	67	70	65	64	60	66	24	20	Maldives
92	23	113	30	46	50	35	31	32	27	39	40	Nepal
...	...	450	46	...	...	...	86	94	76	...	38	Pakistan
...	...	72z	79z	...	...	...	...	...	...	...	22z	Sri Lanka
												Sub-Saharan Africa
...	...	...	...	...	...	...	...	...	...	...	...	Angola
16	23	28	18	58	52	77	72z	70z	82z	53	47	Benin
12	81	13	78	90	81	92	97	96	97	27	25	Botswana
17	25	27	29	...	...	...	88	87	91	49	47	Burkina Faso
12	54	21	55	...	...	...	88	83	91	57	49	Burundi
41	36	62*	40*	...	...	...	63*	59*	68*	52	48*	Cameroon
3	62	3	66	...	...	...	78	71	81	29	26	Cape Verde
...	...	...	...	...	...	...	...	...	...	...	...	Central African Republic
12	9	20	12	...	...	...	27	21	70	68	63	Chad
2	26	3	33	...	...	...	...	...	...	35	35	Comoros

Table 10A (continued)

Country or territory	Teaching staff School year ending in 1999 Total (000)	1999 % F	Teaching staff 2005 Total (000)	2005 % F	Trained teachers (%)[1] School year ending in 1999 Total	1999 Male	1999 Female	Trained teachers (%) 2005 Total	2005 Male	2005 Female	Pupil/teacher ratio[2] School year ending in 1999	2005
Congo	0.6	100	1.1	86	...	...	...	53	−	62	10	22
Côte d'Ivoire	2	96	2*·y	80*·y	...	...	...	100*·y	100*·y	100*·y	23	22*·y
Democratic Rep. of the Congo	...	...	3y	34y	...	...	...	...	...	...	...	23y
Equatorial Guinea	0.4	36	0.6y	80y	...	...	...	36y	46y	33y	43	39y
Eritrea	0.3	97	0.8	97	65	22	66	66	55	66	36	37
Ethiopia	2	93	5	91	63	37	65	79	68	80	36	33
Gabon	...	...	...	...	...	...	...	...	...	...	...	...
Gambia	...	...	0.8z	56z	...	...	...	...	...	...	...	38z
Ghana	26	91	29	91	24	14	25	22	25	22	25	25
Guinea	...	...	2.4	33	...	...	...	...	...	...	...	31
Guinea-Bissau	0.2	73	...	...	...	...	...	...	...	...	21	...
Kenya	44	55	72	87	...	...	...	71	55	73	27	23
Lesotho	...	...	2	95	...	...	...	−	−	−	...	19
Liberia	6	19	...	...	...	...	...	...	...	...	18	...
Madagascar	...	...	3z	91z	...	...	...	...	...	...	...	57z
Malawi	...	...	...	...	...	...	...	...	...	...	...	...
Mali	...	...	1y	73y	...	...	...	...	...	...	...	21y
Mauritius	3	100	3	100	100	.	100	90	.	90	16	15
Mozambique	...	...	...	...	...	...	...	...	...	...	...	...
Namibia	1	88	...	...	77	12	86	...	...	...	27	...
Niger	0.6	98	0.8	97	96	91	96	86z	64z	86z	21	23
Nigeria	...	...	...	...	...	...	...	...	...	...	...	...
Rwanda	...	...	...	...	...	...	...	...	...	...	...	...
Sao Tome and Principe	...	...	0.2y	94y	...	...	...	...	...	...	...	25y
Senegal	1	78	2.2	82	...	...	...	100	100	100	19	36
Seychelles	0.2	100	0.2	100	86	.	86	77y	.y	77y	16	15
Sierra Leone	...	...	...	...	...	...	...	...	...	...	...	...
Somalia	...	...	...	...	...	...	...	...	...	...	...	...
South Africa	6	80	11z	78z	...	...	...	...	...	...	36	34z
Swaziland	...	...	0.5z	75z	...	...	...	...	...	...	...	32z
Togo	0.6	97	0.7z	91z	...	...	...	67y	70y	67y	20	18z
Uganda	3	70	1	84	...	...	...	...	...	...	25	22
United Republic of Tanzania	...	...	15	59	...	...	...	17	10	22	...	46
Zambia	...	...	...	...	...	...	...	...	...	...	...	...
Zimbabwe	...	...	20y	100y	...	...	...	...	...	...	...	23y

	Sum	%F	Sum	%F	Median						Weighted average	
World	5 417	91	6 119	94	...	...	...	...	...	...	21	22
Countries in transition	967	98	927	98	...	...	...	84	90	84	7	8
Developed countries	1 452	94	1 659	93	...	...	...	...	...	...	17	15
Developing countries	2 998	87	3 533	93	...	...	...	...	...	...	27	28
Arab States	117	77	143	86	...	...	...	100	.	100	21	20
Central and Eastern Europe	1 102	99	1 034	99	...	...	...	...	...	...	8	9
Central Asia	143	97	139	97	...	...	...	79	.	79	10	11
East Asia and the Pacific	1 430	94	1 432	96	...	...	...	...	...	...	26	25
East Asia	1 404	94	1 402	96	...	...	...	...	...	...	26	25
Pacific	26	94	30	93	...	...	...	...	...	...	16	17
Latin America and the Caribbean	748	96	894	96	...	...	...	70	−	70	22	21
Caribbean	22	97	26	99	61	40	63	59	.	59	31	31
Latin America	726	96	868	96	...	...	...	...	...	...	22	21
North America and Western Europe	1 100	92	1 332	92	...	...	...	...	...	...	17	15
South and West Asia	601	69	882	93	...	...	...	...	...	...	36	40
Sub-Saharan Africa	177	69	263	74	...	...	...	...	...	...	29	31

1. Data on trained teachers (defined according to national standards) are not collected for countries whose education statistics are gathered through the OECD, Eurostat or the World Education Indicators questionnaires.

2. Based on headcounts of pupils and teachers.
Data in italic are UIS estimates.
Data in bold are for the school year ending in 2006.

(z) Data are for the school year ending in 2004.
(y) Data are for the school year ending in 2003.
(*) National estimates.

PRIMARY EDUCATION

Teaching staff				Trained teachers (%)[1]						Pupil/teacher ratio[2]		Country or territory
School year ending in				School year ending in						School year ending in		
1999		2005		1999			2005			1999	2005	
Total (000)	% F	Total (000)	% F	Total	Male	Female	Total	Male	Female			
5	42	7	45	…	…	…	62^z	57^z	68^z	61	83	Congo
45	20	48*,y	24*,y	…	…	…	100*,y	100*,y	100*,y	43	42*,y	Côte d'Ivoire
155	21	163^y	26^y	…	…	…	…	…	…	26	34^y	Democratic Rep. of the Congo
1	28	2^y	30^y	…	…	…	…	…	…	57	32^y	Equatorial Guinea
6	35	8	40	73	75	69	84	92	71	47	48	Eritrea
69	37	121	45	…	…	…	97	96	98	64	72	Ethiopia
6	42	8^z	45^z	…	…	…	100^y	100^y	100^y	44	36^z	Gabon
5	29	5^z	35^z	72	72	72	58^z	…	…	33	35^z	Gambia
80	32	88	44	72	64	89	56	…	…	30	35	Ghana
16	25	27	24	…	…	…	68	68	68	47	45	Guinea
3	20	…	…	…	…	…	…	…	…	44	…	Guinea-Bissau
148	42	154	45	…	…	…	99^z	98^z	99^z	32	40	Kenya
8	80	10	78	78	68	81	64	46	69	44	42	Lesotho
10	19	…	…	…	…	…	…	…	…	39	…	Liberia
43	58	67	60	…	…	…	36	30	40	47	54	Madagascar
…	…	…	…	…	…	…	…	…	…	…	…	Malawi
15*	23*	28	26	…	…	…	…	…	…	62*	54	Mali
5	54	6	63	100	100	100	100	100	100	26	22	Mauritius
37	25	59	30	…	…	…	60	57	67	61	66	Mozambique
12	67	13	67	29	27	30	92	83	97	32	31	Namibia
13	31	24	37	98	98	98	76^z	78^z	72^z	41	44	Niger
440	47	599	51	…	…	…	50	39	60	41	37	Nigeria
24	55	28	51	49	52	46	82^z	79^z	85^z	54	62	Rwanda
0.7	…	1.0	55	…	…	…	…	…	…	36	31	Sao Tome and Principe
21	23	35	25	…	…	…	100	100	100	49	42	Senegal
0.7	85	0.7	85	82	76	83	78^y	67^y	80^y	15	14	Seychelles
…	…	…	…	…	…	…	…	…	…	…	…	Sierra Leone
…	…	…	…	…	…	…	…	…	…	…	…	Somalia
227	78	209^z	76^z	62	65	61	79^y	77^y	79^y	35	36^z	South Africa
6	75	7^z	73^z	91	89	92	91^z	89^z	91^z	33	32^z	Swaziland
23	13	30	12	…	…	…	37	37	38	41	34	Togo
…	…	140	39	…	…	…	85	84	86	…	52	Uganda
104	45	152	48	…	…	…	100	100	100	40	52	United Republic of Tanzania
33	49	50	48	94	93	95	…	…	…	47	51	Zambia
60	47	61^y	51^y	…	…	…	…	…	…	41	39^y	Zimbabwe

Sum	%F	Sum	%F	Median						Weighted average		
25 724	58	27 048	62	…	…	…	…	…	…	25	25	World
815	93	738	93	…	…	…	98	…	…	19	19	Countries in transition
4 483	81	4 598	83	…	…	…	…	…	…	16	15	Developed countries
20 426	52	21 713	57	…	…	…	…	…	…	27	28	Developing countries
1 554	52	1 802	58	…	…	…	100	100	100	23	22	Arab States
1 363	82	1 247	81	…	…	…	…	…	…	19	18	Central and Eastern Europe
322	84	290	84	…	…	…	84	…	…	21	21	Central Asia
10 094	55	9 734	59	…	…	…	…	…	…	22	20	East Asia and the Pacific
9 934	55	9 554	59	…	…	…	…	…	…	22	20	East Asia
160	70	180	72	…	…	…	…	…	…	21	19	Pacific
2 684	76	2 971	77	…	…	…	82	73	83	26	23	Latin America and the Caribbean
104	50	111	57	76	74	76	80	68	80	24	22	Caribbean
2 580	77	2 861	78	…	…	…	…	…	…	26	23	Latin America
3 443	81	3 653	84	…	…	…	…	…	…	15	14	North America and Western Europe
4 301	35	4 889	45	…	…	…	64	60	66	37	39	South and West Asia
1 964	44	2 461	45	…	…	…	78	72	80	41	45	Sub-Saharan Africa

Table 10B
Teaching staff in secondary and tertiary education

	SECONDARY EDUCATION														
	Teaching staff												Trained teachers (%)[1]		
	Lower secondary				Upper secondary				Total secondary				Total secondary		
	School year ending in				School year ending in				School year ending in				School year ending in		
	1999		2005		1999		2005		1999		2005		2005		
Country or territory	Total (000)	% F	Total (000)	% F	Total (000)	% F	Total (000)	% F	Total (000)	% F	Total (000)	% F	Total	Male	Female
Arab States															
Algeria	...	...	113^z	51^z	...	...	64^z	46^z	...	...	176^z	49^z	...	...	...
Bahrain	...	...	...	...	...	...	...	...	...	...	...	...	...	...	...
Djibouti	0.5	24	...	...	0.2	17	...	...	0.7	22	...	...	...	...	...
Egypt	207	44	222	45	247	38	270	38	454	41	492	41	...	...	...
Iraq	34	77	61	59	23	57	32	56	56	69	93	58	100^z	100^z	100^z
Jordan	...	...	22^y	62^y	10	48	12^y	49^y	...	...	34^y	58^y	...	...	...
Kuwait	11	58	12	53	11	53	12	53	22	56	24	53	100	100	100
Lebanon	27	57	19	60	15	42	22	44	42	51	41	51	...	...	...
Libyan Arab Jamahiriya	...	...	**79**	**82**	...	...	**73**	**71**	...	...	**152**	**77**	...	...	...
Mauritania	1	11	...	...	1	10	...	...	2	10	3	13	100^z	100^z	100^z
Morocco	53	35	60^z	36^z	35	29	40^z	29^z	88	33	100^z	33^z	...	...	...
Oman	7	48	**12**	**54**	5	51	**7**	**48**	13	50	**19**	**52**	**100**	**100**	**100**
Palestinian A. T.	14	49	20	51	3	38	4	37	18	48	25	...	...	...	...
Qatar	2	56	3	54	2	57	2	58	4	57	5	56	...	...	...
Saudi Arabia	...	...	...	...	...	...	...	...	...	...	...	...	...	...	...
Sudan	...	...	30	67	18	47	34	46	...	...	64	56	80	78	82
Syrian Arab Republic	...	...	...	...	...	...	44	46	54	...	...	...	...	...	...
Tunisia	27	46	...	...	30	35	...	...	56	40	72	45	...	...	...
United Arab Emirates	8	54	12	56	8	55	10	53	16	55	22	55	46	47	46
Yemen	29	20	...	...	19	18	...	...	48	19	56^y	21^y	...	...	...
Central and Eastern Europe															
Albania	16	51	...	...	6	54	...	...	22	52	23^z	56^z	...	...	...
Belarus	...	...	...	...	...	...	...	...	107	77	104	80	...	...	...
Bosnia and Herzegovina	...	...	...	...	...	...	...	...	...	...	...	...	...	...	...
Bulgaria	27	76	25	80	29	70	32	75	56	73	57	77	...	...	...
Croatia	16	67	17^y	69^y	18	62	20^y	65^y	33	64	37^y	67^y	100^y	100^y	100^y
Czech Republic[3]	31	76	40	82	41	52	53	56	72	62	93	67	...	...	...
Estonia	5	85	...	...	6	78	...	...	11	81	...	...	...	...	...
Hungary	47	86	50	78	53	59	47	64	100	71	97	71	...	...	...
Latvia	16	83	15	85	9	76	10	81	25	80	25	83	...	...	...
Lithuania	24	81	...	...	12	76	...	...	36	79	43	81	...	...	...
Poland	...	...	131	73	...	...	140	66	...	...	271	69	...	...	...
Republic of Moldova	25	74	23	76	8	68	8	73	33	72	31	75	...	...	...
Romania	104	67	93	68	73	60	68	64	177	64	162	66	...	...	...
Russian Federation	...	...	...	...	...	...	...	...	...	...	1 306	...	93^y	...	...
Serbia and Montenegro	32	60	...	...	27	57	...	...	59	58	...	...	...	...	...
Slovakia	29	77	27	76	25	66	24	69	54	72	51	73	...	...	...
Slovenia	7	77	8	78	9	62	8	64	17	69	16	71	...	...	...
TFYR Macedonia	8	46	9	51	5	53	6	56	13	49	15	53	...	...	...
Turkey	...	...	...	...	...	...	136	41	...	...	...	...	...	...	...
Ukraine	...	...	...	...	...	...	...	...	400	76	349	79	...	...	...
Central Asia															
Armenia	...	...	26	80	...	...	10	85	...	...	36	81	77	75	77
Azerbaijan	...	...	...	...	...	...	...	...	118	63	128	65	100^y	100^y	100^y
Georgia	...	...	...	...	...	...	...	...	58	77	49^y	82^y	...	...	...
Kazakhstan	...	...	...	...	...	...	...	...	...	...	186	85	...	...	...
Kyrgyzstan	...	...	...	...	...	...	...	...	48	68	54	72	76	74	77
Mongolia	8	69	10	73	3	67	5	71	11	69	15	72	...	...	...
Tajikistan	...	...	...	...	...	...	...	...	47	42	60	45	92^z	...	...
Turkmenistan	...	...	...	...	...	...	...	...	...	...	...	...	...	...	...
Uzbekistan	...	...	...	...	...	...	...	...	...	...	...	...	...	...	...
East Asia and the Pacific															
Australia	...	...	...	...	...	...	...	...	...	...	...	...	...	...	...
Brunei Darussalam	2*	48*	2*	58*	1*	47*	2*	58*	3	48	4*	58*	85*	84*	86*
Cambodia	14	28	19^z	33^z	4	24	6^z	26^z	18	27	25^z	31^z	...	...	...
China	3 213	41	**3 661**	**46**	...	...	**2 444**	**43**	...	...	**6 105**	**45**	...	...	...

SECONDARY EDUCATION						TERTIARY EDUCATION				
Pupil/teacher ratio[2]						Teaching staff				
Lower secondary		Upper secondary		Total secondary		School year ending in				
School year ending in		School year ending in		School year ending in		1999		2005		
1999	2005	1999	2005	1999	2005	Total (000)	% F	Total (000)	% F	Country or territory
										Arab States
...	21^z	...	20^z	...	21^z	...	...	25	34	Algeria
...	...	...	...	...	...	...	...	0.8	41	Bahrain
26	...	16	...	23	...	0.0	30	0.1	21	Djibouti
22	20	13	14	17	17	...	...	81^z	...	Egypt
22	19	16	19	20	19	12	31	19	35	Iraq
...	20^y	17	14^y	...	18^y	...	...	8	21	Jordan
12	12	9	9	11	10	2	...	2	27	Kuwait
9	11	8	7	9	9	9	28	21	37	Lebanon
...	5	...	5	...	5	12	13	16^y	...	Libyan Arab Jamahiriya
28	...	24	...	26	31	...	...	0.4	4	Mauritania
19	20^z	14	17^z	17	19^z	16	23	19	24	Morocco
19	13	16	20	18	16	...	...	3	29	Oman
26	28	19	29	24	28	3	13	5	15	Palestinian A. T.
13	11	8	13	10	12	0.7	32	0.7	32	Qatar
...	...	...	...	...	...	20	36	27	33	Saudi Arabia
...	26	22	18	...	22	4	23	...	...	Sudan
...	...	...	10	19	...	...	...	...	...	Syrian Arab Republic
23	...	15	...	19	17	6	41	17	40	Tunisia
14	15	10	11	12	13	...	...	...	...	United Arab Emirates
22	...	21	...	22	25^y	5	1	6	16	Yemen
										Central and Eastern Europe
16	...	17	...	16	18^z	2	36	2^z	41^z	Albania
...	...	...	...	9	9	30	51	42	56	Belarus
...	...	...	...	...	...	...	...	...	...	Bosnia and Herzegovina
13	12	12	12	13	12	24	41	21	45	Bulgaria
14	12^y	11	10^y	12	11^y	7	35	8^y	37^y	Croatia
17	12	9	9	13	10	19	38	24	40	Czech Republic[3]
11	...	10	...	10	...	6	49	7	49	Estonia
11	10	9	10	10	10	21	38	25	39	Hungary
10	11	10	11	10	11	6	52	6	58	Latvia
11	...	11	...	11	10	15	50	13	53	Lithuania
...	13	...	13	...	13	76	...	95	41	Poland
13	12	12	13	13	12	7	50	6	54	Republic of Moldova
12	11	13	16	13	13	26	37	31	43	Romania
...	...	...	...	...	10	...	...	625	54	Russian Federation
14	...	13	...	14	...	13	36	...	...	Serbia and Montenegro
13	13	12	13	13	13	11	38	13	42	Slovakia
14	10	13	12	13	11	2	21	4	33	Slovenia
16	14	16	16	16	15	3	42	3	44	TFYR Macedonia
...	...	...	20	...	...	60	35	82	38	Turkey
...	...	...	...	13	12	133	...	187	...	Ukraine
										Central Asia
...	10	...	10	...	10	9	42	12	46	Armenia
...	...	...	...	8	8	13	36	15	42	Azerbaijan
...	...	...	...	8	9^y	14	49	13	46	Georgia
...	...	...	...	...	11	27	58	42	61	Kazakhstan
...	...	...	...	13	13	8	32	13	54	Kyrgyzstan
19	23	17	21	19	22	6	47	8	55	Mongolia
...	...	...	...	16	16	6	29	7	32	Tajikistan
...	...	...	...	...	...	...	...	...	...	Turkmenistan
...	...	...	...	...	...	...	...	25^z	38^z	Uzbekistan
										East Asia and the Pacific
...	...	...	...	...	...	...	...	...	...	Australia
12*	10*	10*	10*	11	10*	0.5	32	0.6	39	Brunei Darussalam
16	25^z	21	26^z	18	25^z	1	19	2	16	Cambodia
17	17	...	16	...	17	504	...	1 332	51	China

Table 10B (continued)

Country or territory	Lower secondary 1999 Total (000)	% F	Lower secondary 2005 Total (000)	% F	Upper secondary 1999 Total (000)	% F	Upper secondary 2005 Total (000)	% F	Total secondary 1999 Total (000)	% F	Total secondary 2005 Total (000)	% F	Trained teachers (%)[1] Total secondary 2005 Total	Male	Female
Cook Islands	...	...	...	...	...	...	...	...	...	...	0.1^Y	...	...	...	...
DPR Korea	...	...	...	...	...	...	...	...	...	...	...	...	...	...	...
Fiji	...	...	3^Z	50^Z	...	...	1.5^Z	50^Z	...	...	5^Z	50^Z	...	...	...
Indonesia	...	...	751	43	...	...	603	44	...	...	1 354	43	...	...	...
Japan	268	...	258	...	362	...	352	...	630	...	610	...	...	...	...
Kiribati	0.2	59	0.3	52	0.3	38	0.3	42	0.5	46	0.7	47	...	...	...
Lao PDR	9	40	11	41	3.2	40	5	44	12	40	16	42	91	89	92
Macao, China	0.9	59	1	63	0.5	49	0.9	52	1	56	2	58	67	53	76
Malaysia	76	65	87^Z	64^Z	...	...	56^Z	64^Z	...	...	143^Z	64^Z	...	...	...
Marshall Islands	0.1	...	0.2^Y	35^Y	0.2	...	0.2^Y	42^Y	0.3	...	0.4^Y	39^Y	...	...	...
Micronesia	...	...	...	...	...	...	...	...	...	...	...	...	...	...	...
Myanmar	54	77	58	84	14	73	20	78	68	76	78	82	84	84	84
Nauru	...	...	...	...	...	...	...	...	...	...	0.03^Z	53^Z	...	...	...
New Zealand	13	63	17	65	15	54	19	57	28	58	36	61	...	...	...
Niue	0.02	43	...	...	0.00	50	...	...	0.03	44	0.03^Z	68^Z	...	...	...
Palau	0.1	54	...	...	0.1	49	...	...	0.2	51	...	...	...	...	...
Papua New Guinea	6	35	...	...	0.6	30	...	...	7	34	8^Y	37^Y	...	...	...
Philippines	100	76	117	76	50	76	51	77	150	76	168	76	...	...	...
Republic of Korea	90	54	**98**	**64**	102	27	**112**	**39**	192	40	**210**	**51**	...	...	...
Samoa	0.3	76	0.4^Z	74^Z	0.8	49	0.8^Z	53^Z	1	57	1^Z	60^Z	...	...	...
Singapore	9	65	11	67	2	60	3	58	11	64	14	65	...	...	...
Solomon Islands	...	...	...	...	...	...	...	...	1	33	...	...	...	...	...
Thailand	136	58	**109**	**55**	106	62	**84**	**53**	242	60	**194**	**54**	...	...	...
Timor-Leste	...	...	1.8	26	...	...	1	24	...	...	3.2	25	...	...	...
Tokelau	...	...	...	...	...	...	...	...	...	...	0.03^Z	100^Z	...	...	...
Tonga	0.7	49	...	...	0.3	48	...	...	1	48	...	...	...	...	...
Tuvalu	...	...	...	...	...	...	...	...	...	...	...	...	...	...	...
Vanuatu	...	...	...	...	...	...	...	...	0.4	47	...	...	...	...	...
Viet Nam	194	70	295	68	64	51	121	53	258	65	416	64	94	...	...
Latin America and the Caribbean															
Anguilla	...	...	...	...	...	...	...	...	0.1	63	0.08	62	83	81	84
Antigua and Barbuda	...	...	...	...	...	...	...	...	...	...	...	...	...	...	...
Argentina	171	73	110^Y	67^Y	...	...	92^Y	64^Y	...	...	202^Y	66^Y	...	...	...
Aruba	0.2	49	0.2	52	0.2	49	0.3	52	0.4	49	0.5	52	92	91	92
Bahamas	0.6	73	1	77	0.6	75	1	69	1	74	2	73	91	90	91
Barbados	0.7	58	0.8	57	0.5	58	0.6	57	1	58	1	57	60	60	60
Belize	0.7	63	1.3	64	0.2	60	0.4	63	0.9	62	2	64	43^Z	25^Z	53^Z
Bermuda	...	...	0.3	69	...	...	0.4	65	...	...	0.7	67	100	100	100
Bolivia	14	59	19^Y	61^Y	24.5	48	25^Y	47^Y	39	52	44^Y	53^Y	...	...	...
Brazil	703	84	945^Z	87^Z	401	70	625^Z	70^Z	1 104	79	1 571^Z	80^Z	...	...	...
British Virgin Islands	0.2	64	0.1	67	0.0	57	0.1	68	0.2	63	0.2	67	70	70	71
Cayman Islands	0.1	52	0.1	61	0.1	41	0.1	44	0.2	46	0.3	52	100	99	100
Chile	16	78	23	78	29	54	43	54	45	62	66	63	...	...	...
Colombia	138	50	...	...	48	50	...	...	187	50	164	52	...	...	...
Costa Rica	9	51	11^Y	54^Y	4	54	5^Y	55^Y	13	52	16^Y	54^Y	...	...	...
Cuba	40	68	46	64	25	49	38	46	65	60	85	55	79^Z	79^Z	78^Z
Dominica	0.3	68	0.4	57	0.1	67	0.1	62	0.4	68	0.5	58	31	27	34
Dominican Republic	...	...	12	76	14	47	18	52	...	...	31	62	85	77	90
Ecuador	31	49	44	50	23	50	31	48	54	50	75	49	69*^Z	63*^Z	76*^Z
El Salvador	...	...	13	53	...	...	8	44	...	...	21	49	100	100	100
Grenada	...	...	0.6	60	...	...	0.3	57	...	...	0.9	59	35	39	33
Guatemala	20	...	30	...	13	...	18	...	33	...	48	...	...	...	...
Guyana	3	63	3	64	0.9	63	1	63	4	63	4	63	55	46	60
Haiti	...	...	...	...	...	...	...	...	...	...	...	...	...	...	...
Honduras	...	...	11	56	...	...	5	52	...	...	17	55	64^Z	59^Z	69^Z
Jamaica	...	...	...	...	...	...	...	...	...	...	12	68	...	...	...
Mexico	321	46	357	49	198	40	237	43	519	44	593	47	...	...	...
Montserrat	0.02	63	0.02	65	0.01	60	0.01	67	0.03	62	0.03	65	50	11	71
Netherlands Antilles	0.7	46	0.8^Y	58^Y	0.4	66	0.4^Y	49^Y	1	53	1.2^Y	55^Y	...	...	...
Nicaragua	7*	56*	9	56	3.2*	56*	4	59	10*	56*	13	57	53	44	59

Lower secondary 1999	Lower secondary 2005	Upper secondary 1999	Upper secondary 2005	Total secondary 1999	Total secondary 2005	Tertiary 1999 Total (000)	Tertiary 1999 % F	Tertiary 2005 Total (000)	Tertiary 2005 % F	Country or territory
...	...	...	...	...	15[y]	•	•	•	•	Cook Islands
...	...	...	...	...	...	...	...	...	...	DPR Korea
...	22[z]	...	22[z]	...	22[z]	...	...	...	...	Fiji
...	13	...	10	...	12	...	...	271	39	Indonesia
16	14	13	11	14	13	465	...	497	17	Japan
21	21	19	13	20	17	•	•	•	•	Kiribati
20	23	22	28	20	25	1	31	2	31	Lao PDR
24	23	21	21	23	22	0.7	...	2	32	Macao, China
18	17[z]	...	20[z]	...	18[z]	...	...	42[z]	47[z]	Malaysia
28	17[y]	18	17[y]	22	17[y]	...	...	0.05[y]	51[y]	Marshall Islands
...	...	...	...	...	...	0.1	...	...	...	Micronesia
28	33	38	33	30	33	9	76	...	...	Myanmar
...	...	...	...	...	19[z]	•	•	•	•	Nauru
18	15	13	14	15	15	11	43	15	50	New Zealand
6	...	21	...	11	8[z]	•	•	•	•	Niue
14	...	12	...	13	...	...	...	...	...	Palau
22	...	15	...	21	23[y]	1	20	...	...	Papua New Guinea
41	42	21	28	34	38	94	...	113	56	Philippines
22	**21**	23	**16**	23	**18**	127	25	**191**	**31**	Republic of Korea
26	25[z]	17	19[z]	20	21[z]	0.2	41	...	...	Samoa
19	19	14	11	18	17	...	...	...	...	Singapore
...	...	...	...	13	...	•	•	...	...	Solomon Islands
...	**25**	...	**21**	...	**23**	50	53	**70**	...	Thailand
...	28	...	18	...	24	...	...	...	...	Timor-Leste
...	...	...	...	...	7[z]	•	•	•	•	Tokelau
15	...	13	...	15	...	0.1	21	...	...	Tonga
...	...	...	...	...	...	•	•	•	•	Tuvalu
...	...	...	...	23	...	...	...	...	...	Vanuatu
29	23	29	27	29	24	28	37	48	40	Viet Nam
										Latin America and the Caribbean
...	...	...	...	15	12	•	•	0.02	54	Anguilla
...	...	...	...	...	...	•	•	.[z]	.[z]	Antigua and Barbuda
13	19[y]	...	16[y]	...	17[y]	102	54	131[y]	50[y]	Argentina
16	14	16	14	16	14	0.2	43	0.2	45	Aruba
23	17	23	11	23	14	•	•	.[z]	.[z]	Bahamas
18	16	18	16	18	16	0.6	41	...	...	Barbados
24	19	23	16	24	19	...	...	0.1	49	Belize
...	7	...	7	...	7	...	...	...	...	Bermuda
24	24[y]	20	24[y]	21	24[y]	13	...	18[z]	...	Bolivia
23	16[z]	21	16[z]	23	16[z]	174	41	314[z]	44[z]	Brazil
6	10	10	8	7	9	0.1	49	0.1	55	British Virgin Islands
11	12	7	9	9	10	0.0	42	...	...	Cayman Islands
32	26	27	24	29	25	...	...	...	...	Chile
19	...	20	...	19	26	86	34	94	34	Colombia
18	19[y]	18	18[y]	18	19[y]	...	...	4[y]	...	Costa Rica
12	11	10	12	11	11	24	48	91	59	Cuba
21	15	15	16	19	15	•	•	•	•	Dominica
...	26	28	27	...	26	...	...	11[z]	41[z]	Dominican Republic
17	13	17	14	17	13	...	...	...	...	Ecuador
...	25	...	24	...	25	7	32	8	34	El Salvador
...	14	...	18*	...	15*	•	•	•	•	Grenada
15	17	11	14	13	16	...	...	4[y]	...	Guatemala
19	18	19	18	19	18	...	...	0.6	44	Guyana
...	...	...	...	...	...	...	...	...	...	Haiti
...	28	...	45	...	33	...	...	7[z]	38[z]	Honduras
...	...	...	...	...	20	...	...	2[y]	60[y]	Jamaica
18	20	14	15	17	18	192	...	251	...	Mexico
11	11	10	12	10	11	•	•	•	•	Montserrat
12	9[y]	21	19[y]	15	13[y]	0.2	42	...	...	Netherlands Antilles
31*	35	31	32	31	34	...	...	7[y]	46[y]	Nicaragua

Table 10B (continued)

Country or territory	SECONDARY EDUCATION — Teaching staff — Lower secondary — School year ending in 1999 Total (000)	% F	2005 Total (000)	% F	Upper secondary — 1999 Total (000)	% F	2005 Total (000)	% F	Total secondary — 1999 Total (000)	% F	2005 Total (000)	% F	Trained teachers (%)[1] Total secondary 2005 Total	Male	Female
Panama	8	55	10	60	6	55	7	54	14	55	16	57	83	79	86
Paraguay	...	...	20Y	64Y	...	...	23Y	61Y	...	...	43Y	62Y	...	...	...
Peru	...	...	161	44	...	...	...	...	...	...	161	44	...	...	...
Saint Kitts and Nevis	...	...	0.2	60	...	...	0.2	60	...	...	0.4	60	39	47	33
Saint Lucia	0.4	65	0.5	63	0.3	62	0.3	63	0.7	64	0.8	63	58	52	61
St Vincent/Grenad.	...	...	0.4	57	...	...	0.2	60	...	...	0.5	58	55	58	53
Suriname	...	...	2	67	...	...	1	56	...	...	3	62	...	...	...
Trinidad and Tobago	3	61	3	62	2	55	2	62	6	59	6	62	56z	58z	54z
Turks and Caicos Islands	0.1	61	0.1	61	0.0	63	0.1	64	0.1	62	0.2	62	100	100	100
Uruguay	14	75	17Y	...	5	65	6Y	...	19	72	23Y	...	...	...	...
Venezuela	...	...	116	65	...	...	72	60	...	...	188	63	83	76	86
North America and Western Europe															
Andorra	...	...	0.4	61	...	...	0.1	51	...	...	0.5	59	...	...	...
Austria	43	64	42	68	30	49	29	51	73	57	71	61			
Belgium	...	...	42	60	...	...	80	58	...	...	122	58			
Canada	71	68	...	...	68	68	...	...	139	68	...	...			
Cyprus	2	54	...	...	2	49	...	...	5	51	6	60			
Denmark	20	63	...	...	24	30	...	...	44	45	...	...			
Finland	20	71	21	72	...	...	21	57	...	...	42	64			
France	255	...	245z	65z	240	...	267z	53z	495	57	511z	59z			
Germany	365	57	419	60	168	39	177	46	533	51	596	56			
Greece	37	64	43	64	38	49	43	47	75	56	86	56			
Iceland	1.1	78	1z	78z	1	44	2z	50z	3	58	3z	63z			
Ireland	...	...	...	...	...	...	...	...	...	...	...	...			
Israel	19	...	23	77	36	...	...	...	55	...	61	71			
Italy	177	73	183	75	245	59	245	60	422	65	428	66			
Luxembourg	...	...	...	...	...	...	3	45	...	...	3	45			
Malta	3	50	3	60	0.2	31	0.5	36	4	48	4	57			
Monaco	0.2	69	...	...	0.2	54	...	...	0.4	61	0.4z	66z			
Netherlands	...	...	...	...	...	...	...	...	...	...	107	45			
Norway	...	...	20z	73z	26	44	26z	47z	...	...	46z	58z			
Portugal	...	...	...	...	...	...	...	...	...	...	94	69			
San Marino	...	...	0.1z	69z	...	...	...	...	...	...	...	...			
Spain	...	...	160	...	...	...	120	...	...	...	280	56			
Sweden	28	...	38	64	35	50	38	51	63	...	76	58			
Switzerland	...	...	31	48	...	...	9	39	...	...	41	46			
United Kingdom	142	55	153	61	212	56	235	61	355	56	388	61			
United States	764	60	908	68	740	51	727	56	1 504	56	1 635	63			
South and West Asia															
Afghanistan	...	...	32	...	...	...	...	...	...	...	...	...	...	...	...
Bangladesh	136	13	186z	17z	129	13	192z	19z	265	13	378z	18z	32z	31z	35z
Bhutan	0.4	32	1	31	0.2	32	0.4	31	0.6	32	1	31	...	...	...
India[w]	...	...	1 312z	37z	...	...	1 274z	31z	1 995	34	2 586z	34z	...	...	...
Iran, Islamic Republic of	179	45	236	49	143	44	294	47	322	45	530	48	100	100	100
Maldives	0.8	25	1.8Y	34Y	0.1	27	0.3Y	39Y	0.9	25	2Y	35Y	...	...	...
Nepal	22	12	28Y	16Y	18	7	24Y	11Y	40	9	53Y	14Y	...	...	...
Pakistan	...	...	162*,z	54*,z	...	...	36*,z	35*,z	...	...	197*,z	51*,z	...	...	...
Sri Lanka	...	...	67z	64z	...	...	52z	62z	...	...	119z	63z	...	...	...
Sub-Saharan Africa															
Angola	...	...	...	...	...	...	...	...	16	33	...	...	...	...	...
Benin	6	12	10z	11z	3	14	4z	15z	9	12	14z	12z	...	...	...
Botswana	...	...	...	...	...	...	...	...	9	45	12z	47z	93Y	94Y	93Y
Burkina Faso	5	...	...	...	1	...	...	...	6	...	8z	11z	...	...	...
Burundi	...	...	...	...	...	...	...	...	...	...	8z	21z	37Y	39Y	28Y
Cameroon	13	28	...	...	13	28	...	...	26	28	48*	26*	...	...	...
Cape Verde	...	...	2	40	...	...	0.7	40	...	...	2	40	62	60	65
Central African Republic	...	...	...	...	...	...	...	...	...	...	...	...	...	...	...
Chad	2	5	...	...	1	6	...	...	4	5	7	...	...	...	...

SECONDARY EDUCATION						TERTIARY EDUCATION				
Pupil/teacher ratio[2]						Teaching staff				
Lower secondary		Upper secondary		Total secondary						
School year ending in		School year ending in		School year ending in		School year ending in				
1999	2005	1999	2005	1999	2005	1999		2005		
						Total (000)	% F	Total (000)	% F	Country or territory
17	16	15	15	16	16	8	...	11	47	Panama
...	15ʸ	...	9ʸ	...	12ʸ	...	...	...	...	Paraguay
...	12	...	...	...	17	...	...	...	...	Peru
...	10	...	10	...	10	.	.	.	.	Saint Kitts and Nevis
19	17	16	18	18	17	...	...	0.2	48	Saint Lucia
...	17	...	19	...	18	.	.	.	.	St Vincent/Grenad.
...	17	...	10	...	14	...	...	...	...	Suriname
22	16	19	16	21	16	0.5	31	2	33	Trinidad and Tobago
9	9	9	9	9	9	.	.	.	.	Turks and Caicos Islands
12	11ʸ	23	28ʸ	15	15ʸ	11	...	13ᶻ	...	Uruguay
...	12	...	9	...	11	...	...	82*,ᶻ	...	Venezuela
										North America and Western Europe
...	7	...	14	...	8	...	...	0.1	47	Andorra
9	9	12	13	10	11	26	...	30ᶻ	29ᶻ	Austria
...	7	...	7	...	7	...	...	26	41	Belgium
17	...	...	...	...	...	129	41	...	...	Canada
14	...	12	...	13	11	1	34	1	42	Cyprus
10	...	9	...	10	...	...	...	...	...	Denmark
10	10	...	11	...	10	18	46	19	46	Finland
13	13ᶻ	11	10ᶻ	12	11ᶻ	102	40	136ᶻ	39ᶻ	France
15	13	16	16	15	14	272	30	287	34	Germany
10	8	10	9	10	8	17	31	27	36	Greece
11	11ᶻ	14	12ᶻ	13	11ᶻ	1	43	2ᶻ	44ᶻ	Iceland
...	...	...	...	...	...	10	33	12	39	Ireland
12	11	9	...	10	10	...	...	...	...	Israel
10	10	11	11	11	11	73	...	94	34	Italy
...	...	...	5	...	10	...	...	...	...	Luxembourg
...	8	...	20	...	10	0.7	25	0.8	23	Malta
10	...	7	...	8	9ᶻ	.	.	.	.	Monaco
...	...	...	6	...	13	...	...	45	35	Netherlands
...	9ᶻ	8	8ᶻ	...	9ᶻ	14	36	18ᶻ	37ᶻ	Norway
...	...	...	...	...	7	...	...	37	42	Portugal
...	6ᶻ	...	...	...	...	...	...	...	...	San Marino
...	12	...	9	...	11	108	35	145	39	Spain
12	10	18	9	15	10	29	...	38	43	Sweden
...	9	...	29	...	14	8.0	16	34	32	Switzerland
16	15	14	14	15	15	92	32	122	40	United Kingdom
16	15	14	15	15	15	992	41	1 208	43	United States
										South and West Asia
...	14	...	...	...	...	...	...	2ᶻ	12ᶻ	Afghanistan
43	34ᶻ	32	21ᶻ	37	27ᶻ	45	14	52	15	Bangladesh
35	32	27	20	32	28	0.2	...	...	...	Bhutan
...	37ᶻ	...	28ᶻ	34	32ᶻ	...	...	539ᶻ	40ᶻ	India[w]
30	19	31	19	30	19	65	17	115	19	Iran, Islamic Republic of
18	15ʸ	9	8ʸ	17	14ʸ	.	.	0.04ʸ	67ʸ	Maldives
38	40ʸ	24	28ʸ	32	35ʸ	...	...	...	...	Nepal
...	38*,ᶻ	...	32*,ᶻ	...	37*,ᶻ	...	...	69*	17*	Pakistan
...	20ᶻ	...	19ᶻ	...	20ᶻ	...	...	...	...	Sri Lanka
										Sub-Saharan Africa
...	...	...	...	18	...	0.8	20	...	...	Angola
27	27ᶻ	15	16ᶻ	24	24ᶻ	0.6	9	...	...	Benin
...	...	...	...	18	14ᶻ	0.5	28	0.5	37	Botswana
29	...	...	23	28	31ᶻ	0.8	...	2	6	Burkina Faso
...	...	...	...	...	19ᶻ	0.4	...	0.7	14	Burundi
26	...	21	...	24	25*	2.6	...	3	...	Cameroon
...	23	...	23	...	23	...	...	0.5	41	Cape Verde
...	...	...	...	...	...	0.3	5	...	...	Central African Republic
41	...	23	...	34	34	...	...	1.1	3	Chad

Table 10B (continued)

Country or territory	Lower secondary 1999 Total (000)	Lower secondary 1999 % F	Lower secondary 2005 Total (000)	Lower secondary 2005 % F	Upper secondary 1999 Total (000)	Upper secondary 1999 % F	Upper secondary 2005 Total (000)	Upper secondary 2005 % F	Total secondary 1999 Total (000)	Total secondary 1999 % F	Total secondary 2005 Total (000)	Total secondary 2005 % F	Trained teachers (%)[1] Total secondary 2005 Total	Male	Female
Comoros	…	…	2	16	…	…	1	9	…	…	3	13	51[Y]	…	…
Congo	…	…	4[z]	15[z]	…	…	3[z]	11[z]	…	…	7[z]	13[z]	…	…	…
Côte d'Ivoire	13	…	…	…	7	13	…	…	20	…	…	…	…	…	…
Democratic Rep. of the Congo	…	…	…	…	…	…	…	…	89	10	114[Y]	9[Y]	…	…	…
Equatorial Guinea	0.7	5	…	…	0.1	7	…	…	0.9	5	…	…	…	…	…
Eritrea	1	12	2	10	1	11	2	13	2	12	4	11	51	49	67
Ethiopia	38	15	…	…	14	8	…	…	52	13	**96**	**17**	51	51	52
Gabon	2	17	…	…	0.7	15	…	…	3	16	…	…	…	…	…
Gambia	2	16	1[z]	16[z]	0.6	12	0.9[z]	12[z]	2	15	2[z]	14[z]	…	…	…
Ghana	40	24	**56**	**29**	12	16	**17**	**19**	52	22	**74**	**27**	**74**	**83**	**48**
Guinea	4	11	…	…	1	10	…	…	6	11	12	5	…	…	…
Guinea-Bissau	…	…	…	…	…	…	…	…	…	…	…	…	…	…	…
Kenya	…	…	…	…	…	…	…	…	…	…	78	38	…	…	…
Lesotho	2	51	…	…	1	53	…	…	3	51	4	56	81	79	83
Liberia	4	16	…	…	3	16	…	…	7	16	…	…	…	…	…
Madagascar	14	44	…	…	6	44	…	…	20	44	…	…	…	…	…
Malawi	…	…	…	…	…	…	…	…	…	…	…	…	…	…	…
Mali	5*	17*	8	15	3	10	…	…	8*	14*	…	…	…	…	…
Mauritius	…	…	…	…	…	…	…	…	5	47	7	55	…	…	…
Mozambique	…	…	7	19	…	…	2	14	…	…	10	18	…	…	…
Namibia	4	45	…	…	1	49	…	…	5	46	6	50	97	…	…
Niger	2	23	3[z]	21[z]	2	12	2[z]	14[z]	4	18	5[z]	19[z]	30*[,z]	30*[,z]	30*[,z]
Nigeria	…	…	…	…	…	…	…	…	…	…	159	36	…	…	…
Rwanda	…	…	…	…	…	…	…	…	…	…	8	20	…	…	…
Sao Tome and Principe	…	…	…	…	…	…	…	…	…	…	0.4	13	…	…	…
Senegal	6	14	…	…	3	13	…	…	9	14	15	14	51[z]	50[z]	55[z]
Seychelles	0.4	54	…	…	0.2	55	…	…	0.6	54	0.6	56	91[Y]	90[Y]	93[Y]
Sierra Leone	…	…	…	…	…	…	…	…	…	…	…	…	…	…	…
Somalia	…	…	…	…	…	…	…	…	…	…	…	…	…	…	…
South Africa	…	…	…	…	…	…	…	…	145	50	149[z]	52[z]	…	…	…
Swaziland	…	…	…	…	…	…	…	…	…	…	4[z]	49[z]	99[z]	99[z]	99[z]
Togo	5	13	…	…	2	15	…	…	7	13	13	7	47[z]	47[z]	39[z]
Uganda	…	…	…	…	…	…	…	…	…	…	36	22	82[z]	81[z]	86[z]
United Republic of Tanzania	…	…	…	…	…	…	…	…	…	…	…	…	…	…	…
Zambia	4	28	…	…	6	27	…	…	10	27	…	…	…	…	…
Zimbabwe	…	…	…	…	…	…	…	…	31	37	34[Y]	40[Y]	…	…	…

	Sum	% F	Sum	% F	Sum	% F	Sum	% F	Sum	% F	Sum	% F	Median		
World	…	…	…	…	…	…	…	…	24 296	52	28 457	53	…		…
Countries in transition	…	…	…	…	…	…	…	…	2 888	74	2 844	75	…	…	…
Developed countries	…	…	…	…	…	…	…	…	6 296	55	6 564	59	…	…	…
Developing countries	…	…	…	…	…	…	…	…	15 111	47	19 049	47	…	…	…
Arab States	…	…	…	…	…	…	…	…	1 387	46	1 711	49	…	…	…
Central and Eastern Europe	…	…	…	…	…	…	…	…	3 172	72	3 005	74	…	…	…
Central Asia	…	…	…	…	…	…	…	…	972	66	1 069	67	…	…	…
East Asia and the Pacific	…	…	…	…	…	…	…	…	7 704	46	9 116	46	…	…	…
East Asia	…	…	…	…	…	…	…	…	7 476	46	8 867	46	…	…	…
Pacific	…	…	…	…	…	…	…	…	228	57	249	55	…	…	…
Latin America/Caribbean	…	…	…	…	…	…	…	…	2 746	64	3 436	65	69	63	71
Caribbean	…	…	…	…	…	…	…	…	53	44	66	40	58	58	61
Latin America	…	…	…	…	…	…	…	…	2 693	64	3 370	66	…	…	…
N. America/W. Europe	…	…	…	…	…	…	…	…	4 487	56	4 807	60	…	…	…
South and West Asia	…	…	…	…	…	…	…	…	2 956	35	4 142	36	…	…	…
Sub-Saharan Africa	…	…	…	…	…	…	…	…	871	31	1 171	29	…	…	…

1. Data on trained teachers (defined according to national standards) are not collected for countries whose education statistics are gathered through the OECD, Eurostat or the World Education Indicators questionnaires.

2. Based on headcounts of pupils and teachers.
3. Teaching staff in upper secondary includes full- and part-time teachers.

SECONDARY EDUCATION

Pupil/teacher ratio[2]

Lower secondary		Upper secondary		Total secondary		TERTIARY EDUCATION Teaching staff				Country or territory
School year ending in		School year ending in		School year ending in		School year ending in				
1999	2005	1999	2005	1999	2005	1999		2005		
						Total (000)	% F	Total (000)	% F	
...	*16*	...	*11*	...	*14*	0.1	10	*0.1z*	*15z*	Comoros
...	*45z*	...	*18z*	...	*34z*	*0.4*	5	*0.9y*	...	Congo
34	...	*21*	...	29	...	...	...	...	...	Côte d'Ivoire
...	...	...	...	14	15y	4	6	...	...	Democratic Rep. of the Congo
25	...	15	...	23	...	...	...	...	...	Equatorial Guinea
55	57	45	44	51	51	0.2	13	*0.4z*	*14z*	Eritrea
35	...	37	...	36	**54**	2	6	5	10	Ethiopia
28	...	*28*	...	*28*	...	0.6	17	...	...	Gabon
20	*51z*	25	*31z*	22	*42z*	0.1	15	*0.1z*	*16z*	Gambia
20	**18**	19	**21**	20	**19**	*2*	13	**4**	**11**	Ghana
31	...	26	...	30	36	...	...	1	4	Guinea
...	...	...	...	...	...	*0.0*	18	...	...	Guinea-Bissau
...	...	...	...	...	32	...	...	...	...	Kenya
24	...	*17*	...	22	27	0.4	*45*	0.6	...	Lesotho
17	...	18	...	17	...	0.6	15	...	...	Liberia
20	...	*11*	...	*17*	...	1	31	2	31	Madagascar
...	...	...	...	...	...	0.5	25	*0.4z*	*32z*	Malawi
31*	38	24	...	28*	...	1	...	*1*	...	Mali
...	...	...	...	20	17	*0.6*	26	...	...	Mauritius
...	36	...	18	...	32	...	...	3	21	Mozambique
25	...	21	...	24	25	...	...	*0.9y*	*27y*	Namibia
34	*44z*	12	*11z*	24	*31z*	...	...	0.7	6	Niger
...	...	...	...	...	40	52	31	*37z*	*17z*	Nigeria
...	...	...	...	...	26	0.4	10	*2*	*12*	Rwanda
...	...	...	...	...	22	.	.	.	.	Sao Tome and Principe
29	...	*19*	...	25	26	...	...	...	...	Senegal
14	...	*14*	...	14	13	.	.	.	.	Seychelles
...	...	...	...	...	...	...	...	...	...	Sierra Leone
...	...	...	...	...	...	...	...	...	...	Somalia
...	...	...	...	29	*31z*	...	...	43	50	South Africa
...	...	...	...	...	*18z*	0.2	32	0.4	36	Swaziland
40	...	23	...	35	*30*	0.4	10	...	...	Togo
...	...	...	...	...	21	2	17	*4z*	*19z*	Uganda
...	...	...	...	...	...	2	14	3	17	United Republic of Tanzania
29	...	*19*	...	23	...	...	...	...	...	Zambia
...	...	...	...	27	*22y*	...	...	...	...	Zimbabwe

Weighted average						Sum	% F	Sum	% F	
...	...	...	...	18	18	6 476	39	8 812	41	World
...	...	...	...	11	10	797	54	993	53	Countries in transition
...	...	...	...	13	13	2 787	34	3 289	37	Developed countries
...	...	...	...	21	21	2 893	39	4 531	40	Developing countries
...	...	...	...	16	17	205	33	270	34	Arab States
...	...	...	...	12	12	991	50	1 211	50	Central and Eastern Europe
...	...	...	...	10	10	107	44	141	49	Central Asia
...	...	...	...	17	18	1 608	33	2 557	37	East Asia and the Pacific
...	...	...	...	17	18	1 533	33	2 485	37	East Asia
...	...	...	...	15	14	76	44	73	43	Pacific
...	...	...	...	19	17	832	45	1 208	45	Latin America/Caribbean
...	...	...	...	22	19	6	47	8	49	Caribbean
...	...	...	...	19	17	826	45	1 200	45	Latin America
...	...	...	...	14	13	2 043	38	2 492	40	N. America/W. Europe
...	...	...	...	33	29	573	31	784	33	South and West Asia
...	...	...	...	25	28	116	29	149	28	Sub-Saharan Africa

Data in italic are UIS estimates.
Data in bold are for the school year ending in 2006.

(z) Data are for the school year ending in 2004.
(y) Data are for the school year ending in 2003.
(∗) National estimates.

Table 11
Commitment to education: public spending

Country or territory	Total public expenditure on education as % of GNP		Total public expenditure on education as % of total government expenditure		Public current expenditure on education as % of total public expenditure on education		Public current expenditure on primary education as % of public current expenditure on education		Public current expenditure on primary education per pupil (unit cost) at PPP in constant 2004 US$		Public current expenditure on primary education as % of GNP	
	1999	2005	1999	2005	1999	2005	1999	2005	1999	2005	1999	2005
Arab States												
Algeria	...	...	...	...	...	...	...	...	...	672 [y]	...	1.6 [y]
Bahrain	...	...	...	...	...	...	...	...	...	2 926 [x]	...	1.9 [x]
Djibouti	...	7.1	...	27	...	93	...	44	...	983	...	2.9
Egypt	...	...	...	...	...	...	...	...	...	...	...	...
Iraq	...		...		...		...		...		...	
Jordan	5.0	...	21	...	...	...	...	...	537	589 [z]	1.9	1.82 [z]
Kuwait	...	4.5	...	13	...	92	...	21	...	2 910 [z]	...	0.9
Lebanon	2.0	2.7	10	11	...	93	...	33	...	370	...	0.8
Libyan Arab Jamahiriya	...	...	...	...	68	...	12	...	...	...	...	...
Mauritania	3.1	2.4	...	...	...	99	...	62	...	201 [y]	...	1.5
Morocco	6.2	6.8	26	27	91	95	39	45	663	937	2.2	2.9
Oman	4.2	4.3 [z]	21	24	...	89	...	50	1 363	2 142 [z]	1.4	1.8 [z]
Palestinian A. T.	...	...	...	...	...	...	...	...	...	...	...	...
Qatar	...	...	...	...	...	88 [z]	...	...	...	...	...	...
Saudi Arabia	7.0	6.7 [z]	26	28 [z]	...	...	...	...	...	...	...	...
Sudan	...	...	...	...	...	...	...	...	...	...	...	...
Syrian Arab Republic	...	...	...	...	...	...	...	...	412	577 [x]	1.7	2.1 [x]
Tunisia	7.2	7.6	...	21	...	87	...	35	...	1 524	...	2.3
United Arab Emirates	...	1.6*,[z]	...	27	...	...	...	...	1 880	1 601 [z]	0.7	0.4 [z]
Yemen	...	...	...	...	...	...	...	...	...	...	...	...
Central and Eastern Europe												
Albania	...	...	...	...	...	...	...	...	...	...	...	...
Belarus	6.0	6.0	...	11	...	95	...	9	...	1 033	...	0.5
Bosnia and Herzegovina	...	...	...	...	...	...	...	...	...	...	...	...
Bulgaria	...	4.4 [y]	...	...	...	97 [y]	...	19 [y]	...	1 429 [y]	...	0.8 [y]
Croatia	...	4.9 [y]	...	10 [y]	...	93 [y]	...	19 [y]	...	2 246 [y]	...	0.8 [y]
Czech Republic	4.1	4.7 [z]	10	10 [z]	91	90 [z]	18	15 [z]	1 651	2 226 [z]	0.7	0.6 [z]
Estonia	7.0	5.6 [z]	...	15 [z]	...	91 [z]	...	26 [z]	...	2 628 [z]	...	1.3 [z]
Hungary	5.0	5.9 [z]	13	11 [z]	91	94 [z]	20	19 [z]	2 260	3 831 [z]	0.9	1.1 [z]
Latvia	5.8	5.3 [y]	...	15 [y]	...	...	...	...	...	...	...	...
Lithuania	...	5.4 [z]	...	16 [z]	...	95 [z]	...	14 [z]	...	1 879 [z]	...	0.7 [z]
Poland	4.7	5.7 [z]	11	13 [z]	93	95 [z]	...	31 [z]	...	2 865 [z]	...	1.7 [z]
Republic of Moldova	3.9	3.8	...	21	...	94	...	17	...	290	...	0.6
Romania	3.6	3.5 [y]	...	...	...	93 [y]	...	17 [y]	...	919 [y]	...	0.5 [y]
Russian Federation	...	3.6 [z]	...	13 [z]	...	...	...	...	...	...	...	...
Serbia and Montenegro	4.3	...	...	...	...	...	...	...	...	...	...	...
Slovakia	4.3	4.3 [z]	14	11 [z]	96	94 [z]	14	14 [z]	1 190	1 695 [z]	0.6	0.6 [z]
Slovenia	...	6.0 [z]	...	13 [y]	...	92 [z]	...	20 [z]	...	4 866 [z]	...	1.1 [z]
TFYR Macedonia	4.2	3.4 [y]	...	16 [y]	...	...	...	...	...	...	...	...
Turkey	4.0	3.8 [y]	...	...	...	...	...	...	...	...	...	...
Ukraine	3.7	6.5	14	19	...	...	...	...	...	...	...	...
Central Asia												
Armenia	3.1	...	...	...	...	...	...	...	...	...	...	...
Azerbaijan	4.3	2.8	24	20	99	98	...	17	...	337	...	0.5
Georgia	2.0	2.8 [z]	10	13 [z]	...	97 [z]	...	...	...	...	...	...
Kazakhstan	4.0	2.5	14	...	...	...	...	...	...	...	...	...
Kyrgyzstan	3.7	4.6 [y]	...	...	99	...	...	...	...	127 [x]	...	0.7 [x]
Mongolia	6.0	5.4 [z]	...	...	...	94 [z]	...	24 [z]	...	269 [z]	...	1.2 [z]
Tajikistan	2.2	3.6	12	18	90	88	...	27	...	100	...	0.9
Turkmenistan	...	...	...	...	...	...	...	...	...	...	...	...
Uzbekistan	...	...	...	...	...	...	...	...	...	...	...	...
East Asia and the Pacific												
Australia	5.1	4.9 [z]	...	...	96	96 [z]	33	33 [z]	4 311	4 747 [z]	1.6	1.6 [z]
Brunei Darussalam	...	...	9	...	97	...	...	...	...	...	...	...
Cambodia	1.0	2.0 [z]	9	...	...	...	...	...	...	...	...	...
China	1.9	...	13	...	93	...	34	...	...	...	0.6	...
Cook Islands	0.4	...	13	...	99	...	53	...	...	...	0.2	...
DPR Korea	...	...	...	...	...	...	...	...	...	...	...	...

Education for All Global Monitoring Report 2008

Public current expenditure on primary education per pupil as % of GNP per capita		Public current expenditure on secondary education as % of public current expenditure on education		Public current expenditure on secondary education per pupil (unit cost) at PPP in constant 2004 US$		Public current expenditure on secondary education as % of GNP		Public current expenditure on secondary education per pupil as % of GNP per capita		Primary teachers' compensation as % of public current expenditure on primary education		Country or territory
1999	2005	1999	2005	1999	2005	1999	2005	1999	2005	1999	2005	
												Arab States
...	11^y	...	...	...	1 019^y	...	1.9^y	...	17^y	...	...	Algeria
...	16^x	...	...	...	3 273^x	...	1.7^x	...	18^x	...	...	Bahrain
...	45	...	39	...	1 481	...	2.6	...	68	...	54	Djibouti
...	...	...	...	...	...	...	...	...	...	...	...	Egypt
...	...	...	...	...	...	...	...	...	...	...	...	Iraq
13	12^z	...	...	622	712^z	1.8	1.7^z	15	14^z	78	86^z	Jordan
...	11	...	38	...	3 283^z	...	1.6	...	16	...	78	Kuwait
...	7	...	30	...	413	...	0.7	...	7	69	84	Lebanon
...	...	10	...	...	...	...	...	...	...	...	...	Libyan Arab Jamahiriya
...	10	...	33	...	596^y	...	0.8	...	25	...	...	Mauritania
18	22	44	38	1 739	1 620	2.5	2.5	46	38	...	...	Morocco
11	15^z	...	41	2 649	2 039^z	2.0	1.6^z	21	14^z	75	91^z	Oman
...	...	...	...	...	...	...	...	...	...	...	...	Palestinian A. T.
...	...	...	...	...	...	...	...	...	...	...	...	Qatar
...	...	...	...	...	...	...	...	...	...	...	...	Saudi Arabia
...	...	...	...	...	...	...	...	...	...	...	...	Sudan
10	13^x	...	...	132	159^x	1.1	1.3^x	18	20^x	...	...	Syrian Arab Republic
...	20	...	43	...	1 766	...	2.8	...	23	...	...	Tunisia
8	7^z	...	...	2 453	2 070^z	0.7	0.6^z	10	9^z	...	77^z	United Arab Emirates
...	...	...	...	...	...	...	...	...	...	...	...	Yemen
												Central and Eastern Europe
...	...	...	...	...	...	...	...	...	...	...	...	Albania
...	13	...	40	...	1 845	...	2.3	...	24	...	...	Belarus
...	...	...	...	...	...	...	...	...	...	...	...	Bosnia and Herzegovina
...	19^y	...	45^y	...	1 567^y	...	1.9^y	...	21^y	...	61^y	Bulgaria
...	20^y	...	49^y	...	2 838^y	...	2.2^y	...	25^y	...	...	Croatia
11	12^z	50	52^z	3 254	4 190^z	1.9	2.2^z	21	23^z	45	47^z	Czech Republic
...	19^z	...	47^z	...	3 519^z	...	2.4^z	...	26^z	...	...	Estonia
18	24^z	41	42^z	2 352	3 822^z	1.8	2.3^z	19	24^z	...	...	Hungary
...	...	...	...	...	...	...	...	...	...	...	...	Latvia
...	15^z	...	51^z	...	2 666^z	...	2.6^z	...	21^z	...	...	Lithuania
...	23^z	...	35^z	...	2 628^z	...	1.9^z	...	21^z	...	...	Poland
...	14	...	51	...	421	...	1.8	...	20	...	...	Republic of Moldova
...	12^y	...	42^y	...	1 029^y	...	1.4^y	...	13^y	...	...	Romania
...	...	...	...	...	...	...	...	...	...	...	...	Russian Federation
...	...	...	...	...	...	...	...	...	...	...	...	Serbia and Montenegro
10	12^z	56	51^z	2 147	2 421^z	2.3	2.1^z	18	17^z	62	50^z	Slovakia
...	23^z	...	48^z	...	5 904^z	...	2.7^z	...	28^z	...	42^z	Slovenia
...	...	...	...	...	...	...	...	...	...	...	...	TFYR Macedonia
...	...	...	...	...	...	...	...	...	...	...	...	Turkey
...	...	...	...	...	...	...	...	...	...	...	...	Ukraine
												Central Asia
...	...	...	...	...	...	...	...	...	...	...	...	Armenia
...	7	...	52	...	539	...	1.4	...	11	...	...	Azerbaijan
...	...	...	...	...	...	...	...	...	...	...	...	Georgia
...	...	...	...	...	...	...	...	...	...	...	...	Kazakhstan
...	8^x	...	...	...	240^x	...	2.0^x	...	15^x	47	...	Kyrgyzstan
...	13^z	...	32^z	...	249^z	...	1.6^z	...	12^z	...	...	Mongolia
...	8	...	50	...	130	...	1.6	...	11	...	...	Tajikistan
...	...	...	...	...	...	...	...	...	...	...	...	Turkmenistan
...	...	...	...	...	...	...	...	...	...	...	...	Uzbekistan
												East Asia and the Pacific
16	16^z	40	39^z	3 922	4 348^z	1.9	1.8^z	15	...^{z}	60	62^z	Australia
...	...	...	...	...	...	...	...	...	...	...	...	Brunei Darussalam
...	...	...	...	...	...	...	...	...	...	...	...	Cambodia
...	...	38	...	441	...	0.7	...	11	...	...	...	China
...	...	40	...	...	...	0.2	...	...	...	...	...	Cook Islands
...	...	...	...	...	...	...	...	...	...	...	...	DPR Korea

Table 11 (continued)

Country or territory	Total public expenditure on education as % of GNP		Total public expenditure on education as % of total government expenditure		Public current expenditure on education as % of total public expenditure on education		Public current expenditure on primary education as % of public current expenditure on education		Public current expenditure on primary education per pupil (unit cost) at PPP in constant 2004 US$		Public current expenditure on primary education as % of GNP	
	1999	2005	1999	2005	1999	2005	1999	2005	1999	2005	1999	2005
Fiji	5.7	6.4z	18	...	...	97z	...	40z	...	1068z	...	2.5z
Indonesia	...	1.0y	...	...	...	88y	...	39y	...	84y	...	0.3y
Japan	3.5	3.5z	9	11y	...	...	...	...	...	...	...	...
Kiribati	7.7	...	...	...	...	...	...	...	...	...	...	...
Lao PDR	1.0	2.5	...	12	...	44	...	46	...	55	...	0.4
Macao, China	3.6	...	14	14z	...	89z	...	...	...	...	...	...
Malaysia	6.1	6.2z	25	24z	...	88z	...	31z	...	1293z	...	1.7z
Marshall Islands	13.3	9.5z	...	16y	...	...	...	...	...	...	...	...
Micronesia	6.5	...	...	...	...	...	...	...	...	...	...	...
Myanmar	0.6	...	8	...	64	...	...	...	...	...	...	...
Nauru	...	...	...	...	...	...	...	...	...	...	...	...
New Zealand	7.3	7.0	...	21y	95	100	27	26	3720	3853	1.8	1.8
Niue	...	...	...	...	100	...	32	...	...	...	...	...
Palau	...	...	...	...	...	...	...	...	...	...	...	...
Papua New Guinea	...	...	...	...	...	...	...	...	...	...	...	...
Philippines	...	2.5z	...	16z	...	94z	...	55z	...	414z	...	1.3z
Republic of Korea	3.8	4.6z	13	15y	80	88z	44	34z	2564	3254z	1.3	1.4z
Samoa	4.5	...	13	...	99	...	32	...	449	...	1.4	...
Singapore	...	...	...	...	...	...	...	...	...	...	...	...
Solomon Islands	3.3	...	...	...	...	...	...	...	...	...	...	...
Thailand	5.1	4.3	...	25	...	...	...	...	...	...	...	...
Timor-Leste	...	...	...	...	...	...	...	...	...	...	...	...
Tokelau	...	...	...	15y	...	...	...	...	...	...	...	...
Tonga	6.4	4.9z	...	13y	...	...	...	...	...	878x	...	2.2x
Tuvalu	...	...	...	...	...	...	...	...	...	...	...	...
Vanuatu	6.7	10.0y	17	...	84	...	39	...	388	...	2.2	...
Viet Nam	...	...	...	...	...	...	...	...	...	...	...	...
Latin America and the Caribbean												
Anguilla	...	...	...	...	...	41y	...	48y	...	...	...	...
Antigua and Barbuda	3.5	...	...	...	100	...	...	...	...	...	...	...
Argentina	4.6	4.0z	13	13z	94	99z	37	37z	1594	1498z	1.6	1.5z
Aruba	...	...	14	15	90	84	30	30	...	...	...	...
Bahamas	...	...	...	...	...	...	...	...	...	...	...	...
Barbados	5.3	7.2	15	16	92	96	21	28	...	...	1.0	2.0
Belize	5.7	5.9z	17	18y	...	88z	...	47z	...	896z	...	2.5z
Bermuda	...	...	...	...	...	97	...	41	...	...	...	...
Bolivia	5.8	6.6y	16	18y	84	96y	41	46y	286	429y	2.0	2.9y
Brazil	4.4	4.5z	10	...	95	94z	33	32z	855	1071z	1.4	1.4z
British Virgin Islands	...	...	...	12	...	87	...	32	...	...	...	...
Cayman Islands	...	...	...	...	...	...	...	...	...	...	...	...
Chile	4.0	3.8	17	18z	88	95	45	37	1206	1421	1.5	1.4
Colombia	4.5	5.0	17	11	...	99	...	48	...	1478	...	2.4
Costa Rica	5.5	5.1z	...	19z	100	79z	47	56z	1563	1578z	2.6	2.3z
Cuba	7.7	...	14	17	...	86	...	32	...	...	...	...
Dominica	5.5	...	...	...	...	...	...	...	...	...	...	...
Dominican Republic	...	1.9	...	10	...	99	...	65	...	598	...	1.2
Ecuador	2.0	...	10	...	93*	...	...	...	...	...	...	...
El Salvador	2.4	2.8	17	...	...	98	...	51	...	470	...	1.4
Grenada	...	6.0y	...	13y	...	87y	...	35y	...	762y	...	1.8y
Guatemala	...	1.3	...	9	...	100	...	73	...	214	...	0.9
Guyana	9.3	9.1	18	15	...	90	...	34	...	737	...	2.8
Haiti	...	...	...	...	...	...	...	...	...	...	...	...
Honduras	...	...	...	...	...	...	...	...	...	...	...	...
Jamaica	...	5.6	...	9	...	96z	...	31z	...	547	...	1.8
Mexico	4.5	5.5z	23	26z	95	97z	41	40z	1054	1442z	1.8	2.1z
Montserrat	...	...	11	...	47	65z	...	...	...	...	...	...
Netherlands Antilles	...	...	14	...	94	...	...	...	...	...	...	...
Nicaragua	4.0	3.2y	6	...	...	91x	...	68z	...	295z	...	1.5z
Panama	5.1	4.1z	...	9z	...	...	...	...	862	...	1.9	...
Paraguay	4.8	4.3y	9	11y	88	96y	...	46y	...	567y	...	1.9y
Peru	3.5	2.6	21	14	88	97	40	42	355	403	1.2	1.0
Saint Kitts and Nevis	5.6	10.8	13	13y	...	37	...	...	...	987x	...	1.2x

Education for All Global Monitoring Report 2 0 0 8

Public current expenditure on primary education per pupil as % of GNP per capita		Public current expenditure on secondary education as % of public current expenditure on education		Public current expenditure on secondary education per pupil (unit cost) at PPP in constant 2004 US$		Public current expenditure on secondary education as % of GNP		Public current expenditure on secondary education per pupil as % of GNP per capita		Primary teachers' compensation as % of public current expenditure on primary education		Country or territory
1999	2005	1999	2005	1999	2005	1999	2005	1999	2005	1999	2005	
...	19^z	...	33^z	...	991^z	...	2.1^z	...	17^z	...	...	Fiji
...	3^y	...	42^y	...	158^y	...	0.4^y	...	5^y	...	78^y	Indonesia
...	...	...	...	...	...	...	...	...	...	...	...	Japan
...	...	...	...	...	...	...	...	...	...	...	...	Kiribati
...	3	...	23	...	77	...	0.3	...	4	...	...	Lao PDR
...	...	...	...	...	...	...	...	...	...	...	...	Macao, China
...	13^z	...	37^z	...	1877^z	...	2.0^z	...	19^z	70	64^z	Malaysia
...	...	...	...	...	...	...	...	...	...	...	...	Marshall Islands
...	...	...	...	...	...	...	...	...	...	...	...	Micronesia
...	...	...	...	...	...^{y}	...	...	...	...	...	...	Myanmar
...	...	...	...	...	...	...	...	...	...	...	...	Nauru
19	21	40	43	4 634	4 483	2.7	3.0	24	24	...	...	New Zealand
...	...	59	...	...	...	...	...	...	...	...	...	Niue
...	...	...	...	...	...	...	...	...	...	...	...	Palau
...	...	...	...	...	...	...	...	...	...	...	...	Papua New Guinea
...	8^z	...	25^z	...	391^z	...	0.6^z	...	8^z	...	94^z	Philippines
16	16^z	38	43^z	2 130	4 636^z	1.2	1.7^z	13	23^z	78	64^z	Republic of Korea
9	...	27	...	475	...	1.2	...	10	...	...	...	Samoa
...	...	...	...	...	...	...	...	...	...	...	...	Singapore
...	...	...	...	...	...	...	...	...	...	...	...	Solomon Islands
...	...	...	...	...	...	...	...	...	...	...	...	Thailand
...	...	...	...	...	...	...	...	...	...	...	...	Timor-Leste
...	...	...	...	...	...	...	...	...	...	...	...	Tokelau
...	13^x	...	...	...	475^x	...	1.0^x	...	7^x	...	...	Tonga
...	...	...	...	...	...	...	...	...	...	...	...	Tuvalu
12	...	52	...	1 975	...	2.9	...	61	...	94	...	Vanuatu
...	...	...	...	...	...	...	...	...	...	...	...	Viet Nam
												Latin America and the Caribbean
...	...	...	17^y	...	...	...	...	...	...	...	...	Anguilla
...	...	...	...	...	...	...	...	...	...	66	...	Antigua and Barbuda
12	12^z	35	38^z	1 990	2 058^z	1.5	1.5^z	15	16^z	...	63^z	Argentina
...	...	32	32	...	...	...	...	...	...	...	...	Aruba
...	...	...	...	...	...	...	...	...	...	...	...	Bahamas
11	24	31	30	...	...	1.5	2.1	18	26	...	...	Barbados
...	14^z	...	44^z	...	1 298^z	...	2.3^z	...	20^z	...	86^z	Belize
...	...	...	52	...	...	...	...	...	...	...	...	Bermuda
11	17^y	22	25^y	270	345^y	1.1	1.6^y	11	13^y	...	...	Bolivia
11	13^z	36	40^z	775	987^z	1.5	1.7^z	10	12^z	...	...	Brazil
...	...	...	34	...	...	...	...	...	...	...	81	British Virgin Islands
...	...	...	...	...	...	...	...	...	...	...	...	Cayman Islands
13	13	36	39	1 367	1 564	1.3	1.4	15	14	...	85	Chile
...	20	...	36	...	1 364	...	1.8	...	19	91*	76	Colombia
18	17^z	29	34^z	2 263	1 587^z	1.6	1.4^z	26	17^z	...	...	Costa Rica
...	...	...	36	...	...	...	...	...	...	...	69	Cuba
...	...	...	...	...	...	...	...	...	...	...	...	Dominica
...	9	...	29	...	427	...	0.6	...	6	...	71	Dominican Republic
...	...	...	...	...	...	...	...	...	...	...	...	Ecuador
...	9	...	29	...	526	...	0.8	...	11	...	...	El Salvador
...	11^y	...	35^y	...	837^y	...	1.8^y	...	13^y	...	93^y	Grenada
...	5	...	18	...	161	...	0.2	...	4	...	88	Guatemala
...	18	...	13	...	454	...	1.0	...	11	...	75	Guyana
...	...	...	...	...	...	...	...	...	...	...	...	Haiti
...	...	...	...	...	...	...	...	...	...	...	...	Honduras
...	15	...	43^z	...	819	...	2.1	...	22	...	87	Jamaica
12	15^z	...	30^z	...	1 510^z	...	1.6^z	...	15^z	86	88^z	Mexico
...	...	...	...	...	...	...	...	...	...	...	...	Montserrat
...	...	...	...	...	...	...	...	...	...	...	...	Netherlands Antilles
...	8^z	...	31^z	...	309^z	...	0.7^z	...	9^z	...	93	Nicaragua
14	...	...	...	1 229	...	1.5	...	19	...	...	99	Panama
...	12^y	30	28^y	805	642^y	1.3	1.2^y	16	14^y	...	74^y	Paraguay
7	7	28	36	476	520	0.9	0.9	10	9	88	72	Peru
...	8*,^{x}	...	...	...	1 623^x	...	1.3^x	...	15^x	...	68	Saint Kitts and Nevis

Table 11 (continued)

Country or territory	Total public expenditure on education as % of GNP		Total public expenditure on education as % of total government expenditure		Public current expenditure on education as % of total public expenditure on education		Public current expenditure on primary education as % of public current expenditure on education		Public current expenditure on primary education per pupil (unit cost) at PPP in constant 2004 US$		Public current expenditure on primary education as % of GNP	
	1999	2005	1999	2005	1999	2005	1999	2005	1999	2005	1999	2005
Saint Lucia	8.0	6.2	21	17	79	90	*53*	40	*1 151*	909	*3.3*	2.2
St Vincent/Grenad.	*7.2*	8.7	…	16	…	68	…	50	…	1 250	…	2.9
Suriname	…	…	…	…	…	…	…	…	…	…	…	…
Trinidad and Tobago	3.9	…	*16*	…	96	…	40	…	948	…	1.5	…
Turks and Caicos Islands	…	…	17	12	73	88	30	*20*	…	…	…	…
Uruguay	2.8	2.3ʸ	…	8ʸ	92	…	32	…	736	…	0.8	…
Venezuela	…	…	…	…	…	…	…	…	…	…	…	…
North America and Western Europe												
Andorra	…	…	…	…	…	97ᶻ	…	29ᶻ	…	…	…	…
Austria	6.4	5.5ᶻ	12	11ᶻ	*94*	96ᶻ	*19*	19ᶻ	*7021*	7023ᶻ	*1.1*	1.0ᶻ
Belgium	…	6.0ᶻ	…	12ᶻ	…	98ᶻ	…	24ᶻ	…	6127ᶻ	…	1.4ᶻ
Canada	6.0	…	…	…	*98*	…	…	…	…	…	…	…
Cyprus	5.4	6.5ᶻ	…	14ᶻ	86	90ᶻ	34	30ᶻ	3831	5113ᶻ	1.6	1.7ᶻ
Denmark	8.2	8.6ᶻ	15	15ᶻ	…	95ᶻ	…	22ᶻ	*7054*	7358ᶻ	*1.6*	1.8ᶻ
Finland	6.3	6.6ᶻ	12	13ᶻ	*94*	92ᶻ	*21*	20ᶻ	*4404*	4924ᶻ	*1.2*	1.2ᶻ
France	5.7	5.8ᶻ	11	11ᶻ	*91*	91ᶻ	*20*	20ᶻ	*4280*	4837ᶻ	*1.1*	1.0ᶻ
Germany	4.5	4.7ʸ	10	10ʸ	…	…	…	…	…	…	…	…
Greece	3.5	4.3ᶻ	7	8ᶻ	*78*	79ᶻ	*25*	25ᶻ	*2157*	3203ᶻ	*0.7*	0.9ᶻ
Iceland	…	8.3ʸ	…	17ʸ	…	93ʸ	…	35ʸ	…	7718ʸ	…	2.7ʸ
Ireland	5.0	5.6ᶻ	13	14ᶻ	*91*	94ᶻ	*32*	33ᶻ	*3182*	5215ᶻ	*1.5*	1.8ᶻ
Israel	7.5	7.1ᶻ	14	14ʸ	*94*	95ᶻ	*34*	36ᶻ	*4765*	4996ᶻ	*2.4*	2.4ᶻ
Italy	4.8	4.7ᶻ	10	10ᶻ	*94*	95ᶻ	*26*	25ᶻ	*6207*	6571ᶻ	*1.2*	1.1ᶻ
Luxembourg	3.6	…	8	…	…	…	…	…	…	12359ᶻ	…	1.5ᶻ
Malta	4.9	…	…	…	…	…	…	…	…	2443ˣ	…	1.1ˣ
Monaco	…	…	5	…	92	91ᶻ	18	17ᶻ	…	…	…	…
Netherlands	4.8	5.5ᶻ	10	11ᶻ	*96*	93ᶻ	*26*	27ᶻ	*4446*	5441ᶻ	*1.2*	1.4ᶻ
Norway	7.2	7.7ᶻ	16	17ᶻ	90	92ᶻ	25	24ᶻ	*6267*	7013ᶻ	*1.6*	1.7ᶻ
Portugal	*5.7*	5.8ᶻ	*13*	11ᶻ	*93*	98ᶻ	*31*	32ᶻ	*3838*	4762ᶻ	*1.6*	1.8ᶻ
San Marino	…	…	…	…	…	…	…	…	…	…	…	…
Spain	4.4	4.4ʸ	11	11ʸ	*91*	90ʸ	*28*	27ʸ	*3890*	4399ʸ	*1.1*	1.1ʸ
Sweden	7.5	7.3ᶻ	14	13ᶻ	…	100ᶻ	…	27ᶻ	…	7664ᶻ	…	2.0ᶻ
Switzerland	5.0	5.6ʸ	15	13ʸ	90	92ʸ	32	29ʸ	6635	7193ʸ	1.4	1.5ʸ
United Kingdom	4.6	5.4ʸ	11	13ʸ	…	…	…	…	…	…	…	…
United States	5.0	5.6ᶻ	…	15ʸ	…	…	…	…	…	…	…	…
South and West Asia												
Afghanistan	…	…	…	…	…	…	…	…	…	…	…	…
Bangladesh	2.3	2.4	15	14	64	79	39	*35*	63	*106*	0.6	*0.7*
Bhutan	…	…	…	…	…	…	…	…	…	…	…	…
India	4.0	3.8ᶻ	13	11ʸ	*98*	…	30	…	*264*	…	1.2	…
Iran, Islamic Republic of	4.6	4.7	19	23	91	94	…	23	…	599	…	1.0
Maldives	…	7.5	…	15	…	81	…	54	…	…	…	3.3
Nepal	*2.9*	3.4ʸ	*12*	15ʸ	*74*	77ʸ	*53*	49ʸ	*94*	113ʸ	*1.1*	1.3ʸ
Pakistan	2.6	2.4	…	11	89	78	…	…	…	…	…	…
Sri Lanka	…	…	…	…	…	…	…	…	…	…	…	…
Sub-Saharan Africa												
Angola	*3.4*	…	*6*	…	*89*	…	…	…	…	…	…	…
Benin	*2.5*	3.5	…	*14*	*94*	82ᶻ	…	50ᶻ	…	116	…	1.7
Botswana	…	11.0	…	22	…	78	…	25	…	1118	…	2.1
Burkina Faso	…	4.7	…	17	…	96	…	71	…	396	…	3.2
Burundi	3.5	5.2	…	18	94	98	39	52	*76*	120	1.3	2.7
Cameroon	*2.4*	1.8*	*10*	9*	…	85*	…	68*	154	112*	1.2	1.1
Cape Verde	…	7.2	…	25	…	85	…	52	…	1142	…	3.2
Central African Republic	…	…	…	…	…	…	…	…	…	129	…	1.1
Chad	*1.7*	2.5	…	10	…	50	…	48	…	67	…	0.6
Comoros	…	…	…	…	…	…	…	…	…	…	…	…
Congo	6.0	2.8	22	8	93	91	36	27	169	37	2.0	0.7
Côte d'Ivoire	5.6	…	…	…	74	…	43	…	262	…	1.8	*0.1*
D. R. Congo	…	…	…	…	…	…	…	…	…	…	…	…
Equatorial Guinea	…	…	…	4ʸ	…	90ʸ	…	…	…	…	…	…
Eritrea	5.3	5.4	…	…	70	73	…	25	…	111	…	1.0

Public current expenditure on primary education per pupil as % of GNP per capita		Public current expenditure on secondary education as % of public current expenditure on education		Public current expenditure on secondary education per pupil (unit cost) at PPP in constant 2004 US$		Public current expenditure on secondary education as % of GNP		Public current expenditure on secondary education per pupil as % of GNP per capita		Primary teachers' compensation as % of public current expenditure on primary education		Country or territory
1999	2005	1999	2005	1999	2005	1999	2005	1999	2005	1999	2005	
20	16	33	30	1 540	1 166	2.0	1.7	27	20	88	83	Saint Lucia
...	20	...	30	...	1 258	...	1.7	...	20	...	85	St Vincent/Grenad.
...	...	...	...	...	...	...	...	...	...	...	...	Suriname
11	...	31	...	1 089	...	1.2	...	13	...	78	...	Trinidad and Tobago
...	...	40	30	...	...	...	...	...	...	63	...	Turks and Caicos Islands
8	...	37	...	1 081	...	1.0	...	11	...	71	45[y]	Uruguay
...	...	...	...	...	...	...	...	...	...	...	...	Venezuela
												North America and Western Europe
...	...	...	19[z]	...	...	...	...	...	...	...	...	Andorra
23	22[z]	45	48[z]	8 655	8 603[z]	2.7	2.5[z]	29	27[z]	71	68[z]	Austria
...	19[z]	...	43[z]	...	10 364[z]	...	2.5[z]	...	33[z]	...	66[z]	Belgium
...	...	...	...	...	...	...	...	...	...	...	...	Canada
19	23[z]	53	50[z]	6 047	8 323[z]	2.4	2.9[z]	30	37[z]	...	79[z]	Cyprus
24	23[z]	...	35[z]	11 119	10 888[z]	3.0	2.9[z]	37	34[z]	49	52[z]	Denmark
17	17[z]	39	41[z]	6 545	8 948[z]	2.3	2.4[z]	25	30[z]	59	58[z]	Finland
16	16[z]	50	48[z]	6 997	7 680[z]	2.6	2.5[z]	26	26[z]	...	55[z]	France
...	...	...	...	...	...	...	...	...	...	...	...	Germany
12	14[z]	38	36[z]	2 685	4 327[z]	1.0	1.2[z]	15	19[z]	...	...	Greece
...	25[y]	...	34[y]	...	6 753[y]	...	2.6[y]	...	22[y]	...	...	Iceland
12	16[z]	37	35[z]	4 790	7 807[z]	1.7	1.9[z]	18	24[z]	83	77[z]	Ireland
20	21[z]	30	30[z]	5 343	5 282[z]	2.1	2.0[z]	23	22[z]	...	...	Israel
24	23[z]	47	47[z]	7 147	7 556[z]	2.1	2.1[z]	27	27[z]	...	60[z]	Italy
...	20[z]	...	...	...	13 977[z]	...	1.8[z]	...	23[z]	...	75[z]	Luxembourg
...	13[x]	...	...	...	4 244[x]	...	2.0[x]	...	22[x]	...	...	Malta
...	...	51	46[z]	...	...	...	...	...	...	...	...	Monaco
15	17[z]	39	40[z]	6 388	7 495[z]	1.8	2.1[z]	21	24[z]	...	...	Netherlands
17	18[z]	32	35[z]	8 816	10 914[z]	2.1	2.5[z]	24	28[z]	...	...	Norway
20	25[z]	44	41[z]	5 233	7 035[z]	2.3	2.3[z]	28	37[z]	...	87[z]	Portugal
...	...	...	...	...	...	...	...	...	...	...	...	San Marino
17	18[y]	47	41[y]	5 141	5 416[y]	1.9	1.6[y]	23	22[y]	78	76[y]	Spain
...	26[z]	...	37[z]	...	10 299[z]	...	2.7[z]	...	34[z]	50	54[z]	Sweden
...	...	...	...	...	...	...	...	...	...	72	72[y]	Switzerland
19	20[y]	40	37[y]	8 253	8 793[y]	1.8	1.9[y]	24	25[y]	52	50[y]	United Kingdom
...	...	...	...	...	...	...	...	...	...	56	55[z]	United States
												South and West Asia
...	...	...	...	...	...	...	...	...	...	...	...	Afghanistan
4	5	42	47	137	243	0.6	0.9	8	12	...	...	Bangladesh
...	...	...	...	...	...	...	...	...	...	...	...	Bhutan
10	...	38	...	532	...	1.5	...	21	...	79	80[z]	India
...	9	...	35	...	672	...	1.5	...	10	...	...	Iran, Islamic Republic of
...	19	...	22	...	...	...	1.3	...	15[z]	...	...	Maldives
7	8[y]	29	28[y]	147	136[y]	0.6	0.7[y]	11	10[y]	...	...	Nepal
...	...	...	...	...	...	...	...	...	...	...	...	Pakistan
...	...	...	...	...	...	...	...	...	...	...	...	Sri Lanka
												Sub-Saharan Africa
...	...	...	...	...	...	...	...	...	...	...	...	Angola
...	11	...	28[z]	...	...	...	1.0[z]	...	24[z]	...	...	Benin
...	11	...	41	...	3 602	...	3.5	...	37	...	...	Botswana
...	33	...	10	...	250	...	0.5	...	21	...	...	Burkina Faso
12	19	37	33	...	453	1.2	1.7	...	73	...	...	Burundi
8	6*	...	8*	335	31*	0.8	0.1	17	2*	...	...	Cameroon
...	20	...	35	...	1 215	...	2.1	...	21	...	96*	Cape Verde
...	12	...	...	...	...	...	...	...	...	...	...	Central African Republic
...	5	...	29	...	220	...	0.4	...	15	...	...	Chad
...	...	...	...	...	...	...	...	...	...	...	...	Comoros
...	...	...	...	...	...	1.3	1.1	...	...	...	...	Congo
24	5	24	41	...	...	1.5	0.5	42	...	...	...	Côte d'Ivoire
16	...	36	...	711	...	1.5	0.5	...	...	...	...	D. R. Congo
...	...	...	...	...	...	...	...	...	...	...	...	Equatorial Guinea
...	11	...	9	...	75	...	0.4	...	8	...	...	Eritrea

Table 11 (continued)

Country or territory	Total public expenditure on education as % of GNP		Total public expenditure on education as % of total government expenditure		Public current expenditure on education as % of total public expenditure on education		Public current expenditure on primary education as % of public current expenditure on education		Public current expenditure on primary education per pupil (unit cost) at PPP in constant 2004 US$		Public current expenditure on primary education as % of GNP	
	1999	2005	1999	2005	1999	2005	1999	2005	1999	2005	1999	2005
Ethiopia	*3.6*	**6.1**	...	**18**	...	**65**	...	**51**	...	...	...	**2.0**
Gabon	*3.8*	...	...	...	87	...	...	...	...	...	...	...
Gambia	3.1	*2.1z*	14	...	87	*86y*	...	...	...	...	...	...
Ghana	*4.2*	5.5	...	...	...	86	...	34	...	283	...	1.6
Guinea	*2.1*	2.1	...	...	...	...	...	...	...	...	...	...
Guinea-Bissau	5.6	...	12	...	41	...	...	...	...	...	...	...
Kenya	5.4	6.8z	...	29z	95	92z	...	63z	...	240z	...	4.0z
Lesotho	10.2	10.8	26	30	74	85	43	*39*	441	*476*	3.2	*3.6*
Liberia	...	...	...	...	...	...	...	...	...	...	...	...
Madagascar	*2.5*	3.2	...	25	...	84	...	47	...	58	...	1.3
Malawi	4.7	5.9y	25	...	82	82y	...	63y	...	88y	...	3.0y
Mali	*3.0*	4.5	...	15	*90*	81	49	...	131	...	*1.33*	...
Mauritius	4.2	4.5	18	14	91	84	32	30	1 046	1 311	1.2	1.1
Mozambique	*2.5*	3.9z	...	19z	...	94z	...	70z	...	165z	...	2.6z
Namibia	7.9	6.8y	...	...	94	...	59	...	1 444	911y	4.4	3.9y
Niger	*2.1*	2.3z	...	...	...	...	...	...	...	...	...	...
Nigeria	...	...	...	...	...	...	...	...	...	...	...	...
Rwanda	...	3.9	...	12	...	92	...	54	...	*128*	...	1.9
Sao Tome and Principe	...	...	...	...	...	...	...	...	...	...	...	...
Senegal	*3.5*	5.5	...	19	...	83	...	*48*	...	305	...	*2.2*
Seychelles	5.5	*5.7z*	...	...	...	93z	...	31z	...	2 443z	...	*1.6z*
Sierra Leone	...	...	...	...	...	...	...	52y	...	...	...	*2.3y*
Somalia	...	...	...	...	...	...	...	...	...	...	...	...
South Africa	6.2	5.5	22	18	98	97	45	43	1 470*	1 443	2.7	2.3
Swaziland	5.7	6.2z	...	...	100	100z	33	*38z*	430	*472z*	1.9	*2.3z*
Togo	4.3	...	26	...	97	...	*43*	...	155	...	*1.8*	...
Uganda	...	*5.3z*	...	*18z*	...	75z	...	62z	...	106z	...	2.5z
United Republic of Tanzania	*2.2*	...	...	...	...	...	...	...	...	...	...	...
Zambia	2.0	2.2	...	15z	...	99	...	59	...	54	...	...
Zimbabwe	...	...	...	...	...	...	...	...	...	...	...	1.3

	1999	2005	1999	2005	1999	2005	1999	2005	1999	2005	1999	2005
World[1]	4.5	4.9	...	14	...	92	...	34	...	985	...	1.5
Countries in transition	3.7	3.6	...	18	...	...	...	...	...	...	...	...
Developed countries	5.0	5.5	11	13	...	94	...	25	...	4 762	...	1.2
Developing countries	4.4	4.7	...	...	...	89	...	...	...	...	...	1.8
Arab States	...	...	...	...	...	...	...	...	...	960	...	1.9
Central and Eastern Europe	4.3	4.9	...	13	...	94	...	18	...	2 053	...	0.8
Central Asia	3.7	3.2	...	...	...	...	...	...	...	...	...	...
East Asia and the Pacific	4.8	...	...	...	...	...	...	...	...	...	...	...
East Asia	3.5	3.0	11	...	...	...	...	...	...	...	...	...
Pacific	6.4	...	...	...	...	...	...	...	...	...	...	...
Latin America/Caribbean	4.7	5.0	16	13	...	93	...	40	...	...	...	1.8
Caribbean	...	...	...	15	...	87	...	35	...	...	...	...
Latin America	4.5	4.0	15	13	93	96	...	46	862	598	1.6	1.5
N. America/W. Europe	5.0	5.7	12	13	92	93	26	27	4 425	5 441	1.3	1.5
South and West Asia	2.9	3.6	...	15	89	79	...	...	...	...	...	...
Sub-Saharan Africa	3.7	5.0	...	...	...	86	...	50	...	165	...	2.1

1. All regional values shown are medians.
Data in italic are UIS estimates.
Data in bold are for 2006.

(z) Data are for 2004.
(y) Data are for 2003.
(x) Data are for 2002.
(*) National estimates.

Education for All Global Monitoring Report 2 0 0 8

Public current expenditure on primary education per pupil as % of GNP per capita		Public current expenditure on secondary education as % of public current expenditure on education		Public current expenditure on secondary education per pupil (unit cost) at PPP in constant 2004 US$		Public current expenditure on secondary education as % of GNP		Public current expenditure on secondary education per pupil as % of GNP per capita		Primary teachers' compensation as % of public current expenditure on primary education		Country or territory
1999	2005	1999	2005	1999	2005	1999	2005	1999	2005	1999	2005	
...	**16**	...	**10**	...	...	...	**0.4**	...	**6**	...	...	Ethiopia
...	...	...	...	...	...	...	...	...	...	...	...	Gabon
...	...	...	...	...	...	...	...	...	...	...	75z	Gambia
...	12	...	37	...	668	...	1.8	...	29	...	...	Ghana
...	...	...	...	...	...	...	...	...	...	...	...	Guinea
...	...	...	...	...	...	...	...	...	...	...	...	Guinea-Bissau
...	22z	...	25z	...	254z	...	1.6z	...	24z	...	...	Kenya
15	15	24	18	1 288	1 069	1.8	1.7	45	34	84	...	Lesotho
...	...	...	...	...	...	...	...	...	...	...	...	Liberia
...	7	...	23	...	...	...	0.6	...	...	...	...	Madagascar
...	13y	...	10y	...	78y	...	0.5y	...	12y	...	...	Malawi
16	...	34	...	398	...	0.9	...	48	...	...	...	Mali
11	11	37	41	1 544	1 853	1.4	1.6	16	16	...	...	Mauritius
...	14z	...	17z	...	568z	...	0.6z	...	48z	...	93z	Mozambique
21	19y	28	...	2 358	1 100y	2.1	1.6y	34	23y	...	...	Namibia
...	...	...	...	...	...	...	...	...	...	...	...	Niger
...	...	...	...	...	...	...	...	...	...	...	...	Nigeria
...	10	...	11	...	214	...	0.4	...	17	...	...	Rwanda
...	...	...	...	...	...	...	...	...	...	...	...	Sao Tome and Principe
...	18	...	28	...	624	...	1.3	...	36	...	...	Senegal
...	15z	...	30z	...	2 879z	...	1.6z	...	18z	...	62y	Seychelles
...	...	...	27y	...	...	...	1.2y	...	...	...	...	Sierra Leone
...	...	...	...	...	...	...	...	...	...	...	...	Somalia
14*	14	34	33	2 068*	1 823	2.0	1.8	20*	17	...	84	South Africa
9	12z	27	28z	1 216	1 172z	1.5	1.7z	25	31z	...	...	Swaziland
10	...	34	...	498	...	1.4	...	31	...	79	...	Togo
...	9z	...	20z	...	362z	...	0.8z	...	30z	...	...	Uganda
...	...	...	...	...	...	...	...	...	...	...	...	United Republic of Tanzania
...	6	...	15	...	83	...	0.3	...	9	...	93z	Zambia
...	...	...	...	...	...	...	...	...	...	...	...	Zimbabwe
...	14	...	35	...	...	...	1.7	...	20	...	...	World [1]
...	...	...	...	...	...	...	...	...	...	...	...	Countries in transition
...	19	...	42	5 233	5 904	...	2.2	...	24	...	...	Developed countries
...	...	...	...	...	...	...	1.5	...	...	...	...	Developing countries
...	12	...	...	...	1 551	...	1.6	...	17	...	...	Arab States
...	17	...	47	...	2 647	...	2.2	...	22	...	...	Central and Eastern Europe
...	...	...	...	...	...	...	...	...	...	...	...	Central Asia
...	...	...	...	...	...	...	...	...	...	...	...	East Asia and the Pacific
...	...	...	...	...	...	...	...	...	...	...	...	East Asia
...	...	...	...	...	...	...	...	...	...	...	...	Pacific
...	13	...	32	...	...	...	1.5	...	14	...	...	Latin America/Caribbean
...	...	...	31	...	...	...	...	...	...	...	...	Caribbean
12	12	...	33	1 081	642	1.3	1.4	15	13	...	75	Latin America
18	20	42	40	6 467	7 807	2.1	2.3	25	26	...	66	N. America/W. Europe
...	...	...	...	...	...	...	...	...	...	...	...	South and West Asia
...	12	...	27	...	...	...	1.1	...	21	...	...	Sub-Saharan Africa

Table 12
Trends in basic or proxy indicators to measure EFA goals 1, 2, 3, 4 and 5

Country or territory	GOAL 1 Early childhood care and education GROSS ENROLMENT RATIO (GER) IN PRE-PRIMARY EDUCATION (%) School year ending in 1991 Total	1999 Total	2005 Total	GOAL 2 Universal primary education NET ENROLMENT RATIO (NER) IN PRIMARY EDUCATION School year ending in 1991 Total (%)	1991 GPI (F/M)	1999 Total (%)	1999 GPI (F/M)	2005 Total (%)	2005 GPI (F/M)	GOAL 3 Learning needs of all youth and adults YOUTH LITERACY RATE (15-24) 1985-1994[1] Total (%)	1985-1994[1] GPI (F/M)	1995-2004[1] Total (%)	1995-2004[1] GPI (F/M)
Arab States													
Algeria	…	3	6.0	89	0.88	91	0.96	97	0.98	74	0.72*	90	0.92*
Bahrain	29	35	46.8	99	1.00	96	1.02	97	1.00	97	0.99*	97	1.00*
Djibouti	0.6	0.4	1.0	29	0.72	28	0.73	33	0.81	…	…	…	…
Egypt	6	11	16.2	84	0.84	93	0.93	94	0.95	63	0.76*	85	0.88*
Iraq	7	5	5.7	94	0.88	85	0.85	88	0.86	…	…	85	0.91*
Jordan	20	29	30.7	94	1.01	92	1.01	89	1.02	…	…	99	1.00*
Kuwait	31	79	72.9	49	0.93	87	1.01	87	0.99	87	0.93*	100	1.00*
Lebanon	…	67	74.1	73	0.97	94	0.96	92	0.99	…	…	…	…
Libyan Arab Jamahiriya	…	5	**7.6**	96	0.96	…	…	…	…	95	0.92	98	0.97
Mauritania	…	…	1.7	35	0.74	63	0.94	72	1.00	…	…	61	0.82*
Morocco	60	62	53.6	56	0.70	72	0.86	86	0.94	58	0.64*	70	0.75*
Oman	3	6	**8.0**	69	0.95	80	1.00	**73**	**1.02**	…	…	97	0.99*
Palestinian A. T.	14	40	30.1	…	…	97	1.01	80	0.99	…	…	99	1.00*
Qatar	28	25	36.5	89	0.98	94	1.01	96	1.00	90	1.03*	96	1.03*
Saudi Arabia	7	…	10.0	59	0.81	…	…	78	1.03	88	0.86*	96	0.98*
Sudan[2]	18	20	25.5	40	0.75	…	…	…	…	…	…	77	0.84*
Syrian Arab Republic	6	8	10.4	91	0.91	92	0.93	…	…	…	…	92	0.95*
Tunisia	8	14	21.7ʸ	94	0.92	94	0.98	97	1.01	…	…	94	0.96*
United Arab Emirates	55	63	64.3	103	0.98	79	0.99	71	0.97	94	0.96	97	0.98
Yemen	0.7	1	0.9	51	0.38	57	0.59	75ᶻ	0.73ᶻ	60	0.43*	75	0.65
Central and Eastern Europe													
Albania	57	44	49.5ᶻ	95	1.01	99	0.99	94ᶻ	1.00ᶻ	…	…	99	1.00*
Belarus	82	80	104.7	86	0.95	…	…	89	0.97	100	1.00*	100	1.00*
Bosnia and Herzegovina	…	…	…	…	…	…	…	…	…	…	…	100	1.00*
Bulgaria	90	69	79.0	86	0.99	97	0.98	93	0.99	…	…	98	1.00*
Croatia	28	40	46.5ʸ	79	1.00	85	0.98	87ʸ	0.99ʸ	100	1.00*	100	1.00*
Czech Republic	92	94	109.4	87	1.00	97	1.00	92	1.02	…	…	…	…
Estonia	72	90	110.9	100	0.99	96	0.98	95	0.99	100	1.00*	100	1.00*
Hungary	109	80	83.0	91	1.01	88	0.99	89	0.98	…	…	…	…
Latvia	43	53	84.2	92	0.99	…	…	88	1.03	100	1.00*	100	1.00*
Lithuania	58	51	67.6	…	…	95	0.99	89	1.00	100	1.00*	100	1.00*
Poland	48	50	54.3	97	1.00	96	1.00	96	1.00	…	…	…	…
Republic of Moldova[3,4]	72	46	62.4	89	0.99	88	1.00	86	0.99	100	1.00*	100	1.00
Romania	71	63	75.4	81	1.00	96	0.99	93	0.99	99	1.00*	98	1.00*
Russian Federation[5]	73	67	83.9	99	1.00	…	…	92	1.01	100	1.00*	100	1.00*
Serbia and Montenegro[2,3]	…	44	…	…	…	…	…	…	…	99	0.99*	99	1.00*
Slovakia	86	83	94.7	…	…	…	…	92	1.01	…	…	…	…
Slovenia	65	75	79.4	96	1.01	97	0.99	98	0.99	100	1.00*	100	1.00
TFYR Macedonia	…	28	33.4	94	0.99	93	0.98	92	1.00	99	0.99*	99	0.99*
Turkey	4	6	10.0	89	0.92	…	…	89	0.95	93	0.92*	96	0.95*
Ukraine	85	48	85.7	80	1.00	…	…	83	1.00*	…	…	100	1.00*
Central Asia													
Armenia	36	26	33	…	…	…	…	79	1.05	100	1.00*	100	1.00*
Azerbaijan	18	22	29	89	0.99	85	1.01	85	0.98	…	…	100	1.00*
Georgia	58	38	51	97	1.00	…	…	93ᶻ	0.99ᶻ	…	…	…	…
Kazakhstan	71	15	34	89	0.99	…	…	91	0.98	100	1.00*	100	1.00*
Kyrgyzstan	34	10	13	92	1.00	88*	0.99*	87	0.99	…	…	100	1.00*
Mongolia	38	25	40	90	1.02	90	1.04	84	1.03	…	…	98	1.01
Tajikistan	16	8	9	77	0.98	…	…	97	0.96	100	1.00*	100	1.00*
Turkmenistan	…	…	…	…	…	…	…	…	…	…	…	100	1.00*
Uzbekistan	73	…	28ᶻ	78	0.99	…	…	…	…	…	…	…	…
East Asia and the Pacific													
Australia	71	…	104	99	1.00	92	1.01	97	1.00	…	…	…	…
Brunei Darussalam	47	51	52	92	0.98	…	…	93	1.01	98	1.00*	99	1.00*
Cambodia	4	6	9	69	0.84	85	0.91	99	0.98	…	…	83	0.90*

GOAL 4				GOAL 5														Country or territory
Improving levels of adult literacy				Gender parity in primary education						Gender parity in secondary education								
ADULT LITERACY RATE (15 and over)				GROSS ENROLMENT RATIO (GER)						GROSS ENROLMENT RATIO (GER)								
				School year ending in						School year ending in								
1985-1994[1]		1995-2004[1]		1991		1999		2005		1991		1999		2005				
Total (%)	GPI (F/M)	Total (%)	GPI (F/M)	Total (%)	GPI (F/M)	Total (%)	GPI (F/M)	Total (%)	GPI (F/M)	Total (%)	GPI (F/M)	Total (%)	GPI (F/M)	Total (%)	GPI (F/M)			
																		Arab States
50	0.57*	70	0.76*	96	0.85	105	0.91	112	0.93	60	0.79	...	...	83	1.07			Algeria
84	0.87*	87	0.94*	110	1.00	105	1.01	104	0.99	100	1.04	94	1.08	99	1.06			Bahrain
...	...	...	...	35	0.72	35	0.71	40	0.82	11	0.66	15	0.72	24	0.66			Djibouti
44	0.55*	71	0.71*	92	0.83	101	0.91	101	0.94	71	0.79	81	0.91	86	0.92			Egypt
...	...	74	0.76*	108	0.83	92	0.82	98	0.83	44	0.63	34	0.63	45	0.66			Iraq
...	...	91	0.91*	101	1.01	99	1.00	96	1.01	63	1.04	88	1.03	87	1.02			Jordan
74	0.88*	93	0.96*	60	0.95	100	1.01	98	0.98	43	0.98	99	1.02	95	1.06			Kuwait
...	...	...	...	106	0.97	115	0.95	106	0.97	...	...	80	1.10	89	1.10			Lebanon
75	0.70	84	0.81	104	0.94	114	0.98	**106**	**0.99**	86	...	...	...	105	1.21			Libyan Arab Jamahiriya
...	...	51	0.73*	50	0.73	87	0.94	93	1.01	13	0.46	19	0.73	21	0.85			Mauritania
42	0.52*	52	0.60*	64	0.69	87	0.81	105	0.89	35	0.72	37	0.79	50	0.85			Morocco
...	...	81	0.85*	85	0.92	91	0.97	**82**	**1.01**	45	0.81	75	0.99	**88**	**0.96**			Oman
...	...	92	0.91*	...	...	106	1.01	89	0.99	...	...	79	1.04	99	1.07			Palestinian A. T.
76	0.94*	89	0.99*	101	0.93	105	0.96	106	0.99	84	1.06	90	1.07	100	0.98			Qatar
71	0.72*	83	0.87*	73	0.86	...	...	91	1.00	44	0.79	71	...	88	0.96			Saudi Arabia
...	...	61	0.73*	48	0.77	51	0.85	60	0.87	21	0.79	26	...	34	0.94			Sudan[2]
...	...	81	0.84*	101	0.90	102	0.92	124	0.95	48	0.73	40	0.91	68	0.94			Syrian Arab Republic
...	...	74	0.78*	114	0.89	114	0.95	109	0.97	45	0.79	73	1.02	84	1.09			Tunisia
79	0.99	89	0.99	115	0.97	90	0.97	83	0.97	68	1.16	82	1.08	64	1.05			United Arab Emirates
37	0.30*	54	0.47	64	0.35	73	0.56	89	0.74	...	...	41	0.37	47	0.49			Yemen
																		Central and Eastern Europe
...	...	99	0.99*	100	1.00	110	0.98	106z	0.99z	78	0.86	74	0.95	78z	0.96z			Albania
98	0.97*	100	1.00*	96	0.96	109	0.98	101	0.97	95	...	83	1.06	95	1.01			Belarus
...	...	97	0.95*	...	...	...	...	...	...	...	...	...	...	...	...			Bosnia and Herzegovina
...	...	98	0.99*	98	0.97	106	0.97	102	0.99	75	1.04	91	0.98	103	0.95			Bulgaria
...	...	98	0.98*	85	0.99	92	0.98	94y	0.99y	76	1.10	84	1.02	88y	1.02y			Croatia
...	...	...	...	96	1.00	104	0.99	101	0.98	91	0.97	83	1.04	96	1.02			Czech Republic
100	1.00*	100	1.00*	111	0.97	102	0.97	100	0.97	98	1.11	93	1.04	101	1.01			Estonia
...	...	...	...	95	1.00	102	0.98	98	0.98	79	1.01	94	1.02	96	0.99			Hungary
99	0.99*	100	1.00*	97	0.99	99	0.98	92	0.96	91	1.00	89	1.04	98	1.01			Latvia
98	0.99*	100	1.00*	92	0.95	103	0.98	95	1.00	92	...	96	1.01	97	0.99			Lithuania
...	...	...	...	98	0.99	98	0.98	98	0.99	81	1.05	99	0.99	99	0.99			Poland
96	0.96*	99	0.99	93	1.00	95	1.00	92	0.99	80	1.09	84	1.01	82	1.03			Republic of Moldova[3,4]
97	0.96*	97	0.98*	91	1.00	105	0.98	107	0.99	92	0.99	79	1.01	85	1.01			Romania
98	0.97*	99	1.00*	109	1.00	100	0.99	129	1.00	93	1.06	...	...	92	0.99			Russian Federation[5]
92	0.91*	96	0.95*	...	...	104	0.99	...	...	...	...	92	1.01	...	...			Serbia and Montenegro[2,3]
...	...	...	...	...	...	103	0.99	99	0.99	...	...	85	1.02	95	1.01			Slovakia
100	1.00*	100	1.00	100	...	101	0.99	101	0.99	89	...	101	1.02	100	1.00			Slovenia
94	0.94*	96	0.96*	99	0.98	101	0.98	98	1.00	56	0.99	82	0.97	84	0.98			TFYR Macedonia
79	0.76*	87	0.84*	99	0.92	...	...	93	0.95	48	0.63	...	...	75	0.82			Turkey
...	...	99	0.99*	89	1.00	105	0.99	107	1.00	93	...	97	1.02*	89	0.92			Ukraine
																		Central Asia
99	0.99*	99	0.99*	...	...	...	...	94	1.04	...	...	...	...	88	1.03			Armenia
...	...	99	0.99*	111	0.99	94	1.00	96	0.98	88	1.01	76	1.00	83	0.96			Azerbaijan
...	...	...	...	97	1.00	98	1.00	94	1.01	95	0.97	79	0.98	83	1.01			Georgia
98	0.97*	100	1.00*	90	0.99	98	1.00	109	0.99	99	1.04	91	0.99	99	0.97			Kazakhstan
...	...	99	0.99*	...	...	98	0.99	98	0.99	100	1.02	84	1.02	86	1.01			Kyrgyzstan
...	...	98	1.00*	97	1.02	98	1.04	93	1.02	82	1.14	58	1.27	92	1.13			Mongolia
98	0.98*	99	1.00*	91	0.98	98	0.95	101	0.96	102	...	71	0.86	82	0.83			Tajikistan
...	...	99	0.99*	...	...	...	...	...	...	...	...	...	...	...	...			Turkmenistan
...	...	...	...	81	0.98	...	...	100z	0.99z	99	0.91	...	...	95z	0.97z			Uzbekistan
																		East Asia and the Pacific
...	...	...	...	108	0.99	98	1.00	104	0.99	83	1.03	154	1.00	148	0.95			Australia
88	0.89*	93	0.95*	114	0.94	114	0.97	107	1.00	77	1.09	85	1.09	96	1.04			Brunei Darussalam
...	...	74	0.76*	87	0.81	99	0.87	134	0.92	29	0.43	16	0.53	29z	0.69z			Cambodia

Table 12 (continued)

Education for All Global Monitoring Report 2008

Country or territory	GOAL 1 — Early childhood care and education — GROSS ENROLMENT RATIO (GER) IN PRE-PRIMARY EDUCATION (%) 1991 Total	1999 Total	2005 Total	GOAL 2 — Universal primary education — NET ENROLMENT RATIO (NER) IN PRIMARY EDUCATION 1991 Total (%)	1991 GPI (F/M)	1999 Total (%)	1999 GPI (F/M)	2005 Total (%)	2005 GPI (F/M)	GOAL 3 — Learning needs of all youth and adults — YOUTH LITERACY RATE (15-24) 1985-1994[1] Total (%)	1985-1994[1] GPI (F/M)	1995-2004[1] Total (%)	1995-2004[1] GPI (F/M)
China[6]	22	38	**40**	97	0.96	...	...	...	...	94	0.94*	99	0.99*
Cook Islands[3]	...	86	91z	...	...	85	0.96	...	...	...	...	...	...
DPR Korea	...	...	...	...	...	...	...	...	...	...	...	...	...
Fiji	14	17	16	...	...	99	1.01	96	0.99	...	...	...	...
Indonesia	18	24	34	97	0.96	...	...	96	0.96	96	0.98*	99	1.00*
Japan	48	82	85	100	1.00	100	1.00	100	1.00	...	...	...	...
Kiribati[3]	...	...	75z	...	...	97	1.01	...	...	...	...	...	...
Lao PDR	7	8	9	63	0.85	80	0.92	84	0.95	...	...	78	0.90*
Macao, China	88	89	92	81	0.98	85	1.01	91	0.96	...	...	100	1.00*
Malaysia	42	102	119z	...	...	98	0.98	95z	1.00z	96	0.99*	97	1.00*
Marshall Islands	...	59	50y	...	...	...	...	90y	0.99y	...	...	...	...
Micronesia	...	37	...	...	...	...	...	...	...	...	...	...	...
Myanmar	...	2	...	98	0.97	80	0.99	90	1.02	...	...	95	0.98*
Nauru[3]	...	...	71z	...	...	...	...	...	...	...	...	...	...
New Zealand	76	88	93	98	1.00	99	1.01	99	1.00	...	...	...	...
Niue[3]	...	154	100	...	...	99	1.00	...	...	...	...	...	...
Palau[3]	...	63	64	...	...	97	0.94	...	...	...	...	...	...
Papua New Guinea	0.3	35	59y	...	...	...	...	...	...	...	...	67	0.93*
Philippines	12	31	41	96	0.99	92	1.00	94	1.02	97	1.01*	95	1.03*
Republic of Korea	55	80	**96**	104	1.01	94	1.01	**99**	**1.00**	...	...	...	...
Samoa	...	51	49z	...	...	92	0.99	90z	1.00z	99	1.00	99	1.00
Singapore	...	53	...	...	...	82	1.00	...	...	99	1.00*	100	1.00*
Solomon Islands	35	35	41y	...	...	...	...	63y	0.96y	...	...	...	...
Thailand	43	88	**82**	76	0.97	...	...	**88**	**0.96**	...	...	98	1.00*
Timor-Leste	...	...	16	...	...	...	...	98	...	...	...	...	...
Tokelau[3]	...	...	125z	...	...	...	...	...	...	...	...	...	...
Tonga	...	30	23	...	...	91	0.97	95	0.96	...	...	99	1.00*
Tuvalu[3]	...	...	99z	...	...	...	...	...	...	...	...	...	...
Vanuatu	...	49	...	...	...	91	0.99	94	0.98	...	...	...	...
Viet Nam	28	41	60	90	0.92	96	...	88	...	94	0.99*	94	0.99*
Latin America and the Caribbean													
Anguilla	...	...	97	...	...	...	...	89	1.06	...	...	...	...
Antigua and Barbuda	...	...	...	...	...	...	...	...	...	...	...	...	...
Argentina	49	57	64z	...	...	99*	1.00*	99z	0.99z	98	1.00*	99	1.00*
Aruba[3]	...	97	99	...	...	98	1.01	99	1.00	...	...	99	1.00*
Bahamas	...	12	31y	90	1.03	89	0.99	91	1.03	...	...	...	...
Barbados	...	82	93	80	0.99	97	0.99	98	1.00	...	...	...	...
Belize	23	28	33	94	0.99	94	1.00	94	1.03	76	1.01*	...	...
Bermuda[3]	...	...	...	...	...	...	...	98	...	...	...	...	...
Bolivia	32	45	50	...	...	95	1.00	95z	1.01z	94	0.95*	97	0.98*
Brazil	48	58	63z	85	...	91	...	95z	1.00z	...	...	97	1.02*
British Virgin Islands[3]	...	62	90	...	...	96	1.02	95	0.99	...	...	...	...
Cayman Islands	...	...	93	...	...	...	...	81	0.90	...	...	...	...
Chile	72	77	54	89	0.98	...	...	90	0.98	98	1.01*	99	1.00*
Colombia	13	36	39	69	...	88	1.01	87	1.00	91	1.03*	98	1.01*
Costa Rica	65	84	69	87	1.01	...	...	...	...	...	...	98	1.01*
Cuba	102	105	113	93	1.01	98	1.00	97	0.98	...	...	100	1.00*
Dominica[3]	...	80	78	...	...	94	0.98	84	1.02	...	...	...	...
Dominican Republic	...	34	34	57	2.18	84	1.01	88	1.01	...	...	94	1.03*
Ecuador	42	64	77	98	1.01	97	1.01	98z	1.01z	96	0.99*	96	1.00*
El Salvador	21	42	51	...	...	...	...	93	1.00	85	1.00*	88	1.04
Grenada[3]	...	93	81	...	...	...	...	84	0.99	...	...	...	...
Guatemala	25	46	28	...	...	82	0.91	94	0.95	76	0.87*	82	0.91*
Guyana	76	122	107	89	1.00	...	...	...	...	...	...	...	...
Haiti	34	...	...	22	1.05	...	...	...	...	...	...	...	...
Honduras	13	...	33	89	1.02	...	...	91	1.02	...	...	89	1.05*
Jamaica	80	78	95	96	1.00	88	1.00	90	1.00	...	...	...	...
Mexico	63	73	93	98	0.97	98	1.00	98	1.00	95	0.99*	98	1.00*
Montserrat[3]	...	...	105	...	...	...	...	96	...	...	...	...	...
Netherlands Antilles	...	120	113y	...	...	...	...	...	...	97	1.01*	98	1.00

GOAL 4				GOAL 5												Country or territory
Improving levels of adult literacy				Gender parity in primary education						Gender parity in secondary education						
ADULT LITERACY RATE (15 and over)				GROSS ENROLMENT RATIO (GER)						GROSS ENROLMENT RATIO (GER)						
				School year ending in						School year ending in						
1985-1994[1]		1995-2004[1]		1991		1999		2005		1991		1999		2005		
Total (%)	GPI (F/M)	Total (%)	GPI (F/M)	Total (%)	GPI (F/M)	Total (%)	GPI (F/M)	Total (%)	GPI (F/M)	Total (%)	GPI (F/M)	Total (%)	GPI (F/M)	Total (%)	GPI (F/M)	
78	0.78*	91	0.91*	125	0.93	...	...	**112**	**0.98**	49	0.75	62	...	**76**	**1.01**	China[6]
...	...	...	...	...	...	96	0.95	82[z]	0.98[z]	...	...	60	1.08	72[z]	1.02[z]	Cook Islands[3]
...	...	...	...	...	...	...	...	...	...	...	...	...	...	...	...	DPR Korea
...	...	...	...	133	1.00	110	0.99	106	0.98	64	0.95	81	1.11	88	1.07	Fiji
82	0.86*	90	0.92*	114	0.98	...	...	117	0.96	46	0.83	...	...	63	0.99	Indonesia
...	...	...	...	100	1.00	101	1.00	100	1.00	97	1.02	102	1.01	102	1.00	Japan
...	...	...	...	...	...	104	1.01	112	1.02	...	...	84	1.18	87	1.13	Kiribati[3]
...	...	69	0.79*	103	0.79	117	0.85	116	0.88	24*	0.62*	33	0.69	47	0.76	Lao PDR
...	...	91	0.92*	99	0.96	100	0.96	106	0.92	65*	1.11*	76	1.08	97	1.04	Macao, China
83	0.87*	89	0.93*	95	1.00	100	0.98	96[z]	1.00[z]	57	1.05	69	1.10	76[z]	1.14[z]	Malaysia
...	...	...	...	...	...	101	0.98	103	0.96	...	...	...	1.06	76	1.05	Marshall Islands
...	...	...	...	...	...	...	...	115	0.97	...	...	...	...	85	1.07	Micronesia
...	...	90	0.92*	107	0.96	88	0.99	100	1.02	22	0.98	34	1.00	40	0.99	Myanmar
...	...	...	...	...	...	...	...	84[z]	0.99[z]	...	...	...	...	48[z]	1.07[z]	Nauru[3]
...	...	...	...	101	0.99	102	1.01	102	1.00	90	1.02	110	1.06	123	1.07	New Zealand
...	...	...	...	...	...	99	1.00	86	1.24	...	...	98	1.10	99	0.91	Niue[3]
...	...	...	...	...	...	114	0.93	104	0.93	...	...	101	1.07	101	1.08	Palau[3]
...	...	57	0.80*	66	0.88	78	0.93	75[y]	0.88[y]	12	0.61	22	0.76	26[y]	0.79[y]	Papua New Guinea
94	0.99*	93	1.02*	109	0.99	113	1.00	112	0.99	71	1.04	76	1.09	85	1.12	Philippines
...	...	...	...	105	1.01	95	1.01	**104**	**0.99**	90	0.97	100	1.00	**96**	**1.00**	Republic of Korea
98	0.99	99	0.99	124	1.02	99	0.98	100	1.00	33	1.96	80	1.10	80	1.12	Samoa
89	0.87*	93	0.92*	103	0.97	83	1.00	78	1.00	67	0.93	...	1.02	63	1.03	Singapore
...	...	...	...	86	0.86	88	0.93	97	0.95	15	0.61	24	0.75	29	0.83	Solomon Islands
...	...	93	0.95*	98	0.96	94	0.95	**96**	**0.96**	31	0.94	...	...	**71**	**1.05**	Thailand
...	...	...	...	...	...	...	...	151	0.92	...	...	...	...	52	1.00	Timor-Leste
...	...	...	...	...	...	...	...	93[z]	1.35[z]	...	...	...	...	101[z]	0.88[z]	Tokelau[3]
...	...	99	1.00*	112	0.97	112	0.98	115	0.95	99	1.03	101	1.11	98[z]	1.08[z]	Tonga
...	...	...	...	...	...	98	1.02	99[z]	1.07[z]	...	...	...	...	...	...	Tuvalu[3]
...	...	74	...	95	0.96	110	0.98	118	0.97	18	0.80	30	0.88	41[z]	0.86[z]	Vanuatu
88	0.89*	90	0.93*	107	0.93	108	0.93	95	0.94	32	...	62	0.90	76	0.97	Viet Nam
																Latin America and the Caribbean
...	...	...	...	...	...	...	...	91	1.06	...	...	...	...	87	0.97	Anguilla
...	...	...	...	...	...	...	...	...	...	...	...	...	...	...	...	Antigua and Barbuda
96	1.00*	97	1.00*	108	...	117	1.00	113[z]	0.99[z]	72	...	94	1.07	86[z]	1.07[z]	Argentina
...	...	97	1.00*	...	...	112	0.98	114	0.97	...	...	101	1.05	97	1.03	Aruba[3]
...	...	...	...	96	1.03	95	0.98	101	1.00	...	...	115	0.99	90	1.00	Bahamas
...	...	...	...	93	1.00	108	0.98	108	1.00	...	...	104	1.05	113	1.00	Barbados
70	1.00*	...	...	112	0.98	118	0.97	127	0.96	44	1.15	64	1.08	84	1.02	Belize
...	...	...	...	...	...	...	...	102	1.03	...	...	...	...	89	1.09	Bermuda[3]
80	0.82*	87	0.87*	97	0.92	113	0.98	113[z]	1.00[z]	...	...	78	0.93	88[y]	0.97[y]	Bolivia
...	...	89	1.00*	104	...	155	0.94	140[z]	0.93[z]	40	...	99	1.11	106[z]	1.10[z]	Brazil
...	...	...	...	...	...	112	0.97	111	0.96	...	...	99	0.91	104	1.18	British Virgin Islands[3]
...	...	...	...	...	...	...	...	90	0.89	...	...	...	...	102	0.92	Cayman Islands
94	0.99*	96	1.00*	101	0.98	101	0.97	104	0.96	73	1.07	79	1.04	91	1.01	Chile
81	1.00*	93	1.00*	103	1.02	113	1.00	112	0.98	50	1.19	71	1.11	78	1.11	Colombia
...	...	95	1.00*	103	0.99	108	0.98	110	0.99	45	1.06	57	1.09	79	1.06	Costa Rica
...	...	100	1.00*	99	0.97	106	0.96	102	0.95	90	1.14	80	1.06	94	1.00	Cuba
...	...	...	...	...	...	104	0.95	92	0.99	...	...	90	1.35	107	0.97	Dominica[3]
...	...	87	1.00*	94	1.01	113	0.98	113	0.95	...	...	55	1.27	71	1.21	Dominican Republic
88	0.95*	91	0.97*	116	0.99	114	1.00	117	1.00	55*	...	57	1.03	61	1.00	Ecuador
74	0.92*	81	0.96	81	1.01	111	0.96	113	0.96	25	1.22	51	0.98	63	1.03	El Salvador
...	...	...	...	...	...	...	...	93	0.96	...	...	...	...	100	1.03	Grenada[3]
64	0.80*	69	0.84*	81	0.87	101	0.87	114	0.92	23	...	33	0.84	51	0.91	Guatemala
...	...	...	...	94	0.98	119	0.98	132	0.98	79	1.06	81	1.02	102	1.02	Guyana
...	...	...	...	48	0.94	...	...	...	...	21*	0.96*	...	...	...	...	Haiti
...	...	80	1.01*	108	1.04	...	...	113	1.00	33	1.25	...	...	65	1.24	Honduras
...	...	80	1.16*	101	0.99	93	1.00	95	1.00	65	1.06	88	1.02	87	1.03	Jamaica
88	0.94*	92	0.97*	111	0.97	109	0.97	109	0.98	52	1.00	69	1.02	80	1.07	Mexico
...	...	...	...	...	...	...	...	116	1.04	...	...	...	...	116	1.10	Montserrat[3]
95	1.00*	96	1.00	...	...	134	0.94	126[y]	0.98[y]	93	1.19	97	1.16	87[y]	1.09[y]	Netherlands Antilles

Table 13
Trends in basic or proxy indicators to measure EFA goal 6

	GOAL 6 Educational quality						PUPIL/TEACHER RATIO IN PRIMARY EDUCATION[1]		
	SURVIVAL RATE TO GRADE 5								
	School year ending in						School year ending in		
	1991		1999		2004		1991	1999	2005
Country or territory	Total (%)	GPI (F/M)	Total (%)	GPI (F/M)	Total (%)	GPI (F/M)			
Arab States									
Algeria	95	0.99	95	1.02	96	1.03	28	28	25
Bahrain	89	1.01	*97*	*1.01*	99	0.98	19*	...	...
Djibouti	87	1.81	77	1.19	...	...	43	40	*35*
Egypt	...	...	*99*	*1.01*	99y	1.01y	24	*23*	26
Iraq	...	...	66	0.94	81	0.84	25	25	21
Jordan	...	...	98	0.99	99y	1.00y	25	...	20y
Kuwait	...	...	...	...	...	...	18	13	12
Lebanon	...	...	91	1.07	93	1.05	...	14	14
Libyan Arab Jamahiriya	...	...	...	...	...	...	14	...	**5**
Mauritania	75	0.99	*68*	*0.94*	53	1.07	45	47	40
Morocco	75	1.02	82	1.00	79	0.95	27	28	27
Oman	97	0.99	94	1.00	**100**	**1.00**	28	25	**14**
Palestinian Autonomous Territories	...	...	...	...	...	...	...	38	25
Qatar	64	1.02	...	...	...	...	11	13	11
Saudi Arabia	83	1.03	...	...	...	...	16	...	...
Sudan	94	1.09	*84*	*1.10*	79	1.02	34	...	29
Syrian Arab Republic	96	0.98	92	0.99	...	...	25	25	...
Tunisia	86	0.83	92	1.02	97	1.01	28	24	20
United Arab Emirates	80	0.99	92	0.99	97	1.01	18	16	15
Yemen	...	...	*87*	...	73y	0.86y	...	22	...
Central and Eastern Europe									
Albania	...	...	...	...	...	...	19	*23*	21z
Belarus	...	...	...	...	...	...	...	20	16
Bosnia and Herzegovina	...	...	...	...	...	...	...	...	...
Bulgaria	91	0.99	...	...	...	...	15	18	16
Croatia	...	...	...	...	...	...	19	19	18y
Czech Republic	...	...	98	1.01	98	1.01	23	18	16
Estonia	...	...	99	1.01	99	1.01	...	16	...
Hungary	98	1.26	...	...	...	...	12	11	10
Latvia	...	...	...	...	...	...	15	15	12
Lithuania	...	...	...	...	...	...	18	17	14
Poland	98	1.08	99	...	99	...	16	...	12
Republic of Moldova	...	...	...	...	...	...	23	21	18
Romania	...	...	...	...	...	...	22	19	17
Russian Federation	...	...	...	...	...	...	22	*18*	17
Serbia and Montenegro	...	...	...	...	...	...	...	20	...
Slovakia	...	...	...	...	...	...	...	19	18
Slovenia	...	...	...	...	...	...	...	14	15
TFYR Macedonia	...	...	...	...	...	...	21	22	19
Turkey	98	0.99	...	...	97	0.99	30	...	...
Ukraine	98	...	...	...	...	...	22	20	19
Central Asia									
Armenia	...	...	...	...	...	...	...	...	21
Azerbaijan	...	...	...	...	...	...	...	19	13
Georgia	...	...	...	...	...	...	17	17	14y
Kazakhstan	...	...	...	...	...	...	21	...	17
Kyrgyzstan	...	...	...	...	...	...	...	24	24
Mongolia	...	...	...	...	...	...	28	32	34
Tajikistan	...	...	...	...	...	...	21	22	21
Turkmenistan	...	...	...	...	...	...	...	...	...
Uzbekistan	...	...	...	...	...	...	24	...	...
East Asia and the Pacific									
Australia	99	1.01	...	...	...	...	17	*18*	...
Brunei Darussalam	...	...	92	1.00	100	1.01	15	14*	10
Cambodia	...	...	*56*	*0.93*	63	1.05	33	*48*	53

GOAL 6 Educational quality											
% FEMALE TEACHERS IN PRIMARY EDUCATION			**TRAINED PRIMARY-SCHOOL TEACHERS[2] as % of total**		**PUBLIC CURRENT EXPENDITURE ON PRIMARY EDUCATION as % of GNP**			**PUBLIC CURRENT EXPENDITURE ON PRIMARY EDUCATION PER PUPIL (unit cost) at PPP in constant 2004 US$**			
School year ending in			School year ending in		School year ending in			School year ending in			
1991	1999	2005	1999	2005	1991	1999	2005	1991	1999	2005	Country or territory
											Arab States
39	46	50	94	99	...	...	1.6^y	...	...	672^y	Algeria
54*	...	...	...	...	...	...	1.9^x	...	...	2926^x	Bahrain
37	28	27	...	...	...	...	2.9	...	...	983	Djibouti
52	52	55	...	...	...	...	...	...	...	...	Egypt
70	72	72	...	100^z	...	...	...	...	...	...	Iraq
62	...	64^y	...	...	...	1.9	1.8^z	...	537	589^z	Jordan
61	73	86	100	100	1.5	...	0.9	...	...	2910^z	Kuwait
...	82	85	15	14	...	...	0.8	...	...	370	Lebanon
...	...	**82**	...	...	...	...	...	...	...	...	Libyan Arab Jamahiriya
18	26	31	...	100	...	...	1.5	...	...	201^y	Mauritania
37	39	46	...	100	1.6	2.2	2.9	534	663	937	Morocco
47	52	**65**	100	**100**	1.6	1.4	1.8^z	...	1363	2142^z	Oman
...	54	50	100	100	...	...	...	...	...	...	Palestinian Autonomous Territories
72	75	66	...	...	...	...	...	...	...	...	Qatar
48	...	...	...	...	...	...	...	...	...	...	Saudi Arabia
51	...	66	...	58	...	...	...	...	...	...	Sudan
64	65	...	81	...	...	1.7	2.1^x	...	412	577^x	Syrian Arab Republic
45	50	52	...	...	...	...	2.3	...	...	1524	Tunisia
64	73	84	...	60	...	0.7	0.4^z	...	1880	1601^z	United Arab Emirates
...	20	...	...	...	...	...	...	...	...	...	Yemen
											Central and Eastern Europe
55	75	76^z	...	...	...	...	...	...	...	...	Albania
...	99	99	...	100	1.8	...	0.5	...	...	1033	Belarus
...	...	...	...	...	...	...	...	...	...	...	Bosnia and Herzegovina
77	91	93	...	...	2.8	...	0.8^y	...	...	1429^y	Bulgaria
75	89	90^y	100	100^y	...	...	0.8^y	...	...	2246^y	Croatia
...	85	84	...	...	...	0.7	0.6^z	...	1651	2226^z	Czech Republic
...	86	...	...	...	...	...	1.3^z	...	...	2628^z	Estonia
84	85	96	...	...	2.4	0.9	1.1^z	3195	2260	3831^z	Hungary
...	97	97	...	...	...	...	...	...	...	...	Latvia
94	98	98	...	...	...	...	0.7^z	...	...	1879^z	Lithuania
...	...	85	...	...	1.8	...	1.7^z	1231	...	2865^z	Poland
97	96	97	...	...	...	...	0.6	...	...	290	Republic of Moldova
84	86	86	...	...	...	...	0.5^y	...	...	919^y	Romania
99	98	99	...	99^y	...	...	...	...	...	...	Russian Federation
...	82	...	100	...	...	...	...	...	...	...	Serbia and Montenegro
...	93	90	...	...	...	0.6	0.6^z	...	1190	1695^z	Slovakia
...	96	97	...	...	1.0	...	1.1^z	2877	...	4866^z	Slovenia
...	66	70	...	...	...	...	...	...	...	...	TFYR Macedonia
43	...	...	...	...	1.3	...	...	504	...	...	Turkey
98	98	99	...	99.7	...	...	...	...	...	...	Ukraine
											Central Asia
...	...	99	...	77	...	...	...	...	...	...	Armenia
...	83	85	100	100	...	...	0.5	...	...	337	Azerbaijan
92	92	95^y	...	97^y	...	...	...	...	...	...	Georgia
96	...	98	...	...	...	...	...	...	...	...	Kazakhstan
81	95	96	48	58	...	...	0.7^x	...	...	127^x	Kyrgyzstan
90	93	94	...	...	...	...	1.2^z	...	...	269^z	Mongolia
49	56	63	...	84^z	...	...	0.9	...	...	100	Tajikistan
...	...	...	...	...	...	...	...	...	...	...	Turkmenistan
79	...	...	...	...	...	...	...	...	...	...	Uzbekistan
											East Asia and the Pacific
72	...	...	...	...	...	1.6	1.6^z	...	4311	4747^z	Australia
57	66*	71	...	84	0.5	...	...	...	...	...	Brunei Darussalam
31	37	41	...	98	...	...	...	...	...	...	Cambodia

Table 13 (continued)

	GOAL 6 Educational quality								
	SURVIVAL RATE TO GRADE 5						**PUPIL/TEACHER RATIO IN PRIMARY EDUCATION[1]**		
	School year ending in						School year ending in		
	1991		1999		2004		1991	1999	2005
Country or territory	Total (%)	GPI (F/M)	Total (%)	GPI (F/M)	Total (%)	GPI (F/M)			
Nicaragua	44	3.33	48	1.19	54	1.11	36	34	34
Panama	...	...	92	1.01	85	1.01	...	26	24
Paraguay	74	1.02	*78*	*1.05*	81ʸ	1.05ʸ	25	...	28ʸ
Peru	...	...	87	0.98	90	0.99	29	...	23
Saint Kitts and Nevis	...	...	...	...	...	...	22	...	18
Saint Lucia	96	1.02	*90*	...	...	...	29	22	22
Saint Vincent and the Grenadines	...	...	...	...	88ˣ	...	20	...	18
Suriname	...	...	...	...	...	...	22	...	19
Trinidad and Tobago	...	...	...	...	91*	1.03*	26	21	17*
Turks and Caicos Islands	...	...	...	...	46ˣ	1.23ˣ	...	*18*	15
Uruguay	97	1.03	...	...	91ʸ	1.04ʸ	22	20	21ᶻ
Venezuela	86	1.09	91	1.08	91	1.08	23	...	19
North America and Western Europe									
Andorra	...	...	...	...	...	...	...	...	11
Austria	...	...	...	...	...	...	11	13	12
Belgium	91	1.02	...	...	...	...	...	...	11
Canada	97	1.04	...	...	...	...	15	17	...
Cyprus	100	1.00	96	1.03	...	...	21	18	*18*
Denmark	94	1.00	100	1.00	93	1.00	...	10	...
Finland	100	1.00	100	1.00	...	...	...	17	16
France	96	1.37	98	0.99	...	...	...	19	19ᶻ
Germany	...	...	...	...	...	...	...	17	14
Greece	100	1.00	...	...	99	1.02	19	14	11
Iceland	...	...	100	1.00	100ˣ	0.99ˣ	...	*11*	11ᶻ
Ireland	100	1.01	95	1.03	100ʸ	1.00ʸ	27	22	18
Israel	...	...	...	...	...	...	15	13	13
Italy	...	...	97	...	100	1.00	12	11	10
Luxembourg	...	...	*96*	*1.08*	92ˣ	1.02ˣ	13	...	11
Malta	99	1.01	99	0.99	99ˣ	1.01ˣ	21	20	11
Monaco	83	0.81	...	...	...	...	...	16	14ᶻ
Netherlands	...	...	100	1.00	100ˣ	1.00ˣ	17	...	10
Norway	100	1.01	100	1.00	100	1.00	...	...	11ᶻ
Portugal	...	...	...	...	...	...	14	...	11
San Marino	...	...	...	...	...	...	6	...	6ᶻ
Spain	...	...	...	...	*100*	*1.00*	22	15	14
Sweden	100	1.00	...	...	...	...	10	12	10
Switzerland	...	...	...	...	...	...	...	...	13
United Kingdom	...	...	...	...	...	...	20	19	17
United States	...	...	...	...	...	...	...	15	14
South and West Asia									
Afghanistan	...	...	...	...	...	...	...	36	83
Bangladesh	...	...	65	1.16	65ʸ	1.07ʸ	...	56	51ᶻ
Bhutan	...	...	90	1.04	...	...	...	42	31
India	...	...	62	0.95	79ʸ	0.94ʸ	47	35*	...
Iran, Islamic Republic of	90	0.98	...	...	88ˣ	0.99ˣ	31	27	19
Maldives	...	...	...	...	92	1.09	...	24	20
Nepal	51	0.99	58	1.10	**79**	1.10	39	39	**40**
Pakistan	...	...	...	...	70	1.07	...	...	38
Sri Lanka	92	1.01	...	...	...	...	31	...	22ᶻ
Sub-Saharan Africa									
Angola	...	...	...	...	...	...	32	...	...
Benin	55	1.02	...	...	52	0.94	36	53	47
Botswana	84	1.06	87	1.06	*90ʸ*	*1.04ʸ*	30	27	25
Burkina Faso	70	0.96	68	1.05	76	1.01	57	49	47
Burundi	62	0.89	...	...	67	1.03	67	*57*	49
Cameroon	...	...	*81*	...	64ˣ	0.99ˣ	51	52	48*
Cape Verde	...	...	...	...	93	...	...	*29*	26
Central African Republic	23	0.90	...	...	...	...	77	...	...

Education for All Global Monitoring Report

GOAL 6
Educational quality

% FEMALE TEACHERS IN PRIMARY EDUCATION			TRAINED PRIMARY-SCHOOL TEACHERS[2] as % of total		PUBLIC CURRENT EXPENDITURE ON PRIMARY EDUCATION as % of GNP			PUBLIC CURRENT EXPENDITURE ON PRIMARY EDUCATION PER PUPIL (unit cost) at PPP in constant 2004 US$			
School year ending in			School year ending in		School year ending in			School year ending in			
1991	1999	2005	1999	2005	1991	1999	2005	1991	1999	2005	Country or territory
86	83	78	79	77	...	...	1.5z	...	...	295z	Nicaragua
...	75	76	79	90	1.7	1.9	...	645	862	...	Panama
...	...	72y	...	...	...	...	1.9y	...	...	567y	Paraguay
...	...	64	...	...	...	1.2	1.0	...	355	403	Peru
74	...	86	...	58	1.1	...	...	...	...	987x	Saint Kitts and Nevis
83	84	86	...	80	2.5	3.3	2.2	529	1151	909	Saint Lucia
67	...	73	...	74	3.0	...	2.9	737	...	1250	Saint Vincent and the Grenadines
84	...	92	...	...	...	...	...	...	...	...	Suriname
70	76	72*	71	81*,z	...	1.5	...	...	948	...	Trinidad and Tobago
...	92	89	81	82	...	...	...	...	...	...	Turks and Caicos Islands
...	92	...	...	...	0.9	0.8	...	420	736	...	Uruguay
74	...	81	...	84	...	...	...	...	...	...	Venezuela
											North America and Western Europe
...	...	74	...	...	...	...	...	...	...	...	Andorra
82	89	90	...	...	0.9	1.1	1.0z	4359	7021	7023z	Austria
...	...	79	...	...	1.2	...	1.4z	3723	...	6127z	Belgium
69	68	...	...	...	...	...	...	...	...	...	Canada
60	67	83	...	...	1.2	1.6	1.7z	1647	3831	5113z	Cyprus
...	63	...	...	...	...	1.6	1.8z	...	7054	7358z	Denmark
...	71	76	...	...	1.8	1.2	1.2z	3696	4404	4924z	Finland
...	78	81z	...	...	0.9	1.1	1.0z	2624	4280	4837z	France
...	82	84	...	...	...	...	...	...	...	...	Germany
52	57	63	...	...	0.6	0.7	0.9z	1272	2157	3203z	Greece
...	76	78z	...	...	...	...	2.7y	...	...	7718y	Iceland
77	85	84	...	...	1.5	1.5	1.8z	2102	3182	5215z	Ireland
82	...	86	...	...	1.9	2.4	2.4z	2005	4765	4996z	Israel
91	95	96	...	...	0.8	1.2	1.1z	3060	6207	6571z	Italy
51	...	71	...	...	...	...	1.5z	...	...	12359z	Luxembourg
79	87	86	...	...	0.9	...	1.1x	1158	...	2443x	Malta
...	87	80z	...	...	...	...	...	...	...	...	Monaco
53	...	82	...	...	0.9	1.2	1.4z	3072	4446	5441z	Netherlands
...	...	73z	...	...	2.5	1.6	1.7z	9637	6267	7013z	Norway
81	...	82	...	...	1.8	1.6	1.8z	2912	3838	4762z	Portugal
89	...	...	...	...	...	...	...	...	...	...	San Marino
73	68	69	...	...	0.8	1.1	1.1y	1781	3890	4399y	Spain
77	80	81	...	...	3.2	...	2.0z	7185	...	7664z	Sweden
...	...	78	...	...	2.1	1.4	1.5y	10208	6635	7193y	Switzerland
78	76	82	...	...	1.2	...	...	3100	...	...	United Kingdom
...	86	89	...	...	...	...	...	...	...	...	United States
											South and West Asia
...	–	34	...	36	...	...	...	...	...	...	Afghanistan
...	33	34z	64	48z	...	0.6	0.7	...	63	106	Bangladesh
...	32	38	100	94	...	...	...	...	...	...	Bhutan
28	33*	...	...	...	...	1.2	...	...	264	...	India
53	53	61	...	100	...	...	1.0	...	...	599	Iran, Islamic Republic of
...	60	66	67	64	...	...	3.3	...	...	...	Maldives
14	23	*30*	46	31	...	1.1	1.3y	...	94	113y	Nepal
27	...	46	...	86	...	...	...	...	...	...	Pakistan
...	...	79z	...	...	...	...	...	...	...	...	Sri Lanka
											Sub-Saharan Africa
...	...	...	...	...	...	...	...	...	...	...	Angola
25	23	18	58	72z	...	...	1.7	...	...	116	Benin
78	81	78	90	97	...	...	2.1	...	...	1118	Botswana
27	25	29	...	88	...	...	3.2	...	...	396	Burkina Faso
46	54	55	...	88	1.5	1.3	2.7	59	76	120	Burundi
30	36	40*	...	63*	...	1.2	1.1	...	154	112*	Cameroon
...	62	66	...	78	...	...	3.2	...	...	1142	Cape Verde
25	...	...	...	...	1.2	...	1.1	92	...	129	Central African Republic

Table 13 (continued)

Country or territory	GOAL 6 — Educational quality — SURVIVAL RATE TO GRADE 5 — School year ending in 1991 Total (%)	1991 GPI (F/M)	1999 Total (%)	1999 GPI (F/M)	2004 Total (%)	2004 GPI (F/M)	PUPIL/TEACHER RATIO IN PRIMARY EDUCATION[1] — School year ending in 1991	1999	2005
Chad	51	0.74	55	0.86	33	0.94	66	68	63
Comoros	…	…	…	…	*80*	*1.02*	37	35	*35*
Congo	60	1.16	…	…	66ˣ	1.03ˣ	65	61	*83*
Côte d'Ivoire	73	0.93	69	0.89	…	…	37	43	42*,ʸ
Democratic Rep. of the Congo	55	0.86	…	…	…	…	40	26	34ʸ
Equatorial Guinea	…	…	…	…	…	…	…	57	32ʸ
Eritrea	…	…	95	0.95	79	0.89	38	47	48
Ethiopia	18	1.47	…	…	…	…	36	64	**72**
Gabon	…	…	…	…	*69ˣ*	*1.04ˣ*	…	44	36ᶻ
Gambia	…	…	…	…	…	…	31	33	35ᶻ
Ghana	80	0.98	…	…	63ˣ	1.05ˣ	29	30	**35**
Guinea	59	0.76	…	…	76	0.94	40	47	45
Guinea-Bissau	…	…	…	…	…	…	…	44	…
Kenya	77	1.04	…	…	*83*	*1.05*	32	32	*40*
Lesotho	66	1.26	74	1.20	73	…	54	44	42
Liberia	…	…	…	…	…	…	…	39	…
Madagascar	21	0.96	51	1.02	43	1.00	40	47	54
Malawi	64	0.80	49	0.77	42	0.93	61	…	…
Mali	70	0.95	*78*	*0.97*	87	0.93	47	62*	54
Mauritius	97	1.01	99	0.99	97	1.00	21	26	22
Mozambique	34	0.87	43	0.79	62	0.88	55	61	66
Namibia	62	1.08	92	1.02	86	1.04	…	32	31
Niger	62	1.06	…	…	65	0.97	42	41	44
Nigeria	89	…	…	…	*73ʸ*	*1.05ʸ*	39	*41*	37
Rwanda	60	0.97	45	…	46ʸ	1.13ʸ	57	54	62
Sao Tome and Principe	…	…	…	…	76	1.02	…	36	31
Senegal	85	…	…	…	73	0.96	53	49	42
Seychelles	93	1.03	99	1.02	…	…	…	15	14
Sierra Leone	…	…	…	…	…	…	35	…	…
Somalia	…	…	…	…	…	…	…	…	…
South Africa	…	…	65	0.99	82ʸ	1.02ʸ	27	35	*36ᶻ*
Swaziland	77	1.09	80	1.22	77ˣ	1.08ˣ	32	33	32ᶻ
Togo	48	0.80	…	…	75	0.89	58	41	34
Uganda	36	…	…	…	*49*	*0.99*	33	…	52
United Republic of Tanzania	81	1.02	…	…	**85**	**1.03**	36	40	**52**
Zambia	…	…	81	0.94	…	…	…	47	51
Zimbabwe	76	1.12	…	…	*70ˣ*	*1.04ˣ*	39	41	39ʸ

	Median						Weighted average		
World	…	…	…	…	…	…	26	25	25
Countries in transition	…	…	…	…	…	…	22	19	19
Developed countries	…	…	…	…	…	…	17	16	15
Developing countries	…	…	…	…	81	…	29	27	28
Arab States	87	1.00	92	0.99	96	1.03	25	23	22
Central and Eastern Europe	…	…	…	…	…	…	21	19	18
Central Asia	…	…	…	…	…	…	21	21	21
East Asia and the Pacific	…	…	…	…	…	…	23	22	20
East Asia	…	…	…	…	88	0.97	23	22	20
Pacific	…	…	…	…	…	…	18	21	19
Latin America and the Caribbean	…	…	89	1.02	87	1.07	25	26	23
Caribbean	…	…	…	…	…	…	25	24	22
Latin America	80	…	85	0.98	86	…	25	26	23
North America and Western Europe	…	…	…	…	…	…	16	15	14
South and West Asia	…	…	…	…	79	1.02	45	37	39
Sub-Saharan Africa	63	0.93	…	…	73	…	37	41	45

1. Based on headcounts of pupils and teachers.

2. Data on trained teachers (defined according to national standards) are not collected for countries whose education statistics are gathered through the OECD, Eurostat or the World Education Indicators questionnaires.

GOAL 6
Educational quality

% FEMALE TEACHERS IN PRIMARY EDUCATION			TRAINED PRIMARY-SCHOOL TEACHERS[2] as % of total		PUBLIC CURRENT EXPENDITURE ON PRIMARY EDUCATION as % of GNP			PUBLIC CURRENT EXPENDITURE ON PRIMARY EDUCATION PER PUPIL (unit cost) at PPP in constant 2004 US$			
School year ending in			School year ending in		School year ending in			School year ending in			
1991	1999	2005	1999	2005	1991	1999	2005	1991	1999	2005	Country or territory
6	9	12	...	27	0.7	...	0.6	58	...	67	Chad
...	26	*33*	...	...	...	...	...	...	...	...	Comoros
32	42	*45*	...	62z	...	2.0	0.7	...	169	37	Congo
18	20	24*,y	...	100*,y	...	1.8	*0.1*	...	262	...	Côte d'Ivoire
24	21	*26y*	...	...	...	...	...	...	...	...	Democratic Rep. of the Congo
...	28	30y	...	...	...	...	...	...	...	...	Equatorial Guinea
45	35	40	73	84	...	...	1.0	...	...	111	Eritrea
24	37	**45**	...	97	1.5	...	**2.0**	61	...	...	Ethiopia
...	42	*45z*	...	100y	...	...	...	...	...	...	Gabon
31	29	35z	72	58z	1.3	...	...	169	...	...	Gambia
36	32	**44**	72	**56**	...	...	1.6	...	...	283	Ghana
22	25	24	...	68	...	...	...	...	...	...	Guinea
...	20	...	...	...	...	...	...	...	...	...	Guinea-Bissau
38	42	*45*	...	99z	3.2	...	4.0z	196	...	240z	Kenya
80	80	78	78	64	...	3.2	*3.6*	...	441	*476*	Lesotho
...	19	...	...	...	...	...	...	...	...	...	Liberia
...	58	60	...	36	...	...	1.3	...	...	58	Madagascar
31	...	...	...	...	1.1	...	3.0y	...	...	88y	Malawi
25	23*	26	...	...	...	*1.3*	...	...	131	...	Mali
45	54	63	100	100	1.3	1.2	1.1	557	1 046	1 311	Mauritius
23	25	30	...	60	...	...	2.6z	...	...	165z	Mozambique
...	67	67	29	92	...	4.4	3.9y	...	1 444	911y	Namibia
33	31	37	98	76z	...	...	...	...	...	...	Niger
43	*47*	51	...	50	...	...	...	...	...	...	Nigeria
46	55	*51*	49	82z	...	...	1.9	...	...	*128*	Rwanda
...	...	55	...	...	...	...	...	...	...	...	Sao Tome and Principe
27	*23*	25	...	100	1.7	...	*2.2*	157	...	*305*	Senegal
...	85	85	82	78y	...	...	*1.6z*	...	...	*2 443z*	Seychelles
...	...	...	...	61	...	...	*2.3y*	...	...	...	Sierra Leone
...	...	...	...	...	...	...	...	...	...	...	Somalia
58	78	*76z*	62	79y	4.1	2.7	2.3	1 537	1 470*	1 443	South Africa
78	75	*73z*	91	91z	1.4	1.9	*2.3z*	369	430	*472z*	Swaziland
19	13	12	...	37	...	*1.8*	...	155	...	...	Togo
...	...	39	...	85	...	...	*2.5z*	...	...	*106z*	Uganda
40	45	**48**	...	**100**	...	...	...	...	...	...	United Republic of Tanzania
...	49	48	94	...	...	...	1.3	...	...	54	Zambia
40	47	*51y*	...	...	4.3	...	...	...	...	...	Zimbabwe

Weighted average			Median		Median			Median			
56	58	62	...	...	...	...	1.5	...	...	985	World
93	93	93	...	98	...	...	...	...	...	...	Countries in transition
78	81	83	...	...	...	...	1.2	...	...	4 762	Developed countries
49	52	57	...	...	...	...	1.8	...	...	...	Developing countries
52	52	58	...	100	...	...	1.9	...	...	960	Arab States
81	82	81	...	...	...	...	0.8	...	...	2 053	Central and Eastern Europe
85	84	84	...	84	...	...	...	...	...	...	Central Asia
48	55	59	...	...	...	...	...	...	...	...	East Asia and the Pacific
48	55	59	...	...	...	...	...	...	...	...	East Asia
66	70	72	...	...	...	...	...	...	...	...	Pacific
77	76	77	...	82	...	...	1.8	...	...	...	Latin America and the Caribbean
65	50	57	76	80	...	...	...	...	...	...	Caribbean
77	77	78	...	...	...	1.6	1.5	...	862	598	Latin America
80	81	84	...	...	1.2	1.3	1.5	3 060	4 425	5 441	North America and Western Europe
31	35	45	...	64	...	...	...	...	...	...	South and West Asia
40	44	45	...	78	...	...	2.1	...	...	165	Sub-Saharan Africa

Data in italic are UIS estimates.
Data in bold are for the school year ending in 2006.

(z) Data are for the school year ending in 2004.
(y) Data are for the school year ending in 2003.

(x) Data are for the school year ending in 2002.
(∗) National estimates.

Aid tables

Introduction

Most of the data on aid used in this Report are derived from the OECD's International Development Statistics (IDS) database, which records information provided annually by all member countries of the OECD Development Assistance Committee (DAC). The IDS comprises the DAC database, which provides aggregate data, and the Creditor Reporting System, which provides project- and activity-level data. The IDS is available online at www.oecd.org/dac/stats/idsonline. It is updated frequently. The data presented in this Report were downloaded between March and June 2007.

The focus of this section of the annex on aid data is official development assistance. This term and others used in describing aid data are explained below to help in understanding the tables in this section and the data presented in Chapter 4. Private funds are not included.

Aid recipients and donors

Official development assistance (ODA) is public funds provided to developing countries to promote their economic and social development. It is concessional: that is, it takes the form either of a grant or of a loan carrying a lower rate of interest than is available in the market and, usually, a longer than normal repayment period. ODA may be provided directly by a government (bilateral ODA) or through an international agency (multilateral ODA). ODA can include technical cooperation (see below).

Developing countries are those in Part I of the DAC List of Aid Recipients, which essentially comprises all low- and middle-income countries. Twelve central and eastern European countries, including new independent states of the former Soviet Union, plus a set of more advanced developing countries are in Part II of the list, and aid to them is referred to as official aid (OA). The data presented in this Report do not include OA unless indicated.

Bilateral donors are countries that provide development assistance directly to recipient countries. The majority (Australia, Austria, Belgium, Canada, Denmark, Finland, France, Germany, Greece, Ireland, Italy, Japan, Luxembourg, the Netherlands, New Zealand, Norway, Portugal, Spain, Sweden, Switzerland, the United Kingdom and the United States) are members of the DAC, a forum of major bilateral donors established to promote the volume and effectiveness of aid. Non-DAC bilateral donors include the Republic of Korea and some Arab states. Bilateral donors also contribute substantially to the financing of multilateral donors through contributions recorded as multilateral ODA. The financial flows from multilateral donors to recipient countries are also recorded as ODA receipts.

Multilateral donors are international institutions with government membership that conduct all or a significant part of their activities in favour of developing countries. They include multilateral development banks (e.g. the World Bank and the Inter-American Development Bank), United Nations agencies (e.g. UNDP and UNICEF) and regional groupings (e.g. the European Commission and Arab agencies). The development banks also make nonconcessional loans to several middle- and higher-income countries, and these are not counted as part of ODA.

Types of aid

Unallocated aid: some contributions are not susceptible to allocation by sector and are reported as non-sector-allocable aid. Examples are aid for general development purposes (direct budget support), balance-of-payments support, action relating to debt (including debt relief) and emergency assistance.

Basic education: the definition of basic education varies by agency. The DAC defines it as covering primary education, basic life skills for youth and adults, and early childhood education.

Education, level unspecified: the aid to education reported in the DAC database includes basic, secondary and post-secondary education, and a subcategory called 'education, level unspecified'. This subcategory covers aid related to any activity that cannot be attributed solely to the development of a single level of education.

Sector budget funding: funds contributed directly to the budget of a ministry of education are often reported by donors in this subcategory. Although in practice this aid will mainly be used for specific levels of education, such information is not available in the DAC database. This reduces accuracy in assessing the amount of resources made available for each specific level of education.

Technical cooperation (sometimes referred to as technical assistance): according to the DAC Directives, technical cooperation is the provision of know-how in the form of personnel, training, research and associated costs. It includes (a) grants to nationals of aid recipient countries receiving education or training at home or abroad; and (b) payments to consultants, advisers and similar personnel as well as teachers and administrators serving in recipient countries (including the cost of associated equipment). Where such assistance is related specifically to a capital project, it is included with project and programme expenditure and not separately reported as technical cooperation. The aid activities reported in this category vary by donor, as interpretations of the definition are broad.

Debt relief: this includes debt forgiveness, i.e. the extinction of a loan by agreement between the creditor (donor) and the debtor (aid recipient), and other action on debt, including debt swaps, buy-backs and refinancing. In the DAC database, debt forgiveness is reported as a grant. It raises gross ODA but not necessarily net ODA (see below).

Commitments and disbursements: a commitment is a firm obligation by a donor, expressed in writing and backed by the necessary funds, to provide specified assistance to a country or multilateral organization. The amount specified is recorded as a commitment. Disbursement is the release of funds to, or purchase of goods or services for, a recipient; in other words, the amount spent. Disbursements record the actual international transfer of financial resources or of goods or services valued by the donor. As the aid committed in a given year can be disbursed later, sometimes over several years, the annual aid figures based on commitments differ from those based on disbursements.

Gross and net disbursements: gross disbursements are the total aid extended. Net disbursements are the total aid extended minus amounts of loan principal repaid by recipients or cancelled through debt forgiveness.

Current and constant prices: aid figures in the DAC database are expressed in US$. When other currencies are converted into dollars at the exchange rates prevailing at the time, the resulting amounts are at current prices and exchange rates. When comparing aid figures between different years, adjustment is required to compensate for inflation and changes in exchange rates. Such adjustments result in aid being expressed in constant dollars, i.e. in dollars fixed at the value they held in a given reference year, including their external value in terms of other currencies. Thus, amounts of aid for any year and in any currency expressed in 2005 constant dollars reflect the value of that aid in terms of the purchasing power of dollars in 2005. In this Report, most aid data are presented in 2005 constant dollars. The indices used for adjusting currencies and years (called deflators) are derived from Table 36 of the statistical annex of the 2006 DAC Annual Report (OECD-DAC, 2007b). In previous editions of the *EFA Global Monitoring Report*, amounts of aid were based on the constant prices of different years (the 2007 Report used 2003 constant prices), so amounts for a given country for a given year in these editions differ from the amounts presented in this Report for the same year.

For more detailed and precise definitions of terms used in the DAC database, see the DAC Directives, available at www.oecd.org/dac/stats/dac/directives.

Sources: OECD-DAC (2007c).

Table 1: Bilateral and multilateral ODA

	Total ODA (Constant 2005 US$ millions)			ODA disbursements as % of GNI			Sector-allocable ODA (Constant 2005 US$ millions)			Debt relief and other actions relating to debt (Constant 2005 US$ millions)		
	1999–2000 annual average	2004	2005	1999–2000 annual average	2004	2005	1999–2000 annual average	2004	2005	1999–2000 annual average	2004	2005
Australia	1 386	1 302	1 431	0.27	0.25	0.25	1 127	1 037	1 056	10	8	7
Austria	667	393	1 260	0.23	0.23	0.52	357	205	244	213	85	874
Belgium	677	1 323	1 578	0.36	0.41	0.53	448	762	819	62	216	501
Canada	1 509	2 559	2 366	0.25	0.27	0.34	778	1 650	1 436	51	95	470
Denmark	1 125	1 693	1 674	1.06	0.85	0.81	960	1 357	1 446	13	71	66
Finland	280	438	681	0.31	0.37	0.46	174	338	490	24	0	1
France	5 293	7 593	9 400	0.30	0.41	0.47	3 730	3 886	3 868	1 346	2 096	3 761
Germany	4 640	5 684	9 372	0.27	0.28	0.36	3 669	4 310	4 671	321	838	4 035
Greece	0	172	207	0.20	0.16	0.17	0	138	146	0	0	0
Ireland	110	419	483	0.29	0.39	0.42	64	324	336	6	0	0
Italy	984	909	2 218	0.13	0.15	0.29	459	434	445	240	129	1 773
Japan	11 679	11 967	16 563	0.28	0.19	0.28	9 894	8 151	9 446	968	2 444	5 689
Luxembourg	0	162	219	0.71	0.83	0.82	0	99	124	0	0	0
Netherlands	3 260	2 853	4 348	0.84	0.73	0.82	1 509	2 222	3 368	238	30	0
New Zealand	0	188	306	0.25	0.23	0.27	0	132	201	0	0	0
Norway	1 547	1 491	1 948	0.76	0.87	0.94	1 007	1 147	1 503	26	14	2
Portugal	425	1 048	271	0.26	0.63	0.21	221	179	231	183	710	3
Spain	1 537	1 582	1 730	0.22	0.24	0.27	1 059	958	698	100	295	762
Sweden	1 253	2 047	2 694	0.80	0.78	0.94	823	1 097	1 861	0	26	53
Switzerland	1 033	1 265	1 404	0.34	0.41	0.44	613	801	650	0	8	224
United Kingdom	4 745	5 235	9 836	0.32	0.36	0.47	4 021	3 847	4 340	153	787	4 584
United States	11 477	24 160	26 859	0.10	0.17	0.22	7 186	18 644	16 354	115	209	4 219
TOTAL DAC bilateral	**53 627**	**74 484**	**96 848**	...	...	...	**38 098**	**51 718**	**53 734**	**4 069**	**8 061**	**27 026**
African Development Fund	790	1 465	1 519	...	...	...	680	1 382	1 452	1	84	66
Asian Development Fund	1 239	1 575	1 409	...	...	...	1 183	1 503	1 349	0	0	0
European Commission	8 668	9 263	11 355	...	...	...	6 544	7 396	8 983	0	6	0
Fast Track Initiative	0	38	50	...	...	...	0	38	50	0	0	0
International Development Association	6 592	12 253	8 613	...	...	...	6 242	11 701	6 292	0	412	67
Inter-American Development Bank Special Fund	338	336	494	...	...	...	338	333	484	0	0	0
UNICEF	192	676	737	...	...	...	169	404	480	0	0	0
TOTAL multilaterals	**18 514**	**26 985**	**25 732**	...	...	...	**15 806**	**24 119**	**20 646**	**1**	**502**	**133**
TOTAL all donors	**72 141**	**101 469**	**122 581**	...	...	...	**53 904**	**75 838**	**74 380**	**4 070**	**8 563**	**27 160**

Notes:
(···) indicates that data are not available.
Data for sector-allocable aid include general budget support.
All data represent commitments unless otherwise specified.
Sources: CRS online database (OECD-DAC, 2007c); DAC online database, Table 1 (OECD-DAC, 2007c).

Table 2: Bilateral and multilateral aid to education

	Total aid to education — Constant 2005 US$ millions			Total aid to basic education — Constant 2005 US$ millions			Direct aid to education — Constant 2005 US$ millions			Direct aid to basic education — Constant 2005 US$ millions			Secondary education — Constant 2005 US$ millions		
	1999–2000 annual average	2004	2005	1999–2000 annual average	2004	2005	1999–2000 annual average	2004	2005	1999–2000 annual average	2004	2005	1999–2000 annual average	2004	2005
Australia	239	116	138	63	77	37	239	116	137	40	51	21	21	9	15
Austria	122	84	95	5	4	4	122	83	95	3	3	2	40	6	1
Belgium	89	164	146	15	34	36	87	157	143	5	21	23	10	5	17
Canada	95	200	246	48	158	189	93	179	232	27	136	146	16	3	3
Denmark	69	145	129	42	94	71	63	117	125	34	54	33	19	2	20
Finland	26	79	52	12	52	28	26	71	50	3	33	10	1	2	1
France	1548	1578	1496	354	321	236	1515	1547	1461	91	273	196	284	149	149
Germany	829	1103	416	119	130	161	826	1091	405	96	107	115	97	93	83
Greece	0	23	38	0	3	6	0	22	38	0	0	0	0	0	0
Ireland	17	59	62	9	38	38	17	53	58	4	28	22	1	4	3
Italy	53	86	···	15	39	···	50	85	···	1	21	···	11	13	···
Japan	517	1238	855	213	298	264	330	1237	841	46	209	155	36	71	49
Luxembourg	0	23	29	0	11	13	0	23	29	0	11	3	0	11	6
Netherlands	272	419	721	176	274	476	235	392	618	127	254	361	10	4	11
New Zealand	0	50	67	0	14	48	0	46	62	0	11	44	0	4	3
Norway	137	165	207	85	117	116	134	140	185	72	85	78	8	6	6
Portugal	36	56	65	9	6	10	35	55	64	4	3	4	4	2	6
Spain	225	126	184	68	45	73	225	123	183	21	30	48	31	24	34
Sweden	68	85	173	44	68	63	44	71	144	24	59	1	1	1	5
Switzerland	45	46	24	19	26	5	45	36	24	14	18	3	20	7	7
United Kingdom	435	956	336	320	830	249	316	794	257	233	737	164	15	1	1
United States	355	600	744	194	530	596	331	598	694	174	510	509	43	15	39
TOTAL DAC bilateral	**5180**	**7401**	**6222**	**1811**	**3170**	**2719**	**4732**	**7037**	**5844**	**1019**	**2654**	**1937**	**670**	**435**	**458**
African Development Fund	74	158	123	46	49	62	68	129	66	18	2	0	0	61	0
Asian Development Fund	125	305	311	9	123	33	125	304	282	0	123	18	104	181	264
European Commission	709	576	949	451	227	474	503	429	720	332	102	310	60	61	61
Fast Track Initiative	0	38	50	0	38	50	0	38	50	0	38	50	0	0	0
International Development Association	787	2126	584	406	1377	268	609	1624	559	143	1032	84	53	316	19
Inter-American Development Bank Special Fund	5	48	22	3	29	0	5	42	22	0	10	0	0	0	22
UNICEF	28	60	68	28	59	67	28	60	68	28	59	67	0	0	1
TOTAL multilaterals	**1734**	**3311**	**2106**	**945**	**1903**	**954**	**1343**	**2625**	**1768**	**522**	**1366**	**529**	**217**	**619**	**368**
TOTAL all donors	**6914**	**10712**	**8328**	**2756**	**5074**	**3672**	**6076**	**9662**	**7612**	**1541**	**4020**	**2466**	**887**	**1054**	**826**

Notes:
(···) indicates that data are not available.
Data for sector-allocable aid include general budget support.
All data represent commitments unless otherwise specified.
Sources: CRS online database (OECD-DAC, 2007c); DAC online database, Table 1 (OECD-DAC, 2007c).

Post-secondary education (Constant 2005 US$ millions)			Education, level unspecified (Constant 2005 US$ millions)			Share of education in total ODA (%)			Share of education in total sector-allocable ODA (%)			Share of basic education in total aid to education (%)			
1999–2000 annual average	2004	2005	1999–2000 annual average	2004	2005	1999–2000 annual average	2004	2005	1999–2000 annual average	2004	2005	1999–2000 annual average	2004	2005	
132	5	71	45	50	31	17	9	10	21	11	13	26	66	26	Australia
75	72	89	4	3	2	18	21	8	34	41	39	4	5	4	Austria
53	111	80	19	21	24	13	12	9	20	21	18	17	21	25	Belgium
10	18	12	40	22	72	6	8	10	12	12	17	51	79	77	Canada
0	10	1	10	51	71	6	9	8	7	11	9	61	65	55	Denmark
4	5	4	17	30	35	9	18	8	15	23	11	44	66	54	Finland
647	1 059	1 070	493	66	45	29	21	16	41	41	39	23	20	16	France
591	856	127	42	35	80	18	19	4	23	26	9	14	12	39	Germany
0	18	26	0	4	11	…	13	18	…	17	26	…	11	15	Greece
2	9	4	11	12	29	16	14	13	27	18	19	51	63	62	Ireland
13	14	…	24	37	…	5	9	…	12	20	…	29	46	…	Italy
99	782	433	149	176	204	4	10	5	5	15	9	41	24	31	Japan
0	0	0	0	1	20	…	14	13	…	23	23	…	49	44	Luxembourg
37	122	119	61	12	127	8	15	17	18	19	21	65	65	66	Netherlands
0	29	11	0	2	3	…	26	22	…	38	33	…	28	73	New Zealand
32	10	47	22	38	54	9	11	11	14	14	14	62	71	56	Norway
18	44	43	8	6	11	9	5	24	16	31	28	26	11	16	Portugal
79	42	53	94	27	48	15	8	11	21	13	26	30	36	39	Spain
2	6	43	17	5	95	5	4	6	8	8	9	65	81	37	Sweden
1	4	9	10	7	5	4	4	2	7	6	4	43	57	21	Switzerland
13	32	0	54	25	92	9	18	3	11	25	8	74	87	74	United Kingdom
98	34	22	16	38	125	3	2	3	5	3	5	55	88	80	United States
1 907	3 280	2 264	1 137	668	1 184	10	10	6	14	14	12	35	43	44	TOTAL DAC
0	0	0	49	66	66	9	11	8	11	11	8	62	31	50	African Development Fund
4	0	0	17	0	0	10	19	22	11	20	23	7	40	10	Asian Development Fund
79	163	248	32	104	100	8	6	8	11	8	11	64	39	50	European Commission
0	0	0	0	0	0	…	100	100	…	100	100	…	100	100	Fast Track Initiative
65	88	112	348	188	344	12	17	7	13	18	9	52	65	46	International Development Association
0	0	0	5	31	0	2	14	4	2	14	5	50	61	0	Inter-American Development Bank Special Fund
0	0	0	0	0	0	14	9	9	16	15	14	100	99	99	UNICEF
148	251	361	456	389	511	9	12	8	11	14	10	55	57	45	TOTAL multilaterals
2 056	3 531	2 624	1 592	1 058	1 695	10	11	7	13	14	11	40	47	44	TOTAL all donors

Education for All Global Monitoring Report 2 0 0 8

Table 4: Recipients of aid to education

	Total aid to education (Constant 2005 US$ millions)			Total aid to basic education (Constant 2005 US$ millions)			Total aid to basic education per primary school-age child (Constant 2005 US$)			Direct aid to education (Constant 2005 US$ millions)			Direct aid to basic education (Constant 2005 US$ millions)		
	1999–2000 annual average	2004	2005	1999–2000 annual average	2004	2005	1999–2000 annual average	2004	2005	1999–2000 annual average	2004	2005	1999–2000 annual average	2004	2005
Arab States	1 057	1 383	1 283	309	496	457	8	13	11	1 032	1 372	1 194	141	454	341
unallocated within the region	*24*	*10*	*23*	*6*	*2*	*14*	*…*	*…*	*…*	*24*	*10*	*23*	*4*	*2*	*7*
Algeria	119	191	185	36	22	21	9	5	6	119	191	185	0	22	9
Bahrain	1	0	0	0	0	0	0	0	0	1	0	0	0	0	0
Djibouti	46	44	53	13	4	32	126	32	254	44	44	53	1	0	30
Egypt	144	72	95	38	39	76	5	5	8	144	72	95	36	38	71
Iraq	8	185	130	1	163	90	0	37	20	8	182	130	0	153	89
Jordan	26	50	56	2	31	33	3	38	39	22	50	18	0	30	13
Lebanon	41	54	48	8	1	5	18	2	11	41	54	48	1	1	1
Libyan Arab Jamahiriya	2	0	2	0	0	0	0	0	0	2	0	2	0	0	0
Mauritania	39	35	38	11	9	25	25	19	53	32	35	38	1	8	19
Morocco	255	315	233	62	10	33	15	3	9	255	315	233	11	6	30
Oman	1	1	1	0	0	0	0	0	0	1	1	1	0	0	0
Palestinian A. T.	55	35	101	28	12	50	77	29	114	54	28	70	18	3	20
Saudi Arabia	2	4	4	0	0	1	0	0	0	2	4	4	0	0	0
Sudan	20	36	37	5	21	20	1	4	4	13	34	36	1	19	7
Syrian Arab Republic	38	69	22	4	1	1	2	1	1	38	69	22	0	1	0
Tunisia	172	90	210	44	1	16	37	1	14	171	90	191	28	1	4
Yemen	64	193	43	48	179	41	15	50	11	63	193	43	40	172	40
Central and Eastern Europe	396	382	295	126	80	27	10	7	2	360	345	291	84	24	11
unallocated within the region	*14*	*13*	*21*	*2*	*3*	*2*	*…*	*…*	*…*	*13*	*13*	*21*	*0*	*0*	*0*
Albania	31	38	20	11	6	4	41	27	16	24	32	20	2	1	2
Belarus	0	0	8	0	0	1	0	0	1	0	0	8	0	0	0
Bosnia and Herzegovina	35	40	33	11	3	2	54	16	13	27	40	33	2	2	1
Croatia	19	21	13	0	4	0	2	21	1	19	21	13	0	4	0
Republic of Moldova	9	12	9	3	4	1	12	19	…	3	12	9	0	4	0
Serbia and Montenegro	39	75	43	6	21	8	…	…	…	38	51	43	1	6	5
Slovenia	7	0	0	0	0	0	2	0	0	7	0	0	0	0	0
TFYR Macedonia	25	21	17	11	4	4	87	33	39	12	17	13	4	1	2
Turkey	215	160	101	81	33	4	10	4	1	215	157	101	76	6	0
Ukraine	0	0	30	0	0	0	0	0	0	0	0	30	0	0	0
Central Asia	104	211	118	26	70	58	4	11	10	84	193	103	9	43	43
unallocated within the region	*0*	*0*	*6*	*0*	*0*	*3*	*…*	*…*	*…*	*0*	*0*	*0*	*0*	*0*	*0*
Armenia	10	36	7	2	14	1	8	101	9	9	29	5	0	8	0
Azerbaijan	7	6	9	2	1	5	3	2	8	6	6	5	0	0	2
Georgia	20	32	7	4	5	2	15	13	6	13	25	6	0	0	1
Kazakhstan	16	16	10	2	4	3	2	4	3	16	16	10	2	0	0
Kyrgyzstan	9	28	18	4	12	13	8	26	28	3	26	18	0	7	11
Mongolia	15	46	30	6	18	20	23	81	76	13	46	30	4	17	19
Tajikistan	8	19	15	3	13	9	5	19	14	7	17	13	1	9	8
Turkmenistan	4	3	3	1	0	0	2	1	1	3	3	3	0	0	0
Uzbekistan	14	25	12	2	3	2	1	1	1	14	25	12	1	1	1
East Asia and the Pacific	1 252	1 728	1 265	361	324	431	2	2	3	1 059	1 656	1 207	128	193	275
unallocated within the region	*23*	*39*	*39*	*9*	*16*	*18*	*…*	*…*	*…*	*14*	*39*	*39*	*4*	*2*	*4*
Cambodia	38	44	55	14	18	28	7	9	14	32	44	55	7	14	11
China	164	883	326	26	13	10	0	0	0	164	883	326	16	8	4
Cook Islands	0	4	2	0	1	1	…	…	…	0	4	2	0	0	0
DPR Korea	12	3	2	5	1	1	3	1	1	1	1	1	0	0	0
Fiji	6	31	6	1	14	1	9	129	13	6	31	6	1	0	1
Indonesia	301	155	241	121	74	83	5	3	3	193	155	211	55	56	51

Direct aid to secondary education — Constant 2005 US$ millions			Direct aid to post-secondary education — Constant 2005 US$ millions			Aid to education, level unspecified — Constant 2005 US$ millions			Share of education in total ODA (%)			Share of education in total sector-allocable ODA (%)			Share of basic education in total aid to education (%)		
1999–2000 annual average	2004	2005	1999–2000 annual average	2004	2005	1999–2000 annual average	2004	2005	1999–2000 annual average	2004	2005	1999–2000 annual average	2004	2005	1999–2000 annual average	2004	2005
201	**121**	**108**	**378**	**726**	**602**	**311**	**71**	**143**	**16**	**8**	**5**	**20**	**10**	**11**	**29**	**36**	**36**
2	*6*	*0*	*13*	*1*	*2*	*5*	*0*	*14*	...	...	...	...	...	...	...	...	...
5	2	1	42	166	150	72	0	25	48	31	33	54	61	41	30	12	12
0	0	0	0	0	0	0	0	0	97	24	9	97	71	9	2	0	0
12	23	4	9	13	16	21	8	3	46	63	55	48	78	64	29	9	60
44	1	1	58	31	13	6	2	9	9	5	10	10	7	12	27	54	80
0	2	36	7	10	4	1	17	1	7	2	1	46	2	2	8	88	69
4	0	0	17	19	3	1	1	2	4	9	9	6	10	10	10	61	58
10	9	6	16	43	33	14	1	8	29	33	20	33	39	22	20	2	10
0	0	0	1	0	2	0	0	0	87	...	47	93	...	54	11	...	2
6	0	0	13	25	8	12	1	11	16	10	15	18	16	29	28	26	65
59	39	10	83	262	187	103	7	7	28	24	26	30	30	27	24	3	14
0	0	0	1	0	0	0	0	0	8	6	6	8	8	7	12	8	5
9	4	4	7	9	18	20	12	28	9	6	11	11	8	13	52	35	49
0	1	2	1	3	1	1	0	1	55	30	49	55	49	50	12	5	17
1	1	2	10	11	2	1	4	26	7	3	1	20	11	4	26	60	55
1	28	0	30	40	20	7	1	1	30	45	21	31	51	22	10	1	4
49	2	42	65	87	141	29	0	4	26	16	45	26	19	47	25	1	7
1	1	1	6	5	1	16	15	2	14	40	12	18	48	17	75	93	94
47	**47**	**27**	**181**	**199**	**226**	**48**	**75**	**27**	**7**	**10**	**5**	**11**	**11**	**6**	**32**	**21**	**9**
1	*3*	*2*	*9*	*4*	*14*	*3*	*6*	*4*	...	...	...	...	...	...	...	...	...
3	8	0	9	18	14	11	5	3	5	10	6	7	11	6	34	17	18
0	0	0	0	0	6	0	0	1	...	...	14	...	...	15	...	...	7
0	13	12	16	24	18	8	2	2	3	7	7	5	7	9	30	7	7
0	0	1	19	16	11	1	1	1	21	11	6	25	12	7	2	20	2
0	0	0	3	7	8	0	1	0	6	8	4	6	9	6	37	38	7
1	10	9	26	30	23	11	6	6	2	6	3	4	6	4	17	27	19
0	0	0	6	0	0	0	0	0	18	...	...	20	...	...	2	...	...
2	4	0	5	9	10	1	3	0	4	6	9	8	7	9	43	19	26
40	9	1	88	91	91	11	51	8	26	30	6	34	32	7	38	20	4
0	0	0	0	0	29	0	0	1	...	...	5	...	...	5	...	...	1
23	**21**	**7**	**38**	**94**	**37**	**14**	**35**	**16**	**5**	**12**	**5**	**7**	**13**	**6**	**25**	**33**	**49**
0	*0*	*0*	*0*	*0*	*0*	*0*	*0*	*0*	...	...	...	...	...	...	...	...	...
0	8	1	7	7	4	1	5	1	4	12	2	4	13	2	15	40	17
0	0	0	2	5	2	3	1	0	2	4	2	3	4	2	32	17	51
0	0	0	12	23	4	0	2	1	7	11	2	8	14	3	22	15	29
9	0	0	5	9	5	1	7	5	8	14	7	8	14	8	11	22	27
1	6	0	1	6	4	0	7	3	4	13	8	5	14	11	38	42	69
1	0	0	6	26	7	2	3	4	5	28	20	10	35	26	39	40	68
2	0	1	0	2	3	3	6	1	5	8	6	9	10	8	40	69	62
3	0	0	0	3	3	0	0	0	17	23	15	18	28	16	18	9	11
7	6	4	3	14	5	3	4	2	9	8	9	9	8	9	16	12	18
207	**139**	**101**	**450**	**1 134**	**576**	**273**	**190**	**256**	**9**	**15**	**9**	**10**	**16**	**11**	**29**	**19**	**34**
1	*4*	*1*	*8*	*5*	*6*	*1*	*27*	*28*	...	...	...	...	...	...	...	...	...
3	2	1	13	20	10	9	8	34	7	8	10	9	9	11	38	42	50
10	17	4	118	848	304	19	11	13	6	35	17	6	36	20	16	1	3
0	1	0	0	2	0	0	1	2	3	47	15	3	47	18	0	21	38
0	0	0	1	1	1	0	0	0	6	3	3	20	14	9	46	30	37
0	0	1	5	3	3	0	27	2	28	49	14	30	54	15	15	45	23
54	4	8	59	59	118	25	36	34	15	7	5	19	8	9	40	48	34

Table 4 (continued)

	Total aid to education (Constant 2005 US$ millions)			Total aid to basic education (Constant 2005 US$ millions)			Total aid to basic education per primary school-age child (Constant 2005 US$)			Direct aid to education (Constant 2005 US$ millions)			Direct aid to basic education (Constant 2005 US$ millions)		
	1999–2000 annual average	2004	2005	1999–2000 annual average	2004	2005	1999–2000 annual average	2004	2005	1999–2000 annual average	2004	2005	1999–2000 annual average	2004	2005
Kiribati	7	3	1	3	0	0	…	…	…	7	3	1	0	0	0
Lao PDR	31	63	20	5	19	8	7	25	10	29	63	20	2	15	4
Malaysia	91	33	18	1	6	2	0	2	1	91	33	18	0	0	0
Marshall Islands	4	12	13	2	6	6	…	…	…	0	12	13	0	1	0
Micronesia	0	0	0	0	0	0	0	0	0	0	0	0	0	0	0
Myanmar	3	16	14	2	3	6	0	1	1	3	16	14	1	3	4
Nauru	0	0	1	0	0	0	…	…	…	0	0	1	0	0	0
Niue	0	1	4	0	1	2	…	…	…	0	1	1	0	0	0
Palau	2	4	3	1	2	2	…	…	…	0	1	1	0	1	1
Papua New Guinea	92	17	67	48	5	58	67	5	61	87	17	67	29	0	51
Philippines	177	80	56	63	53	35	6	5	3	175	80	56	5	46	30
Republic of Korea	28	0	0	4	0	0	1	0	0	28	0	0	0	0	0
Samoa	7	11	12	3	1	10	122	26	306	7	11	12	1	0	9
Solomon Islands	12	8	23	4	7	21	48	90	277	7	8	23	0	6	21
Thailand	47	46	37	13	4	3	2	1	1	24	46	37	0	2	0
Timor-Leste	8	20	15	2	12	4	17	97	34	7	19	14	1	10	1
Tokelau	0	3	3	0	1	1	…	…	…	0	0	0	0	0	0
Tonga	2	5	5	0	0	3	18	31	194	2	5	5	0	0	2
Tuvalu	1	4	2	0	0	1	…	…	…	1	4	2	0	0	0
Vanuatu	11	7	17	1	1	4	16	31	113	11	6	17	0	1	3
Viet Nam	187	238	282	35	67	124	4	8	15	170	175	265	6	26	76
Latin America and the Caribbean	**576**	**729**	**660**	**259**	**341**	**263**	**5**	**6**	**4**	**548**	**669**	**637**	**175**	**232**	**164**
unallocated within the region	*72*	*62*	*117*	*31*	*19*	*19*	…	…	…	*70*	*62*	*117*	*15*	*16*	*10*
Anguilla	3	0	0	0	0	0	…	…	…	3	0	0	0	0	0
Antigua and Barbuda	1	0	3	1	0	0	…	…	…	1	0	3	0	0	0
Argentina	16	19	28	2	2	14	1	0	3	16	19	28	0	1	13
Aruba	0	0	0	0	0	0	…	…	…	0	0	0	0	0	0
Barbados	0	0	0	0	0	0	1	0	1	0	0	0	0	0	0
Belize	1	1	1	1	0	0	21	10	10	1	1	1	1	0	0
Bolivia	40	127	85	29	106	39	23	77	29	38	118	85	26	94	6
Brazil	45	47	37	11	5	7	1	0	1	45	47	37	5	2	3
Chile	19	12	12	3	1	2	1	0	1	19	12	12	1	0	1
Colombia	33	30	27	11	4	4	2	1	1	33	30	27	4	3	3
Costa Rica	4	5	3	0	2	1	1	5	2	4	5	3	0	2	1
Cuba	9	12	4	1	3	0	1	3	1	8	12	4	0	3	0
Dominica	1	1	1	0	0	0	…	…	…	0	0	1	0	0	0
Dominican Republic	21	13	12	7	9	6	6	8	5	21	13	12	6	8	2
Ecuador	10	22	14	2	4	3	1	3	2	10	22	14	1	4	2
El Salvador	14	10	10	7	5	5	9	6	5	14	10	10	5	4	2
Grenada	0	1	12	0	0	12	…	…	…	0	0	12	0	0	12
Guatemala	30	18	39	19	10	28	10	5	14	30	18	39	17	8	25
Guyana	6	12	0	1	7	0	7	83	2	5	6	0	0	4	0
Haiti	30	21	65	18	9	21	14	7	17	27	21	52	11	9	7
Honduras	23	88	42	13	55	32	12	50	29	20	70	42	5	27	27
Jamaica	21	12	5	17	8	4	52	24	12	15	6	5	14	5	3
Mexico	21	27	22	4	2	3	0	0	0	21	27	22	1	1	2
Montserrat	2	0	0	1	0	0	…	…	…	0	0	0	0	0	0
Nicaragua	74	120	48	60	66	36	74	78	43	72	101	41	52	26	31
Panama	13	3	3	1	1	0	3	2	1	13	3	3	1	0	0
Paraguay	4	8	14	2	4	4	3	4	5	4	8	14	2	3	3
Peru	27	41	29	9	14	10	3	4	3	27	41	26	6	11	6
Saint Kitts and Nevis	0	0	0	0	0	0	…	…	…	0	0	0	0	0	0
Saint Lucia	2	1	1	1	0	1	60	20	24	1	1	1	0	0	0
St Vincent/Grenad.	1	3	0	1	1	0	…	45	11	1	3	0	0	0	0
Suriname	1	2	17	0	1	8	1	10	144	1	2	17	0	0	0
Trinidad and Tobago	1	1	0	0	0	0	0	0	0	1	1	0	0	0	0
Turks and Caicos Islands	2	0	0	2	0	0	…	…	…	2	0	0	2	0	0
Uruguay	5	4	2	1	1	0	2	4	1	5	4	2	0	1	0
Venezuela	24	8	7	3	0	0	1	0	0	21	8	7	0	0	0

Direct aid to secondary education (Constant 2005 US$ millions)			Direct aid to post-secondary education (Constant 2005 US$ millions)			Aid to education, level unspecified (Constant 2005 US$ millions)			Share of education in total ODA (%)			Share of education in total sector-allocable ODA (%)			Share of basic education in total aid to education (%)		
1999–2000 annual average	2004	2005	1999–2000 annual average	2004	2005	1999–2000 annual average	2004	2005	1999–2000 annual average	2004	2005	1999–2000 annual average	2004	2005	1999–2000 annual average	2004	2005
0	0	0	1	3	1	6	0	0	29	10	4	29	10	4	43	6	18
3	24	2	20	17	7	4	7	7	14	27	6	16	28	7	15	30	38
2	1	1	87	20	12	2	12	4	7	44	2	7	46	2	1	18	13
0	0	1	0	0	0	0	11	12	7	23	25	9	24	26	45	50	50
0	0	0	0	0	0	0	0	0	...	...	...	...	...	...	...	...	...
0	0	0	1	12	4	1	0	6	5	13	10	8	25	19	58	21	47
0	0	0	0	0	0	0	0	1	51	1	8	51	5	9	0	3	27
0	0	0	0	0	1	0	0	0	32	8	14	38	12	14	0	45	49
0	0	0	0	0	0	0	0	0	4	14	11	5	15	11	40	54	55
8	4	1	16	4	1	33	9	13	18	3	26	19	3	27	52	29	86
33	3	6	22	19	12	115	12	8	11	15	11	11	17	12	36	66	61
0	0	0	20	0	0	8	0	0	83	...	...	89	...	...	14	...	...
1	5	1	1	5	1	4	1	1	24	19	18	24	21	18	44	8	81
1	0	0	4	1	2	1	0	0	11	8	15	11	9	15	29	80	89
5	3	1	17	36	29	2	5	6	3	8	6	3	8	7	27	9	9
0	1	4	5	6	5	1	3	4	3	12	8	4	13	9	29	58	27
0	0	0	0	0	0	0	0	0	93	21	18	93	21	19	0	45	44
0	1	0	2	3	1	0	1	1	11	19	28	11	19	33	14	9	55
0	2	0	0	1	1	1	0	1	16	52	11	16	55	11	34	3	35
5	3	10	5	3	2	1	0	1	27	17	22	30	24	23	4	15	23
80	66	58	43	65	52	41	18	78	8	8	10	9	8	10	19	28	44
56	**57**	**79**	**176**	**222**	**219**	**140**	**158**	**176**	**6**	**8**	**8**	**8**	**11**	**11**	**45**	**47**	**40**
2	*1*	*3*	*23*	*38*	*85*	*30*	*7*	*19*	...	...	...	...	...	...	...	...	...
2	0	0	0	0	0	0	0	0	52	0	1	54	0	1	12	...	0
0	0	3	0	0	0	1	0	0	16	0	96	16	0	98	50	8	0
3	1	2	8	16	10	4	2	2	13	22	26	26	27	29	15	8	52
0	0	0	0	0	0	0	0	0	0	...	...	0	...	...	...	...	...
0	0	0	0	0	0	0	0	0	4	0	3	4	0	3	23	0	25
0	0	0	0	0	0	0	0	0	3	4	3	3	5	4	77	73	65
1	2	7	6	7	5	4	15	66	4	10	14	6	19	17	73	83	46
4	4	2	24	35	23	11	7	9	18	10	12	19	10	13	24	11	20
3	1	1	12	10	8	4	1	2	27	13	17	29	15	20	13	6	17
2	3	4	12	22	18	15	2	1	4	3	3	4	4	4	35	13	15
1	0	0	2	2	2	0	0	1	6	12	3	8	14	4	11	49	28
2	0	1	4	9	3	1	0	0	12	17	6	16	20	8	14	24	13
0	0	0	0	0	0	0	0	0	5	8	2	5	8	2	48	32	20
10	2	2	3	1	1	1	1	6	6	6	10	7	6	11	33	69	48
2	6	5	5	11	5	2	2	2	5	7	7	7	8	8	19	20	21
2	2	1	3	2	1	4	2	5	7	7	4	8	8	5	51	53	48
0	0	0	0	0	0	0	0	0	1	3	46	1	10	53	47	48	99
2	2	2	6	4	6	4	3	6	8	7	12	10	8	16	64	54	72
5	1	0	0	0	0	0	0	0	4	7	0	5	8	0	10	63	29
2	3	22	4	8	7	11	1	15	11	5	7	15	8	10	59	45	33
1	1	1	2	4	3	13	38	10	2	13	3	4	16	7	55	63	76
0	0	0	1	0	0	0	0	2	18	7	7	20	9	13	81	69	78
1	1	1	14	24	17	5	2	2	9	12	8	10	12	8	17	7	14
0	0	0	0	0	0	0	0	0	4	2	0	5	2	0	54	50	...
3	13	5	3	2	2	14	60	3	10	8	7	14	17	10	81	55	75
1	0	1	11	1	1	0	1	1	37	6	6	38	7	7	7	29	12
0	1	7	1	2	1	2	3	3	2	10	22	9	11	24	55	51	30
5	10	7	10	13	9	5	7	4	2	8	7	3	9	10	32	34	34
0	0	0	0	0	0	0	0	0	0	2	0	0	2	0	5	0	0
0	0	0	0	0	0	0	0	0	8	3	2	8	4	2	58	64	64
0	2	0	0	0	0	1	1	0	9	20	6	9	22	6	50	22	40
0	0	0	1	1	2	0	0	16	3	2	30	3	2	30	6	31	45
0	0	0	1	1	0	0	0	0	9	4	1	11	5	1	9	0	3
0	0	0	0	0	0	0	0	0	35	7	37	35	7	37	100	100	100
1	0	0	2	2	1	1	1	0	28	16	4	28	20	4	16	35	11
1	1	1	17	7	5	3	0	1	17	12	17	20	13	20	13	5	5

Table 4 (continued)

	Total aid to education (Constant 2005 US$ millions)			Total aid to basic education (Constant 2005 US$ millions)			Total aid to basic education per primary school-age child (Constant 2005 US$)			Direct aid to education (Constant 2005 US$ millions)			Direct aid to basic education (Constant 2005 US$ millions)		
	1999–2000 annual average	2004	2005	1999–2000 annual average	2004	2005	1999–2000 annual average	2004	2005	1999–2000 annual average	2004	2005	1999–2000 annual average	2004	2005
North America and Western Europe	3	55	1	0	27	0	…	…	…	3	55	0	0	0	0
unallocated within the region	*2*	*55*	*1*	*0*	*27*	*0*	…	…	…	*2*	*55*	*0*	*0*	*0*	*0*
Malta	1	0	0	0	0	0	1	0	0	1	0	0	0	0	0
South and West Asia	812	2750	1101	431	2141	537	3	13	3	798	2564	1060	328	1972	365
unallocated within the region	*0*	*0*	*0*	*0*	*0*	*0*	…	…	…	*0*	*0*	*0*	*0*	*0*	*0*
Afghanistan	7	199	227	2	159	165	0	33	33	7	186	213	1	143	151
Bangladesh	129	928	308	79	696	101	4	42	6	129	887	308	75	671	77
Bhutan	5	3	7	1	2	1	…	…	…	5	3	7	0	1	0
India	446	1034	82	284	946	19	3	8	0	432	983	82	197	918	17
Iran, Islamic Republic of	77	57	19	4	1	1	0	0	0	77	57	19	0	1	0
Maldives	15	16	8	0	1	1	7	20	19	15	16	8	0	1	1
Nepal	56	199	19	47	190	11	15	54	3	56	199	18	46	188	9
Pakistan	26	256	295	9	141	197	0	7	10	26	176	273	5	46	104
Sri Lanka	50	56	136	4	6	42	3	3	26	50	56	133	4	3	6
Sub-Saharan Africa	2279	2900	2810	1149	1451	1504	11	13	13	1765	2235	2337	631	990	956
unallocated within the region	*42*	*54*	*50*	*23*	*42*	*10*	…	…	…	*41*	*52*	*49*	*18*	*34*	*2*
Angola	21	16	66	8	5	57	5	3	31	21	16	66	3	3	54
Benin	37	59	69	18	32	26	16	24	19	28	45	68	8	24	8
Botswana	13	1	64	0	0	32	1	1	102	13	1	64	0	0	0
Burkina Faso	67	160	153	35	135	87	17	63	39	52	140	81	25	124	43
Burundi	6	18	21	2	8	11	2	7	9	4	5	11	0	1	2
Cameroon	115	141	72	31	23	29	13	9	11	92	141	72	6	22	21
Cape Verde	26	37	45	7	4	9	105	57	122	21	33	37	2	2	1
C. A. R.	28	13	17	7	2	10	11	3	15	21	10	14	2	1	9
Chad	30	27	19	11	14	11	8	9	7	22	20	14	6	9	9
Comoros	7	11	28	3	1	10	27	11	83	6	11	27	0	0	0
Congo	16	52	30	7	17	7	13	25	11	16	43	22	0	10	3
Côte d'Ivoire	126	39	37	45	5	10	17	2	3	110	39	37	22	5	10
D. R. Congo	14	123	40	6	80	16	1	9	2	14	79	36	3	50	12
Equatorial Guinea	9	7	8	4	4	5	71	60	73	9	7	8	3	3	3
Eritrea	33	2	95	27	1	80	53	2	137	33	2	95	25	1	66
Ethiopia	52	222	61	25	106	33	2	13	4	51	118	43	18	49	18
Gabon	50	42	24	15	8	3	81	39	16	50	42	24	10	8	3
Gambia	11	10	1	9	10	1	48	46	3	10	10	1	8	10	1
Ghana	119	194	103	86	80	61	28	24	18	88	144	71	70	44	30
Guinea	41	20	45	19	9	24	15	7	16	41	20	45	16	9	14
Guinea-Bissau	13	5	17	5	1	7	26	5	28	8	5	16	2	1	1
Kenya	63	110	64	39	56	49	6	11	9	33	78	64	22	15	45
Lesotho	16	22	3	2	20	1	5	60	4	16	20	2	1	17	0
Liberia	2	4	3	1	4	3	3	6	5	2	4	3	1	3	3
Madagascar	73	102	144	26	49	81	12	20	31	41	68	130	1	23	45
Malawi	136	39	94	94	23	49	48	10	21	104	25	61	67	12	22
Mali	84	119	74	44	96	37	24	44	16	72	111	52	20	91	13
Mauritius	24	16	17	3	0	2	25	0	15	24	16	17	0	0	2
Mozambique	151	135	262	81	77	180	32	21	47	109	62	205	32	38	111
Namibia	25	8	5	17	5	4	48	11	9	25	8	5	14	4	3
Niger	31	79	80	13	72	49	7	33	21	18	75	48	3	68	30
Nigeria	70	70	13	40	56	8	2	3	0	69	70	13	23	56	8
Rwanda	76	27	42	36	11	17	29	8	12	39	14	27	5	2	3
Sao Tome and Principe	5	10	4	1	2	1	…	94	23	5	10	4	0	1	0
Senegal	138	142	242	75	59	29	48	32	16	129	120	242	41	46	23
Seychelles	1	0	1	1	0	0	…	…	…	1	0	1	0	0	0
Sierra Leone	23	20	26	11	12	15	16	16	18	2	9	9	0	7	3

Education for All Global Monitoring Report 2008

Direct aid to secondary education			Direct aid to post-secondary education			Aid to education, level unspecified			Share of education in total ODA			Share of education in total sector-allocable ODA			Share of basic education in total aid to education		
Constant 2005 US$ millions			Constant 2005 US$ millions			Constant 2005 US$ millions			(%)			(%)			(%)		
1999–2000 annual average	2004	2005	1999–2000 annual average	2004	2005	1999–2000 annual average	2004	2005	1999–2000 annual average	2004	2005	1999–2000 annual average	2004	2005	1999–2000 annual average	2004	2005
0	0	0	2	1	0	0	54	0	4	16	0	4	16	0	6	49	50
0	0	0	2	1	0	0	54	0	…	…	…	…	…	…	…	…	…
0	0	0	1	0	0	0	0	0	39	…	…	40	…	…	7	…	…
110	263	247	170	177	144	190	152	304	12	21	8	15	24	10	53	78	49
0	0	0	0	0	0	0	0	0	…	…	…	…	…	…	…	…	…
0	11	5	5	14	42	1	19	15	4	7	7	14	8	8	22	80	73
38	182	171	8	25	12	9	9	48	6	35	15	8	43	16	61	75	33
2	0	4	1	1	2	2	1	1	8	6	9	8	6	9	21	56	13
12	6	6	63	55	55	160	4	4	20	26	2	22	26	3	64	91	23
0	5	1	69	52	17	8	0	1	51	28	30	61	68	41	5	1	4
10	14	6	4	0	0	0	1	1	47	56	10	47	57	48	3	8	15
4	1	0	5	7	6	1	3	3	12	28	4	12	30	4	83	95	56
1	4	0	12	16	5	9	110	163	3	18	10	7	19	18	35	55	67
43	40	52	2	8	6	1	4	69	8	5	8	9	7	17	9	10	31
215	398	236	396	591	523	523	257	622	12	10	8	15	15	14	50	50	54
4	1	2	10	2	29	10	15	17	…	…	…	…	…	…	…	…	…
1	1	0	7	8	7	10	4	5	6	1	15	11	9	26	38	29	86
5	0	6	5	19	20	10	2	34	9	10	13	10	12	15	47	54	37
2	0	0	11	0	0	0	0	63	30	2	54	35	2	57	3	47	50
9	5	2	12	9	20	6	2	16	11	26	16	13	29	18	53	84	57
0	0	0	2	3	2	2	0	6	3	3	7	6	5	14	32	45	50
4	28	1	54	89	34	29	2	16	18	15	15	24	35	38	27	16	40
3	5	1	11	25	26	5	1	10	18	31	13	20	39	14	26	12	21
9	4	0	7	6	6	2	0	0	19	16	16	22	18	19	24	16	59
2	2	0	13	5	5	2	4	0	8	9	4	9	15	6	36	52	60
1	1	0	0	7	7	5	2	20	23	25	43	29	28	51	45	12	37
0	9	0	2	20	19	13	4	0	12	25	2	39	26	21	44	32	24
22	3	0	36	30	27	31	1	0	19	12	14	32	32	33	36	14	27
1	1	8	4	11	12	7	17	5	8	6	2	13	12	5	46	65	40
2	1	0	1	1	1	3	2	4	29	14	20	33	35	35	47	56	58
3	0	0	2	0	0	3	0	28	13	1	29	23	2	66	80	63	85
4	7	2	17	50	11	12	12	12	6	10	3	13	13	6	47	48	54
17	12	0	13	21	20	9	0	0	45	25	32	60	34	50	30	20	15
0	0	0	0	0	0	1	0	0	18	20	1	19	22	1	84	96	61
10	39	4	7	39	7	1	22	31	12	8	7	14	16	13	72	41	59
8	0	0	11	11	10	6	0	21	15	7	22	17	13	33	46	46	54
1	1	1	4	3	4	1	0	11	14	8	21	18	10	38	37	24	41
2	4	5	5	9	7	4	50	8	6	7	6	8	9	7	61	51	76
13	0	0	1	0	0	1	2	2	17	25	3	18	27	3	12	89	56
0	0	0	0	0	0	1	1	0	4	1	1	8	4	3	67	89	81
8	1	0	15	25	26	17	19	60	12	8	11	15	17	19	35	48	56
15	5	6	1	0	12	20	8	21	20	9	10	23	11	11	69	59	52
10	6	0	7	12	12	34	2	27	14	16	8	16	20	9	52	81	50
0	0	0	18	16	15	6	0	0	51	41	35	51	74	37	13	0	11
7	6	4	13	11	9	56	6	81	9	11	18	13	12	20	54	57	69
3	2	1	3	1	1	5	1	1	20	3	5	21	3	5	67	62	68
5	0	7	3	4	5	6	3	6	11	17	12	13	33	16	42	90	61
3	5	1	10	9	4	33	1	1	12	5	0	12	5	1	57	80	61
4	1	1	4	6	10	27	5	14	15	6	7	19	7	10	48	42	40
1	3	0	2	3	3	1	3	0	12	22	22	13	24	27	21	21	12
9	11	149	21	58	59	59	5	11	16	12	25	21	23	35	54	42	12
0	0	0	0	0	0	1	0	0	18	4	5	18	6	5	47	23	36
0	1	0	1	1	0	0	0	5	8	5	7	11	6	8	49	62	55

Education for All Global Monitoring Report 2008

Table 4 (continued)

	Total aid to education (Constant 2005 US$ millions)			Total aid to basic education (Constant 2005 US$ millions)			Total aid to basic education per primary school-age child (Constant 2005 US$)			Direct aid to education (Constant 2005 US$ millions)			Direct aid to basic education (Constant 2005 US$ millions)		
	1999–2000 annual average	2004	2005	1999–2000 annual average	2004	2005	1999–2000 annual average	2004	2005	1999–2000 annual average	2004	2005	1999–2000 annual average	2004	2005
Somalia	5	19	6	2	12	5	1	8	3	5	19	6	0	5	4
South Africa	83	80	149	39	10	104	6	1	14	83	80	149	34	5	83
Swaziland	1	1	25	0	0	25	1	2	126	1	1	25	0	0	25
Togo	13	14	17	5	0	6	7	1	6	12	14	17	2	0	6
Uganda	147	147	178	89	83	107	18	14	18	99	48	148	47	32	84
U. R. Tanzania	80	372	95	41	137	36	6	20	5	31	299	41	15	99	6
Zambia	134	104	194	90	74	157	44	33	68	72	96	158	53	54	130
Zimbabwe	23	6	5	8	2	1	3	1	1	23	6	5	1	2	1
unallocated by countries	*435*	*574*	*794*	*94*	*144*	*394*	…	…	…	*428*	*574*	*782*	*44*	*111*	*312*
Total	6 914	10 712	8 328	2 756	5 074	3 672	5	9	6	6 076	9 662	7 612	1 541	4 020	2 466

Total upper middle income countries	659	546	542	170	98	191	4	2	4	651	539	540	128	32	121
Total low middle income countries	2 152	3 097	2 461	650	771	731	3	4	3	1 947	2 995	2 320	289	568	460
Total high income countries	38	0	0	4	0	0	1	0	0	38	0	0	0	0	0
Unallocated by income	602	723	1 022	161	213	446	…	…	…	590	721	1 004	84	165	334
Total least developed countries	2 041	3 935	3 115	1 054	2 477	1 658	10	23	15	1 590	3 307	2 652	599	2 046	1 116
Total low income countries	3 464	6 346	4 303	1 770	3 992	2 303	6	13	8	2 850	5 406	3 748	1 039	3 255	1 552
Total middle income countries	2 810	3 643	3 003	820	869	923	3	3	3	2 598	3 535	2 859	417	600	580
Total	6 914	10 712	8 328	2 756	5 074	3 672	5	9	6	6 076	9 662	7 612	1 541	4 020	2 466

Arab States	1 057	1 383	1 283	309	496	457	8	13	11	1 032	1 372	1 194	141	454	341
Central and Eastern Europe	396	382	295	126	80	27	10	7	2	360	345	291	84	24	11
Central Asia	104	211	118	26	70	58	4	11	10	84	193	103	9	43	43
East Asia and the Pacific	1 252	1 728	1 265	361	324	431	2	2	3	1 059	1 656	1 207	128	193	275
Latin America and the Caribbean	576	729	660	259	341	263	5	6	4	548	669	637	175	232	164
North America and Western Europe	3	55	1	0	27	0	5	…	…	3	55	0	0	0	0
South and West Asia	812	2 750	1 101	431	2 141	537	3	13	3	798	2 564	1 060	328	1 972	365
Sub-Saharan Africa	2 279	2 900	2 810	1 149	1 451	1 504	11	13	13	1 765	2 235	2 337	631	990	956
Unallocated by region	*435*	*574*	*794*	*94*	*144*	*394*	…	…	…	*428*	*574*	*782*	*44*	*111*	*312*
Total	6 914	10 712	8 328	2 756	5 074	3 672	5	9	6	6 076	9 662	7 612	1 541	4 020	2 466

Notes:
(···) indicates that data are not available.
Data for sector-allocable aid include general budget support.
All data represent commitments unless otherwise specified.
Sources: CRS online database (OECD-DAC, 2007c); DAC online database, Table 1 (OECD-DAC, 2007c); annex, Statistical Tables 1 and 5.

| Direct aid to secondary education | | | Direct aid to post-secondary education | | | Aid to education, level unspecified | | | Share of education in total ODA | | | Share of education in total sector-allocable ODA | | | Share of basic education in total aid to education | | |
| Constant 2005 US$ millions | | | Constant 2005 US$ millions | | | Constant 2005 US$ millions | | | (%) | | | (%) | | | (%) | | |
1999–2000 annual average	2004	2005	1999–2000 annual average	2004	2005	1999–2000 annual average	2004	2005	1999–2000 annual average	2004	2005	1999–2000 annual average	2004	2005	1999–2000 annual average	2004	2005
0	0	0	0	0	0	4	13	2	4	10	4	11	33	12	51	63	76
11	23	17	28	41	8	11	10	40	16	13	15	17	13	16	47	13	70
1	0	0	0	0	0	0	0	0	5	3	47	7	4	49	7	90	99
0	0	0	3	13	11	6	0	0	12	22	24	16	29	32	41	3	33
2	10	6	15	3	42	34	2	17	13	10	13	15	12	17	60	56	60
6	192	6	7	5	22	3	3	7	6	18	5	8	22	6	51	37	38
4	4	5	3	5	5	13	33	19	12	10	10	16	16	21	67	71	81
3	0	0	5	3	3	13	1	1	10	4	3	11	6	4	35	38	26
27	*9*	*21*	*265*	*388*	*297*	*93*	*66*	*151*	…	…	…	…	…	…	…	…	…
887	**1 054**	**826**	**2 056**	**3 531**	**2 624**	**1 592**	**1 058**	**1 695**	**10**	**11**	**7**	**13**	**14**	**11**	**40**	**47**	**44**

Direct aid to secondary education			Direct aid to post-secondary education			Aid to education, level unspecified			Share of education in total ODA			Share of education in total sector-allocable ODA			Share of basic education in total aid to education		
94	64	40	352	317	241	77	126	139	17	19	10	19	21	11	26	18	35
373	230	230	767	1 894	1 228	518	303	402	8	10	6	10	11	11	30	25	30
0	0	0	29	0	0	8	0	0	28	24	9	30	71	9	11	0	0
36	23	30	327	439	434	142	94	206	…	…	…	…	…	…	…	…	…
222	543	439	310	485	477	459	232	620	11	13	9	14	19	13	52	63	53
382	737	527	581	880	722	848	534	948	11	13	8	14	18	12	51	63	54
468	294	269	1 119	2 211	1 469	594	429	541	10	11	6	12	12	11	29	24	31
887	**1 054**	**826**	**2 056**	**3 531**	**2 624**	**1 592**	**1 058**	**1 695**	**10**	**11**	**7**	**13**	**14**	**11**	**40**	**47**	**44**

Direct aid to secondary education			Direct aid to post-secondary education			Aid to education, level unspecified			Share of education in total ODA			Share of education in total sector-allocable ODA			Share of basic education in total aid to education		
201	121	108	378	726	602	311	71	143	16	8	5	20	10	11	29	36	36
47	47	27	181	199	226	48	75	27	7	10	5	11	11	6	32	21	9
23	21	7	38	94	37	14	35	16	5	12	5	7	13	6	25	33	49
207	139	101	450	1 134	576	273	190	256	9	15	9	10	16	11	29	19	34
56	57	79	176	222	219	140	158	176	6	8	8	8	11	11	45	47	40
0	0	0	2	1	0	0	54	0	4	16	0	4	16	0	6	49	50
110	263	247	170	177	144	190	152	304	12	21	8	15	24	10	53	78	49
215	398	236	396	591	523	523	257	622	12	10	8	15	15	14	50	50	54
27	*9*	*21*	*265*	*388*	*297*	*93*	*66*	*151*	…	…	…	…	…	…	…	…	…
887	**1 054**	**826**	**2 056**	**3 531**	**2 624**	**1 592**	**1 058**	**1 695**	**10**	**11**	**7**	**13**	**14**	**11**	**40**	**47**	**44**

Public enrolment. Number of students enrolled in institutions that are controlled and managed by public authorities or agencies (national/federal, state/provincial or local), whatever the origins of their financial resources.

Public expenditure on education. Total current and capital expenditure on education by local, regional and national governments, including municipalities (household contributions are excluded). It covers public expenditure for both public and private institutions. Current expenditure includes expenditure for goods and services that are consumed within a given year and have to be renewed the following year, such as staff salaries and benefits; contracted or purchased services; other resources, including books and teaching materials; welfare services; and items such as furniture and equipment, minor repairs, fuel, telecommunications, travel, insurance and rent. Capital expenditure includes expenditure for construction, renovation and major repairs of buildings, and the purchase of heavy equipment or vehicles.

Pupil. A child enrolled in pre-primary or primary education. Youth and adults enrolled at more advanced levels are often referred to as students.

Pupil/teacher ratio (PTR). Average number of pupils per teacher at a specific level of education, based on headcounts for both pupils and teachers.

Pupil/trained-teacher ratio. Average number of pupils per **trained teacher** at a specific level of education, based on headcounts for both pupils and trained teachers.

Purchasing power parity (PPP). An exchange rate that accounts for price differences among countries, allowing international comparisons of real output and incomes.

Quintile. In statistics, one of five equal groups into which a population can be divided according to the distribution of values of a variable.

Repetition rate by grade. Number of **repeaters** in a given grade in a given school year, expressed as a percentage of enrolment in that grade the previous school year.

Repeaters. Number of pupils enrolled in the same grade or level as the previous year, expressed as a percentage of the total enrolment in that grade or level.

School life expectancy (SLE). Number of years a child of school entrance age is expected to spend at school or university, including years spent on repetition. It is the sum of the age-specific enrolment ratios for primary, secondary, post-secondary non-tertiary and tertiary education.

School-age population. Population of the age group officially corresponding to a given level of education, whether enrolled in school or not.

Secondary education (ISCED levels 2 and 3). Programme comprising lower secondary and upper secondary education. Lower secondary education (ISCED 2) is generally designed to continue the basic programmes of the primary level but the teaching is typically more subject-focused, requiring more specialized teachers for each subject area. The end of this level often coincides with the end of compulsory education. In upper secondary education (ISCED 3), the final stage of secondary education in most countries, instruction is often organized even more along subject lines and teachers typically need a higher or more subject-specific qualification than at ISCED level 2.

Sector-wide programme. A programme in which all significant funding for the sector supports a single sector policy and expenditure programme, under the leadership of the government, adopting common approaches across the sector and progressing towards relying on government procedures to disburse and account for all funds.

Stunting. Proportion of under-5s falling below minus 2 and minus 3 standard deviations from the median height-for-age of the reference population. Low height for age is a basic indicator of malnutrition.

Survival rate by grade. Percentage of a cohort of students who are enrolled in the first grade of an education cycle in a given school year and are expected to reach a specified grade, regardless of repetition.

Teacher compensation. A teacher's base salary plus all bonuses. Base salary refers to the minimum scheduled gross annual salary for a full-time teacher who has the minimum training necessary to be qualified at the beginning of his or her teaching career. Reported base salaries are defined as the total sum of money paid by the employer for the labour supplied minus the employer's contribution to social security and pension funding. Bonuses that are a regular part of the annual salary (e.g a thirteenth month of pay or a holiday bonus) are generally included in the base salary.

Teachers/teaching staff. Number of persons employed full time or part time in an official capacity to guide and direct the learning experience of pupils and students, irrespective of their qualifications or the delivery mechanism, i.e. face-to-face and/or at a distance. Excludes educational personnel who have no active teaching duties (e.g. headmasters, headmistresses or principals who do not teach) and persons who work occasionally or in a voluntary capacity.

Technical and vocational education and training (TVET). Programmes designed mainly to prepare students for direct entry into a particular occupation or trade, or class of occupations or trades. Successful completion of such programmes normally leads to a labour-market-relevant vocational qualification recognized by the relevant authorities (ministry of education, employers' associations) in the country in which it is obtained.

Tertiary or higher education (ISCED levels 5 and 6). Programmes with an educational content more advanced than what is offered at ISCED levels 3 and 4. The first stage of tertiary education, ISCED level 5, includes level 5A, composed of largely theoretically based programmes intended to provide sufficient qualifications for gaining entry to advanced research programmes and professions with high skill requirements; and level 5B, where programmes are generally more practical, technical and/or occupationally specific. The second stage of tertiary education, ISCED level 6, comprises programmes devoted to advanced study and original research, leading to the award of an advanced research qualification.

Total debt service. Sum of principal repayments and interest paid in foreign currency, goods or services on long-term debt, or interest paid on short-term debt, as well as repayments (repurchases and charges) to the International Monetary Fund.

Total fertility rate. Average number of children that would be born to a woman if she were to live to the end of her childbearing years (15 to 49) and bear children at each age in accordance with prevailing age-specific fertility rates.

Total primary net enrolment ratio (TNER). Enrolment of children of the official primary school age group in either primary or secondary school, expressed as a percentage of the population in that age group.

Trained teacher. Teacher who has received the minimum organized teacher training normally required for teaching at the relevant level in a given country.

Transition rate to secondary education. New entrants to the first grade of secondary education in a given year, expressed as a percentage of the number of pupils enrolled in the final grade of primary education the previous year.

Undernutrition/malnutrition. The condition of people whose dietary energy intake is below that needed for maintaining a healthy life and carrying out light physical activity. Malnutrition refers to food deficiencies in terms of either quantity or quality (lack of specific nutrients or vitamins).

Upper-secondary education (ISCED level 3). See **secondary education**.

Variance. A measure of dispersion of a given distribution.

Youth literacy rate. Number of literate persons aged 15 to 24, expressed as a percentage of the total population in that age group.

References[*]

Abadzi, H. 2006. *Efficient Learning for the Poor: Insights from the Frontier of Cognitive Neuroscience.* Washington, DC, World Bank. (Directions in Development.)

—— 2007. *Absenteeism and Beyond: Loss and Cost of Instructional Time in Schools.* Washington, DC, IEGSG. (Draft.)

Academy for Education Development and USAID Ethiopia. 2001. *Ethiopian National Learning Assessment of Grade 4 Students.* Addis Ababa, National Organization of Examinations.

—— 2004. *Ethiopian Second National Learning Assessment of Grade 4 Students.* Addis Ababa, National Organization of Examinations.

Africa Network Campaign on Education for All. 2007. *African Civil Society Involvement in Policy Dialogue and EFA Processes: A Study Conducted for the Collective Consultation of NGOs in Education (CCNGO).* Dakar, ANCEFA.

African Development Bank. 2007. *Selected Statistics on African Countries.* Tunis, ADB, Statistics Department.

Aga Khan Foundation. 2007. Non-state providers and public-private-community partnerships in education - contributions towards achieving EFA: A critical review of challenges, opportunities and issues. Background paper for *EFA Global Monitoring Report 2008.*

Ahmed, A. U. 2004. *Impact of Feeding Children in School: Evidence from Bangladesh.* Washington, DC, International Food Policy Research Institute.

—— 2005. *Comparing Food and Cash Incentives for Schooling in Bangladesh.* Washington, DC, International Food Policy Research Institute. (Linking Research and Action: Strengthening Food Assistance and Food Policy Research.)

—— 2006. *Conditional Cash and Food Transfer Programs for Education in Bangladesh.* Third International Conference on Conditional Cash Transfers, Istanbul, Turkey, World Bank, 26–30 June.

Ahmed, A. U. and Arends-Kuenning, M. 2006. Do crowded classrooms crowd out learning? Evidence from the food for education program in Bangladesh. *World Development,* Vol. 34, No. 4, pp. 665–84.

Ahmed, F. B. 2006. Male bias in school texts. *The Tribune Online Edition* No. 26 February. http://www.tribuneindia.com/2006/20060226/society.htm#2 (Accessed 26 July 2007.)

Ahmed, S. S. 2005. *Delivery Mechanisms of Cash Transfer Programs to the Poor in Bangladesh.* Washington, DC, World Bank, Human Development Network, Social Protection Unit. (Social Protection Discussion Paper Series, 0520.)

Aitchison, J. 2007. South Africa non-formal education country profile. Background paper for *EFA Global Monitoring Report 2008.*

Al-Samarrai, S. and Zaman, H. 2006. *Abolishing School Fees in Malawi: The Impact on Education Access and Equity.* Munich, Germany, Munich Personal RePEc Archive. (MPRA Paper, 130.)

Albania Ministry of Education and Science. 2005. *Education for All/Fast Track Initiative (EFA/FTI) Proposal.* Washington, DC/Tirana, World Bank/Albania Ministry of Education and Science, Policy Analysis and Planning Department.

Alcázar, L., Rogers, F. H., Chaudhury, N., Hammer, J., Kremer, M. and Muralidharan, K. 2006. *Why Are Teachers Absent? Probing Service Delivery in Peruvian Primary Schools.* Washington, DC, World Bank.

Allard, A. 2004. Speaking of gender: teachers' metaphorical constructs of male and female students. *Gender and Education,* Vol. 16, No. 3, pp. 347–63.

American Association of University Women. 1992. *How Schools Shortchange Girls. The AAUW: A Study of Major Findings on Girls and Education.* Washington, DC, AAUW.

Anderson-Levitt, K., Bloch, M. and Soumaré, A. 1998. Inside classrooms in Guinea: girls' experiences. Bloch, M., Beoku-Betts, J. and Tabachnick, R. (eds), *Women and Education in Sub-Saharan Africa.* Boulder, Col., Lynne Rienner, pp. 99–130.

Angrist, J. and Lavy, V. 2002. New evidence on classroom computers and pupil learning. *The Economic Journal,* Vol. 112, No. 482, pp. 735–65.

Anis, K. 2007. Ethiopia non-formal education country profile. Background paper for *EFA Global Monitoring Report 2008.*

Arab Network for Literacy and Adult Education. 2007. *Summary Regional Report: A Study Conducted for the Collective Consultation of NGOs in Education (CCNGO).* Giza, Egypt, ANLAE.

Aradhya, N. and Kashyap, A. 2006. *The 'Fundamentals': Right to Education in India.* Bangalore, India, Books for Change. (Education.)

Araujo, M. C. and Schady, N. 2006. *Cash Transfers, Conditions, School Enrollment, and Child Work: Evidence from a Randomized Experiment in Ecuador.* Washington, DC, World Bank. (Policy Research Working Paper, 3930.)

Archer, D. 2007. Civil society education coalitions. Background paper for *EFA Global Monitoring Report 2008.*

Armecin, G., Behrman, J. R., Duazo, P., Ghuman, S., Gualtiano, S., King, E. M. and Lee, N. 2006. *Early Childhood Development through an Integrated Program: Evidence from the Philippines.* Washington, DC, World Bank. (Policy Research Working Paper Series, 3922.)

Ashcraft, C. 2006. 'Girl, you better go get you a condom': popular culture and teen sexuality as resources for critical multicultural curriculum. *Teachers College Record,* Vol. 108, No. 1, pp. 2145–86.

* All background papers for *EFA Global Monitoring Report 2008* are available at www.efareport.unesco.org

Asia South Pacific Bureau of Adult Education. 2007. *Collective Consultation of NGOs Survey on Civil Society Engagement on Education Policy Dialogue Since Dakar 2000: Report of Survey Findings.* Maharashtra, India, ASPBAE.

Asian Development Bank. 2006. *2006 Annual Evaluation Review.* Mandaluyong City, Philippines, Asian Development Bank, Operations Evaluation Department. (RPE: OTH 2006-11.)

— 2007. *Key Indicators 2007: Inequality in Asia.* Manila, Asian Development Bank.

Attanasio, O., Battistin, E., Fitzsimons, E., Meghir, C., Mesnard, A. and Vera-Hernandez, M. 2004. *Evaluación del Impacto del Programa Familias en Acción - Subsidos Condicionados de la Red de Apoyo Social: Informe del Primer Seguimiento.* London, Institute for Fiscal Studies.

Attanasio, O., Fitzsimons, E., Gomez, A., Lopez, D., Meghir, C. and Mesnard, A. 2006. *Child Education and Work Choices in the Presence of a Conditional Cash Transfer Programme in Rural Colombia.* London, Institute for Fiscal Studies. (Working Paper, 06/13.)

Aydagül, B. 2007. Turkey case study. Background paper for *EFA Global Monitoring Report 2008.*

Balagun, P. 2005. *Evaluating Progress towards Harmonisation.* London, UK Department for International Development. (Working Paper, 15.)

Balázsi, I. 2007. Results of the national assessment of basic competencies in Hungary. Background paper for *EFA Global Monitoring Report 2008.*

Bankov, K., Mikova, D. and Smith, T. M. 2006. Assessing between-school variation in educational resources and mathematics and science achievement in Bulgaria. *Prospects: Quarterly Review of Comparative Education,* Vol. 36, No. 4, pp. 447–73.

Bano, M. 2007. Progress since Dakar: Pakistan country review. Background paper for *EFA Global Monitoring Report 2008.*

Barrera-Osorio, F. 2007. *The Impact of Private Provision of Public Education: Empirical Evidence from Bogotá's Concession Schools.* Washington, DC, World Bank. (4121.)

Barrera-Osorio, F., Linden, L. L. and Urquiola, M. 2007. *The Effects of User Fee Reductions on Enrollment: Evidence from a Quasi-Experiment.* Paper presented at the Quality of Education in Latin America and the Caribbean, Mexico City, 2–3 February.

Barrett, A. M., Ali, S., Clegg, J., Hinostroza, J. E., Lowe, J., Nikel, J., Novelli, M., Oduro, G., Pillay, M., Tikly, L. and Yu, G. 2007. Initiatives to improve the quality of teaching and learning: what really matters? Background paper for *EFA Global Monitoring Report 2008.*

Batbaatar, M., Bold, T., Marshall, J., Oyuntsetseg, D., Tamir, C. and Tumennast, G. 2005. *Children on the Move: Rural-Urban Migration and Access to Education in Mongolia.* London, Childhood Poverty Research and Policy Centre. (CHIP Report, 17.)

Baucal, A., Pavlovic-Babic, D. and Willms, J. D. 2006. Differential selection into secondary schools in Serbia. *Prospects: Quarterly Review of Comparative Education,* Vol. 36, No. 4, pp. 539–46.

Baudino, C. 2007. Review of recent literature on gender inequalities in teaching methods and peer relationship management in the French-speaking area. Background paper for *EFA Global Monitoring Report* 2008.

Beckmann, S. and Rai, P. 2004. *HIV/AIDS, Work and Development in the United Republic of Tanzania.* Geneva, International Labour Office. (Country profile produced within the ILO-GTZ partnership.)

Behrman, J. R., Parker, S. W. and Todd, P. E. 2007. *Do School Subsidy Programs Generate Lasting Benefits? A Five-Year Follow-Up of Oportunidades Participants.* Mexico City/Philadelphia, Penn., Instituto Nacional de Salud Publica/Andrew W. Mellon Foundation/University of Pennsylvania Population Studies Center.

Bella, N. and Mputu, H. 2004. Dropout in primary and secondary: a global issue and an obstacle to the achievement of the Education for All goals. *The International Journal on School Disaffection,* Vol. 2, No. 2, pp. 14–30.

Benavot, A. 2004. A global study of intended instructional time and official school curricula, 1980–2000. Background paper for *EFA Global Monitoring Report 2005.*

— 2006. *The Diversification of Secondary Education: School Curricula in Comparative Perspective.* Geneva, Switzerland, UNESCO International Bureau of Education. (Working Paper on Curriculum Issues, 6.)

— 2007. Adhoc consultation on the literate environment: selected highlights. Background paper for *EFA Global Monitoring Report 2008.*

Benavot, A. and Gad, L. 2004. Actual instructional time in African primary schools: factors that reduce school quality in developing countries. *Prospects: Quarterly Review of Comparative Education,* Vol. 34, No. 3, pp. 291–310.

Benavot, A. and Tanner, E. 2007. Mapping national learning assessments in the world, 1995–2006. Background paper for *EFA Global Monitoring Report 2008.*

Benbenishty, R. and Astor, R. 2005. *School Violence in Context. Culture, Neighborhoods, Family, School and Gender.* New York, Oxford University Press.

Bender, P., Diarra, A., Edoh, K. and Ziegler, M. 2007. *Evaluation of the World Bank Assistance to Primary Education in Mali. A Country Case Study.* Washington, DC, World Bank, Independent Evaluation Group.

Benemérita Universidad Autónoma de Puebla. 2006. *CONAFE: Evaluación 2006 Programas Compensatorios (PAREIB).* Puebla, Mexico, Benemérita Universidad Autónoma de Puebla.

Benin Ministry of Primary and Secondary Education. 2004. *Document de Contribution. La Gestion des Enseignants non-Fonctionnaires* [Contribution Document. Management of Contract Teachers]. Paper presented at the Conférence sur les Enseignantes non-Fonctionnaires, Bamako, Ministry of Primary and Secondary Education, 21–23 November. (In French.)

Bentaouet-Kattan, R. 2005. Primary school fees: an update. Background paper for *EFA Global Monitoring Report 2006*.

— 2006. *Implementation of Free Basic Education Policy*. Washington, DC, World Bank. (Education Working Paper Series, 7.)

Benveniste, L. 2002. The political structuration of assessment: negotiating state power and legitimacy. *Comparative Education Review*, Vol. 46, No. 1, pp. 89–118.

Berlinski, S. and Galiani, S. 2005. *The Effect of a Large Expansion of pre-Primary School Facilities on Preschool Attendance and Maternal Employment*. London, Institute for Fiscal Studies. (Working Paper, 04/30.)

Besley, T. and Cord, L. J. (eds). 2007. *Delivering on the Promise of Pro-Poor Growth: Insights and Lessons from Country Experiences*. Washington, DC, Palgrave Macmillan and World Bank.

Betcherman, G., Fares, J., Luinstra, A. and Prouty, R. 2004. *Child Labor, Education, and Children's Rights*. Washington, DC, World Bank, Human Development Network, Social Protection Unit. (Social Protection Discussion Paper Series, 0412.)

Bines, H. 2007. Education for all in Ethiopia: policy and progress, 2000–2006. Country case study. Background paper for *EFA Global Monitoring Report 2008*.

Bloom, D. E., Canning, D. and Sevilla, J. 2003. *The Demographic Dividend: A New Perspective on the Economic Consequences of Population Change*. Santa Monica, Calif., RAND. (Monograph Report.)

Blumberg, R. L. 2007. Gender bias in textbooks: a hidden obstacle on the road to equality in education. Background paper for *EFA Global Monitoring Report 2008*.

Boissiere, M. 2004. *Determinants of Primary Education Outcomes in Developing Countries: Background Paper for the Evaluation of the World Bank's Support to Primary Education*. Washington, DC, World Bank.

Boler, T. and Jellema, A. 2005. *Deadly Inertia: A Cross-country Study of Educational Responses to HIV/AIDS*. Brussels, Global Campaign for Education.

Bonnet, G. 2007. What do recent evaluations tell us about the state of teachers in sub-Saharan countries? Background paper for *EFA Global Monitoring Report 2008*.

Boone, P. 1996. Politics and the effectiveness of foreign aid. *European Economic Review*, Vol. 40, pp. 289–329.

Bosch, A., Rhodes, R. and Kariuki, S. 2002. Interactive radio instruction: an update from the field. Haddad, W. D. and Draxler, A. (eds), *Technologies for Education: Potentials, Parameters, and Prospects*. Paris/Washington, DC, UNESCO/Academy for Educational Development.

Bourdon, J., Frölich, M. and Michaelowa, K. 2007. *Teacher Shortages, Teacher Contracts and Their Impact on Education in Africa*. St Gallen, Switzerland, Universität St Gallen, Department of Economics. (2007-20.)

Boyle, S., Brock, A., Mace, J. and Sibbons, M. 2002. *Reaching the Poor. The 'Costs' of Sending Children to School: A Six Country Comparative Study*. London, UK Department for International Development. (Education Research Report, 47.)

Bracho, T. 2007. Mexico country case study. Background paper for *EFA Global Monitoring Report 2008*.

Bratton, M., Alderfer, P., Browser, G. and Temba, J. 1999. The effects of civic education on political culture: evidence from Zambia. *World Development*, Vol. 27, No. 5, pp. 807–24.

Bray, M. 2006. Private supplementary tutoring: comparative perspectives on patterns and implications. *Compare: A Journal of Comparative Education*, Vol. 36, No. 4, pp. 515–30.

Bray, M. and Mukundan, M. V. 2003. Management and governance for EFA: is decentralisation really the answer? Background paper for *EFA Global Monitoring Report 2003/4*.

Brazil Federal Senate. 2007. *Constituição da República Federativa do Brasil. Texto Consolidado até a Emenda Constitucional nº 53 de 19 de Dezembro de 2006* [Constitution of the Federative Republic of Brazil. Consolidated text up to the Constitutional Amendment number 53 of 19 December 2006]. Brasilia, Federal Senate.

Brazil Ministry of Social Development and Fight against Hunger. 2005. *Levantamento de Beneficiários do Programa de Erradicação do Trabalho Infantil* [Analysis of Beneficiaries of the Child Labour Erradication Programme]. Brasilia, Ministry of Social Development and Fight against Hunger. (25.) (In Portuguese.)

— 2007. *Resultados na área de Educação* [Results in the Area of Education]. Brasilia, Ministry of Social Development and Fight against Hunger. http://www.mds.gov.br/bolsafamilia/condicionalidades/resultados-na-area-de-educacao (In Portuguese.)

Brenner, M. 1998. Gender and classroom interactions in Liberia. Bloch, M., Beoku-Betts, J. and Tabachnick, R. (eds), *Women and Education in Sub-Saharan Africa*. Boulder, Colo., Lynne Rienner, pp. 131–56.

Briller, V. 2007. Country case study Tajikistan. Background paper for *EFA Global Monitoring Report 2008*.

Brock-Utne, B. (ed.). 2000. *Whose Education for All? The Recolonization of the African Mind*. New York, Falmer Press.

Bruneforth, M. 2007. The distribution of out-of-school children by school exposure. Background paper for *EFA Global Monitoring Report 2008*.

Bundy, D. A. P., Shaeffer, S., Jukes, M., Beegle, K., Gillespie, A., Drake, L., Frances Lee, S.-h., Hoffman, A.-M., Jones, J., Mitchell, A., Barcelona, D., Camara, B., Golmar, C., Savioli, L., Sembene, M., Takeuchi, T. and Wright, C. 2006. School-Based Health and Nutrition Programs. Jamison, D. T., Breman, J. G., Measham, A. R., Alleyne, G., Claeson, M., Evans, D. B., Jha, P., Mills, A. and Musgrove, P. (eds), *Disease Control Priorities in Developing Countries*. New York, Oxford University Press and The World Bank, pp. 1091–108.

Buonomo Zabaleta, M. 2007. *A Dynamic Analysis of the Effects of Child Labor on Educational Attainments in Nicaragua*. Doctoral dissertation, The George Washington University, Washington, DC.

Burnside, C. and Dollar, D. 2000. Aid, Policies and Growth. *American Economic Review*, Vol. 90, pp. 847–68.

Caillaud, F. 2007. *Gender Inequality in Education and Economic Development*. Ph.D. dissertation, Université d'Aix-Marseille, France.

Caillods, F. and Hallak, J. 2004. *Education and PRSPs: A Review of Experiences*. Paris, UNESCO International Institute for Educational Planning.

Cambodia Ministry of Education, Youth and Sport. 2005. *Education Strategic Plan 2006–2010*. Phnom Penh, Ministry of Education, Youth and Sport.

Cameron, L. A., Dowling, J. M. and Worswick, C. 2001. Education and labor market participation of women in Asia: evidence from five countries. *Economic Development and Cultural Change*, Vol. 49, No. 3, pp. 460–77.

Campaña Latinoamericana por el Derecho a la Educación and Consejo de Educación de Adultos de América Latina. 2007. *Study on Civil Society Involvement in Education Policy Dialogue and the EFA Process*. São Paulo, Brazil/Panama City, CLADE/CEAAL.

Caoli-Rodriguez, R. B. 2007. Country case study: the Philippines. Background paper for *EFA Global Monitoring Report 2008*.

Cardoso, E. and Souza, A. P. 2003. *The Impact of Cash Transfers on Child Labor and School Attendance in Brazil*. São Paulo, Brazil, University of São Paulo, Department of Economics.

Cardoso, F. H. 2003. *Civil Society and Global Governance*. Paper presented at the UN Secretary-General's High Level Panel on UN-Civil Society, New York, United Nations, 2–3 June.

Carlson, S. and Gadio, C. T. 2002. Teacher professional development in the use of technology. Haddad, W. D. and Draxler, A. (eds), *Technologies for Education: Potentials, Parameters, and Prospects*. Paris/Washington, DC, UNESCO/Academy for Educational Development.

Carr-Hill, R. and Peart, E. 2005. *The Education of Nomadic Peoples in East Africa: Djibouti, Eritrea, Ethiopia, Kenya, Tanzania and Uganda. Review of Relevant Literature*. Tunis Belvédère, Tunisia/Paris, African Development Bank/UNESCO International Institute for Educational Planning.

Case, A., Hosegood, V. and Lund, F. 2005. The reach and impact of child support grants: evidence from KwaZulu-Natal. *Development Southern Africa*, Vol. 22, No. 4, pp. 467–82.

Cassidy, T. 2006. *Education Management Information Systems (EMIS) in Latin America and the Caribbean: Lessons and Challenges*. Washington, DC, Inter-American Development Bank, Integration and Regional Programs Department, Sustainable Development Department. (Work Document. Study prepared for the VIII Regional Policy Dialogue Meeting, Education Network.)

Castro, L. 2006. *Nicaragua: Social Protection Network*. Paper presented at the Third International Conference on Conditional Cash Transfers, Istanbul, Turkey, 26–30 June.

Center for Global Development. 2007. *Does the IMF Constrain Health Spending in Poor Countries? Evidence and an Agenda for Action*. Washington, DC, Center for Global Development. (Report of the Working Group on IMF Programs and Health Spending.)

Chabbott, C. and Ramirez, F. O. 2000. Development and education. Hallinan, M. (ed.), *Handbook of the Sociology of Education*. New York, Kluwer Academic, pp. 163–88.

Chan, M. 2007. *Health Diplomacy in the 21st Century*. Address to Directorate for Health and Social Affairs, Oslo, 13 February.

Châtaigner, J.-M. and Gaulme, F. 2005. *Agir en Faveur des Acteurs et des Sociétés Fragiles: Pour une Vision Renouvelée des Enjeux de l'Aide au Développement dans la Prévention et la Gestion de Crises* [Acting in Favour of Actors and Fragile States: For a Renewed Vision of Development Aid Stakes in Crisis Prevention and Management]. Paris, French Development Agency, Research Department. (Working Document.)(In French.)

Chaudhury, N., Hammer, J., Kremer, M., Muralidharan, K. and Rogers, F. H. 2006. Missing in action: teacher and health worker absence in developing countries. *The Journal of Economic Perspectives*, Vol. 20, No. 1, pp. 91–116.

Chaudhury, N. and Parajuli, D. 2006. *Conditional Cash Transfers and Female Schooling: The Impact of the Female School Stipend Program on Public School Enrollments in Punjab, Pakistan*. Washington, DC, World Bank. (Policy Research Working Paper, 4102.)

Chauvet, L. and Collier, P. 2007. Education in fragile states. Background paper for *EFA Global Monitoring Report 2008*.

Chen, D. H. C. 2004. *Gender Equality and Economic Development: The Role for Information and Communication Technologies*. Washington, DC, World Bank, The Knowledge for Development Program. (World Bank Policy Research Working Paper, 3285.)

Chilisa, B. 2002. National policies on pregnancy in education systems in sub-Saharan Africa: the case of Botswana. *Gender and Education*, Vol. 14, No. 1, pp. 31–5.

Chitrakar, R. 2007. Nepal non-formal education country profile. Background paper for *EFA Global Monitoring Report 2008*.

Clemens, M., Radelet, S. and Bhavnani, R. 2004. *Counting Chickens When They Hatch: The Short-Term Effect of Aid on Growth*. Washington, DC, Center for Global Development. (Working Paper, 44.)

Cohen, E. 1986. On the sociology of the classroom. Hannaway, J. and Lockheed, M. (eds), *The Contributions of the Social Sciences to Educational Policy and Practice: 1965–1985*. Berkeley, Calif., McCutchan.

Collier, P., Elliott, V. L., Hegre, H., Hoeffler, A., Reynal-Querol, M. and Sambanis, N. 2003. *Breaking the Conflict Trap: Civil War and Development Policy*. Washington, DC, World Bank and Oxford University Press. (World Bank Policy Research Report.)

Colombia Agencia Presidencial para la Acción Social y la Cooperación Internacional. 2007. *Familias en Acción* [Families in Action]. Bogota, Agencia Presidencial para la Acción Social y la Cooperación Internacional. http://www.accionsocial.gov.co/contenido/contenido.aspx?catID=204&conID=157&pagID=264 (Accessed 4 October 2007.) (In Spanish)

Committee on the Rights of the Child, UNICEF and Bernard van Leer Foundation. 2006. *A Guide to General Comment 7: 'Implementing Child Rights in Early Childhood'*. The Hague, Netherlands.

Condie, R. and Munro, B. 2007. *The Impact of ICT in Schools – A Landscape Review*. Coventry, UK, BECTA.

Consultative Group on Early Childhood Care and Development. 2003. *Advocacy*. Toronto, Ont., CGECCD. (Coordinators Notebook: An International Resource for Early Childhood Development, 27.)

Cornejo B., A., Escobar, D., Nuñez A., R., Reyes V., G. and Rojas P., K. 2003. *Evaluación de Impacto del Programa de Alimentación Escolar de JUNAEB* [Impact Evaluation of JUNAEB's School Feeding Programme]. Santiago, Gobierno de Chile, Junta Nacional de Auxilio Escolar y Becas. (In Spanish.)

Cromer, S. and Brugeilles, C. 2006. Manuels scolaires et égalité des sexes [Textbooks and sex equality]. *Administration et Éducation*, Vol. 110, p. 95. (In French.)

Crouch, L. 2004. *The Hard Slog of Implementation: South African Reforms from Early Post-apartheid to the Future*. Conference 'Governance and Accountability in Social Sector Decentralisation', Washington, DC, World Bank, 18–19 February.

Crouch, L. and Fasih, T. 2004. *Patterns of Educational Development: Implications for Further Efficiency Analysis*. Washington, DC, World Bank.

Cueto, S. and Secada, W. 2004. Oportunidades de aprendizaje y rendimiento en matemática de niños y niñas Aimara, Quechua y Castellano hablantes en escuelas bilingües y monolingües en Puno, Perú [Learning opportunities and mathematics achievement of Aymara-, Quechua- and Spanish-speaking boys and girls in bilingual and monolingual schools in Puno, Peru]. Winkler, D. R. and Cueto, S. (eds), *Etnicidad, Raza, Género y Educación en América Latina*. Santiago, Programa de Promoción de la Reforma Educativa en América Latina y el Caribe, pp. 315–53. (In Spanish.)

Dalgaard, C.-J., Hansen, H. and Tarp, F. 2004. On the empirics of foreign aid and growth. *The Economic Journal*, Vol. 114, June, pp. F191–F216.

Dang, H.-A. 2006. *The Determinants and Impact of Private Tutoring Classes in Vietnam*. St. Paul, Minn., University of Minnesota, Department of Applied Economics.

Das, J., Dercon, S., Habyarimana, J. and Krishnan, P. 2005. *Teacher Shocks and Student Learning: Evidence from Zambia*. Washington, DC, World Bank. (Policy Research Working Paper, 3602.)

Davies, P. 1999. *Student Retention in Further Education: A Problem of Quality or of Student Finance?* Paper presented at the British Educational Research Association Annual Conference, Brighton, UK, University of Sussex, 2–5 September.

Davoodi, H. R., Tiongson, E. and Asawanuchit, S. S. 2003. *How Useful are Benefit Incidence Analyses of Public Education and Health Spending*. Washington, DC, International Monetary Fund. (Working Paper, 03/227.)

De Silva, I. 2006. Demographic and social trends affecting families in the South and Central Asian region. New York, United Nations, Department of Economic and Social Affairs, Division for Social Policy and Development, Program on the Family. http://www.un.org/esa/socdev/family/Publications/mtdesilva.pdf. (Accessed 7 October 2007.)

Dee, T. 2004. Are there civic returns to education? *Journal of Public Economics*, Vol. 88, No. 9, pp. 1697–720.

Degenhart, E. R. (ed.). 1990. *Thirty Years of International Research. An Annotated Bibliography of IEA Publications (1960–1990)*. The Hague, Netherlands, International Association for the Evaluation of Educational Achievement.

Deininger, K. 2003. Does cost of schooling affect enrollment by the poor? Universal primary education in Uganda. *Economics of Education Review*, Vol. 22, No. 3, pp. 291–305.

Dembélé, M. 2005. Breaking the mold: teacher development for pedagogical renewal. Verspoor, A. M. (ed.), *The Challenge of Learning: Improving the Quality of Basic Education in sub-Saharan Africa*. Paris, Association for the Development of Education in Africa, pp. 167–94.

Desse, J. 2005. *Evaluation des Acquis Scolaires* [School achievement evaluation]. Port-au-Prince, Ministry of National Education, Youth and Sports; Support Programme for the Strengthening of Education Quality in Haiti. (In French.)

DFID. 2005. *DFID's Medium Term Action Plan on Aid Effectiveness: Our Response to the Paris Declaration*. London, UK Department for International Development, Poverty Reduction Strategies and Aid Harmonisation Team, Policy Division.

Di Gropello, E. 2006. *A Comparative Analysis of School-Based Management in Central America*. Washington, DC, World Bank. (Working Paper, 72.)

Dreher, A., Nunnenkamp, P. and Thiele, R. 2006. *Does Aid for Education Educate Children? Evidence from Panel Data*. Zürich, Switzerland, KOF - Swiss Institute for Business Cycle Research, Swiss Federal Institute of Technology (ETH Zürich). (Working Paper, 146.)

Drèze, J. and Kingdon, G. G. 2001. School participation in rural India. *Review of Development Economics*, Vol. 5, No. 1, pp. 1–24.

Drudy, S. and Chatáin, M. 2002. Gender effects in classroom interaction: data collection, self-analysis and reflection. *Evaluation and Research in Education*, Vol. 16, No. 1, pp. 35–50.

du Plessis, J. 2003. *Rainbow Charts and Coconuts: Teacher Development for Continuous Assessment in Malawi Classrooms*. Washington, DC, American Institutes for Research.

Duflo, E. and Breierova, L. 2002. *The Impact of Education on Fertility and Child Mortality: Do Fathers Really Matter less than Mothers?* Cambridge, Mass., Massachusetts Institute of Technology, Department of Economics. (Working Paper.)

Dulger, I. 2004. *Turkey: Rapid Coverage for Compulsory Education – The 1997 Basic Education Program.* Washington, DC, World Bank.

Dunne, M. and Leach, F. 2005. *Gendered School Experiences: The Impact on Retention and Achievement in Botswana and Ghana.* London, UK Department for International Development.

Dutcher, N. 1997. *The Use of First and Second Languages in Education: A Review of International Experience.* Washington, DC, World Bank.

Duthilleul, Y. 2005. *Lessons Learnt in the Use of 'Contract' Teachers.* Paris, UNESCO International Institute for Educational Planning.

Easterly, W. R. 2001. *The Elusive Quest for Growth: Economists' Adventures and Misadventures in the Tropics.* Cambridge, Mass., MIT Press.

—— 2002. *The Cartel of Good Intentions: Bureaucracy versus Markets in Foreign Aid.* Washington, DC, Center for Global Development. (Working Paper, 4.)

—— 2003. *Can Foreign Aid Buy Growth?* New York, New York University.

—— 2006. *The White Man's Burden: Why the West's Efforts to Aid the Rest Have Done So Much Ill and So Little Good.* New York, Penguin Press.

Ecuador Ministry of Social Welfare. 2007. *Bono de Desarrollo Humano* [Human Development Voucher]. Quito, Ministry of Social Welfare, Social Protection Programme. http://www.pps.gov.ec/PPS/PPS/BDH/INF/BaseLegal.aspx (Accessed 4 October 2007.) (In Spanish.)

Education International. 2006. *Education International Report to the Expert Committee on the Application of the 1966 ILO/UNESCO Recommendation on the Status of Teachers and 1997 UNESCO Recommendation on the Status of Higher Education Teaching Personnel.* Brussels, Education International.

Education Policy and Data Center. 2007*a*. Global series of enrolment projections for primary school. Background paper for *EFA Global Monitoring Report 2008.*

—— 2007*b*. Non-formal educational attainment. EPDC summary report for GMR. Background paper for *EFA Global Monitoring Report 2008.*

—— 2007*c*. Past and future school participation around the world: comparisons by school level, sub-national region and over time. Background paper for *EFA Global Monitoring Report 2008.*

Education Support Program. 2006. *Education in a Hidden Marketplace: Monitoring of Private Tutoring. Overview and Country Reports. Azerbaijan, Bosnia and Herzegovina, Croatia, Georgia, Lithuania, Mongolia, Poland, Slovakia, Ukraine.* Budapest, Open Society Institute, Education Support Program, Network of Education Policy Centers.

—— 2007. *Monitoring School Dropouts: Albania, Kazakhstan, Latvia, Mongolia, Slovakia and Tajikistan.* Budapest, Open Society Institute, Education Support Program, Network Education Policy Centers.

Eide, A. H. and Loeb, M. E. 2006. *Living Conditions among People with Activity Limitations in Zambia. A National Representative Study.* Oslo, Zambian Federation for the Disabled/University of Zambia, Institute on Economic and Social Research/Zambia Central Statistical Office/SINTEF. (Report, A262.)

Eide, A. H., Nhiwathiwa, S., Muderedzi, J. and Loeb, M. E. 2003. *Living Conditions among People with Activity Limitations in Zimbabwe. A National Representative Study.* Oslo, SINTEF Unimed.

Eilor, J., Okurut, H. E., Opolot, M. J., Mulyalya, C., Nansamba, J. F., Nakayenga, J., Zalwango, C., Omongin, O., Nantume, O. and Apolot, F. 2003. *Country Case Study: Uganda. Impact of Primary Education Reform Program (PERP) on the Quality of Basic Education in Uganda.* Paper presented at the ADEA Biennal Meeting, Grand Baie, Mauritius, 3–6 December.

Einarsson, C. and Granström, K. 2004. Gender-biased interaction in the classroom: the influence of gender and age in the relationship between teacher and pupil. *Scandinavian Journal of Educational Research,* Vol. 46, No. 2, pp. 117–27.

Ejrnæs, M. and Pörtner, C. C. 2004. Birth order and the intrahousehold allocation of time and education. *Review of Economics and Statistics,* Vol. 86, No. 4, pp. 1008–19.

Elley, W. B. 1992. *How in the World do Students Read? IEA Study of Reading Literacy.* The Hague, Netherlands, International Association for the Evaluation of Educational Achievement.

Emerson, P. M. and Souza, A. P. 2002. *Bargaining Over Sons and Daughters: Child Labor, School Attendance and Intra-household Gender Bias in Brazil.* Nashville, Tenn., Vanderbilt University, Department of Economics. (0213.)

Encinas-Martin, M. 2006. A global survey of educational evaluation: international, regional and national assessments of student learning. Background paper for *EFA Global Monitoring Report 2007.*

Espinosa, G. 2006. El currículo y la equidad de género en la primaria: estudio de tres escuelas estatales de Lima [The curriculum and gender equity in primary education: study of three state schools in Lima]. Ames, P. (ed.), *Las Brechas Invisibles: Desafíos para una Equidad de Género en la Educación.* Lima, Peruvian Studies Institute, pp. 103–47. (In Spanish.)

Ethiopia Ministry of Education. 2005. *Education Sector Development Program III (ESDP-III): 2005/2006 – 2010/2011 (1998 EFY – 2002 EFY). Program Action Plan (PAP).* Addis Ababa, Ministry of Education. (Final Draft.)

— 2006. *Ethiopia Education Sector Development Programme III: 1998 E.C. – 2002 E.C. (2005/06 G.C. – 2009/10 G.C.). Joint Review Mission: 20th October – 10th November 2006 G.C. Final Report.* Addis Ababa, Ministry of Education.

European Commission. 2005. *Eurostat: European Labor Force Survey 2005 Microdata.* Brussels, European Commission. http://epp.eurostat.ec.europa.eu/portal/page?_pageid=1913,47567825,1913_47568351&_dad=portal&_schema=PORTAL#B

— 2007. *Keeping our Promises on Education.* Brussels, European Commission. http://ec.europa.eu/development/services/events/promises-edu/index.htm (Accessed 3 October 2007.)

European Monitoring Centre on Racism and Xenophobia. 2006a. *The Annual Report on the Situation regarding Racism and Xenophobia in the Member States of the EU.* Vienna, EUMC:

— 2006b. *Roma and Travellers in Public Education: An overview of the Situation in the EU Member States.* Vienna, EUMC.

European Roma Rights Centre. 2004. *Stigmata: Segregated Schooling of Roma in Central and Eastern Europe.* Budapest, ERRC.

— 2007. *The Impact of Legislation and Policies on School Segregation of Romani Children: A Study of Anti-Discrimination Law and Government Measures to Eliminate Segregation in Education in Bulgaria, Czech Republic, Hungary, Romania and Slovakia.* Budapest, ERRC.

Farrell, G., Isaacs, S. and Trucano, M. 2007. *The NEPAD e-Schools Demonstration Project: A Work in Progress.* A Public Report. Vancouver, BC/Washington, DC, Commonwealth of Learning/infoDEV, World Bank. (ICT and Education Series.)

Farrell, G. M. 2003. An overview of developments and trends in the application of information and communication technologies in education. Farrell, G. M. and Wachholz, C. (eds), *Meta-Survey on the Use of Technologies in Education in Asia and the Pacific.* Bangkok, UNESCO-Bangkok.

Farrell, G. M. and Isaacs, S. Forthcoming. *Survey of ICT and Education in Africa: A Synthesis Report Based on 53 Country Surveys.* Washington, DC, InfoDev. (ICT and Education Series. Draft.)

Farrell, G. M. and Wachholz, C. (eds). 2003. *Meta-Survey on the Use of Technologies in Education in Asia and the Pacific 2003–2004.* Bangkok, UNESCO-Bangkok.

Fauci, A. S. 2001. Infectious diseases: considerations for the 21st century. *Clinical Infectious Diseases,* Vol. 32, No. 1, pp. 675–85.

Fennema, F. and Peterson, P. 1985. Autonomous learning behaviors: a possible explanation of gender-related differences in mathematics. Wilkinson, L. and Marrett, C. (eds), *Gender Influences in Classroom Interaction.* Orlando, Fla., Academy Press, pp. 17–35.

Ferreira, W. 2005. *Brazilian Experience: B. SC. for the Deaf.* Brasilia, Brazil Ministry of Education, Secretariat of Special Education.

Ferrer, G. 2006. *Educational Assessment Systems in Latin America: Current Practice and Future Challenges.* Washington, DC, Partnership for Educational Revitalization in the Americas.

Filmer, D. 2005. *Disability, Poverty and Schooling in Developing Countries: Results from 11 Household Surveys.* Washington, DC, World Bank, Development Research Group. (Social Protection Discussion Paper, 0539.)

Filmer, D. and Schady, N. 2006. *Getting Girls into School: Evidence from a Scholarship Program in Cambodia.* Washington, DC, World Bank. (Policy Research Working Paper, 3910.)

Fomba, C. O. 2006. *Evaluation du Niveau d'Acquisition en Français, en Mathématiques et en Sciences des Elèves des Ecoles Traditionnelles du Cycle de Base 1* [Evaluation of Achievement Level in French, Mathematics and Sciences of Students in Traditional Basic Cycle 1 Schools]. Niamey, Niger Ministry of Basic Education and Literacy/Exams and Examinations Direction/Division of Evaluation and Monitoring of Student Achievement. (In French.)

Fredriksen, B. 2005. *Building Capacity in the Education Sector in Africa: The Need to Strengthen External Agencies' Capacity to Help.* Paper presented at the seminar on Building Capacity for the Education Sector in Africa, Oslo, 13–14 October.

Freedom House. 2007. *Freedom in the World Historical Ratings, 1973–2007.* Washington, DC, Freedom House. http://www.freedomhouse.org/uploads/fiw/FIWAllScores.xls (Accessed 3 May 2007.)

FTI Secretariat. 2007. *Quality Assurance in the Education for All - Fast Track Initiative.* Washington, DC, Fast Track Initiative Secretariat.

Fuller, B. and Clarke, P. 1994. Raising school effects while ignoring culture? Local conditions and the influence of classroom tools, rules and pedagogy. *Review of Educational Research,* Vol. 64, No. 1, pp. 119–57.

Fundación Cisneros. 2006. *AME Report 2006.* Caracas, Fundación Cisneros.

Fuwa, N. 2006. *The Net Impact of the Female Secondary Stipend Program in Bangladesh.* Washington, DC, World Bank. (Working Paper Series.)

Fyfe, A. 2006. *The Use of Contract Teachers in Developing Countries: Trends and Impact.* Geneva, ILO/UNESCO. (Prepared for the Joint ILO/UNESCO Committee of Experts on the Application of the Recommendations concerning Teaching Personnel. Ninth Session, Geneva, 30 October-3 November 2006. Working Group on Employment and Careers, CEART/9/2006/WG-EC-2.)

Gajardo, M. 2007. Dominican Republic: The search for a quality Education for All. Background paper for *EFA Global Monitoring Report 2008.*

Galiani, S., Gertler, P. and Schargrodsky, E. 2005. *School Decentralization: Helping the Good Get Better, but Leaving the Rest Behind.* Washington, DC, World Bank.

Gambell, T. and Hunter, D. 2000. Surveying gender differences in Canadian school literacy. *Journal of Curriculum Studies,* Vol. 32, pp. 689–719.

Genito, D., Roces, L. and Somerset, A. 2005. *Reducing Disparities in Teacher Provision in the Philippines: Progress and Constraints.* Paper presented at the 8th UKFIET Oxford International Conference on Education and Development, Oxford, UK, University of Oxford, 13–15 September.

Georges, H. 2000. *Rapport final de Synthèse* [Final Synthesis Report]. Niamey, Niger Ministry of National Education, SEDEP/Evaluation Unit, Direction of Education Projects. (In French.)

Gertler, P., Patrinos, H. and Rubio-Codina, M. 2006. *Empowering Parents to Improve Education: Evidence from Rural Mexico.* Washington, DC, World Bank. (3935.)

Geske, A., Grinfelds, A., Dedze, I. and Zhang, Y. 2006. Family background, school quality and rural-urban disparities in student learning achievement in Latvia. *Prospects: Quarterly Review of Comparative Education,* Vol. XXXVI, No. 4, pp. 419–32.

Geva, E. and Ryan, E. B. 1993. Linguistic and cognitive correlates of academic skills in first and second languages. *Language Learning,* Vol. 43, No. 1, pp. 5–42.

Glewwe, P. and Kremer, M. 2005. Schools, teachers, and education outcomes in developing countries. Hanushek, E. and Welch, F. (eds), *Handbook of the Economics of Education,* Vol. 2. Oxford, UK, North-Holland. (Handbooks in Economics, 26.)

Glewwe, P. and Olinto, P. 2004. *Evaluating of the Impact of Conditional Cash Transfers on Schooling: An Experimental Analysis of Hondura's PRAF Program.* Minneapolis, Minn./Washington, DC, University of Minnesota/International Food Policy Research Institute, Food Consumption and Nutrition Division. (Final Report for USAID.)

Global Campaign for Education. 2005. *Deadly Intertia: A Cross-Country Study of Educational Responses to HIV/AIDS.* Brussels, Global Campaign for Education.

Gökalp, Y. 2006. *Conditional Cash Transfers in Turkey: Motivation, Design, Achievements, Challenges, and the Way Forward.* Paper presented at the Third International Conference on Conditional Cash Transfers, Istanbul, Turkey, World Bank, 26–30 June.

Goody, E. and Bennett, J. 2001. Literacy for Gonja and Birifor children in Northern Ghana. Olson, D. R. and Torrance, N. (eds), *The Making of Literate Societies.* Oxford, UK, Blackwell, pp. 178–200.

Gordon, N. and Vegas, E. 2005. Educational finance equalization, spending, teacher quality, and student outcomes: the case of Brazil's FUNDEF. Vegas, E. (ed.), *Incentives to Improve Teaching: Lessons from Latin America.* Washington, DC, World Bank, pp. 151–86.

GTZ. 2007. *Social Cash Transfers in Zambia: Setup, Lessons Learned and Challenges.* Paper presented at the Africa Regional Workshop on Cash Transfers, Mombasa, Kenya, German Technical Cooperation, 26–28 February.

Government of Yemen. 2007. *Progress of Allocations of the Yemen Consultative Group and Post-Consultative Group Pledges.* Paper presented at the 1st Post CG Follow up Meeting between the Government of Yemen and its Development Partners, Sana'a.

Govinda, R. 2007. Education for all in India: assessing progress towards Dakar goals. Background paper for *EFA Global Monitoring Report 2008.*

Grigorenko, E. L., Sternberg, R. J., Jukes, M., Alcock, K., Lambo, J., Ngorosho, D., Nokes, C. and Bundy, D. A. P. 2006. Effects of antiparasitic treatment on dynamically and statically tested cognitive skills over time. *Journal of Applied Developmental Psychology,* Vol. 27, No. 6, pp. 499–526.

Grin, F. 2005. *The Economics of Language Policy Implementation: Identifying and Measuring Costs.* Mother Tongue-Based Bilingual Education in Southern Africa: The Dynamics of Implementation, Cape Town, South Africa, Volkswagen Foundation and Project for the Study of Alternative Education in South Africa, 16–19 October.

Grindle, M. S. 2007. *Going Local: Decentralization, Democratization, and the Promise of Good Governance.* Princeton, NJ, Princeton University Press.

Group of 8. 2005. *G8 Gleneagles 2005: Africa.* Gleneagles, UK, G8.

Guarcello, L., Lyon, S. and Rosati, F. C. 2006a. *Child Labour and Education for All: An Issue Paper.* Rome, ILO/UNICEF/World Bank, Understanding Children's Work. (Working Paper Series.)

—— 2006b. *Promoting School Enrolment, Attendance and Retention among Disadvantaged Children in Yemen: The Potential of Conditional Cash Transfers.* Rome, ILO/UNICEF/World Bank, Understanding Children's Work.

Guarcello, L. and Rosati, F. C. 2007. *Does School Quality Matter for Working Children?* Rome, ILO/UNICEF/World Bank, Understanding Children's Work. (Draft.)

Guatemala Government and World Bank. 2000. *Encuesta Nacional Sobre Condiciones de Vida 2000* [National Survey on Living Standards 2000]. Guatemala City/Washington, DC, Guatemala Government/World Bank. (In Spanish.)

Guo, L. and Zhou, Z. 2002. Children, gender, and language teaching materials. *Chinese Education and Society,* Vol. 35, No. 5, pp. 34–52.

Haddad, W. D. and Draxler, A. 2002. *Technologies for Education: Potentials, Parameters, and Prospects.* Paris/Washington, DC, UNESCO/Academy for Educational Development.

Hall, G. and Patrinos, H. A. 2006. *Indigenous Peoples, Poverty and Human Development in Latin America.* London, Palgrave Macmillan.

Hampden-Thompson, G. and Johnston, J. S. 2006. *Variation in the Relationship Between Non-school Factors and Student Achievement on International Assessments.* Washington, DC, US Department of Education, Institute of Education Science, National Center for Education Statistics. (NCES 2006014.)

Hannum, E. 2002. Ethnic differences in basic education in reform-era rural China. *Demography*, Vol. 39, No. 1, pp. 95–117.

Hannum, E. and Buchmann, C. 2004. Global educational expansion and socio-economic development: an assessment of findings from the social sciences. *World Development*, Vol. 33, No. 3, pp. 1–22.

Hansen, H. and Tarp, F. 2001. Aid and growth regressions. *Journal of Development Economics*, Vol. 64, No. 2, pp. 547–70.

Hanushek, E. A. 2004. Economic analysis of school quality. Background paper for the *EFA Global Monitoring Report 2005*.

Hanushek, E. A. and Kimko, D. 2000. Schooling, labor force quality, and the growth of nations. *American Economic Review*, Vol. 90, No. 5, pp. 1184–208.

Hanushek, E. A. and Wößmann, L. 2007. *The Role of Education Quality in Economic Growth*. Washington, DC, World Bank, Human Development Network, Education Team. (Policy Research Working Paper, 4122.)

Hddigui, E. M. 2007a. Evaluation of student achievement in Marocco. Background paper for *EFA Global Monitoring Report 2008*.

—— 2007b. Morocco country case study. Background paper for *EFA Global Monitoring Report 2008*.

Hedges, J. 2002. The importance of posting and interaction with the education bureaucracy in becoming a teacher in Ghana. *International Journal of Educational Development*, Vol. 22, No. 3–4, pp. 353–66.

Henaff, N., Lange, M.-F. and Trân, T. K. T. 2007. Country study: Viet Nam. Background paper for *EFA Global Monitoring Report 2008*.

Hepp, P., Hinostroza, J. E. and Laval, E. 2004. A systematic approach to educational renewal with new technologies: empowering learning communities in Chile. Brown, A. and Davis, N. (eds), *World Yearbook of Education 2004: Digital Technology, Communities and Education*. London, Routledge Falmer, pp. 299–311.

Heugh, K. 2003. *Language Policy and Democracy in South Africa: The Prospects of Equality within Rights-Based Policy and Planning*. Stockholm, Stockholm University Centre for Research on Bilingualism.

Hexagrama Consultora. 2006. *Equidad de Género y Reformas Educativas: Argentina, Chile, Colombia, Peru* [Gender Equity and Education Reforms: Argentina, Chile, Colombia, Peru]. Santiago, Hexagrama Consultora, FLACSO-Buenos Aires and Instituto de Estudios Sociales Contemporáneos. (In Spanish.)

Heyneman, S. P. 2006. The role of textbooks in a modern system of education. Braslavsky, C. (ed.), *Textbooks and Quality Learning for All*. Geneva, UNESCO International Bureau of Education, pp. 31–92.

Heyneman, S. P. and Jamison, D. 1980. Student learning in Uganda: textbook availability and other determinants. *Comparative Education Review*, Vol. 24, No. 2, pp. 108–18.

High-Level Forum on the Health MDGs. 2005. *Fiscal Space and Sustainability from the Perspective of the Health Sector*, Paris, High-Level Forum on the Health MDGs, 14–15 November.

Hinostroza, J. E., Hepp, P., Cox, C. and Guzmán, A. 2003. National policies and practices on ICT in education: Chile (Enlaces). Plomp, T., Anderson, R. E., Law, N. and Quale, A. (eds), *Cross-National Policies and Practices on Information and Communication Technology in Education*. Greenwich, Conn., Information Age Publishing, pp. 97–113.

Hoppers, W. 2007. Meeting the learning needs of all young people and adults: an exploration of successful policies and strategies in non-formal education. Background paper for *EFA Global Monitoring Report 2008*.

Horn, D., Balázsi, I., Takács, S. and Zhang, Y. 2006. Tracking and inequality of learning outcomes in Hungarian secondary schools. *Prospects: Quarterly Review of Comparative Education*, Vol. XXXVI, No. 4, pp. 433–46.

Howe, E. R. 2006. Exemplary teacher induction: an international review. *Educational Philosophy and Theory*, Vol. 38, No. 3, pp. 287–97.

Hull, G. and Schultz, K. 2001. Literacy and learning out of school: a review of theory and research. *Review of Educational Research*, Vol. 71, No. 4, pp. 575–611.

Human Security Centre. 2006. *Human Security Brief 2006*. Vancouver, BC, University of British Columbia.

Hussein, A. 2006. *Conditional Cash Transfers in Low Income Countries: Applicability and Challenges – Kenya*. Paper presented at the Third International Conference on Conditional Cash Transfers, Istanbul, Turkey, World Bank, 26–30 June.

IDA/IMF. 2006. *Heavily Indebted Poor Countries Initiative (HIPC) and Multilateral Debt Relief Initiative (MDRI) – Status of Implementation*. Washington, DC, International Development Association/International Monetary Fund.

ILO. 1958. *Convention No. 111 concerning Discrimination in Respect of Employment and Occupation*. Geneva, Switzerland, International Labour Organization. (Adopted by the General Conference of the ILO on 25 June 1958.)

—— 1989. *Convention No. 169 concerning Indigenous and Tribal Peoples in Independent Countries*. Geneva, Switzerland, International Labour Organization.

—— 1999. *Convention No. 182 concerning the Prohibition and Immediate Action for the Elimination of the Worst Forms of Child Labour*. Geneva, Switzerland, International Labour Organization.

—— 2006a. *Changing Patterns in the World of Work*. Geneva, ILO. (Report of the Director-General, International Labour Conference, 95th Session 2006, Report I [C].)

—— 2006b. *Every Child Needs a Teacher: Education for All (EFA) Global Action Week 24–30 April 2006*. Pretoria, South Africa, ILO.

—— 2007. *Global Employment Trends for Women*. Geneva, Switzerland, International Labour Organization. (Brief.)

ILO/UNESCO. 2006. *Joint ILO/UNESCO Committee of Experts on the Application of the Recommendations concerning Teaching Personnel. Report. Ninth Session*. Geneva, Switzerland, International Labour Organization/UNESCO.

IMF. 2005. *Uganda: Poverty Reduction Strategy Paper*. Washington, DC, International Monetary Fund/Uganda Ministry of Finance, Planning and Economic Development. (IMF Country Report, 05/307.)

IMF Independent Evaluation Office. 2007. *An Evaluation of the IMF and Aid to Sub-Saharan Africa*. Washington, DC, International Monetary Fund, Independent Evaluation Group.

Institute for the Promotion of Teaching Science and Technology. 2005. *Students' Achievement (Learning Outcome) in Thailand*. Bangkok, IPST.

Ireland, T. 2007. Brazil non-formal education country profile. Background paper for *EFA Global Monitoring Report 2008*.

Isaacs, S. 2005. 'Against all odds': reflections on the challenges of SchoolNet Africa. Bracey, B. and Culver, T. (eds), *Harnessing the Potential of ICT for Education: A Multistakeholder Approach*. Proceedings from the Dublin Global Forum of the United Nations ICT Task Force. New York, United Nations ICT Task Force. (ICT Task Force Series, 9.)

Istrate, O., Noveanu, G. and Smith, T. M. 2006. Exploring sources of variation in Romanian science achievement. *Prospects: Quarterly Review of Comparative Education*, Vol. XXXVI, No. 4, pp. 475–96.

Jamaica National Poverty Eradication Programme. 2007. *The National Poverty Eradication Programme: Annual Report 2005/2006*. Kingston, NPEP.

Jamison, D., Searle, B., Galda, K. and Heyneman, S. 1981. Improving elementary mathematics education in Nicaragua: an experimental study of the impact of textbooks and radio on achievement. *Journal of Educational Psychology*, Vol. 73, pp. 556–67.

Jha, J. and Jhingran, D. 2005. *Elementary Education for the Poorest and Other Deprived Groups*. New Delhi, Manohar Publishers.

Jha, J. and Kelleher, F. 2006. *Boys' Underachievement in Education. An Exploration in Selected Commonwealth Countries*. Vancouver, BC, Commonwealth Secretariat/Commonwealth of Learning.

Jones, S. and Dindia, K. 2004. A meta-analytic perspective on sex equity in the classroom. *Review of Education Research*, Vol. 74, No. 4, pp. 443–71.

Jukes, M. and Desai, K. 2005. Education and HIV/AIDS. Background paper for *EFA Global Monitoring Report 2006*.

Karatnycky, A. 2002. *Freedom in the World 2002: The Democracy Gap*. Budapest, Freedom House.

Karatnycky, A. and Ackerman, P. 2005. *How Freedom is Won: From Civic Resistance to Durable Democracy*. New York, Freedom House.

Katz, E. 2003. The changing role of women in the rural economies of Latin America. Davis, B. (ed.), *Food, Agriculture and Rural Development: Current and Emerging Issues for Economic Analysis*, Vol. 1, Latin America and the Caribbean. Rome, Food and Agriculture Organization.

Keeves, J. P. 1995. *The World of School Learning: Selected Key Findings from 35 Years of IEA Research*. The Hague, Netherlands, International Association for the Evaluation of Educational Achievement.

Kefaya, N. 2007. Country case study: Yemen. Background paper for *EFA Global Monitoring Report 2008*.

Kellaghan, T. and Greaney, V. 2003. *Monitoring Performance: Assessment and Examinations in Africa*. Paper presented at the ADEA Biennial Meeting 2003, Grand Baie, Mauritius, Association for the Development of Education in Africa, 3–6 December.

Kenya National Bureau of Statistics. 2007. *Kenya National Adult Literacy Survey (KNALS) Report*. Nairobi, National Bureau of Statistics.

Khandker, S., Pitt, M. and Fuwa, N. 2003. *Subsidy to Promote Girls' Secondary Education: The Female Stipend Program in Bangladesh*. Washington, DC, World Bank.

Kim, M. 2007. *School Choice and Private Supplementary Education in South Korea*. Paper presented at the IIEP Policy Forum 'Confronting the shadow education system: What government policies for what private tutoring?' Paris, 5–6 July.

Kirby, D., Laris, B. A. and Rolleri, L. 2005. *Impact of Sex and HIV Education Programs on Sexual Behaviors of Youth in Developing and Developed Countries*. Research Triangle Park, NC, Family Health International, Youth Net Program/USAID/ETR Associates. (Youth Research Working Paper Series, 2.)

Kirschner, P. A., Sweller, J. and Clark, R. E. 2006. Why minimal guidance during instruction does not work: an analysis of the failure of constructivist, discovery, problem-based, experiential, and inquiry-based teaching. *Educational Psychologist*, Vol. 41, No. 2, pp. 75–86.

Klein, S. S., Kramarae, C. and Richardson, B. 2007. Examining the achievement of gender equity in and through education. Klein, S. S. (ed.), *Handbook for Achieving Gender Equity through Education*, 2nd edn. Mahwah, NJ, Lawrence Erlbaum Associates, pp. 1–13.

Kristensen, K., Omagor-Loican, M., Onen, N. and Okot, D. 2006. Opportunities for inclusion? The education of learners with special education needs and disabilities in special schools in Uganda. *British Journal of Special Education*, Vol. 33, No. 3, pp. 139–47.

Krueger, A. B. and Lindahl, M. 2001. Education for growth: why and for whom? *Journal of Economic Literature*, Vol. 39, No. 4, pp. 1101–36.

Lao People's Democratic Republic Ministry of Education. 2001. *Lao National Literacy Survey 2001: Final Report*. Bangkok, UNESCO Asia and Pacific Bureau for Education.

Lawson, A., Booth, D., Msuya, M., Wangwe, S. and Williamson, T. 2005. *Does General Budget Support Work? Evidence from Tanzania*. London/Dar es Salaam, Overseas Development Institute/Daima Associates.

Leach, F. 2006. Researching gender violence in schools: methodological and ethical considerations. *World Development*, Vol. 34, No. 6, pp. 1129–47.

Leithwood, K. and Menzies, T. 1998. A review of research concerning the implementation of site-based management. *School Effectiveness and School Improvement*, Vol. 9, No. 3, pp. 233–85.

LeVine, R. A., LeVine, S. E., Richman, A., Uribe, F. M. T., Correa, C. S. and Miller, P. M. 1991. Women's schooling and child care in the demographic transition: a Mexican case study. *Population and Development Review*, Vol. 17, pp. 459–96.

LeVine, R. A., LeVine, S. E., Rowe, M. L. and Schnell-Anzola, B. 2004. Maternal literacy and health behavior: a Nepalese case study. *Social Science and Medicine*, Vol. 58, pp. 866–77.

LeVine, R. A., LeVine, S. E. and Schnell, B. 2001. Improve the women: mass schooling, female literacy, and worldwide social change. *Harvard Education Review*, Vol. 71, pp. 1–50.

Levy, D. and Ohls, J. 2007. *Evaluation of Jamaica's PATH Program: Final Report*. Washington, DC, Mathematica Policy Research, Inc.

Levy, S. 2006. *Progress against Poverty: Sustaining Mexico's Progresa-Oportunidades Program*. Washington, DC, Brookings Institution Press.

Lewin, K. M. and Sayed, Y. 2005. *Non-Government Secondary Schooling in sub-Saharan Africa: Exploring the Evidence in South Africa and Malawi*. London, UK Department for International Development. (Researching the Issues, 59.)

Lewis, M. A. and Lockheed, M. E. 2006. *Inexcusable Absence: Why 60 Million Girls Still Aren't in School and What To Do about It*. Washington, DC, Center for Global Development.

Liberia Ministry of Education. 2007. *Liberian Primary Education Recovery Program*. Monrovia, Liberia Ministry of Education. (Prepared for the Fast Track Initiative.)

Limage, L. 2005. The political economy and recent history of book publishing and print materials. Background paper for *EFA Global Monitoring Report 2006*.

Linden, L., Banerjee, A. and Duflo, E. 2003. *Computer-Assisted Learning: Evidence from a Randomized Experiment*. Cambridge, Mass., Massachusetts Institute of Technology, Poverty Action Lab. (Draft, 5.)

Linehan, S. 2004. Language of instruction and the quality of basic education in Zambia. Background paper for *EFA Global Monitoring Report 2005*.

Lockheed, M. and Hanushek, E. 1988. Improving educational efficiency in developing countries: what do we know? *Compare*, Vol. 18, No. 1, pp. 21–38.

Lockheed, M. and Verspoor, A. 1991. *Improving Primary Education in Developing Countries*. Oxford, UK, Oxford University Press.

Loeb, M. E. and Eide, A. H. 2004. *Living Conditions among People with Activity Limitations in Malawi. A National Representative Study*. Oslo, SINTEF Health Research.

López, N., Pereyra, A. and Sourrouille, F. 2007. Urban and rural disparities in Latin America: some implications for educational access. Background paper for *EFA Global Monitoring Report 2008*. (Through UNESCO International Institute for Educational Planning-Buenos Aires.)

Luciak, M. 2004. *Migrants, Minorities and Education: Documenting Discrimination and Integration in 15 Member States of the European Union*. Luxembourg, European Communities. (On behalf of the European Monitoring Centre on Racism and Xenophobia.)

Lyon, S. and Rosati, F. C. 2006. *Non-Formal Education Approaches for Child Labourers: An Issue Paper*. Rome, ILO/UNICEF/World Bank, Understanding Children's Work.

Ma, X. 2007. Gender differences in learning outcomes. Background paper for *EFA Global Monitoring Report 2008*.

MacGregor, K. 2007. The good news: global trends in the media and its role in Education for All. Background paper for *EFA Global Monitoring Report 2008*.

Machona, P. E. and Chilala, M. M. 2004. *The Role of Assessment in the Implementation of National Education Policies in Zambia*. Paper presented at the 22nd African Association for Education Assessment Meeting, Gabarone, 13–17 September.

Mackay, K. 2006. *Institutionalization of Monitoring and Evaluation Systems to Improve Public Sector Management*. Washington, DC, World Bank, Independent Evaluation Group and the Thematic Group for Poverty Analysis, Monitoring and Impact Evaluation. (ECD Working Paper Series, 15.)

Macpherson, I. 2007. Tanzania non-formal education country profile. Background paper for *EFA Global Monitoring Report 2008*.

Malawi National Statistics Office and ORC Macro. 2003. *Malawi DHS EdData Survey 2002: Education Data for Decision-making*. Calverton, Md., Malawi National Statistics Office/ORC Macro.

Mali Ministry of Education, UNESCO Pôle de Dakar and World Bank. 2006. *Eléments de Diagnostic du Système Éducatif Malien: Le Besoin d'une Politique Éducative Nouvelle pour l'Atteinte des Objectifs du Millénaire et la Réduction de la Pauvreté* [Elements for a Diagnostic of the Education System in Mali: The Need for a New Education Policy to Reach the Millenium Goals and Poverty Reduction]. Dakar, Mali Ministry of Education/UNESCO Pôle de Dakar/World Bank. (In French.)

Maluccio, J. A. and Flores, R. 2004. *Impact Evaluation of a Conditional Cash Transfer Program: The Nicaraguan Red de Protección Social*. Washington, DC, International Food Policy Research Institute. (184.)

Marphatia, A. A., Moussié, R., Ainger, A.-M. and Archer, D. 2007. *Confronting the Contradictions: The IMF, Wage Bill Caps and the Case for Teachers*. Johannesburg, South Africa, Action Aid.

Marshall, J. H. 2004. *EQIP School Grants Program Evaluation: Final Report*. Phnom Penh, Cambodia Ministry of Education, Youth and Sports.

Mason, A. 2006. *Changing Age Structures and their Implications for Development*. Paper presented at the Challenges of World Population in the 21st Century: The Changing Age Structure of Population and its Consequences for Development, New York, 12 October 2006.

Mason, K. and Longsworth, N. 2005. *Belize Report: Hemispheric Project for the Preparation of Polices and Strategies for the Prevention of School Failure*. Belmopan, Belize Ministry of Education Youth, Sports and Culture, Quality Assurance and Development Services.

McKenzie, D. J. 2007. *A Profile of the World's Developing Country Migrants*. Bonn, Germany, Institute for the Study of Labor. (Discussion paper, 2948.)

Mchazime, H. 2003. *Integrating Primary School Curriculum and Continuous Assessment in Malawi. Learner Assessment for Improved Educational Quality: An Exchange of Current Ideas and Best Practices*. Paper presented at the sub-Regional Conference on Assessment, Livingstone, Zambia, USAID.

Meana, T. 2003. Estamos ocultas, escondidas tras los masculinos [We are hidden, hiding behind the males]. *Emakunde*, Vol. 52, pp. 24–5. (In Spanish.)

Menezes-Filho, N. and Pazello, E. 2006. *Do Teachers' Wages Matter for Proficiency? Evidence from a Funding Reform in Brazil*. Paper presented at the International Conference Economics of Education: Major Contributions and Future Directions, Dijon, France, Université de Bourgogne - Pôle AAFE, Institut de Recherche sur l'Education Sociologie et Economie de l'Education–Centre National de la Recherche Scientifique, 20–23 June.

Mere, K., Reiska, P. and Smith, T. M. 2006. Impact of SES on Estonian students' science achievement across different cognitive domains. *Prospects: Quarterly Review of Comparative Education,* Vol. XXXVI, No. 4, pp. 497–516.

Michaelowa, K. 2004. *Aid Effectiveness Reconsidered: Panel Data Evidence for the Education Sector*. Hamburg, Germany, Hamburg Institute of International Economics. (HWWA Discussion Paper, 264.)

Michaelowa, K. and Weber, A. 2007*a*. Aid Effectiveness in Primary, Secondary and Tertiary Education. Background paper for the *EFA Global Monitoring Report 2008*.

—— 2007*b*. Aid effectiveness in the education sector: a dynamic panel analysis. Lahiri, S. (ed.), *Theory and Practice of Foreign Aid*. Amsterdam, Elsevier, pp. 357–85.

Michaelowa, K. and Wechtler, A. 2006. *The Cost-Effectiveness of Inputs in Primary Education: Insights from the Literature and Recent Student Surveys for sub-Saharan Africa*. Paper presented at the ADEA Biennale, Libreville, Association for the Development of Education in Africa, 27–31 March.

Mickelson, R. A., Nkomo, M. and Smith, S. S. 2001. Education, ethnicity, gender and social transformation in Israel and South Africa. *Comparative Education Review*, Vol. 45, No. 1, pp. 1–28.

Miguel, E. and Kremer, M. 2004. Worms: identifying impact on education and health in the presence of treatment externalities. *Econometrica*, Vol. 72, No. 1, pp. 159–218.

Milligan, K., Moretti, E. and Oreopoulos, P. 2003. Does education improve citizenship? Evidence from the US and the UK. *Journal of Public Economics*, Vol. 88, No. 9–10, pp. 1667–95.

Mingat, A. 2003. *Management of Education Systems in sub-Saharan African Countries: A Diagnostic and Ways toward Improvement in the Context of the EFA-FTI*. Washington, DC/Dakar, World Bank/UNESCO Pôle de Dakar.

—— 2004. *La Rémunération des Enseignants de l'Enseignement Primaire dans les Pays Francophones d'Afrique sub-Saharienne* [Salary of primary teachers in Francophone countries of sub-Saharan Africa]. Paper presented at the Conférence sur les Enseignantes non-Fonctionnaires, Bamako, Ministry of Education, Direction of Education Volunteers Project, 21–23 November. (In French.)

Minow, M. 2002. Education for Co-Existence. Isaac Marks Memorial Lecture. *Arizona Law Review*, Vol. 44, No. 1, pp. 1–29.

Mirembe, R. and Davies, L. 2001. Is schooling a risk? Gender, power relations and school culture in Uganda. *Gender and Education*, Vol. 13, No. 4, pp. 401–16.

Mkhonta, L. 2003. *Continuous Assessment at Primary School in Swaziland. Learner Assessment for Improved Educational Quality: An Exchange of Current Ideas and Best Practices*. Paper presented at the Sub-Regional Conference on Assessment, Livingstone, Zambia, USAID.

Mongolia National Statistical Office. 2004. *Main Report of Household Income and Expenditure Survey/Living Standards Measurement Survey 2002–2003*. Ulaan Baatar, Mongolia National Statistical Office.

Montagnes, I. 2001. *Thematic Studies: Textbooks and Learning Materials 1990–99*. Dakar, UNESCO, World Education Forum. (Education for All 2000 Assessments; Co-ordinated by the UK Department for International Development and UNESCO.)

Montoya, M. 2003. *La educación sexual desde el Ministerio de Educación Pública* [Sex education from the Ministry of Public Education]. Paper presented at the Colloquium on Gender and Social Equity for All, Lima, Catholic University of Peru, School of Education. (In Spanish.)

Moon, B. 2007. *Research Analysis: Attracting, Developing and Retaining Effective Teachers: A Global Overview of Current Policies and Practices*. Paris, UNESCO. (Working Paper, ED/HED/TED/2007/ME/20.)

Morgan, P. 2006. *The Concept of Capacity, Draft Version*. Maastricht, Netherlands, European Centre for Development Policy Management. (Study on Capacity, Change and Performance.)

Morgan, W. J., Sives, A. and Appleton, S. 2006. *Teacher Mobility, 'Brain Drain', Labour Markets and Educational Resources in the Commonwealth.* London, Department for International Development. (Knowledge and Research.)

Morley, S. and Coady, D. 2003. *From Social Assistance to Social Development: Targeted Education Subsidies in Developing Countries.* Washington, DC, Center for Global Development.

Motala, S. 2007. *Education Transformation in South Africa: The Impact of Finance Equity Reforms in Public Schooling after 1998.* Ph.D. Dissertation, University of the Witwatersrand, Johannesburg.

Mozambique Ministry of Education. 2005. *Education Sector Strategic Plan II (ESSPII) 2005 – 2009.* Maputo, Ministry of Education.

Muito, M. 2004. *Gender Quality in the Classroom. Reflections on Practice.* Nairobi, Forum for African Women Educationalists.

Mulkeen, A. 2006. *Policy, Planning, Utilization and Management of Rural Primary School Teachers in Africa: Lesotho, Malawi, Mozambique, Tanzania, Uganda. Country Reports of the Maseru Workshop 2005.* Washington, DC, World Bank.

Mullis, I. V. S., Martin, M. O., Gonzalez, E. J. and Chrostowski, S. J. 2004. *TIMSS 2003 International Mathematics Report: Findings from IEA's Trends in International Mathematics and Science Study at the Fourth and Eighth Grades.* Chestnut Hill, Mass., TIMSS & PIRLS International Study Center, Boston College, Lynch School of Education.

Mullis, I. V. S., Martin, M. O., Gonzalez, E. J. and Kennedy, A. M. 2003. *PIRLS 2001 International Report: IEA's Study of Reading Literacy Achievement in Primary Schools in 35 Countries.* Chestnut Hill, Mass., International Association for the Evaluation of Educational Achievement and International Study Center, Boston College, Lynch School of Education.

Mundy, K. 2006. *Civil Society Participation and the Governance of Educational Systems in the Context of Sector-wide Approaches to Basic Education.* Toronto, Ont., Ontario Institute for Studies in Education.

Mungai, A. 2002. *Growing up in Kenya: Rural Schooling and Girls.* New York, Peter Lang.

Muñoz Villalobos, V. 2007. *Implementation of General Assembly Resolution 60/251 of 15 March 2006 Entitled 'Human Rights Council'. The Right to Education of Persons with Disabilities. Report by the Special Rapporteur on the Right to Education.* New York, United Nations. (A/HRC/4/29.)

Murillo, L. 2007. Analysis of Achievement Results from National Assessments in Latin America. Background paper for *EFA Global Monitoring Report 2008.* (Through UNESCO Regional Bureau for Education in Latin America and the Caribbean.)

Nadoo, K. 2003. Civil society at a time of uncertainty. *OECD Observer,* OECD No. 237. http://www.oecdobserver.org/news/fullstory.php/aid/1012/Civil_society_at_a_time_of_global_uncertainty.html (Accessed 20 September 2007.)

Neri, M. and Buchmann, G. 2007. Monitoring the Dakar education goals: evaluation of the Brazilian case. Background paper for *EFA Global Monitoring Report 2008.*

Netherlands Ministry of Foreign Affairs. 2006. *From Project Aid to Sector Support: An Evaluation of the Sector-Wide Approach in Dutch Bilateral Aid 1998–2005.* The Hague, Policy Operations and Evaluation Department. (IOB Evaluations, 301.)

Ngom, E. H. 2007. Evolution of apprenticeship results in Senegal based on national evaluations. Background paper for *EFA Global Monitoring Report 2008.*

Niane, B. and Robert, F. 2007. Country case study: Senegal. Background paper for *EFA Global Monitoring Report 2008.*

Nicaragua National Statistics and Census Institute and World Bank. 2001. *Encuesta Nacional de Hogares sobre Medición de Nivel de Vida 2001* [2001 National Household Living Standards Measurement Survey]. Managua/Washington, DC, Nicaragua National Statistics and Census Institute/World Bank. (In Spanish.)

Nigeria National Population Commission and ORC Macro. 2004. *Nigeria DHS EdData Survey 2004: Education Data for Decision-Making.* Calverton, Md., National Population Commission/ORC Macro.

Nilsson, P. 2003. *Education for All: Teacher Demand and Supply in South Asia.* Brussels, Education International. (13.)

Nishimura, M., Yamano, T. and Sasaoka, Y. 2005. *Impacts of the Universal Primary Education Policy on Educational Attainment and Private Costs in Rural Uganda.* New York/Tokyo, Columbia University, Teachers College/ Foundation for Advanced Studies on International Development/National Graduate Institute for Policy Studies.

Nordtveit, H. 2005. Public-private partnerships and outsourcing. Background paper for *EFA Global Monitoring Report 2006.*

O'Malley, B. 2007. *Education under Attack: A Global Study on Targeted Political and Military Violence against Education Staff, Students, Teachers, Union and Government Officials and Institutions.* Paris, UNESCO.

OECD-DAC. 2005. *Paris Declaration on Aid Effectiveness: Harmonization, Alignment, Results and Mutual Accountability.* High Level Forum on Aid Effectiveness, Paris, Organisation for Economic Co-operation and Development, Development Co-operation Directorate, Development Assistance Committee, 28 February–2 March.

—— 2006a. *The Challenge of Capacity Development: Working Towards Good Practice.* Paris, Organisation for Economic Co-operation and Development, Development Co-operation Directorate, Development Assistance Committee, Network on Governance. (DCD/DAC/GOVNET [2005]5/REV1.)

—— 2006b. *Development Co-operation Report 2005.* Paris, Organisation for Economic Co-operation and Development, Development Co-operation Directorate, Development Assistance Committee. (OECD Journal on Development.)

—— 2006c. *Monitoring Resource Flows to Fragile States: 2005 Report.* Paris, Organisation for Economic Co-operation and Development, Development Co-operation Directorate, Development Assistance Committee, Fragile States Group.

—— 2006d. *Monitoring Resource Flows to Fragile States: 2006 Report. DAC Meeting, 15 November 2006*. Paris, Organisation for Economic Co-operation and Development, Development Co-operation Directorate, Development Assistance Committee, Fragile States Group. (DCD/DAC[2006]52.)

—— 2007a. *DAC List of ODA Recipients: Effective from 2006 for Reporting on Flows in 2005, 2006 and 2007*. Paris, Organisation for Economic Co-operation and Development, Development Co-operation Directorate, Development Assistance Committee. www.oecd.org/dac/stats/daclist (Accessed 5 October 2007.)

—— 2007b. *Development Co-operation Report 2006*. Paris, Organisation for Economic Co-operation and Development, Development Co-operation Directorate, Development Assistance Committee. (OECD Journal on Development.)

—— 2007c. *International Development Statistics: Online Databases on Aid and Other Resource Flows*. Paris, Organisation for Economic Co-operation and Development, Development Co-operation Directorate, Development Assistance Committee. www.oecd.org/dac/stats/idsonline (Accessed 13 July 2007.)

OECD. 2001. *Knowledge and Skills for Life. First Results from PISA 2000*. Paris, Organisation for Economic Co-operation and Development.

—— 2004a. *Early Childhood Education and Care Policy: Country Note for Mexico*. Paris, Organisation for Economic Co-operation and Development, Directorate for Education.

OECD. 2004b. *Education at a Glance: OECD Indicators - 2004*. Paris, Organisation for Economic Co-operation and Development.

—— 2004c. *Learning for Tomorrow's World: First Results from PISA 2003*. Paris, Organisation for Economic Co-operation and Development, Programme for International Student Assessment.

—— 2006. *Where Immigrants Succeed: A Comparative Review of Performance and Engagement in PISA 2003*. Paris, Organisation for Economic Co-operation and Development.

—— 2007a. *Development Committee Meeting, Washington, 15 April 2007, Statement by Mr Angel Gurría, OECD Secretary-General, and Mr Richard Manning, Chairman, OECD Development Assistance Committee (DAC)*. Paris, Organisation for Economic Co-operation and Development.

—— 2007b. *Understanding the Brain: The Birth of a Learning Science*. Paris, Organisation for Economic Co-operation and Development.

—— 2007c. *Understanding the Social Outcomes of Learning*. Paris, Organisation for Economic Co-operation and Development, Centre for Educational Research and Innovation.

OECD and Statistics Canada. 2000. *Literacy in the Information Age: Final Report of the International Adult Literacy Survey*. Paris, Organisation for Economic Co-operation and Development.

Open Society Institute. 2007. *Equal Access to Quality Education for Roma: Bulgaria, Hungary, Romania, Serbia*. Budapest, OSI/EU Monitoring and Advocacy Program, Education Support Program, Roma Participation Program. (Volume 1.)

Organisation Internationale de la Francophonie, CONFEMEN and Chad Ministry of National Education. 2006. *La Qualité de l'Éducation au Tchad: Quels Espaces et Facteurs d'Ameloration* [Education Quality in Chad: What Room and Factors for Improvement]. Dakar, CONFEMEN. (In French.)

Ortega Goodspeed, T. 2006. *Using Report Cards to Promote Better Education Policy in Latin America: PREAL's Experience*. Santiago, Partnership for Educational Revitalization in the Americas.

Ouane, A. 2003. *Towards a Multicultural Culture of Education*. Hamburg, Germany, UNESCO Institute for Education.

Overseas Development Institute. 2006. *PSABH - A Good News Case Study: Primary School Action for Better Health Projects in Kenya (PSABH)*. London, ODI. http://www.odi.org.uk/RAPID/Tools/Case_studies/PSABH.html (Accessed 2 October 2007.)

Oxenham, J. 2004. The quality of programmes and policies. Background paper for *EFA Global Monitoring Report 2005*.

Oxfam. 2007. *Paying for People: Financing the Skilled Workers Needed to Deliver Health and Education Services for All*. Oxford, UK, Oxfam. (Briefing Paper, 98.)

Packer, S. 2007. International EFA architecture. Lessons and prospects: a preliminary assessment. Background paper for *EFA Global Monitoring Report 2008*.

Paes de Souza, R. 2006. *Bolsa Família Program Effects on Health and Education Services: Catching Unusual Suspects*. Brasilia, Brazil Ministry of Social Development and Fight against Hunger. http://siteresources.worldbank.org/SAFETYNETSANDTRANSFERS/Resources/281945-1131468287118/1876750-1162923802334/CCT_Brazil_Romulo_10-30-06.pdf (Accessed 4 October 2007.)

Panama Government and World Bank. 2003. *2003 Panama Encuesta de Niveles de Vida* [2003 Panama Living Standards Household Survey]. Panama City/Washington, DC, Panama Government/World Bank. (In Spanish.)

Paris Club. 2007. *Description of the Paris Club*. Paris, Paris Club. http://www.clubdeparis.org/sections/qui-sommes-nous

Parker, S. W., Rubalcava, L. and Teruel, G. 2005. Schooling inequality and language barriers. *Economic Development and Cultural Change*, Vol. 54, No. 1, pp. 71–94.

Patchen, T. 2006. Engendering participation, deliberating dependence: inner-city adolescents' perceptions of classroom practice. *Teachers College Record*, Vol. 108, No. 10, pp. 2053–79.

Pearson, R. and Alviar, C. 2007. *The Evolution of the Government of Kenya Cash Transfer Programme for Vulnerable Children between 2002 to 2006 and Prospects for Nationwide Scale-Up*. Nairobi, UNICEF Kenya.

MNON

Pelgrum, W. J. 2001. Obstacles to the integration of ICT in education: results from a worldwide educational assessment. *Computers & Education*, Vol. 37, No. 2, pp. 163–78.

Phamotse, P., Mapetla, P., Phatela, M., Khechane, N. and Monaheng-Mariti, P. 2006. *Lesotho Country Report*. Maseru Workshop 2005, World Bank.

Pinheiro, P. S. 2006. *World Report on Violence against Children*. Geneva, United Nations Secretary-General's Study on Violence against Children.

Plaatjies, D. 2006. *Conditional Cash Transfer Programs in South Africa*. Paper presented at the Third International Conference on Conditional Cash Transfers, Istanbul, Turkey, World Bank, June 26–30.

Porta, E. and Laguna, J. R. 2007a. *Equidad de la Educación en Guatemala* [Education Equity in Guatemala]. Guatemala City, USAID Guatemala and Academy for Educational Development. (Vol. 4.)(In Spanish.)

—— 2007b. Present state of education for all: the case of Guatemala. Background paper for *EFA Global Monitoring Report 2008*.

—— 2007c. Present state of education for all: the case of Nicaragua. Background paper for *EFA Global Monitoring Report 2008*.

Postlethwaite, T. N. 2004. *Monitoring Educational Achievement*. Paris, UNESCO International Institute for Educational Planning. (Fundamentals of Educational Planning, 81.)

Price, M. and Benton-Short, L. 2007. *Counting Immigrants in Cities across the Globe*. Washington, DC, Migration Policy Institute. (Migration Information Source.)

Pridmore, P. 2007. *Impact of Health on Education Access and Achievement: A Cross-National Review of the Research Evidence*. Brighton, UK Department for International Development; Consortium for Research on Educational Access, Transitions & Equity.

Primo Braga, C. A. and Brokhaug, K. 2005. *Services and the Doha Development Agenda*. Washington, DC, World Bank. (Prepared for the Working Group on Trade of the Parliamentary Network on the World Bank.)

Pritchett, L. 2004. *Towards a New Consensus for Addressing the Global Challenge of the Lack of Education*. Washington, DC, Center for Global Development. (Working Paper, 43.)

Project Ploughshares. 2007. *Armed Conflicts Report 2007*. Waterloo, Ont., Project Ploughshares. http://www.ploughshares.ca/libraries/ACRText/ACR-TitlePageRev.htm (Accessed 5 October 2007.)

Qureshi, M. 2004. Globalization - Friend or foe of the developing world? UNESCO and United Nations University (eds), *International Conference 'Globalization with a Human Face - Benefitting All'. 30 - 31 July 2003, Tokyo, Japan*. Paris, UNESCO, pp. 58–67.

Ramirez, F. O., Luo, X., Schofer, E. and Meyer, J. W. 2006. Student achievement and national economic growth. *American Journal of Education*, Vol. 113, pp. 1–29.

Ravallion, M. and Wodon, Q. T. 1999. *Does Child Labor Displace Schooling? Evidence on Behavioral Responses to an Enrollment Subsidy*. Washington, DC, World Bank, Development Research Group. (Policy Research Working Paper, 2116.)

Razquin, P. 2003. *Teacher Career Incentives and Sanctions*. Stanford, Calif., Research Triangle Institute International, Literacy Enhancement Assistance Project. (Final Report.)

Reh, M. 1981. *Problems of Linguistic Communication in Africa*, Vol. 1. Hamburg, Germany, Helmut Buske. (African linguistic bibliographies.)

Reimers, F., DeShano da Silva, C. and Trevino, E. 2006. *Where is the 'Education' in Conditional Cash Transfers in Education?* Montreal, Qué, UNESCO Institute for Statistics. (4.)

Riddell, A. 2007a. The new modalities of aid to education: the view from some development agencies' headquarters. Background paper for *EFA Global monitoring Report 2008*.

—— 2007b. The new modalities of aid to education: the view from within some recipient countries. Background paper for *EFA Global Monitoring Report 2008*.

Riddell, R. C. 2007. *Does Foreign Aid Really Work?* Oxford, UK, Oxford University Press.

Roodman, D. 2004. *The Anarchy of Numbers: Aid, Development and Cross-country Empirics*. Washington, DC, Center for Global Development. (Working Paper, 32.)

Rosati, F. C. and Rossi, M. 2007. *Impact of School Quality on Child Labor and School Attendance: The Case of CONAFE Compensatory Education Program in Mexico*. Rome, ILO/UNICEF/World Bank, Understanding Children's Work. (21.)

Rose, P. 2002. *Is the Non-State Education Sector Serving the Needs of the Poor? Evidence from East and Southern Africa*. Paper presented at the workshop Making Services Work for Poor People, Oxford, United Kingdom, World Development Report 2003/04 Workshop, 4–5 November.

—— 2006. Collaborating in Education for All? Experiences of government support for non-state provision of basic education in South Asia and sub-Saharan Africa. *Public Administration and Development*, Vol. 26, No. 3, pp. 219–30.

—— 2007. *Review of Absorptive Capacity and Education in the Context of Scaling-up Aid*. Brighton, UK, Global Campaign for Education/France Ministry of Foreign Affairs/UK Department for International Development. (68.)

Ross, H., Lou, J., Yang, L., Rybakova, O. and Wakhunga, P. 2005. China country study. Background paper for *EFA Global Monitoring Report 2006*.

Rus, C. 2004. *The Training of Roma/Gypsy School Mediators and Assistants*. Timifloara, Romania, Conseil de l'Europe. (Timifloara/Romania Seminar, 1–4 April 2004. Organized in cooperation with Institutul Intercultural Timifloara.)

Sabri, A. 2007. Egypt non-formal education country profile. Background paper for *EFA Global Monitoring Report 2008*.

Sachs, J. D. 2005. *The End of Poverty: Economic Possibilities for Our Time*. New York, The Penguin Press.

Save the Children. 2007a. Children in crisis: education rights for children in conflict affected and fragile states. Background paper for *EFA Global Monitoring Report 2008*.

— 2007b. Education rights for children in conflict affected and fragile states. Background paper for *EFA Global Monitoring Report 2008*.

Scheerens, J. 2004. Review of school and instructional effectiveness research. Background paper for *EFA Global Monitoring Report 2005*.

Scheerens, J. and Visscher, A. J. 2004. *School Factors Related to Quality and Equity*. Paris, OECD. (PISA Thematic Report.)

Schmidt, P. 2006. *Budget Support in the EC's Development Cooperation*. Bonn, Germany, German Development Institute. (Studies, 20.)

School Fee Abolition Initiative. Forthcoming. *Lessons Learned from Abolishing School Fees in Ethiopia, Ghana, Kenya, Malawi and Mozambique*. New York/Washington, DC, UNICEF/World Bank.

Schubert, B. and Huijbregts, M. 2006. *The Malawi Social Cash Transfer Pilot Scheme: Preliminary Lessons Learned*. Paper presented at the Conference on Social Protection Initiatives for Children, Women and Families: An Analysis of Recent Experiences, New York, UNICEF, 30–31 October.

Schulmeyer, A. 2004. Estado actual de la evaluación docente en trece países de América Latina [Current state of teacher evaluation in thirteen Latin American countries]. Pearlman, M., Schulmeyer, A., Tedesco, J. C., Tenti, E., Aguerrondo, I., Vaillant, D., Rego, T., Avalos, B., Namo de Mello, G., Chezzi Dallan, E. M., Rama, G., Navarro, J. C., Liang, X., Herrán, C. A., Uribe, C., Mizala, A. and Romaguera, P. (eds), *Maestros en América Latina: Nuevas Perspectivas sobre su Formación y Desempeño*. Santiago, PREAL/Inter-American Development Bank, pp. 25–64. (In Spanish.)

Schultz, P. T. 2002. Why governments should invest more to educate girls. *World Development*, Vol. 30, No. 2, pp. 207–25.

Schwille, J. and Dembélé, M. 2007. *Global Perspectives on Teacher Learning: Improving Policy and Practice*. Paris, UNESCO International Institute for Educational Planning. (Fundamentals of Educational Planning, 84.)

Scribner, S. and Cole, M. 1981. *The Psychology of Literacy*. Cambridge, Mass., Harvard University Press.

Seel, A. 2007. Reaching the unreached: progress and challenges in EFA in East Asia, focusing on China, Viet Nam, Cambodia, Philippines and Indonesia. Background paper for *EFA Global Monitoring Report 2008*.

Shapiro, J. and Trevino, J. M. 2004. *Compensatory Education for Disadvantaged Mexican Students: An Impact Evaluation Using Propensity Score Matching*. Washington, DC, World Bank. (3334.)

Sherman, J. D. and Poirier, J. M. 2007. Sub-national disparities in participation in quality primary education: draft report. Background paper for *EFA Global Monitoring Report 2008*. (Through the American Institutes for Research.)

Shi, J. and Ross, H. 2002. Guest editors' introduction. *Chinese Education and Society*, Vol. 35, No. 5, pp. 3–13.

Shockley, R., Guglielmino, P. and Watlington, E. 2006. *The Costs of Teacher Attrition*. Paper presented at The International Congress for School Effectiveness and Improvement, Fort Lauderdale, Fla., Florida Atlantic University, 5 January.

Sida. 2007. *Progress in Educational Development*. Stockholm, Swedish International Development Cooperation Agency. (Sida's Contributions 2006.)

Silova, I., Johnson, M. S. and Heyneman, S. P. 2007. Education and the crisis of social cohesion in Azerbaijan and Central Asia. *Comparative Education Review*, Vol. 52, No. 2, pp. 159–80.

Singh, K. 2007. Emerging understanding of the right to education. Background paper for *EFA Global Monitoring Report 2008*.

Sirias, T. 2007. Su primer decreto: muerte a la autonomia [Its first decree: death to autonomy]. *El Nuevo Diario*, 12 January, Section: National.

Skelton, C. 2005. Boys and girls in the elementary school. Kelton, C., Francis, B. and Smulyan, L. (eds), *The SAGE Handbook of Gender and Education*. London, SAGE Publications.

Skoufias, E. and Shapiro, J. 2006. *The Pitfalls of Evaluating a School Grants Program Using Non-Experimental Data*. Washington, DC, World Bank.

Smith, G., Kippax, S., Aggleton, P. and Tyrer, P. 2003. HIV/AIDS school-based education in selected Asia-Pacific countries. *Sex Education*, Vol. 3, No. 1, pp. 3–21.

Smith, M. T., Miguel Langa, R. and Marizane, K. 2006. *Mozambique Country Report*. Maseru Workshop 2005, World Bank.

Smits, J., Huisman, J. and Webbink, E. 2007. *Family Background, District and National Determinants of Primary School Enrollment in 62 Developing Countries*. Paper presented at the XIII World Congress of Comparative Education Societies, Sarajevo, 3–7 September.

South African Democratic Teachers Union. 2003. *Matric 2002: Results of a Survey of the Impressions of SADTU Education Desk Leaders. The Educators Voice*. Johannesburg, South Africa, SADTU.

Souza, A. P. and Emerson, P. M. 2002. *Birth Order, Child Labor and School Attendance in Brazil*. Nashville, Tenn., Vanderbilt University, Department of Economics. (0212.)

Stash, S. and Hannum, E. 2001. Who goes to school? Educational stratification by gender, caste and ethnicity in Nepal. *Comparative Education Review*, Vol. 45, pp. 354–78.

Steiner-Khamsi, G. 2007. Mongolia country case study. Background paper for *EFA Global Monitoring Report 2008*.

Straková, J., Tomásek, V. and Willms, J. D. 2006. Educational inequalities in the Czech Republic. *Prospects: Quarterly Review of Comparative Education*, Vol. XXXVI, No. 4, pp. 517–28.

Stromquist, N. P. 2007. The gender socialization process in schools: a cross-national comparison. Background paper for *EFA Global Monitoring Report 2008*.

Tajikistan Goscomstat and World Bank. 2003. *2003 Tajikistan LSMS Survey*. Dushanbe/Washington, DC, Tajikistan Goscomstat/World Bank.

Temple, J. 2001. Growth effects of education and social capital in the OECD countries. *OECD Economic Studies*, No. 33, pp. 57–101.

The Economist. 2007. Rich man, poor man. Brazil special report. *The Economist*, 14 April, p. 11.

The Guardian. 2007. Dubai's ruler gives £5bn to improve region's education. *The Guardian*, 14 June.

Theobald, D., Umar, A., Ochekpe, S. and Sanni, K. 2007. Nigeria country case study. Background paper for *EFA Global Monitoring Report 2008*.

Thiele, R., Nunnenkamp, P. and Dreher, A. 2006. *Sectoral Aid Priorities: Are Donors Really Doing their Best to Achieve the Millennium Development Goals?* Zürich, Switzerland, KOF - Swiss Institute for Business Cycle Research, Swiss Federal Institute of Technology (ETH Zürich). (Working Papers, 124.)

Tidemand, P., Steffensen, J. and Olsen, H. B. 2007. *Local Level Service Delivery, Decentralisation and Governance: A Comparative Study of Uganda, Kenya and Tanzania Education, Health and Agriculture Sectors*. Copenhagen, Dege Consult.

Timor-Leste National Statistics Directorate and World Bank. 2001. *2001 Timor-Leste LSMS Survey*. Dili/Washington, DC, National Statistics Directorate/World Bank.

Tinio, V. L. 2003. *ICT in Education*. New York, United Nations Development Programme.

Tomasevski, K. 2003. *Education Denied: Costs and Remedies*. London, Zed Books.

—— 2006. *The State of the Right to Education Worldwide. Free or Fee: 2006 Global Report*. Copenhagen.

Topel, R. 1999. Labor markets and economic growth. Ashenfelt, O. and Card, D. (eds), *Handbook of Labor Economics*, Vol. 3C. Amsterdam, North Holland, pp. 2943–84.

Uganda Bureau of Statistics and ORC Macro. 2001. *Uganda DHS EdData Survey 2001: Education Data for Decision-making*. Calverton, Md., Bureau of Statistics and ORC Macro.

Uganda National Examinations Board. 2006. *The Achievements of Primary School Pupils in Uganda in English Literacy and Numeracy*. Kampala, Ministry of Education.

UIS. 2005. *Global Education Digest 2005: Comparing Education Statistics across the World*. Montreal, Qué, UNESCO Institute for Statistics.

—— 2006a. *Education Counts. Benchmarking Progress in 19 WEI Countries. World Education indicators – 2006*. Montreal, Qué, UNESCO Institute for Statistics.

—— 2006b. *Global Education Digest 2006: Comparing Education Statistics across the World*. Montreal, Qué, UNESCO Institute for Statistics.

—— 2006c. *Teachers and Educational Quality: Monitoring Global Needs for 2015*. Montreal, Qué, UNESCO Institute for Statistics.

UIS/OECD. 2003. *Financing Education: Investments and Returns. Analysis of the World Education Indicators 2002*. Montreal, Qué/Paris, UNESCO Institute for Statistics/OECD.

UN-HABITAT. 2006. *The State of the World's Cities Report 2006/7: The Millennium Development Goals and Urban Sustainability; 30 Years of Shaping the Habitat Agenda*. Nairobi, United Nations Human Settlements Programme.

UN News Service. 2007. *Security Council Urges Greater Protection of Civilians in Armed Conflict*. New York, UN News Service. http://www.un.org/apps/news/story.asp?NewsID=23014&Cr=civilian&Cr1=conflict# (Accessed 3 October 2007.)

UN Population Division. 2005. *UN Population Prospects: The 2004 Revision Population Database*. New York, United Nations.

—— 2007. *World Population Prospects: The 2006 Revision. Highlights*. New York, United Nations, Department of Economic and Social Affairs, Population Division. (Economic & Social Affairs, Working Paper, ESA/P/WP.202.)

UNAIDS. 2006. *2006 Report on the Global AIDS Epidemic. A UNAIDS 10th Anniversary Special Edition*. Geneva, Switzerland, Joint United Nations Program on HIV/AIDS.

UNAIDS Interagency Task Team on Education. 2005. *Report on the Education Sector Global HIV/AIDS Readiness Survey 2004: Policy Implications for Education & Development. An Integration of Perspectives from Ministries of Education and Civil Society Organizations*. Paris, UNESCO.

UNDP. 2006. *Human Development Report 2006. Beyond Scarcity: Power, Poverty and the Global Water Crisis*. New York, United Nations Development Programme.

UNESCO-Bangkok. 2006. *Equivalency Programmes (EPs) for Promoting Lifelong Learning*. Bangkok, UNESCO.

—— 2007a. *Advocacy Kit for Promoting Multilingual Education: Including the Excluded. Language in Education Policy and Practice in Asia and the Pacific*. Bangkok, UNESCO-Bangkok.

—— 2007b. *Strengthening Community Learning Centres through Linkages and Networks. A Synthesis of Six Country Reports*. Bangkok, UNESCO.

UNESCO-BREDA. 2007. *Education for All in Africa 2007. Dakar+7 Report*. Dakar, UNESCO Regional Office for Education in Africa and Pôle de Dakar. (EFA: Top Priority for Integrated Sector-Wide Policies.)

UNESCO-IBE. 2007*a*. A compilation of background information about educational materials and equipment worldwide (prepared by Nhung Truong and Massimo Amadio). Background paper for *EFA Global Monitoring Report 2008*.

—— 2007*b*. Pre-service training programmes for 'basic education' teachers: an initial exploration of minimum qualification standards worldwide (prepared by Massimo Amadio and Nhung Truong). Background paper for *EFA Global Monitoring Report 2008*.

—— 2007*c*. Recent estimates of intended instructional time over the first nine years of schooling (prepared by Massimo Amadio). Background paper for *EFA Global Monitoring Report 2008*.

—— 2007*d*. Worldwide tendencies in the use of the term 'basic education' in K-12 educational programmes at the start of the twenty-first century (prepared by Massimo Amadio and Nhung Truong). Background paper for *EFA Global Monitoring Report 2008*.

UNESCO-IIEP. 2004. *Summer School, Educational Reconstruction in Post-Conflict Situations: Access and Inclusion. Module on Policies for Inclusive Access: Curriculum*. Paris, UNESCO International Institute for Educational Planning.

—— 2005. Country templates synthesis report. Background paper for *EFA Global Monitoring Report 2006*.

UNESCO-OREALC. 2007. *The State of Education in Latin America and the Caribbean: Guaranteeing Quality Education for All. A Regional Report, Reviewing and Assessing the Progress of Latin America and the Caribbean toward Education for All within the Framework of the Regional Education Project (EFA/PRELAC)*. Santiago, UNESCO Regional Bureau for Education in Latin America and the Caribbean.

UNESCO-UNEVOC/UIS. 2006. *Participation in Formal and Vocational Education and Training Programmes Worldwide. An Initial Statistical Study*. Bonn, Germany, UNESCO-UNEVOC International Centre for Technical and Vocational Education and Training/UNESCO Institute for Statistics.

UNESCO. 1960. *Convention against Discrimination in Education. Adopted by the General Conference at its Eleventh Session, Paris, 14 December 1960*. Paris, UNESCO.

—— 1990. *World Declaration on Education for All and Framework for Action to Meet Basic Learning Needs. Adopted by the World Conference on Education for All 'Meeting Basic Learning Needs'*, Jomtien, Thailand, UNESCO, 5–9 March.

—— 1997. *International Standard Classification of Education (ISCED) 1997*. Paris, UNESCO. (BPE.98/WS/1.)

—— 2000*a*. *The Dakar Framework for Action: Education for All - Meeting our Collective Commitments*. World Education Forum, Dakar, UNESCO.

—— 2000*b*. *Education for All. Status and Trends 2000: Assessing Learning Achievement*. Paris, UNESCO. (Published for the International Consultative Forum on Education for All.)

—— 2003*a*. *Education in a Multilingual World*. Paris, UNESCO. (Education Position Paper.)

—— 2003*b*. *EFA Global Monitoring Report 2003/4. Gender and Education for All: The Leap to Equality*. Paris, UNESCO.

—— 2004*a*. *Civil Society Engagement in EFA in the Post-Dakar Period: A Self-Reflective Review*. Paris, UNESCO. (Working document for the Fifth EFA Working Group Meeting, ED/EFA/2006/12.)

—— 2004*b*. *EFA Global Monitoring Report 2005. Education for All: The Quality Imperative*. Paris, UNESCO.

—— 2005*a*. *EFA Global Monitoring Report 2006. Education for All: Literacy for Life*. Paris, UNESCO.

—— 2005*b*. *Implementing Education for All: Teacher and Resource Management in the Context of Decentralization*. Paris, UNESCO. (Education Policies and Strategies, 8.)

—— 2006*a*. *EFA Global Monitoring Report 2007. Strong Foundations: Early Childhood Care and Education*. Paris, UNESCO.

—— 2006*b*. *UNESS Egypt*. Paper presented at the UNESS (UNECO National Education Support Strategy) Pilot Evaluation Workshop, Paris, UNESCO, 27–29 September.

—— 2007*a*. *From Access to Success: Meeting on Improving Learning*. Paris, UNESCO. http://portal.unesco.org/education/en/ev.php-URL_ID=52857&URL_DO=DO_TOPIC&URL_SECTION=201.html

—— 2007*b*. *UNESCO's Teacher Training Initiative for sub-Saharan Africa (TTISSA). Meeting on TTISSA at IIEP*. Paris, UNESCO. http://portal.unesco.org/education/en/ev.php-URL_ID=53121&URL_DO=DO_TOPIC&URL_SECTION=201.html

UNFPA. 2007. *State of World Population 2007: Unleashing the Potential of Urban Growth*. New York, United Nations Population Fund.

UNICEF. 2001. *A Decade of Transition*. Florence, Italy, United Nations Children's Fund, Innocenti Research Centre. (MONEE Project Regional Monitoring Report, 8.)

—— 2004. *The Framework for the Protection, Care and Support of Orphans and Vulnerable Children Living in a World with HIV and AIDS*. New York, United Nations Children's Fund.

—— 2005*a*. *Gender Achievement and Prospects in Education. The GAP Report*. New York, United Nations Children's Fund.

—— 2005*b*. *Joint Press Release: Women, Water and Hygiene are Key to Change in Africa*. New York, United Nations Children's Fund. http://www.unicef.org/media/media_28260.html

—— 2005*c*. *Progress for Children: A Report Card on Immunization*. New York, United Nations Children's Fund.

—— 2005*d*. *The State of the World's Children 2005: Childhood Under Threat*. New York, United Nations Children's Fund.

—— 2006. *The State of the World's Children 2007. Woman and Children: The Double Dividend of Gender Equality*. New York, United Nations Children's Fund.

UNICEF/UNAIDS/WHO. 2007. *Children and AIDS: A Stocktaking Report. Actions and Progress during the First Year of Unite for Children, Unite against AIDS.* New York, United Nations Children's Fund, the Joint United Nations Program on HIV/AIDS, World Health Organization.

United Nations. 1948. *Universal Declaration of Human Rights.*New York, United Nations. (Adopted and Proclaimed by General Assembly Resolution 217 A [III] of 10 December 1948.)

—— 1965. *International Convention on the Elimination of All Forms of Racial Discrimination.* (Adopted and Opened for Signature and Ratification by General Assembly Resolution 2106 [XX] of 21 December 1965.)

—— 1966a. *International Covenant on Civil and Political Rights.* (Adopted and Opened for Signature, Ratification and Accession by General Assembly Resolution 2200A [XXI] of 16 December 1966.)

—— 1966b. *International Covenant on Economic, Social and Cultural Rights.* (Adopted and Opened for Signature, Ratification and Accession by General Assembly Resolution 2200A [XXI] of 16 December 1966.)

—— 1979. *Convention on the Elimination of All Forms of Discrimination against Women.* (Adopted and Opened for Signature, Ratification and Accession by General Assembly Resolution 34/180 of 18 December 1979.)

—— 1989. *Convention on the Rights of the Child.* (Adopted and Opened for Signature, Ratification and Accession by General Assembly Resolution 44/25 of 20 November 1989. Entry into Force 2 September 1990, in Accordance with Article 49.)

—— 1990. *International Convention on the Protection of the Rights of All Migrant Workers and Members of their Families.* (Adopted by General Assembly Resolution 45/158 of 18 December 1990.)

—— 2000. *Optional Protocol to the Convention on the Rights of the Child on the Involvement of Children in Armed Conflict.* (Adopted and Opened for Signature, Ratification and Accession by General Assembly Resolution A/RES/54/263 of 25 May 2000.)

—— 2001a. *General Assembly Resolution. Road Map towards the Implementation of the United Nations Millennium Declaration. Fifty-sixth Session. Item 40 of the Provisional Agenda. Follow-up to the Outcome of the Millennium Summit.* New York, United Nations. (Report of the Secretary-General, A/56/326.)

—— 2001b. *Resolution Adopted by the General Assembly. Twenty-Sixth Special Session, Agenda Item 8. Declaration of Commitment on HIV/AIDS.* New York, United Nations. (A/RES/S-26/2.)

—— 2006a. *Convention on the Rights of Persons with Disabilities.* New York, United Nations. (Adopted by the Sixty-First Session Item 67 [b]. Human Rights Questions: Human Rights Questions, Including Alternative Approaches for Improving the Effective Enjoyment of Human Rights and Fundamental Freedoms.)

—— 2006b. *Major Trends Affecting Families: A Background Document.* New York, United Nations, Department of Economic and Social Affairs, Division for Social Policy and Development, Program on the Family.

—— 2006c. *World Migrant Stock: The 2005 Revision Population Database.* New York, United Nations, Department of Economic and Social Affairs, Population Division. http://esa.un.org/migration (Accessed 5 March 2007.)

—— 2006d. *World Report on Violence Against Children.* Geneva, United Nations.

—— 2006e. *World Urbanization Prospects: The 2005 Revision.* New York, United Nations, Department of Economic and Social Affairs, Population Division. (Working Paper, ESA/P/WP/200.)

—— 2007. *World Population Prospects: The 2006 Revision. Highlights.* New York, United Nations, Department of Economic and Social Affairs, Population Division. (Economic & Social Affairs, Working Paper, ESA/P/WP.202.)

United Nations System. 2004. *5th Report on the World Nutrition Situation: Nutrition for Improved Development Outcomes.* Geneva, Switzerland, United Nations System, Standing Committee on Nutrition.

Us-Sabur, Z. 2007. Bangladesh non-formal education country profile. Background paper for *EFA Global Monitoring Report 2008.*

US Fund for UNICEF. 2007. *UNICEF's Low-cost, High-impact Water and Sanitation Programs Save Lives.* New York, US Fund for UNICEF. http://www.unicefusa.org/site/c.duLRI8OOH/b.2557515/k.A3E4/Water__Sanitation.htm

US Social Security Administration. 2005. *Social Security Programs throughout the World: Africa, 2005.* Washington, DC, Office of Policy; Office of Research, Evaluation and Statistics. (SSA Publication, 13-11803.)

—— 2006a. *Social Security Programs throughout the World: Europe, 2006.* Washington, DC, Office of Policy; Office of Research, Evaluation and Statistics. (SSA Publication, 13-11801.)

—— 2006b. *Social Security Programs Throughout the World: The Americas, 2005.* Washington, DC, Office of Policy; Office of Research, Evaluation and Statistics. (SSA Publication, 13-11803.)

—— 2007. *Social Security Programs throughout the World: Asia and the Pacific, 2006.* Washington, DC, Office of Policy; Office of Research, Evaluation and Statistics. (SSA Publication, 13-11802.)

USAID. 2003. *Unsafe Schools: A Literature Review of School-Related Gender-Based Violence in Developing Countries.* Washington, DC, USAID, Office of Women in Development.

USAID South Africa. 2006. *Integrated Education Program Analysis of the Impact on Pupil Performance of the District Development Support Programme (DDSP).* Pretoria, USAID South Africa. (Prepared by Eric Schollar for RTI International.)

Vachon, P. 2007. Country case studies: Burkina Faso. Background paperfor *EFA global Monitoring Report 2008.*

Valdivia, B. 2006. El rol del docente en la orientación y elección vocacionales en la secundaria técnica [Teacher's role in vocational guidance and choice in technical education]. Ames, P. (ed.), *Las Brechas Invisibles: Desafíos para una Equidad de Género en la Educación.* Lima, Peruvian Studies Institute, pp. 194–79. (In Spanish.)

Vally, S. 2003. Education policy and implementation developments, June to August 1998. Chisholm, L., Motala, S. and Vally, S. (eds), *South African Education Policy Review*. Sandown, South Africa, Heinemann Publishers, pp. 465–95.

van de Walle, N. 2005. *Overcoming Stagnation in Aid-Dependent Countries*. Washington, DC, Center for Global Development.

Vermeersch, C. 2003. *School Meals, Educational Achievement and School Competition: Evidence from a Randomized Experiment*. Oxford, UK, Oxford University. (Working Paper.)

Vermeersch, C. and Kremer, M. 2004. *School Meals, Educational Achievement, and School Competition: Evidence from a Randomized Evaluation*. Washington, DC, World Bank. (Policy Research Working Paper, 3523.)

Villegas-Reimers, E. 2003. *Teacher Professional Development: An International Review of the Literature*. Paris, UNESCO International Institute for Educational Planning.

Wade Diagne, A. and Aw Sall, B. R. 2006. *State-of-the Art of the Outsourcing Strategy of Literacy Programs*. ADEA Biennale on Education in Africa, Libreville, Association for the Development of Education in Africa, 27–31 March.

Wagstaff, A. and van Doorslaer, E. 2003. Catastrophe and impoverishment in paying for health care: with applications to Vietnam 1993–1998. *Health Economics*, Vol. 12, No. 11, pp. 921–34.

Walters, P. B. 2000. The limits of growth: expansion and school reform in historical perspective. Hallinan, M. (ed.), *Handbook of the Sociology of Education*. New York, Kluwer Academic, pp. 163–87.

Watkins, K. 2000. *The Oxfam Education Report*. London, Oxfam.

Watson, D. and Yohannes, L. 2005. *Capacity Building for Decentralised Education Service Delivery in Ethiopia*. Maastricht, Netherlands, European Centre for Development Policy Management. (Study of Capacity, Change and Performance.)

Weber, A. 2006. *Aid Effectiveness in the Education Sector: The Role of Policies Reassessed*. Goethe-University, Frankfurt, Germany.

Whitehead, M., Dahlgren, G. and Evans, T. 2001. Equity and health sector reforms: can low-income countries escape the medical poverty trap? *The Lancet*, Vol. 358, pp. 833–6.

WHO. 2007. *WHO Report 2007. Global Tuberculosis Control: Surveillance, Planning, Financing*. Geneva, Switzerland, World Health Organization.

WHO/UNICEF. 2005. *World Malaria Report*. Geneva, Switzerland, World Health Organization, Roll Back Malaria Department, and United Nations Children's Fund.

Wils, A. 2002. *On Accelerating the Global Literacy Transition*. Cambridge, Mass., Harvard University, Kennedy School of Government, Belfer Center for Science and International Affairs, Environment and Natural Resources Program. (BCSIA Research and Assessment Systems for Sustainability Program Discussion Paper, 2002-18.)

Winkler, D. R. and Gershberg, A. I. 2003. *Education Decentralization in Africa: A Review of Recent Policy and Practice*. Washington, DC, World Bank.

Woldehanna, T. and Jones, N. 2006. *How Pro-Poor is Ethiopia's Education Expansion? A Benefit Incidence Analysis of Education since 1995/96*. London, Save the Children, Young Lives. (Working Paper, 23.)

Wolff, L., de Moura Castro, C., Navarro, J. C. and Garcia, N. 2002. Television for secondary education: experience of Mexico and Brazil. Haddad, W. D. and Draxler, A. (eds), *Technologies for Education: Potentials, Parameters, and Prospects*. Paris/New York, UNESCO/Academy for Educational Development.

Woods, E. 2007a. Education for All in Eritrea: policy and progress, 2000–2006. Country case study. Background paper for *EFA Global Monitoring Report 2008*.

—— 2007b. Education for All in Rwanda: policy and progress, 2000–2006. Country case study. Background paper for *EFA Global Monitoring Report 2008*.

—— 2007c. Education for All in the United Republic of Tanzania: policy and progress, 2000–2006. Country case study. Background paper for *EFA Global Monitoring Report 2008*.

World Bank. 2002. *User Fees in Primary Education*. Washington, DC, World Bank. (Mimeograph, review draft.)

—— 2004a. *Books, Buildings and Learning Outcomes: An Impact Evaluation of World Bank Support to Basic Education in Ghana*. Washington, DC, World Bank.

—— 2004b. *Cost, Financing and School Effectiveness of Education in Malawi: A Future of Limited Choices and Endless Opportunities*. Washington, DC, World Bank Human Development Sector Africa Region.

—— 2004c. *Education in Indonesia: Managing the Transition to Decentralization*. Washington, DC, World Bank. (29506.)

—— 2004d. *Republic of Niger: Public Expenditure Management and Financial Accountability Review (PEMFAR)*. Washington, DC, World Bank, Africa Region, PREM 3. (29752-NE.)

—— 2005a. *Cambodia: Quality Basic Education for All*. Washington, DC, World Bank, East Asia and the Pacific Region, Human Development Sector Unit. (Human Development Sector Reports, 32619-KH.)

—— 2005b. *Education in Ethiopia: Strengthening the Foundation for Sustainable Progress*. Washington, DC, World Bank.

—— 2005c. *Education in the Democratic Republic of Congo. Priorities and Options for Regeneration*. Washington, DC, World Bank. (Country Studies, 0-8213-6121-X.)

—— 2005d. *Expanding Opportunities and Building Competencies for Young People: A New Agenda for Secondary Education*. Washington, DC, World Bank.

—— 2005e. *Global Economic Prospects 2006: Economic Implications of Remittances and Migration*. Washington, DC, World Bank.

— 2005f. *Implementation Completion Report: Republic of Albania Education Reform Project.* Washington, DC, World Bank. (31861.)

— 2005g. *Mozambique Poverty and Social Impact Analysis: Primary School Enrollment and Retention - The Impact of School Fees.* Washington, DC, World Bank, Human Development Africa Region. (29423-MZ.)

— 2005h. *Primary and Secondary Education in Lesotho: A Country Status Report for Education.* Washington, DC, World Bank Africa Region Human Development. (101.)

— 2005i. *Reshaping the Future: Education and Postconflict Reconstruction.* Washington, DC, World Bank.

— 2006a. *A Decade of Measuring the Quality of Governance. Governance Matters 2006: Worldwide Governance Indicators, 1996–2006. Annual Indicators and Underlying Data.* Washington, DC, World Bank.

— 2006b. *Global Monitoring Report 2006.* Washington, DC, World Bank.

— 2006c. *Third International Conditional Cash Transfers Conference, June 26–30 2006, Istanbul-Turkey. Conference Sessions.* Istanbul, Turkey, World Bank. http://info.worldbank.org/etools/icct06/agenda.htm (Accessed 2 October 2007.)

— 2007a. *2005 IDA Resource Allocation Index (IRAI).* Washington, DC, World Bank. http://go.worldbank.org/FHNU4A23U0

— 2007b. *Africa Regional Workshop on Cash Transfer Programs for the Vulnerable Groups.* Mombasa, Kenya, World Bank. http://web.worldbank.org/WBSITE/EXTERNAL/WBI/WBIPROGRAMS/SPLP/0,contentMDK:21270980~menuPK:461671~pagePK:64156158~piPK:64152884~theSitePK:461654,00.html (Accessed 2 October 2007.)

— 2007c. *Country Classification.* Washington, DC, World Bank. http://web.worldbank.org/WBSITE/EXTERNAL/DATASTATISTICS/0,contentMDK:20420458~menuPK:64133156~pagePK:64133150~piPK:64133175~theSitePK:239419,00.html (Accessed 3 October 2007.)

— 2007d. *Global Monitoring Report 2007: Confronting the Challenges of Gender Equality and Fragile States.* Washington, DC, World Bank.

— 2007e. *Investing in Indonesia's Education: Allocation, Equity, and Efficiency of Public Expenditures.* Jakarta, World Bank, Poverty Reduction and Economic Management Unit, East Asia and Pacific Region.

— 2007f. *World Development Indicators.* Washington, DC, World Bank.

World Bank and Government of Kenya. 2005. *Kenya Public Expenditure Review 2004. Report on the Structure and Management of Public Spending.* Washington, DC, World Bank. (29421-KE.)

World Bank Development Research Group. 2006. *Le Système Éducatif Guinéen: Diagnostic et Perspectives pour la Politique Éducative dans le Contexte de Contraintes Macro-économiques Fortes et de Réduction de la Pauvreté* [The Guinean Education System: Diagnostic and Perspectives for Education Policy in the Context of Strong Macro-Economic Constraints and Poverty Reduction]. Conakry, World Bank, Africa Region Human Development. (Working Paper Series, 33644.)(In French.)

World Bank Independent Evaluation Group. 2006a. *Debt Relief for the Poorest: An Evaluation Update of the HIPC Initiative.* Washington, DC, World Bank.

— 2006b. *From Schooling Access to Learning Outcomes: An Unfinished Agenda. An Evaluation of World Bank Support to Primary Education.* Washington, DC, World Bank. (Conference Edition.)

World Food Programme. 2006. *Food for Education Works: A Review of WFP FFE Programme Monitoring and Evaluation 2002–2006.* Rome, World Food Programme.

Yap, Y.-T., Sedlacek, G. and Orazem, P. F. 2001. *Limiting Child Labor through Behavior-Based Income Transfers: An Experimental Evaluation of the PETI Program in Rural Brazil.* Washington, DC, World Bank.

Yi, J. 2002. A discussion on the form of elementary school social teaching materials from the angle of gender analysis. *Chinese Education and Society,* Vol. 35, No. 5, pp. 63–76.

Yizengaw, T. 2006. Government-donor relations in the preparations and implementation of the education sector development programs of Ethiopia. Background paper for *EFA Global Monitoring Report 2007.*

Yonggong, L. and He, L. 2006. Developing skills for the poor: developing skills for rural populations in China. *International Institute for Educational Planning Newsletter,* Vol. XXIV, No. 3, pp. 4.

Young, M. E. and Richardson, L. M. (eds). 2007. *Early Child Development from Measurement to Action: A Priority for Growth and Equity.* Washington, DC, World Bank.

Zafeirakou, A. 2007. Teacher policies for serving the underserved populations: a synthesis of selected policies. Background paper for *EFA Global Monitoring Report 2008.*

Zambia Central Statistics Office and ORC Macro. 2003. *Zambia DHS EdData Survey 2002: Education Data for Decision-Making.* Calverton, Md., Central Statistics Office and ORC Macro.

Zambia Ministry of Community Development and Social Services and GTZ. 2005. *Pilot Social Cash Transfer Scheme: Kalomo District, Zambia.* Lusaka/Eschborn, Germany, Ministry of Community Development and Social Services, Public Welfare Assistance Scheme/German Technical Cooperation. (Monitoring Report 2nd Edition.)

Zelmanova, O., Korsnakova, P., Tramonte, L. and Willms, J. D. 2006. Education inequality in Slovakia: the effects of early selection. *Prospects: Quarterly Review of Comparative Education,* Vol. XXXVI, No. 4, pp. 529–38.

Zhao, J. and Wenbin, H. 2007. EFA case study: China. Background paper for *EFA Global Monitoring Report 2008.*

Abbreviations

ADB	Asian Development Bank
AfDF	African Development Fund
AME	Actualización de Maestros en Educación
AsDF	Asian Development Fund
ASEAN	Association of Southeast Asia Nations
CA	Continuous Assessment
CAQ	Custo Aluno Qualidade (Brazil)
CCT	Conditional cash transfer
CIDA	Canadian International Development Agency
CLADE	Campaña Latinoamericana por el Derecho a la Educación
CONFEMEN	Conférence des Ministres de l'Éducation des pays ayant le français en partage
CPIA	Country Policy and Institutions Assessment
CSO	Civil society organization
DAC	Development Assistance Committee (OECD)
DPT	Diphtheria Pertussis Tetanus vaccine
DFID	Department for International Development (United Kingdom)
E-9	Nine high-population countries (Bangladesh, Brazil, China, Egypt, India, Indonesia, Mexico, Nigeria, Pakistan)
EC	European Commission
ECCE	Early childhood care and education
EDI	Education for All Development Index
EFA	Education for All
EMIS	Education Management Information System(s)
ESDP	Education Sector Development Programme (Ethiopia)
ESSP	Education Sector Strategic Plan (Mozambique)
EU	European Union
FRESH	Focusing Resources on Effective School Health
FTI	Fast Track Initiative
FUNDEB	Fundo de Manutenção e Desenvolvimento da Educação Básica e de Valorização dos Profissionais da Educação (Brazil)
FUNDEF	Fundo de Manutenção e Desenvolvimento do Ensino Fundamental e de Valorização do Magistério (Brazil)
G8	Group of Eight (Canada, France, Germany, Italy, Japan, Russian Federation, United Kingdom and United States, plus EU representatives)
GCE	Global Campaign for Education
GDP	Gross domestic product
GNP	Gross national product
GEI	Gender-specific EFA Index
GER	Gross enrolment ratio
GIR	Gross intake rate
GNP	Gross national product
GPI	Gender parity index

HIPC	Heavily Indebted Poor Countries
HIV/AIDS	Human immuno-deficiency virus/acquired immune deficiency syndrome
IALS	International Adult Literacy Survey
IBE	International Bureau of Education (UNESCO)
IBRD	International Bank for Reconstruction and Development (World Bank)
ICT	Information and communication technology
IDA	International Development Association (World Bank)
IDB	Inter-American Development Bank
IEA	International Association for the Evaluation of Educational Achievement
IIEP	International Institute for Educational Planning (UNESCO)
ILO	International Labour Organization
IMF	International Monetary Fund
INEE	Inter-Agency Network for Education in Emergencies
INGO	International non-governmental organization
IRC	International Resource Committee
IRI	Interactive Radio Instruction
ISCED	International Standard Classification of Education
LAMP	Literacy Assessment and Monitoring Programme
LDCs	Least developed countries
LGA	Local Government Area (Nigeria)
LLECE	Laboratorio Latinamericano de Evaluación de la Calidad de la Educación
MDG	Millennium Development Goal
MDRI	Multilateral Debt Reduction Initiative
MICS	Multiple Indicator Cluster Surveys (UNICEF)
NBTL	New Breakthrough to Literacy (Zambia)
NCERT	National Council of Educational Research and Training (India)
NER	Net enrolment ratio
NEPAD	New Partnership for Africa's Development
NFE	Non-formal education
NGO	Non-government organization
NIR	Net intake rate
ODA	Official development assistance
OECD	Organisation for Economic Co-operation and Development
OHCHR	Office of the United Nations High Commissioner for Human Rights
OREALC	UNESCO Regional Bureau for Education in Latin America and the Caribbean
OVC	Orphans and vulnerable children
PAP	Priority Action Programme (Cambodia)
PASEC	Programme d'analyse des systèmes éducatifs de la CONFEMEN
PETI	Programa de Erradicação do Trabalho Infantil (Brazil)
PDDEB	Plan Décennal de Développement de l'Education de Base (Burkina Faso)
PEDP	Primary Education Development Programme (Bangladesh)
PIRLS	Progress in Reading Literacy Study
PISA	Programme for International Student Assessment

PPP	Purchasing power parity
PREAL	Programa de Promoción de la Reforma Educativa de América Latina y el Caribe
PRONADE	Programa Nacional de Autogestión para el Desarrollo Educativo (Guatemala)
PRSP	Poverty Reduction Strategy Paper
PTA	Parent-teacher association
PTR	Pupil/teacher ratio
SACMEQ	Southern and Eastern Africa Consortium on Monitoring Educational Quality
SECAD	Secretariat of Continuing Literacy and Diversity (Brazil)
SETA	Sectoral Education and Training Authorities (South Africa)
Sida	Swedish International Development Cooperation Agency
SMC	School Management Committees (Nigeria)
SNA	SchoolNet Africa
SWAPs	Sector-wide approach
TIMSS	Trends in International Mathematics and Science Study
TNER	Total primary net enrolment ratio
TTISSA	Teacher Training Initiative for sub-Saharan Africa
TVET	Technical and vocational education and training
UIL	UNESCO Institute for Lifelong Learning
UIS	UNESCO Institute for Statistics
UN	United Nations
UN-HABITAT	United Nations Human Settlements Programme
UNAIDS	Joint United Nations Programme on HIV/AIDS
UNDP	United Nations Development Programme
UNESCO	United Nations Educational, Scientific and Cultural Organization
UNEVOC	International Centre for Technical and Vocational Training (UNESCO)
UNFPA	United Nations Population Fund
UNICEF	United Nations Children's Fund
UNPD	United Nations Population Division
UPC	Universal primary completion
UPE	Universal primary education
USAID	United States Agency for International Development
WEI	World Education Indicators
WHO	World Health Organization

Index

This index is in word-by-word order and covers chapters 1 to 5. Page numbers in *italics* indicate figures and tables; those in **bold** refer to material in boxes. The letter 'n' following a page number indicates information in a note at the side of the page; the letter 'm' indicates a map. Definitions of terms can be found in the glossary, and additional information on countries can be found in the statistical annex.

A

absenteeism, teachers 19, **76**
abuse, in schools 86
academic achievement
    see school achievement
access to education
    see also poverty
  basic education 58
  boys 81
  ECCE programmes 39, 95
  and ethnicity 23, 48, 120
  expansion 23, 108-23
  at expense of quality 186
  girls 13, 34, 80-1
  non-formal programmes 61
  policies improving 112-17
  pre-primary education 33, 95
  primary education 41, 53, *54*, 80-1, 109
  and quality 137
  and school costs 153
  tertiary education 59
  textbooks 66, 68, 73, 73-4, 125-6
accountability, education sector 141, 172
acquired immune deficiency syndrome
    see HIV/AIDS
adolescents *see* young people
Adopt-a-School (Philippines) **110**
adult education *see* learning and life skills; teacher training; tertiary education
adult literacy (EFA goal)
    see also youth literacy
  aid 160
  assessment **62**, *62*, 69, *69*
  definition 62, 62n
  EDI indicator 92, 95
  government responsibilities 192, *193*
  monitoring 62, **62**, 63, 66
  multilingual activities 131-2
  non-state providers 122-3
  programmes 60, 121-3, **133**
  progress towards 33, 62-6, *182*, 190
  trends 64, *64*, 181-2
Afghanistan
  adult literacy 64, *64m*, 65n
  effect of conflict 74
  EDI 93n
  education aid 159, *159*, 165, 189, 189n, *190*
  gender parity/disparity 81, *82m*, *85m*
  non-formal learning 60
  out-of-school children 50n
  post-conflict education **137**
  pre-primary education *37m*, 38, *38-9*
  primary education 42, 78, *113m*
  teaching staff 75, 77, *78*
Africa
  see also Sub-Saharan Africa; individual countries
  distance learning 134
  EFA coalitions **103**
  gender parity/disparity *82m*, *85m*, 88
  use of ICT 136
  school networking **135**

Africa Action Plan 191
Africa Network Campaign on Education for All **102**
African Development Bank **163**
African Development Fund *161*, *162*
agriculture 18n, 19-20
aid 21-3, 154-72, 173-5
    see also education aid; ODA
aid commitments and disbursements 21, *21*, *23*, 154, 156, *157*, *158*, *159*, 160
aid effectiveness 169-72
aid flows 189
AIDS *see* HIV/AIDS
Albania
  abolition of school fees *112m*
  adult literacy *64m*, 182
  basic education 26
  compulsory education 25
  EDI *94*, 95
  education costs 151, 152
  education plans 100, 100n
  gender parity/disparity *82m*, *85m*, 184
  learning assessments 133
  out-of-school children *50m*
  pre-primary education *37m*, *38-9*
  primary education 45, *55m*, *113m*, 180
  tertiary education 92
Algeria
  abolition of school fees *112m*
  adult literacy 63, *64m*, 182, 190
  child mortality rate 35n
  civil society organizations 102n
  EDI 93
  gender parity/disparity *82m*, 83, *85m*, 184
  out-of-school children *50m*
  pre-primary education *37m*, *38-9*
  primary education *43*, 45, 53, *55m*, 56, 78, *113m*, 180
  teaching staff 78
America *see* Latin America; North America; *individual countries*
Andorra
  gender parity/disparity *82m*, *85m*
  out-of-school children *50m*
  pre-primary education *37m*
  primary education *43*
  tertiary education 92
Angola
  abolition of school fees *112m*
  adult literacy *64m*, 65n, 182
  EDI 93n
  education aid 165
  out-of-school children 50n
Anguilla
  gender parity/disparity *82m*, *85m*, 184
  out-of-school children *50m*
  pre-primary education *37m*, 39, 40
  primary education *43*, *55m*, 56, 78, 180
  teaching staff 78
Antigua and Barbuda
  abolition of school fees *112m*
  compulsory education 24
Arab Network for Literacy and Adult Education **103**
Arab States
  see also individual countries
  adult literacy 63, *63*, 65, 181
  child mortality rate 35
  civil society organizations **103**
  ECCE programmes 179
  EDI 93, *93*, 94
  education aid 22, **163**, *163*
  education expenditure 140, 142, *142*, 143, 146, *146*, 148, *149*, *157*, 172
  fragile states *21*
  GDP *185*
  gender parity/disparity 79, *80*, 81, *81*, 83, *83*, 84, *84*, *86*, 89, 183
  immigration 18n
  learning assessments 69, *69*, 71

learning environment 72, 125
  ODA *22*
  out-of-school children 49, *49*, *50m*, 51
  pre-primary education 33, 35, 36, *36*, *37m*, *38-9*, 40
  primary education 41, *41*, 42, *42*, **43**, *43*, 44, *44*, 45, 53, *54*, *55m*, 56, 73, 80, 83, 179
  private education 36-7
  secondary education 56-7, **57**, 58, *58*, *59*, 80, 84
  teaching staff 75, *76*, 77, *78*, 87, 185, *185*
  tertiary education 59, 80, 86, 92
Argentina
  abolition of school fees *112m*
  adult literacy *64m*, 182
  basic education 26
  child mortality rate 35n
  decentralization 107
  distance learning 134
  ECCE programmes 108
  EDI 94
  education costs 150
  education expenditure *144-5*, 147, 148, *150*
  gender parity/disparity *82m*, *85m*, 184
  learning assessments 67, 72, *72*
  out-of-school children *50m*
  pre-primary education *37m*, *38-9*
  primary education *43*, 45, 46, *46*, 47, *55m*, *113m*, 180
  tertiary education 92
armed conflict *see* conflicts
Armenia
  abolition of school fees *112m*
  adult literacy *64m*, 182
  gender parity/disparity *82m*, *85m*, 89, 90, 184
  out-of-school children *50m*
  pre-primary education *37m*, 38, *38-9*
  primary education *55m*, 78, 180
  teaching staff 78
Aruba
  adult literacy *64m*, 182
  compulsory education 25
  EDI 94
  gender parity/disparity *82m*, 83, *85m*, 184
  out-of-school children *50m*
  pre-primary education *37m*, 40
  primary education *43*, *55m*, 56, 78, *113m*, 180
  teaching staff 78
  tertiary education 92
Asia
    see also Central Asia; East Asia; South and West Asia; *individual countries*
  distance learning 135
  immigration 18n
  inclusive education 121
  multilingual education 131
Asian Development Bank **163**, 168, 171
Asian Development Fund *161*, *162*
assessment
    see also monitoring
  literacy **62**, *62*
  of student learning 67-72, 133-4
attendance *see* school attendance
Australia
  abolition of school fees *112m*
  education aid donor *161*, *162*, 168, 187
  education expenditure *144-5*, *150*
  gender parity/disparity *82m*, 84, *85m*, 87, 184
  out-of-school children *50m*
  pre-primary education *37m*
  primary education *43*, 45, *113m*, 180
  secondary education 57
  teaching staff 87
  tertiary education 92

Austria
  abolition of school fees *112m*
  adult literacy *64m*
  education aid donor *161*, *162*, 187
  education expenditure *144-5*, *150*
  gender parity/disparity *82m*, *85m*, 90, 184
  learning assessments 67
  out-of-school children *50m*
  pre-primary education *37m*
  primary education *55m*, *113m*, 180
  tertiary education 92
auxiliary teachers (contract) 78-9, *79*, 127-8
Azerbaijan
  abolition of school fees *112m*
  adult literacy *64m*, 182
  compulsory education 24
  EDI 93n, *94*
  education costs 151
  education expenditure 142, 144, *144-5*
  gender parity/disparity *82m*, *85m*, 184
  out-of-school children *50m*
  pre-primary education *37m*, *38-9*, 40
  primary education 42, *43*, 45, *55m*, 56, 78, *113m*, 180
  teaching staff 78

B

Backward Region Grant Fund (India) 111
Bahamas
  child mortality rate 35n
  gender parity/disparity *82m*, *85m*, 184
  out-of-school children *50m*
  pre-primary education *37m*, *38-9*
  primary education *43*, 45, 52n, 78, *113m*, 180
  teaching staff 78
Bahrain
  abolition of school fees *112m*
  adult literacy *64m*, 182
  compulsory education 25
  EDI 93n, *94*
  gender parity/disparity *82m*, *85m*, 90, 90, 91, 184
  out-of-school children *50m*
  pre-primary education 36, *37m*, *38-9*
  primary education *43*, *55m*, *113m*, 180
  private education 37
  tertiary education 92
Bangladesh
  abolition of school fees *112m*
  adult literacy 64, *64m*, 182
  cash transfers 114, *115*, 117
  child labour 119
  child mortality rate 35n
  civil society organizations 102n, 103, **103**
  compulsory education 24
  distance learning 134
  EDI 93, *94*
  education aid 159, *159*, 160, 161, 165, 166, 167, 168, 174, *175*
  education costs 152
  education expenditure 142, *144-5*, 146, 147
  ethnic populations 120
  gender parity/disparity *82m*, 83, *85m*, 184
  effect of health and nutrition programmes 124
  HIV/AIDS 18n
  household size 18n
  learning environment 87
  non-formal learning 60, 61, 122
  non-government schools 104, 105
  out-of-school children 48, *50m*, 51, 152
  pre-primary education 36, *37m*, *38-9*, 40

primary education 45, 46, 46, 46n, 47,
    48, 54, 55m, 56, 113m, 179, 180
teaching staff 75, 128, 129
Barbados
    abolition of school fees 112m
    education expenditure 144, 144-5
    gender parity/disparity 82m, 85m, 184
    out-of-school children 50m
    pre-primary education 37m, 40
    primary education 43, 52n, 55m, 56,
        78, 113m, 180
    teaching staff 78
Barbuda see Antigua and Barbuda
barriers see access to education
basic education
    see also lower secondary education;
        pre-primary education; primary
        education; universal primary
        education
    access 58
    aid
    commitments and disbursements 156,
        157, 158, 194
    components 155, 165, 165
    donors 161, 174, 188
    use and effect 141, 156, 157-8, 157
    effective utilization 191
    geographic distribution 189
    impact of 169-72, 186-7
    low-income countries 141, 165, 186-7,
        189, 190
    programmatic support 166
    proportion of education aid 155, 157,
        159, 160, 160, 161
    prospects 187-8, 187
    share of total aid 187
    trends 13, 154-5, 160-1
    benefits 24
    Dakar Framework 100
    definitions 25, 26, 192
    enrolment 110
    see also enrolment, primary education;
        enrolment, secondary education
    expansion to disadvantaged areas 192
    funding 99, 111
    government expenditure 25, 140, 149,
        164, 186
    government policies 58, 99
    needs 14
    programmes 60
    progress towards EFA goals 58, 172,
        192
Basic Education for Hard-to-Reach Urban
    Working Children (Bangladesh) 119
Basic Education Sub-sector Investment
    Programme (Zambia) 133
behavioural problems, and educational
    achievement 67
Belarus
    abolition of school fees 112m
    adult literacy 64m, 182
    compulsory education 25
    EDI 93n
    education expenditure 142, 144-5, 147
    gender parity/disparity 82m, 85m, 184
    out-of-school children 50m
    pre-primary education 37m, 40
    primary education 43, 55m, 56, 78,
        113m, 180
    teaching staff 78
    tertiary education 92
Belgium
    abolition of school fees 112m
    compulsory education 24
    education aid donor 161, 162, 187
    education expenditure 150
    gender parity/disparity 82m, 85m, 88,
        184
    out-of-school children 50m
    pre-primary education 37m
    primary education 113m, 180

secondary education 58-9
teaching staff 88
tertiary education 92
Belize
    abolition of school fees 112m
    education expenditure 144-5
    gender parity/disparity 82m, 85m, 90,
        90, 184
    learning assessments 70, 71, 72, 72
    out-of-school children 50m
    pre-primary education 37m, 38-9
    primary education 43, 45, 113m, 180
    private education 36-7
Benin
    abolition of school fees 112m
    adult literacy 64, 64m, 65n, 182
    EDI 93
    education aid 165, 175, 189
    education expenditure 144, 144-5, 174
    education plans 100n
    gender parity/disparity 81, 82, 82m, 83,
        84, 85m, 184
    geographic disparity 111
    non-government schools 104
    out-of-school children 50m, 51
    poverty reduction programmes 164
    pre-primary education 37m, 38-9, 39
    primary education 43, 44, 45, 46, 46,
        47, 47, 53, 54, 55m, 56, 113m, 180
    secondary education 57
    teaching staff 77, 79, 79
Bermuda
    gender parity/disparity 82m, 85m, 184
    out-of-school children 50m
    primary education 52n, 55m, 78, 180
    teaching staff 78
Bhutan
    abolition of school fees 112m
    basic education 26
    compulsory education 25
    education aid 165
    primary education 43, 78
    private education 36-7
    teaching staff 77, 78
bias see discrimination; gender bias
bilateral donors
    commitments and disbursements 156,
        161, 162
    education strategies 160, 166, 191
    increase in aid 21, 194
    projected aid 187-8
bilingual learning environments 120, 131-
    2
Bolivia
    abolition of school fees 112m
    adult literacy 64m, 182
    child labour 119
    EDI 94
    education aid 157-8, 158, 159, 166
    education expenditure 142, 144-5, 147
    education plans 100n
    ethnic populations 120
    gender parity/disparity 82m, 85m, 184
    learning environment 73
    non-formal learning 61
    out-of-school children 50m
    poverty reduction programmes 164
    pre-primary education 37m, 38-9
    primary education 43, 45, 46, 47, 47,
        48, 55m, 56, 113m, 180
Bolsa Escola (Brazil) 115
Bolsa Família (Brazil) 115, 116, 153
Bono de Desarrollo Humano (Ecuador)
    116
Bosnia and Herzegovina
    abolition of school fees 112m
    adult literacy 64m, 182
    effect of conflict 74
    gender parity/disparity 82m, 85m
    out-of-school children 50m
    post-conflict education 137

pre-primary education 37m
primary education 55m, 113m
Botswana
    abolition of school fees 112m
    adult literacy 64m, 65, 133, 182
    basic education 26
    cash transfers 117
    child mortality rate 35
    education aid 158
    education expenditure 142, 143
    education management 101
    gender parity/disparity 82m, 83, 84,
        85m, 88, 90, 184
    governance 20
    learning assessments 68n
    learning environment 125
    primary education 45, 55m, 56, 78,
        113m, 180
    teaching staff 78
boys
    see also 'gender' entries; men
    access to education 81
    experience of violence 86
    performance 89, 89, 90, 91
    pre-primary participation 38
    primary education 81-3, 83
    school attendance 49
    secondary education 34, 83, 84
    teacher expectations 87, 91
Brazil
    abolition of school fees 112m
    adult literacy 64, 64m, 122, 182
    basic education 26
    cash transfers 115, 116
    child labour 119
    civil society organizations 102n, 103
    distance learning 135
    ECCE programmes 108
    education aid 189
    education expenditure 25, 144-5, 149,
        153
    gender parity/disparity 82m, 85m, 184
    geographic disparity 111
    inclusive education 121
    learning assessments 67, 70, 71, 133
    learning environment 73
    non-formal learning 60, 61
    out-of-school children 50m, 51
    pre-primary education 37m, 38-9
    primary education 45, 45, 46, 46, 47,
        47, 48, 53, 54, 55m, 113m, 180
    secondary education 57
    teaching staff 76, 126
    tertiary education 92
bridging courses, for child workers 119
Brigada Eskwela (Philippines) 110
British Virgin Islands
    gender parity/disparity 82m, 83, 85m,
        184
    out-of-school children 50m
    pre-primary education 37m
    primary education 43, 78, 113m, 180
    teaching staff 78
Brunei Darussalam
    adult literacy 64m, 182
    compulsory education 25
    curriculum 132
    gender parity/disparity 82m, 85m, 184
    out-of-school children 50m
    pre-primary education 37m, 38-9, 40
    primary education 43, 55, 55m, 56, 78,
        180
    teaching staff 78
    tertiary education 92
Bulgaria
    abolition of school fees 112m
    adult literacy 64m, 182
    compulsory education 25
    EDI 94
    education aid 189
    ethnic populations 120

gender parity/disparity 82m, 85m, 184
governance 20
out-of-school children 50m
pre-primary education 37m, 38-9
primary education 45, 55m, 113m, 180
tertiary education 92
Bureau of Non-Formal Education
    (Bangladesh) 122
Burkina Faso
    abolition of school fees 112m
    adult literacy 63, 64, 64m, 65n, 182,
        190
    basic education 26
    civil society organizations 103
    debt relief 164
    decentralization 106
    ECCE programmes 108
    EDI 93
    education aid 158, 159, 159, 165, 189,
        189n, 190
    education expenditure 148
    education management 102
    education plans 100n
    gender parity/disparity 81, 82m, 85m,
        90, 117, 118, 183, 184
    geographic disparity 111
    multilingual education 132
    non-formal learning 60, 123
    out-of-school children 48, 50, 50m, 51
    pre-primary education 37m, 38-9
    primary education 41, 42, 43, 43, 45,
        46, 46, 47, 47, 48, 55m, 78, 113m,
        180
    teaching staff 78, 79
Burundi
    abolition of school fees 112m
    adult literacy 64m, 182
    basic education 26
    compulsory education 25
    effect of conflict 74
    EDI 93n
    education aid 158, 158, 165, 175, 189,
        189n, 190
    education expenditure 144, 144-5, 145,
        148
    gender parity/disparity 82m, 83, 84,
        85m, 184
    non-formal learning 61, 61
    out-of-school children 48, 50m, 50n
    poverty reduction programmes 164
    pre-primary education 36, 37m, 38-9,
        39, 40
    primary education 42, 43, 46, 53, 54,
        55, 55m, 56, 78, 113m, 180, 181n
    teaching staff 40, 77, 78

C

Caicos Islands see Turks and Caicos
    Islands
Cambodia
    abolition of school fees 112m
    adult literacy 64m, 66, 182, 182, 190
    cash transfers 114, 115
    civil society organizations 103
    curriculum 132
    decentralization 106
    ECCE programmes 109
    EDI 93
    education aid 165, 166, 175
    education costs 151
    education expenditure 142, 144, 144-5,
        174
    education plans 100n
    gender parity/disparity 82m, 83, 84,
        85m, 184
    geographic disparity 111
    multilingual education 132
    non-formal learning 60
    out-of-school children 48, 50m, 50n
    post-conflict education 136
    pre-primary education 37m, 38-9

primary education *43*, 44, 45, 46, 46,
46n, 47, 53, 54, *54*, *55m*, *78*, *113m*,
179, *180*
quality of education **123**
school expansion 109
secondary education 57
teaching staff 75, 77, 78, *78*, 78n, 128
tertiary education *92*
Cameroon
abolition of school fees *112m*
adult literacy *64m*
basic education 26
compulsory education 25
education aid *165*, *175*
education expenditure 142, 143, 144,
144-5, 146, *174*
gender parity/disparity *82m*, *85m*, 89,
184
non-formal learning 61
out-of-school children *48*
pre-primary education 36, *37m*, *38-9*,
40
primary education 41, *42*, 47, 48, 53,
54, *55m*, *56*, *78*, *113m*
secondary education 57
teaching staff 40, *78*, *78*, *79*, 127
Canada
abolition of school fees *112m*
education aid donor 23, *160*, *161*, *162*,
166, *168*, *187*
education expenditure *150*
primary education *180*
Canadian International Development
Agency 103
capacity building
education aid *164-5*, *170*, *171*, *195*
for education monitoring 101
for EFA 27, *192*, 193-4
Cape Verde
abolition of school fees *112m*
adult literacy *63*, *64m*, *182*
basic education 26
child mortality rate 35n
EDI *93*
education aid *165*
education expenditure 142, 143, 148
gender parity/disparity *82m*, *85m*, *184*
pre-primary education *37m*, *38-9*, *40*
primary education *42*, **43**, *45*, *55m*, *56*,
78, *113m*, *179*, *180*
teaching staff 40, *78*
capitation grants 153
CAQ, education quality tool (Brazil) **103**
carers/caregivers *see* mothers
Caribbean *see* Latin America and the
Caribbean; *individual countries*
Cash for Education (Bangladesh) 115
cash transfer programmes 114-17,
115-16, 153-4
Catalytic Fund 160, 188-9, 191
see also Fast Track Initiative
Cayman Islands
gender parity/disparity *82m*, *85m*, *184*
out-of-school children *50m*
pre-primary education *37m*, *40*
primary education *42*, **43**, *55m*, *78*, *180*
teaching staff *78*
Central African Republic
abolition of school fees *112m*
adult literacy 64, *64m*, 65n, *182*
EDI 93n
education aid *165*, 189, 189n, *190*
gender parity/disparity 81, 82, *82m*
non-formal learning 61
out-of-school children 50n
pre-primary education *37m*, *38-9*
primary education 41, *42*, 53
Central Asia
see also individual countries
adult literacy *63*, 65, 181
ECCE programmes 35

EDI *93*
education aid **163**, *163*
education expenditure 142, 143, 146,
146, 148
fragile states 21
GDP *185*
gender parity/disparity 79, *80*, 81, 83,
84, 86
governance 20
learning assessments 69
learning environment 72, 74
out-of-school children 49, *50m*, 51
pre-primary education 35, *36*, *37m*,
38-9, 40
primary education 41, *41*, *42*, **43**, 44,
44, 45, 53, 54, *55m*, *56*, 73, *80*, 83
secondary education 56-7, 57, 58, *58*,
59, *80*, 84
teaching staff 75, *75*, *76*, 77, *78*, 87, *185*
tertiary education *59*, *80*, 86, *92*
Central and Eastern Europe
see also individual countries
adult literacy *63*, 181
EDI *93*
education aid **163**
education expenditure 142, *142*, 146,
146, 148
gender parity/disparity 79, *80*, 81, 84,
86, 183
governance 20
learning assessments **68**, 69, *69*
learning environment 72
out-of-school children 49, *50m*, 51
pre-primary education *36*, *37m*, *38-9*,
40, 179
primary education 41, *42*, **43**, 44, 44,
45, 53, 54, *55m*, *56*, 73, *80*, 83
secondary education 56-7, 57, 58, *58*,
59, *80*, 84
teaching staff 75, *75*, *76*, *78*, 87, *185*
tertiary education *59*, *80*, 86, *92*
Chad
abolition of school fees *112m*
adult literacy 64, *64m*, 65n, *182*, 190
EDI 93, 93n, 94, 95
education aid 158, *158*, *165*, *175*, 189,
189n, *190*
education expenditure 142, *144-5*
gender parity/disparity 81, 82, *82m*, 83,
84, *85m*, 90, *184*
learning environment 74
non-formal learning 61, *61*, 123
out-of-school children *48*, *50m*, 50n,
51
post-conflict education 136
pre-primary education *37m*, 38, *38-9*
primary education 41, *42*, 45, 46, 47,
47, 48, 53, 54, *54*, *55m*, *78*, *113m*,
180, 181n
teaching staff 75, 77, *78*, *78*, *79*
child abuse, in schools 86
child health and nutrition, programmes
18-19, 23, 35, 124
child labour 114, 118-20, *119*, 193
child mortality rate 32, 35
child soldiers 136, **137**
Child Support Grant (South Africa) 116
Chile
abolition of school fees *112m*
adult literacy *64m*, *182*
child mortality rate 35n
education costs 150
education expenditure *144-5*, *150*
education management 101
gender parity/disparity *82m*, **84**, *85m*,
88, *90*, *184*
effect of health and nutrition
programmes 124
use of ICT 135
learning assessments 70, *71*, 133
learning environment 73

non-formal learning 61
non-government schools 105
out-of-school children *50m*
pre-primary education *36*, *37m*, *38-9*
primary education *42*, 47, 48, *55m*,
113m
teaching staff 126
tertiary education *92*
China
abolition of school fees *112m*
adult literacy 64, *64m*, 65, 122, *182*
basic education 26
curriculum 131, **132**
distance learning 134
education aid 159
education aid donor 162
education costs 152
education management 101
education policies 20n
ethnic minorities 23
ethnic populations 120
gender parity/disparity *82m*, 84, *85m*,
89, *184*
HIV/AIDS 18n
non-formal learning 60, 61
out-of-school children 50, 152
pre-primary education *37m*, *38-9*
primary education *42*, 45, 46, 46, 47, **51**
private education 36-7
school expansion 109
teaching staff 127, 128
violence and abuse 86
China-Africa Development Fund 162
civil rights **16**, *20*
civil society organizations (CSOs) 194
and democracy 20
funding of capital costs **110**
partnerships with *99*, 101-4, **102**, **103**,
110, 173-4, 193
CLADE **103**
Classroom Galang sa Mamamayang
Pilipino Abroad (Philippines) **110**
classroom shortages 110
Classrooms from Filipinos Overseas
(Philippines) **110**
cluster-based mentoring, teacher
programme **130**
coalitions *see* national education
coalitions; partnerships
cohort completion rates 54-5, 54n, *56*
Colombia
abolition of school fees *112m*, 114
adult literacy *182*
cash transfers 115
distance learning 134
education expenditure *144-5*, 154
gender parity/disparity *82m*, 83, *83*,
85m, *184*
learning assessments 67, 70, *71*, 72,
72
learning environment 73
non-formal learning 61
non-government schools 104
out-of-school children *50m*
pre-primary education *37m*, *38-9*
primary education 45, 46, 46, 47, 54,
55m, *56*, *113m*, *180*
tertiary education *92*
Committee on the Rights of the Child 17
Commonwealth of Independent States
(CIS) 19
community financing 110
community involvement, programmes to
improve gender parity 117
community learning centres 60-1
community teachers (contract) 78-9, *79*,
127-8
Comoros
abolition of school fees *112m*
education aid *165*, 189, 189n, *190*

gender parity/disparity *82m*, 83, *85m*,
184
non-formal learning *61*
out-of-school children 50n
pre-primary education *37m*, *38-9*
primary education 41, *42*, 53, *55m*,
113m
tertiary education *92*
compensatory programmes **107**
completion rates *see* school completion
compulsory education 17, 24, 35, 58, 93,
109, 110
see also universal primary education
concession school programme (Colombia)
104-5
conditional cash transfer (CCT)
programmes 153-4
conflicts
see also fragile states
and education 33, 74, 99, 136-7, 136n
Congo
abolition of school fees *112m*
adult literacy *64m*, *182*
EDI 93n
education aid 158, *158*, *165*, *175*
education expenditure 142, 143, 144,
144-5, *145*, 146, 147, 148
gender parity/disparity *82m*, 84, *85m*,
184
out-of-school children *50m*, 50n
pre-primary education 36, *37m*, 39, 40
primary education 41, *42*, 53, 54, *55m*,
113m
teaching staff 40, *40*, 77, *78*, *79*
Congo, Democratic Republic *see*
Democratic Republic of the Congo
construction costs, school buildings 110
continuing education, teachers 127, 130
continuous assessment 133-4
contract teachers 78-9, *79*, 127-8
Convention on the Elimination of All
Forms of Discrimination against
Women (1979) **16**
Convention on the Rights of the Child
(CRC) (1989) **16**, 17, 24
Convention on the Rights of Persons with
Disabilities (2006) **16**, 120-1
Cook Islands
gender parity/disparity *82m*, *85m*, *184*
pre-primary education *37m*
primary education *42*, *113m*
corporal punishment 86
corruption 20, 172
Costa Rica
abolition of school fees *112m*
adult literacy *64m*, *182*
distance learning 134
education expenditure *144-5*
gender parity/disparity *82m*, 83, *85m*,
184
learning assessments 71
non-formal learning 61
pre-primary education 36, *37m*, *38-9*,
39, 40
primary education 47, *55m*, *56*, *78*,
113m
teaching staff *78*
tertiary education *92*
Côte d'Ivoire
abolition of school fees *112m*
adult literacy 64, *64m*, 65n, *182*
compulsory education 25
debt relief 164
education aid 158, *158*, *165*, 189, 189n,
190
gender parity/disparity 81, 82, *82m*, 89,
184
non-formal learning 61, *61*, 123
out-of-school children 50, *50m*, 50n, *51*
pre-primary education *37m*, *38-9*, 40

primary education 41, *42, 45, 46,*
113m, 180, 181n
teaching staff *79*
countries in transition *see* transition
countries
CRC (Convention on the Rights of the
Child) **16**, 17, 24
crisis situations *see* conflicts; fragile
states
Croatia
abolition of school fees *112m*
adult literacy *64m, 182*
child mortality rate 35n
EDI *94*
ethnic populations 120
gender parity/disparity *82m, 85m, 184*
out-of-school children *50m*
pre-primary education *37m, 38-9*
primary education *42, 45, 55m, 113m,*
180
tertiary education *92*
cross-cultural studies, education 23
Cuba
abolition of school fees *112m*
adult literacy *64m, 182*
child mortality rate 35n
EDI *94*
education policies 20n
gender parity/disparity *82m, 85m, 184*
out-of-school children *50m*
pre-primary education *37m, 40*
primary education *43,* 48, *55m, 59, 78,*
113m, 180
teaching staff *78, 126*
curriculum
child-centred and outcome-oriented
130-1, **132**
gender neutrality 88, 89-90, *90*
inclusive 193
national assessments of learning 69
secondary education **57**
Cyprus
abolition of school fees *112m*
adult literacy *64m, 182*
EDI *94*
education expenditure *144-5*
gender parity/disparity *82m, 85m, 184*
out-of-school children *50m*
pre-primary education *37m, 38-9*
primary education *55m, 113m, 180*
tertiary education *92*
Czech Republic
abolition of school fees *112m*
adult literacy *64m*
education aid donor 162
education expenditure *144-5, 150*
ethnic populations 120
gender parity/disparity *82m, 85m, 184*
learning assessments **68**
out-of-school children *50m*
pre-primary education *37m*
primary education *45, 55m, 113m*
tertiary education *92*
Czechoslovakia *see* Czech Republic;
Slovakia

D

Dakar Framework for Action 98-100, *99,*
141
see also EFA goals
initiatives 27
key elements 14-15, **15**, 26-7
progress towards 172-5
Dakar World Education Forum
see also EFA goals
agencies 14n
EFA conception 12, **14**
goals and strategies 14-15, **15**, 26-7,
98-100, *99,* **99**
debt relief
decline 141, 187

increase 22, 154, 162, 164, 173
decentralization, education management
106-7
democracy 20, 24
Democratic People's Republic of Korea
abolition of school fees *112m*
compulsory education *25*
education aid *165*
education policies 20n
Democratic Republic of the Congo
abolition of school fees *112m*
adult literacy *64m,* 65n, *182*
basic education *26*
debt relief 164
EDI 93n
education aid *165,* 189, 189n, *190*
education costs 152
gender parity/disparity 81, 82, *82m,*
85m, 184
non-formal learning *61*
out-of-school children 50n
pre-primary education *37m, 38-9*
primary education 41, *42, 113m*
Denmark
abolition of school fees *112m*
education aid donor 160, *161, 162, 166,*
187
education expenditure 52n, *144-5, 150,*
150
gender parity/disparity *82m, 85m,* 90,
184
out-of-school children *50m*
pre-primary education *37m*
primary education *55m, 113m, 180*
tertiary education *92*
Department for International Development
(DFID) 166-7
deprivation *see* disadvantage; exclusion;
household wealth; inequality;
inequity; marginalization; poverty
developed countries
see also OECD countries
educational achievement 68-9
gender parity 79
industrial relocation 20
literacy 63
out-of-school children 51
pre-primary education 36, 40
primary education *41,* 44, 49, 53
secondary education 58, *58*
teaching staff *75, 76*
tertiary education 59, *59*
developing countries
see also least developed countries;
low-income countries; middle-
income developing countries
aid projections *187*
diseases 18
see also HIV/AIDS
effect of economic growth 19
education aid 156, *156,* 165, *165*
education expenditure 150
educational achievement 67, 68-9
literacy 63, 64-5
low quality of education 34
ODA *see* ODA
out-of-school children 49, *51*
population growth 17-18
pre-primary education 36-7, *36, 40*
primary education 17, 18, *41,* 44
secondary education *58*
teaching staff *75, 76,* **76**
tertiary education 59, *59*
under-5 mortality rate 35
deworming programmes 23, 124
Directorate for the Promotion of Girls'
Education (Burkina Faso) 118
disabilities
rights **16**, 120-1
and school attendance 48-9, *48*
disadvantage

see also access to education; ethnicity;
exclusion; inclusive education;
inequality; inequity; marginalization;
poverty
effect on girls 34, 81-2
inclusive policies 192, 192-3
and provision of private education 104
targeted programmes 114-17, *115,*
115-16, 118
disbursements of ODA 21, *21, 22,* 154,
156, *157,* 160, 187
discrimination
see also gender bias; stereotyping
ethnic 120
human rights legislation **16**
diseases
see also HIV/AIDS
effect on education 18, 19
disparity *see* disadvantage; educational
disparity; gender parity/disparity;
geographic disparity; inequity
distance education 134-5, **134**
Djibouti
abolition of school fees *112m*
basic education *26*
compulsory education *25*
education aid *158,* 165
education expenditure 142
gender parity/disparity 81, *82m,* 84,
85m, 184
out-of-school children *50m,* 50n
pre-primary education *37m, 38-9, 39,*
40
primary education 41, 42, *43,* 44, 45,
46, 53, *113m, 180,* 181n
secondary education 57
teaching staff 77
domestic expenditure on education *see*
governments, education
expenditure
Dominica
gender parity/disparity *82m, 85m, 184*
out-of-school children *50m*
pre-primary education *37m, 38-9, 40*
primary education *42, 43, 45, 54, 55m,*
56, 78, 113m, 180
teaching staff *78*
Dominican Republic
abolition of school fees *112m*
adult literacy *64m, 182*
compulsory education *25*
distance learning 134
EDI *94*
education expenditure 142, 143, 147
gender parity/disparity *82m,* 83, *85m,*
184
non-formal learning *61*
out-of-school children *50m*
pre-primary education *37m, 38-9, 40*
primary education *43, 45, 47, 54, 55m,*
78, 113m, 179, 180
teaching staff *78*
violence and abuse 86
donors
aid to basic education *161,* 174
and capacity building 164-5, 170, 171
commitments and disbursements 21-
2, *21, 23,* 154, 156, *157, 158, 159,*
160, *161, 162*
education strategies 160, 166, 191
funding of fee abolition 153
increase in aid 21, 194
influences on 159
partnerships 174, 186
projected aid 187-8
reduction in aid 160-1
relationship with governments 141,
166, 170
role 186-7
strategies 160-1, 164-9
dropout

see also out-of-school children; school
completion; school participation
from primary education 50, *52, 52,* 55,
152
from secondary education **84**

E

E-9 initiative 93n
early childhood care and education (ECCE)
see also pre-primary education
access 95, 192
neglect of 13, 194
participation 43, 44, 179
programmes 34-7, 36, 108-9
progress towards 28, 32-40, 95
research 23
trends 179
East Asia and the Pacific
see also individual countries
adult literacy 33, 63, *63,* 65, 181
child mortality rate 35
ECCE programmes 108
economic growth 19
EDI 93, *93,* 94
education aid **163**, *163,* 171
education expenditure 142, *142,* 143,
146, *146,* 148, 149, 157
EFA coalitions **103**
fragile states *21*
GDP *185*
gender parity/disparity 79, 80, 81, 83,
83, 84, *84,* 86, 90, 183
learning assessments 69, *69,* 71
learning environment 72, 125
monitoring EFA 101n
ODA *22*
out-of-school children 49, *50m,* 51
pre-primary education 33, 35, *36, 37m,*
38-9, 40
primary education 41, *41, 42, 43, 43,*
44, *44,* 45, 52n, 53, 54, 55m, 56, 73,
80, 83
secondary education 34, 56-7, 57, 58,
58, 59, 80, 84
teaching staff 75, *75,* 76, 78, 87, 185,
185
tertiary education 59, 80, 86, *92*
Eastern Europe *see* Central and Eastern
Europe; *individual countries*
economic development, impact of aid 169
economic growth 19
Ecuador
abolition of school fees *112m*
adult literacy *64m, 182*
basic education *26*
cash transfers *115*
child mortality rate 35n
distance learning 134
EDI 93, *94*
ethnic populations 120
gender parity/disparity *82m, 85m, 184*
learning environment 73
out-of-school children *50m*
pre-primary education *37m, 38-9,* 39
primary education *43,* 48, *55m,* 56,
113m, 180
teaching staff 127
EDI 91-5, *93,* 94-5
education
see also early childhood care and
education; pre-primary education;
primary education; 'school' *entries*;
secondary education; tertiary
education
access *see* access to education
aid *see* education aid
expenditure *see* education expenditure;
governments, education
expenditure
quality *see* quality of education

education aid 154-72, **155**, *156, 157, 165,*
  186-91
  see also basic education, aid
  capacity building 164-5, 170, 171
  countries receiving most *159*
  donors *see* donors, aid
  integrated strategies 188-9
  monitoring 165
  need for increase 194
  new modalities 164-9
  non-formal education programmes 60
  pre-primary 160
  primary 114-17, *115-16,* 160, 169, 190
  programmatic approach 169
  proportion of education expenditure
    174
  prospects *187*
  for secondary and tertiary education
    191
  share of total aid 173
  textbook provision 74
education costs
  policies reducing 78
  share of household expenditure 149-
    54, *150,* 151-2, *152,* 153, 159-64,
    172, 193
education expenditure
  governments *see* governments,
    education expenditure
  by households 149-54, *150,* 151-2, *152,*
    153, 159-64, 172, 195
Education for All *see* EFA
Education for All: The Quality Imperative
  28
education laws 107
education management 101, 101n, 106-7
Education Management Information
  Systems (EMIS) 101, 101n
education plans 100-1, 167, 173, 174, 194
education report cards **104**
Education Sector Development
  Programmes (Ethiopia) 117
education sector plans 100-1, 167, 173,
  174, 194
education trends 22-7
educational attainment
  see also school achievement
  through non-formal learning 61, *61*
  trends 70-1, *71*
educational disparity 13, 33, 44-9, **52,** 68,
  68, 95
educational outcomes *see* learning
  outcomes
educational reform 13
EDUSAT (India) **134**
EFA
  attempts at global approach 27
  conception 12, 13, **14**
  global priorities 191-2
  goals *see* EFA goals
  international architecture 26-7, 192
  responsibility of governments 192
  strategies 14-15, **15,** 98-100, *99,* **99**
  World Declaration **14**
EFA Assessment 13
EFA coalitions **103**
EFA Development Index 91-5, *93,* 94-5
EFA goals 14, **15,** 32-3
  goal 1, early childhood care and
    education 32-3, 34-40, 95, 179
  access 95, 192
  neglect of 13, 194
  participation 43, 44, 179
  programmes 34-7, 36, 108-9
  progress towards 28, 32-40, 95
  research 23
  trends 179
  goal 2, universal primary education
  see also compulsory education;
    primary education
  aid 190

  in EFA priorities 192
  Millennium Development Goal 14
  monitoring **51**
  progress towards 41-59, 92, 93, 95,
    180
  trends 179-81
  goal 3, learning and life skills
    monitoring **60**
  neglect 13, 33
  programmes 60-1, 119, 121-3, 193
  progress towards 59-61, 95
  trends 181
  goal 4, adult literacy
  see also youth literacy
  aid 160
  definition 62, 62n
  EDI indicator 95
  government responsibilities 192, 193
  learning assessments **62**, *62,* 69, *69*
  monitoring 62, **62,** *63,* 66
  multilingual activities 131-2
  non-state providers 122-3
  programmes 60, 121-3, **133**
  progress towards 33, 62-6, *182,* 190
  trends 181-2
  goal 5, gender parity
  adult literacy *63,* 65
  curriculum subjects 89-90, *90*
  EDI indicator 95
  use of female teachers 128, **128**
  and gender equality 23, 28, 117-18
  government responsibilities 192, 193
  learning outcomes 95
  Millennium Development Goal 14
  missed target 12, 33-4
  pre-primary education 37-9
  primary education 33, 80-3, *80*
  progress towards 28, 79-92, 95
  secondary education 33, 83-4
  tertiary education 84
  trends 183, *184*
  goal 6, quality of education
  benefits 24
  EDI indicator 93
  government responsibilities 192, 193,
    194
  improving 25-6, 123-36, **123**
  in non-state schools 105
  progress towards 28, 34, 66-9, 95
  trends 183-5
  and education expenditure 186
  and education plans 100, 194
  progress towards 32-4, 33, **51,** 92-5,
    99, 108, 191
  secondary education 56
  tertiary education 56
  trends 17-23, 178-85
EFA strategies 14-15, **15,** 98-100, *99,* **99**
Egypt
  abolition of school fees *112m*
  adult literacy 63, 64, *64m, 182,* 190
  child mortality rate 35n
  compulsory education *25*
  EDI 93
  education costs 151
  gender parity/disparity *82m, 85m, 184*
  non-formal learning 60
  out-of-school children *48, 50m*
  pre-primary education *37m, 38-9*
  primary education 41, *42, **43,** 45, 46,*
    47, 47, 48, *55m, 113m, 179, 180*
  school expansion 109
  school networking **135**
El Salvador
  abolition of school fees *112m*
  adult literacy *64m,* 65, *182*
  civil society organizations 102n
  EDI 93
  education expenditure 142, *144-5*
  gender parity/disparity *82m, 83, 85m,*
    90, 184

  learning assessments 70, *71,* 72, *72*
  out-of-school children *50m*
  pre-primary education *37m, 38-9,* 40
  primary education *43, 47, 55m, 56, 78,*
    106, *113m, 180*
  teaching staff *78,* 126
  tertiary education *92*
emergency contexts *see* conflicts
EMIS 101, 101n
employment, women 23, 87, *87,* 129, **129**
Enciclomedia (Mexico) 126
Enhanced Heavily Indebted Poor Countries
  (HIPC) Initiative 153, 162-3, 164
Enlaces (Chile) 135
enrolment
  and abolition of school fees 111-13,
    113m
  effect of aid 114-17, *115-16,* 160, 169
  basic education 110
  and classroom shortages 110
  and education expenditure 148, 152
  effect of expansion 109, 149
  factors affecting 18, 35, 124, 152
  and gender parity 81
  out-of-school children *51*
  post-secondary education *57*
  pre-primary education 32-3, 35, *36, 37,*
    38-9, 104, 109
  effect of aid 160
  private programmes 36-7
  primary education
  change in 17
  and decentralization 106
  and funding 110, 111-12
  geographic disparity 46, *46,* 47
  grade 1 41
  increases 42-4, **43,** *44, 45,* 50, 54, 127
  trends 93, 179, *180,* 186
  progress towards goals 12-13
  and pupil/teacher ratio 40, 75, 109
  secondary education 33, 56-7, *58, 59,*
    84, **84,** *85*
  tertiary 59, *59*
  TVET programmes 58
entrants to primary school 41, *41, **43,** 44*
  see also gross intake rate
environments
  learning 28, 72-4, 86-7, *99,* 108, 125-6
  literate 28, 65-6
equality *see* equity; gender equality;
  inequality
Equatorial Guinea
  abolition of school fees *112m*
  adult literacy *64m, 182*
  compulsory education 24
  education aid *165*
  education expenditure 143
  gender parity/disparity 81, *82m*
  out-of-school children *50m*
  pre-primary education *37m,* 38, *38-9*
  primary education *45,* 53, *113m, 180*
  teaching staff 77
equity
  see also gender equality; gender
    parity/disparity; inequality; inequity
  challenges 13
  in education expenditure 148-9, *149,*
    149
  importance of goal 34
  in land ownership 18n
equivalency education programmes 60
Eritrea
  abolition of school fees *112m*
  curriculum 131
  EDI 93n
  education aid *158, 165, 175,* 189, 189n,
    190
  education expenditure *144-5,* 147
  ethnic populations 120
  gender parity/disparity *82m, 83, 85m,*
    184

  out-of-school children *50m,* 50n
  pre-primary education 36, *37m, 38-9,*
    40
  primary education 41, *42, **43,** 45, 46,*
    46, 47, 53, 54, *54, 55m, 56, 78,*
    113m, 180, 181n
  school expansion 110
  teaching staff 40, *76,* 77, *78*
  tertiary education *92*
Estonia
  abolition of school fees *112m*
  adult literacy *64m, 182*
  EDI 94
  education expenditure *144-5*
  gender parity/disparity *82m, 85m, 184*
  out-of-school children *50m*
  pre-primary education *37m*
  primary education *55m, 113m, 180*
  tertiary education *92*
Ethiopia
  abolition of school fees *112m*
  adult literacy 64, *64m,* 65n
  basic education *26*
  compulsory education *25*
  curriculum **132**
  debt relief 164
  decentralization 106
  ECCE programmes 108
  EDI *94,* 95
  education aid *165,* 167, 168, *175,* 187,
    189, 189n, *190*
  education expenditure 142, 144, *144-5,*
    145, 149, 174
  ethnic populations 120
  gender parity/disparity 81, *82m, 85m,*
    117, *184*
  geographic disparity 111
  inclusive education 121
  learning assessments 70, *71,* 133
  learning environment 125
  non-formal learning 60
  out-of-school children *48,* 50, *50m,* 51
  pre-primary education *37m, 38-9*
  primary education 41, *42, **43,** 44, 44n,*
    45, 45, 46, 46, *47, 47,* 48, 53, 54,
    55m, 78, 113m, 180
  private education 36-7
  school expansion 109, 110
  secondary education 57, 75
  teaching staff 77, *78,* 126, 128, 129, **129**
  tertiary education *92*
ethnicity
  barrier to education 23, 48, 120
  and migration 18
Europe
  see also Central and Eastern Europe;
    North America and Western
    Europe; *individual countries*
  GDP *185*
European Commission, education aid
  donor 160, *161, 162,* 167
European Union, ODA *23*
evaluation *see* monitoring
exclusion
  see also access to education;
    disadvantage; ethnicity; inclusive
    education; inequality; inequity;
    marginalization
  education policies addressing 120-1
  and literacy 65
extreme poverty rate 19

F

'faire-faire' Senegalese literacy model
  122-3
Familias en Acción (Colombia) *115,* 153
Family Allowance Programme (Honduras)
  115, 116
family structure, changes 18
Fast Track Initiative
  allocation of aid 160

commitments *161, 162*
coordination of donors 27
development 188-9
and education plans 167, 173, 174
limitations 13
measurement of quality 26
female, *see also* girls; mothers; women
Female Secondary School Stipend
  (Bangladesh) *115*
Female Secondary School Stipend
  (Pakistan) *116*
female teachers 87, *87*, 129, **129**
feminization
  of agriculture 18n
  of HIV/AIDS 18n
Fiji
  abolition of school fees *112m*
  EDI *94*
  education expenditure *144-5*
  gender parity/disparity *82m, 85m, 184*
  out-of-school children *50m*
  pre-primary education *37m, 38-9*
  primary education *43, 55m, 113m, 180*
  private education 36-7
finance
  see also education aid; funding
  for EFA 192, 194
financial incentives
  to reduce child labour 118-19
  for teachers 126, 128, 129
Finland
  abolition of school fees *112m*
  education aid donor 160, *161, 162*, 166,
    187
  education expenditure *144-5*, 150, *150*
  ethnic populations 120
  gender parity/disparity *82m, 85m*, 183,
    184
  out-of-school children *50m*
  pre-primary education *37m, 38-9*
  primary education *43, 55m, 113m, 180*
  tertiary education *92*
flexible schooling 119, 120
Focusing Resources on Effective School
  Health (FRESH) 124-5, 125n
for-profit sector *see* private education
former Yugoslav Republic of Macedonia
  see the former Yugoslav Republic of
  Macedonia
fragile states 21, *21*, 33, 157, 192
  see also conflicts
  EDI 93, 93n
  education aid 189
  educational programmes 136-7
  gender parity 81
  increase in aid 194
  learning assessments 69
  out-of-school children 50
  UPE 179, 181
  utilization of aid 191
Framework for Action *see* Dakar
  Framework for Action
France
  abolition of school fees *112m*
  education aid donor 23, 159, 160, 161,
    161, 162, 187
  education expenditure *144-5, 150*
  gender parity/disparity *82m, 85m*, 87,
    184
  out-of-school children *50m*
  pre-primary education *37m*
  primary education *113m, 180*
  teaching staff 87, 88
Free Education for Normal University
  Students (China) 128
free primary education 24
  see also education costs
FRESH, healthy school environments 124-
  5, 125n
FTI *see* Fast Track Initiative

Fund for the Maintenance and
  Development of Basic Education
  and Valorization of Teaching
  (FUNDEB) 108, 111
FUNDEF 111
funding
  basic education *99*, 111
  capital costs 110
  education 24-5, 153, **163**, 194
  see also education aid
further education *see* learning and life
  skills; post-secondary non-tertiary
  education; tertiary education

G

G8 summits 14, 22, 27
Gabon
  abolition of school fees *112m*
  adult literacy *64m, 182*
  gender parity/disparity *82m, 83*
  primary education 42, 53, 54, *55m, 113m*
  teaching staff 77n
Gambia
  abolition of school fees *112m*
  compulsory education 25
  EDI 93n
  education aid *165, 175*, 189, 189n, *190*
  education expenditure 142, 144, *144-5,
    145, 146, 174*
  education plans 100n
  gender parity/disparity 81, *82m, 84,
    85m, 183, 184*
  geographic disparity 111
  non-formal learning 61, *61*, 123
  out-of-school children *50m, 50n*
  poverty reduction programmes 164
  pre-primary education 36, *37m, 38-9*
  primary education 42, 45, 46, *46, 47,
    113m, 180*
  private education 36-7
  tertiary education *92*
Gates Foundation 162
GCE (Global Campaign for Education) 102,
  102
GDP
  debt service ratio 162
  education expenditure share 162
  growth rate 19, *185*
GEI (gender-specific EFA index) 92
gender bias
  see also stereotyping
  in schools 34, 87, **89**, 90-1
  textbooks 88-9
*Gender and Education for All: The Leap to
  Equality* 28
gender equality
  and abuse in schools 125
  and EFA goals 34, 193
  and gender parity 23, 28
  and MDG 14
  requirements for 85-91
  strategies in education *99*
gender inequality
  and agriculture 18n
  employment 23
gender parity/disparity (EFA goal)
  adult literacy *63*, 65
  curriculum subjects 89-90, *90*
  EDI indicator 92, 95
  use of female teachers 128, **128**
  and gender equality 23, 28, 117-18
  government responsibilities 192, 193
  learning outcomes 95
  Millennium Development Goal 14
  missed target 12, 33-4
  pre-primary education 37-9
  primary education 33, 80-3, *80*
  progress towards 79-92, 95
  secondary education 33, 83-4
  tertiary education 84
  trends 183, *184*

gender parity index
  adult literacy *63*, 65
  pre-primary education 37
  primary education *80, 81*
  secondary education *80, 84*
  tertiary education *80*, 84
gender roles/stereotyping
  in early education 34
  and learning outcomes 91
gender-specific EFA index 92
geographic disparity 45-6, *46, 47, 70, 72,
  72, 107*, 111-12
Georgia
  abolition of school fees *112m*
  compulsory education 25
  education expenditure 142, *144-5*
  gender parity/disparity *82m, 85m, 184*
  out-of-school children *50m*
  pre-primary education 36, *37m*, 38,
    38-9
  primary education *43, 55m, 113m, 180*
  tertiary education 92
GER *see* gross enrolment ratio
Germany
  abolition of school fees *112m*
  compulsory education 24
  education aid donor 23, 159, 160, 161,
    162, 187, 188
  education expenditure *144-5, 150*
  gender parity/disparity *82m, 85m, 184*
  learning assessments 67
  pre-primary education *37m*
  primary education *55m, 113m*
Ghana
  abolition of school fees *112m*
  adult literacy *64m*, **133**, *182*, 190
  compulsory education 25
  debt relief 164
  decentralization 107
  education aid 153, *159*, 160, *165*, 167,
    175, 189, 189n, *190*
  education expenditure 144, *144-5*, 174
  gender parity/disparity 81, *82m, 83,
    85m, 90, 184*
  governance 20
  learning environment 125
  non-formal learning 60
  out-of-school children 48, *50m*, 51
  poverty reduction programmes 164
  pre-primary education 36, *37m, 38-9,
    40*
  primary education 41, 42, **43**, 45, 46,
    46, 47, 48, *55m*, 56, 78, *113m*, 179,
    180
  teaching staff 40, **76**, *78*, 126
  tertiary education *92*
  violence and abuse 86
Gini coefficient 19
GIR (gross intake rate) 41, *41, 42*
girls
  see also 'gender' entries; women
  access to education 13, 34, 80-1
  benefit from education expenditure
    149
  effect of cash transfer programmes
    114, *115-16*
  effect of disadvantaged backgrounds
    34
  experience of violence 86
  effect of female teachers 128, **128**
  gender parity programmes 117-18,
    137
  effect of nutrition programmes 124
  performance 70, 89, *89*, 91
  pre-primary education 37-8
  primary education 81-3, *83*
  school attendance 49, 86-7, 153
  secondary education 83, **84**
  teacher expectations 87
Girls' Education Advisory Committees
  (Ethiopia) 125

Gleneagles Summit 14, 22, *23*
global action plan for EFA 27
Global Action Week 26, **102**
Global Campaign for Education (GCE) 102,
  102
Global Monitoring Reports 27, 28, 101,
  107
global population 17-18
global trends, affecting education 17-22
GMR 27, 28, 101, 107
GNP (gross national product) 141-6, *142,
  143, 145, 146, 147, 148, 172, 174,
  174, 186*
governance
  education *99*
  progress 20
governments
  basic education policies 58, *99*
  and donor aid 141, 166, 170
  early childhood provision 34-7, 36, 95,
    108-9
  education expenditure 140, 141-9, *142,
    144-5, 146*, 149, 173, 186
  funding arrangements 150, *150, 151*
  growth 174-5, *175*
  and IMF 171
  and poverty reduction measures 19,
    99, 162, 163-4
  effect of school fee abolition 153-4
  trends 185-6, *185*
  education programmes *see*
    programmes
  exclusion, policies on 120-1
  focus for Framework for Action 192-4
  partnerships with non-state providers
    104-5, 122-3
  relationship with CSOs *99*, 101-4, **102**,
    103, **110**, 173-4
  responsibility for EFA 194
  school fee policies 112-14
GPI *see* gender parity index
grade 1 *see* entrants to primary school
grade 5 *see* survival rate to last grade
grade repetition
  see also school progression
  and achievement 70
  primary schools 52-3, **52**
  reduction **107**
Greece
  abolition of school fees *112m*
  adult literacy *64m*, 181, *182*
  education aid donor *161, 162, 187*
  education expenditure *144-5, 150*
  ethnic populations 120
  gender parity/disparity *82m, 85m, 184*
  learning assessments 67
  out-of-school children *50m*
  pre-primary education *37m, 38-9*
  primary education *43, 45, 55m, 113m,
    180*
  tertiary education *92*
Grenada
  abolition of school fees *112m*
  gender parity/disparity *82m, 85m*
  out-of-school children *50m*
  pre-primary education *37m, 38-9, 39,
    40*
  primary education 55, *55m*, 56, 78, *180*
  teaching staff 78
Grenadines *see* Saint Vincent and the
  Grenadines
gross enrolment ratio
  pre-primary education 35, 36, *36, 37,
    38-9*
  primary education 44, 81, *113m*, 127,
    149
  secondary education 59, 84
  tertiary education 59
gross intake rate, primary education 41,
  41, 42

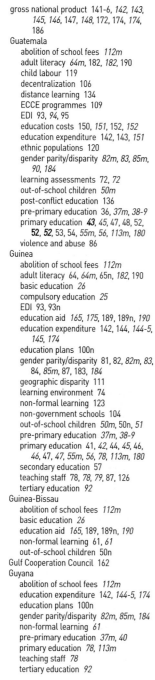

gross national product 141-6, *142, 143,*
145, 146, 147, *148,* 172, 174, *174,*
186
Guatemala
abolition of school fees *112m*
adult literacy *64m,* 182, *182,* 190
child labour 119
decentralization 106
distance learning 134
ECCE programmes 109
EDI 93, *94,* 95
education costs 150, *151,* 152, *152*
education expenditure 142, 143, *151*
ethnic populations 120
gender parity/disparity *82m, 83, 85m,*
90, 184
learning assessments 72, *72*
out-of-school children *50m*
post-conflict education 136
pre-primary education 36, *37m, 38-9*
primary education *43, 45,* 47, 48, 52,
52, *52,* 53, 54, *55m,* 56, *113m, 180*
violence and abuse 86
Guinea
abolition of school fees *112m*
adult literacy 64, *64m,* 65n, *182,* 190
basic education 26
compulsory education *25*
EDI 93, 93n
education aid 165, *175,* 189, 189n, 190
education expenditure 142, 144, *144-5,*
145, 174
education plans 100n
gender parity/disparity 81, 82, *82m, 83,*
84, 85m, 87, *183, 184*
geographic disparity 111
learning environment 74
non-formal learning 123
non-government schools 104
out-of-school children *50m,* 50n, 51
pre-primary education *37m, 38-9*
primary education 41, *42, 44, 45, 46,*
46, 47, 47, 55m, 56, *78, 113m, 180*
secondary education 57
teaching staff 78, *78, 79,* 87, 126
tertiary education *92*
Guinea-Bissau
abolition of school fees *112m*
basic education 26
education aid 165, *189,* 189n, *190*
non-formal learning 61, *61*
out-of-school children 50n
Gulf Cooperation Council 162
Guyana
abolition of school fees *112m*
education expenditure 142, *144-5, 174*
education plans 100n
gender parity/disparity *82m, 85m, 184*
non-formal learning *61*
pre-primary education *37m, 40*
primary education *78, 113m*
teaching staff *78*
tertiary education *92*

H

Haiti
abolition of school fees *112m*
basic education 26
compulsory education *25*
EDI 93n
education aid 165, *189,* 189n, *190*
gender parity/disparity *90*
learning assessments 70
out-of-school children 50n
primary education *47, 47*
health *see* child health and nutrition;
HIV/AIDS
Herzegovina *see* Bosnia and Herzegovina
Hewlett Foundation 162
high-income countries

education expenditure 142, *143,* 147,
147, 172
gender disparity 118
service industries 20
higher education *see* tertiary education
HIPC Initiative 153, 162-3, 164
HIV/AIDs
curriculum for **132**
and education programmes *99*
and mortality rate 18
effect on school participation 19
effect on teaching staff 19, **76**
effect on women 18, 18n
holistic policies, for ECCE 28
home-based classrooms **137**
Honduras
abolition of school fees *112m*
adult literacy *64m,* 65, *182*
cash transfers *115,* 116
EDI 93
education aid 166
education expenditure 154
education plans 100n
gender parity/disparity *82m, 83, 83,*
85m, 90
learning assessments 70, 71, 72
out-of-school children *50m*
pre-primary education *37m, 38-9*
primary education *43,* 47, *55m,* 106
teaching staff 126
tertiary education *92*
violence and abuse 86
hours of instruction *see* instructional time
household costs
education expenditure 149-54, *150,*
151-2, *152,* 153, 159-64, 172, 193
and school attendance 112, *115-16,*
141, 152
household structures 18
household surveys, literacy 66
household wealth
see also disadvantage; household
costs; poverty
and ECCE participation 33
and educational attainment 61
and literacy 65
Human Development Voucher (Ecuador)
115
human immunodeficiency virus *see*
HIV/AIDS
human rights 16, **16,** *20,* 24
Hungary
abolition of school fees *112m*
adult literacy *64m*
EDI *94*
education expenditure *144-5, 150*
ethnic populations 120
gender parity/disparity *82m, 85m, 90,*
184
learning assessments 67, 68, 70
out-of-school children *50m*
pre-primary education *37m, 38-9*
primary education *43, 45, 55m, 113m,*
180
tertiary education *92*

I

Iceland
abolition of school fees *112m*
education expenditure 147, *150*
gender parity/disparity *82m, 85m, 89,*
90, 184
out-of-school children *50m*
pre-primary education *37m*
primary education *43,* 52n, *55m, 113m,*
180
tertiary education *92*
ICT, use in education 126, 134-6
IDA 160, *161, 162,* 188
IDB *161, 162, 163*
illiteracy *see* adult literacy

illness *see* disease
ILO Convention concerning Discrimination
in Respect of Employment and
Occupation (1958) 16
ILO Convention No. 169 concerning
Indigenous and Tribal Peoples in
Independent Countries (1989) 16
ILO Convention No. 182 concerning the
Prohibition and Immediate Action
for the Elimination of the Worst
Forms of Child Labour (1999) **16**
IMF 164, 171
immigrants
see also migration
education in European Union 120
immunization 19, 32, 35
incentives
see also financial incentives
to reduce child labour 118-19, *119,* 193
inclusive education 120-1, 192, 192-3
income *see* household wealth
India
abolition of school fees *112m*
adult literacy 64, *64m,* 65n, 182, *182*
child labour 119
civil society organizations **103**
distance learning 134, *134,* 135
ECCE programmes 109
EDI 93
education aid 159, *159,* 161, 165, 167,
174, *175,* 187, 189
education costs 149, 152
education expenditure *144-5,* 146, 150,
150
education plans 100n
education rights 24
ethnic populations 120
gender parity/disparity 81, *82m, 83,*
85m, 89, 117, 118, *184*
geographic disparity 111, 111-12
HIV/AIDS 18n
household size 18n
multilingual education 132-3
non-formal learning 60, 122
non-government schools 104
out-of-school children 49, *50m,* 51
pre-primary education 36, *37m, 38-9*
primary education 46, *46, 47, 54, 54,*
55m, 113m, 179, 180
school networking 135
teaching staff 77, 78n, 127, 128
indigenous populations
see also ethnicity
educational disparity 48
Indonesia
abolition of school fees *112m*
adult literacy 64, *64m, 182*
child mortality rate 35n
curriculum **132**
decentralization 106, 107
distance learning 134
education aid *159*
education costs 152
education expenditure 25, 142, *150*
education plans 100n
gender parity/disparity *82m, 83, 85m,*
184
HIV/AIDS 18n
learning assessments 67
non-formal learning 60, 61
out-of-school children 48, *50m,* 152
pre-primary education *37m, 38-9*
primary education *43, 43,* 45, 46, *46,*
47, 48, *55m, 179,* 180
private education 36-7
INEE 136
inequality
see also equity; inequity
and economic growth 19
and education expansion 23

inequity
see also access to education;
disadvantage; educational disparity;
equity; gender parity/disparity;
geographic disparity; inequality
in educational opportunity 13, 33, 44-9,
52, 68, **68,** 95
infants *see* under-3s
information and communication
technology (ICT), use in education
126, 134-6
infrastructure 74, 109, **110**
instructional time for learning 28, 67, 72,
73, **76,** 125
Inter-Agency Network for Education in
Emergencies (INEE) 136
Inter-American Development Bank (IDB)
Special Fund 161, 162, 163
Interactive Radio Instruction (IRI) 135
International Adult Literacy Survey (IALS)
66
international aid *see* education aid; ODA
International Bank for Reconstruction and
Development (IBRD) **163**
International Bill of Human Rights 16, **16,**
24
International Convention on the
Elimination of All Forms of Racial
Discrimination (1965) 16
International Convention on the Protection
of the Rights of All Migrant Workers
and Members of their Families
(1990) 16
International Covenant on Civil and
Political Rights (1966) 16
International Covenant on Economic,
Social and Cultural Rights (1966) **16**
International Development Association
(IDA) 160, *161, 162,* 188
international learning assessments 34,
67-8, 67n
International Monetary Fund (IMF) 164, 171
International Rescue Committee (IRC),
home-based classrooms **137**
Internet, school access **135**
Internship Programme for the Support of
Rural Schools (China) 128
investment projects 165
Iran *see* Islamic Republic of Iran
Iraq
adult literacy *64m, 182*
effect of conflict 74
EDI *94,* 95
education aid 22, *159*
gender parity/disparity *82m, 83, 85m,*
184
out-of-school children *50m,* 51
pre-primary education *37m, 38-9*
primary education 45, 46, *55m,* 56,
179, 180
tertiary education *92*
IRC, home based classrooms **137**
Ireland
abolition of school fees *112m*
education aid donor 160, *161, 162,* 187
education expenditure *144-5, 150*
gender parity/disparity *82m, 85m, 183,*
184
out-of-school children *50m*
primary education 45, **57,** *113m, 180*
ISCED
level 4 enrolments **57**
level 5 and 6 91
level 2 57-8, 59
level 3 58
and vocational education 58-9
Islamic Development Bank 162
Islamic Republic of Iran
abolition of school fees *112m*
adult literacy 63, *64m, 182*
child mortality rate 35n

compulsory education 24
education expenditure 143, *144-5*, 146
gender parity/disparity 81, *82m*, *85m*, 90, *90*, 184
learning assessments 67
out-of-school children *50m*, 51
pre-primary education 36, *37m*, 38, *38-9*
primary education *42*, **43**, 45, 46, *55m*, 78, *113m*, 180
teaching staff *78*
tertiary education *92*
Israel
abolition of school fees *112m*
education expenditure *144-5*
gender parity/disparity 23, *82m*, *85m*, 184
out-of-school children *50m*
pre-primary education *37m*
primary education *55m*, *113m*, 180
tertiary education *92*
Italy
abolition of school fees *112m*
adult literacy *64m*, *182*
EDI 94
education aid donor 23, *161*, 162, 187
education expenditure *144-5*, *150*
gender parity/disparity *82m*, *85m*, 184
learning assessments 67
out-of-school children *50m*
pre-primary education *37m*
primary education *55m*, *113m*, 180
tertiary education *92*
Ivory Coast *see* Cote d'Ivoire

J

Jamaica
abolition of school fees *112m*
adult literacy *64m*, 65
cash transfers *115*
compulsory education *25*
education costs *150*
education expenditure 143, *150*, *150*
gender parity/disparity *82m*, *83*, 84, *85m*, 184
out-of-school children 48, *50m*
pre-primary education *37m*
primary education *42*, **43**, 45, *55m*, *113m*, 180
Japan
abolition of school fees *112m*
education aid donor 23, 160, *161*, *162*, 168, 187, 188
education costs 151
education expenditure *144-5*, *150*
gender parity/disparity *82m*, *85m*, 184
out-of-school children *50m*
pre-primary education *37m*, *38-9*
primary education *113m*, 180
tertiary education *92*
Jomtien Conference 13, **14**, **144**, 145
Jordan
abolition of school fees *112m*
adult literacy *64m*, *182*
education expenditure *150*, *150*
gender parity/disparity 82, *82m*, *85m*, *90*, 91, 184
out-of-school children *50m*
pre-primary education *37m*, *38-9*
primary education 41, *42*, **43**, 45, *55m*, *113m*, 179, *180*
private education 37
tertiary education *92*
Jornada Ampliada (Brazil) 119

K

Kasturba Gandhi Balika Vidyalaya (India) 118
Kazakhstan
abolition of school fees *112m*
adult literacy *64m*, *182*
education costs 152
education expenditure 142, 144, *144-5*
gender parity/disparity *82m*, *85m*, 184
out-of-school children *50m*
pre-primary education 36, *37m*, *38-9*
primary education **43**, *55m*, 56, **57**, *113m*, 180
Kenya
abolition of school fees *112m*, 113
adult literacy **62**, *64m*, 66, *182*
basic education 26
cash transfers 115, 116, **117**
child labour 119
civil society organizations 102n, 103, **103**
curriculum **132**
ECCE programmes 105
education aid 153, *165*, *175*, 189, 189n, *190*
education costs 151
education expenditure 142, 143, 144, *144-5*, *145*, 148, 153, 154, *174*
education plans 100n
gender parity/disparity *82m*, *85m*, 87, *90*, 184
geographic disparity 111
health programmes 23
learning assessments 68n
non-formal learning 61
orphans **117**
out-of-school children 48, 50, *50m*, 51
pre-primary education *37m*, *38-9*, 40
primary education 44n, 45, 46, *46*, 47, *47*, 48, *55m*, 56, *113m*, 179, 180
teaching staff **76**, 78n, 87
Kiribati
compulsory education *25*
education aid *165*
gender parity/disparity *82m*, *83*, *85m*, 184
out-of-school children 50n
pre-primary education *37m*, *38-9*
primary education 52n, *55m*, *113m*, 180
knowledge economy 20
Korea *see* Democratic People's Republic of Korea
Kosovo, effect of conflict 74
Kuwait
abolition of school fees *112m*
adult literacy 63, *64m*, *182*
gender parity/disparity *82m*, *85m*, 90, *90*, 184
learning assessments 67
out-of-school children *50m*
pre-primary education 36, *37m*, *38-9*, 40
primary education *42*, **43**, 44n, 45, *55m*, 56, 57, 78, *113m*, 180
teaching staff *78*
tertiary education *92*
Kyrgyzstan
abolition of school fees *112m*
adult literacy *64m*, *182*
compulsory education *25*
EDI 94
education aid *165*, *175*, 189
education expenditure *144-5*, *174*
gender parity/disparity *82m*, *85m*, 184
out-of-school children *50m*
pre-primary education *37m*, *38-9*, 40
primary education **43**, 45, *55m*, 56, 78, *113m*, 180
teaching staff *78*
tertiary education *92*

L

language development 91
languages, educational achievement 69, 89, *89*, *90*
Lao People's Democratic Republic
abolition of school fees *112m*
adult literacy *64m*, 66, 182, *182*
compulsory education 24, *25*
EDI 93n
education aid *165*, 166, *175*, 189
education expenditure 142, 144, *144-5*, 146
ethnic populations 120
gender parity/disparity *82m*, *85m*, 184
multilingual education 132
non-formal learning 61
out-of-school children *50m*, 50n
pre-primary education *37m*, *38-9*, 40
primary education **43**, 45, 53, *55m*, 56, 78, *113m*, 180
teaching staff *78*
late enrolment, primary education **43**, 50
Latin America and the Caribbean
see also individual countries
adult literacy 63, *63*, 65, 181, 182
child mortality rate 35
debt relief 162
distance learning 135
ECCE programmes 35, 108
economic growth 19
EDI 93, *93*
education aid 162, **163**, *163*, 174
education expenditure 142, *142*, 143, 145, 146, *146*, 148, 154, 157, 172
fragile states 21
GDP 185
gender parity/disparity 79, 80, *80*, 81, 82, 83, *83*, 84, 86, 88, 118, 183
inclusive education 121
learning assessments 69, *69*, *71*, 134
learning environment 72, 125
monitoring EFA 101n
ODA 22
out-of-school children 49, *49*, *50m*, 51
pre-primary education 33, 35, 36, *37m*, *38-9*, 40
primary education 41, 42, **43**, *43*, 44, *44*, 45, 49, 52n, 53, 54, *55m*, 56, 73, 80, *83*, 179
secondary education 34, 57, 58, *58*, 59, 80, 84
teaching staff 75, *75*, *76*, 77, 78, 87, 185
tertiary education 59, 80, 86, *92*
Latin American Campaign for the Right to Education (CLADE) 103
latrines, in schools 86-7
Latvia
abolition of school fees *112m*
adult literacy *64m*, *182*
EDI 93n
education costs 152
education expenditure *144-5*
gender parity/disparity *82m*, *85m*, 184
learning assessments **68**
out-of-school children *50m*
pre-primary education *37m*, *38-9*
primary education *42*, *55m*, *113m*
tertiary education *92*
laws *see* legislation
LDCs *see* least developed countries
learning assessments 67-72, *69*, *71*
learning environment 28, 72-4, 86-7, *99*, 108, 125-6, 193
learning and life skills (EFA goal)
monitoring **60**
neglect 13, 33
programmes 60-1, 119, 121-3, 193
progress towards 59-61, 95
trends 181
learning materials 66, 68, 73-4

learning outcomes
and aid 141
compensatory programmes **107**
and decentralization 106
disparities 183
gender parity 89-91, *90*, 95
need for improvement 26, 34
least developed countries
see also developing countries; low-income countries
debt relief 162
education aid *156*, *165*, *165*, 173
education expenditure 172
Millennium Development Goals 14
ODA *156*
population growth 17
Lebanon
abolition of school fees *112m*
education expenditure 142, *144-5*, 146
gender parity/disparity *82m*, *83*, *85m*, 184
out-of-school children *50m*
pre-primary education *37m*, *38-9*, 40
primary education **43**, 44n, 45, *55m*, 78, *113m*, 180
teaching staff 40, 77, *78*
tertiary education *92*
legislation
on child labour 118, *119*
compulsory education 24-5, 24n, *25*, 110
for decentralization 106, 107
for ECCE 108
for education expenditure 24-5
human rights **16**, 17
learning and life skills 122
safety in school 125
special needs 121
lenders *see* donors
Lesotho
abolition of school fees *112m*, 114
adult literacy *64m*, 65
cash transfers **117**
compulsory education *25*
EDI 93, 94, 95
education aid *165*, *175*
education expenditure 142, 143, *144-5*, *145*, 146, *174*
gender parity/disparity *82m*, *85m*, 184
learning assessments 68n
learning environment 74, 126
non-formal learning 61
out-of-school children *50m*
pre-primary education 36, *37m*, *38-9*
primary education **43**, 44, 45, 53, *55m*, 56, 78, *113m*, 180
private education 36-7
teaching staff **76**, *78*, 126, 128, 129
tertiary education *92*
Liberia
abolition of school fees *112m*
adult literacy *64m*, 65, *182*
effect of conflict 74
EDI 93n
education aid 162, *165*, 189, 189n, *190*
out-of-school children 50n
Liberian campaign network **103**
Libyan Arab Jamahiriya
abolition of school fees *112m*
adult literacy *64m*, *182*
gender parity/disparity *82m*, *85m*
pre-primary education *37m*, *38-9*
primary education *113m*
Liechtenstein, gender parity/disparity 90, *90*
life skills *see* learning and life skills
literacy *see* adult literacy; youth literacy
Literacy for Life 28
Literate Brazil 122
literate environments 28, 65-6

Lithuania
  abolition of school fees *112m*
  adult literacy *64m, 182*
  EDI *94,* 95
  gender parity/disparity *82m, 85m, 184*
  out-of-school children *50m*
  pre-primary education *37m, 38-9*
  primary education *45, 55m, 113m, 180*
  tertiary education *92*
livelihoods programmes 60
low-income countries
  see also developing countries; least
      developed countries
  education aid **155**, 186-7, 189
  basic education 141, 165, 186-7, 189,
      190
  donors 164, 165, 174
  trends 154, 156, *156, 157, 173, 175*
  education expenditure 142, *143,* 147,
      147
  educational achievement 67
  GDP *185*
  ODA 22, *156, 157*
  service industries 20
  UPE 179, 181
lower secondary education *26, 57-8, 59,
    152, 152*
  see also basic education
Luxembourg
  abolition of school fees *112m*
  education aid donor *161, 162, 187*
  gender parity/disparity *82m, 83, 85m,
      183, 184*
  learning assessments 67
  out-of-school children *50m*
  pre-primary education *37m, 38-9*
  primary education *55m, 113m, 180*

M

Macao, China
  abolition of school fees *112m*
  adult literacy *64m, 182*
  basic education *26*
  gender parity/disparity *82m,* 84, *85m,
      90, 184*
  out-of-school children *50m*
  pre-primary education *37m, 40*
  primary education *42, **43**, 45, 78,
      113m, 180*
  teaching staff *78*
  tertiary education *92*
Madagascar
  abolition of school fees *112m*
  adult literacy *64m, 182,* 190
  education aid *165, 175,* 189
  education expenditure 143, *144-5, 174*
  gender parity/disparity *82m,* 90
  out-of-school children *48, 50m,* 51
  pre-primary education 36, *37m, 38-9*
  primary education 41, ***43,** 44, 45, 46,
      47, 48, 53, 54, 54, 55m, 56, 78,
      113m, 180*
  teaching staff *77, 78, 78, 79*
  tertiary education *92*
Madrasa Early Childhood Programme
    (East Africa) 105
mainstreaming (inclusive education) 120-
    1, *192,* 192-3
Making a School (Brazil) 122
malaria 18
Malawi
  abolition of school fees *112m,* 113
  adult literacy 63, *64m,* **133,** *182,* 190
  cash transfers 116
  compulsory education *25*
  EDI 93, *94,* 95
  education aid *159, 160, 165, 175,* 189
  education costs 151
  education expenditure 144, *144-5, 145,
      151,* 153, 154

gender parity/disparity 81, *82m, 83,
    85m,* 87, *184*
learning assessments 68n, 133
learning environment 74
non-government schools 105
out-of-school children 48, *50m*
poverty reduction programmes 164
primary education *45, 47, 48, 53, 54,
    55m, 113m, 180*
teaching staff **76,** 87, 126, 128
violence and abuse 86
Malaysia
  abolition of school fees *112m*
  adult literacy *64m, 182*
  curriculum **132**
  education expenditure 142, 143, *144-5*
  gender parity/disparity *82m, 85m, 184*
  multilingual education 132
  out-of-school children *50m*
  pre-primary education *37m,* 38
  primary education *52n, 55m, 113m,
      180*
  tertiary education *92*
Maldives
  abolition of school fees *112m*
  adult literacy *64m, 182*
  basic education *26*
  child mortality rate 35n
  compulsory education *25*
  education aid *165*
  gender parity/disparity 81, *82m, 85m,
      184*
  out-of-school children *50m*
  pre-primary education *37m, 38-9,* 40
  primary education 41, 42, *45,* 78,
      113m, 180
  teaching staff *78*
male *see* boys; men
Mali
  abolition of school fees *112m*
  adult literacy 64, *64m,* 65n, *182*
  civil society organizations 103
  EDI 93
  education aid *158, 158, 165,* 166, *175,
      189, 189n, 190*
  education expenditure 144, *144-5,* 164,
      174
  gender parity/disparity 82, *82m, 83,
      85m, 90, 184*
  geographic disparity 111
  non-government schools 104
  out-of-school children 50, *50m,* 51
  pre-primary education *37m, 38-9*
  primary education 41, 42, *42,* **43,** *43,* 44,
      *45, 46, 46, 47, 47, 53, 54, 54, 55m,
      56, 113m, 180*
  teaching staff 77, *79,* 127, 128
malnutrition 19, 35
  see also child health and nutrition
Malta
  abolition of school fees *112m*
  adult literacy *64m,* 65, 181, *182*
  gender parity/disparity *82m, 85m, 184*
  out-of-school children *50m*
  pre-primary education *37m*
  primary education *42, 45, 55m, 113m,
      180*
  tertiary education *92*
management capacity 101, **102,** 193
marginalization 108
  see also access to education;
      disadvantage; ethnicity; exclusion;
      inclusive education; inequality;
      inequity
Marshall Islands
  education expenditure 143, *144-5*
  gender parity/disparity *82m, 85m, 184*
  out-of-school children *50m*
  pre-primary education 36, *37m, 38-9*
  primary education *52n*

Master of Education for Rural Schools
    (China) 128
mathematics, educational achievement
    67, 69, *69,* 70, 70, 89, *89, 90,* 91
Mauritania *190*
  abolition of school fees *112m*
  adult literacy *64m, 182*
  compulsory education *25*
  EDI *94,* 95
  education aid *165, 175,* 189, 189n
  education expenditure 142, 143, *144-5,
      146,* 147, *174*
  education plans 100n
  gender parity/disparity 82, *82m, 83,
      85m, 184*
  geographic disparity 111
  learning environment 74
  non-government schools 104
  out-of-school children *50m*
  poverty reduction programmes 164
  pre-primary education *37m, 38-9*
  primary education ***43,** 44, 45, 46, 46,
      47, 53, 54, 54, 55m, 56, 78, 113m,
      180*
  teaching staff 75, 77, *78, 79*
Mauritius
  abolition of school fees *112m*
  adult literacy *64m, 182*
  compulsory education *25*
  EDI *94*
  education expenditure *144-5, 145,* 146
  gender parity/disparity *82m, 85m, 184*
  learning assessments 68n
  learning environment 74
  out-of-school children *50m*
  pre-primary education *37m,* 40
  primary education ***43,** 45, 55m, 78,
      113m, 180*
  teaching staff *78*
  tertiary education *92*
MDRI 164
media, use in education 135
medical poverty trap 19
men
  see also boys
  literacy *62, 63*
  non-formal learning 61
  tertiary education 84
Mexico
  abolition of school fees *112m*
  adult literacy *64m, 182*
  basic education *26*
  cash transfers 114, *115,* 116
  child labour 119
  child mortality rate 35n
  compensatory programmes **107**
  decentralization 107
  distance learning 134, 135
  ECCE programmes 108
  education expenditure 25, 143, 144,
      144-5, 150, 154
  education management 101
  ethnic populations 120
  gender parity/disparity *82m,* 84, *85m,
      90, 184*
  impact of education 23
  learning assessments 67, 70, 71, 72, *72*
  non-formal learning 60
  out-of-school children *50m*
  pre-primary education *37m,* 109
  primary education ***43,** 45, 46, 47, 55m,
      113m, 180*
  teaching staff 126
  tertiary education *92*
  violence and abuse 86
Micronesia, gender parity/disparity *82m,
    85m*
Middle East
  see also Arab States; Islamic Republic
      of Iran; Israel; *individual countries*
  education aid *163*

middle-income developing countries
  see also developing countries
  education aid *157, 165,* 189
  education expenditure 84, 142, *143,
      147, 147, 153-4, 172*
  educational achievement 67
  gender parity 118
  ODA 22, *157*
  primary education 53
  service industries 20
  tertiary education 59
  UPE 179
migration
  see also immigrants
  rights of migrants **16**
  to urban areas 18, 111, **111**
Miith Akolda Curriculum (Sudan) **137**
Millennium Development Goals 13, 14,
    84n, 170
minorities *see* disadvantage; ethnicity;
    exclusion; marginalization
Moldova *see* Republic of Moldova
Mongolia
  abolition of school fees *112m*
  adult literacy *64m, 182*
  curriculum **132**
  EDI *94*
  education aid 157-8, *158, 165, 175,* 189
  education costs 152
  education expenditure *144-5, 151, 174*
  ethnic populations 120
  gender parity/disparity *82m, 83, 85m,
      184*
  out-of-school children 48, *50m*
  pre-primary education *37m,* 38, *38-9*
  primary education *45,* 48, *54, 55m, 56,
      113m, 180*
  rural-urban migration **111**
  tertiary education *92*
monitoring
  see also assessment
  education aid 165
  education expenditure 141
  education progress 101-2
  EFA goals 33, **51,** 92-5, *99,* 193
  learning and life skills 33, 61
  literate environments 65-6
  UPE **51**
Montenegro *see* Serbia and Montenegro
Montserrat
  compulsory education *25*
  gender parity/disparity *82m,* 83, *85m*
  out-of-school children *50m*
  pre-primary education *37m,* 40
  primary education ***43,** *43,* 78, *180*
  teaching staff *78*
Morocco
  abolition of school fees *112m*
  adult literacy 64, *64m,* 65n, *182*
  child mortality rate 35n
  compulsory education *25*
  curriculum 131
  decentralization 106
  education aid *159*
  education expenditure 142, *144-5, 146,*
      147
  education management 101
  ethnic populations 120
  gender parity/disparity 81, *82m, 83,
      85m,* 117, *184*
  geographic disparity 111
  learning assessments 67, 70, 71, 133
  out-of-school children 48, *50m,* 51
  pre-primary education 36, *37m,* 38,
      38-9, 40
  primary education ***43,** 44, 45, 46, 46,
      46n, 47, 47, 48, 53, 55m, 56, 78,
      113m, 180*
  private education 37
  school expansion 109
  teaching staff **76,** *78*

tertiary education *92*
mortality rate 18, 32, 35
mother tongue 28, 131n, 132-3, 193
mothers, effect of education on school
    participation 52
Mozambique
    abolition of school fees *112m*, 113, 114
    adult literacy 64, *64m*, 65n, *182*, 190
    basic education 26
    civil society organizations 103
    compulsory education *25*
    effect of conflict 74
    debt relief 164
    EDI *94*, 95
    education aid 153, 159, *159*, 165, 166,
        175, 189, 189n, *190*
    education costs 151, 152
    education expenditure 144, *144-5*, 174
    education plans 100n
    gender parity/disparity *82m*, 83, *85m*,
        184
    geographic disparity 111
    governance 20
    learning assessments 68n
    out-of-school children 48, *50m*, 51
    primary education *43*, 44, 44n, *45*, 46,
        46, 46n, 47, 48, 53, 54, 54, *55m*, *78*,
        113m, 179, 180
    secondary education 57
    teaching staff 75, **76**, 77, *78*, 126, 128
    tertiary education *92*
multicultural education programmes 137
Multilateral Debt Reduction Initiative
    (MDRI) 164
multilateral donors
    basic education aid 188
    commitments and disbursements *21*,
        161, 162
    education strategies 160, 166, 191
    increase in aid 194
multilingual education 131-2, 193
multisectoral programmes 193
Myanmar
    abolition of school fees *112m*
    adult literacy *64m*, *182*
    basic education 26
    compulsory education 24
    curriculum **132**
    EDI 93
    education aid *165*, 189
    gender parity/disparity *82m*, 83, *85m*,
        184
    non-formal learning 61, *61*
    out-of-school children *50m*, 50n, 51
    primary education *43*, 45, 46, *55m*, 56,
        78, *113m*, 180
    teaching staff *78*

N

Namibia
    abolition of school fees *112m*
    adult literacy *64m*, **133**, *182*
    cash transfers **117**
    compulsory education *25*
    EDI *94*
    education aid 189
    education expenditure 142, 143, *144-5*,
        145, 148
    gender parity/disparity *82m*, 83, *85m*,
        184
    learning assessments 68n, 133
    non-formal learning 60
    out-of-school children *50m*
    pre-primary education 36, *37m*, 38,
        38-9
    primary education 42, **43**, 45, 47, *47*,
        55m, 56, *78*, *113m*, 180
    private education 36-7
    teaching staff 77, *78*
    tertiary education *92*
    violence and abuse 86n

National Campaign for the Right to
    Education (Brazil) **103**
national education coalitions **102**, **103**
National Education Plan (Brazil) 108
National Girls' Education Strategy (Yemen)
    117
National Institute of Open Schooling (India)
    60
national learning assessments 34, 68-72,
    69, *71*, *90*, 133-4, 193
National Programme on Girls' Education
    at Elementary Level (India) 118
Nauru
    compulsory education *25*
    gender parity/disparity *82m*, *85m*, 184
    pre-primary education *37m*, *38-9*
NEPAD **135**
Nepal
    abolition of school fees *112m*
    adult literacy 63, 64, *64m*, 65n, *182*
    compulsory education 24, *25*
    EDI *94*, 95
    education aid *159*, 165, 167, *175*, 189n,
        190
    education costs 152
    education expenditure 146, 147
    ethnic minorities 23
    ethnic populations 120
    gender parity/disparity 81, *82m*, *83*, 84,
        85m, 184
    household size 18n
    impact of education 23
    non-formal learning 60
    out-of-school children *50m*, 51, 152
    post-conflict education 136
    pre-primary education *37m*, *38-9*
    primary education 44, 45, 46, 47, 53,
        54, *54*, *55m*, 56, *78*, *113m*
    teaching staff 77, *78*
NER *see* net enrolment ratio
net enrolment ratio
    EDI indicator 93, 95
    primary education
    and decentralization 106
    and funding 110, 111-12
    geographic disparity 46, *46*, 47
    increases 42-3, 44, *44*, 45, 50, 54
    total primary NER 179, *180*, 186
Netherlands
    abolition of school fees *112m*
    compulsory education 24
    education aid donor 160, *161*, 162, 166,
        168, 172, *187*
    education expenditure *144-5*, 150
    gender parity/disparity *82m*, *85m*, 184
    out-of-school children *50m*
    pre-primary education *37m*
    primary education 52n, *55m*, *113m*, 180
    secondary education 59
    tertiary education *92*
Netherlands Antilles
    adult literacy *64m*, *182*
    gender parity/disparity *82m*, *85m*, 184
    pre-primary education *37m*
    primary education *113m*
Nevis *see* Saint Kitts and Nevis
New Breakthrough to Literacy (Zambia)
    133
New Partnership for Africa's Development
    (NEPAD) **135**
New Zealand
    abolition of school fees *112m*
    education aid donor 160, *161*, 162, *187*
    education expenditure *144-5*, 150
    gender parity/disparity *82m*, *85m*, 90,
        90, 183, 184
    out-of-school children *50m*
    pre-primary education *37m*
    primary education **43**, *113m*, 180
    private education 36-7
    tertiary education *92*

NGOs
    see also civil society organizations
        (CSOs); non-state providers
    ECCE programmes 104
Nicaragua
    abolition of school fees *112m*
    adult literacy *64m*, 65, 182, *182*, 190
    basic education 26
    cash transfers 114, *116*
    child labour 119
    compulsory education *25*
    decentralization 106
    distance learning 135
    ECCE programmes 109
    EDI 93, *94*
    education aid 157-8, *158*, *159*, 165, *175*
    education costs 151, *151*, 152, *152*
    education expenditure *144-5*, *151*, 174
    education plans 100, 100n
    gender parity/disparity *82m*, 83, *83*,
        85m, 90, 184
    out-of-school children *50m*
    poverty reduction programmes 164
    pre-primary education *37m*, *38-9*, 40
    primary education *43*, *43*, 45, 47, 48,
        53, *54*, *55m*, 56, *78*, 106, *113m*, 180
    teaching staff *78*, 78n
    violence and abuse 86
Niger
    abolition of school fees *112m*
    adult literacy 64, *64m*, 65n, *182*, 190
    basic education 26
    civil society organizations **103**
    compulsory education *25*
    EDI 93, 93n
    education aid 158, *158*, 165, *175*, 189,
        189n, *190*
    education expenditure 142, *144-5*, *145*,
        174
    education plans 100n
    gender parity/disparity 81, 82, *82m*, 83,
        85m, 90, 184
    geographic disparity 111
    learning assessments 71, 72, *72*
    non-formal learning 61, *61*, 123
    out-of-school children 50, *50m*, 50n,
        51
    poverty reduction programmes 164
    pre-primary education *37m*, *38-9*
    primary education 41, 42, **43**, 45, 46,
        46, 47, 53, *54*, 55, *55m*, 56, *113m*,
        180, 181n
    teaching staff 78, 79, *79*, 127
Nigeria
    abolition of school fees *112m*
    adult literacy 64, *64m*, *182*
    compulsory education *25*
    ECCE programmes 108
    EDI 93n
    education aid 158, *158*, 165, 189, 189n,
        190
    education costs 151, *151*
    education expenditure 149
    gender parity/disparity 82, *82m*, 83, 84,
        85m, 184
    non-government schools 105
    out-of-school children 48, 49, *50m*,
        50n, 51
    pre-primary education *37m*, *38-9*
    primary education *43*, 45, *45*, 46, *46*,
        47, 48, *55m*, 59, *78*, *113m*, 180, 181n
    teaching staff 77, 77n, *78*, 129
Niue
    gender parity/disparity *82m*, *85m*, 184
    pre-primary education *37m*
    primary education 42, 52n, *113m*
nomadic populations 120
non-concessional loans **163**
non-formal learning 33, 59-61, *61*, 95
    programmes 60-1, 119, 121-3, 193
non-government organizations *see* NGOs

non-state providers of education 104-6,
    122-3
    see also civil society organizations
        (CSOs); NGOs; private education
North America and Western Europe
    see also individual countries
    adult literacy 63, 65
    ECCE programmes 35
    EDI 93, *93*
    education expenditure 142, *142*, 143,
        146, *146*, 148, 150
    gender parity/disparity 79, *80*, 81, 82,
        83, 84, *86*, 90, 118, 183
    learning assessments 69, *69*
    learning environment 72, 125
    out-of-school children 49, *49*, *50m*, 51
    pre-primary education 36, *37m*, *38-9*,
        40
    primary education 41, *41*, 42, *42*, 43-4,
        43, 44, 45, 52n, 54, *55m*, 73, 80, 83
    secondary education 56-7, 57, 58, *58*,
        59, 80, 84
    teaching staff 75, *75*, 76, 87, 185
    tertiary education 59, *59*, 80, 86, *92*
Norway
    abolition of school fees *112m*
    child mortality rate 35n
    education aid donor 160, *161*, 162, 166,
        168, *187*
    education expenditure *144-5*, 149, *150*
    gender parity/disparity *82m*, *85m*, 90,
        184
    out-of-school children *50m*
    pre-primary education *37m*, *38-9*
    primary education 52n, *55m*, *113m*,
        180
    tertiary education *92*
numeracy *62*, **62**, 69, *69*
nutrition policies 19, 124
    see also child health and nutrition

O

ODA
    debt relief 22, 141, 154, 162, 164, 173,
        187
    disbursements *21*, *21*, *22*, 154, 156,
        157, 160, 187
    for education 154-62, **155**, *156*, *157*, 169
    see also education aid
    increase 21
    new modalities 164-9
    projections 188
OECD countries
    see also developed countries
    democracy and education 24
    education expenditure 149, 150, *150*
    gender parity 84, 91
    literacy 66
    secondary education 84
    tertiary education 91
    UPE 179
    vocational education 57
official development assistance *see* ODA
Oman
    abolition of school fees *112m*
    adult literacy *64m*, *182*
    basic education 26
    compulsory education *25*
    education expenditure *144-5*, 146
    gender parity/disparity 82, *82m*, *85m*,
        184
    out-of-school children *50m*
    pre-primary education *37m*, *38-9*, 40
    primary education 41, 42, **43**, 45, 53,
        54, *55m*, *113m*, 180
    private education 37
open learning 134-5, **134**
Optional Protocol to the Convention on
    the Rights of the Child on the
    Involvement of Children in Armed
    Conflict (2000) **16**

orphans/orphanhood
cash transfers *115*, **117**
from HIV/AIDS 18n, 19
in special education 121
out-of-school children 49-52, *49*, *50*, *51*
see also dropout; school attendance
and education aid 157-8, *158*
and EFA goals 33
over-age entry **43**, 50

P

Pakistan
abolition of school fees *112m*
adult literacy 64, *64m*, 181, *182*
cash transfers 114, *116*
child labour 119
civil society organizations 102n
compulsory education 24, *25*
decentralization 106
distance learning 134
EDI 93
education aid 159, *159*, *165*, 174, *175*, 189, 189n, *190*
education expenditure 142, *144-5*, 146
ethnic populations 120
gender parity/disparity 81, *82m*, *83*, *85m*, *184*
HIV/AIDS 18n
household size 18n
non-government schools 104
out-of-school children 49, *50m*, 51
post-conflict education 136
pre-primary education *37m*, *38-9*
primary education *43*, 44, 46, *46*, 55, *55m*, 56, *78*, 179, *180*
teaching staff *78*, 130, **130**
Palau
compulsory education 24, *25*
gender parity/disparity *82m*, *85m*, *184*
pre-primary education *37m*, *38-9*
primary education *42*
Palestinian Autonomous Territories
adult literacy *64m*, *182*
civil society organizations 102n
education aid *158*, 189
gender parity/disparity *82m*, *85m*, 91, *184*
out-of-school children *50m*
pre-primary education 36, *37m*, *38-9*, *40*
primary education 41, *42*, **43**, 44, 45, *55m*, *78*, *113m*, 179, *180*
private education 37
teaching staff *78*
tertiary education *92*
Panama
abolition of school fees *112m*
adult literacy *64m*, *182*
basic education *26*
distance learning 134
EDI *94*
education costs 150, 151, *151*, *152*
education expenditure 143, *144-5*, 151
gender parity/disparity *82m*, *85m*, *184*
learning environment 73
out-of-school children *50m*
pre-primary education *37m*, *38-9*, *40*
primary education *43*, 48, *55m*, 56, *78*, *113m*, *180*
teaching staff *78*
tertiary education *92*
violence and abuse 86
Papua New Guinea
abolition of school fees *112m*
adult literacy *64m*, *182*
civil society organizations **103**
compulsory education *25*
curriculum **132**
education aid *159*, *165*, 189n, *190*
gender parity/disparity *82m*, *85m*, *184*
HIV/AIDS 18n

out-of-school children *50n*
pre-primary education 36, *37m*, *38-9*
primary education 52n, *55m*, *113m*
para-teachers (contract) 78-9, *79*, 127-8
Paraguay
abolition of school fees *112m*
adult literacy *64m*, *182*
EDI *94*
education expenditure *144-5*, *150*
education plans 100n
gender parity/disparity *82m*, *83*, *85m*, *184*
learning assessments 72, *72*
out-of-school children *50m*
pre-primary education *37m*, *38-9*
primary education 45, 47, *47*, 48, *55m*, *113m*
parents *see* mothers
Paris Declaration on Aid Effectiveness 164, 168, 173, 194-5
participation
see also school participation
ECCE 33, 179
tertiary education 59
Partnership for Education Revitalization in the Americas **104**
partnerships
with donors 174, 186
between governments and CSOs 99, 101-4, *102*, **103**, *110*, 173-4
between governments and non-state providers 104-5, 122-3
pastoral populations 120
peace education programmes 137
per-pupil expenditure, primary education 147-8, *148*, *148*, *151*
Peru
abolition of school fees *112m*
adult literacy *64m*, *182*
basic education *26*
child labour 119
civil society organizations **103**
distance learning 134
education expenditure 142, *144-5*, *150*
gender parity/disparity *82m*, 84, *85m*, 87, 88, *90*, *184*
learning assessments 70, *71*, 72, *72*
learning environment 73, 86
non-formal learning 61
out-of-school children 48, *50m*
pre-primary education *37m*, *38-9*, 39
primary education *43*, 45, 46, *47*, 48, *55m*, *113m*, 179, *180*
teaching staff 87, 88, 127
Philippines
abolition of school fees *112m*
adult literacy *64m*, *182*
basic education *26*
child labour 119
child mortality rate 35n
civil society organizations 102n, **103**, **110**
curriculum **132**
ECCE programmes 109
EDI 93
education aid *159*
education expenditure 142, *150*
education management 101
gender parity/disparity *82m*, *83*, *85m*, 89, 90, *90*, 91, *184*
non-formal learning 60, 61
out-of-school children 48, *50m*, 51
pre-primary education *37m*, *38-9*
primary education *43*, 45, 46, *46*, 47, 48, *55m*, 110, *113m*, *180*
school networking **135**
teaching staff 128, 129, **129**, 130
physical punishment 86
physical safety, in schools 86, 124-5
plans (education plans) 100-1, 167, 173, 174, 194

out-of-school children *50n*
Poland
abolition of school fees *112m*
compulsory education 24
education costs 151
education expenditure *144-5*, *150*
ethnic populations 120
gender parity/disparity *82m*, *85m*, *184*
out-of-school children *50m*
pre-primary education *37m*, *38-9*, 39
primary education *55m*, *113m*, *180*
tertiary education *92*
political and civil rights **16**, *20*
population growth 17-18
Portugal
abolition of school fees *112m*
adult literacy *64m*, 181, *182*
basic education *26*
education aid donor *161*, *162*, 187
education expenditure *144-5*, 150, *150*
gender parity/disparity *82m*, *85m*, *184*
learning assessments 67
out-of-school children *50m*
pre-primary education *37m*, *38-9*
primary education 53, *113m*, *180*
tertiary education *92*
post-secondary non-tertiary education *57*
see also learning and life skills; tertiary education
poverty 19
see also disadvantage
effect on literacy 65
effect on pre-primary participation 33
in rural areas 111
effect on school participation 47-8, *48*, 52, 152
poverty reduction programmes 19, *99*, *162*, 163-4
Poverty Reduction Strategy Papers (PRSPs) 100-1
pre-primary education
see also early childhood care and education
access 33, 95
aid 160
as basic education *26*
duration 35
and EFA goals 32-3
enrolment *see* enrolment, pre-primary education
evaluation 109
expenditure on *147*
gender disparity 37-8
gender stereotyping 34
private 36-7
programmes 109
teaching staff 32, 39-40
primary education 41-55
see also basic education; universal primary education (EFA goal)
access 41, 53, *54*, 80-1, 109
aid *190*
completion rates 170
curriculum 130-1
duration 44n
enrolment *see* enrolment, primary education
expenditure on 146, 147, *147*, 148-9, *148*, 150-1, *151*
gender parity 34, 80-3, *80*, 183
gross intake rates *42*
improving quality 123-36, **123**
teacher shortages 34, 74-8
teaching hours 34, 67, 72, *73*
teaching staff 74-8, *75*, *78*
Primary Education Development Plan (United Republic of Tanzania) 153
Primary Education Development Programme (Bangladesh) 168
Priority Action Programme (Cambodia) **123**

private education
see also non-state providers of education
and achievement 70
pre-primary education 36-7
primary schools, pupil/teacher ratios 39, 77
secondary schools, household expenditure 151
private foundations, education aid 162
Programa de Asignación Familiar (Honduras) 154
programmatic approach to aid 169
see also sector wide aid programmes
Programme of Advancement through Health and Education (Jamaica) *115*
programmes
see also education plans
adult literacy 60, 121-3, **133**
aid *see* education aid
basic education 60
cash transfers 114-17, *115-16*, 153-4
child health and nutrition 18-19, 23, 35, 124
ECCE 34-7, 95, 108-9
improving gender parity 117-18, **137**
improving quality of education 123, **123**
for inclusive education 120-1
learning outcomes **107**
multicultural education 137
non-formal learning 60-1, 119, 121-3
pre-primary education 36-7, 109
primary education 34, 43, 109-21, **110**, *112*, *115-16*, **117**, *119*
secondary education *57*
SWAps 149, 164, *165*, 166-8, 171-2, 173
targeting child labour 119, 193
Progresa-Oportunidades (Mexico) *115*, *116*, 154
progression *see* school progression
PRONADE (Guatemala) 106
PRSPs 100-1
psychological violence, in schools 86
PTR *see* pupil/teacher ratio
public expenditure *see* governments, education expenditure
public schools (state schools), pupil/teacher ratios 39, 40, 77
punishment, corporal 86
pupil/teacher ratio 32, *76*, *78*, *113m*, 127
and enrolment 40, 75, 109
in pre-primary programmes 39, 40, *40*
and teacher shortages 77, 128
pupil/textbook ratio 73
pupils, support from schools 55

Q
Qatar
abolition of school fees *112m*
adult literacy *64m*, *182*
compulsory education 25
gender parity/disparity *82m*, *85m*, *184*
out-of-school children *50m*
pre-primary education 36, *37m*, *38-9*
primary education *43*, 45, *113m*, *180*
tertiary education *92*
qualifications *see* teacher training
quality of education (EFA goal)
benefits 24
EDI indicator 92
government responsibilities 192, 193, 194
improving 25-6, 123-36, **123**
in non-state schools 105
progress towards 28, 34, 66-9, 95
trends 183-5

R

radio, use in education 135
Rainbow Spectrum initiative (Philippines) 129, **129**
ratification of treaties 17
reading assessments 67
reading materials, for literacy 66
regional learning assessments 67-8
registration, non-state schools 105
regulation
  non-state education providers 104-5
  in school-based management 106
religious training **57**
remote areas
  see also rural areas
  access to education 120
repetition *see* grade repetition
report cards **104**
Republic of the Congo *see* Democratic Republic of the Congo
Republic of Korea
  abolition of school fees *112m*
  basic education 26
  child mortality rate *35n*
  education aid donor 162
  education costs 151
  education expenditure *144-5, 150*
  gender parity/disparity 23, *82m, 85m,* 90, *90,* 184
  learning environment 125
  out-of-school children *50m*
  pre-primary education *37m*
  primary education *43,* 45, *52n, 55m,* 59, *113m, 180*
  tertiary education *92*
Republic of Moldova
  abolition of school fees *112m*
  adult literacy *64m, 182*
  EDI *94,* 95
  education aid *165, 175*
  education expenditure 143, *144-5,* 147, *174*
  gender parity/disparity *82m, 85m,* 89, 90, *90,* 184
  non-formal learning *61*
  out-of-school children *50m*
  pre-primary education 36, *37m, 38-9,* 40
  primary education *42, 43,* 45, *55m, 113m, 180*
research, benefits of education 23-4
resources *see* aid; funding; school resources
restricted range disparity index 45-6
right to education 16, 24
rights 16, **16,** *20,* 24
Roma communities 120
Romania
  abolition of school fees *112m*
  adult literacy *64m, 182*
  compulsory education *25*
  EDI *94*
  education expenditure *144-5*
  ethnic populations 120
  gender parity/disparity *82m, 85m, 184*
  governance 20
  learning assessments **68**
  out-of-school children *48, 50m*
  post-conflict education 137
  pre-primary education *37m, 38-9*
  primary education *42,* 45, *55m, 113m, 180*
  teaching staff 130
  tertiary education *92*
ROSEN network (Niger) **103**
rural areas
  see also remote areas; urban areas
  and education expenditure 149
  educational achievement 72, *72*
  effects of poverty 111
  non-formal learning *61*

out-of-school children 52
school attendance 46-7, *47,* **107**
teacher shortages 128
rural-urban migration 18, 111, **111**
Russian Federation
  abolition of school fees *112m*
  adult literacy *64m, 182*
  education aid donor 23
  gender parity/disparity *82m, 85m, 184*
  HIV/AIDS *18n*
  learning assessments 67
  out-of-school children *50m*
  pre-primary education 36, *37m, 38-9*
  primary education *42, 113m, 180*
Rwanda
  abolition of school fees *112m*
  adult literacy *64m, 182*
  compulsory education *25*
  decentralization 106
  ECCE programmes 108
  education aid *165, 166, 167, 189, 189n, 190*
  education plans 100
  gender parity/disparity 82, *82m, 83, 85m,* 87, *184*
  non-formal learning *61*
  out-of-school children 48, *50m*
  primary education *43, 46, 47,* 48, 53, 54, *55m,* 56, *113m, 180*
  school expansion 110
  teacher training 126
  teaching staff 75, *75n,* 77, 87

S

safety in schools 86, 124-5
Saint Kitts and Nevis
  abolition of school fees *112m*
  compulsory education 24
  education expenditure 144, *144-5*
  gender parity/disparity *82m, 85m, 184*
  out-of-school children *50m*
  pre-primary education *37m,* 40
  primary education *42, 43, 52n, 78*
  teaching staff *78*
Saint Lucia
  abolition of school fees *112m*
  basic education 26
  EDI *94*
  education expenditure *144-5,* 147, 148
  gender parity/disparity *82m,* 83, *85m, 184*
  out-of-school children *50m*
  pre-primary education *37m, 38-9,* 40
  primary education *43,* 45, *55m, 78, 113m, 180*
  teaching staff *78*
Saint Vincent and the Grenadines
  abolition of school fees *112m*
  education expenditure 144, *144-5*
  gender parity/disparity *82m,* 83, *85m, 184*
  out-of-school children *50m*
  pre-primary education *37m, 38-9,* 40
  primary education *43, 55m, 78, 180*
  teaching staff *78*
salaries, teaching staff 75, 79, 126
Samoa
  adult literacy *64m, 182*
  education aid *165*
  gender parity/disparity *82m, 85m, 184*
  out-of-school children *50m*
  pre-primary education *37m, 38-9*
  primary education 45, *113m, 180*
sanitation, and school attendance 86-7
Sao Tome and Principe
  abolition of school fees *112m*
  adult literacy *64m, 182*
  compulsory education *25*
  EDI *93*
  education aid *165*
  gender parity/disparity 81, *82m, 85m*

non-formal learning *61*
out-of-school children *50m, 50n*
pre-primary education *37m, 38-9*
primary education 45, 53, *55m, 113m, 180*
Sarva Shiksha Abhiyan (India) 118
Saudi Arabia
  abolition of school fees *112m*
  adult literacy *64m, 182*
  compulsory education 25
  education expenditure 142, 143, *144-5,* 146
  gender parity/disparity 81, 82, *82m, 83, 85m,* 91, *184*
  out-of-school children *50m,* 51
  pre-primary education *37m, 38-9*
  primary education *42, 43, 55m,* 179, *180*
  tertiary education *92*
Scholarship for girls (Cambodia) 115
school achievement
  assessment 67-72, 133-4
  boys 89, 91
  gender equality 34
  girls *70,* 89, 91
  languages 69, 89, *89,* 90
  mathematics 67, 69, *69,* 70, *70,* 89, *90,* 91
  and nutrition 35, 124
  science 67, 89, *89,* 90, 91
school attendance
  see also dropout; early childhood care and education (ECCE); participation; enrolment; out-of-school children; school participation
  boys 49
  effect of cash transfer programmes 114
  and child labour 118, *119*
  and disability 48-9, *48*
  girls 49, 86-7, 153
  effect of HIV/AIDS 19
  and household costs 112, *115-16,* 141, 153
  and poverty 47-8, 48, 52, 152-3
  in rural areas 46-7, *47,* **107**
school-based literate environments 66
school-based management 106
school buildings 74, 109, **110**
school completion 33, 35, 54-5, *54n,* **62,** 170
school costs *see* education costs
school curriculum *see* curriculum
school environment *see* learning environment
school fees *46m,* 112-14, *112m, 113m,* 150-1, 153-4, 172, 192
school meals 23, **123,** 124
school participation
  see also enrolment; out-of-school children; school attendance
  effect of HIV/AIDS 19
  effect of poverty 47-8, *48,* 52, 152
  primary 42-4, 81-2
    see also universal primary education
  secondary 58
  effect of socio-economic background **84**
school places, provision 109
school progression 33, 82-3
  see also grade repetition
school resources 66, 68, 73-4
school retention 95
  see also school completion; survival rate to last grade
school self-management 106
school-site management 106
school uniforms 150-1
school violence 86, 124-5
SchoolNet Africa **135**
SchoolNets **135**

schools *see* education; pre-primary education; primary education; secondary education
science, educational achievement 67, 89, *89, 90,* 91
scorecards **104**
Scotland (UK), gender parity/disparity *90*
'second chance' programmes 60
secondary education
  see also basic education
  aid 168
  costs 152
  and EFA goals 56
  enrolment 33, 56-7, *58,* 84, *85*
  expansion 56-7, **57,** 186
  expenditure on *147, 147,* 148, 150, 152
  gender parity 80, *80,* 83, 84, **84,** 183
  teaching staff 75, *75*
  transition to 114
  TVEI 58-9
sector aid 154, 155, **155,** 165
sector-wide approaches (SWAps) 149, 164, *165,* 166-8, 171-2, 173
sectoral strategies 99
Senegal
  abolition of school fees *112m*
  adult literacy 64, *64m, 65n, 182,* 190
  civil society organizations 103
  debt relief 164
  decentralization 106
  education aid 159, *159,* 160, *165, 175,* 189, *189n, 190*
  education expenditure 144, *144-5, 145, 174*
  gender parity/disparity *82m,* 83, *85m,* 90, *184*
  governance 20
  learning assessments 70, *71*
  non-formal learning 60, 61, *61,* 122
  out-of-school children 48, *50m,* 51
  pre-primary education 36, *37m,* 38, *38-9,* 39, 40
  primary education 41, *42, 43,* 45, 46, *46, 47, 47,* 48, 55, *55m,* 56, 78, *113m, 180*
  teaching staff 77, 78, *78,* 79, *79,* 128, 129
Serbia and Montenegro
  abolition of school fees *112m*
  adult literacy *64m, 182*
  compulsory education *25*
  gender parity/disparity *82m, 85m*
  out-of-school children *50m*
  pre-primary education *37m*
  primary education *55m, 113m, 180*
service industries 19-20
sex education, gender bias **89**
sexual abuse/harassment 86
Seychelles
  abolition of school fees *112m*
  adult literacy *64m*
  education expenditure *144-5, 145*
  gender parity/disparity 81, *82m, 85m,* 90, *90, 184*
  learning assessments *68n*
  learning environment 74
  out-of-school children *50m*
  pre-primary education *37m*
  primary education *52n, 55m,* **57,** *113m, 180*
Sida 166, 171
Sierra Leone
  abolition of school fees *112m*
  adult literacy 64, *64m, 65n, 182*
  civil society organizations **103**
  EDI *93n*
  education aid *165, 189, 189n, 190*
  non-formal learning *61*
  out-of-school children *50n*
  teaching staff 77

Singapore
  abolition of school fees *112m*
  adult literacy *64m, 182*
  compulsory education *25*
  gender parity/disparity *82m, 85m,* 91, *184*
  primary education *113m*
single-parent families 18
Slovakia
  abolition of school fees *112m*
  adult literacy *64m*
  education costs 152
  education expenditure *144-5, 150*
  ethnic populations 120
  gender parity/disparity *82m, 85m, 184*
  out-of-school children *50m*
  pre-primary education *37m*
  primary education *55m, 113m*
  tertiary education *92*
Slovenia
  abolition of school fees *112m*
  adult literacy *64m, 182*
  basic education *26*
  education expenditure 142
  gender parity/disparity *82m, 85m, 184*
  out-of-school children *50m*
  pre-primary education *37m, 38-9*
  primary education *55m, 113m, 180*
  tertiary education *92*
slums 18n, 47
Social Cash Transfer (Zambia) *116*
Social Risk Mitigation Project (Turkey) *116*
Social Safety Net (Nicaragua) *116, 116*
socio-economic background, effect on learning 67, **68, 84**
socio-economic inequalities 19
Solomon Islands
  education aid *165, 189, 189n, 190*
  gender parity/disparity *82m, 85m, 184*
  out-of-school children *50m, 50n*
  pre-primary education *37m, 38-9*
  primary education *113m*
Somalia
  abolition of school fees *112m*
  compulsory education *25*
  EDI *93n*
  education aid *165, 189, 189n, 190*
  out-of-school children 50n
Soros Foundation 162
South Africa
  abolition of school fees *112m,* 114
  adult literacy 181, *182*
  cash transfers *116*
  child mortality rate 35
  curriculum 131
  decentralization 106
  EDI *94, 95*
  education aid 162
  education expenditure 144, *144-5, 145,* 146, 149
  gender parity/disparity 23, *82m, 83, 85m, 90, 184*
  learning assessments 68n, 69, 70, *71,* 133
  non-formal learning 60, 122
  non-government schools 104, 105
  out-of-school children 50, *50m,* 51
  pre-primary education 36, *37m, 38-9*
  primary education *43, 43,* 44, 45, 46, 54, *55m, 113m,* 179, *180*
  school networking **135**
  teaching staff 126
  tertiary education *92*
South America *see* Latin America; *individual countries*
South and West Asia
  see also individual countries
  adult literacy 33, 63, *63,* 65
  economic growth 19
  EDI 93, *93, 94*
  education aid 159, **163,** *163,* 171, 173

education expenditure 142, *142,* 143, 146, *146, 148, 157,* 172
  fragile states *21*
  GDP *185,* 186
  gender parity/disparity 79, 80, *80,* 81, *81,* 83, *83,* 84, *84, 86*
  learning assessments 69, *69*
  learning environment 72, 125
  learning and life skills 181
  ODA *22*
  out-of-school children 49, *49, 50m,* 51
  pre-primary education 33, 35, 36, *36, 37m, 38-9,* 40
  primary education 41, *41,* 42, *42,* **43**, 44, *44,* 45, 53, 54, *55m,* 56, 73, 80, 83, 108, 127, 178
  secondary education 56-7, 58, *58,* 59, *80, 84*
  teaching staff 34, 75, *75,* 76, 77, 78, 87, 127, 128, 185, *185*
  tertiary education *59, 80, 86,* 92
Spain
  abolition of school fees *112m*
  education aid donor *161, 162, 187*
  education expenditure *144-5, 150*
  ethnic populations 120
  gender parity/disparity *82m, 85m,* 183, *184*
  learning assessments 67
  out-of-school children *50m*
  pre-primary education *37m*
  primary education *55m, 113m, 180*
  tertiary education *92*
special needs, inclusive education 121
  see also disabilities
Sri Lanka
  abolition of school fees *112m*
  adult literacy *64m, 182*
  civil society organizations **103**
  gender parity/disparity *82m, 85m, 184*
  out-of-school children *50m*
  primary education 42, **43**, *180*
  teaching staff 127
staff *see* teaching staff
state *see* governments
stereotyping
  see also discrimination; gender bias
  attitudes of teachers 91
  in early education 34
stigmatization *see* discrimination; gender bias
Strong Foundations: Early Childhood Care and Education 28
students, support from schools 55
stunted children 35
Sub-Saharan Africa
  see also individual countries
  adult literacy 33, 63, *63,* 65, 181, 182, 190
  cash transfers 116-17
  child mortality rate 35
  debt relief 162
  disease 18, 18n
  distance learning 135
  ECCE programmes 179
  economic growth 19
  EDI 93, *93, 94*
  education aid 22, 157, 158, 159, **163,** *163,* 171, 173, 174
  education expenditure 142, *142,* 143, **144,** 145, 146, *146,* 147, 148, *148,* 149, *149, 157,* 172
  EFA goals 22
  fragile states *21*
  GDP *185,* 186
  gender parity/disparity 79, 80, *80,* 81, *81,* 82, 83, *83,* 84, *84, 86,* 183
  governance 20
  inclusive education 121
  learning assessments 69, *71*
  learning environment 72, 86, 125

learning and life skills 181
  monitoring EFA 101n
  ODA 22, *22,* 23
  orphans 117
  out-of-school children 49, *49, 50m,* 51
  effect of population growth 17
  pre-primary education 33, 35, 36, *36, 37m, 38-9,* 40
  primary education 41, *41,* 42, *42,* **43**, *43,* 44, *44,* 45, 52n, 53, 54, *55m,* 56, 73, 80, 83, 108, 127, 178
  secondary education 56-7, 57, 58, *58, 59, 80, 84*
  teaching staff 34, 75, *75, 76,* **76**, 77, 77n, *78, 79,* 87, 127, 128, 148, 185, *185*
  tertiary education 59, *59, 80, 86,* 92
Sudan
  abolition of school fees *112m*
  adult literacy *64m, 182*
  compulsory education *25*
  EDI *93n*
  education aid *165,* 189, *189n,* 190
  education plans 100n
  gender parity/disparity 82, *82m, 85m, 184*
  non-formal learning *61*
  out-of-school children 50n
  post-conflict education **137**
  pre-primary education *37m, 38-9,* 40
  primary education 41, 42, 53, 54, *55m,* 78, *113m*
  teaching staff 40, *78*
support for pupils 55
Suriname
  abolition of school fees *112m*
  adult literacy *64m, 182*
  compulsory education *25*
  gender parity/disparity *82m,* 83, *85m, 184*
  out-of-school children *50m*
  pre-primary education *37m, 38-9*
  primary education *43,* 53
survival rate to last grade **52,** 53-5, *54,* 55, 56, 83, *83,* 95
SWAps 149, 164, *165,* 166-8, 171-2, 173
Swaziland
  abolition of school fees *112m*
  adult literacy *64m, 182*
  child mortality rate 35
  compulsory education *25*
  EDI 94
  education aid *158,* 159
  education expenditure 142, *144-5, 145*
  gender parity/disparity *82m,* 83, *85m, 184*
  learning assessments 68n, 133
  non-formal learning *61*
  out-of-school children *50m*
  pre-primary education *37m, 38-9*
  primary education 45, *55m,* 56, *113m,* 179, *180*
  tertiary education *92*
  violence and abuse 86n
Sweden
  abolition of school fees *112m*
  education aid donor *161, 162,* 166, 168, 187
  education expenditure *144-5, 150, 150*
  gender parity/disparity *82m, 85m,* 87, *184*
  out-of-school children *50m*
  pre-primary education *37m, 38-9*
  primary education 42, *113m, 180*
  teaching staff 87
  tertiary education *92*
Swedish International Development Cooperation Agency (Sida) 166, 171
Switzerland
  abolition of school fees *112m*
  education aid donor *161, 162, 187*

education expenditure *144-5*
  gender parity/disparity *82m, 85m,* 88, 183, *184*
  out-of-school children *50m*
  pre-primary education *37m*
  primary education 42, 45, *113m, 180*
  teaching staff 88
  tertiary education *92*
Syrian Arab Republic
  abolition of school fees *112m*
  adult literacy *64m, 182*
  child mortality rate 35n
  gender parity/disparity *82m, 85m, 184*
  pre-primary education *37m, 38-9,* 40
  primary education *43,* 54, *55m, 113m,* 180
  secondary education 57
  teaching staff 40
system assessments *see* national learning assessments

T

Tajikistan
  abolition of school fees *112m*
  adult literacy *64m, 182*
  child labour 118
  compulsory education *25*
  effect of conflict 74
  education aid *165,* 175
  education costs 151, *151,* 152, *152*
  education expenditure 144, *144-5, 151, 174*
  gender parity/disparity *82m,* 83, *85m, 184*
  non-formal learning *61*
  out-of-school children *50m,* 50n
  pre-primary education *37m, 38-9,* 40
  primary education *55m,* 56, *113m, 180*
take-home rations 124
Tanzania *see* United Republic of Tanzania
targeting
  child labour programmes 119
  for disadvantage 114-17, *115, 115-16,* 118
  of fee reductions 114
  for gender parity 118
  literacy programmes 122
teacher absenteeism 19, **76**
teacher attrition 130
teacher migration 75n
teacher-pupil interactions 87-8
teacher training 34, **57**, 77n, 79, 126
  distance education 134-5
  gender issues 88
  HIV/AIDs curriculum **132**
  ICT 134-5, 136
  mentoring **130**
  professional development 127, 130
  special needs 121
teachers *see* teaching staff
teaching conditions *see* learning environment
teaching hours *see* instructional time
teaching materials *see* information and communication technology; learning environment; textbooks
teaching staff
  see also 'teacher' entries
  absenteeism 19, **76**
  contract 78-9, *79,* 127-8
  deployment 128-9
  gender biased attitudes 34, 87, 90, 91
  government responsibilities 193
  incentives 126, 128, 129
  and increased enrolment *113m,* 114
  leaving profession 130
  as role models 87, 90
  needed for quality of education 183-5, *185*
  for nomadic and pastoralist schools 120

pre-primary education 32, 39-40
primary education 74-8, *75*, *78*
professional development 127, 130
recruitment 126, 128, 129, **129**
secondary education 75, *75*
shortage 32, 34, 39-40, 75-9, *75*, 75n, 128
status, morale and professionalism 99
trained 40, 77-8, *78*
training *see* teacher training
unqualified 40
technical cooperation 165
technical and vocational education and training (TVET) 58-9
teenagers *see* young people
Telesecundaria (Mexico) 135
television, use in education 135
temporary teachers (contract) 78-9, *79*, 127-8
Ten-Year Development Plan for Basic Education (Burkina Faso) 111, 118
tertiary education
    education expenditure 147, *147*, 148, 150
    enrolment 59, *59*
    expansion 24, 186
    gender parity 80, *80*, 84, 91, 92
textbooks
    access to 66, 68, 73-4, 125-6, 193
    gender bias 88-9
Thailand
    abolition of school fees *112m*
    adult literacy *64m*, *182*
    basic education 26
    compulsory education 25
    curriculum **132**
    education costs 150
    education expenditure 143, *144-5*, 150, *150*
    gender parity/disparity *82m*, *85m*, *184*
    learning assessments 67, 71, 72
    non-formal learning 60, 122
    out-of-school children *50m*
    pre-primary education 36, *37m*, *38-9*
    primary education 46, *113m*
the former Yugoslav Republic of Macedonia
    abolition of school fees *112m*
    adult literacy *64m*, *182*
    compulsory education 25
    EDI 94
    education expenditure *144-5*
    gender parity/disparity *82m*, *85m*, *184*
    out-of-school children *50m*
    post-conflict education 137
    pre-primary education *37m*, *38-9*
    primary education 45, *55m*, *113m*, *180*
    tertiary education 92
Third World *see* developing countries; least developed countries; low-income countries; middle income developing countries
time for learning *see* instructional time
Timor-Leste
    abolition of school fees *112m*, 113
    compulsory education 25
    effect of conflict 74
    education aid 165
    education costs 151, *151*, 152
    gender parity/disparity *82m*, *85m*
    out-of-school children *50m*, 50n
    pre-primary education *37m*, *38-9*
    primary education **43**, *43*, *113m*, *180*
Tobago *see* Trinidad and Tobago
toddlers *see* under-3s
Togo
    abolition of school fees *112m*
    adult literacy *64m*, 65n, *182*
    cash transfers **117**
    EDI 93n
    education aid *165*, 189

gender parity/disparity 82, *82m*, *83*, 84, *85m*, 89, *184*
non-formal learning 61
out-of-school children *50m*, 50n
pre-primary education *37m*, *38-9*
primary education 42, **43**, 45, 53, *55m*, *56*, *78*, *113m*, *180*
teaching staff 77n, *78*, *78*, *79*, 127
Tokelau
    gender parity/disparity *82m*, *85m*, *184*
    pre-primary education *37m*
    primary education 42, 52n
Tonga
    adult literacy *64m*, *182*
    EDI 93
    education expenditure 143, *144-5*
    gender parity/disparity *82m*, *85m*, *184*
    out-of-school children *50m*, 50n
    pre-primary education *37m*, *38-9*
    primary education 45, *113m*, *180*
total primary net enrolment ratio (TNER) 179, *180*
training, *see also* teacher training
Training Young Farmers for the 21st Century (China) 60
transaction costs, aid 194
transition
    back to school for child workers 119
    to secondary education 114
    upper primary school 118
transition countries
    diseases 18
    effect of economic growth 19
    education expenditure 149
    educational achievement 68-9
    entrants into primary education 41, 44
    gender parity 79
    literacy 63
    out-of-school children 49
    pre-primary education 35, 36, 40
    primary education 53
    secondary education 58, *58*
    teaching staff 75, 76
    tertiary education 59, *59*
Trinidad and Tobago
    abolition of school fees *112m*
    adult literacy *64m*, *182*
    gender parity/disparity *82m*, *83*, *85m*, *184*
    out-of-school children *50m*
    pre-primary education *37m*, *38-9*
    primary education *43*, 45, *55m*, *113m*, *180*
    teaching staff 126
    tertiary education 92
tuberculosis 18
tuition fees *see* school fees
Tunisia
    abolition of school fees *112m*
    adult literacy *64m*, *182*, 190
    basic education 26
    EDI 93
    education expenditure 142, *144-5*
    ethnic populations 120
    gender parity/disparity *82m*, *85m*, 89, 90, *184*
    out-of-school children *50m*
    pre-primary education *37m*, *38-9*
    primary education *43*, 45, *55m*, *113m*, *180*
    teaching staff **76**
Turkey
    abolition of school fees *112m*
    adult literacy *64m*, *182*
    cash transfers 116
    curriculum 131
    decentralization 106
    education aid *159*
    education aid donor 162
    education expenditure *144-5*, 150, *150*
    ethnic populations 120

gender parity/disparity 82, *82m*, *85m*, *184*
learning assessments 67
out-of-school children *50m*, 51
pre-primary education *37m*, *38-9*
primary education 42, **43**, *55m*, 179, *180*
teaching staff 128
Turkmenistan
    abolition of school fees *112m*
    adult literacy *64m*, *182*
Turks and Caicos Islands
    gender parity/disparity *82m*, *83*, *85m*
    out-of-school children *50m*
    pre-primary education *37m*, 40
    primary education 42, **43**, 53, 54, *55m*, *78*
    teaching staff *78*
Tuvalu
    compulsory education 25
    education aid 165
    gender parity/disparity *82m*
    pre-primary education *37m*
    primary education 42, 52n, *113m*
TV, use in education 135
TVET 58-9
two parent families 18

U

Uganda
    abolition of school fees *112m*, 113
    adult literacy *64m*, **133**, *182*
    cash transfers **117**
    civil society organizations **103**
    debt relief 164
    decentralization 106
    ECCE programmes 105
    education aid 153, 159, *159*, 165
    education costs 151, 152
    education expenditure 151
    education plans 100n
    gender parity/disparity 82, *82m*, 84, *85m*, 90, *184*
    inclusive education 121
    learning assessments 68n, 69, 70, 72
    learning environment 74, 86-7
    non-government schools 105
    out-of-school children 152
    post-conflict education 136
    pre-primary education 36, *37m*, *38-9*
    primary education **43**, 47, 53, 54, *55m*, *113m*
    private education 36-7
    secondary education 57
    teaching staff 77, 126, 128
    tertiary education 92
    violence and abuse 86, 86n
Ukraine
    abolition of school fees *112m*
    adult literacy *64m*, *182*
    compulsory education 25
    education aid 189
    education expenditure 142, 144, *144-5*
    gender parity/disparity *82m*, *85m*, *184*
    HIV/AIDS 18n
    out-of-school children *50m*
    pre-primary education *37m*, *38-9*
    primary education 42, **43**, *78*, *113m*, *180*
    teaching staff *78*
under-3s, ECCE provision 32, 34-5, 179
under-5 mortality rate 35
under-age entry **43**
underdeveloped countries *see* developing countries; least developed countries; low-income countries; middle income developing countries
undernutrition 35
    see also child health and nutrition
UNESCO
    role in EFA 26, 27

Global Monitoring Reports 27, 28, 101, 107
UNESCO Convention against Discrimination in Education (1960) **16**
UNICEF, education aid donor *161*, *162*, 168
United Arab Emirates
    abolition of school fees *112m*
    adult literacy *64m*, *182*
    compulsory education 25
    EDI 94
    education expenditure 142
    gender parity/disparity *82m*, *85m*, *184*
    out-of-school children *50m*
    pre-primary education *37m*, *38-9*, 40
    primary education 42, *43*, **43**, 44, 44n, 45, *55m*, *56*, *78*, *113m*, *180*
    teaching staff *78*
United Kingdom
    abolition of school fees *112m*
    distance learning 134
    education aid donor 23, 159, 160, *161*, *162*, 167, 187
    education expenditure *144-5*, 150
    gender parity/disparity *82m*, *85m*, 90, *184*
    out-of-school children *50m*
    pre-primary education *37m*, *38-9*
    primary education 52n, *113m*, *180*
    teaching staff 126
    tertiary education 92
United Nations Convention on the Rights of Persons with Disabilities **16**, 120-1
United Nations Convention on the Rights of the Child (CRC) **16**, 17, 24
United Nations Universal Declaration of Human Rights 16, **16**, 24
United Republic of Tanzania
    abolition of school fees *112m*, 113
    adult literacy *64m*, *182*, 190
    child mortality rate 35n
    civil society organizations 102n, 103, **103**
    debt relief 164
    decentralization 106
    education aid 153, 159, *159*, 165, 166, 167-8, 187
    education plans 100n
    gender parity/disparity 82, *82m*, *83*, 90
    geographic disparity 111
    governance 20
    effect of health and nutrition programmes 124
    learning assessments 68n
    learning environment 74
    out-of-school children 48, *50m*, 51
    pre-primary education *37m*, *38-9*, 39, 40
    primary education 41, 42, **43**, 44, 45, 46, 46, 46n, 47, *47*, 48, *55m*, *78*, *113m*, *180*
    school expansion 110
    teaching staff 40, **76**, 77, 77n, *78*, 126, 128
United States
    abolition of school fees *112m*
    compulsory education 25
    distance learning 134
    education aid donor 23, 159, 160, 161, *161*, *162*, 167, *187*, 188
    education expenditure *144-5*, 150
    gender parity/disparity *82m*, *85m*, 87, *184*
    out-of-school children *50m*
    pre-primary education *37m*, *38-9*
    primary education **43**, 45, *113m*
    teaching staff 87
Universal Declaration of Human Rights (1948) 16, **16**, 24

universal literacy target 181, *182*
universal pre-primary education 109
universal primary education (EFA goal) 33
  see also compulsory education;
    primary education
  aid 190
  in EFA priorities 192
  Millennium Development Goal 14
  monitoring **51**
  progress towards 33, 41-59, 92, 93, 95,
    179-81, *180*
  trends 179-81, *180*
UPE *see* universal primary education
upper secondary education *26*, 58, *59*
urban areas 18, 67, 72, *72*
urbanization 18
Uruguay
  abolition of school fees *112m*
  adult literacy *64m*, *182*
  ECCE programmes 108
  education expenditure 142, 143, *144-5*,
    150, *150*
  gender parity/disparity *82m*, 83, *83*,
    85m, *184*
  out-of-school children *50m*
  pre-primary education *37m*, *38-9*
  primary education *45*, *55m*, *113m*
USSR *see* Armenia; Azerbaijan; Belarus;
    Estonia; Georgia; Kazakhstan;
    Kyrgyzstan; Latvia; Lithuania;
    Republic of Moldova; Russian
    Federation; Turkmenistan; Ukraine;
    Uzbekistan.
Uzbekistan
  abolition of school fees *112m*
  compulsory education *25*
  education aid *165*
  education plans 100n
  gender parity/disparity *82m*, *85m*, *184*
  multilingual education 132
  non-formal learning *61*
  out-of-school children 50n
  pre-primary education *37m*, *38-9*
  primary education 52n, *55m*

V

vaccination campaigns 19, 32, 35
Vanuatu
  abolition of school fees *112m*
  adult literacy *64m*
  child mortality rate 35n
  compulsory education *25*
  education aid *165*, *175*
  education expenditure 144, *144-5*
  gender parity/disparity *82m*, *85m*, *184*
  out-of-school children *50m*, 50n
  primary education *45*, *55m*, *113m*, *180*
Venezuela
  abolition of school fees *112m*
  adult literacy *64m*, *182*
  compulsory education *25*
  distance learning 134
  EDI *94*
  gender parity/disparity *82m*, 83, *83*,
    85m, *184*
  impact of education 23
  learning environment 73
  out-of-school children *50m*
  pre-primary education *37m*, *38-9*, 40
  primary education **43**, *45*, *55m*, 56, *78*,
    113m, *180*
  teaching staff *78*
vernacular education 28, 131n, 132-3, 193
Viet Nam
  abolition of school fees *112m*
  adult literacy *64m*, *182*
  curriculum **132**
  EDI *94*
  education aid *159*, *165*, *167*, 189
  education cost 151

education plans 100n
ethnic populations 120
gender parity/disparity *82m*, 84, *85m*,
    184
HIV/AIDS 18n
learning assessments 133
non-formal learning 60, *61*
out-of-school children 48, *50m*, *51*
pre-primary education 36, *37m*, *38-9*
primary education 41, *42*, 44, 44n, *45*,
    46, *47*, 48, *55m*, *78*, *113m*, *180*
teaching staff *78*
tertiary education *92*
violence, in school 86, 124-5
vocational education
  post-secondary level **57**
  TVET 58-9
voluntary teachers (contract) 78-9, *79*,
    127-8
vouchers, for education 150

W

wages, teaching staff 75, *79*, 126
Western Europe *see* North America and
    Western Europe; *individual
    countries*
women
  see also 'gender' *entries*; girls
  career opportunities 20, 91
  employment 23
  as teachers 87, *87*, 129, **129**
  and HIV/AIDS 18, 18n
  literacy 33, **62**, *63*, 65
  non-formal learning 61
  tertiary education 84, 91, *92*
workplace environments, and literacy 66
World Bank
  education aid donor 161-2, 164, 168,
    188, 191
  governance report 20n
  success of projects 170-1
World Education Forum, Dakar *see* Dakar
    World Education Forum
world population 17-18

Y

Yemen
  abolition of school fees *112m*
  adult literacy 63, *64m*, 65n, *182*, 190
  EDI *94*, 95
  education aid *159*, 162, *165*, 187, 189,
    189n, *190*
  education costs 152
  education management 101
  education plans 100, 100n
  gender parity/disparity 81, *82m*, *83*, 84,
    85m, 117, *184*
  out-of-school children *50m*, *51*, 152
  pre-primary education *37m*, 38, *38-9*
  primary education 41, *42*, 44, *45*, 54,
    55m, *113m*, 179, *180*
  teaching staff 129, **129**
young children *see* early childhood care
    and education; pre-primary
    education
young people
  see also learning and life skills
  educational attainment 61
  educational programmes 60-1, 119,
    121-3, 193
  informal education 33, 60, 121-3, 181
youth literacy 65
Yugoslavia *see* Bosnia and Herzegovina;
    Croatia; Serbia and Montenegro;
    Slovenia; the former Yugoslav
    Republic of Macedonia

Z

Zambia
  abolition of school fees *112m*, 113
  adult literacy *64m*, **133**, *182*, 190
  cash transfers 116, *116*, **117**
  civil society organizations 103
  compulsory education *25*
  debt relief 164
  education aid *159*, *165*, *167*, *175*, 187,
    189
  education costs 151, *151*, 152
  education expenditure 142, *144-5*, *145*,
    151
  education plans 100n
  gender parity/disparity *82m*, *85m*, *184*
  geographic disparity 111
  impact of education 23
  learning assessments 68n, 133
  learning environment 74
  multilingual education 132
  out-of-school children *50m*, *51*
  primary education 41, *42*, **43**, 44, *45*,
    46, *46*, *47*, 47, 48, *113m*, *180*
  teaching staff **76**
  violence and abuse 86n
Zanzibar
  see also United Republic of Tanzania
  ECCE programmes 105
  learning environment 74
Zimbabwe
  abolition of school fees *112m*
  adult literacy *64m*, *182*
  basic education *26*
  child mortality rate 35
  education aid *165*, 189
  gender parity/disparity *82m*, *85m*, *184*
  learning assessments 68n
  out-of-school children *50m*, 50n
  pre-primary education *37m*, *38-9*
  primary education *45*, *46*, *46*, *47*, 47,
    48, *55m*, *113m*, 179, *180*
  teaching staff 77n
  violence and abuse 86